MORE PRAISE FROM ACROSS THE NATION
FOR THE JOBBANK SERIES...

"If you are looking for a job ... before you go to the newspapers and the help-wanted ads, listen to Bob Adams, publisher of *The Metropolitan New York JobBank*."
-Tom Brokaw, *NBC*

"For those graduates whose parents are pacing the floor, conspicuously placing circled want ads around the house and typing up resumes, [*The Carolina JobBank*] answers job-search questions."
-Greensboro News and Record

"A timely book for Chicago job hunters follows books from the same publisher that were well received in New York and Boston ... [*The Chicago JobBank* is] a fine tool for job hunters ..."
-Clarence Peterson, *Chicago Tribune*

"Because our listing is seen by people across the nation, it generates lots of resumes for us. We encourage unsolicited resumes. We'll always be listed [in *The Chicago JobBank*] as long as I'm in this career."
-Tom Fitzpatrick, Director of Human Resources
Merchandise Mart Properties, Inc.

"Job-hunting is never fun, but this book can ease the ordeal ... [*The Los Angeles JobBank*] will help allay fears, build confidence, and avoid wheel-spinning."
-Robert W. Ross, *Los Angeles Times*

"*The Florida JobBank* is an invaluable job-search reference tool. It provides the most up-to-date information and contact names available for companies in Florida. I should know -- it worked for me!"
-Rhonda Cody, Human Resources Consultant
Aetna Life and Casualty

"*The Boston JobBank* provides a handy map of employment possibilities in greater Boston. This book can help in the initial steps of a job search by locating major employers, describing their business activities, and for most firms, by naming the contact person and listing typical professional positions. For recent college graduates, as well as experienced professionals, *The Boston JobBank* is an excellent place to begin a job search."
-Juliet F. Brudney, Career Columnist
Boston Globe

"No longer can jobseekers feel secure about finding employment just through want ads. With the tough competition in the job market, particularly in the Boston area, they need much more help. For this reason, *The Boston JobBank* will have a wide and appreciative audience of new graduates, job changers, and people relocating to Boston. It provides a good place to start a search for entry-level professional positions."

> *-Journal of College Placement*

"*The Phoenix JobBank* is a first-class publication. The information provided is useful and current."

> **-Lyndon Denton**
> **Director of Human Resources and Materials Management**
> **Apache Nitrogen Products, Inc.**

"*The Seattle JobBank* is an essential resource for job hunters."

> **-Gil Lopez, Staffing Team Manager**
> **Battelle Pacific Northwest Laboratories**

"I read through the 'Basics of Job Winning' and 'Resumes' sections [in *The Dallas-Fort Worth JobBank*] and found them to be very informative, with some positive tips for the job searcher. I believe the strategies outlined will bring success to any determined candidate."

> **-Camilla Norder, Professional Recruiter**
> **Presbyterian Hospital of Dallas**

"Through *The Dallas-Fort Worth JobBank,* we've been able to attract high-quality candidates for several positions."

> **-Rob Bertino, Southern States Sales Manager**
> **CompuServe**

"Packed with helpful contacts, *The Houston JobBank* empowers its reader to launch an effective, strategic job search in the Houston metropolitan area."

> **-Andrew Ceperley, Director**
> **College of Communication Career Services**
> **The University of Texas at Austin**

"*The San Francisco Bay Area JobBank* ... is a highly useful guide, with plenty of how-to's ranging from resume tips to interview dress codes and research shortcuts."

> **-A.S. Ross, *San Francisco Examiner***

"[*The Atlanta JobBank* is] one of the best sources for finding a job in Atlanta!"

> **-Luann Miller, Human Resources Manager**
> **Prudential Preferred Financial Services**

What makes the JobBank series the nation's premier line of employment guides?

With vital employment information on thousands of employers across the nation, the JobBank series is the most comprehensive and authoritative set of career directories available today.

Each book in the series provides information on **dozens of different industries** in a given city or area, with the primary employer listings providing contact information, telephone and fax numbers, e-mail addresses, Websites, a summary of the firm's business, internships, and in many cases descriptions of the firm's typical professional job categories.

All of the reference information in the JobBank series is as up-to-date and accurate as possible. Every year, the entire database is thoroughly researched and verified by mail and by telephone. Adams Media Corporation publishes **more local employment guides more often** than any other publisher of career directories.

The JobBank series offers **28 regional titles**, from Minneapolis to Houston, and from Boston to San Francisco as well as **two industry-specific titles**. All of the information is organized geographically, because most people look for jobs in specific areas of the country.

A condensed, but thorough, review of the entire job search process is presented in the chapter **The Basics of Job Winning**, a feature which has received many compliments from career counselors. In addition, each JobBank directory includes a section on **resumes and cover letters** the *New York Times* has acclaimed as "excellent."

The JobBank series gives job hunters the most comprehensive, timely, and accurate career information, organized and indexed to facilitate your job search. An entire career reference library, JobBank books are designed to help you find optimal employment in any market.

Top career publications from Adams Media Corporation

The JobBank Series:
each JobBank book is $16.95

The Atlanta JobBank, 14th Ed.
The Austin/San Antonio JobBank, 3rd Ed.
The Boston JobBank, 19th Ed.
The Carolina JobBank, 6th Ed.
The Chicago JobBank, 18th Ed.
The Colorado JobBank, 13th Ed.
The Connecticut JobBank, 2nd Ed.
The Dallas-Fort Worth JobBank, 13th Ed.
The Detroit JobBank, 9th Ed.
The Florida JobBank, 15th Ed.
The Houston JobBank, 11th Ed.
The Indiana JobBank, 3rd Ed.
The Las Vegas JobBank, 2nd Ed.
The Los Angeles JobBank, 17th Ed.
The Minneapolis-St. Paul JobBank, 11th Ed.
The Missouri JobBank, 3rd Ed.
The New Jersey JobBank, 1st Ed.
The Metropolitan New York JobBank, 18th Ed.
The Ohio JobBank, 10th Ed.
The Greater Philadelphia JobBank, 14th Ed.
The Phoenix JobBank, 8th Ed.
The Pittsburgh JobBank, 2nd Ed.
The Portland JobBank, 3rd Ed.
The San Francisco Bay Area JobBank, 16th Ed.
The Seattle JobBank, 12th Ed.
The Tennessee JobBank, 5th Ed.
The Virginia JobBank, 3rd Ed.
The Metropolitan Washington DC JobBank, 15th Ed.

The JobBank Guide to Computer & High-Tech Companies, 2nd Ed. ($17.95)
The JobBank Guide to Health Care Companies, 2nd Ed. ($17.95)

The National JobBank, 2003 (Covers the entire U.S.: $450.00 hc)

Other Career Titles:
The Adams Cover Letter Almanac ($12.95)
The Adams Internet Job Search Almanac, 6th Ed. ($12.95)
The Adams Executive Recruiters Almanac, 2nd Ed. ($17.95)
The Adams Job Interview Almanac ($12.95)
The Adams Jobs Almanac, 8th Ed. ($16.95)
The Adams Resume Almanac ($10.95)
Business Etiquette in Brief ($7.95)
Campus Free College Degrees, 8th Ed. ($16.95)
Career Tests ($12.95)
Closing Techniques, 2nd Ed. ($8.95)
Cold Calling Techniques, 4th Ed. ($8.95)
College Grad Job Hunter, 4th Ed. ($14.95)
The Complete Resume & Job Search Book for College Students, 2nd Ed. ($12.95)
Cover Letters That Knock 'em Dead, 5th Ed. ($12.95)
Every Woman's Essential Job Hunting & Resume Book ($11.95)
The Everything Cover Letter Book ($12.95)
The Everything Get-A-Job Book ($12.95)
The Everything Hot Careers Book ($12.95)
The Everything Job Interview Book ($12.95)
The Everything Online Business Book ($12.95)
The Everything Online Job Search Book ($12.95)
The Everything Resume Book ($12.95)
The Everything Selling Book ($12.95)
First Time Resume ($7.95)
How to Start and Operate a Successful Business ($9.95)
Knock 'em Dead, 2003 ($14.95)
Knock 'em Dead Business Presentations ($12.95)
Market Yourself and Your Career, 2nd Ed. ($12.95)
The New Professional Image ($12.95)
The 150 Most Profitable Home Businesses for Women ($9.95)
The Resume Handbook, 3rd Ed. ($7.95)
Resumes That Knock 'em Dead, 5th Ed. ($12.95)
The Road to CEO ($20.00 hc)
The 250 Job Interview Questions You'll Most Likely Be Asked ($9.95)
Your Executive Image ($10.95)

If you cannot find these titles at your favorite book outlet, you may order them directly from the publisher. **BY PHONE:** Call 800/872-5627 (in Massachusetts 508/427-7100). We accept Visa, Mastercard, and American Express. $4.95 will be added to your total for shipping and handling. **BY MAIL:** Write out the full titles of the books you'd like to order and send payment, including $4.95 for shipping and handling to: Adams Media Corporation, 57 Littlefield Street, Avon MA 02322. 30-day money back guarantee. **BY FAX:** 800/872-5628.
Discounts available for standing orders.

18th Edition
THE Metropolitan
New York
JobBank

Reference Editor:	Christie L. Barros
Assistant Reference Editor:	Lisa A. Geraghty
Production Manager:	Michelle Roy Kelly

Adams Media Corporation
AVON, MASSACHUSETTS

Published by Adams Media Corporation
57 Littlefield Street, Avon, MA 02322 U.S.A.
www.adamsmedia.com

ISBN: 1-58062-816-8
ISSN: 1098-979X
Manufactured in Canada.

Because addresses and telephone numbers of smaller companies change rapidly, we recommend you call each company and verify the information before mailing to the employers listed in this book. Mass mailings are not recommended.

While the publisher has made every reasonable effort to obtain and verify accurate information, occasional errors are possible due to the magnitude of the data. Should you discover an error, or if a company is missing, please write the editors at the above address so that we may update future editions.

"This publication is designed to provide accurate and authoritative information with regard to the subject matter covered. It is sold with the understanding that the publisher is not engaged in rendering legal, accounting, or other professional advice. If legal advice or other expert assistance is required, the services of a competent professional person should be sought."

--From a *Declaration of Principles* jointly adopted by a Committee of the American Bar Association and a Committee of Publishers and Associations

This book is available on standing order and at quantity discounts for bulk purchases.
For information, call 800/872-5627 (in Massachusetts, 508/427-7100).

TABLE OF CONTENTS

Automotive/87
- Automotive Repair Shops
- Automotive Stampings
- Industrial Vehicles and Moving Equipment
- Motor Vehicles and Equipment
- Travel Trailers and Campers

Banking/Savings and Loans/88

Biotechnology, Pharmaceuticals, and Scientific R&D/95
- Clinical Labs
- Lab Equipment Manufacturers
- Pharmaceutical Manufacturers and Distributors

Business Services and Non-Scientific Research/102
- Adjustment and Collection Services
- Cleaning, Maintenance, and Pest Control Services
- Credit Reporting Services
- Detective, Guard, and Armored Car Services/Security Systems Services
- Miscellaneous Equipment Rental and Leasing
- Secretarial and Court Reporting Services

Charities and Social Services/108
- Job Training and Vocational Rehabilitation Services

Chemicals/Rubber and Plastics/114
- Adhesives, Detergents, Inks, Paints, Soaps, Varnishes
- Agricultural Chemicals and Fertilizers
- Carbon and Graphite Products
- Chemical Engineering Firms
- Industrial Gases

Communications: Telecommunications and Broadcasting/117
- Cable/Pay Television Services
- Communications Equipment
- Radio and Television Broadcasting Stations
- Telephone, Telegraph, and Other Message Communications

Computer Hardware, Software, and Services/124
- Computer Components and Hardware Manufacturers
- Consultants and Computer Training Companies
- Internet and Online Service Providers
- Networking and Systems Services
- Repair Services/Rental and Leasing
- Resellers, Wholesalers, and Distributors
- Software Developers/Programming Services

Educational Services/135
- Business/Secretarial/Data Processing Schools
- Colleges/Universities/Professional Schools
- Community Colleges/Technical Schools/Vocational Schools
- Elementary and Secondary Schools
- Preschool and Child Daycare Services

Electronic/Industrial Electrical Equipment/141
- Electronic Machines and Systems
- Semiconductor Manufacturers

Environmental and Waste Management Services/150
- Environmental Engineering Firms
- Sanitary Services

Fabricated/Primary Metals and Products/152
- Aluminum and Copper Foundries
- Die-Castings
- Iron and Steel Foundries/Steel Works, Blast Furnaces, and Rolling Mills

Financial Services/154
- Consumer Financing and Credit Agencies

- *Investment Specialists*
- *Mortgage Bankers and Loan Brokers*
- *Security and Commodity Brokers, Dealers, and Exchanges*

Food and Beverages/Agriculture/164
- *Crop Services and Farm Supplies*
- *Dairy Farms*
- *Food Manufacturers/Processors and Agricultural Producers*
- *Tobacco Products*

Government/168
- *Courts*
- *Executive, Legislative, and General Government*
- *Public Agencies (Firefighters, Military, Police)*
- *United States Postal Service*

Health Care: Services, Equipment, and Products/169
- *Dental Labs and Equipment*
- *Home Health Care Agencies*
- *Hospitals and Medical Centers*
- *Medical Equipment Manufacturers and Wholesalers*
- *Offices and Clinics of Health Practitioners*
- *Residential Treatment Centers/Nursing Homes*
- *Veterinary Services*

Hotels and Restaurants/179
Insurance/183
Legal Services/191
Manufacturing: Miscellaneous Consumer/194
- *Art Supplies*
- *Batteries*
- *Cosmetics and Related Products*
- *Household Appliances and Audio/Video Equipment*
- *Jewelry, Silverware, and Plated Ware*
- *Miscellaneous Household Furniture and Fixtures*
- *Musical Instruments*
- *Tools*
- *Toys and Sporting Goods*

Manufacturing: Miscellaneous Industrial/201
- *Ball and Roller Bearings*
- *Commercial Furniture and Fixtures*
- *Fans, Blowers, and Purification Equipment*
- *Industrial Machinery and Equipment*
- *Motors and Generators/Compressors and Engine Parts*
- *Vending Machines*

Mining/Gas/Petroleum/Energy Related/207
- *Anthracite, Coal, and Ore Mining*
- *Mining Machinery and Equipment*
- *Oil and Gas Field Services*
- *Petroleum and Natural Gas*

Paper and Wood Products/209
- *Forest and Wood Products and Services*
- *Lumber and Wood Wholesale*
- *Millwork, Plywood, and Structural Members*
- *Paper and Wood Mills*

Printing and Publishing/211
- *Book, Newspaper, and Periodical Publishers*
- *Commercial Photographers*
- *Commercial Printing Services*
- *Graphic Designers*

SECTION FOUR: PRIMARY EMPLOYERS (Northern New Jersey)

The Employers/246

The Metropolitan New York JobBank *is organized according to industry. Many listings include the address and phone number of each major firm listed, along with a description of the company's basic product lines and services, and, in many cases, a contact name and other relevant hiring information.*

Automotive/262
- Automotive Repair Shops
- Automotive Stampings
- Industrial Vehicles and Moving Equipment
- Motor Vehicles and Equipment
- Travel Trailers and Campers

Banking/Savings and Loans/264

Biotechnology, Pharmaceuticals, and Scientific R&D/267
- Clinical Labs
- Lab Equipment Manufacturers
- Pharmaceutical Manufacturers and Distributors

Business Services and Non-Scientific Research/281
- Adjustment and Collection Services
- Cleaning, Maintenance, and Pest Control Services
- Credit Reporting Services
- Detective, Guard, and Armored Car Services/Security Systems Services
- Miscellaneous Equipment Rental and Leasing
- Secretarial and Court Reporting Services

Charities and Social Services/284
- Job Training and Vocational Rehabilitation Services

Chemicals/Rubber and Plastics/285
- Adhesives, Detergents, Inks, Paints, Soaps, Varnishes
- Agricultural Chemicals and Fertilizers
- Carbon and Graphite Products
- Chemical Engineering Firms
- Industrial Gases

Communications: Telecommunications and Broadcasting/292
- Cable/Pay Television Services
- Communications Equipment
- Radio and Television Broadcasting Stations
- Telephone, Telegraph, and Other Message Communications

Computer Hardware, Software, and Services/295
- Computer Components and Hardware Manufacturers
- Consultants and Computer Training Companies
- Internet and Online Service Providers
- Networking and Systems Services
- Repair Services/Rental and Leasing
- Resellers, Wholesalers, and Distributors
- Software Developers/Programming Services

Educational Services/306
- Business/Secretarial/Data Processing Schools
- Colleges/Universities/Professional Schools
- Community Colleges/Technical Schools/Vocational Schools
- Elementary and Secondary Schools
- Preschool and Child Daycare Services

Electronic/Industrial Electrical Equipment/308
- Electronic Machines and Systems
- Semiconductor Manufacturers

Environmental and Waste Management Services/314
- Environmental Engineering Firms
- Sanitary Services

Fabricated/Primary Metals and Products/317
- Aluminum and Copper Foundries
- Die-Castings
- Iron and Steel Foundries/Steel Works, Blast Furnaces, and Rolling Mills

Financial Services319/
- Consumer Financing and Credit Agencies

- *Investment Specialists*
- *Mortgage Bankers and Loan Brokers*
- *Security and Commodity Brokers, Dealers, and Exchanges*

Food and Beverages/Agriculture/322
- *Crop Services and Farm Supplies*
- *Dairy Farms*
- *Food Manufacturers/Processors and Agricultural Producers*
- *Tobacco Products*

Government/326
- *Courts*
- *Executive, Legislative, and General Government*
- *Public Agencies (Firefighters, Military, Police)*
- *United States Postal Service*

Health Care: Services, Equipment, and Products/327
- *Dental Labs and Equipment*
- *Home Health Care Agencies*
- *Hospitals and Medical Centers*
- *Medical Equipment Manufacturers and Wholesalers*
- *Offices and Clinics of Health Practitioners*
- *Residential Treatment Centers/Nursing Homes*
- *Veterinary Services*

Hotels and Restaurants/334
Insurance/336
Legal Services/341
Manufacturing: Miscellaneous Consumer/343
- *Art Supplies*
- *Batteries*
- *Cosmetics and Related Products*
- *Household Appliances and Audio/Video Equipment*
- *Jewelry, Silverware, and Plated Ware*
- *Miscellaneous Household Furniture and Fixtures*
- *Musical Instruments*
- *Tools*
- *Toys and Sporting Goods*

Manufacturing: Miscellaneous Industrial/351
- *Ball and Roller Bearings*
- *Commercial Furniture and Fixtures*
- *Fans, Blowers, and Purification Equipment*
- *Industrial Machinery and Equipment*
- *Motors and Generators/Compressors and Engine Parts*
- *Vending Machines*

Mining/Gas/Petroleum/Energy Related/360
- *Anthracite, Coal, and Ore Mining*
- *Mining Machinery and Equipment*
- *Oil and Gas Field Services*
- *Petroleum and Natural Gas*

Paper and Wood Products/362
- *Forest and Wood Products and Services*
- *Lumber and Wood Wholesale*
- *Millwork, Plywood, and Structural Members*
- *Paper and Wood Mills*

Printing and Publishing/364
- *Book, Newspaper, and Periodical Publishers*
- *Commercial Photographers*
- *Commercial Printing Services*
- *Graphic Designers*

INTRODUCTION

HOW TO USE THIS BOOK

Right now, you hold in your hands one of the most effective job-hunting tools available anywhere. In *The Metropolitan New York JobBank*, you will find valuable information to help you launch or continue a rewarding career. But before you open to the book's employer listings and start calling about current job openings, take a few minutes to learn how best to use the resources presented in *The Metropolitan New York JobBank*.

The Metropolitan New York JobBank will help you to stand out from other jobseekers. While many people looking for a new job rely solely on newspaper help-wanted ads, this book offers you a much more effective job-search method — direct contact. The direct contact method has been proven twice as effective as scanning the help-wanted ads. Instead of waiting for employers to come looking for you, you'll be far more effective going to them. While many of your competitors will use trial and error methods in trying to set up interviews, you'll learn not only how to get interviews, but what to expect once you've got them.

In the next few pages, we'll take you through each section of the book so you'll be prepared to get a jump-start on your competition.

Basics of Job Winning

Preparation. Strategy. Time management. These are three of the most important elements of a successful job search. *Basics of Job Winning* helps you address these and all the other elements needed to find the right job.

One of your first priorities should be to define your personal career objectives. What qualities make a job desirable to you? Creativity? High pay? Prestige? Use *Basics of Job Winning* to weigh these questions. Then use the rest of the chapter to design a strategy to find a job that matches your criteria.

In *Basics of Job Winning,* you'll learn which job-hunting techniques work, and which don't. We've reviewed the pros and cons of mass mailings, help-wanted ads, and direct contact. We'll show you how to develop and approach contacts in your field; how to research a prospective employer; and how to use that information to get an interview and the job.

Also included in *Basics of Job Winning*: interview dress code and etiquette, the "do's and don'ts" of interviewing, sample interview questions, and more. We also deal with some of the unique problems faced by those jobseekers who are currently employed, those who have lost a job, and college students conducting their first job search.

Resumes and Cover Letters

The approach you take to writing your resume and cover letter can often mean the difference between getting an interview and never being noticed. In this section, we discuss different formats, as well as what to put on (and what to leave off) your resume. We review the benefits and drawbacks of professional resume writers, and the importance of a follow-up letter. Also included in this section are sample resumes and cover letters which you can use as models.

The Employer Listings

Employers are listed alphabetically by industry. When a company does business under a person's name, like "John Smith & Co.," the company is usually listed by the surname's spelling (in this case "S"). Exceptions occur when a company's name is widely recognized, like "JCPenney" or "Howard Johnson Motor Lodge." In those cases, the company's first name is the key ("J" and "H" respectively).

The Metropolitan New York JobBank covers a very wide range of industries. Each company profile is assigned to one of the industry chapters listed below.

Accounting and Management Consulting	*Fabricated/Primary Metals and Products*
Advertising, Marketing, and Public Relations	*Financial Services*
Aerospace	*Food and Beverages/Agriculture*
Apparel, Fashion, and Textiles	*Government*
Architecture, Construction, and Engineering	*Health Care: Services, Equipment, and*
Arts, Entertainment, Sports, and Recreation	*Products*
Automotive	*Hotels and Restaurants*
Banking/Savings and Loans	*Insurance*
Biotechnology, Pharmaceuticals, and	*Legal Services*
Scientific R&D	*Manufacturing: Miscellaneous Consumer*
Business Services and Non-Scientific	*Manufacturing: Miscellaneous Industrial*
Research	*Mining/Gas/Petroleum/Energy Related*
Charities and Social Services	*Paper and Wood Products*
Chemicals/Rubber and Plastics	*Printing and Publishing*
Communications: Telecommunications and	*Real Estate*
Broadcasting	*Retail*
Computer Hardware, Software, and Services	*Stone, Clay, Glass, and Concrete Products*
Educational Services	*Transportation/Travel*
Electronic/Industrial Electrical Equipment	*Utilities: Electric/Gas/Water*
Environmental and Waste Management	*Miscellaneous Wholesaling*
Services	

Many of the company listings offer detailed company profiles. In addition to company names, addresses, and phone numbers, these listings also include contact names or hiring departments, and descriptions of each company's products and/or services. Many of these listings also feature a variety of additional information including:

Common positions - A list of job titles that the company commonly fills when it is hiring, organized in alphabetical order from Accountant to X-ray Technician. Note: Keep in mind that *The Metropolitan New York JobBank* is a directory of major employers in the area, not a directory of openings currently available. Many of the companies listed will be hiring, others will not. However, since most professional job openings are filled without the placement of help-wanted ads, contacting the employers in this book directly is still a more effective method than browsing the Sunday papers.

Special programs - Does the company offer training programs, internships, or apprenticeships? These programs can be important to first time jobseekers and college students looking for practical work experience. Many employer profiles will include information on these programs.

Parent company - If an employer is a subsidiary of a larger company, the name of that parent company will often be listed here. Use this information to supplement your company research before contacting the employer.

Number of employees - The number of workers a company employs.

Company listings may also include information on other U.S. locations and any stock exchanges the firm may be listed on.

A note on all employer listings that appear in *The Metropolitan New York JobBank*: This book is intended as a starting point. It is not intended to replace any effort that you, the jobseeker, should devote to your job hunt. Keep in mind that while a great deal of effort has been put into collecting and verifying the company profiles provided in this book, addresses and contact names change regularly. Inevitably, some contact names listed herein have changed even before you read this. We recommend you contact a company before mailing your resume to ensure nothing has changed.

Index

The Metropolitan New York JobBank index is organized alphabetically by industry.

THE JOB SEARCH

THE BASICS OF JOB WINNING: A CONDENSED REVIEW

This chapter is divided into four sections. The first section explains the fundamentals that every jobseeker should know, especially first-time jobseekers. The next three sections deal with special situations faced by specific types of jobseekers: those who are currently employed, those who have lost a job, and college students.

THE BASICS:
Things Everyone Needs to Know

Career Planning

The first step to finding your ideal job is to clearly define your objectives. This is better known as career planning (or life planning if you wish to emphasize the importance of combining the two). Career planning has become a field of study in and of itself.

If you are thinking of choosing or switching careers, we particularly emphasize two things. First, choose a career where you will enjoy most of the day-to-day tasks. This sounds obvious, but most of us have at some point found the idea of a glamour industry or prestigious job title attractive without thinking of the key consideration: Would we enjoy performing the everyday tasks the position entails?

The second key consideration is that you are not merely choosing a career, but also a lifestyle. Career counselors indicate that one of the most common problems people encounter in jobseeking is that they fail to consider how well-suited they are for a particular position or career. For example, some people, attracted to management consulting by good salaries, early responsibility, and high-level corporate exposure, do not adapt well to the long hours, heavy travel demands, and constant pressure to produce. Be sure to ask yourself how you might adapt to the day-to-day duties and working environment that a specific position entails. Then ask yourself how you might adapt to the demands of that career or industry as a whole.

Choosing Your Strategy

Assuming that you've established your career objectives, the next step of the job search is to develop a strategy. If you don't take the time to develop a plan, you may find yourself going in circles after several weeks of randomly searching for opportunities that always seem just beyond your reach.

The most common jobseeking techniques are:

- following up on help-wanted advertisements (in the newspaper or online)
- using employment services
- relying on personal contacts
- contacting employers directly (the Direct Contact method)

Each of these approaches can lead to better jobs. However, the Direct Contact method boasts twice the success rate of the others. So unless you have specific reasons to employ other strategies, Direct Contact should form the foundation of your job search.

If you choose to use other methods as well, try to expend at least half your energy on Direct Contact. Millions of other jobseekers have already proven that Direct Contact has been twice as effective in obtaining employment, so why not follow in their footsteps?

Setting Your Schedule

Okay, so now that you've targeted a strategy it's time to work out the details of your job search. The most important detail is setting up a schedule. Of course, since job searches aren't something most people do regularly, it may be hard to estimate how long each step will take. Nonetheless, it is important to have a plan so that you can monitor your progress.

When outlining your job search schedule, have a realistic time frame in mind. If you will be job-searching full-time, your search could take at least two months or more. If you can only devote part-time effort, it will probably take at least four months.

You probably know a few people who seem to spend their whole lives searching for a better job in their spare time. Don't be one of them. If you are presently working and don't feel like devoting a lot of energy to jobseeking right now, then wait. Focus on enjoying your present position, performing your best on the job, and storing up energy for when you are really ready to begin your job search.

> **The first step in beginning your job search is to clearly define your objectives.**

Those of you who are currently unemployed should remember that *job-hunting is tough work, both physically and emotionally*. It is also intellectually demanding work that requires you to be at your best. So don't tire yourself out by working on your job campaign around the clock. At the same time, be sure to discipline yourself. The most logical way to manage your time while looking for a job is to keep your regular working hours.

If you are searching full-time and have decided to choose several different strategies, we recommend that you divide up each week, designating some time for each method. By trying several approaches at once, you can evaluate how promising each seems and alter your schedule accordingly. Keep in mind that the *majority of openings are filled without being advertised*. Remember also that positions advertised on the Internet are just as likely to already be filled as those found in the newspaper!

If you are searching part-time and decide to try several different contact methods, we recommend that you try them sequentially. You simply won't have enough time to put a meaningful amount of effort into more than one method at once. Estimate the length of your job search, and then allocate so many weeks or months for each contact method, beginning with Direct Contact. The purpose of setting this schedule is not to rush you to your goal but to help you periodically evaluate your progress.

The Direct Contact Method

Once you have scheduled your time, you are ready to begin your search in earnest. Beginning with the Direct Contact method, the first step is to develop a checklist for categorizing the types of firms for which you'd like to work. You might categorize firms by product line, size, customer type (such as industrial or consumer), growth prospects, or geographical location. Keep in mind, the shorter the list the easier it will be to locate a company that is right for you.

Next you will want to use this *JobBank* book to assemble your list of potential employers. Choose firms where *you* are most likely to be able to find a job. Try matching your skills with those that a specific job demands. Consider where your skills might be in demand, the degree of competition for employment, and the employment outlook at each company.

Separate your prospect list into three groups. The first 25 percent will be your primary target group, the next 25 percent will be your secondary group, and the remaining names will be your reserve group.

After you form your prospect list, begin working on your resume. Refer to the Resumes and Cover Letters section following this chapter for more information.

Once your resume is complete, begin researching your first batch of prospective employers. You will want to determine whether you would be happy working at the firms you are researching and to get a better idea of what their employment needs might be. You also need to obtain enough information to sound highly informed about the company during phone conversations and in mail correspondence. But don't go all out on your research yet! You probably won't be able to arrange interviews with some of these firms, so save your big research effort until you start to arrange interviews. Nevertheless, you should plan to spend several hours researching each firm. Do your research in batches to save time and energy. Start with this book, and find out what you can about each of the firms in your primary target group. For answers to specific questions, contact any pertinent professional associations that may be able to help you learn more about an employer. Read industry publications looking for articles on the firm. (Addresses of associations and names of important publications are listed after each section of employer listings in this book.) Then look up the company on the Internet or try additional resources at your local library. Keep organized, and maintain a folder on each firm.

> **The more you know about a company, the more likely you are to catch an interviewer's eye. (You'll also face fewer surprises once you get the job!)**

Information to look for includes: company size; president, CEO, or owner's name; when the company was established; what each division does; and benefits that are important to you. An abundance of company information can now be found electronically, through the World Wide Web or commercial online services. Researching companies online is a convenient means of obtaining information quickly and easily. If you have access to the Internet, you can search from your home at any time of day.

You may search a particular company's Website for current information that may be otherwise unavailable in print. In fact, many companies that maintain a site update their information daily. In addition, you may also search articles written about the company online. Today, most of the nation's largest newspapers, magazines, trade publications, and regional business periodicals have online versions of their publications. To find additional resources, use a search engine like Yahoo! or Alta Vista and type in the keyword "companies" or "employers."

If you discover something that really disturbs you about the firm (they are about to close their only local office), or if you discover that your chances of getting a job there are practically nil (they have just instituted a hiring freeze), then cross them off your prospect list. If possible, supplement your research efforts by contacting individuals who know the firm well. Ideally you should make an informal contact with someone at that particular firm, but often a direct competitor or a major customer will be able to supply you with just as much information. At the very least, try to obtain whatever printed information the company has available — not just annual reports, but product brochures, company profiles, or catalogs. This information is often available on the Internet.

Getting the Interview

Now it is time to make Direct Contact with the goal of arranging interviews. If you have read any books on job-searching, you may have noticed that most of these books tell you to avoid the human resources office like the plague. It is said that the human resources office never hires people; they screen candidates. Unfortunately, this is often the case. If you can identify the appropriate manager with the authority to hire you, you should try to contact that person directly.

The obvious means of initiating Direct Contact are:

- Mail (postal or electronic)
- Phone calls

Mail contact is a good choice if you have not been in the job market for a while. You can take your time to prepare a letter, say exactly what you want, and of course include your resume. Remember that employers receive many resumes every day. Don't be surprised if you do not get a response to your inquiry, *and don't spend weeks waiting for responses that may never come.* If you do send a letter, follow it up (or precede it) with a phone call. This will increase your impact, and because of the initial research you did, will underscore both your familiarity with and your interest in the firm. Bear in mind that your goal is to make your name a familiar one with prospective employers, so that when a position becomes available, your resume will be one of the first the hiring manager seeks out.

DEVELOPING YOUR CONTACTS: NETWORKING

Some career counselors feel that the best route to a better job is through somebody you already know or through somebody to whom you can be introduced. These counselors recommend that you build your contact base beyond your current acquaintances by asking each one to introduce you, or refer you, to additional people in your field of interest.

The theory goes like this: You might start with 15 personal contacts, each of whom introduces you to three additional people, for a total of 45 additional contacts. Then each of these people introduces you to three additional people, which adds 135 additional contacts. Theoretically, you will soon know every person in the industry.

Of course, developing your personal contacts does not work quite as smoothly as the theory suggests because some people will not be able to introduce you to anyone. The further you stray from your initial contact base, the weaker your references may be. So, if you do try developing your own contacts, try to begin with as many people that you know personally as you can. Dig into your personal phone book and your holiday greeting card list and locate old classmates from school. Be particularly sure to approach people who perform your personal business such as your lawyer, accountant, banker, doctor, stockbroker, and insurance agent. These people develop a very broad contact base due to the nature of their professions.

If you send a fax, always follow with a hard copy of your resume and cover letter in the mail. Often, through no fault of your own, a fax will come through illegibly and employers do not often have time to let candidates know.

Another alternative is to make a "cover call." Your cover call should be just like your cover letter: concise. Your first statement should interest the employer in you. Then try to subtly mention your familiarity with the firm. Don't be overbearing; keep your introduction to three sentences or less. Be pleasant, self-confident, and relaxed. This will greatly increase the chances of the person at the other end of the line developing the conversation. But don't press. If you are asked to follow up with "something in the mail," this signals the conversation's natural end. Don't try to prolong the conversation once it has ended, and don't ask what they want to receive in the mail. Always send your resume and a highly personalized follow-up letter, reminding the addressee of the phone conversation. *Always* include a cover letter if you are asked to send a resume, and treat your resume and cover letter as a total package. Gear your letter toward the specific position you are applying for and prove why you would be a "good match" for the position.

> **Always include a cover letter if you are asked to send a resume.**

Unless you are in telephone sales, making smooth and relaxed cover calls will probably not come easily. Practice them on your own, and then with your friends or relatives.

DON'T BOTHER WITH MASS MAILINGS OR BARRAGES OF PHONE CALLS

Direct Contact does not mean burying every firm within a hundred miles with mail and phone calls. Mass mailings rarely work in the job hunt. This also applies to those letters that are personalized -- but dehumanized -- on an automatic typewriter or computer. Don't waste your time or money on such a project; you will fool no one but yourself.

The worst part of sending out mass mailings, or making unplanned phone calls to companies you have not researched, is that you are likely to be remembered as someone with little genuine interest in the firm, who lacks sincerity -- somebody that nobody wants to hire.

If you obtain an interview as a result of a telephone conversation, be sure to send a thank-you note reiterating the points you made during the conversation. You will appear more professional and increase your impact. However, unless specifically requested, don't mail your resume once an interview has been arranged. Take it with you to the interview instead.

You should never show up to seek a professional position without an appointment. Even if you are somehow lucky enough to obtain an interview, you will appear so unprofessional that you will not be seriously considered.

HELP WANTED ADVERTISEMENTS

Only a small fraction of professional job openings are advertised. Yet the majority of jobseekers -- and quite a few people not in the job market -- spend a lot of time studying the help wanted ads. As a result, the competition for advertised openings is often very severe.

A moderate-sized employer told us about their experience advertising in the help wanted section of a major Sunday newspaper:

It was a disaster. We had over 500 responses from this relatively small ad in just one week. We have only two phone lines in this office and one was totally knocked out. We'll never advertise for professional help again.

If you insist on following up on help wanted ads, then research a firm before you reply to an ad. Preliminary research might help to separate you from all of the other professionals responding to that ad, many of whom will have only a passing interest in the opportunity. It will also give you insight about a particular firm, to help you determine if it is potentially a good match. That said, your chances of obtaining a job through the want ads are still much smaller than they are with the Direct Contact method.

Preparing for the Interview

As each interview is arranged, begin your in-depth research. You should arrive at an interview knowing the company upside-down and inside-out. You need to know the company's products, types of customers, subsidiaries, parent company, principal locations, rank in the industry, sales and profit trends, type of ownership, size, current plans, and much more. By this time you have probably narrowed your job search to one industry. Even if you haven't, you should still be familiar with common industry terms, the trends in the firm's industry, the firm's principal competitors and their relative performance, and the direction in which the industry leaders are headed.

Dig into every resource you can! Surf the Internet. Read the company literature, the trade press, the business press, and if the company is public, call your stockbroker (if you have one) and ask for additional information. If possible, speak to someone at the firm before the interview, or if not, speak to someone at a competing firm. The more time you spend, the better. Even if you feel extremely pressed for time, you should set aside several hours for pre-interview research.

> **You should arrive at an interview knowing the company upside-down and inside-out.**

If you have been out of the job market for some time, don't be surprised if you find yourself tense during your first few interviews. It will probably happen every time you re-enter the market, not just when you seek your first job after getting out of school.

Tension is natural during an interview, but knowing you have done a thorough research job should put you more at ease. Make a list of questions that you think might be asked in each interview. Think out your answers carefully and practice them with a friend. Tape record your responses to the problem questions. (See also in this chapter: Informational Interviews.) If you feel particularly unsure of your interviewing skills, arrange your first interviews at firms you are not as interested in. (But remember it is common courtesy to seem enthusiastic about the possibility of working for any firm at which you interview.) Practice again on your own after these first few interviews. Go over the difficult questions that you were asked.

Take some time to really think about how you will convey your work history. Present "bad experiences" as "learning experiences." Instead of saying "I hated my position as a salesperson because I had to bother people on the phone," say "I realized that cold-calling was not my strong suit. Though I love working with people, I decided my talents would be best used in a more face-to-face atmosphere." Always find some sort of lesson from previous jobs, as they all have one.

Interview Attire

How important is the proper dress for a job interview? Buying a complete wardrobe, donning new shoes, and having your hair styled every morning are not enough to guarantee you a career position as an investment banker. But on the other hand, if you can't find a clean, conservative suit or won't take the time to wash your hair, then you are just wasting your time by interviewing at all.

Personal grooming is as important as finding appropriate clothes for a job interview. Careful grooming indicates both a sense of thoroughness and self-confidence. This is not the time to make a statement – take out the extra earrings and avoid any garish hair colors not found in nature. Women should not wear excessive makeup, and both men and women should refrain from wearing any perfume or cologne (it only takes a small spritz to leave an allergic interviewer with a fit of sneezing and a bad impression of your meeting). Men should be freshly shaven, even if the interview is late in the day, and men with long hair should have it pulled back and neat.

Men applying for any professional position should wear a suit, preferably in a conservative color such as navy or charcoal gray. It is easy to get away with wearing the same dark suit to consecutive interviews at the same company; just be sure to wear a different shirt and tie for each interview.

Women should also wear a business suit. Professionalism still dictates a suit with a skirt, rather than slacks, as proper interview garb for women. This is usually true even at companies where pants are acceptable attire for female employees. As much as you may disagree with this guideline, the more prudent time to fight this standard is after you land the job.

The final selection of candidates for a job opening won't be determined by dress, of course. However, inappropriate dress can quickly eliminate a first-round candidate. So while you shouldn't spend a fortune on a new wardrobe, you should be sure that your clothes are adequate. The key is to dress at least as formally or slightly more formally and more conservatively than the position would suggest.

What to Bring

Be complete. Everyone needs a watch, a pen, and a notepad. Finally, a briefcase or a leather-bound folder (containing extra, unfolded, copies of your resume) will help complete the look of professionalism.

Sometimes the interviewer will be running behind schedule. Don't be upset, be sympathetic. There is often pressure to interview a lot of candidates and to quickly fill a demanding position. So be sure to come to your interview with good reading material to keep yourself occupied and relaxed.

The Interview

The very beginning of the interview is the most important part because it determines the tone for the rest of it. Those first few moments are especially crucial. Do you smile when you meet? Do you establish enough eye contact, but not too much? Do you walk into the office with a self-assured and confident stride? Do you shake hands firmly? Do you make small talk easily without being garrulous? It is

---

BE PREPARED:
Some Common Interview Questions

Tell me about yourself.

Why did you leave your last job?

What excites you in your current job?

Where would you like to be in five years?

How much overtime are you willing to work?

What would your previous/present employer tell me about you?

Tell me about a difficult situation that you
faced at your previous/present job.

What are your greatest strengths?

What are your weaknesses?

Describe a work situation where you took initiative
and went beyond your normal responsibilities.

Why should we hire you?

---

human nature to judge people by that first impression, so make sure it is a good one. But most of all, try to be yourself.

Often the interviewer will begin, after the small talk, by telling you about the company, the division, the department, or perhaps, the position. Because of your detailed research, the information about the company should be repetitive for you, and the interviewer would probably like nothing better than to avoid this regurgitation of the company biography. So if you can do so tactfully, indicate to the interviewer that you are very familiar with the firm. If he or she seems intent on providing you with background information, despite your hints, then acquiesce.

But be sure to remain attentive. If you can manage to generate a brief discussion of the company or the industry at this point, without being forceful, great. It will help to further build rapport, underscore your interest, and increase your impact.

> # The interviewer's job is to find a reason to turn you down; your job is to not provide that reason.
>
> -John L. LaFevre, author,
> *How You Really Get Hired*
>
> Reprinted from the 1989/90 *CPC Annual,* with permission of the National Association of Colleges and Employers (formerly College Placement Council, Inc.), copyright holder.

Soon (if it didn't begin that way) the interviewer will begin the questions, many of which you will have already practiced. This period of the interview usually falls into one of two categories (or somewhere in between): either a structured interview, where the interviewer has a prescribed set of questions to ask; or an unstructured interview, where the interviewer will ask only leading questions to get you to talk about yourself, your experiences, and your goals. Try to sense as quickly as possible in which direction the interviewer wishes to proceed. This will make the interviewer feel more relaxed and in control of the situation.

Remember to keep attuned to the interviewer and make the length of your answers appropriate to the situation. If you are really unsure as to how detailed a response the interviewer is seeking, then ask.

As the interview progresses, the interviewer will probably mention some of the most important responsibilities of the position. If applicable, draw parallels between your experience and the demands of the position as detailed by the interviewer. Describe your past experience in the same manner that you do on your resume: emphasizing results and achievements and not merely describing activities. But don't exaggerate. Be on the level about your abilities.

The first interview is often the toughest, where many candidates are screened out. If you are interviewing for a very competitive position, you will have to make an impression that will last. Focus on a few of your greatest strengths that are relevant to the position. Develop these points carefully, state them again in different words, and then try to summarize them briefly at the end of the interview.

Often the interviewer will pause toward the end and ask if you have any questions. Particularly in a structured interview, this might be the one chance to really show your knowledge of and interest in the firm. Have a list prepared of specific questions that are of real interest to you. Let your questions subtly show your research and your knowledge of the firm's activities. It is wise to have an extensive list of questions, as several of them may be answered during the interview.

Do not turn your opportunity to ask questions into an interrogation. Avoid reading directly from your list of questions, and ask questions that you are fairly certain the interviewer can answer (remember how you feel when you cannot answer a question during an interview).

Even if you are unable to determine the salary range beforehand, do not ask about it during the first interview. You can always ask later. Above all, don't ask about fringe benefits until you have been offered a position. (Then be sure to get all the details.)

Try not to be negative about anything during the interview, particularly any past employer or any previous job. Be cheerful. Everyone likes to work with someone who seems to be happy. Even if you detest your current/former job or manager, do not make disparaging comments. The interviewer may construe this as a sign of a potential attitude problem and not consider you a strong candidate.

Don't let a tough question throw you off base. If you don't know the answer to a question, simply say so – do not apologize. Just smile. Nobody can answer every question – particularly some of the questions that are asked in job interviews.

Before your first interview, you may be able to determine how many rounds of interviews there usually are for positions at your level. (Of course it may differ quite a bit even within the different levels of one firm.) Usually you can count on attending at least two or three interviews, although some firms are known to give a minimum of six interviews for all professional positions. While you should be more relaxed as you return for subsequent interviews, the pressure will be on. The more prepared you are, the better.

Depending on what information you are able to obtain, you might want to vary your strategy quite a bit from interview to interview. For instance, if the first interview is a screening interview, then be sure a few of your strengths really stand out. On the other hand, if later interviews are primarily with people who are in a position to veto your hiring, but not to push it forward, then you should primarily focus on building rapport as opposed to reiterating and developing your key strengths.

If it looks as though your skills and background do not match the position the interviewer was hoping to fill, ask him or her if there is another division or subsidiary that perhaps could profit from your talents.

After the Interview

Write a follow-up letter immediately after the interview, while it is still fresh in the interviewer's mind (see the sample follow-up letter format found in the Resumes and Cover Letters chapter). Not only is this a thank-you, but it also gives you the chance to provide the interviewer with any details you may have forgotten (as long as they can be tactfully added in). If you haven't heard back from the interviewer within a week of sending your thank-you letter, call to stress your continued interest in the firm and the position. If you lost any points during the interview for any reason, this letter can help you regain footing. Be polite and make sure to stress your continued interest and competency to fill the position. Just don't forget to proofread it thoroughly. If you are unsure of the spelling of the interviewer's name, call the receptionist and ask.

THE BALANCING ACT:
Looking for a New Job While Currently Employed

For those of you who are still employed, job-searching will be particularly tiring because it must be done in addition to your normal work responsibilities. So don't overwork yourself to the point where you show up to interviews looking exhausted or start to slip behind at your current job. On the other hand, don't be tempted to quit your present job! The long hours are worth it. Searching for a job while you have one puts you in a position of strength.

Making Contact

If you must be at your office during the business day, then you have additional problems to deal with. How can you work interviews into the business day? And if you work in an open office, how can you even call to set up interviews? Obviously, you should keep up the effort and the appearances on your present job. So maximize your use of the lunch hour, early mornings, and late afternoons for calling. If you keep trying, you'll be surprised how often you will be able to reach the executive you are trying to contact during your out-of-office hours. You can catch people as early as 8 a.m. and as late as 6 p.m. on frequent occasions.

Scheduling Interviews

Your inability to interview at any time other than lunch just might work to your advantage. If you can, try to set up as many interviews as possible for your lunch hour. This will go a long way to creating a relaxed atmosphere. But be sure the interviews don't stray too far from the agenda on hand.

Lunchtime interviews are much easier to obtain if you have substantial career experience. People with less experience will often find no alternative to taking time off for interviews. If you have to take time off, you have to take time off. But try to do this as little as possible. Try to take the whole day off in order to avoid being blatantly obvious about your job search, and try to schedule two to three interviews for the same day. (It is very difficult to maintain an optimum level of energy at more than three interviews in one day.) Explain to the interviewer why you might have to juggle your interview schedule; he/she should honor the respect you're showing your current employer by minimizing your days off and will probably appreciate the fact that another prospective employer is interested in you.

> **Try calling as early as 8 a.m. and as late as 6 p.m. You'll be surprised how often you will be able to reach the executive you want during these times of the day.**

References

What do you tell an interviewer who asks for references from your current employer? Just say that while you are happy to have your former employers contacted, you are trying to keep your job search confidential and would rather that your current employer not be contacted until you have been given a firm offer.

IF YOU'RE FIRED OR LAID OFF:
Picking Yourself Up and Dusting Yourself Off

If you've been fired or laid off, you are not the first and will not be the last to go through this traumatic experience. In today's changing economy, thousands of professionals lose their jobs every year. Even if you were terminated with just cause, do not lose heart. Remember, being fired is not a reflection on you as a person. It is usually a reflection of your company's staffing needs and its perception of your recent job performance and attitude. And if you were not performing up to par or enjoying your work, then you will probably be better off at another company anyway.

> **Be prepared for the question "Why were you fired?" during job interviews.**

A thorough job search could take months, so be sure to negotiate a reasonable severance package, if possible, and determine to what benefits, such as health insurance, you are still legally entitled. Also, register for unemployment compensation immediately. Don't be surprised to find other professionals collecting unemployment compensation – it is for everyone who has lost their job.

Don't start your job search with a flurry of unplanned activity. Start by choosing a strategy and working out a plan. Now is not the time for major changes in your life. If possible, remain in the same career and in the same geographical location, at least until you have been working again for a while. On the other hand, if the only industry for which you are trained is leaving, or is severely depressed in your area, then you should give prompt consideration to moving or switching careers.

Avoid mentioning you were fired when arranging interviews, but be prepared for the question "Why were you fired?" during an interview. If you were laid off as a result of downsizing, briefly explain, being sure to reinforce that your job loss was not due to performance. If you were in fact fired, be honest, but try to detail the reason as favorably as possible and portray what you have learned from your mistakes. If you are confident one of your past managers will give you a good reference, tell the interviewer to contact that person. Do not to speak negatively of your past employer and try not to sound particularly worried about your status of being temporarily unemployed.

Finally, don't spend too much time reflecting on why you were let go or how you might have avoided it. Think positively, look to the future, and be sure to follow a careful plan during your job search.

THE COLLEGE STUDENT:
Conducting Your First Job Search

While you will be able to apply many of the basics covered earlier in this chapter to your job search, there are some situations unique to the college student's job search.

THE GPA QUESTION

You are interviewing for the job of your dreams. Everything is going well: You've established a good rapport, the interviewer seems impressed with your qualifications, and you're almost positive the job is yours. Then you're asked about your GPA, which is pitifully low. Do you tell the truth and watch your dream job fly out the window?

Never lie about your GPA (they may request your transcript, and no company will hire a liar). You can, however, explain if there is a reason you don't feel your grades reflect your abilities, and mention any other impressive statistics. For example, if you have a high GPA in your major, or in the last few semesters (as opposed to your cumulative college career), you can use that fact to your advantage.

Perhaps the biggest problem college students face is lack of experience. Many schools have internship programs designed to give students exposure to the field of their choice, as well as the opportunity to make valuable contacts. Check out your school's career services department to see what internships are available. If your school does not have a formal internship program, or if there are no available internships that appeal to you, try contacting local businesses and offering your services. Often, businesses will be more than willing to have an extra pair of hands (especially if those hands are unpaid!) for a day or two each week. Or try contacting school alumni to see if you can "shadow" them for a few days, and see what their daily duties are like.

Informational Interviews

Although many jobseekers do not do this, it can be extremely helpful to arrange an informational interview with a college alumnus or someone else who works in your desired industry. You interview them about their job, their company, and their industry with questions you have prepared in advance. This can be done over the phone but is usually done in person. This will provide you with a contact in the industry who may give you more valuable information – or perhaps even a job opportunity -- in the future. Always follow up with a thank you letter that includes your contact information.

> *The goal is to try to begin building experience and establishing contacts as early as possible in your college career.*

What do you do if, for whatever reason, you weren't able to get experience directly related to your desired career? First, look at your previous jobs and see if there's anything you can highlight. Did you supervise or train other employees? Did you reorganize the accounting system, or boost productivity in some way? Accomplishments like these demonstrate leadership, responsibility, and innovation - - qualities that most companies look for in employees. And don't forget volunteer activities and school clubs, which can also showcase these traits.

On-Campus Recruiting

Companies will often send recruiters to interview on-site at various colleges. This gives students a chance to interview with companies that may not have interviewed them otherwise. This is particularly true if a company schedules "open" interviews, in which the only screening process is who is first in line at the sign-ups. Of course, since many more applicants gain interviews in this format, this also means that many more people are rejected. The on-campus interview is generally a screening interview, to see if it is worth the company's time to invite you in for a second interview. So do everything possible to make yourself stand out from the crowd.

The first step, of course, is to check out any and all information your school's career center has on the company. If the information seems out of date, check out the company on the Internet or call the company's headquarters and ask for any printed information.

Many companies will host an informational meeting for interviewees, often the evening before interviews are scheduled to take place. DO NOT MISS THIS MEETING. The recruiter will almost certainly ask if you attended. Make an effort to stay after the meeting and talk with the company's representatives. Not only does this give you an opportunity to find out more information about both the company and the position, it also makes you stand out in the recruiter's mind. If there's a particular company that you had your heart set on, but you weren't able to get an interview with them, attend the information session anyway. You may be able to persuade the recruiter to squeeze you into the schedule. (Or you may discover that the company really isn't the right fit for you after all.)

Try to check out the interview site beforehand. Some colleges may conduct "mock" interviews that take place in one of the standard interview rooms. Or you may be able to convince a career counselor (or even a custodian) to let you sneak a peek during off-hours. Either way, having an idea of the room's setup will help you to mentally prepare.

Arrive at least 15 minutes early to the interview. The recruiter may be ahead of schedule, and might meet you early. But don't be surprised if previous interviews have run over, resulting in your 30-minute slot being reduced to 20 minutes (or less). Don't complain or appear anxious; just use the time you do have as efficiently as possible to showcase the reasons *you* are the ideal candidate. Staying calm and composed in these situations will work to your advantage.

LAST WORDS

A parting word of advice. Again and again during your job search you will face rejection. You will be rejected when you apply for interviews. You will be rejected after interviews. For every job offer you finally receive, you probably will have been rejected many times. Don't let rejections slow you down. Keep reminding yourself that the sooner you go out, start your job search, and get those rejections flowing in, the closer you will be to obtaining the job you want.

RESUMES AND COVER LETTERS

When filling a position, an employer will often have 100-plus applicants, but time to interview only a handful of the most promising ones. As a result, he or she will reject most applicants after only briefly skimming their resumes.

Unless you have phoned and talked to the employer – which you should do whenever you can – you will be chosen or rejected for an interview entirely on the basis of your resume and cover letter. *Your cover letter must catch the employer's attention, and your resume must hold it.* (But remember – a resume is no substitute for a job search campaign. *You* must seek a job. Your resume is only one tool, albeit a critical one.)

RESUME FORMAT:
Mechanics of a First Impression

The Basics

Employers dislike long resumes, so unless you have an unusually strong background with many years of experience and a diversity of outstanding achievements, keep your resume length to one page. If you must squeeze in more information than would otherwise fit, try using a smaller typeface or changing the margins. Watch also for "widows" at the end of paragraphs. You can often free up some space if you can shorten the information enough to get rid of those single words taking up an entire line. Another tactic that works with some word processing programs is to decrease the font size of your paragraph returns and changing the spacing between lines.

Print your resume on standard 8 1/2" x 11" paper. Since recruiters often get resumes in batches of hundreds, a smaller-sized resume may be lost in the pile. Oversized resumes are likely to get crumpled at the edges, and won't fit easily in their files.

First impressions matter, so make sure the recruiter's first impression of your resume is a good one. Never hand-write your resume (or cover letter)! Print your resume on quality paper that has weight and texture, in a conservative color such as white, ivory, or pale gray. Good resume paper is easy to find at many stores that sell stationery or office products. It is even available at some drug stores. Use *matching* paper and envelopes for both your resume and cover letter. One hiring manager at a major magazine throws out all resumes that arrive on paper that differs in color from the envelope!

Do not buy paper with images of clouds and rainbows in the background or anything that looks like casual stationery that you would send to your favorite aunt. Do not spray perfume or cologne on your resume. Do not include your picture with your resume unless you have a specific and appropriate reason to do so.

Another tip: Do a test print of your resume (and cover letter), to make sure the watermark is on the same side as the text so that you can read it. Also make sure it is right-side up. As trivial as this may sound, some recruiters check for this! One recruiter at a law firm in New Hampshire sheepishly admitted this is the first thing he checks. *"I open each envelope and check the watermarks on the resume and cover letter. Those candidates that have it wrong go into a different pile."*

Getting it on Paper

Modern photocomposition typesetting gives you the clearest, sharpest image, a wide variety of type styles, and effects such as italics, bold-facing, and book-like justified margins. It is also too expensive for many jobseekers. The quality of today's laser printers means that a computer-generated resume can look just as impressive as one that has been professionally typeset.

A computer with a word processing or desktop publishing program is the most common way to generate your resume. This allows you the flexibility to make changes almost instantly and to store different drafts on disk. Word processing and desktop publishing programs also offer many different fonts to choose from, each taking up different amounts of space. (It is generally best to stay between 9-point and 12-point font size.) Many other options are also available, such as bold-facing or italicizing for emphasis and the ability to change and manipulate spacing. It is generally recommended to leave the right-hand margin unjustified as this keeps the spacing between the text even and therefore easier to read. It is not wrong to justify both margins of text, but if possible try it both ways before you decide.

For a resume on paper, the end result will be largely determined by the quality of the printer you use. Laser printers will generally provide the best quality. Do not use a dot matrix printer.

Many companies now use scanning equipment to screen the resumes they receive, and certain paper, fonts, and other features are more compatible with this technology. White paper is preferable, as well as a standard font such as Courier or Helvetica. You should use at least a 10-point font, and avoid bolding, italics, underlining, borders, boxes, or graphics.

Household typewriters and office typewriters with nylon or other cloth ribbons are *not* good enough for typing your resume. If you don't have access to a quality word processing program, hire a professional with the resources to prepare your resume for you. Keep in mind that businesses such as Kinko's (open 24 hours) provide access to computers with quality printers.

Don't make your copies on an office photocopier. Only the human resources office may see the resume you mail. Everyone else may see only a copy of it, and copies of copies quickly become unreadable. Furthermore, sending photocopies of your resume or cover letter is completely unprofessional. Either print out each copy individually, or take your resume to a professional copy shop, which will generally offer professionally-maintained, extra-high-quality photocopiers and charge fairly reasonable prices. You want your resume to represent you with the look of polished quality.

Proof with Care

Whether you typed it or paid to have it produced professionally, mistakes on resumes are not only embarrassing, but will usually remove you from consideration (particularly if something obvious such as your name is misspelled). No matter how much you paid someone else to type, write, or typeset your resume, *you* lose if there is a mistake. So proofread it as carefully as possible. Get a friend to help you. Read your draft aloud as your friend checks the proof copy. Then have your friend read aloud while you check. Next, read it letter by letter to check spelling and punctuation.

If you are having it typed or typeset by a resume service or a printer, and you don't have time to proof it, pay for it and take it home. Proof it there and bring it back later to get it corrected and printed.

If you wrote your resume with a word processing program, use the built-in spell checker to double-check for spelling errors. Keep in mind that a spell checker will not find errors such as "to" for "two" or "wok" for "work." Many spell check programs do not recognize missing or misused punctuation, nor are they set to check the spelling of capitalized words. It's important that you still proofread your resume to check for grammatical mistakes and other problems, even after it has been spellchecked. If you find mistakes, do not make edits in pen or pencil or use white-out to fix them on the final copy!

Electronic Resumes

As companies rely increasingly on emerging technologies to find qualified candidates for job openings, you may opt to create an electronic resume in order to remain competitive in today's job market. Why is this important? Companies today sometimes request that resumes be submitted by e-mail, and many hiring managers regularly check online resume databases for candidates to fill unadvertised job openings. Other companies enlist the services of electronic employment database services, which charge jobseekers a nominal fee to have their resumes posted to the database to be viewed by potential employers. Still other companies use their own automated applicant tracking systems, in which case your resume is fed through a scanner that sends the image to a computer that "reads" your resume, looking for keywords, and files it accordingly in its database.

Whether you're posting your resume online, e-mailing it directly to an employer, sending it to an electronic employment database, or sending it to a company you suspect uses an automated applicant tracking system, you must create some form of electronic resume to take advantage of the technology. Don't panic! An electronic resume is simply a modified version of your conventional resume. An electronic resume is one that is sparsely formatted, but filled with keywords and important facts.

In order to post your resume to the Internet – either to an online resume database or through direct e-mail to an employer – you will need to change the way your resume is formatted. Instead of a Word, WordPerfect, or other word processing document, save your resume as a plain text, DOS, or ASCII file. These three terms are basically interchangeable, and describe text at its simplest, most basic level, without the formatting such as boldface or italics that most jobseekers use to make their resumes look more interesting. If you use e-mail, you'll notice that all of your messages are written and received in this format. First, you should remove all formatting from your resume including boldface, italics, underlining, bullets, differing font sizes, and graphics. Then, convert and save your resume as a plain text file. Most word processing programs have a "save as" feature that allows you to save files in different formats. Here, you should choose "text only" or "plain text."

Another option is to create a resume in HTML (hypertext markup language), the text formatting language used to publish information on the World Wide Web. However, the real usefulness of HTML resumes is still being explored. Most of the major online databases do not accept HTML resumes, and the vast majority of companies only accept plain text resumes through their e-mail.

Finally, if you simply wish to send your resume to an electronic employment database or a company that uses an automated applicant tracking system, there is no need to convert your resume to a plain text file. The only change you need to make is to organize the information in your resume by keywords. Employers are likely to do keyword searches for information, such as degree held or knowledge of particular types of software. Therefore, using the right keywords or key phrases in your resume is critical to its ultimate success. Keywords are usually nouns or short phrases that the computer searches for which refer to experience, training, skills, and abilities. For example, let's say an employer searches an employment database for a sales representative with the following criteria:

BS/BA
exceeded quota
cold calls
high energy
willing to travel

Even if you have the right qualifications, neglecting to use these keywords would result in the computer passing over your resume. Although there is no way to know for sure which keywords employers are most likely to search for, you can make educated guesses by checking the help-wanted ads or online job postings for your type of job. You should also arrange keywords in a keyword summary, a paragraph listing your qualifications that immediately follows your name and address (see sample letter in this chapter). In addition, choose a nondecorative font with clear, distinct characters, such as Helvetica or Times. It is more difficult for a scanner to accurately pick up the more unusual fonts. Boldface and all capital letters are best used only for major section headings, such as "Experience" and "Education." It is also best to avoid using italics or underlining, since this can cause the letters to bleed into one another.

For more specific information on creating and sending electronic resumes, see *The Adams Internet Job Search Almanac.*

Types of Resumes

The most common resume formats are the functional resume, the chronological resume, and the combination resume. (Examples can be found at the end of this chapter.) A functional resume focuses on skills and de-emphasizes job titles, employers, etc. A functional resume is best if you have been out of the work force for a long time or are changing careers. It is also good if you want to highlight specific skills and strengths, especially if all of your work experience has been at one company. This format can also be a good choice if you are just out of school or have no experience in your desired field.

Choose a chronological format if you are currently working or were working recently, and if your most recent experiences relate to your desired field. Use reverse chronological order and include dates. To a recruiter your last job and your latest schooling are the most important, so put the last first and list the rest going back in time.

A combination resume is perhaps the most common. This resume simply combines elements of the functional and chronological resume formats. This is used by many jobseekers with a solid track record who find elements of both types useful.

Organization

Your name, phone number, e-mail address (if you have one), and a complete mailing address should be at the top of your resume. Try to make your name stand out by using a slightly larger font size or all capital letters. Be sure to spell out everything. Never abbreviate St. for Street or Rd. for Road. If you are a college student, you should also put your home address and phone number at the top.

Change your message on your answering machine if necessary – RUSH blaring in the background or your sorority sisters screaming may not come across well to all recruiters. If you think you may be moving within six months then include a second address and phone number of a trusted friend or relative who can reach you no matter where you are.

Remember that employers will keep your resume on file and may contact you months later if a position opens that fits your qualifications. All too often, candidates are unreachable because they have moved and had not previously provided enough contact options on their resume.

Next, list your experience, then your education. If you are a recent graduate, list your education first, unless your experience is more important than your education. (For example, if you have just graduated from a teaching school, have some business experience, and are applying for a job in business, you would list your business experience first.)

Keep everything easy to find. Put the dates of your employment and education on the left of the page. Put the names of the companies you worked for and the schools you attended a few spaces to the right of the dates. Put the city and state, or the city and country, where you studied or worked to the right of the page.

The important thing is simply to break up the text in some logical way that makes your resume visually attractive and easy to scan, so experiment to see which layout works best for your resume. However you set it up, *stay consistent.* Inconsistencies in fonts, spacing, or tenses will make your resume look sloppy. Also, be sure to use tabs to keep your information vertically lined up, rather than the less precise space bar.

RESUME CONTENT:
Say it with Style
Sell Yourself

You are selling your skills and accomplishments in your resume, so it is important to inventory yourself and know yourself. If you have achieved something, say so. Put it in the best possible light, but avoid subjective statements, such as "I am a hard worker" or "I get along well with my coworkers." Just stick to the facts.

While you shouldn't hold back or be modest, don't exaggerate your achievements to the point of misrepresentation. <u>Be honest</u>. Many companies will immediately drop an applicant from consideration (or fire a current employee) upon discovering inaccurate or untrue information on a resume or other application material.

Write down the important (and pertinent) things you have done, but do it in as few words as possible. Your resume will be scanned, not read, and short, concise phrases are much more effective than long-winded sentences. Avoid the use of "I" when emphasizing your accomplishments. Instead, use brief phrases beginning with action verbs.

While some technical terms will be unavoidable, you should try to avoid excessive "technicalese." Keep in mind that the first person to see your resume may be a human resources person who won't necessarily know all the jargon – and how can they be impressed by something they don't understand?

Keep it Brief

Also, try to hold your paragraphs to six lines or less. If you have more than six lines of information about one job or school, put it in two or more paragraphs. A short resume will be examined more carefully. Remember: Your resume usually has between eight and 45 seconds to catch an employer's eye. So make every second count.

Job Objective

A functional resume may require a job objective to give it focus. One or two sentences describing the job you are seeking can clarify in what capacity your skills will be best put to use. Be sure that your stated objective is in line with the position you're applying for.

Examples:

>An entry-level editorial assistant position in the publishing industry.
>A senior management position with a telecommunications firm.

Don't include a job objective on a chronological resume unless your previous work experiences are <u>completely</u> unrelated to the position for which you're applying. The presence of an overly specific job objective might eliminate you from consideration for other positions that a recruiter feels are a better match for your qualifications. But even if you don't put an objective on paper, having a career goal in mind as you write can help give your resume a solid sense of direction.

USE ACTION VERBS

How you write your resume is just as important as *what* you write. In describing previous work experiences, the strongest resumes use short phrases beginning with action verbs. Below are a few you may want to use. (This list is not all-inclusive.)

achieved	developed	integrated	purchased
administered	devised	interpreted	reduced
advised	directed	interviewed	regulated
arranged	distributed	launched	represented
assisted	established	managed	resolved
attained	evaluated	marketed	restored
budgeted	examined	mediated	restructured
built	executed	monitored	revised
calculated	expanded	negotiated	scheduled
collaborated	expedited	obtained	selected
collected	facilitated	operated	served
compiled	formulated	ordered	sold
completed	founded	organized	solved
computed	generated	participated	streamlined
conducted	headed	performed	studied
consolidated	identified	planned	supervised
constructed	implemented	prepared	supplied
consulted	improved	presented	supported
controlled	increased	processed	tested
coordinated	initiated	produced	trained
created	installed	proposed	updated
determined	instructed	published	wrote

Some jobseekers may choose to include both "Relevant Experience" and "Additional Experience" sections. This can be useful, as it allows the jobseeker to place more emphasis on certain experiences and to de-emphasize others.

Emphasize continued experience in a particular job area or continued interest in a particular industry. De-emphasize irrelevant positions. It is okay to include one opening line providing a general description of each company you've worked at. Delete positions that you held for less than four months (unless you are a very recent college grad or still in school). Stress your results and your achievements, elaborating on how you contributed in your previous jobs. Did you increase sales, reduce costs, improve a product, implement a new program? Were you promoted? Use specific numbers (i.e., quantities, percentages, dollar amounts) whenever possible.

Education

Keep it brief if you have more than two years of career experience. Elaborate more if you have less experience. If you are a recent college graduate, you may choose to include any high school activities that are directly relevant to your career. If you've been out of school for a while you don't need to list your education prior to college.

Mention degrees received and any honors or special awards. Note individual courses or projects you participated in that might be relevant for employers. For example, if you are an English major applying for a position as a business writer, be sure to mention any business or economics courses. Previous experience such as Editor-in-Chief of the school newspaper would be relevant as well.

If you are uploading your resume to an online job hunting site such as CareerCity.com, action verbs are still important, but the key words or key nouns that a computer would search for become more important. For example, if you're seeking an accounting position, key nouns that a computer would search for such as "Lotus 1-2-3" or "CPA" or "payroll" become very important.

Highlight Impressive Skills

Be sure to mention any computer skills you may have. You may wish to include a section entitled "Additional Skills" or "Computer Skills," in which you list any software programs you know. An additional skills section is also an ideal place to mention fluency in a foreign language.

Personal Data

This section is optional, but if you choose to include it, keep it brief. A one-word mention of hobbies such as fishing, chess, baseball, cooking, etc., can give the person who will interview you a good way to open up the conversation.

Team sports experience is looked at favorably. It doesn't hurt to include activities that are somewhat unusual (fencing, Akido, '70s music) or that somehow relate to the position or the company to which you're applying. For instance, it would be worth noting if you are a member of a professional organization in your industry of interest. Never include information about your age, alias, date of birth, health, physical characteristics, marital status, religious affiliation, or political/moral beliefs.

References

The most that is needed is the sentence "References available upon request" at the bottom of your resume. If you choose to leave it out, that's fine. This line is not really necessary. It is understood that references will most likely be asked for and provided by you later on in the interviewing process. Do not actually send references with your resume and cover letter unless specifically requested.

HIRING A RESUME WRITER:
Is it the Right Choice for You?

If you write reasonably well, it is to your advantage to write your own resume. Writing your resume forces you to review your experiences and figure out how to explain your accomplishments in clear, brief phrases. This will help you when you explain your work to interviewers. It is also easier to tailor your resume to each position you're applying for when you have put it together yourself.

If you write your resume, everything will be in your own words; it will sound like you. It will say what you want it to say. If you are a good writer, know yourself well, and have a good idea of which parts of your background employers are looking for, you should be able to write your own resume better than someone else. If you decide to write your resume yourself, have as many people as possible review and proofread it. Welcome objective opinions and other perspectives.

When to Get Help

If you have difficulty writing in "resume style" (which is quite unlike normal written language), if you are unsure which parts of your background to emphasize, or if you think your resume would make your case better if it did not follow one of the standard forms outlined either here or in a book on resumes, then you should consider having it professionally written.

Even some professional resume writers we know have had their resumes written with the help of fellow professionals. They sought the help of someone who could be objective about their background, as well as provide an experienced sounding board to help focus their thoughts.

If You Hire a Pro

The best way to choose a writer is by reputation: the recommendation of a friend, a personnel director, your school placement officer, or someone else knowledgeable in the field.

Important questions:
- "How long have you been writing resumes?"
- "If I'm not satisfied with what you write, will you go over it with me and change it?"
- "Do you charge by the hour or a flat rate?"

There is no sure relation between price and quality, except that you are unlikely to get a good writer for less than $50 for an uncomplicated resume and you shouldn't have to pay more than $300 unless your experience is very extensive or complicated. There will be additional charges for printing. Assume nothing no matter how much you pay. It is your career at stake if there are mistakes on your resume!

Few resume services will give you a firm price over the phone, simply because some resumes are too complicated and take too long to do for a predetermined price. Some services will quote you a price that applies to almost all of their customers. Once you decide to use a specific writer, you should insist on a firm price quote *before* engaging their services. Also, find out how expensive minor changes will be.

COVER LETTERS:
Quick, Clear, and Concise

Always mail a cover letter with your resume. In a cover letter you can show an interest in the company that you can't show in a resume. You can also point out one or two of your skills or accomplishments the company can put to good use.

Make it Personal

The more personal you can get, the better, so long as you keep it professional. If someone known to the person you are writing has recommended that you contact the company, get permission to include his/her name in the letter. If you can get the name of a person to send the letter to, address it directly to that person (after first calling the company to verify the spelling of the person's name, correct title, and mailing address). Be sure to put the person's name and title on both the letter and the envelope. This will ensure that your letter will get through to the proper person, even if a new person now occupies this position. It will not always be possible to get the name of a person. Always strive to get at least a title.

Be sure to mention something about why you have an interest in the company - - *so many candidates apply for jobs with no apparent knowledge of what the company does!* This conveys the message that they just want any job.

Type cover letters in full. Don't try the cheap and easy ways, like using a computer mail merge program or photocopying the body of your letter and typing in the inside address and salutation. You will give the impression that you are mailing to a host of companies and have no particular interest in any one.

Print your cover letter on the same color and same high-quality paper as your resume.

Cover letter basic format

<u>Paragraph 1:</u> State what the position is that you are seeking. It is not always necessary to state how you found out about the position – often you will apply without knowing that a position is open.

<u>Paragraph 2:</u> Include what you know about the company and why you are interested in working there. Mention any prior contact with the company or someone known to the hiring person if relevant. Briefly state your qualifications and what you can offer. (Do not talk about what you cannot do).

<u>Paragraph 3:</u> Close with your phone number and where/when you can be reached. Make a request for an interview. State when you will follow up by phone (or mail or e-mail if the ad requests no phone calls). Do not wait long – generally five working days. If you say you're going to follow up, then actually do it! This phone call can get your resume noticed when it might otherwise sit in a stack of 225 other resumes.

Cover letter do's and don'ts

- *Do* keep your cover letter brief and to the point.
- *Do* be sure it is error-free.
- *Do* accentuate what you can offer the company, not what you hope to gain.
- *Do* be sure your phone number and address is on your cover letter just in case it gets separated from your resume (this happens!).
- *Do* check the watermark by holding the paper up to a light – be sure it is facing forward so it is readable – on the same side as the text, and right-side up.
- *Do* sign your cover letter (or type your name if you are sending it electronically). Blue or black ink are both fine. Do not use red ink.
- *Don't* just repeat information verbatim from your resume.
- *Don't* overuse the personal pronoun "I."
- *Don't* send a generic cover letter – show your personal knowledge of and interest in that particular company.

THANK YOU LETTERS:
Another Way to Stand Out

As mentioned earlier, *always* send a thank you letter after an interview (see the sample later in this section). So few candidates do this and it is yet another way for you to stand out. Be sure to mention something specific from the interview and restate your interest in the company and the position.

It is generally acceptable to handwrite your thank you letter on a generic thank you card (but *never* a postcard). Make sure handwritten notes are neat and legible. However, if you are in doubt, typing your letter is always the safe bet. If you met with several people it is fine to send them each an individual thank you letter. Call the company if you need to check on the correct spelling of their names.

Remember to:
- Keep it short.
- Proofread it carefully.
- Send it *promptly.*

FUNCTIONAL RESUME

C.J. RAVENCLAW
129 Pennsylvania Avenue
Washington DC 20500
202/555-6652
e-mail: ravenclaw@dcpress.net

Objective
A position as a graphic designer commensurate with my acquired skills and expertise.

Summary
Extensive experience in plate making, separations, color matching, background definition, printing, mechanicals, color corrections, and personnel supervision. A highly motivated manager and effective communicator. Proven ability to:

- **Create Commercial Graphics**
- **Produce Embossed Drawings**
- **Color Separate**
- **Control Quality**
- **Resolve Printing Problems**
- **Analyze Customer Satisfaction**

Qualifications
Printing:
Knowledgeable in black and white as well as color printing. Excellent judgment in determining acceptability of color reproduction through comparison with original. Proficient at producing four- or five-color corrections on all media, as well as restyling previously reproduced four-color artwork.

Customer Relations:
Routinely work closely with customers to ensure specifications are met. Capable of striking a balance between technical printing capabilities and need for customer satisfaction through entire production process.

Specialties:
Practiced at creating silk screen overlays for a multitude of processes including velo bind, GBC bind, and perfect bind. Creative design and timely preparation of posters, flyers, and personalized stationery.

Personnel Supervision:
Skillful at fostering atmosphere that encourages highly talented artists to balance high-level creativity with maximum production. Consistently beat production deadlines. Instruct new employees, apprentices, and students in both artistry and technical operations.

Experience
Graphic Arts Professor, Ohio State University, Columbus OH (1992-1996).
Manager, Design Graphics, Washington DC (1997-present).

Education
Massachusetts Conservatory of Art, Ph.D. 1990
University of Massachusetts, B.A. 1988

CHRONOLOGICAL RESUME

HARRY SEABORN
557 Shoreline Drive
Seattle, WA 98404
(206) 555-6584
e-mail: hseaborn@centco.com

EXPERIENCE

THE CENTER COMPANY   Seattle, WA
Systems Programmer   1996-present
- Develop and maintain customer accounting and order tracking database using a Visual Basic front end and SQL server.
- Plan and implement migration of company wide transition from mainframe-based dumb terminals to a true client server environment using Windows NT Workstation and Server.
- Oversee general local and wide area network administration including the development of a variety of intranet modules to improve internal company communication and planning across divisions.

INFO TECH, INC.   Seattle, WA
Technical Manager   1994-1996
- Designed and managed the implementation of a network providing the legal community with a direct line to Supreme Court cases across the Internet using SQL Server and a variety of Internet tools.
- Developed a system to make the entire library catalog available on line using PERL scripts and SQL.
- Used Visual Basic and Microsoft Access to create a registration system for university registrar.

EDUCATION

SALEM STATE UNIVERSITY   Salem, OR
    M.S. in Computer Science.   1993
    B.S. in Computer Science.   1991

COMPUTER SKILLS

- Programming Languages: Visual Basic, Java, C++, SQL, PERL
- Software: SQL Server, Internet Information Server, Oracle
- Operating Systems: Windows NT, UNIX, Linux

FUNCTIONAL RESUME

Donna Hermione Moss
703 Wizard's Way
Chicago, IL 60601
(312) 555-8841
e-mail: donna@cowfire.com

OBJECTIVE:
To contribute over five years of experience in promotion, communications, and administration to an entry-level position in advertising.

SUMMARY OF QUALIFICATIONS:
- Performed advertising duties for small business.
- Experience in business writing and communications skills.
- General knowledge of office management.
- Demonstrated ability to work well with others, in both supervisory and support staff roles.
- Type 75 words per minute.

SELECTED ACHIEVEMENTS AND RESULTS:
Promotion:
Composing, editing, and proofreading correspondence and public relations materials for own catering service. Large-scale mailings.

Communication:
Instruction; curriculum and lesson planning; student evaluation; parent-teacher conferences; development of educational materials. Training and supervising clerks.

Computer Skills:
Proficient in MS Word, Lotus 1-2-3, Excel, and Filemaker Pro.

Administration:
Record-keeping and file maintenance. Data processing and computer operations, accounts receivable, accounts payable, inventory control, and customer relations. Scheduling, office management, and telephone reception.

PROFESSIONAL HISTORY:
Teacher; Self-Employed (owner of catering service); Floor Manager; Administrative Assistant; Accounting Clerk.

EDUCATION:
Beloit College, Beloit, WI, BA in Education, 1991

CHRONOLOGICAL RESUME

PERCY ZIEGLER
16 Josiah Court
Marlborough CT 06447
203/555-9641 (h)
203/555-8176, x14 (w)

EDUCATION
Keene State College, Keene NH
Bachelor of Arts in Elementary Education, 1998
- Graduated *magna cum laude*
- English minor
- Kappa Delta Pi member, inducted 1996

EXPERIENCE
September 1998-
Present
Elmer T. Thienes Elementary School, Marlborough CT
Part-time Kindergarten Teacher
- Instruct kindergartners in reading, spelling, language arts, and music.
- Participate in the selection of textbooks and learning aids.
- Organize and supervise class field trips and coordinate in-class presentations.

Summers
1995-1997
Keene YMCA, Youth Division, Keene NH
Child-care Counselor
- Oversaw summer program for low-income youth.
- Budgeted and coordinated special events and field trips, working with Program Director to initiate variations in the program.
- Served as Youth Advocate in cooperation with social worker to address the social needs and problems of participants.

Spring 1997
Wheelock Elementary School, Keene NH
Student Teacher
- Taught third-grade class in all elementary subjects.
- Designed and implemented a two-week unit on Native Americans.
- Assisted in revision of third-grade curriculum.

Fall 1996
Child Development Center, Keene NH
Daycare Worker
- Supervised preschool children on the playground and during art activities.
- Created a "Wishbone Corner," where children could quietly look at books or take a voluntary "time-out."

ADDITIONAL INTERESTS
Martial arts, Pokemon, politics, reading, skiing, writing.

ELECTRONIC RESUME

GRIFFIN DORE
69 Dursley Drive
Cambridge, MA 02138
(617) 555-5555

KEYWORD SUMMARY

Senior financial manager with over ten years experience in Accounting and Systems Management, Budgeting, Forecasting, Cost Containment, Financial Reporting, and International Accounting. MBA in Management. Proficient in Lotus, Excel, Solomon, and Windows.

EXPERIENCE

COLWELL CORPORATION, Wellesley, MA
Director of Accounting and Budgets, 1990 to present
    Direct staff of twenty in General Ledger, Accounts Payable, Accounts Receivable, and International Accounting.
    Facilitate month-end closing process with parent company and auditors.
    Implemented team-oriented cross-training program within accounting group, resulting in timely month-end closings and increased productivity of key accounting staff.
    Developed and implemented a strategy for Sales and Use Tax Compliance in all fifty states.
    Prepare monthly financial statements and analyses.

FRANKLIN AND DELANEY COMPANY, Melrose, MA
Senior Accountant, 1987-1990
    Managed Accounts Payable, General Ledger, transaction processing, and financial reporting. Supervised staff of five.

Staff Accountant, 1985-1987
    Managed Accounts Payable, including vouchering, cash disbursements, and bank reconciliation.
    Wrote and issued policies.
    Maintained supporting schedules used during year-end audits.
    Trained new employees.

EDUCATION

MBA in Management, Northeastern University, Boston, MA, 1989
BS in Accounting, Boston College, Boston, MA, 1985

ASSOCIATIONS

National Association of Accountants

GENERAL MODEL
FOR A COVER LETTER

Your mailing address
Date

Contact's name
Contact's title
Company
Company's mailing address

Dear Mr./Ms. _____:

Immediately explain why your background makes you the best candidate for the position that you are applying for. Describe what prompted you to write (want ad, article you read about the company, networking contact, etc.). Keep the first paragraph short and hard-hitting.

Detail what you could contribute to this company. Show how your qualifications will benefit this firm. Describe your interest in the corporation. Subtly emphasizing your knowledge about this firm and your familiarity with the industry will set you apart from other candidates. Remember to keep this letter short; few recruiters will read a cover letter longer than half a page.

If possible, your closing paragraph should request specific action on the part of the reader. Include your phone number and the hours when you can be reached. Mention that if you do not hear from the reader by a specific date, you will follow up with a phone call. Lastly, thank the reader for their time, consideration, etc.

Sincerely,

(signature)

Your full name (typed)

Enclosure (use this if there are other materials, such as your resume, that are included in the same envelope)

SAMPLE COVER LETTER

16 Josiah Court
Marlborough CT 06447
January 16, 2000

Ms. Leona Malfoy
Assistant Principal
Laningham Elementary School
43 Mayflower Drive
Keene NH 03431

Dear Ms. Malfoy:

Toby Potter recently informed me of a possible opening for a third grade teacher at Laningham Elementary School. With my experience instructing third-graders, both in schools and in summer programs, I feel I would be an ideal candidate for the position. Please accept this letter and the enclosed resume as my application.

Laningham's educational philosophy that every child can learn and succeed interests me, since it mirrors my own. My current position at Elmer T. Thienes Elementary has reinforced this philosophy, heightening my awareness of the different styles and paces of learning and increasing my sensitivity toward special needs children. Furthermore, as a direct result of my student teaching experience at Wheelock Elementary School, I am comfortable, confident, and knowledgeable working with third-graders.

I look forward to discussing the position and my qualifications for it in more detail. I can be reached at 203/555-9641 evenings or 203/555-8176, x14 weekdays. If I do not hear from you before Tuesday of next week, I will call to see if we can schedule a time to meet. Thank you for your time and consideration.

Sincerely,

Percy Ziegler

Percy Ziegler

Enclosure

GENERAL MODEL FOR A
THANK YOU/FOLLOW-UP LETTER

Your mailing address
Date

Contact's name
Contact's title
Company
Company's mailing address

Dear Mr./Ms._____:

Remind the interviewer of the reason (i.e., a specific opening, an informational interview, etc.) you were interviewed, as well as the date. Thank him/her for the interview, and try to personalize your thanks by mentioning some specific aspect of the interview.

Confirm your interest in the organization (and in the opening, if you were interviewing for a particular position). Use specifics to re-emphasize that you have researched the firm in detail and have considered how you would fit into the company and the position. This is a good time to say anything you wish you had said in the initial meeting. Be sure to keep this letter brief; a half page is plenty.

If appropriate, close with a suggestion for further action, such as a desire to have an additional interview, if possible. Mention your phone number and the hours you can be reached. Alternatively, you may prefer to mention that you will follow up with a phone call in several days. Once again, thank the person for meeting with you, and state that you would be happy to provide any additional information about your qualifications.

Sincerely,

(signature)

Your full name (typed)

PRIMARY EMPLOYERS
(Includes: New York City, Long Island, Rockland County, Westchester County)

ACCOUNTING AND MANAGEMENT CONSULTING

You can expect to find the following types of companies in this chapter:

Consulting and Research Firms • Industrial Accounting Firms •
Management Services • Public Accounting Firms •
Tax Preparation Companies

ARTHUR ANDERSEN LLP
1345 Avenue of the Americas, New York NY 10105. 212/708-4000.
Contact: Recruiting. **E-mail address:** new.york.careers@andersen.com.
World Wide Web address: http://www.andersen.com. **Description:** One of
the largest certified public accounting firms in the world. Arthur Andersen's
four key practice areas include Audit and Business Advisory, Tax and
Business Advisory, Business Consulting, and Economic and Financial
Consulting. **NOTE:** This firm does not accept unsolicited resumes. Please
check the Website for available positions. **Common positions include:**
Accountant/Auditor; Actuary; Consultant; Economist; Financial Analyst;
Systems Analyst. **Corporate headquarters location:** Chicago IL. **Other U.S.
locations:** Nationwide. **Operations at this facility include:** Business
Services; Management Consulting.

CAP GEMINI ERNST & YOUNG
5 Times Square, 9th Floor, New York NY 10036. 917/934-8000. **Contact:**
Human Resources. **World Wide Web address:** http://www.cgey.com.
Description: Provider of management consulting services including
business strategy, operations, and people and information management.
Services include systems integration; application design, development, and
documentation; systems conversions and migrations; and information
technology consulting. **NOTE:** Jobseekers are encouraged to apply online.
Other U.S. locations: Nationwide. **International locations:** Worldwide.
Number of employees nationwide: 3,000.

CAP GEMINI ERNST & YOUNG
1114 Avenue of the Americas, 29th Floor, New York NY 10036. 212/944-
6464. **Contact:** Human Resources Department. **World Wide Web address:**
http://www.usa.capgemini.com. **Description:** Provider of management
consulting services including business strategy, operations, and people and
information management. Services include systems integration; application
design, development, and documentation; systems conversions and
migrations; and information technology consulting. **NOTE:** Jobseekers are
encouraged to apply online. **Other U.S. locations:** Nationwide.
International locations: Worldwide. **Number of employees nationwide:**
3,000.

DELOITTE & TOUCHE
1633 Broadway, New York NY 10019-6754. 212/489-1600. **Contact:**
Human Resources. **World Wide Web address:** http://www.us.deloitte.com.
Description: An international firm of certified public accountants providing
professional accounting, auditing, tax, and management consulting services
to widely diversified clients. The company has a specialized program
consisting of national industry groups and functional groups that cross
industry lines. Groups are involved in various disciplines including

accounting, auditing, taxation management advisory services, small and growing businesses, mergers and acquisitions, and computer applications. **Corporate headquarters location:** Wilton CT. **Other U.S. locations:** Nationwide. **Parent company:** Deloitte Touche Tohmatsu International is a global leader with nearly 90,000 employees in over 130 countries.

ERNST & YOUNG LLP
5 Times Square, New York NY 10036-6530. 212/773-3000. **Contact:** Human Resources. **World Wide Web address:** http://www.ey.com. **Description:** A certified public accounting firm that also provides management consulting services. Services include data processing, financial modeling, financial feasibility studies, production planning and inventory management, management sciences, health care planning, human resources, cost accounting, and budgeting systems. **Other U.S. locations:** Nationwide. **International locations:** Worldwide.

FIND/SVP, INC.
625 Sixth Avenue, 2nd Floor, New York NY 10011. 212/645-4500. **Fax:** 212/645-7681. **Contact:** Mr. Tom McGillis, Human Resources Generalist. **E-mail address:** careers@findsvp.com. **World Wide Web address:** http://www.findsvp.com. **Description:** Provides business and management consulting, research, and advisory services. The company also offers seminars, conferences, and publications. Founded in 1969. **Corporate headquarters location:** This location.

KPMG
345 Park Avenue, New York NY 10154. 212/909-5000. **Contact:** Human Resources. **World Wide Web address:** http://www.kpmgcareers.com. **Description:** This location houses offices of the company's legal department as well as the top management staff. KPMG delivers a wide range of value-added assurance, tax, and consulting services. **Common positions include:** Accountant/Auditor. **Corporate headquarters location:** Montvale NJ. **Other U.S. locations:** Nationwide. **Parent company:** KPMG International is a professional services firm with more than 85,000 employees worldwide including 6,500 partners and 60,000 professionals, serving clients in 844 cities throughout 155 countries. KPMG International is a leader among professional services firms engaged in capturing, managing, assessing, and delivering information to create knowledge that will help its clients maximize shareholder value.

MERCER HUMAN RESOURCE CONSULTING
1166 Avenue of the Americas, New York NY 10036. 212/345-7000. **Contact:** Recruiting Coordinator. **World Wide Web address:** http://www.mercerhr.com. **Description:** One of the world's largest actuarial and human resources management consulting firms. The company offers advice to organizations on all aspects of employee/management relationships. Services include retirement, health and welfare, performance and rewards, communication, investment, human resources administration, risk, finance and insurance, and health care provider consulting. **Corporate headquarters location:** This location. **Other U.S. locations:** Nationwide. **International locations:** Worldwide. **Parent company:** Marsh & McLennan Companies, Inc. **Listed on:** New York Stock Exchange. **Stock exchange symbol:** MMC.

PRICEWATERHOUSECOOPERS
1301 Avenue of the Americas, New York NY 10019. 646/471-4000. **Contact:** Human Resources Department. **World Wide Web address:**

http://www.pwcglobal.com. **Description:** One of the largest certified public accounting firms in the world. PricewaterhouseCoopers provides public accounting, business advisory, management consulting, and taxation services. **Corporate headquarters location:** This location. **Other U.S. locations:** Nationwide.

PRICEWATERHOUSECOOPERS
1177 Avenue of the Americas, New York NY 10036. 646/471-4000. **Contact:** Human Resources Department. **World Wide Web address:** http://www.pwcglobal.com. **Description:** One of the largest certified public accounting firms in the world. PricewaterhouseCoopers provides public accounting, business advisory, management consulting, and taxation services. **Corporate headquarters location:** New York NY. **Other U.S. locations:** Nationwide. **International locations:** Worldwide.

TOWERS PERRIN
100 Summit Lake Drive, Valhalla NY 10595. 914/745-4000. **Contact:** Human Resources. **World Wide Web address:** http://www.towers.com. **Description:** A management consulting firm. **Common positions include:** Actuary. **Corporate headquarters location:** New York NY. **Operations at this facility include:** Administration; Regional Headquarters; Research and Development; Service.

TOWERS PERRIN
335 Madison Avenue, New York NY 10017-4605. 212/309-3400. **Contact:** Recruiting Coordinator. **World Wide Web address:** http://www.towers.com. **Description:** A management consulting firm. **Corporate headquarters location:** This location.

ADVERTISING, MARKETING, AND PUBLIC RELATIONS

You can expect to find the following types of companies in this chapter:

Advertising Agencies • Direct Mail Marketers •
Market Research Firms • Public Relations Firms

ASSOCIATED MERCHANDISING CORPORATION (AMC)

500 Seventh Avenue, New York NY 10018. 212/819-6600. **Contact:** Roger Bush, Human Resources Department. **World Wide Web address:** http://www.theamc.com. **Description:** Performs retail product development and international apparel sourcing services for retail clients. **Common positions include:** Accountant/Auditor; Buyer; Commercial Artist; Computer Programmer; Customer Service Representative; Operations/Production Manager; Product Manager; Quality Control Supervisor. **Corporate headquarters location:** Minneapolis MN. **Other U.S. locations:** Miami FL; Minneapolis MN. **Parent company:** Target Corporation. **Operations at this facility include:** Administration; Research and Development; Service. **Listed on:** New York Stock Exchange. **Stock exchange symbol:** TGT. **Number of employees nationwide:** 400.

BBDO WORLDWIDE INC.

1285 Avenue of the Americas, New York NY 10019. 212/459-5000. **Recorded jobline:** 212/459-JOBS. **Contact:** Manager of Human Resources Department. **E-mail address:** nyhrmanagerrecruiting@bbdo.com. **World Wide Web address:** http://www.bbdo.com. **Description:** Operates a worldwide network of advertising agencies with related businesses in public relations, direct marketing, sales promotion, graphic design, graphic arts, and printing. BBDO Worldwide operates 83 subsidiaries, affiliates, and associates in advertising and related operations. **Corporate headquarters location:** This location. **Other U.S. locations:** Nationwide. **International locations:** Worldwide.

BATES USA

498 Seventh Avenue, New York NY 10018. 212/297-7000. **Contact:** Human Resources. **World Wide Web address:** http://www.batesusa.com. **Description:** One of the largest advertising and public relations agencies in the United States. **Corporate headquarters location:** This location.

BLAIR TELEVISION

3 East 54th Street, New York NY 10022. 212/603-5000. **Contact:** Human Resources. **World Wide Web address:** http://www.petrymedia.com/blair. **Description:** Provides the media industry with national sales, marketing, and research services. Blair Television represents 140 TV stations and provides services to advertising agency/buying accounts and spot TV advertisers. **Common positions include:** Researcher; Sales Executive. **Corporate headquarters location:** This location. **Other U.S. locations:** Nationwide. **Operations at this facility include:** Administration; Research and Development; Sales. **Number of employees at this location:** 250. **Number of employees nationwide:** 500.

BOZELL WORLDWIDE
40 West 23rd Street, New York NY 10010. 212/727-5000. **Fax:** 212/463-8419. **Contact:** Personnel. **E-mail address:** bozellhr@newyork.bozell.com. **World Wide Web address:** http://www.bozell.com. **Description:** A full-service advertising agency. Bozell also offers public relations services such as corporate relations, marketing support, employee relations, financial relations, government affairs, and community relations. **Corporate headquarters location:** New York NY. **Other U.S. locations:** Nationwide. **International locations:** Worldwide. **Parent company:** The Interpublic Group of Companies. **Listed on:** New York Stock Exchange. **Stock exchange symbol:** IPG.

BURSON-MARSTELLER
230 Park Avenue South, New York NY 10003. 212/614-4000. **Contact:** Human Resources. **World Wide Web address:** http://www.bm.com. **Description:** A public relations agency. **Common positions include:** Public Relations Specialist. **Special programs:** Internships. **Corporate headquarters location:** This location. **Other U.S. locations:** Los Angeles CA; Sacramento CA; San Diego CA; San Francisco CA; Washington DC; Miami FL; Chicago IL; Pittsburgh PA; Dallas TX. **Subsidiaries include:** Cohn & Wolfe, Public Relations. **Parent company:** Young & Rubicam, Inc. **Listed on:** Privately held. **Number of employees at this location:** 350. **Number of employees worldwide:** 2,000.

CITIGATE DEWE ROGERSON
1440 Broadway, 16th Floor, New York NY 10018. 212/688-6840. **Fax:** 212/838-3393. **Contact:** Ms. Jody Johnson, Director of Human Resources Department. **E-mail address:** jjohnson@dewerogerson.com. **World Wide Web address:** http://www.dewerogerson.com. **Description:** A public relations agency specializing in financial communications, market research, media relations, and shareholder intelligence. Founded in 1968. **NOTE:** Entry-level positions are offered. **Common positions include:** Account Representative; Administrative Assistant; Fund Manager; Graphic Artist; Graphic Designer; Marketing Manager; Marketing Specialist; Multimedia Designer; Online Content Specialist; Public Relations Specialist. **Special programs:** Internships. **Office hours:** Monday - Friday, 9:00 a.m. - 5:00 p.m. **Corporate headquarters location:** This location. **Other U.S. locations:** San Francisco CA; Chicago IL. **International locations:** Worldwide. **Parent company:** Incepta Group plc. **Listed on:** Privately held.

DDB WORLDWIDE, INC.
437 Madison Avenue, New York NY 10022. 212/415-2000. **Contact:** Wendy Raye, Human Resources Manager. **World Wide Web address:** http://www.ddbn.com. **Description:** A full-service, international advertising agency. **Common positions include:** Advertising Executive; Media Specialist. **Special programs:** Internships. **Corporate headquarters location:** This location. **Other U.S. locations:** Los Angeles CA; Chicago IL. **Parent company:** Omnicom Group, Inc. (also at this location, 212/415-3600) is a holding company that provides advertising, marketing, media buying, and interactive media services through its subsidiaries. **Listed on:** New York Stock Exchange. **Stock exchange symbol:** OMC. **Number of employees at this location:** 400.

R.H. DONNELLEY
One Manhattanville Road, Purchase NY 10577. 914/933-6800. **Contact:** Human Resources. **E-mail address:** info@rhdonnelley.com. **World Wide Web address:** http://www.rhdonnelley.com. **Description:** Engaged in selling

advertising space in Yellow Pages directories. R.H. Donnelley also provides telemarketing services. **Common positions include:** Accountant/Auditor; Claim Representative; Commercial Artist; Computer Programmer; Credit Manager; Customer Service Representative; Department Manager; Draftsperson; Financial Analyst; General Manager; Human Resources Manager; Marketing Specialist; Operations/Production Manager; Purchasing Agent/Manager; Sales Representative; Systems Analyst. **Corporate headquarters location:** This location. **Other U.S. locations:** FL; IL; NC; NV; PA; VA. **Listed on:** New York Stock Exchange. **Stock exchange symbol:** RHD.

DOREMUS & COMPANY, INC.
200 Varick Street, 11th Floor, New York NY 10014. 212/366-3000. **Contact:** Ms. Kristin Mooney, Director of Human Resources Department. **E-mail address:** kmooney@doremus.com. **World Wide Web address:** http://www.doremus.com. **Description:** An agency specializing in corporate and financial advertising. Founded in 1903. **NOTE:** Entry-level positions are offered. **Common positions include:** Advertising Executive; Graphic Artist; Sales Executive. **Special programs:** Internships. **Corporate headquarters location:** This location. **Other U.S. locations:** San Francisco CA. **International locations:** London, England; Tokyo, Japan. **Parent company:** Omnicom Group. **Annual sales/revenues:** More than $100 million. **Number of employees at this location:** 100.

EARLE PALMER BROWN
685 Third Avenue, 2nd Floor, New York NY 10017. 212/986-4122. **Contact:** Barbara Clinton, Human Resources Representative. **World Wide Web address:** http://www.epb.com. **Description:** An agency offering advertising, public relations, marketing research, *Yellow Pages* advertising, direct marketing, and sales promotions. Founded in 1952. **Corporate headquarters location:** Bethesda MD. **Other U.S. locations:** St. Petersburg FL; Philadelphia PA; Richmond VA.

FCB WORLDWIDE
150 East 42nd Street, 12th Floor, New York NY 10017. 212/885-3000. **Contact:** Judith Kemp, Director of Personnel. **E-mail address:** careersny@fcb.com. **World Wide Web address:** http://www.fcb.com. **Description:** An international advertising agency. FCB/LKP offers additional services including direct marketing, design and production of sales promotion programs; market and product research; package design; and trademark and trade name development. The company operates offices throughout Europe, Asia, and Latin America. **Corporate headquarters location:** Chicago IL. **International locations:** Worldwide. **Parent company:** Foote, Cone & Belding Communications.

GOTHAM INC.
100 Fifth Avenue, New York NY 10011. 212/414-7000. **Contact:** Human Resources Department. **E-mail address:** info@gothaminc.com. **World Wide Web address:** http://www.gothaminc.com. **Description:** Specializes in creating start-up brands with an emphasis on fashion and beauty advertising. Founded in 1994. **International locations:** Paris, France. **Parent company:** The Interpublic Group of Companies. **Listed on:** New York Stock Exchange. **Stock exchange symbol:** IPG. **CEO:** Stone Roberts.

HILL AND KNOWLTON INC.
466 Lexington Avenue, 3rd Floor, New York NY 10017. 212/885-0300. **Contact:** Sharon James, Director of Human Resources Department. **World**

Wide Web address: http://www.hillandknowlton.com. **Description:** One of the largest public relations/public affairs counseling firms in the world. **Corporate headquarters location:** This location. **Other U.S. locations:** San Francisco CA; Washington DC. **International locations:** Worldwide.

THE INTERPUBLIC GROUP OF COMPANIES, INC.
1271 Avenue of the Americas, 44th Floor, New York NY 10020. 212/399-8000. **Contact:** Doris Weil, Director of Corporate Human Resources. **E-mail address:** hr@interpublic.com. **World Wide Web address:** http://www.interpublic.com. **Description:** An advertising agency. The company plans, creates, and implements advertising campaigns in various media through either its own subsidiaries or contracts with local agencies. Other activities include publishing, market research, public relations, product development, and sales promotion. Interpublic's international business groups include McCann-Erickson WorldGroup and The Lowe Group. **Corporate headquarters location:** This location. **Listed on:** New York Stock Exchange. **Stock exchange symbol:** IPG.

THE KAPLAN THALER GROUP, LTD.
World Wide Plaza, 825 Eighth Avenue, New York NY 10019. 212/474-5000. **Contact:** Manager of Human Resources Department. **E-mail address:** kaplanthalergroup@kaplanthaler.com. **World Wide Web address:** http://www.kaplanthaler.com. **Description:** A national advertising agency. **Corporate headquarters location:** Chicago IL. **Other U.S. locations:** Nationwide. **International locations:** Worldwide. **Parent company:** Bcom3. **Number of employees nationwide:** 1,275.

KATZ MEDIA
125 West 55th Street, 21st Floor, Manhattan NY 10019-5366. 212/424-6000. **Fax:** 212/424-6110. **Contact:** Human Resources Department. **World Wide Web address:** http://www.katz-media.com. **Description:** An advertising agency. **Corporate headquarters location:** San Antonio TX. **Parent company:** Clear Channel Communications. **Listed on:** New York Stock Exchange. **Stock exchange symbol:** CCU.

LOWE
885 Second Avenue, New York NY 10017. 212/605-8000. **Contact:** Human Resources. **E-mail address:** info@loweworldwide.com. **World Wide Web address:** http://www.loweworldwide.com. **Description:** An advertising agency. **Corporate headquarters location:** This location. **Parent company:** The Interpublic Group of Companies, Inc. **Listed on:** New York Stock Exchange. **Stock exchange symbol:** IPG. **Number of employees at this location:** 700.

LYONS LAVEY NICKEL SWIFT INC.
220 East 42nd Street, 3rd Floor, New York NY 10017. 212/771-3000. **Fax:** 212/771-3016. **Contact:** Human Resources Manager. **E-mail address:** jobs@hmcny.com. **World Wide Web address:** http://www.llns.com. **Description:** An advertising agency for pharmaceutical firms. Founded in 1972. **NOTE:** Entry-level positions are offered. **Common positions include:** Administrative Assistant; Advertising Clerk; Advertising Executive; Art Director; Computer Support Technician; Computer Technician; Copywriter; Customer Service Representative; Editor; Human Resources Manager; MIS Specialist; Secretary. **Special programs:** Summer Jobs. **Office hours:** Monday - Friday, 9:00 a.m. - 5:00 p.m. **Corporate headquarters location:** New York NY. **Parent company:** Omnicom Group, Inc. operates advertising agencies and also offers marketing consultation, consumer

research, promotion programs, and public relations services. **Listed on:** New York Stock Exchange. **Stock exchange symbol:** OMC. **President:** Al Nickel. **Number of employees at this location:** 200.

McCANN-ERICKSON WORLDWIDE

622 Third Avenue, New York NY 10017. 646/865-2000. **Contact:** Human Resources. **World Wide Web address:** http://www.mccann.com. **Description:** An advertising agency. **Corporate headquarters location:** This location. **Other U.S. locations:** Atlanta GA; Chicago IL; Louisville KY; Houston TX; Seattle WA. **Parent company:** The Interpublic Group of Companies, Inc. **Listed on:** New York Stock Exchange. **Stock exchange symbol:** IPG.

ARNOLD McGRATH WORLDWIDE

110 Fifth Avenue, New York NY 10011. 212/463-1000. **Fax:** 212/463-1628. **Contact:** Chris Martin, Director of Personnel. **E-mail address:** cmartin@arnny.com. **World Wide Web address:** http://www.arnny.com. **Description:** An advertising agency. Founded in 1980. **NOTE:** Entry-level positions are offered. **Common positions include:** Account Manager; Administrative Assistant; Advertising Executive; Designer; Graphic Artist; Graphic Designer; Market Research Analyst; Video Production Coordinator. **Special programs:** Internships; Apprenticeships; Training. **Corporate headquarters location:** This location. **Operations at this facility include:** Service. **Annual sales/revenues:** $21 - $50 million. **Number of employees at this location:** 330.

THE MEDICUS GROUP

1675 Broadway, New York NY 10019-5809. 212/468-3100. **Fax:** 212/468-3208. **Contact:** Emilie Schaum, Director of Human Resources. **World Wide Web address:** http://www.medicusgroup.com. **Description:** Markets a wide range of pharmaceutical and consumer health products and services to health care professionals, patients, and consumers. Services include advertising and promotions, direct-to-consumer marketing, interactive media, medical education, public relations, publication planning, and sales training. **NOTE:** Entry-level positions are offered. **Common positions include:** Administrative Assistant; Advertising Executive; Art Director; Copywriter; Graphic Artist; Public Relations Specialist; Technical Writer/Editor. **Special programs:** Internships. **Office hours:** Monday - Friday, 9:00 a.m. - 5:00 p.m. **Corporate headquarters location:** This location. **International locations:** Worldwide. **Parent company:** D'Arcy Masius Benton & Bowles (also at this location, 212/468-3622) is an international advertising agency whose other subsidiaries include Brainwaves; Highway One; Telewest. **Operations at this facility include:** Administration; Regional Headquarters. **Listed on:** Privately held. **CEO:** Glenn DeSimone. **Annual sales/revenues:** $51 - $100 million. **Number of employees at this location:** 150. **Number of employees worldwide:** 530.

MICKELBERRY COMMUNICATIONS

405 Park Avenue, Suite 1003, New York NY 10022. 212/832-0303. **Contact:** Human Resources Department. **World Wide Web address:** http://www.mickelberry.com. **Description:** A holding company for three marketing companies and a commercial printing group. **Parent company:** Union Capital Corporation.

MOSS DRAGOTI
437 Madison Avenue, New York NY 10022. 212/415-2900. **Contact:** Director of Personnel. **World Wide Web address:** http://www.ddb.com. **Description:** An advertising agency. **Parent company:** DDB Worldwide.

THE NPD GROUP, INC.
900 West Shore Road, Port Washington NY 11050. 516/625-0700. **Contact:** Human Resources Department. **E-mail address:** hr@npd.com. **World Wide Web address:** http://www.npd.com. **Description:** A market research firm offering a full line of custom and syndicated consumer research services including point-of-sale computerized audits, purchase panels, mail panels, telephone research, mathematical modeling, and consulting. Industries covered include consumer packaged goods, apparel, toys, electronics, automotive, sports, books, and food consumption. **Common positions include:** Account Manager; Administrative Assistant; Administrative Manager; Computer Programmer; Data Entry Clerk; Economist; Researcher; Statistician; Technical Writer/Editor. **Special programs:** Internships. **Corporate headquarters location:** This location. **Other U.S. locations:** Chicago IL; Hyattsville MD; Greensboro NC; Cincinnati OH; Houston TX. **Number of employees nationwide:** 800.

NIELSEN MEDIA RESEARCH COMPANY
299 Park Avenue, New York NY 10171. 212/708-7500. **Fax:** 212/708-7533. **Contact:** Kimberly Baglia-Fortner, Human Resources Representative. **World Wide Web address:** http://www.nielsenmedia.com. **Description:** Nielsen Media Research measures television show audience sizes and provides this information to broadcast networks and advertising agencies. **Common positions include:** Economist; Financial Analyst. **Other U.S. locations:** CA; FL; GA; IL; TX. **Operations at this facility include:** Administration; Divisional Headquarters; Research and Development; Sales; Service. **Number of employees at this location:** 195. **Number of employees nationwide:** 3,500.

OGILVY & MATHER
309 West 49th Street, New York NY 10019. 212/237-6000. **Contact:** Joy Mauerhoff, Senior Partner/Development and Administration. **World Wide Web address:** http://www.ogilvy.com. **Description:** An advertising agency. **Other U.S. locations:** Nationwide. **International locations:** Worldwide.

POSTERLOID CORPORATION
48-62 36th Street, Long Island City NY 11101. 718/729-1050. **Contact:** Human Resources. **Description:** Manufactures and markets indoor menu board display systems for the fast-food and convenience store industries and changeable magnetic display signage used primarily by banks to display interest rates and other information. These displays are custom manufactured for ceiling hanging or for window or counter displays. **Corporate headquarters location:** New York NY. **Parent company:** Alpine Group, Inc. is active in the defense and commercial electronics and telecommunications wire and cable industries through subsidiaries, Alpine Polyvision, Inc. and DNE Technologies, Inc., both of which operate out of CT, and Superior TeleTec Inc. in Atlanta GA. **Listed on:** New York Stock Exchange. **Stock exchange symbol:** AGI. **Number of employees at this location:** 55.

PUBLISHERS CLEARING HOUSE
382 Channel Drive, Port Washington NY 11050. 516/883-5432. **Contact:** Human Resources. **World Wide Web address:** http://www.pch.com.

Description: A direct mail marketing company. Publishers Clearing House is one of the largest sources of new magazine subscribers. The company also conducts continuing research to develop effective promotions for other products and services. **Common positions include:** Accountant/Auditor; Advertising Clerk; Computer Programmer; Customer Service Representative; Financial Analyst; Industrial Engineer; Marketing Specialist; Systems Analyst. **Corporate headquarters location:** This location. **Subsidiaries include:** Campus Subscriptions.

RUDER-FINN, INC.
301 East 57th Street, New York NY 10022. 212/593-6400. **Contact:** Human Resources. **E-mail address:** careers@ruderfinn.com. **World Wide Web address:** http://www.ruderfinn.com. **Description:** Offers a wide range of services in the public relations field. **Corporate headquarters location:** This location. **Other U.S. locations:** CA; DC. **International locations:** China; France; Israel; Singapore; United Kingdom.

SAATCHI & SAATCHI ADVERTISING
375 Hudson Street, New York NY 10014. 212/463-2304. **Contact:** Human Resources. **World Wide Web address:** http://www.saatchi-saatchi.com. **Description:** An advertising agency. **Company slogan:** Nothing is impossible. **Office hours:** Monday - Friday, 9:00 a.m. - 5:00 p.m. **Corporate headquarters location:** This location. **Other U.S. locations:** Nationwide. **International locations:** Worldwide. **Number of employees at this location:** 500.

SUDLER & HENNESSEY INC.
230 Park Avenue South, New York NY 10003-1566. 212/614-4100. **Contact:** Rose Lombardo, Human Resources. **World Wide Web address:** http://www.sudler.com. **Description:** An advertising agency. **Corporate headquarters location:** This location.

SYSTEMAX INC.
22 Harbor Park Drive, Port Washington NY 11050. 516/608-7000. **Fax:** 516/608-7111. **Contact:** Human Resources Department. **World Wide Web address:** http://www.systemax.com. **Description:** A direct marketer of brand-name and private-label computer, office, and industrial products targeting mid-range and major corporate accounts, small office/home customers, and value-added resellers. Founded in 1949. **NOTE:** Entry-level positions are offered. **Common positions include:** Account Representative; Accountant; Administrative Assistant; Advertising Executive; Applications Engineer; Auditor; Buyer; Computer Operator; Computer Programmer; Computer Support Technician; Computer Technician; Customer Service Representative; Database Administrator; Database Manager; Desktop Publishing Specialist; Graphic Artist; Industrial Engineer; Internet Services Manager; Market Research Analyst; Marketing Manager; Marketing Specialist; MIS Specialist; Network/Systems Administrator; Sales Representative; Software Engineer; Systems Analyst; Technical Writer/Editor; Transportation/Traffic Specialist; Webmaster. **Special programs:** Internships; Summer Jobs. **Corporate headquarters location:** This location. **Other U.S. locations:** CA; FL; GA; IL; NJ; NC; OH. **Subsidiaries include:** Global Computer Supplies; Midwest Micro Corp.; Misco America, Inc.; Misco Canada Inc.; TigerDirect Inc. **Listed on:** New York Stock Exchange. **Stock exchange symbol:** SYX. **Annual sales/revenues:** More than $100 million. **Number of employees at this location:** 500. **Number of employees nationwide:** 2,000. **Number of employees worldwide:** 4,000.

TBWA/CHIAT/DAY

488 Madison Avenue, 7th Floor, New York NY 10022. 212/804-1000. **Fax:** 212/804-1200. **Contact:** Manager of Human Resources Department. **E-mail address:** resumes@tbwachiat.com. **World Wide Web address:** http://www.tbwachiat.com. **Description:** An advertising agency.

J. WALTER THOMPSON COMPANY

466 Lexington Avenue, New York NY 10017. 212/210-7000. **Contact:** Human Resources. **E-mail address:** nygetajob@jwt.com. **World Wide Web address:** http://www.jwt.com. **Description:** A full-service advertising agency. **Corporate headquarters location:** This location. **Other U.S. locations:** Nationwide. **International locations:** Worldwide. **Parent company:** WPP Group. **Listed on:** NASDAQ. **Stock exchange symbol:** WPPGY.

VIACOM OUTDOOR

405 Lexington Avenue, 14th Floor, New York NY 10174. 212/297-6400. **Contact:** Human Resources Department. **World Wide Web address:** http://www.viacom-outdoor.com. **Description:** An advertising agency specializing in the design of billboards and posters. **Common positions include:** Accountant/Auditor; Artist; Controller; Credit Manager; Department Manager; General Manager; Market Research Analyst; Sales Executive. **Special programs:** Internships. **Other U.S. locations:** Nationwide. **Operations at this facility include:** Administration; Divisional Headquarters; Financial Offices; Marketing; Research and Development; Sales; Service.

JANE WESMAN PUBLIC RELATIONS, INC.

928 Broadway, Suite 903, New York NY 10010. 212/598-4440. **Fax:** 212/598-4590. **Contact:** Human Resources. **World Wide Web address:** http://www.wesmanpr.com. **Description:** Provides book publicity services including press kits, author tours, radio and print publicity, and media training. **Corporate headquarters location:** This location.

WUNDERMAN

675 Avenue of the Americas, 4th Floor, New York NY 10010-5104. 212/941-3700. **Contact:** Human Resources. **World Wide Web address:** http://www.wunderman.com. **Description:** Provides communications and database technologies for the marketing industry through the company's international research and development marketing lab. **International locations:** Worldwide. **President/CEO:** David Sable.

YOUNG & RUBICAM, INC.

285 Madison Avenue, 9th Floor, New York NY 10017. 212/210-3000. **Fax:** 212/210-5007. **Contact:** Human Resources. **World Wide Web address:** http://www.yandr.com. **Description:** An international advertising agency. The company operates through three divisions: Young & Rubicam International; Marsteller Inc., a worldwide leader in business-to-business and consumer advertising; and Young & Rubicam USA, with 14 consumer advertising agencies operating through four regional groups, and five specialized advertising and marketing agencies. **Common positions include:** Advertising Clerk; Financial Analyst; Human Resources Manager; Market Research Analyst; Systems Analyst. **Special programs:** Internships. **Corporate headquarters location:** This location. **Other U.S. locations:** Nationwide. **Subsidiaries include:** Burson-Marsteller provides public relations services throughout the world.

AEROSPACE

You can expect to find the following types of companies in this chapter:

Aerospace Products and Services • Aircraft Equipment and Parts

AEROFLEX INC.
35 South Service Road, Plainview NY 11807. 516/293-8686. **Contact:** Jane Brady, Vice President of Personnel. **World Wide Web address:** http://www.aeroflex.com. **Description:** Manufactures custom-designed hybrid microcircuits for use in applications including electrical systems used in aircraft maintenance, flight and navigational systems, sonar systems, satellite experimentation systems, missile firing systems, power supply systems, computer testing systems, television camera and radio receiver systems, and other applications using miniaturized components. Founded in 1937. **Common positions include:** Electrical/Electronics Engineer; Mechanical Engineer. **Corporate headquarters location:** This location. **Listed on:** NASDAQ. **Stock exchange symbol:** ARXX.

CPI AEROSTRUCTURES, INC.
200-A Executive Drive, Edgewood NY 11717. 631/586-5200. **Contact:** Linda Coradino, Personnel Manager. **World Wide Web address:** http://www.cpiaero.com. **Description:** Engaged in contract production of structural aircraft parts and subassemblies for the commercial and military sectors of the aircraft industry. The company also provides engineering, technical, and program management services. **Corporate headquarters location:** This location. **Listed on:** AMEX. **Stock exchange symbol:** CVU.

ELLANEF MANUFACTURING CORPORATION
97-11 50th Avenue, Corona NY 11368. 718/699-4000. **Contact:** Ernest Constantine, Human Resources Manager. **World Wide Web address:** http://www.malaero.com. **Description:** Manufactures a wide range of aircraft components for major aerospace OEMs and airlines operating nationwide. **Common positions include:** Aerospace Engineer; Cost Estimator; Customer Service Representative; Electrician; General Manager; Industrial Production Manager; Machinist; Operations/Production Manager; Purchasing Agent/Manager; Quality Control Supervisor. **Corporate headquarters location:** This location. **Parent company:** Magellan Aerospace Corporation. **Operations at this facility include:** Manufacturing. **Number of employees at this location:** 500.

K&F INDUSTRIES INC.
600 Third Avenue, 27th Floor, New York NY 10016. 212/297-0900. **Contact:** Human Resources. **Description:** A holding company for two divisions that manufacture aircraft braking systems.

NORTHROP GRUMMAN CORPORATION
South Oyster Bay Road, M/S A02005, Bethpage NY 11714. 516/575-0574. **Contact:** Human Resources Department. **World Wide Web address:** http://www.northgrum.com. **Description:** Manufactures military aircraft, commercial aircraft parts, and electronic systems. Northrop Grumman manufactures the B-2 Spirit Stealth Bomber, as well as parts for the F/A-18 and the 747, and radar equipment. Other operations include computer systems development for management and scientific applications.

Corporate headquarters location: Los Angeles CA. **Listed on:** New York Stock Exchange. **Stock exchange symbol:** NOC.

PARKER HANNIFIN CORPORATION

300 Marcus Boulevard, P.O. Box 9400, Smithtown NY 11787. 631/231-3737. **Contact:** Human Resources Manager. **World Wide Web address:** http://www.parker.com. **Description:** This location manufactures and distributes aerospace instrumentation and equipment including fuel flow instruments. Overall, Parker Hannifin makes motion control products including fluid power systems, electromechanical controls, and related components. The Motion and Control Group makes hydraulic pumps, power units, control valves, accumulators, cylinders, actuators, and automation devices to remove contaminants from air, fuel, oil, water, and other fluids. The Fluid Connectors Group makes connectors, tube and hose fittings, hoses, and couplers that transmit fluid. The Seal Group makes sealing devices, gaskets, and packing that insure leak-proof connections. The Automotive and Refrigeration Groups make components for use in industrial and automotive air conditioning and refrigeration systems. Principal products of the aerospace segment are hydraulic, pneumatic, and fuel systems and components. **Corporate headquarters location:** Cleveland OH. **Listed on:** New York Stock Exchange. **Stock exchange symbol:** PH.

STELLEX MONITOR AEROSPACE CORPORATION

1000 New Horizons Boulevard, Amityville NY 11701-1181. 631/957-2300. **Contact:** Human Resources Department. **World Wide Web address:** http://www.monair.com. **Description:** Manufactures precision structural aerospace parts and assemblies for commercial and military aircraft. **Parent company:** Stellex Aerostructures, Inc.

APPAREL, FASHION, AND TEXTILES

You can expect to find the following types of companies in this chapter:
Broadwoven Fabric Mills • Knitting Mills • Curtains and Draperies • Footwear • Nonwoven Fabrics • Textile Goods and Finishing • Yarn and Thread Mills

ABERDEEN SPORTSWEAR, INC.
350 Fifth Avenue, Suite 2828, New York NY 10118. 212/244-5100. **Contact:** Thomas Jackson, Controller. **Description:** Manufactures a line of sport jackets. **Corporate headquarters location:** This location.

ALKAHN LABELS, INC.
111 West 40th Street, 13th Floor, New York NY 10018. 212/398-0200. **Fax:** 646/562-2001. **Contact:** Human Resources Department. **World Wide Web address:** http://www.alkahn.com. **Description:** Manufactures cloth labels for clothing manufacturers. Alkahn offers a complete line of products including care labels, specialty weaves, and printed items. Founded in 1906. **Other U.S. locations:** Los Angeles CA; Chicago IL; Cowpens SC. **International locations:** Hong Kong.

AMERICAN TROUSER
350 Fifth Avenue, Suite 3200, New York NY 10118. 212/244-0900. **Contact:** John Rossi, Senior Vice President of Merchandise. **World Wide Web address:** http://www.american-trouser.com. **Description:** This location provides administrative services. Overall, American Trouser manufactures men's pants. **Corporate headquarters location:** Columbus MS.

ARIS INDUSTRIES, INC.
463 Seventh Avenue, New York NY 10018. 646/473-4200. **Contact:** Human Resources. **Description:** Engaged in the licensing and sale of men's and young men's sportswear and outerwear and ladies' sportswear.

BEST MANUFACTURING, INC.
1633 Broadway, 18th Floor, New York NY 10019. 212/974-1100. **Fax:** 212/245-0385. **Contact:** Human Resources. **World Wide Web address:** http://www.bestmfg.com. **Description:** A manufacturer of textiles and washable service apparel. Founded in 1914. **Common positions include:** Customer Service Representative; Management Trainee. **Corporate headquarters location:** This location. **Other U.S. locations:** Nationwide. **Operations at this facility include:** Administration. **Listed on:** Privately held. **Number of employees at this location:** 85. **Number of employees nationwide:** 1,100.

CHF INDUSTRIES, INC.
One Park Avenue, 9th Floor, New York NY 10016. 212/951-7800. **Contact:** Human Resources. **Description:** Engaged in the production, export, and import of comforters, curtains, towels, and other textile goods. **Corporate headquarters location:** Charlotte NC.

CELANESE ACETATE TEXTILES
3 Park Avenue, 37th Floor, New York NY 10016. 212/251-8000. **Contact:** Human Resources. **World Wide Web address:** http://www.celanese.com.

Description: Manufactures acetate products including acetate yarn and Micro Safe fiber. Primary customers include the apparel, furnishings, and industrial markets. **Other U.S. locations:** Nationwide. **International locations:** Worldwide. **Parent company:** Celanese AG is an industrial chemical company. **Listed on:** New York Stock Exchange. **Stock exchange symbol:** CZ.

JOSEPHINE CHAUS, INC.
530 Seventh Avenue, 18th Floor, New York NY 10018. 212/354-1280. **Contact:** Human Resources Department. **World Wide Web address:** http://www.bernardchaus.com. **Description:** Designs, manufactures, and markets women's apparel. Career casual sportswear is marketed under the Chaus, Chaus Woman, and Chaus Petite labels and blouses are marketed under the Josephine label. Weekend casual sportswear bears the Chaus Sport and Chaus Jeanswear labels. Dresses are marketed under the Chaus Dresses, Chaus Woman Dresses, and Chaus Petite Dresses labels.

CONCORD FABRICS INC.
1359 Broadway, 3rd Floor, New York NY 10018. 212/760-0300. **Contact:** Personnel. **World Wide Web address:** http://www.concordfabrics.com. **Description:** Designs, develops, and manufactures woven and knitted fabrics for sale to manufacturers and retailers. Concord Fabrics is one of the nation's largest independent textile converters. **Common positions include:** Clerical Supervisor; Computer Programmer; Designer; Systems Analyst. **Special programs:** Internships. **Corporate headquarters location:** This location. **Other U.S. locations:** CA; GA. **Operations at this facility include:** Administration; Sales. **Number of employees at this location:** 200. **Number of employees nationwide:** 700.

CROSCILL HOME FASHIONS
261 Fifth Avenue, 25th Floor, New York NY 10016. 212/689-7222. **Contact:** Richard Wold, Controller. **E-mail address:** jobapps@croscill.com. **World Wide Web address:** http://www.croscill.com. **Description:** Manufactures curtains, draperies, and other textile products. **Corporate headquarters location:** Durham NC.

CYGNE DESIGNS INC.
1410 Broadway, Suite 1002, New York NY 10018. 212/997-7767. **Contact:** Office Manager. **Description:** Cygne Designs is a private-label designer, merchandiser, and manufacturer of women's apparel, serving retailers including Ann Taylor, The Limited Stores, Express, Lane Bryant, Victoria's Secret Stores, Lerner, and Casual Corner. The company's products include a broad range of woven and knit career, casual, and intimate women's apparel.

DAN RIVER, INC.
1325 Avenue of the Americas, New York NY 10019. 212/554-5531. **Contact:** Human Resources Department. **World Wide Web address:** http://www.danriver.com. **Description:** This location is the sales and marketing headquarters. Overall, Dan River, Inc. is a manufacturer and marketer of textile products for the home fashions and apparel fabrics markets. Dan River manufactures a coordinated line of home fashions consisting of packaged bedroom furnishings such as comforters, sheets, pillowcases, shams, bedskirts, decorative pillows, and draperies. The company also manufactures a broad range of woven and knit cotton and cotton-blend apparel fabrics, and is a domestic supplier of men's dress shirt fabrics, primarily oxford and pinpoint oxford cloth. **Common positions**

include: Administrative Manager; Budget Analyst; Claim Representative; Clerical Supervisor; Cost Estimator; Credit Manager; Customer Service Representative; Designer; General Manager; Human Resources Manager; Management Trainee; Merchandiser; Product Manager; Production Manager; Purchasing Agent/Manager; Sales Manager. **Corporate headquarters location:** Danville VA. **Other U.S. locations:** CA; GA; IL; MA; MN; NJ; NC; PA; SC; TX. **Subsidiaries include:** Dan River Factory Stores, Inc. operates 12 factory outlet stores in the Midwest and the Southeast. **Operations at this facility include:** Administration; Divisional Headquarters; Sales; Service. **Listed on:** New York Stock Exchange. **Stock exchange symbol:** DRF. **Number of employees at this location:** 90.

DANSKIN INC.
530 Seventh Avenue, Floor M1, New York NY 10018. 212/764-4630. **Contact:** Human Resources Department. **World Wide Web address:** http://www.danskin.com. **Description:** Danskin designs, manufactures, and markets several brands of women's activewear, dancewear, tights, and sheer hosiery. Brand names include Danskin, Dance France, Round-the-Clock, Givenchy, and Anne Klein. **Corporate headquarters location:** This location. **Other U.S. locations:** Nationwide. **Subsidiaries include:** Pennaco (Grenada MS). **Number of employees nationwide:** 1,550.

DARLINGTON FABRICS CORPORATION
1359 Broadway, Suite 1404, New York NY 10018. 212/279-7733. **Contact:** Personnel. **World Wide Web address:** http://www.darlingfabrics.com. **Description:** This location is a sales office. Overall, Darlington Fabrics Corporation is a wide-warp knit elastic knitting company. **NOTE:** Resumes should be sent to Human Resources, 36 Beach Street, Westerly RI 02891. 401/596-2816. **Listed on:** Privately held.

DONNKENNY, INC.
1411 Broadway, 10th Floor, New York NY 10018. 212/730-7770. **Contact:** Human Resources. **Description:** A sportswear manufacturer. Three distinct and expanding divisions make up Donnkenny: Donnkenny Classics, Mickey & Co., and Lewis Frimel/Flirts. **Corporate headquarters location:** This location.

EVERLAST WORLDWIDE, INC.
1350 Broadway, Suite 2300, New York NY 10018. 212/239-0990. **Contact:** Mr. George Horowitz, President. **World Wide Web address:** http://www.everlast.com. **Description:** Everlast Worldwide, Inc. designs, manufactures, and sells activewear and sportswear. **Corporate headquarters location:** This location. **Listed on:** NASDAQ. **Stock exchange symbol:** EVST.

FAB INDUSTRIES, INC.
200 Madison Avenue, 7th Floor, New York NY 10016. 212/592-2700. **Contact:** Ms. Marsha Cohen, Office Manager. **E-mail address:** fabindus@mindspring.com. **World Wide Web address:** http://www.fab-industries.com. **Description:** Fab Industries is a manufacturer of knitted textile fabrics, laces, and related finished home products, as well as polyurethane coated fabrics. The company markets its products to the apparel, home furnishings, industrial, retail, and other specialty markets. Fab operates eight manufacturing plants at five locations in North Carolina and New York. **Corporate headquarters location:** This location. **Listed on:** American Stock Exchange. **Stock exchange symbol:** FIT. **Number of employees nationwide:** 1,800.

FORSTMANN COMPANY
498 Seventh Avenue, 15th Floor, New York NY 10018-6791. 212/642-6900. **Contact:** Personnel Department. **World Wide Web address:** http://www.forstmann.com. **Description:** Designs, manufactures, and markets woolen, worsted, and other fabrics primarily used in the production of brand-name and private label apparel for men and women, as well as specialty fabrics for use in billiard and gaming tables, sports caps, and career uniforms. **Corporate headquarters location:** Dublin GA.

G-III APPAREL GROUP, LTD.
512 Seventh Avenue, New York NY 10018-4202. 212/944-6230. **Contact:** Andrea Shaffer, Human Resources Department. **World Wide Web address:** http://www.g-iii.com. **Description:** G-III Apparel Group, Ltd. designs, manufactures, imports, and markets an extensive range of apparel including coats, jackets, pants, skirts, and other sportswear items under its G-III, Siena, Siena Studio, Colebrook and Co., Kenneth Cole, and Nine West labels, and under private retail and licensed labels. The company also manufactures and markets a full line of women's leather apparel in junior, miss, and half sizes; and an outerwear line of men's leather apparel at a wide range of retail sales prices. The company's products also include textile outerwear, woolen coats, and sportswear. **Corporate headquarters location:** This location. **Listed on:** NASDAQ. **Stock exchange symbol:** GIII.

GALEY & LORD, INC.
980 Sixth Avenue, 4th Floor, New York NY 10018-5401. 212/465-3000. **Fax:** 212/465-3081. **Contact:** Human Resources. **Description:** This location houses executive offices. Overall, Galey & Lord is a leading manufacturer and marketer of apparel fabric sold to clothing manufacturers. The company is a major producer of wrinkle-free cotton fabrics for uniforms and for sportswear manufacturers and printed fabrics for the home. Galey & Lord also manufactures denim. **Corporate headquarters location:** This location. **Other U.S. locations:** Greensboro NC. **Subsidiaries include:** G&L Service Company provides marketing services for Galey & Lord. Galey & Lord Home Fashion Fabrics manufactures and distributes fabrics used in home decorating and furnishing. Klopman International is a supplier of fabrics used in career wear. Swift Denim manufactures and distributes a wide variety of denim products. **President/CEO:** Arthur C. Wiener.

GARAN INC.
350 Fifth Avenue, 19th Floor, New York NY 10118. 212/563-2000. **Contact:** Ms. Dana Gleason, Personnel Manager. **Description:** Garan designs, manufactures, and sells apparel for children, women, and men. Products include shirts, sweatshirts, sweaters, trousers, skirts, shorts, and overalls. Trade names, trademarks, and licensed names include Garanimals, Garan by Marita, Bobbie Brooks, Garan Mountain Lion, Long Gone, Team Rated, National Football League, National Basketball Association, National Hockey League, Major League Baseball, and Disney. **Corporate headquarters location:** This location. **Listed on:** New York Stock Exchange. **Stock exchange symbol:** GAN.

JLM COUTURE, INC.
225 West 37th Street, 5th Floor, New York NY 10018. 212/921-7058. **Contact:** Human Resources Department. **World Wide Web address:** http://www.jlmcouture.com. **Description:** Designs, manufactures, and markets bridal gowns, bridesmaid gowns, veils, and related accessories.

JORDACHE ENTERPRISES
1400 Broadway, Suite 1411, New York NY 10018. 212/643-8400. **Contact:** Human Resources. **World Wide Web address:** http://www.jordache.com. **Description:** Distributes designer jeans and other fashion apparel products.

KENNETH COLE PRODUCTIONS
603 West 50th Street, New York NY 10019. 212/265-1500. **Fax:** 212/830-7422. **Contact:** Personnel. **E-mail address:** nyjobs@kennethcole.com. **World Wide Web address:** http://www.kencole.com. **Description:** Manufactures men's and women's shoes, bags, scarves, watches, belts, and other accessories. **Corporate headquarters location:** This location. **Listed on:** New York Stock Exchange. **Stock exchange symbol:** KCP.

THE LESLIE FAY COMPANIES, INC.
1412 Broadway, 3rd Floor, New York NY 10018. 212/221-4000. **Contact:** Human Resources. **Description:** Engaged in the design, manufacture, and sale of a diversified line of women's dresses, sportswear, blouses, and intimate apparel. **Corporate headquarters location:** This location.

LIZ CLAIBORNE
1441 Broadway, New York NY 10018. 212/354-4900. **Contact:** Jorge Figueredo, Human Resources Director. **E-mail address:** staffing@liz.com. **World Wide Web address:** http://www.lizclaiborne.com. **Description:** One of America's leading apparel companies. Liz Claiborne is comprised of 18 apparel and accessories divisions and several licenses. Products are sold under the company brand names and private labels. **NOTE:** Entry-level positions are offered. **Common positions include:** Account Manager; Account Representative; Administrative Assistant. **Special programs:** Internships. **Corporate headquarters location:** This location. **Listed on:** New York Stock Exchange. **Stock exchange symbol:** LIZ. **CEO:** Paul Charron. **Number of employees worldwide:** 7,000.

J.B. MARTIN COMPANY
10 East 53rd Street, Suite 3100, New York NY 10022. 212/421-2020. **Contact:** David Budd, Director of Sales. **World Wide Web address:** http://www.jbmartin.com. **Description:** Manufactures velvet. **Corporate headquarters location:** This location.

MILLIKEN & COMPANY
1045 Sixth Avenue, New York NY 10018. 212/819-4200. **Contact:** Personnel. **World Wide Web address:** http://www.milliken.com. **Description:** Manufactures a wide range of textile yarns and fabrics, apparel, and related chemical and packaging products. Products range from tire cord to yarn and fashion fabrics to women's wear and men's wear. Milliken & Company has also developed several products and industrial processes used in textile products manufacturing.

MOVIE STAR, INC.
1115 Broadway, New York NY 10010. 212/684-3400. **Contact:** Human Resources. **World Wide Web address:** http://www.moviestarinc.com. **Description:** A diversified apparel manufacturer. The company operates through three divisions. The largest division, Sanmark, designs, manufactures, and sells private label sleepwear, robes, loungewear, leisurewear, daywear, and undergarments to mass merchants, as well as to national and regional chains. Cinema Etoile is also an intimate apparel producer. The Irwin B. Schwabe division produces private label work and leisure shirts for chain stores and mail order catalogs as well as shirts that

are sold under the Private Property brand name. The 25 Movie Star factory stores carry an assortment of merchandise, some of which is supplied by the three manufacturing divisions, as well as sportswear and accessories. **Corporate headquarters location:** This location. **Other U.S. locations:** GA; MI. **Listed on:** American Stock Exchange. **Stock exchange symbol:** MSI.

NATIONAL SPINNING COMPANY INC.
111 West 40th Street, 28th Floor, New York NY 10018. 212/382-6400. **Contact:** Human Resources Department. **World Wide Web address:** http://www.natspin.com. **Description:** Engaged in the manufacturing, marketing, and distribution of yarn products to knitwear manufacturers. The company also produces hand-knitting yarn and rug kits for distribution to retail chains throughout the United States. **Corporate headquarters location:** This location.

NINE WEST GROUP
Nine West Plaza, 1129 Westchester Avenue, White Plains NY 10604-3529. 914/640-6400. **Fax:** 914/640-3499. **Contact:** Melissa Tavino, Human Resources Department. **E-mail address:** jobs@ninewest.com. **World Wide Web address:** http://www.ninewest.com. **Description:** A manufacturer and retailer of women's shoes. **Office hours:** Monday - Thursday, 9:00 a.m. - 5:00 p.m.; Friday, 8:30 a.m. - 3:00 p.m. **Parent company:** Jones Apparel Group. **Listed on:** New York Stock Exchange. **Stock exchange symbol:** JNY.

PHILLIPS-VAN HEUSEN CORPORATION
200 Madison Avenue, 10th Floor, New York NY 10016-3908. 212/381-3500. **Contact:** Betty Chaves, Director of Human Resources Department. **World Wide Web address:** http://www.pvh.com. **Description:** Manufactures, wholesales, and retails men's and women's apparel. **Common positions include:** Accountant/Auditor; Buyer; Designer; Human Resources Manager; Manufacturer's/Wholesaler's Sales Rep.; Purchasing Agent/Manager; Systems Analyst. **Corporate headquarters location:** This location. **Other U.S. locations:** AL; NJ. **Listed on:** New York Stock Exchange. **Stock exchange symbol:** PVH. **Number of employees nationwide:** 14,000.

POLO RALPH LAUREN
650 Madison Avenue, New York NY 10022. 212/318-7000. **Fax:** 212/318-7200. **Contact:** Personnel. **E-mail address:** jobs@poloralphlauren.com. **World Wide Web address:** http://www.polo.com. **Description:** This location is an administrative office. Overall, Polo Ralph Lauren manufactures clothing and shoes for women and men. **Corporate headquarters location:** This location. **Listed on:** New York Stock Exchange. **Stock exchange symbol:** RL.

SALANT CORPORATION
1114 Avenue of the Americas, 36th Floor, New York NY 10036. 212/221-7500. **Contact:** Human Resources. **Description:** Designs, manufactures, imports, and markets a broad line of men's, children's, and women's apparel and accessories to retailers. Menswear is the company's largest sales category, with a focus on sportswear, dress shirts, neckwear, slacks, and jeans marketed under the Perry Ellis, J.J. Farmer, Thomson, John Henry, Gant, Manhattan, AXXA, Liberty of London, UNICEF, Peanuts, and Save the Children brand names. The company's children's brands include Joe Boxer, Dr. Denton, Power Rangers, certain Disney characters, and OshKosh B'Gosh. Women's wear includes sportswear marketed under the Made in the Shade brand name. The company's products are sold through

department and specialty stores, major discounters, and mass volume retailers. Salant operates six domestic manufacturing facilities and five distribution centers. **Corporate headquarters location:** This location. **Number of employees worldwide:** 4,200.

F. SCHUMACHER & COMPANY
79 Madison Avenue, New York NY 10016. 212/213-7900. **Contact:** Ms. Gail Maddox, Director of Employment. **World Wide Web address:** http://www.fschumacher.com. **Description:** A textile wholesaler specializing in rug and fabric trading. **Corporate headquarters location:** This location. **Other U.S. locations:** Nationwide.

SPRINGS INDUSTRIES, INC.
104 West 40th Street, New York NY 10018. 212/556-6000. **Contact:** Peggy Rampulla, Human Resources Manager. **World Wide Web address:** http://www.springs.com. **Description:** Produces a wide range of finished apparel fabrics, consumer fashion fabrics, and retail and specialty fabrics. **Common positions include:** Administrator; Manufacturer's/Wholesaler's Sales Rep.; Marketing Specialist. **Corporate headquarters location:** Fort Mills SC. **Operations at this facility include:** Divisional Headquarters; Regional Headquarters; Sales. **Number of employees worldwide:** 23,500.

TOTE ISOTONER INC.
420 Fifth Avenue, 3rd Floor, New York NY 10018. 212/944-1129. **Contact:** Human Resources. **Description:** Produces a wide range of gloves and related accessories including nationally distributed Isotoner products.

THE WARNACO GROUP, INC.
90 Park Avenue, New York NY 10016. 212/661-1300. **Contact:** Human Resources Department. **Description:** A manufacturer, designer, and marketer of women's intimate apparel, men's wear, and men's accessories under brand names including Calvin Klein, Fruit of the Loom, Warner's, Olga, and Chaps by Ralph Lauren. Warnaco markets its products through a chain of 48 retail outlets, as well as department stores and mass merchandisers in North America and Europe. **Corporate headquarters location:** This location.

WEST MILL CLOTHES INC.
57-07 31st Avenue, Woodside NY 11377. 718/204-6640. **Contact:** Clifford Goodman, Personnel Officer. **Description:** Manufactures formalwear. **Corporate headquarters location:** This location.

WEST POINT STEVENS, INC.
1185 Avenue of the Americas, New York NY 10036. 212/930-2050. **Contact:** Lisa Brier, Director of Human Resources Department. **World Wide Web address:** http://www.westpointstevens.com. **Description:** A major worldwide marketing and manufacturing organization. The company's core products are fabrics made from both natural and man-made fibers and yarns for a broad range of end uses including products for the home and apparel. **Common positions include:** Account Manager; Administrative Assistant; Attorney; Customer Service Representative; Designer; Graphic Artist; Manufacturer's/Wholesaler's Sales Rep.; Receptionist; Secretary. **Corporate headquarters location:** This location. **Operations at this facility include:** Administration; Design; Marketing; Sales; Service. **Number of employees at this location:** 250. **Number of employees nationwide:** 19,000.

ARCHITECTURE, CONSTRUCTION, AND ENGINEERING

You can expect to find the following types of companies in this chapter:

Architectural and Engineering Services • Civil and Mechanical Engineering Firms • Construction Products, Manufacturers, and Wholesalers • General Contractors/ Specialized Trade Contractors

AMEC
1633 Broadway, 24th Floor, New York NY 10019. 212/484-0300. **Fax:** 212/484-0580. **Contact:** Ann Sue Mushnick, Senior Vice President of Human Resources. **World Wide Web address:** http://www.amec.com. **Description:** One of the largest construction management companies in the world offering a wide range of services including construction management, contracting program management, consulting, and design and construction. Founded in 1936. **Common positions include:** Accountant/Auditor; Attorney; Civil Engineer; Claim Representative; Computer Programmer; Construction and Building Inspector; Construction Contractor; Cost Estimator; Human Resources Manager; Mechanical Engineer; MIS Specialist; Paralegal; Structural Engineer; Systems Analyst; Technical Writer/Editor. **Special programs:** Internships. **Corporate headquarters location:** This location. **Operations at this facility include:** Divisional Headquarters; Regional Headquarters. **Annual sales/revenues:** More than $100 million. **Number of employees at this location:** 140. **Number of employees nationwide:** 500.

ACME STEEL PARTITION COMPANY, INC.
513 Porter Avenue, Brooklyn NY 11222. 718/384-7800. **Contact:** Human Resources. **Description:** Manufacturers of steel doors, frames, and movable steel partitions.

AMMANN AND WHITNEY
96 Morton Street, New York NY 10014-3326. 212/462-8500. **Contact:** Ruth Darvie, Personnel Director. **E-mail address:** rdarvie@ammann-whitney.com. **World Wide Web address:** http://www.ammann-whitney.com. **Description:** An engineering consulting firm. **Common positions include:** Architect; Civil Engineer; Construction Engineer; Design Engineer; Electrical/Electronics Engineer; Mechanical Engineer; Structural Engineer. **Other U.S. locations:** Wethersfield CT; Washington DC; Boston MA; Hoboken NJ; Philadelphia PA; Richmond VA.

DREW INDUSTRIES INC.
200 Mamaroneck Avenue, Suite 301, White Plains NY 10601. 914/428-9098. **Contact:** Harvey Kaplan, Secretary and Treasurer. **World Wide Web address:** http://www.drewindustries.com. **Description:** Drew Industries is the holding company of Kinro, Inc. Kinro is one of the leading producers of aluminum and vinyl windows for manufactured homes, and windows and doors for recreational vehicles. Kinro has nine domestic manufacturing plants. **Corporate headquarters location:** This location. **Listed on:** American Stock Exchange. **Stock exchange symbol:** DW.

FOSTER WHEELER LTD.
9431 Foster Wheeler Road, Dansville NY 14437. 716/335-3131. **Contact:** Human Resources. **World Wide Web address:** http://www.fwc.com. **Description:** Engaged in three business segments: process plants segment, consisting primarily of the design, engineering, and construction of process plants and fired heaters for oil refiners and chemical producers; a utility and engine segment, consisting primarily of the design and fabrication of steam generators, condensers, feedwater heaters, electrostatic precipitators, and other pollution abatement equipment; and an industrial segment that supplies pressure vessels and internals, electrical copper products, industrial insulation, welding wire, and electrodes. **Corporate headquarters location:** Clinton NJ. **Other U.S. locations:** Nationwide. **International locations:** Worldwide. **Listed on:** New York Stock Exchange. **Stock exchange symbol:** FWC.

HUDSON-SHATZ PAINTING COMPANY INC.
429 West 53rd Street, New York NY 10019. 212/757-6363. **Contact:** Human Resources Department. **Description:** A painting contractor. **Corporate headquarters location:** This location.

INDUSTRIAL ACOUSTICS COMPANY (IAC)
1160 Commerce Avenue, Bronx NY 10462. 718/931-8000. **Contact:** Human Resources. **E-mail address:** info@industrialacoustics.com. **World Wide Web address:** http://www.industrialacoustics.com. **Description:** IAC is an international company with engineering and manufacturing capabilities serving the architectural, air conditioning, industrial, medical and life sciences, power plant, and military/commercial aviation markets. The company develops and markets noise control products, turnkey systems for air conditioning and air handling units, jet engine aircraft hush-house test facilities, detention cells, acoustical ceilings for correctional institutions, and other special purpose ceilings. Founded in 1949. **International locations:** Germany; United Kingdom.

KSW MECHANICAL SERVICES
3716 23rd Street, Long Island City NY 11101. 718/361-6500. **Contact:** Human Resources. **Description:** A mechanical contracting firm engaged in the installation of heating, ventilation, and air conditioning systems in commercial buildings. **Corporate headquarters location:** This location.

PARAMOUNT ELECTRONICS COMPANY
57 Willoughby Street, Brooklyn NY 11201. 718/237-8730. **Contact:** Human Resources Department. **Description:** Provides contract drafting services. **Corporate headquarters location:** This location.

PARSONS BRINCKERHOFF INC.
One Penn Plaza, New York NY 10119. 212/465-5000. **Contact:** Ed Swartz, Vice President of Personnel. **World Wide Web address:** http://www.pbworld.com. **Description:** Provides total engineering and construction management services, including the development of major bridges, tunnels, highways, marine facilities, buildings, industrial complexes, and railroads. **Corporate headquarters location:** This location. **International locations:** Worldwide. **Subsidiaries include:** Parsons Brinckerhoff Construction Services; Parsons Brinckerhoff Development Corporation; Parsons Brinckerhoff International; Parsons Brinckerhoff Quade & Douglas.

SLANT/FIN CORPORATION
100 Forest Drive, Greenvale NY 11548. 516/484-2600. **Contact:** Edward F. Sliwinski, Personnel Manager. **E-mail address:** info@slantfin.com. **World Wide Web address:** http://www.slantfin.com. **Description:** Engaged in the manufacture and sale of heating and cooling equipment for both domestic and foreign markets. **NOTE:** Edward F. Sliwinski is the Personnel Manager for the factory. Contact the company regarding employment in other departments. **Corporate headquarters location:** This location. **International locations:** Canada.

SLATTERY SKANSKA INC.
16-16 Whitestone Expressway, Whitestone NY 11357. 718/767-2600. **Fax:** 718/767-2668. **Contact:** Larry Bolyard, Director of Human Resources Department. **E-mail address:** larry.bolyard@slattery.skanska.com. **World Wide Web address:** http://www.slatteryskanska.com. **Description:** A heavy construction firm engaged in large-scale projects such as mass transit, sewage treatment plants, highways, bridges, and tunnels. **Common positions include:** Accountant/Auditor; Civil Engineer; Cost Estimator; Draftsperson; Environmental Engineer; Mechanical Engineer; Structural Engineer. **Office hours:** Monday - Friday, 8:00 a.m. - 4:30 p.m. **Corporate headquarters location:** This location. **Parent company:** Skanska USA. **Operations at this facility include:** Administration. **Listed on:** Privately held. **Number of employees at this location:** 1,000.

STROBER BROTHERS, INC.
Pier 3, Furman Street, Brooklyn NY 11201. 718/875-9700. **Fax:** 718/246-3080. **Contact:** Human Resources. **World Wide Web address:** http://www.strober.com. **Description:** Strober Organization, Inc. is a supplier of building materials to professional building contractors in the residential, commercial, and renovation construction markets. The company operates 10 building centers across four states, offering a broad selection of gypsum wallboard and other drywall products, lumber, roofing, insulation and acoustical materials, plywood, siding products, metal specialties, hardware and tools, waterproofing, masonry, and steel decking products. The building centers also offer a full spectrum of millwork. Founded in 1912. **Corporate headquarters location:** This location.

TAMS CONSULTANTS
655 Third Avenue, New York NY 10017. 212/867-1777. **Contact:** Human Resources. **World Wide Web address:** http://www.tamsconsultants.com. **Description:** An engineering consulting firm.

TESTWELL LABORATORIES, INC.
47 Hudson Street, Ossining NY 10562. 914/762-9000. **Fax:** 914/762-9638. **Contact:** Human Resources Director. **World Wide Web address:** http://www.testwelllabs.com. **Description:** Provides construction materials and environmental testing, inspection, and consulting services for the construction, environmental, and real estate industries. **Common positions include:** Chemical Engineer; Chemist; Civil Engineer; Clerical Supervisor; Geologist/Geophysicist; Services Sales Representative; Structural Engineer. **Corporate headquarters location:** This location. **Other area locations:** Albany NY. **Other U.S. locations:** Miami FL; Mays Landing NJ. **Operations at this facility include:** Administration; Regional Headquarters; Sales; Service. **Listed on:** Privately held. **Number of employees at this location:** 90. **Number of employees nationwide:** 400.

TURNER CORPORATION
375 Hudson Street, New York NY 10014. 212/229-6000. **Contact:** Human Resources. **World Wide Web address:** http://www.turnerconstruction.com. **Description:** A holding company involved in construction, general building, contract management, and real estate development. **Corporate headquarters location:** This location. **Subsidiaries include:** Turner Construction Company; Turner Medical Building Services.

WELSBACH ELECTRIC CORPORATION
P.O. Box 560252, 111-01 14th Avenue, College Point NY 11356-0252. 718/670-7900. **Contact:** Human Resources Department. **World Wide Web address:** http://www.welsbachelectric.com. **Description:** An electrical contractor engaged in the installation and maintenance of streetlights and traffic signals. **Corporate headquarters location:** This location. **Parent company:** EMCOR Group, Inc. **Listed on:** New York Stock Exchange. **Stock exchange symbol:** EME. **President:** Fred Goodman.

ARTS, ENTERTAINMENT, SPORTS, AND RECREATION

You can expect to find the following types of companies in this chapter:

Botanical and Zoological Gardens • Entertainment Groups • Motion Picture and Video Tape Production and Distribution • Museums and Art Galleries • Physical Fitness Facilities • Professional Sports Clubs • Public Golf Courses • Racing and Track Operations • Sporting and Recreational Camps • Theatrical Producers

A&E TELEVISION NETWORKS
235 East 45th Street, New York NY 10017. 212/210-1400. **Contact:** Human Resources. **World Wide Web address:** http://www.aande.com/corporate. **Description:** A media corporation that provides magazine and book publishing services, distributes home videos, and operates Websites and the A&E and History Channel cable stations. **Corporate headquarters location:** This location.

AMERIC DISC
11 Oval Drive, Islandia NY 11749. 631/234-0200. **Contact:** Human Resources. **World Wide Web address:** http://www.americdisc.com. **Description:** Americ Disc is one of the nation's leading independent multimedia manufacturing companies offering CD-audio and CD-ROM mastering and replication; videocassette and audiocassette duplication; laser video disc recording; off-line and online video editing; motion picture film processing; film-to-tape and tape-to-film transfers; and finishing, packaging, warehousing, and fulfillment services. **Corporate headquarters location:** Quebec, Canada.

THE AMERICAN KENNEL CLUB
260 Madison Avenue, 4th Floor, New York NY 10016. 212/696-8304. **Recorded jobline:** 919/816-3896. **Contact:** Human Resources. **World Wide Web address:** http://www.akc.org. **Description:** An independent, nonprofit organization devoted to the advancement of purebred dogs. The American Kennel Club adopts and enforces rules and regulations governing dog shows, obedience trials, and field trials, and fosters and encourages interest in the health and welfare of purebred dogs. The club also offers a wide range of books and magazines for national distribution. Founded in 1884. **NOTE:** Entry-level positions are offered. Resumes should be sent to P.O. Box 37905, Raleigh NC 27627-7905. **Common positions include:** Accountant; Administrative Assistant; Desktop Publishing Specialist; Editor; Editorial Assistant; Financial Analyst; Graphic Designer. **Office hours:** Monday - Friday, 8:30 a.m. - 4:15 p.m. **Corporate headquarters location:** This location. **Other U.S. locations:** Raleigh NC. **Listed on:** Privately held. **President/CEO:** Al Cheaure. **Annual sales/revenues:** $21 - $50 million. **Number of employees at this location:** 75. **Number of employees nationwide:** 450.

AMERICAN MUSEUM OF NATURAL HISTORY
Central Park West at 79th Street, New York NY 10024-5192. 212/769-5000. **Contact:** Richard MacKewice, Director of Human Resources. **World Wide Web address:** http://www.amnh.org. **Description:** A museum of

anthropology, astronomy, mineralogy, and zoology. The museum has a research library and 38 exhibition halls and offers educational and research programs. The museum also publishes several in-house and nationally distributed magazines based on research conducted there. Founded in 1869. **Corporate headquarters location:** This location.

AMERICAN SYMPHONY ORCHESTRA LEAGUE
33 West 60th Street, 5th Floor, New York NY 10023. 212/262-5161. **Fax:** 212/262-5198. **Contact:** Director of Human Resources. **E-mail address:** hr@symphony.org. **World Wide Web address:** http://www.symphony.org. **Description:** A national service organization for America's professional, symphony, chamber, youth, and college orchestras. Founded in 1942. **Common positions include:** Marketing Manager; Marketing Specialist; Network/Systems Administrator; Public Relations Specialist; Web Advertising Specialist; Webmaster; Website Developer. **Office hours:** Monday - Friday, 9:00 a.m. - 5:30 p.m. **Other U.S. locations:** Washington DC.

APOLLO THEATRE
253 West 125th Street, New York NY 10027. 212/531-5300. **Contact:** Human Resources. **Description:** A nonprofit performing arts theater owned and operated by the Apollo Theatre Foundation. Performances take place year-round.

ARISTA RECORDS, INC.
6 West 57th Street, 2nd Floor, New York NY 10019. 212/489-7400. **Fax:** 212/830-2107. **Contact:** Human Resources Department. **World Wide Web address:** http://www.arista.com. **Description:** Provides sales, promotional, and artist and repertoire activities for Arista Records and its contracted artists. **Corporate headquarters location:** This location. **Parent company:** BMG Music. **Operations at this facility include:** Administration; Sales.

BROADWAY VIDEO INC.
1619 Broadway, 10th Floor, New York NY 10019. 212/265-7600. **Contact:** Personnel. **World Wide Web address:** http://www.broadwayvideo.com. **Description:** An entertainment production company offering editing, design, sound, and related services for all types of media. **Corporate headquarters location:** This location. **Founder:** Mr. Lorne Michaels.

BROOKLYN ACADEMY OF MUSIC
30 Lafayette Avenue, Brooklyn NY 11217. 718/636-4111. **Contact:** Human Resources. **World Wide Web address:** http://www.bam.org. **Description:** A nonprofit arts showcase offering dance, opera, and theatrical performances, as well as performances by the Brooklyn Philharmonic Orchestra. Founded in 1859. **Special programs:** Internships.

BROOKLYN BOTANIC GARDEN
1000 Washington Avenue, Brooklyn NY 11225. 718/623-7200. **Contact:** Human Resources Department. **E-mail address:** personnel@bbg.org. **World Wide Web address:** http://www.bbg.org. **Description:** Exhibits over 10,000 plants in the Steinhardt Conservatory. Brooklyn Botanic Garden also offers programs teaching hands-on gardening to children ages three to 17. Brooklyn Botanic Garden offers special events such as the Cherry Blossom Festival, student art exhibitions, tours of the Japanese Hill-and-Pond Garden, and the Annual Spring Plant Sale. Founded in 1910.

CINE MAGNETICS VIDEO & DIGITAL LABORATORIES
100 Business Park Drive, Armonk NY 10504-1750. 914/273-7500. **Contact:** Personnel. **World Wide Web address:** http://www.cinemagnetics.com. **Description:** Cine Magnetics is involved in video and film duplication and photo finishing. **Corporate headquarters location:** This location. **Other U.S. locations:** Culver City CA.

CITY CENTER OF MUSIC AND DRAMA INC. (CCMD)
70 Lincoln Center Plaza, 4th Floor, New York NY 10023-6580. 212/870-4266. **Fax:** 212/870-4286. **Contact:** Cynthia Herzegovitch, Human Resources Administrator. **Description:** Organizational and management offices for the nonprofit cultural organization with activities that include plays, ballets, and operas. The center operates the New York State Theater, the New York City Opera, the New York Ballet, and City Center Special Productions. **Common positions include:** Accountant/Auditor; Clerical Supervisor; Computer Programmer; Health Services Manager; Human Resources Manager; MIS Specialist. **Corporate headquarters location:** This location. **Operations at this facility include:** Administration. **Number of employees nationwide:** 2,000.

THE CLOISTERS
Fort Tryon Park, New York NY 10040. 212/650-2280. **Contact:** Assistant Museum Educator. **World Wide Web address:** http://www.metmuseum.org. **Description:** A museum devoted to the art of medieval Europe. The collection includes architectural fragments, sculptures, frescoes, illuminated manuscripts, tapestries, stained glass, and paintings. Established in 1938. **Special programs:** Internships. **Parent company:** The Metropolitan Museum of Art.

COMEDY CENTRAL
1775 Broadway, 9th Floor, New York NY 10019. 212/767-8600. **Contact:** Human Resources. **World Wide Web address:** http://www.comcentral.com. **Description:** Operates the Comedy Central network, which produces such shows as *The Daily Show*, *South Park*, and *Dr. Katz*. **Corporate headquarters location:** This location.

COURT TV
600 Third Avenue, 2nd Floor, New York NY 10016. 212/973-2800. **Contact:** Personnel. **World Wide Web address:** http://www.courttv.com. **Description:** A cable network providing coverage of some of the country's most widely publicized legal battles. **Corporate headquarters location:** This location.

DUART FILM AND VIDEO
245 West 55th Street, New York NY 10019. 212/757-4580. **Contact:** Supervisor. **World Wide Web address:** http://www.duart.com. **Description:** Involved in motion picture services and television broadcasting.

HBO (HOME BOX OFFICE)
1100 Avenue of the Americas, New York NY 10036. 212/512-1000. **Contact:** Human Resources Department. **World Wide Web address:** http://www.hbo.com. **Description:** Operates HBO, HBO HDTV, and Cinemax, television networks dedicated to movies. Divisions of HBO include: MoreMAX, ThrillerMAX, and ActionMAX. **Other U.S. locations:** Los Angeles CA. **Parent company:** AOL Time Warner Inc. **Listed on:** New York Stock Exchange. **Stock exchange symbol:** AOL.

THE HUDSON RIVER MUSEUM OF WESTCHESTER
ANDRUS PLANETARIUM
511 Warburton Avenue, Yonkers NY 10701. 914/963-4550. **Contact:** Human Resources. **World Wide Web address:** http://www.hrm.org. **Description:** A museum of art, history, and science. Collections include 19th-century fine and decorative arts, and 19th- and 20th-century paintings. Andrus Planetarium is the only public planetarium in Westchester County.

JUNIPER GROUP, INC.
111 Great Neck Road, Suite 604, Great Neck NY 11021. 516/829-4670. **Fax:** 516/829-4691. **Contact:** Human Resources. **World Wide Web address:** http://www.junipergroup.com. **Description:** Juniper Group operates in two segments: health care and entertainment. The company's principal revenues are generated from health care, which consists of management for hospitals and health care cost containment for health care payers. The entertainment segment acquires and distributes film rights to various media including home video, pay-per-view, pay television, cable television, networks, ad-hoc networks, and independent syndicated television stations. Founded in 1989. **Corporate headquarters location:** This location. **Subsidiaries include:** Juniper Medical Systems, Inc. with subsidiaries that include Diversified Health Affiliates, Inc. and Juniper Healthcare Containment Systems, Inc. Diversified Health Affiliates operates Juniper Group's management business while Juniper Healthcare Containment Systems conducts health care cost containment service operations. **Listed on:** NASDAQ. **Stock exchange symbol:** JUNI.

LINCOLN CENTER FOR THE ARTS, INC.
NEW YORK CITY BALLET
70 Lincoln Center Plaza, New York NY 10023. 212/875-5000. **Fax:** 212/875-5185. **Contact:** Manager of Human Resources Department. **E-mail address:** humanresources@lincolncenter.org. **World Wide Web address:** http://www.lincolncenter.org. **Description:** An international center for performing arts.

MGM/UNITED ARTISTS
ORION PICTURES CORPORATION
1350 Avenue of the Americas, 24th Floor, New York NY 10019. 212/708-0300. **Contact:** Human Resources Department. **World Wide Web address:** http://www.mgm.com. **Description:** One of the nation's largest film distribution companies. **Common positions include:** Attorney; Branch Manager; Computer Programmer; Customer Service Representative; Department Manager; Human Resources Manager; Public Relations Specialist; Systems Analyst. **Special programs:** Internships. **Corporate headquarters location:** Santa Monica CA. **Operations at this facility include:** Administration; Sales; Service. **Listed on:** New York Stock Exchange. **Stock exchange symbol:** MGM. **Number of employees at this location:** 250.

MADISON SQUARE GARDEN, L.P.
2 Penn Plaza, 16th Floor, New York NY 10121. 212/465-6330. **Recorded jobline:** 212/465-6335. **Contact:** Manager of Human Resources Department. **E-mail address:** msghr@thegarden.com. **World Wide Web address:** http://www.thegarden.com. **Description:** Operates sports and entertainment events in the Arena, Rotunda, and Paramount Theatre. Professional sports teams include the NBA's New York Knicks, the WNBA's New York Liberty, and the NHL's New York Rangers. Madison Square Garden also operates the MSG Network (one of the nation's oldest regional

cable television sports networks). In addition, Madison Square Garden operates its own restaurants, catering, fast food, and merchandise divisions. This location also hires seasonally. **NOTE:** Part-time jobs are offered. **Common positions include:** Budget Analyst; Computer Programmer; Customer Service Representative; Financial Analyst; Human Resources Manager; MIS Specialist; Public Relations Specialist; Radio/TV Announcer/Broadcaster; Restaurant/Food Service Manager; Systems Analyst; Typist/Word Processor. **Special programs:** Internships. **Internship information:** Madison Square Garden has a college internship program that runs during the fall, spring, and summer semesters. For application information, call 212/465-6258. **Corporate headquarters location:** This location. **Operations at this facility include:** Administration; Sales.

THE METROPOLITAN MUSEUM OF ART
1000 Fifth Avenue, New York NY 10028. 212/879-5500. **Contact:** Peggy Saldok, Human Resources Representative. **World Wide Web address:** http://www.metmuseum.org. **Description:** A museum containing one of the most extensive art collections in the world. Permanent exhibits range from ancient art to modern art. Operations include conservation and curatorial departments, education services, libraries, concerts and lectures, internships, fellowships, publications and reproductions, and exhibitions. The museum also operates The Cloisters in Fort Tryon Park. **Common positions include:** Accountant/Auditor; Administrative Assistant; Educational Specialist; Librarian; Researcher.

THE METROPOLITAN OPERA
Lincoln Center, New York NY 10023. 212/799-3100. **Fax:** 212/870-7405. **Contact:** Lisa Fuld, Personnel. **E-mail address:** resumes@mail.metopera.org. **World Wide Web address:** http://www.metopera.org. **Description:** One of the world's largest nonprofit arts organizations, producing approximately 25 operas per year. The opera tours internationally and performs free outdoor concerts in New York area parks. Founded in 1883. **NOTE:** Entry-level positions, part-time jobs, and second and third shifts are offered. **Common positions include:** Accountant; Actor/Actress/Performer; Administrative Assistant; Administrative Manager; Applications Engineer; Blue-Collar Worker Supervisor; Budget Analyst; Cashier; Commercial Artist; Computer Programmer; Computer Technician; Customer Service Representative; Database Administrator; Department Manager; Designer; Electrical/Electronics Engineer; Employment Interviewer; Financial Analyst; Help-Desk Technician; Human Resources Manager; Marketing Manager; Mechanical Engineer; Operations Manager; Secretary; Telecommunications Manager. **Corporate headquarters location:** This location. **Operations at this facility include:** Administration; Manufacturing; Sales; Service. **Number of employees at this location:** 1,000.

MULTIMEDIA TUTORIAL SERVICES, INC.
205 Kings Highway, Brooklyn NY 11223. 718/234-0404. **Contact:** Human Resources. **Description:** Produces and markets tutorial education programs, primarily in videotape and also CD-ROM formats, for use by adults and children in homes, work, schools, libraries, and other locales. Principal products consist of a series of 92 videotapes and supplemental materials on mathematics and an interactive, audio-visual, CD-ROM based system for language instruction. The company's videotapes include colorful computer graphics and real life vignettes. **Corporate headquarters location:** This location.

MUSEUM OF MODERN ART
11 West 53rd Street, New York NY 10019. 212/708-9400. **Contact:** Human Resources Manager. **World Wide Web address:** http://www.moma.org. **Description:** Houses one of the world's foremost collections of modern art. **Common positions include:** Administrative Worker/Clerk; Secretary. **Special programs:** Internships. **Corporate headquarters location:** This location. **Number of employees at this location:** 550.

NEW LINE CINEMA
888 Seventh Avenue, 19th Floor, New York NY 10106. 212/649-4900. **Contact:** Human Resources Department. **World Wide Web address:** http://www.newline.com. **Description:** Produces and distributes low-budget theatrical motion pictures (generally action/adventure and comedy films targeted at the younger market). The company also acquires distribution rights to films produced by others, and has agreements with distributors in ancillary markets such as home video, pay television, and free television.

THE NEW YORK BOTANICAL GARDEN
200th Street & Kazimiroff Boulevard, Bronx NY 10458-5126. 718/817-8744. **Contact:** Human Resources. **E-mail address:** hr@nybg.org. **World Wide Web address:** http://www.nybg.org. **Description:** An internationally recognized center for botanical research offering 47 gardens and plant collections. The New York Botanical Garden is dedicated to environmental education and the conservation of plant diversity. Founded in 1891. **Common positions include:** Administrator; Fundraising Specialist. **Special programs:** Internships. **Corporate headquarters location:** This location. **Operations at this facility include:** Education; Research and Development.

THE NEW YORK RACING ASSOCIATION
P.O. Box 90, Jamaica NY 11417. 718/641-4700. **Contact:** Human Resources. **World Wide Web address:** http://www.nyracing.com. **Description:** A state-franchised, nonprofit racing association that owns, operates, and manages three horseracing tracks: Aqueduct, Belmont Park, and Saratoga, where pari-mutuel wagering is conducted. These facilities are the site of some of America's most prestigious stakes races: The Wood Memorial, and The Belmont and Travers Stakes.

NEW YORK SHAKESPEARE FESTIVAL
425 Lafayette Street, New York NY 10003. 212/539-8500. **Contact:** General Manager. **Description:** A nonprofit organization involved in many productions: year-round on-Broadway, off-Broadway, on tour around the country, television specials of theatrical works, free Shakespearean productions in Central Park each summer, and the development of new works.

OXYGEN MEDIA, INC.
75 9th Avenue, 7th Floor, New York City NY 10011. 212/651-2000. **Contact:** Human Resources. **E-mail address:** jobs@oxygen.com. **World Wide Web address:** http://www.oxygen.com. **Description:** Produces and broadcasts television programs and Websites geared toward women viewers.

PARAMOUNT CENTER FOR THE ARTS
1008 Brown Street, Peekskill NY 10566. 914/739-2333. **Contact:** Human Resources. **World Wide Web address:** http://www.paramountcenter.org. **Description:** A former vaudeville house revived as a performing arts facility offering programs in music, theater, film, and dance.

RADIO CITY ENTERTAINMENT
1260 Avenue of the Americas, New York NY 10020. 212/247-4777.
Contact: Human Resources Department. **World Wide Web address:**
http://www.radiocity.com. **Description:** A diversified entertainment
production company. **Common positions include:** Advertising Manager;
Attorney; Customer Service Representative; Emergency Medical Technician;
Human Resources Manager; Operations/Production Manager; Public
Relations Specialist; Purchasing Agent/Manager; Systems Analyst. **Special
programs:** Internships. **Corporate headquarters location:** This location.
Parent company: Madison Square Garden, L.P.

RIOT MANHATTAN
545 Fifth Avenue, 5th Floor, New York NY 10017. 212/687-4000. **Contact:**
Human Resources. **E-mail address:** info@rioting.com. **World Wide Web
address:** http://www.riotingmanhattan.com. **Description:** Provides post
production and creative services. **Corporate headquarters location:** This
location.

ROUNDABOUT THEATRE COMPANY, INC.
231 West 39th Street, Suite 1200, New York NY 10018. 212/719-9393.
Fax: 212/869-8817. **Contact:** Human Resources Department. **World Wide
Web address:** http://www.roundabouttheatre.org. **Description:** A theater
presenting revivals of classic plays. Founded in 1965. **Common positions
include:** Administrative Assistant; Fundraising Specialist; General Manager;
Ticket Agent. **Special programs:** Internships. **Number of employees at this
location:** 50.

SHOWTIME NETWORKS INC.
1633 Broadway, New York NY 10019. 212/708-1600. **Contact:** Human
Resources. **World Wide Web address:** http://www.showtimeonline.com.
Description: Operates a number of premium cable networks including
SHOWTIME, SHO2, SHO3, Showtime Extreme, Showtime Beyond, The
Movie Channel, The Movie Channel 2, Sundance, and FLIX. **Corporate
headquarters location:** This location. **Parent company:** Viacom
International Inc. **Listed on:** New York Stock Exchange. **Stock exchange
symbol:** VIA.

SHUBERT ORGANIZATION, INC.
234 West 44th Street, 7th Floor, New York NY 10036. 212/944-3700.
Contact: Elliot H. Greene, Vice President of Finance. **Description:** Owns 16
Broadway theatres, the National Theatre in Washington DC, and the
Shubert Theatre in Los Angeles CA. The Shubert Organization also
produces plays. **Common positions include:** Accountant/Auditor;
Administrative Worker/Clerk; Management Trainee. **Corporate
headquarters location:** This location. **Operations at this facility include:**
Administration; Sales.

SONY PICTURES ENTERTAINMENT
550 Madison Avenue, 7th Floor, New York NY 10022. 212/833-8500. **Fax:**
212/833-6249. **Recorded jobline:** 212/833-6526. **Contact:** Kathleen
Alvarez, Human Resources Supervisor. **World Wide, Web address:**
http://www.sonypictures.com. **Description:** Sony Pictures is involved in
motion pictures, television, theatrical exhibitions, and studio facilities and
technology. The motion picture business distributes movies produced by
Columbia TriStar Pictures. The television business, which encompasses
Columbia TriStar Television, Columbia TriStar Television Distribution, and
Columbia TriStar International Television, is involved with numerous cable

channels and distributes and syndicates television programs such as *Days of Our Lives* and *Dawson's Creek*. Loews Cineplex Entertainment operates state-of-the-art theaters in 385 locations with 2,926 screens in 15 states. Sony Pictures Imageworks specializes in motion picture special effects and production planning through previsualization sequences. **NOTE:** Entry-level positions are offered. **Common positions include:** Account Representative; Administrative Assistant; Sales Manager; Sales Representative; Secretary. **Special programs:** Internships. **Internship information:** Sony Pictures Entertainment offers various fall, spring, and summer internships in its Manhattan and Inwood, Long Island offices. Students must be available to work 15 to 21 hours per week. Majors in film, communications, management, and marketing are a plus, but all majors are welcome. Applicants must have basic office experience, excellent writing skills, and good interpersonal skills. Most internships are for academic credit, but some offer pay or a weekly stipend. Interested jobseekers should mail or fax a resume and cover letter to Samantha Rothman, Human Resources. **Corporate headquarters location:** Culver City CA. **Parent company:** Sony Corporation of America. **Operations at this facility include:** Administration; Sales. **Listed on:** New York Stock Exchange. **Stock exchange symbol:** SNE. **Number of employees at this location:** 100.

SOUTH STREET SEAPORT MUSEUM
207 Front Street, New York NY 10038. 212/748-8600. **Fax:** 212/748-8610. **Contact:** Melissa Clark, Director of Human Resources Department. **World Wide Web address:** http://www.southstseaport.org. **Description:** A maritime history museum. Through educational programs, exhibitions, and the preservation of buildings and ships, the museum interprets the role of the seaport in the development of the city, state, and nation. Founded in 1967.

STATEN ISLAND INSTITUTE OF ARTS AND SCIENCES
75 Stuyvesant Place, Staten Island NY 10301. 718/727-1135. **Fax:** 718/273-5683. **Contact:** Human Resources. **Description:** An organization that focuses on Staten Island and its people with strong collections in arts and sciences. Founded in 1881.

TIME WARNER CABLE
One Cablevision Center, 2nd Floor, Suite 2, Ferndale NY 12734. 845/295-2650. **Fax:** 845/295-2451. **Contact:** Kerry Madison, Director of Human Resources. **World Wide Web address:** http://www.twcnyc.com. **Description:** Time Warner Cable is one of the largest cable television operators in the United States. The company owns or manages 64 cable television systems in 18 states, serving a total of 1.3 million subscribers. The company owns and operates 50 cable television systems in 15 states, principally in New York, Pennsylvania, Massachusetts, Florida, California, North Carolina, South Carolina, and Louisiana. The company's systems offer subscribers packages of basic and cable programming services consisting of television signals available off-air; a limited number of television signals from distant cities; numerous satellite-delivered, nonbroadcast channels such as CNN, MTV, USA Network, ESPN, A&E, TNT, and Nickelodeon; displays of information such as time, news, weather and stock market reports; and public, governmental, and educational access channels. **Common positions include:** Customer Service Representative; Installer; Marketing Specialist; Sales Executive; Technician. **Special programs:** Summer Jobs. **Parent company:** AOL Time Warner, Inc. **Listed on:** New York Stock Exchange. **Stock exchange symbol:** AOL. **Number of employees at this location:** 380.

USA INTERACTIVE
152 West 57th Street, New York NY 10019. 212/314-7300. **Contact:** Personnel. **World Wide Web address:** http://www.usainteractive.com. **Description:** An e-commerce and entertainment company operating one of the nation's largest cable television networks. **Corporate headquarters location:** This location.

UNIVERSAL MUSIC GROUP
825 Eighth Avenue, 28th Floor, New York NY 10019. 212/333-8000. **Contact:** Human Resources Department. **World Wide Web address:** http://www.universalstudios.com/music. **Description:** Produces and markets popular and classical records and is active in the areas of film development, production, and distribution, as well as event television, video theater, merchandising, touring, and music publishing. **Subsidiaries include:** MCA; Universal Concerts. **Parent company:** The Seagram Company Ltd.

WARNER BROS. INC.
1325 Avenue of the Americas, 31st Floor, New York NY 10019. 212/636-5000. **Contact:** Manager of Human Resources Department. **World Wide Web address:** http://www.warnerbros.com. **Description:** Offices of the diversified entertainment company. **Parent company:** AOL Time Warner. **Listed on:** New York Stock Exchange. **Stock exchange symbol:** AOL.

WILDLIFE CONSERVATION SOCIETY (WCS)
BRONX ZOO
2300 Southern Boulevard, Bronx NY 10460. 718/220-5100. **Fax:** 718/220-2464. **Contact:** Mariam Benitez, Human Resources Director. **World Wide Web address:** http://www.wcs.org/home/zoos/bronxzoo. **Description:** Operates the Aquarium for Wildlife Conservation, the Bronx Zoo, the Central Park Wildlife Center, the Prospect Park Wildlife Center, and the Queens Wildlife Center. Wildlife Conservation Society (WCS) also manages the St. Catherine Wildlife Survival Center off the coast of Georgia and nearly 300 international field projects in over 50 nations. Additionally, WCS conducts environmental education programs at local, national, and international levels. **Common positions include:** Collection Manager; Curator; Graphic Artist; Horticulturist; Wildlife Keeper. **Office hours:** Monday - Friday, 9:00 a.m. - 5:00 p.m.

WILLIAM MORRIS AGENCY, INC.
1325 6th Avenue, New York NY 10019. 212/903-1110. **Fax:** 212/903-1474. **Contact:** Ms. Pat Galloway, Director of Human Resources. **World Wide Web address:** http://www.wma.com. **Description:** One of the largest talent and literary agencies in the world. Founded in 1898. **NOTE:** Entry-level positions are offered. **Common positions include:** Administrative Assistant; Agent Trainee. **Special programs:** Training. **Corporate headquarters location:** Beverly Hills CA. **Other U.S. locations:** Nashville TN. **Operations at this facility include:** Regional Headquarters. **Listed on:** Privately held. **Number of employees at this location:** 200. **Number of employees nationwide:** 700. **Number of employees worldwide:** 750.

YONKERS RACEWAY
810 Central Park Avenue, Yonkers NY 10704. 914/968-4200. **Contact:** Anita Tripo, Director of Human Resources. **Description:** Operates a major harness racing facility, as well as a convention and meeting facility. **Common positions include:** Accountant/Auditor; Food and Beverage Service Worker; Market Research Analyst; Public Relations Specialist. **Corporate headquarters location:** This location.

AUTOMOTIVE

You can expect to find the following types of companies in this chapter:

Automotive Repair Shops • Automotive Stampings • Industrial Vehicles and Moving Equipment • Motor Vehicles and Equipment • Travel Trailers and Campers

ARLEN CORPORATION

505 Eighth Avenue, Suite 300, New York NY 10018. 212/736-8100. **Contact:** Human Resources. **Description:** Manufactures and distributes steering wheels, physical security devices, interior accessories, and composite plastic and acrylic molded styling accessories for the automotive aftermarket and for automotive and marine original equipment manufacturers. The company also manufactures and distributes metal trim and accessories for the light-truck and sport-utility market.

AUDIOVOX CORPORATION

150 Marcus Boulevard, Hauppauge NY 11788. 631/231-7750. **Contact:** Elizabeth O'Connell, Manager of Human Resources Department. **E-mail address:** employment@audiovox.com. **World Wide Web address:** http://www.audiovox.com. **Description:** Engaged in the sale and distribution of a variety of automotive electronic components including car radios, speakers, alarm systems, and cellular phones. **Common positions include:** Accountant/Auditor; Branch Manager; Budget Analyst; Computer Programmer; Customer Service Representative; Draftsperson; Electrical/Electronics Engineer; Financial Analyst; Marketing Manager; Mechanical Engineer; Payroll Clerk; Purchasing Agent/Manager; Quality Control Supervisor; Secretary; Services Sales Representative; Stock Clerk; Systems Analyst; Travel Agent. **Special programs:** Internships. **Corporate headquarters location:** This location. **Other U.S. locations:** CA; FL; GA; IL; KY; LA; NC; OH; PA; SC; TN; VA. **Subsidiaries include:** Quintex Mobile Communications. **Operations at this facility include:** Administration; Divisional Headquarters; Regional Headquarters; Research and Development; Sales; Service. **Listed on:** NASDAQ. **Stock exchange symbol:** VOXX. **Number of employees at this location:** 350.

STANDARD MOTOR PRODUCTS INC.

37-18 Northern Boulevard, Long Island City NY 11101. 718/392-0200. **Contact:** Vincent Ruggiero, Employment Manager. **World Wide Web address:** http://www.smpcorp.com. **Description:** Engaged primarily in the manufacture of electrical and fuel system automotive replacement parts sold internationally under the Standard Blue Streak, Hygrade, Champ, and Four Seasons brand names. Products include ignition parts, automotive wire and cable parts, carburetor parts and kits, general service auto parts (radio antennas, gasoline cans, brooms and brushes, polishing cloths, fuses, and other auto accessories), and automotive heating and air conditioning systems. **Common positions include:** Accountant/Auditor; Buyer; Computer Programmer; Draftsperson; Electrical/Electronics Engineer; Financial Analyst; Industrial Designer; Industrial Engineer; Mechanical Engineer; Purchasing Agent/Manager; Quality Control Supervisor; Statistician; Systems Analyst; Technical Writer/Editor. **Corporate headquarters location:** This location. **Listed on:** New York Stock Exchange. **Stock exchange symbol:** SMP. **Number of employees worldwide:** 3,500.

BANKING/SAVINGS AND LOANS

You can expect to find the following types of companies in this chapter:

Banks • Bank Holding Companies and Associations •
Lending Firms/Financial Services Institutions

APPLE BANK FOR SAVINGS
122 East 42nd Street, New York NY 10168. 212/224-6400. **Toll-free phone:** 800/722-6888. **Fax:** 212/224-6592. **Contact:** Human Resources. **World Wide Web address:** http://www.theapplebank.com. **Description:** Operates a full-service savings bank serving New York City, Long Island, and Westchester with a total of 43 branches. **NOTE:** Entry-level positions are offered. **Common positions include:** Account Representative; Administrative Assistant; Advertising Clerk; Assistant Manager; Auditor; Bank Officer/Manager; Bank Teller; Computer Operator; Computer Programmer; Customer Service Representative; Insurance Agent/Broker; Marketing Specialist; MIS Specialist; Sales Executive; Sales Manager; Sales Representative; Secretary. **Corporate headquarters location:** This location. **Listed on:** Privately held. **Annual sales/revenues:** More than $100 million. **Number of employees at this location:** 900.

ASTORIA FEDERAL SAVINGS BANK
1150 Franklin Avenue, Garden City NY 11530. 516/746-0700. **Contact:** Human Resources. **E-mail address:** hr@astoriafederal.com. **World Wide Web address:** http://www.astoriafederal.com. **Description:** Provides a full range of banking and related financial services. **NOTE:** Hiring is conducted through the parent company. Interested jobseekers should address all inquiries to Manager of Human Resources, Astoria Financial Corporation, One Astoria Federal Plaza, Lake Success NY 11042-1085. **Corporate headquarters location:** Lake Success NY. **Parent company:** Astoria Financial Corporation. **Listed on:** NASDAQ. **Stock exchange symbol:** ASFC.

ASTORIA FEDERAL SAVINGS BANK
451 Fifth Avenue, Brooklyn NY 11215. 718/965-7500. **Contact:** Human Resources Department. **E-mail address:** hr@astoriafederal.com. **World Wide Web address:** http://www.astoriafederal.com. **Description:** A savings bank offering a complete range of traditional banking and mortgage services. **NOTE:** Hiring is conducted through the parent company. Interested jobseekers should address all inquiries to Manager of Human Resources, Astoria Financial Corporation, One Astoria Federal Plaza, Lake Success NY 11042-1085. **Common positions include:** Accountant/Auditor; Bank Officer/Manager; Branch Manager; Buyer; Department Manager; Financial Analyst; Human Resources Manager; Management Trainee; Purchasing Agent/Manager; Systems Analyst. **Parent company:** Astoria Financial Corporation. **Operations at this facility include:** Administration. **Listed on:** NASDAQ. **Stock exchange symbol:** ASFC.

ASTORIA FINANCIAL CORPORATION
ASTORIA FEDERAL SAVINGS & LOAN ASSOCIATION
One Astoria Federal Plaza, Lake Success NY 11042-1085. 516/327-3000. **Toll-free phone:** 800/ASTORIA. **Fax:** 516/327-7610. **Contact:** Manager of Recruiting and Employee Relations. **E-mail address:** hr@astoriafederal.com. **World Wide Web address:** http://www.astoriafederal.com. **Description:** A bank holding company. Founded in 1888. **Common positions include:**

Accountant; Adjuster; Assistant Manager; Auditor; Branch Manager; Customer Service Representative; Management Trainee; Typist/Word Processor. **Corporate headquarters location:** This location. **Subsidiaries include:** With 87 banking offices, Astoria Federal Savings & Loan Association provides a range of financial services and products to over 700,000 customers throughout the Long Island and New York City metropolitan areas. **Listed on:** NASDAQ. **Stock exchange symbol:** ASFC. **CEO:** George L. Engelke, Jr. **Number of employees at this location:** 400. **Number of employees nationwide:** 2,000.

BANK OF NEW YORK

101 Barclay Street, Floor 1-E, New York NY 10286. 212/815-4984. **Contact:** Human Resources Department. **World Wide Web address:** http://www.bankofny.com. **Description:** A bank that serves individuals, corporations, foreign and domestic banks, governments, and other institutions through banking offices in New York City and foreign branches, representative offices, subsidiaries, and affiliates. **Common positions include:** Bank Officer/Manager. **Corporate headquarters location:** New York NY. **Parent company:** The Bank of New York Company, Inc. **Listed on:** New York Stock Exchange. **Stock exchange symbol:** BK. **Number of employees nationwide:** 12,000.

BANK OF NEW YORK

One Wall Street, 13th Floor, New York NY 10286. 212/635-7703. **Contact:** Human Resources. **World Wide Web address:** http://www.bankofny.com. **Description:** A bank that serves individuals, corporations, foreign and domestic banks, governments, and other institutions through banking offices in New York City and foreign branches, representative offices, subsidiaries, and affiliates. **Common positions include:** Accountant/Auditor; Bank Officer/Manager; Branch Manager; Computer Programmer; Customer Service Representative; Financial Analyst; Systems Analyst. **Special programs:** Internships. **Corporate headquarters location:** This location. **Parent company:** Bank of New York Company, Inc. **Listed on:** New York Stock Exchange. **Stock exchange symbol:** BK. **Number of employees nationwide:** 12,000.

BANK OF TOKYO MITSUBISHI

1251 Sixth Avenue, New York NY 10020-1104. 212/766-3400. **Contact:** Human Resources. **World Wide Web address:** http://www.btmny.com. **Description:** One of the 50 largest commercial banks in the United States. The company operates five offices throughout the New York metropolitan area, as well as in London and the Bahamas. **Corporate headquarters location:** This location. **Parent company:** The Bank of Tokyo Ltd. (Tokyo, Japan).

BARCLAYS BANK

222 Broadway, 10th Floor, New York NY 10038. 212/412-4000. **Contact:** Human Resources. **World Wide Web address:** http://www.barclays.co.uk. **Description:** An international banking institution with more than 5,000 offices in 60 countries including most international trade centers. International banking services include commercial loans, foreign exchange services, drafts and money transfers, foreign collections, leasing, stock and security custodial services, and economic information and publications. Barclays Bank also operates a global investment bank through its BZW Group subsidiary. **Parent company:** Barclays plc. **Corporate headquarters location:** London, England. **Other U.S. locations:** San Francisco CA. **Listed on:** New York Stock Exchange. **Stock exchange symbol:** BCS.

BRIDGEHAMPTON NATIONAL BANK

P.O. Box 3005, Bridgehampton NY 11932-3005. 631/537-1000. **Contact:** Human Resources. **World Wide Web address:** http://www.bridgenb.com. **Description:** One of the oldest independent commercial banks headquartered on the South Fork of Long Island. The bank operates six full-service banking offices located in Bridgehampton, East Hampton, Mattituck, Montauk, Southampton, and Southold NY, as well as a residential mortgage and loan center in Riverhead NY. **Parent company:** Bridge Bancorp, Inc.

CITIBANK

One EAB Plaza, Uniondale NY 11555. 516/627-3999. **Contact:** Human Resources. **World Wide Web address:** http://www.citibank.com. **Description:** A full-service commercial bank offering a range of services through more than 80 branch banking offices in metropolitan New York and Long Island. **Corporate headquarters location:** New York NY. **Parent company:** Citigroup, Inc. **Listed on:** New York Stock Exchange. **Stock exchange symbol:** C.

CITIBANK, N.A.

399 Park Avenue, New York NY 10043-0001. 212/559-1000. **Contact:** Search and Staffing. **World Wide Web address:** http://www.citibank.com. **Description:** Operates a global, full-service consumer franchise encompassing branch banking, credit and charge cards, and private banking. In branch banking, Citibank services almost 20 million accounts in 41 countries and territories. In global card products, Citibank is one of the world's largest bankcard and charge card issuers. In addition, Citibank issues and services approximately 5 million private-label cards for department stores and retail outlets. Citibank Private Bank offices in 31 countries and territories provide a full-range of wealth management services and serve as a window that gives clients access to the full range of Citibank's global capabilities. **Corporate headquarters location:** This location. **Parent company:** Citigroup, Inc., with its subsidiaries and affiliates, is a global financial services organization serving individuals, businesses, governments, and financial institutions in 100 countries and territories. **Listed on:** New York Stock Exchange. **Stock exchange symbol:** C. **Number of employees nationwide:** 36,000.

DIME SAVINGS BANK OF WILLIAMSBURG

1000 Port Washington Boulevard, Port Washington NY 11050. 516/883-8100. **Contact:** Human Resources. **Description:** A full-service bank.

EMIGRANT SAVINGS BANK

5 East 42nd Street, New York NY 10017. 212/850-4000. **Contact:** Edward Tully, Senior Vice President of Human Resources. **World Wide Web address:** http://www.emigrant.com. **Description:** Offers a wide range of traditional banking services. Emigrant Savings Bank has locations in Manhattan, Brooklyn, and Queens, as well as in Nassau, Suffolk, and Westchester Counties. Founded in 1850. **Corporate headquarters location:** This location.

FINANCIAL FEDERAL CREDIT INC.

733 Third Avenue, 7th Floor, New York NY 10017. 212/599-8000. **Fax:** 212/286-5885. **Contact:** Human Resources Department. **World Wide Web address:** http://www.financialfederal.com. **Description:** Provides financing of leases and capital loans on industrial, commercial, and professional equipment to middle market customers in a variety of industries. Founded in 1989. **Corporate headquarters location:** This location. **Other U.S.**

locations: Mesa AZ; Union City GA; Westmont IL; Charlotte NC; Teaneck NJ; Houston TX. **Listed on:** New York Stock Exchange. **Stock exchange symbol:** FIF. **Annual sales/revenues:** $51 - $100 million. **Number of employees nationwide:** 130.

FIRST OF LONG ISLAND CORPORATION
30 Glen Head Road, Glen Head NY 11545-1411. 516/671-4900. **Fax:** 516/656-3971. **Contact:** Director of Human Resources Department. **E-mail address:** humres@optonline.net. **World Wide Web address:** http://www.firstofli.com. **Description:** First of Long Island Corporation is the holding company for First National Bank of Long Island, a full-service commercial bank that provides a broad range of financial services to individual, professional, corporate, institutional, and government customers through its 14 branch system on Long Island. **Subsidiaries include:** First of Long Island Agency sells insurance, primarily fixed-annuity products. **Listed on:** NASDAQ. **Stock exchange symbol:** FLIC.

GREENPOINT BANK
211-11 Northern Boulevard, Bayside NY 11360. 718/423-6500. **Contact:** Human Resources. **World Wide Web address:** http://www.greenpoint.com. **Description:** A full-service savings bank. **Other area locations:** Albertson NY; Brooklyn NY; Great Neck NY; Hicksville NY; Kew Gardens NY; Ridgewood NY; Sunnyside NY. **Corporate headquarters location:** New York NY. **Parent company:** GreenPoint Financial Corporation. **Listed on:** New York Stock Exchange. **Stock exchange symbol:** GPT.

HSBC BANK USA
452 Fifth Avenue, 12th Floor, New York NY 10018. 212/525-5000. **Fax:** 877/248-4722. **Recorded jobline:** 888/HRHELP4. **Contact:** Human Resources. **World Wide Web address:** http://www.banking.us.hsbc.com. **Description:** An international banking institution that provides a wide range of individual and commercial services. **Corporate headquarters location:** London, England. **Parent company:** HSBC Holdings plc. **Listed on:** New York Stock Exchange. **Stock exchange symbol:** HBC.

INDEPENDENCE COMMUNITY BANK
195 Montague Street, Brooklyn NY 11201. 718/722-5300. **Contact:** Human Resources. **World Wide Web address:** http://www.myindependence.com. **Description:** A savings bank that offers a wide range of traditional banking services as well as specialized financial services, loans, and insurance services. **Corporate headquarters location:** This location. **Listed on:** NASDAQ. **Stock exchange symbol:** ICBC.

INDEPENDENCE COMMUNITY BANK
7500 Fifth Avenue, Brooklyn NY 11209. 718/745-6100. **Contact:** Human Resources. **World Wide Web address:** http://www.myindependence.com. **Description:** A savings bank that offers a wide range of traditional banking services as well as specialized financial services, loans, and insurance services. **Listed on:** NASDAQ. **Stock exchange symbol:** ICBC.

JEFFERSONVILLE BANCORP
THE FIRST NATIONAL BANK OF JEFFERSONVILLE
300 Main Street, P.O. Box 398, Jeffersonville NY 12748. 845/482-4000. **Contact:** Human Resources. **E-mail address:** jeffbank@jeffbank.com. **World Wide Web address:** http://www.jeffbank.com. **Description:** Owns and operates full-service banks. Founded in 1913. **Corporate headquarters location:** This location. **Other area locations:** Eldred NY; Liberty NY; Loch

Sheldrake NY; Monticello NY; Wurtsboro NY. **Subsidiaries include:** The First National Bank of Jeffersonville (also at this location). **Listed on:** NASDAQ. **Stock exchange symbol:** JFBC. **President:** Arthur Keesler.

M&T BANK
350 Park Avenue, 5th Floor, New York NY 10022. 212/350-2500. **Contact:** Human Resources. **World Wide Web address:** http://www.mandtbank.com. **Description:** A full-service savings bank providing cooperative apartment loans, home improvement loans, mortgage loans, pension plans, retirement accounts, life insurance, student loans, and other traditional banking services. **Common positions include:** Accountant/Auditor; Bank Officer/Manager; Branch Manager; Customer Service Representative; Department Manager; Financial Analyst; Human Resources Manager; Management Trainee; Marketing Specialist; Mortgage Banker; Operations/Production Manager; Services Sales Representative. **Corporate headquarters location:** Buffalo NY. **Operations at this facility include:** Administration; Divisional Headquarters. **Listed on:** New York Stock Exchange. **Stock exchange symbol:** MTB.

NORTH FORK BANCORPORATION, INC.
NORTH FORK BANK
275 Broad Hollow Road, Melville NY 11747. 631/844-1000. **Contact:** Personnel. **World Wide Web address:** http://www.northforkbank.com. **Description:** A commercial bank holding company. The principal subsidiary, North Fork Bank (also at this location), is one of the largest independent commercial banks headquartered on Long Island. **Corporate headquarters location:** This location. **Listed on:** New York Stock Exchange. **Stock exchange symbol:** NFB.

RIDGEWOOD SAVINGS BANK
71-02 Forest Avenue, Ridgewood NY 11385. 718/240-4800. **Contact:** Norman McNamee, Human Resources Representative. **World Wide Web address:** http://www.ridgewoodbank.com. **Description:** A full-service savings bank. **Common positions include:** Accountant/Auditor; Assistant Manager; Bank Officer/Manager; Branch Manager; Credit Manager; Customer Service Representative; Department Manager; Instructor/Trainer; Insurance Agent/Broker; Management Trainee; Marketing Specialist; Purchasing Agent/Manager; Systems Analyst. **Corporate headquarters location:** This location. **Operations at this facility include:** Administration; Service. **Number of employees at this location:** 550.

ROSLYN SAVINGS BANK
One Jericho North Plaza, Jericho NY 11753. 516/942-6000. **Contact:** Human Resources. **World Wide Web address:** http://www.roslyn.com. **Description:** Operates a full-service mutual savings bank. Roslyn Savings offers a full range of commercial and savings bank services through 12 offices including locations in Brooklyn, Queens, Deer Park, and Nassau County. Founded in 1895. **Corporate headquarters location:** This location. **Parent company:** Roslyn Bancorp Inc. **Listed on:** NASDAQ. **Stock exchange symbol:** RSLN.

THE ROYAL BANK OF CANADA
12 East 49th Street 40th Floor, New York NY 10006-1404. 212/428-6200. **Contact:** Personnel. **World Wide Web address:** http://www.royalbank.com. **Description:** One of North America's largest banks. **Listed on:** New York Stock Exchange. **Stock exchange symbol:** RY.

STERLING NATIONAL BANK & TRUST COMPANY

145 East 40th Street, New York NY 10016-1797. 212/490-9809. **Fax:** 212/490-8852. **Contact:** Manager of Human Resources Department. **E-mail address:** hrresumes@sterlingbancorp.com. **World Wide Web address:** http://www.sterlingbancorp.com. **Description:** A full-service commercial bank offering a complete range of corporate and individual services. **Corporate headquarters location:** This location. **Parent company:** Sterling Bancorp. **Listed on:** New York Stock Exchange. **Stock exchange symbol:** STL.

SUFFOLK BANCORP

P.O. Box 9000, 6 West Second Street, Riverhead NY 11901. 631/727-2700. **Contact:** Human Resources. **E-mail address:** info@scnb.com. **World Wide Web address:** http://www.suffolkbancorp.com. **Description:** Suffolk Bancorp is engaged in the commercial banking business through its subsidiary, Suffolk County National Bank. The bank is one of the largest independent banks headquartered on Long Island. Founded in 1890. **Subsidiaries include:** Island Computer Corporation.

U.S. FEDERAL RESERVE BANK OF NEW YORK

33 Liberty Street, New York NY 10045-0001. 212/720-5000. **Contact:** Human Resources. **World Wide Web address:** http://www.ny.frb.org. **Description:** One of 12 regional Federal Reserve banks that, along with the Federal Reserve Board in Washington DC and the Federal Open Market Committee, comprise the Federal Reserve System, the nation's central bank. Responsibilities include monetary policy, banking supervision and regulation, and processing payments. **Common positions include:** Accountant/Auditor; Attorney; Bank Officer/Manager; Budget Analyst; Computer Programmer; Economist; Human Resources Manager; Librarian; Paralegal; Systems Analyst. **Special programs:** Internships. **Other U.S. locations:** San Francisco CA; Washington DC; Atlanta GA; Chicago IL; Boston MA; Minneapolis MN; Kansas City MO; St. Louis MO; Cleveland OH; Philadelphia PA; Dallas TX; Richmond VA. **Operations at this facility include:** Administration; Regional Headquarters; Research and Development. **Number of employees at this location:** 3,200.

WACHOVIA CORPORATION

202 Mamaroneck Avenue, White Plains NY 10601. 914/682-7416. **Recorded jobline:** 800/FUNHIRE. **Contact:** Human Resources. **World Wide Web address:** http://www.wachovia.com. **Description:** A bank. **Parent company:** Wachovia Corporation is one of the nation's largest bank holding companies with subsidiaries operating over 1,330 full-service bank branches in the south Atlantic states. These subsidiaries provide retail banking, retail investment, and commercial banking services. The corporation provides other financial services including mortgage banking, home equity lending, leasing, insurance, and securities brokerage services from 222 branch locations. The corporation also operates one of the nation's largest ATM networks.**Corporate headquarters location:** Charlotte NC. **Listed on:** New York Stock Exchange. **Stock exchange symbol:** WB.

WASHINGTON MUTUAL, INC.

1304 Broadway, Hewlett NY 11557. 631/234-9992. **Contact:** Human Resources. **World Wide Web address:** http://www.wamu.com. **Description:** Washington Mutual, Inc. is a financial services company that, through its subsidiaries, engages in the following lines of business: consumer banking, mortgage banking, commercial banking, financial services and consumer finance. **Corporate headquarters location:** Seattle WA. **Listed on:** New York Stock Exchange. **Stock exchange symbol:** WM.

WASHINGTON MUTUAL, INC.

EAB Plaza, 14th Floor, Uniondale NY 11556. 516/745-2980. **Contact:** Human Resources. **World Wide Web address:** http://www.wamu.com. **Description:** Washington Mutual, Inc. is a financial services company that, through its subsidiaries, engages in the following lines of business: consumer banking, mortgage banking, commercial banking, financial services and consumer finance. **Common positions include:** Account Representative; Accountant/Auditor; Bank Officer/Manager; Branch Manager; Computer Programmer; Credit Manager; Customer Service Representative; Financial Analyst; Sales Executive; Services Sales Representative; Systems Analyst. **Corporate headquarters location:** Seattle WA. **Listed on:** New York Stock Exchange. **Stock exchange symbol:** WM.

BIOTECHNOLOGY, PHARMACEUTICALS, AND SCIENTIFIC R&D

You can expect to find the following types of companies in this chapter:

Clinical Labs • Lab Equipment Manufacturers •
Pharmaceutical Manufacturers and Distributors

AMERICAN BIOGENETIC SCIENCES, INC. (ABS)
1375 Akron Street, Copiague NY 11726. 631/789-2600. **Contact:** Human Resources Department. **World Wide Web address:** http://www.mabxa.com. **Description:** A biopharmaceutical company developing monoclonal, antibody-based products to diagnose, image, and treat thrombosis and arteriosclerosis. The company also develops therapeutic compounds to treat epilepsy and neuroprotective compounds that cross the blood-brain barrier and mimic the action of nerve growth factors for the treatment of neurodegenerative disorders such as Alzheimer's, Parkinson's disease, and ALS.

AMERICAN STANDARDS TESTING BUREAU INC.
P.O. Box 583, New York NY 10274-0583. 212/943-3160. **Physical address:** 40 Water Street, New York NY 10004. **Fax:** 212/825-2250. **Contact:** John Zimmerman, Director, Professional Staffing. **Description:** Offers lab consulting and forensic services to the government and various industries. The company specializes in biotechnology, environmental sciences, forensics, engineering, failure analysis, and products liability. **Common positions include:** Administrative Manager; Aerospace Engineer; Agricultural Engineer; Architect; Attorney; Biomedical Engineer; Chemical Engineer; Chemist; Civil Engineer; Clerical Supervisor; Construction Contractor; Credit Manager; Editor; Electrical/Electronics Engineer; Environmental Engineer; Financial Analyst; Food Scientist/Technologist; General Manager; Industrial Engineer; Management Analyst/Consultant; Management Trainee; Manufacturer's/Wholesaler's Sales Rep.; Materials Engineer; Mechanical Engineer; Metallurgical Engineer; MIS Specialist; Paralegal; Petroleum Engineer; Public Relations Specialist; Science Technologist; Services Sales Representative; Structural Engineer; Technical Writer/Editor; Typist/Word Processor; Video Production Coordinator. **Corporate headquarters location:** This location. **Other U.S. locations:** Nationwide. **Operations at this facility include:** Administration; Divisional Headquarters; Research and Development; Sales. **Listed on:** Privately held. **Annual sales/revenues:** More than $100 million. **Number of employees at this location:** 470.

BARR LABORATORIES, INC.
2 Quaker Road, P.O. Box 2900, Pomona NY 10970-0519. 845/362-1100. **Contact:** Human Resources Department. **World Wide Web address:** http://www.barrlabs.com. **Description:** This location operates two facilities. The first facility houses the development and production laboratories. The second building is comprised of office and manufacturing space, which houses the research and development administrative staff and pharmacy operations team. Overall, Barr Laboratories is a leading independent developer, manufacturer, and marketer of off-patent pharmaceuticals. **Corporate headquarters location:** This location. **Listed on:** New York Stock Exchange. **Stock exchange symbol:** BRL.

BIOSPECIFICS TECHNOLOGIES CORPORATION

35 Wilbur Street, Lynbrook NY 11563. 516/593-7000. **Fax:** 516/593-7039. **Contact:** Human Resources Department. **World Wide Web address:** http://www.biospecifics.com. **Description:** An industry leader in the production and development of enzyme pharmaceuticals used for wound healing, tissue regeneration, and tissue remodeling. Biospecifics Technologies Corporation produces Collagenase Santyl ointment, an enzyme used for the treatment of chronic wounds and dermal ulcers. **NOTE:** Part-time jobs are offered. **Common positions include:** Accountant; Administrative Assistant; Biochemist; Biological Scientist; Chemical Engineer; Chemist; Chief Financial Officer; Clinical Lab Technician; Human Resources Manager; Secretary; Statistician. **Office hours:** Monday - Friday, 9:00 a.m. - 5:00 p.m. **Corporate headquarters location:** This location. **Listed on:** New York Stock Exchange. **Stock exchange symbol:** BSTC. **President/CEO:** Edwin H. Wegman.

BRISTOL-MYERS SQUIBB COMPANY

345 Park Avenue, New York NY 10154-0037. 212/546-4000. **Contact:** Human Resources. **World Wide Web address:** http://www.bms.com. **Description:** This location manufactures pharmaceuticals. Overall, Bristol-Myers Squibb is a manufacturer of pharmaceuticals, medical devices, nonprescription drugs, toiletries, and beauty aids. The company's pharmaceutical products include cardiovascular drugs, anti-infective agents, anticancer agents, AIDS therapy treatments, central nervous system drugs, diagnostic agents, and other drugs. The company's line of nonprescription products includes formulas, vitamins, analgesics, remedies, and skin care products sold under the brand names Bufferin, Excedrin, Nuprin, and Comtrex. Beauty aids include Clairol and Ultress hair care, Nice 'n Easy hair colorings, hair sprays, gels, and deodorants. **Common positions include:** Biological Scientist; Chemical Engineer; Chemist; Financial Analyst; Mechanical Engineer. **Corporate headquarters location:** This location. **Listed on:** New York Stock Exchange. **Stock exchange symbol:** BMY.

DARBY GROUP COMPANIES

865 Merrick Avenue, Westbury NY 11590. 516/683-1800. **Contact:** Personnel. **World Wide Web address:** http://www.darbygroup.com. **Description:** A manufacturer and distributor of over-the-counter drugs, pharmaceuticals, and vitamins. **Corporate headquarters location:** This location. **Other U.S. locations:** Nationwide.

DAXOR CORPORATION

The Empire State Building, 350 Fifth Avenue, Suite 7120, New York NY 10118. 212/244-0555. **Fax:** 212/244-0806. **Contact:** Human Resources. **World Wide Web address:** http://www.daxor.com. **Description:** Promotes the safety of the American Blood Banking System. The company's Idant Division also researches cryobiology for artificial insemination purposes and operates one of the largest sperm banks in the United States. **Corporate headquarters location:** This location. **Listed on:** American Stock Exchange. **Stock exchange symbol:** DXR.

DEL LABORATORIES, INC.

178 EAB Plaza, West Tower, 8th Floor, Uniondale NY 11556. 516/844-2020. **Fax:** 631/293-7091. **Contact:** Human Resources. **E-mail address:** resume@dellabs.com. **World Wide Web address:** http://www.dellabs.com. **Description:** A fully-integrated manufacturer and marketer of packaged consumer products including cosmetics, toiletries, beauty aids, and

proprietary pharmaceuticals. Products are distributed to chain and independent drug stores, mass merchandisers, and supermarkets. Divisions include Commerce Drug Company, Del International, Natural Glow, La Cross, La Salle Laboratories, Nutri-Tonic, Naturistics, Rejuvia, and Sally Hansen. **NOTE:** Entry-level positions and second and third shifts are offered. **Common positions include:** Account Manager; Account Representative; Accountant; Administrative Assistant; Advertising Clerk; AS400 Programmer Analyst; Blue-Collar Worker Supervisor; Budget Analyst; Buyer; Chemist; Clerical Supervisor; Computer Operator; Customer Service Representative; Database Administrator; Electrician; Environmental Engineer; Event Planner; Financial Analyst; Graphic Artist; Help-Desk Technician; Industrial Engineer; Internet Services Manager; Intranet Developer; Manufacturing Engineer; Marketing Manager; Media Planner; MIS Specialist; Network/Systems Administrator; Production Manager; Public Relations Specialist; Quality Control Supervisor; Sales Manager; Sales Representative; Secretary; Systems Analyst; Systems Manager; Webmaster; Website Developer. **Corporate headquarters location:** This location. **Other area locations:** Farmingdale NY. **Other U.S. locations:** Rocky Point NC. **Operations at this facility include:** Administration; Divisional Headquarters; Manufacturing; Regional Headquarters; Research and Development; Service. **Listed on:** American Stock Exchange. **Stock exchange symbol:** DLI. **Annual sales/revenues:** More than $100 million.

E-Z-EM INC.
717 Main Street, Westbury NY 11590. 516/333-8230. **Fax:** 516/333-1392. **Contact:** Kathy Hahl, Administrative Assistant. **E-mail address:** hr@ezem.com. **World Wide Web address:** http://www.ezem.com. **Description:** E-Z-EM is a worldwide producer of barium sulfate contrast systems for use in GI tract X-ray examinations. The company operates in two industry segments: diagnostic products and surgical products. The diagnostic products segment includes both contrast systems, consisting of barium sulfate formulations and related apparatus used in X-ray, CT-scanning, and other imaging examinations; and noncontrast systems, which include interventional radiology products, custom contract pharmaceuticals, gastrointestinal cleansing laxatives, X-ray protection equipment, and immunoassay tests. **Corporate headquarters location:** This location. **Listed on:** American Stock Exchange. **Stock exchange symbol:** EZM.

EMISPHERE TECHNOLOGIES INC.
765 Old Saw Mill River Road, Tarrytown NY 10591-6751. 914/347-2220. **Fax:** 914/593-8166. **Contact:** Human Resources. **World Wide Web address:** http://www.emisphere.com. **Description:** Researches and develops oral drug delivery systems. **Corporate headquarters location:** This location. **Listed on:** NASDAQ. **Stock exchange symbol:** EMIS.

ENZO CLINICAL LABS
60 Executive Boulevard, Farmingdale NY 11735. 516/496-8080. **Contact:** Debbie Sohmer, Human Resources Department. **World Wide Web address:** http://www.enzobio.com. **Description:** Engaged in the research, development, marketing, and manufacturing of health care products. Enzo's products and services are sold to scientists and medical personnel worldwide. The company has proprietary technologies and expertise in manipulating and modifying genetic material and other biological molecules. Founded in 1976. **Subsidiaries include:** Enzo Therapeutics, Inc. is developing antisense genetic medicines to combat cancer, viral, and other diseases. Enzo Diagnostics, Inc. develops and markets proprietary DNA probe-based products to clinicians and researchers. EnzoLabs, Inc.

provides diagnostic testing services to the New York medical community. **Corporate headquarters location:** This location. **Parent company:** Enzo Biochem. **Listed on:** New York Stock Exchange. **Stock exchange symbol:** ENZ.

EON LABS MANUFACTURING, INC.
227-15 North Conduit Avenue, Laurelton NY 11413. 718/276-8600. **Contact:** Maria Sinnott, Human Resources Department. **World Wide Web address:** http://www.eonlabs.com. **Description:** Manufacturers of generic pharmaceuticals, both prescription and over-the-counter.

FOREST LABORATORIES, INC.
909 Third Avenue, 24th Floor, New York NY 10022. 212/224-6741. **Toll-free phone:** 800/947-5227. **Fax:** 212/750-9152. **Contact:** Bernard McGovern, Vice President of Personnel. **E-mail address:** staffing@frx.com. **World Wide Web address:** http://www.frx.com. **Description:** Develops, manufactures, and sells branded and generic prescription drugs for the treatment of cardiovascular, central nervous system, pulmonary, and women's health problems. In the United States, Forest Laboratories' ethical specialty products and generics are marketed directly by the company's subsidiaries Forest Pharmaceuticals and Inwood Laboratories. In the United Kingdom, Ireland, and certain export markets, Forest Laboratories products are marketed directly by the company's subsidiaries, Pharmax Ltd. and Tosara Group. **NOTE:** Entry-level positions are offered. **Common positions include:** Analytical Engineer; Biochemist; Biological Scientist; Business Development Manager; Clinical Applications Specialist; Clinical Lab Technician; Contract/Grant Administrator; Financial Analyst; Market Research Analyst; Marketing Manager; Pharmacist; Product Manager; Quality Assurance Engineer; Regulatory Affairs Director; Research and Development Engineer; Research Scientist; Safety Specialist; Sales Representative; Technical Writer/Editor; Toxicologist. **Special programs:** Internships; Co-ops; Summer Jobs. **Office hours:** Monday - Friday, 9:00 a.m. - 5:00 p.m. **Corporate headquarters location:** This location. **Other U.S. locations:** St. Louis MO; Jersey City NJ; Commack NY; Farmingdale NY; Inwood NY; Cincinnati OH. **International locations:** Ireland; United Kingdom. **Subsidiaries include:** Forest Pharmaceuticals; Inwood Laboratories, Inc.; Pharmax Ltd.; Tosara Group. **Operations at this facility include:** Accounting/Auditing; Administration; Financial Offices; Marketing; Sales. **Listed on:** New York Stock Exchange. **Stock exchange symbol:** FRX. **President:** Howard Solomon. **Annual sales/revenues:** More than $100 million. **Number of employees at this location:** 250. **Number of employees nationwide:** 1,700.

E. FOUGERA & COMPANY
SAVAGE LABORATORIES
60 Baylis Road, Melville NY 11747. 631/454-6996. **Contact:** Human Resources Manager. **World Wide Web address:** http://www.fougera.com. **Description:** Manufactures various multisource topicals and ophthalmics. Products include surgical lubricants, antifungal creams, hydrocortisone ointments, and other generic pharmaceuticals. **Corporate headquarters location:** This location. **Parent company:** Altana, Inc. also owns Savage Laboratories (also at this location), which manufactures ethical pharmaceuticals.

GERICARE
5 Odell Plaza, Yonkers NY 10701. 914/476-6500. **Contact:** Human Resources. **Description:** A supplier of pharmaceuticals and related products to long-term care facilities, hospitals, and assisted living communities.

HI-TECH PHARMACAL CO., INC.
369 Bayview Avenue, Amityville NY 11701. 631/789-8228. **Contact:** Personnel. **World Wide Web address:** http://www.hitechpharm.com. **Description:** Develops, manufactures, and markets generic drugs. Hi-Tech Pharmacal manufactures more than 100 generic products; the majority of these liquid and semisolid pharmaceuticals are marketed under the company's own brand names. **Corporate headquarters location:** This location. **Subsidiaries include:** Health Care Products manufactures branded items marketed under the H-T, Sooth-It, and Diabetic Tussin brands. **Listed on:** NASDAQ. **Stock exchange symbol:** HITK.

IMCLONE SYSTEMS INC.
180 Varick Street, 6th Floor, New York NY 10014-4606. 212/645-1405. **Fax:** 212/645-2054. **Contact:** Lisa Cammy, Human Resources Director. **World Wide Web address:** http://www.imclone.com. **Description:** Engaged primarily in the research and development of therapeutic products for the treatment of cancer and cancer-related diseases. **Listed on:** NASDAQ. **Stock exchange symbol:** IMCL.

NOVO NORDISK OF NORTH AMERICA
405 Lexington Avenue, Suite 6400, New York NY 10174. 212/878-9600. **Fax:** 212/867-0298. **Contact:** Human Resources Department. **World Wide Web address:** http://www.novonordisk-us.com. **Description:** This location is the corporate service office for North America. Overall, Novo Nordisk is a holding company whose divisions produce insulin, industrial enzymes, and other drugs and bioindustrial items. The Health Care Group is the diabetes care division that develops and manufactures insulin and delivery systems related to the treatment of diabetes. The Biopharmaceuticals division develops, produces, and markets products for the treatment of coagulation and other blood disorders as well as growth disorders. The Bioindustrial division consists of detergents, providing enzymes to the detergent industry. **NOTE:** Human Resources is located at 100 Overlook Center, Suite 200, Princeton NJ 08540. 609/987-5800. **Common positions include:** Administrative Assistant; Attorney; Finance Director; Financial Analyst; Intellectual Property Lawyer; Public Relations Specialist. **Other U.S. locations:** Davis CA; Clayton NC; Franklinton NC; Princeton NJ; Seattle WA. **Parent company:** Novo Nordisk A/S (Baysvaerd, Denmark). **Listed on:** New York Stock Exchange. **Stock exchange symbol:** NVO. **Number of employees at this location:** 25. **Number of employees nationwide:** 1,000. **Number of employees worldwide:** 13,000.

NUTRITION 21
4 Manhattanville Road, Purchase NY 10577-2197. 914/701-4500. **Fax:** 914/696-0860. **Contact:** Human Resources Department. **World Wide Web address:** http://www.nutrition21.com. **Description:** Develops and markets nutrition products. The company focuses on products with medical value for consumers concerned with cardiovascular health and diabetes. Founded in 1982. **Common positions include:** Chemist; Food Scientist/Technologist; Marketing Manager; Nutritionist; Product Manager. **Corporate headquarters location:** This location. **Listed on:** NASDAQ. **Stock exchange symbol:** NXXI.

OSI PHARMACEUTICALS, INC.

58 South Service Road, Suite 110, Melville NY 11747. 631/962-2000. **Contact:** Personnel. **World Wide Web address:** http://www.osip.com. **Description:** A biopharmaceutical company utilizing proprietary technologies to discover and develop products for the treatment and diagnosis of human diseases. The company conducts a full range of drug discovery activities from target identification through clinical candidates for its own products and in collaborations and co-ventures with other major pharmaceutical companies. **Corporate headquarters location:** This location. **Listed on:** NASDAQ. **Stock exchange symbol:** OSIP. **President:** Dr. Colin Goddard.

PDK LABS INC.

145 Ricefield Lane, Hauppauge NY 11788. 631/273-2630. **Contact:** Human Resources. **E-mail address:** info@pdklabs.com. **World Wide Web address:** http://www.pdklabs.com. **Description:** PDK Labs manufactures and distributes over-the-counter pharmaceutical products and vitamins. The company's line of products primarily consists of nonprescription caffeine products, pain relievers, decongestants, diet aids, and a broad line of vitamins, nutritional supplements, and cosmetics. The company markets its products through direct mail, regional distributors, and private label manufacturing.

PRECISION PHARMA

155 Duryea Road, Melville NY 11747. 631/752-7314. **Contact:** Human Resources. **Description:** Precision Pharma is a leader in the field of pathogen inactivation of blood products. The company's technologies are designed to address the risk of viral contamination of blood products. Founded in 1995. **NOTE:** Second and third shifts are offered. **Common positions include:** Accountant; Administrative Assistant; Biochemist; Biological Scientist; Budget Analyst; Chemical Engineer; Computer Support Technician; Database Manager; Financial Analyst; Help-Desk Technician; Human Resources Manager; Manufacturing Engineer; Production Manager; Purchasing Agent/Manager; Quality Assurance Engineer; Quality Control Supervisor; Sales Manager; Secretary.

QUEST DIAGNOSTICS INCORPORATED

575 Underhill Boulevard, Syosset NY 11791. 516/677-3800. **Contact:** Personnel. **World Wide Web address:** http://www.questdiagnostics.com. **Description:** This location is a clinical laboratory. Overall, Quest Diagnostics is one of the largest clinical laboratories in North America, providing a broad range of clinical laboratory services to health care clients that include physicians, hospitals, clinics, dialysis centers, pharmaceutical companies, and corporations. The company offers and performs tests on blood, urine, and other bodily fluids and tissues to provide information for health and well-being. **Corporate headquarters location:** Teterboro NJ. **Listed on:** New York Stock Exchange. **Stock exchange symbol:** DGX.

REGENERON PHARMACEUTICALS, INC.

777 Old Saw Mill River Road, Suite 10, Tarrytown NY 10591. 914/345-7400. **Fax:** 914/345-7790. **Contact:** Human Resources Representative. **E-mail address:** jobs@regeneron.com. **World Wide Web address:** http://www.regeneron.com. **Description:** A research company that develops pharmaceuticals to treat neurological, oncological, inflammatory, allergic, and bone disorders as well as muscle atrophy. **Corporate headquarters location:** This location. **Listed on:** NASDAQ. **Stock exchange symbol:** REGN.

SCIENTIFIC INDUSTRIES, INC.

70 Orville Drive, Airport International Plaza, Bohemia NY 11716. 631/567-4700. **Contact:** Human Resources Department. **World Wide Web address:** http://www.scientificindustries.com. **Description:** Manufactures and markets laboratory equipment including vortex mixers and miscellaneous laboratory apparatuses including timers, rotators, and pumps. The company develops and sells computerized control and data logging systems for sterilizers and autoclaves. Scientific Industries' products are used by hospital laboratories, clinics, research laboratories, pharmaceutical manufacturers, and medical device manufacturers. **Corporate headquarters location:** This location.

STERIS-ISOMEDIX SERVICES

23 Elizabeth Drive, Chester NY 10918. 845/469-4087. **Contact:** Human Resources. **Description:** Provides contract sterilization services to manufacturers of prepackaged health care and consumer products.

UNDERWRITERS LABORATORIES INC.

1285 Walt Whitman Road, Melville NY 11747-3801. 631/271-6200. **Fax:** 631/271-8259. **Contact:** Employment Coordinator. **E-mail address:** melville@us.ul.com. **World Wide Web address:** http://www.ul.com. **Description:** An independent, nonprofit organization that specializes in product safety testing and certification worldwide. **Common positions include:** Clerk; Computer Programmer; Electrical/Electronics Engineer; Electronics Technician. **Special programs:** Summer Jobs. **Corporate headquarters location:** Northbrook IL. **Other U.S. locations:** Santa Clara CA; Research Triangle Park NC; Camas WA. **Number of employees at this location:** 800. **Number of employees worldwide:** 4,000.

WATSON LABORATORIES

33 Ralph Avenue, Copiague NY 11726-1297. 631/842-8383. **Contact:** Personnel Director. **Description:** Manufactures brand-name and generic pharmaceuticals in the areas of dermatology, women's health, neuropsychiatry, and primary care.

WYETH

401 North Middletown Road, Pearl River NY 10965-1299. 845/732-5000. **Contact:** Personnel Director. **World Wide Web address:** http://www.wyeth.com. **Description:** Manufactures both prescription and nonprescription pharmaceutical and hospital products including pharmaceuticals for the treatment of infectious diseases, mental illness, cancer, arthritis, skin disorders, glaucoma, tuberculosis, and other diseases; adult and pediatric vaccines; vitamin, multivitamin, and mineral products; and Davis & Geck surgical sutures, wound closure devices, and other hospital products.

BUSINESS SERVICES AND NON-SCIENTIFIC RESEARCH

You can expect to find the following types of companies in this chapter:

Adjustment and Collection Services • Cleaning, Maintenance, and Pest Control Services • Credit Reporting • Detective, Guard, and Armored Car Services • Miscellaneous Equipment Rental and Leasing • Secretarial and Court Reporting Services

ADT SECURITY SERVICES
335 West 16th Street, New York NY 10011. 646/336-2300. **Contact:** Personnel. **World Wide Web address:** http://www.adtsecurityservices.com. **Description:** Designs, programs, markets, and installs protective systems to safeguard life and property from hazards such as burglary, hold-up, and fire. ADT Security Services has over 180,000 customers in the United States, Canada, and Western Europe. Founded in 1874. **Corporate headquarters location:** Boca Raton FL. **Parent company:** Tyco International Ltd. **Listed on:** New York Stock Exchange. **Stock exchange symbol:** TYC.

ADECCO
175 Broad Hollow Road, Melville NY 11747. 631/844-7800. **Contact:** Human Resources. **World Wide Web address:** http://www.adecco.com. **Description:** Provides a wide variety of job search and placement services, from temporary placements to executive recruitment. **Corporate headquarters location:** This location. **Listed on:** New York Stock Exchange. **Stock exchange symbol:** ADO.

ALLIED SECURITY
14 East 39th Street, 2nd Floor, New York NY 10016. 212/532-1744. **Contact:** Human Resources Department. **World Wide Web address:** http://www.alliedsecurity.com. **Description:** A full-service corporate security firm that provides contract guard services, electronic security, and investigative services. **Corporate headquarters location:** King of Prussia PA.

AMERICAN CLAIMS EVALUATION, INC.
One Jericho Plaza, 3rd Floor, Wing B, Jericho NY 11753. 516/938-8000. **Contact:** Human Resources. **Description:** American Claims Evaluation, Inc. is a health care cost containment services company that verifies the accuracy of hospital bills submitted to its clients for payment. Such clients include commercial health insurance companies, third-party administrators, health maintenance organizations, and self-insured corporate clients. The company also provides a full range of vocational rehabilitation and disability management services through its wholly-owned subsidiaries. **Corporate headquarters location:** This location. **Listed on:** NASDAQ. **Stock exchange symbol:** AMCE.

AMERICAN STUDENT LIST COMPANY, LLC
330 Old Country Road, Mineola NY 11501. 516/248-6100. **Contact:** Human Resources. **World Wide Web address:** http://www.studentlist.com. **Description:** A leading provider of direct marketing information of preschool children and students from elementary schools, high schools, colleges, and post-graduate schools throughout the United States. Lists are

rented primarily to various colleges, educational institutions, financial institutions, magazine publishers, and national organizations. Lists are available for all geographic areas of the United States and are provided to customers in the form of mailing labels, magnetic tape, or computer diskettes. **Other U.S. locations:** Boca Raton FL. **Parent company:** Havas Advertising. **Listed on:** NASDAQ. **Stock exchange symbol:** HADV.

C.T. CORPORATION
111 Eighth Avenue, 13th Floor, New York NY 10011. 212/894-8940. **Contact:** Human Resources Department. **World Wide Web address:** http://www.ctcorporation.com. **Description:** C.T. Corporation provides research and accounting services for attorneys.

CASCADE LINEN SERVICES
835 Myrtle Avenue, Brooklyn NY 11206. 718/963-9600. **Contact:** Human Resources. **Description:** Provides commercial linen supply and rental services for hotels, restaurants, and medical institutions. **Corporate headquarters location:** This location.

CENDANT CORPORATION
9 West 57th Street, 37th Floor, New York NY 10019. 212/413-1800. **Contact:** Human Resources Department. **World Wide Web address:** http://www.cendant.com. **Description:** Provides a wide range of business services including dining services, hotel franchise management, mortgage programs, and timeshare exchanges. Cendant Corporation's Real Estate Division offers employee relocation and mortgage services through Century 21, Coldwell Banker, ERA, Cendant Mortgage, and Cendant Mobility. The Travel Division provides car rentals, vehicle management services, and vacation timeshares through brand names including Avia, Days Inn, Howard Johnson, Ramada, Travelodge, and Super 8. The Membership Division offers travel, shopping, auto, dining, and other financial services through Travelers Advantage, Shoppers Advantage, Auto Vantage, Welcome Wagon, Netmarket, North American Outdoor Group, and PrivacyGuard. Founded in 1997. **NOTE:** Resumes should be sent to Human Resources, Cendant Corporation, One Campus Drive, Parsippany NJ 07054. **Corporate headquarters location:** This location. **Listed on:** New York Stock Exchange. **Stock exchange symbol:** CD. **Number of employees worldwide:** 28,000.

COLIN SERVICE SYSTEMS INC.
One Brockway Place, White Plains NY 10601. 914/328-0800. **Fax:** 914/328-3385. **Contact:** Human Resources Department. **World Wide Web address:** http://www.colin.com. **Description:** A maintenance firm specializing in commercial cleaning services. **Common positions include:** Accountant/Auditor; Administrative Manager; Blue-Collar Worker Supervisor; Claim Representative; Computer Programmer; Customer Service Representative; Environmental Engineer; Financial Analyst; Human Resources Manager; Operations/Production Manager; Systems Analyst. **Corporate headquarters location:** This location. **Operations at this facility include:** Administration. **Listed on:** Privately held.

COMFORCE
415 Crossways Park Drive, P.O. Box 9006, Woodbury NY 11797. 516/437-3300. **Fax:** 516/470-2298. **Contact:** Human Resources Department. **World Wide Web address:** http://www.comforce.com. **Description:** A temporary staffing company that operates a network of 63 offices. Comforce supplies prescreened and experienced temporary staffers for the general and automated office, medical support, MIS, technical, lab support, accounting,

marketing, and light industrial services. **Corporate headquarters location:** This location. **Subsidiaries include:** LabForce provides laboratory professionals including chemists, biologists, engineers, and all types of scientific support personnel. THISCO and Brentwood provide unlimited financing and total back-office administrative services, payroll preparation, and billing for independent temporary staffing services. Payroll Options Unlimited provides outsourcing solutions for companies utilizing 1099 Independent Contractors, returning retirees, and consultants. **Listed on:** American Stock Exchange. **Stock exchange symbol:** CFS.

COMMAND SECURITY CORPORATION (CSC)
P.O. Box 340, Lexington Park, Lagrangeville NY 12540. 845/454-3703. **Contact:** Human Resources. **Description:** CSC principally provides uniformed and nonuniformed security services from its 16 operating offices to commercial, financial, industrial, aviation, and government clients. Security services include providing guards for access control, theft prevention, surveillance, vehicular and foot patrol, and crowd control. **Corporate headquarters location:** This location. **Other U.S. locations:** CA; CT; FL; IL; MA; NJ; PA. **Number of employees nationwide:** 5,000.

CORPORATE LANGUAGE SERVICES
18 John Street, Suite 300, New York NY 10038. 212/240-0274. **Toll-free phone:** 800/788-0450. **Fax:** 212/349-0964. **Contact:** Human Resources Supervisor. **World Wide Web address:** http://www.alsintl.com. **Description:** A translation and interpreting company serving a worldwide, diversified clientele. **NOTE:** Entry-level positions and part-time jobs are offered. **Common positions include:** Account Representative; Accountant; Administrative Assistant; Advertising Executive; Customer Service Representative; Database Administrator; Desktop Publishing Specialist; ESL Teacher; Human Resources Manager; Multimedia Designer; Webmaster. **Corporate headquarters location:** This location. **Other U.S. locations:** Washington DC; Kansas City MO. **Parent company:** ALS International. **Listed on:** Privately held. **Number of employees at this location:** 80. **Number of employees nationwide:** 100.

CYBERDATA, INC.
20 Max Avenue, Hicksville NY 11801. 516/942-8000. **Fax:** 516/942-0800. **Contact:** Personnel Department. **E-mail address:** jobs@cyberdata.com. **World Wide Web address:** http://www.cyberdata.com. **Description:** Provides an array of information-based services for client companies including information management, storage, and dissemination. CyberData, Inc. offers a mass fax service through a large number of modems.

ESQUIRE DEPOSITION SERVICES
216 East 45th Street, 8th Floor, New York NY 10017. 212/687-8010. **Contact:** Human Resources Department. **World Wide Web address:** http://www.esquirecom.com/deposition. **Description:** A court reporting firm using state-of-the-art technology to provide printed and computerized transcripts, video recordings of testimony from depositions, and speech recognition systems to the legal profession primarily in metropolitan New York City and Southern California. The company's technologies include real-time transcription, interactive real-time transcription, full-text search and retrieval programs, compressed transcripts, and multimedia technology systems.

THE GREAT BRIDAL EXPO GROUP INC.

P.O. Box 337, West Islip NY 11795. 631/669-1200. **Contact:** Human Resources Department. **E-mail address:** info@greatbridalexpo.com. **World Wide Web address:** http://www.greatbridalexpo.com. **Description:** Produces and presents trade-show expositions in major cities in the United States. These expositions introduce prospective brides and grooms and their families to products and services they may need to plan their weddings, honeymoons, and homes.

GUARDIAN CLEANING INDUSTRIES

170 Varick Street, 3rd Floor, New York NY 10013. 212/645-9500. **Contact:** Mr. Samuel Herzfeld, President. **World Wide Web address:** http://www.guardian.baweb.com. **Description:** An industrial/commercial maintenance firm providing cleaning and exterminating services. **Corporate headquarters location:** This location.

HEALTH MANAGEMENT SYSTEMS, INC. (HMS, INC.)

401 Park Avenue South, New York NY 10016. 212/685-4545. **Fax:** 212/889-8776. **Contact:** Personnel. **E-mail address:** recruit@hmsy.com. **World Wide Web address:** http://www.hmsy.com. **Description:** HMS, Inc. provides financial systems, consulting, and data processing services to major hospitals and government agencies (Medicaid/Medicare) throughout the country. **Common positions include:** Management Analyst/Consultant; Systems Analyst; Technical Writer/Editor. **Corporate headquarters location:** This location. **Other U.S. locations:** Los Angeles CA. **Subsidiaries include:** Quality Medical Adjudication (QMA, Inc.). **Listed on:** NASDAQ. **Stock exchange symbol:** HMSY.

HEALTHPLEX INC.

60 Charles Lindbergh Boulevard, Uniondale NY 11553. 516/794-3000. **Contact:** Human Resources Department. **World Wide Web address:** http://www.healthplex.com. **Description:** Provides administrative services, primarily claims processing and related electronic data processing services. **Subsidiaries include:** Dentcare Delivery Systems, Inc.; International Healthcare Services, Inc.; OASYS Corporation.

INTERPOOL, INC.

633 Third Avenue, 27th Floor, New York NY 10017. 212/916-3261. **Contact:** Personnel. **World Wide Web address:** http://www.interpool.com. **Description:** Leases containers and chassis, primarily to container shipping lines. The company is one of the world's leading lessors of intermodal dry cargo containers and one of the largest lessors of intermodal container chassis in the United States. **Corporate headquarters location:** Princeton NJ. **International locations:** Worldwide. **Subsidiaries include:** Interpool Limited conducts the international container leasing business. Founded in 1968. **Listed on:** New York Stock Exchange. **Stock exchange symbol:** IPX.

JOHN C. MANDEL SECURITY

611 Jackson Avenue, Bronx NY 10455. 718/402-5002. **Contact:** Personnel Department. **Description:** Provides security services through armed and unarmed guards on an around-the-clock basis. Clients range from private housing developments and projects to a wide range of commercial and industrial customers.

NASSAU LIBRARY SYSTEM

900 Jerusalem Avenue, Uniondale NY 11553. 516/292-8920. **Contact:** Personnel. **World Wide Web address:** http://www.nassaulibrary.org.

Description: An association of autonomous local public libraries and a central service center, with 54 libraries in the system. The system office supports local library service through a wide range of supplementary and complementary services, collections, specialized staff, and professional programming; provides effective and economical centralized services; initiates legislation beneficial to library service; and develops, promotes, and maintains standards of library service within Nassau County. The system also provides extensive technical services to member libraries. **Common positions include:** Administrative Worker/Clerk; Data Entry Clerk; Librarian; Purchasing Agent/Manager. **Corporate headquarters location:** This location.

ONESOURCE FACILITY SERVICES
429 West 53rd Street, New York NY 10019. 212/408-6200. **Contact:** Personnel. **World Wide Web address:** http://www.2onesource.com. **Description:** Provides a variety of services including janitorial, landscaping, and pest control to public institutions, retail stores, schools, industrial facilities, and commercial buildings. **Corporate headquarters location:** Atlanta GA.

SANBORN MAP COMPANY
629 Fifth Avenue, Pelham NY 10803. 914/738-1649. **Fax:** 914/738-1680. **Contact:** General Manager. **E-mail address:** pelham@sanborn.com. **World Wide Web address:** http://www.sanbornmap.com. **Description:** A mapping and geographical information service, Sanborn Map Company is a data source for AM/FM, GIS, and environmental investigations. Sanborn's operations are organized through three units: Mapping, Custom Databases, and Environmental Data Services. Mapping involves building footprint maps showing street addresses and building details based on actual field inspections. Sanborn's Environmental Data Services operation uses an archive of maps dating back to 1867 to show building and land use including underground tanks and pipes, types of material stored, and owners and occupants of properties. The company's Custom Databases operation produces databases and designed digital map files based on Sanborn's existing map collection and its current field survey services. Information collected from the field survey services include land and building uses, housing unit counts, building vacancy status, building construction details, and building condition. **Common positions include:** Draftsperson; Geographer; Researcher; Surveyor. **Corporate headquarters location:** This location. **Operations at this facility include:** Administration; Manufacturing; Research and Development; Sales. **Listed on:** Privately held. **Number of employees at this location:** 35.

SUFFOLK COOPERATIVE LIBRARY SYSTEM
627 North Sunrise Service Road, Bellport NY 11713. 631/286-1600. **Contact:** Dorothy Curto, Human Resources Specialist. **Description:** A county-chartered library association that provides a variety of support services to the 52 libraries comprising the Suffolk County library system. **Corporate headquarters location:** This location.

TEMCO SERVICE INDUSTRIES INC.
One Park Avenue, 1st Floor, New York NY 10016. 212/889-6353. **Contact:** Human Resources. **Description:** Offers a wide variety of maintenance, security, and related services through a workforce directed by a network of experienced managers. The company operates in the following areas: Building Maintenance Services; Engineering Maintenance Services; Extermination and Security Services; and Incineration and Heat Recovery

Systems. **Common positions include:** Accountant/Auditor; Blue-Collar Worker Supervisor; Branch Manager; Computer Programmer; Financial Analyst; General Manager; Mechanical Engineer; Operations/Production Manager; Services Sales Representative. **Corporate headquarters location:** This location. **International locations:** Belgium. **Operations at this facility include:** Administration; Sales; Service.

TRIZETTO GROUP, INC.
1700 Broadway, New York NY 10019. 212/765-8500. **Contact:** Human Resources Department. **World Wide Web address:** http://www.trizetto.com. **Description:** Develops health management software for insurance agencies and health care providers. **NOTE:** Interested jobseekers should send resumes to 1085 Morris Avenue, Union NJ 07083. **Corporate headquarters location:** Newport Beach CA. **Listed on:** NASDAQ. **Stock exchange symbol:** TZIX.

WESTCHESTER LIBRARY SYSTEM
410 Saw Mill River Road, Ardsley NY 10502. 914/674-3600. **Fax:** 914/674-4185. **Contact:** Human Resources Department. **World Wide Web address:** http://www.wls.lib.ny.us. **Description:** Provides a wide range of buying, distribution, and other support services to the 38 member libraries in the Westchester County library system. **Corporate headquarters location:** This location.

WINFIELD SECURITY
35 West 35th Street, New York NY 10001. 212/947-3700. **Contact:** Human Resources. **World Wide Web address:** http://www.winfieldsecurity.com. **Description:** Provides security guard services for office buildings, schools, businesses, and manufacturers. **Corporate headquarters location:** This location. **Other area locations:** Bronx NY; Brooklyn NY; Queens NY. **Other U.S. locations:** Bloomfield NJ.

WINSTON RESOURCES, INC.
535 Fifth Avenue, Suite 701, New York NY 10017. 212/557-5000. **Contact:** Human Resources. **Description:** Winston Resources is a network of recruiting companies. Winston Resources has seven owned offices and 21 offices licensed or franchised under various names. Businesses include Winston Personnel, which recruits entry-level to management personnel in a wide range of industries; Winston Staffing Services, which provides temporary personnel in a broad range of job categories; Winston Temporaries, which provides clerical, word processing, secretarial, technical, and other support personnel; Winston Data Services, which provides data entry, computer operations, programming, systems analysis, and technical support staff; Winston Medical Temporaries, which provides lab, X-ray, and other technicians as well as physicians and nurses; Winston Nurse Staffing, which provides 24-hour staffing and bedside care in hospitals; Accountants Today, which provides accounting and financial personnel; Winston Interim Professional, which provides professional and managerial staff in human resources, mortgage underwriting, purchasing, and marketing; Fisher-Todd Associates, which is a national executive recruitment agency; Winston Advertising Agency, which provides a full range of advertising services as well as recruitment advertising placement; and Winston Franchise, which markets, sells, and manages personnel recruitment and temporary services franchises under the names Roth Young, Alpha Temps, Winston Personnel, and Winston Interim Professionals. Founded in 1967. **Corporate headquarters location:** This location.

CHARITIES AND SOCIAL SERVICES

You can expect to find the following types of organizations in this chapter:

Social and Human Service Agencies • Job Training and Vocational Rehabilitation Services • Nonprofit Organizations

AFS INTERCULTURAL PROGRAMS, INC.
198 Madison Avenue, 8th Floor, New York NY 10016. 212/299-9000. **Fax:** 212/299-9090. **Contact:** Human Resources Department. **World Wide Web address:** http://www.afs.org/usa. **Description:** An international exchange organization that provides intercultural learning opportunities for high school students, families, and teachers. The agency operates programs in approximately 55 countries via an international network of volunteers. **Common positions include:** Accountant/Auditor; Admissions Officer; Communications Specialist; Computer Programmer; Fundraising Specialist; Marketing Specialist; Public Relations Specialist.

ALCOHOLICS ANONYMOUS (A.A.)
P.O. Box 459, Grand Central Station, New York NY 10163. 212/870-3400. **Physical address:** 475 Riverside Drive, 11th Floor, New York NY 10115. **Contact:** Human Resources. **World Wide Web address:** http://www.aa.org. **Description:** Alcoholics Anonymous (A.A.) is a fellowship of men and women who share their experiences with each other so that they may work on their common problems and help others to recover from alcoholism. A.A. consists of 89,000 local groups in 141 countries. Founded in 1935. **Corporate headquarters location:** This location. **Subsidiaries include:** A.A. World Services, Inc. operates at this location with 100 employees coordinating with local groups, with A.A. groups in treatment and correctional facilities, and with members and groups overseas. A.A. literature is prepared, published, and distributed through this office. The A.A. Grapevine, Inc. publishes the *A.A. Grapevine,* the fellowship's monthly international journal. The magazine has a circulation of about 119,000 in the United States, Canada, and other countries. A.A. Grapevine, Inc. also produces a selection of cassette tapes and anthologies of magazine articles.

AMERICAN FOUNDATION FOR THE BLIND
11 Penn Plaza, Suite 300, New York NY 10001. 212/502-7600. **Toll-free phone:** 800/AFB-LINE. **Contact:** Kelly Bleach, Director of Personnel. **E-mail address:** afbinfo@afb.net. **World Wide Web address:** http://www.afb.org. **Description:** A nonprofit organization. The American Foundation for the Blind (AFB) is a leading national resource for people who are blind or visually impaired, the organizations that serve them, and the general public. AFB operates through four primary areas of activity: development, collection, and dissemination of information; identification, analysis, and resolution of critical issues; education of the public and policymakers on the needs and capabilities of people who are blind or visually impaired; and production and distribution of talking books and other audio materials. Founded in 1921.

AMERICAN SOCIETY FOR THE PREVENTION OF CRUELTY TO ANIMALS
424 East 92nd Street, New York NY 10128. 212/876-7700. **Fax:** 212/876-0014. **Contact:** Human Resources. **E-mail address:** hr@aspca.org. **World Wide Web address:** http://www.aspca.org. **Description:** The society is

involved in six primary areas: animals as pets; humane education; animals for sport and entertainment; experimentation on animals; animal industries; and protection of wild animals and endangered species. Founded in 1866.

BEDFORD STUYVESANT RESTORATION CORPORATION
1368 Fulton Street, Brooklyn NY 11216-2630. 718/636-6900. **Contact:** Human Resources. **E-mail address:** info@restorationplaza.org. **World Wide Web address:** http://www.restorationplaza.org. **Description:** One of the nation's oldest and largest nonprofit community development corporations. The company promotes the economic revitalization of Bedford Stuyvesant.

THE BOYS' CLUB OF NEW YORK (BCNY)
287 East 10th Street, New York NY 10009. 212/677-1109. **Contact:** Hiring. **World Wide Web address:** http://www.bcny.org. **Description:** Provides a variety of services to young men in the New York City area. BCNY's educational program has helped hundreds of young men to attend leading prep schools and colleges, offering support and counseling to help them succeed. BCNY's job training program offers teenage members their first work experience in top-flight New York companies. The club offers a year-round program serving boys between 6 and 17 years old. Founded in 1876. **Corporate headquarters location:** This location.

CATHOLIC CHARITIES OF THE DIOCESE OF BROOKLYN & QUEENS
191 Joralemon Street, Brooklyn NY 11201. 718/722-6000. **Contact:** Thomas DeStefano, Executive Director. **World Wide Web address:** http://www.ccbq.org. **Description:** A network of private social service organizations that provides food, shelter, and clothing to disadvantaged individuals. **Common positions include:** Accountant/Auditor; Administrator; Case Manager; Counselor; Program Manager; Social Worker. **Corporate headquarters location:** Alexandria VA. **Other U.S. locations:** Nationwide. **Number of employees nationwide:** 1,800.

CHILDREN'S AID SOCIETY
105 East 22nd Street, New York NY 10010. 212/949-4800. **Contact:** Human Resources Manager. **World Wide Web address:** http://www.childrensaidsociety.org. **Description:** Provides early, intensive, and long-term support to thousands of city children and their families through various programs and services including medical and dental care, foster care, group homes, adoption, homemakers, emergency assistance, food distribution, Head Start, tutoring, mentors, community centers, community schools, counseling, court diversion programs, camps, sports, arts, dance, theater, chorus, internships, jobs, teen pregnancy prevention, leadership projects, college and prep/college scholarships, and services to the homeless. Founded in 1853. **Corporate headquarters location:** This location. **Operations at this facility include:** Administration; Regional Headquarters.

CHILDREN'S VILLAGE
Westmore Hall, 1st Floor, Dobbs Ferry NY 10522. 914/693-0600. **Contact:** Human Resources. **E-mail address:** recruiter@childrensvillage.org. **World Wide Web address:** http://www.childrensvillage.org. **Description:** A nonprofit organization that operates a residential treatment center for emotionally disturbed children. **Corporate headquarters location:** This location.

COMMUNITY COUNSELING SERVICES COMPANY

Empire State Building, 350 Fifth Avenue, Suite 7210, New York NY 10118. 212/695-1175. **Contact:** Human Resources Department. **World Wide Web address:** http://www.ccsfundraising.com. **Description:** A nationwide fundraising company that organizes campaigns for nonprofit clients.

COMMUNITY SERVICE SOCIETY OF NEW YORK

105 East 22nd Street, New York NY 10010. 212/254-8900. **Contact:** Personnel Manager. **E-mail address:** info@cssny.org. **World Wide Web address:** http://www.cssny.org. **Description:** A nonprofit, social advocacy organization that conducts policy analysis and research, provides training and technical assistance to strengthen community-based organizations, and develops service programs that respond to the complex problems faced by the poor in New York City.

THE FORD FOUNDATION

320 East 43rd Street, New York NY 10017. 212/573-5000. **Fax:** 212/351-3677. **Contact:** Human Resources. **World Wide Web address:** http://www.fordfound.org. **Description:** One of the largest philanthropic organizations in the United States. This private, nonprofit institution donates funds for educational, developmental, research, and experimental efforts designed to produce significant advances in a wide range of social problems. The company also operates several overseas field offices in Asia, Latin America, the Middle East, and Africa. **Common positions include:** Accountant/Auditor; Administrator; Assistant Program Officer; Attorney; Economist; Human Resources Manager; Program Officer; Systems Analyst. **Corporate headquarters location:** This location.

FOSTER HOME SERVICES

JEWISH CHILD CARE ASSOCIATION

120 Wall Street, 12th Floor, New York NY 10005. 212/558-9943. **Contact:** Personnel. **World Wide Web address:** http://www.jewishchildcareny.org. **Description:** Provides social services for children including the placement of abused children in foster homes, as well as training programs for future foster parents. **Common positions include:** Registered Nurse; Social Worker. **Corporate headquarters location:** This location. **Operations at this facility include:** Administration; Service.

GIRL SCOUTS OF THE UNITED STATES OF AMERICA

420 Fifth Avenue, New York NY 10018-2798. 212/852-8000. **Toll-free phone:** 800/GSU-SA4U. **Contact:** Staffing Department. **World Wide Web address:** http://www.girlscouts.org. **Description:** Girl Scouts is a national scouting organization for girls. **Corporate headquarters location:** This location.

HENRY STREET SETTLEMENT

265 Henry Street, New York NY 10002. 212/766-9200. **Contact:** Human Resources. **Description:** Provides various social services including daycare, home care, housekeeping, Meals on Wheels, work training for 16- to 21-year-olds, after-school homework help, shelter for battered women, and care for pregnant teenagers.

JEWISH COMMUNITY CENTER ASSOCIATION

15 East 26th Street, 10th Floor, New York NY 10010-1579. 212/532-4949. **Contact:** C. Carlson, Personnel Manager. **E-mail address:** info@jcca.org. **World Wide Web address:** http://www.jcca.org. **Description:** The nonprofit, national coordinating body for the Jewish Community Center

movement in North America. The association has more than 50 area locations.

JUST ONE BREAK, INC.
120 Wall Street, 20th Floor, New York NY 10005. 212/785-7300. **Fax:** 212/785-4513. **Contact:** Recruiter. **E-mail address:** jobs@justonebreak.com. **World Wide Web address:** http://www.justonebreak.com. **Description:** A nonprofit organization that helps people with disabilities find employment. Founded in 1947. **Common positions include:** Accountant; Administrative Assistant; Bank Officer/Manager; Clerical Supervisor; Computer Operator; Counselor; Customer Service Manager; Database Manager; Graphic Artist; Management Trainee; MIS Specialist; Operations Manager; Paralegal; Project Manager; Sales Representative; Secretary; Social Worker; Systems Analyst; Systems Manager; Telecommunications Manager.

LIGHTHOUSE INTERNATIONAL
111 East 59th Street, New York NY 10022-1202. 212/821-9200. **Toll-free phone:** 800/829-0500. **Fax:** 212/821-9708. **Recorded jobline:** 212/821-9419. **Contact:** Recruiting. **E-mail address:** info@lighthouse.org. **World Wide Web address:** http://www.lighthouse.org. **Description:** Enables people who are blind or partially blind to lead independent lives through education, research, information, career and social services, and vision rehabilitation. Lighthouse International serves more than 5,000 persons. **Common positions include:** Accountant/Auditor; Accounting Clerk; Administrative Assistant; Development Officer; Early Childhood Teacher; Mail Distributor; Optician; Physical Therapist; Public Relations Specialist; Registered Nurse; Rehabilitation Teacher; Social Worker; Speech-Language Pathologist; Teacher Aide; Teacher/Professor. **Special programs:** Internships. **Other area locations:** Medford NY; Poughkeepsie NY; Queens NY; White Plains NY. **Operations at this facility include:** Administration; Education; Research and Development; Service. **Number of employees at this location:** 305. **Number of employees nationwide:** 375.

LITTLE FLOWER CHILDREN'S SERVICES OF NEW YORK
186 Joralemon Street, Brooklyn NY 11201. 718/875-3500. **Contact:** Carol A. Huck, Human Resources Director. **E-mail address:** hr@littleflowerny.org. **World Wide Web address:** http://www.littleflowerny.org. **Description:** Provides foster care and adoption services, group homes, residential treatment units, shelter cottages, intermediate care facilities for mentally handicapped children, and therapeutic foster boarding homes. Little Flower Children's Services cares for approximately 2,600 children annually. **Corporate headquarters location:** This location. **Operations at this facility include:** Administration. **Number of employees nationwide:** 650.

LITTLE FLOWER CHILDREN'S SERVICES OF NEW YORK
2450 North Wading River Road, Wading River NY 11792. 631/929-6200. **Fax:** 631/929-6121. **E-mail address:** hr@littleflowerny.org. **World Wide Web address:** http://www.littleflowerny.org. **Contact:** Human Resources Director. **Description:** Provides adoption and foster care services, foster homes for individuals who are mentally handicapped, intermediate care facilities, residential treatment facilities, and therapeutic foster boarding homes. Little Flower Children's Services cares for more than 2,600 children annually. **Common positions include:** Child Care Worker; Nurse; Secretary; Social Worker. **Special programs:** Internships. **Corporate headquarters location:** Brooklyn NY. **Operations at this facility include:** Administration; Regional Headquarters. **Number of employees at this location:** 400. **Number of employees nationwide:** 650.

LOWER WEST SIDE HOUSEHOLD SERVICES CORPORATION
250 West 57th Street, Suite 1511, New York NY 10107-1511. 212/307-7107. **Fax:** 212/956-2308. **Contact:** Brenda Franklin, Assistant Program Manager. **World Wide Web address:** http://www.homecareny.org. **Description:** A nonprofit company that provides home health care services to the elderly, infants, toddlers, and adults living in the five boroughs of New York City and Westchester County. Services include nursing, custodial care, nutrition, social work, and arrangements for medical equipment. The agency also provides free custodial care for individuals and families infected with HIV/AIDS. **NOTE:** Second and thirds shifts are offered. Founded in 1969. **Common positions include:** Accountant; Administrative Assistant; Computer Scientist; Home Health Aide; Licensed Practical Nurse; Marketing Specialist; Occupational Therapist; Physical Therapist; Social Worker; Speech-Language Pathologist; Web Advertising Specialist; Website Developer. **Special programs:** Training. **Office hours:** Monday - Friday, 8:00 a.m. - 5:00 p.m. **Corporate headquarters location:** This location. **Other U.S. locations:** Westchester NY. **Number of employees at this location:** 250.

MARCH OF DIMES
1275 Mamaroneck Avenue, White Plains NY 10605. 914/428-7100. **Contact:** Human Resources Department. **World Wide Web address:** http://www.modimes.org. **Description:** The organization operates the Campaign for Healthier Babies, which includes programs of research, community service, education, and advocacy. Birth defects are the primary focus of March of Dimes research efforts. March of Dimes chapters across the country work with their communities to determine and meet the needs of women, children, and families. Through specially designed programs, women are provided with access to prenatal care. **Corporate headquarters location:** This location. **Other U.S. locations:** Nationwide.

MARYKNOLL FATHERS AND BROTHERS
P.O. Box 302, Maryknoll NY 10545. 914/941-7590. **Contact:** Human Resources. **World Wide Web address:** http://www.maryknoll.org. **Description:** This location houses administrative and fundraising offices. Overall, Maryknoll Fathers and Brothers is an international order of religious missionaries. **NOTE:** Entry-level positions and part-time jobs are offered. **Common positions include:** Controller; Graphic Artist; Help-Desk Technician; Internet Services Manager; Managing Editor; Network/Systems Administrator; Radio/TV Announcer/Broadcaster; Registered Nurse; Reporter; Technical Writer/Editor; Video Production Coordinator; Webmaster. **Special programs:** Summer Jobs. **Corporate headquarters location:** This location. **Facilities Manager:** Peter Murray. **Information Systems Manager:** Jim Combes. **Number of employees at this location:** 370. **Number of employees nationwide:** 425.

U.S. FUNDS FOR UNICEF
333 East 38th Street, 6th Floor, New York NY 10016. 212/686-5522. **Contact:** Roslyn Carnege, Director of Human Resources. **World Wide Web address:** http://www.unicefusa.org. **Description:** Organized for educational and charitable purposes, U.S. Funds for UNICEF aims to increase awareness of the needs of children around the world. **Common positions include:** Accountant/Auditor; Administrator; Budget Analyst; Computer Programmer; Customer Service Representative; Editor; Education Administrator; Financial Analyst; Human Resources Manager; Marketing Specialist; Public Relations Specialist; Purchasing Agent/Manager; Systems Analyst. **Special programs:** Internships. **Corporate headquarters location:** This location. **Other U.S.**

locations: Los Angeles CA; Washington DC; Atlanta GA; Chicago IL; Boston MA; Houston TX. **Operations at this facility include:** Administration; Divisional Headquarters. **Listed on:** Privately held. **Number of employees at this location:** 100.

UNITED CEREBRAL PALSY ASSOCIATIONS OF NEW YORK STATE
330 West 34th Street, 14th Floor, New York NY 10001. 212/947-5770. **Fax:** 212/290-8475. **Contact:** Human Resources Department. **World Wide Web address:** http://www.cerebralpalsynys.org. **Description:** A nonprofit health care organization that provides services to persons with developmental disabilities. **NOTE:** Entry-level positions are offered. **Common positions include:** Nurse Practitioner; Occupational Therapist; Physician; Preschool Worker; Psychologist; Registered Nurse; Social Worker; Speech-Language Pathologist. **Special programs:** Internships. **Corporate headquarters location:** Washington DC. **Other area locations:** Bronx NY; Brooklyn NY; Queens NY; Staten Island NY. **Operations at this facility include:** Administration; Divisional Headquarters. **Annual sales/revenues:** $51 - $100 million. **Number of employees at this location:** 1,700.

UNITED WAY OF NEW YORK CITY
2 Park Avenue South, 2nd Floor, New York NY 10016-1601. 212/251-2500. **Contact:** Human Resources. **World Wide Web address:** http://www.uwnyc.org. **Description:** A nonprofit organization that offers referral and crisis intervention services for pregnant women and parents.

WESTCHESTER COMMUNITY OPPORTUNITY PROGRAM
2269 Saw Mill River Road, Building 3, Suite G-16, Elmsford NY 10523-3833. 914/592-5600. **Contact:** Paulette Warren, Personnel Director. **Description:** A county-sponsored, nonprofit social services agency operating through numerous community action programs that provide clinical services, employment training programs, energy programs, and a wide range of other community services. **Corporate headquarters location:** This location.

YWCA
610 Lexington Avenue, New York NY 10022. 212/755-4500. **Contact:** Human Resources. **E-mail address:** info@ywcanyc.org. **World Wide Web address:** http://www.ywcanyc.org. **Description:** Provides counseling, physical fitness activities, a shelter, and daycare facilities for women and their children. **Corporate headquarters location:** This location. **Other U.S. locations:** Nationwide.

CHEMICALS/RUBBER AND PLASTICS

You can expect to find the following types of companies in this chapter:

Adhesives, Detergents, Inks, Paints, Soaps, Varnishes • Agricultural Chemicals and Fertilizers • Carbon and Graphite Products • Chemical Engineering Firms • Industrial Gases

ACETO CORPORATION
One Hollow Lane, Suite 201, Lake Success NY 11042. 516/627-6000. **Contact:** Ms. Pat Miller, Office Manager. **E-mail address:** hr@aceto.com. **World Wide Web address:** http://www.aceto.com. **Description:** Manufactures chemicals for a wide variety of uses in agricultural markets, color producing industries, and pharmaceutical and health care industries. The chemicals are used to synthesize colors used in photography, textiles, plastics, paints, and printing inks. In the pharmaceutical industry, the company supplies bulk pharmaceuticals and specialty chemicals for use as raw materials to synthesize pharmaceuticals and antibiotics. Aceto also manufactures plastics, surface coatings, and other specialty performance chemicals including antioxidants for plastics, adhesion promoters for automotive finishes, and catalysts for use in the manufacture of certain resins. **Corporate headquarters location:** This location. **Listed on:** NASDAQ. **Stock exchange symbol:** ACET.

BALCHEM CORPORATION
P.O. Box 175, Slate Hill NY 10973-0175. 845/355-5300. **Contact:** Human Resources. **World Wide Web address:** http://www.balchem.com. **Description:** A leader in the manufacturing and marketing of encapsulated food ingredients for a variety of industries. The company is also a leading supplier of ethylene oxide, a packaging sterilant. Founded in 1967. **Corporate headquarters location:** This location. **Listed on:** American Stock Exchange. **Stock exchange symbol:** BCP.

CHEMPRENE INC.
P.O. Box 471, Beacon NY 12508. 845/831-2800. **Physical address:** 483 Fishkill Avenue, Beacon NY 12508. **Fax:** 845/831-5967. **Contact:** Human Resources. **Description:** Chemprene produces a wide range of specialty industrial diaphragms, belting, and coated fabrics by spread coating, dip coating, and calendering methods. **Common positions include:** Blue-Collar Worker Supervisor; Chemist; Customer Service Representative; Designer; Draftsperson; Electrician; Industrial Production Manager; Mechanical Engineer. **Corporate headquarters location:** This location. **Operations at this facility include:** Administration; Manufacturing; Research and Development; Sales. **Listed on:** Privately held. **Number of employees at this location:** 180.

CIBA SPECIALTY CHEMICALS
540 White Plains Road, Tarrytown NY 10591-9005. 914/785-2000. **Contact:** Human Resources. **E-mail address:** careers@cibasc.com. **World Wide Web address:** http://www.cibasc.com. **Description:** This location manufactures chemical additives. Overall, the company manufactures specialty chemicals through five divisions: additives, colors, consumer care, performance polymers, and water treatments. **Operations at this facility**

include: Regional Headquarters. **Listed on:** New York Stock Exchange. **Stock exchange symbol:** CSB.

INTERNATIONAL FLAVORS & FRAGRANCES INC.
521 West 57th Street, New York NY 10019. 212/765-5500. **Contact:** Human Resources. **World Wide Web address:** http://www.iff.com. **Description:** Creates and manufactures flavors and fragrances used by other manufacturers in a wide variety of consumer products. Fragrance products are sold principally to manufacturers of perfumes, cosmetics, personal care items, soaps, detergents, air fresheners, and household products. Flavor products are sold principally to manufacturers of dairy, meat, processed foods, beverages, pharmaceuticals, snacks, baked goods, confectioneries, tobacco products, oral care products, and animal foods. **Common positions include:** Accountant/Auditor; Chemist; Computer Programmer; Customer Service Representative; Human Resources Manager; Marketing Specialist; Secretary; Systems Analyst. **Corporate headquarters location:** This location. **Other U.S. locations:** Hazlet NJ; South Brunswick NJ; Union Beach NJ. **Operations at this facility include:** Administration; Regional Headquarters; Sales; Service. **Listed on:** New York Stock Exchange. **Stock exchange symbol:** IFF.

PAWLING CORPORATION
157 Charles Colman Boulevard, Pawling NY 12564. 845/855-1000. **Contact:** Human Resources Manager. **World Wide Web address:** http://www.pawling.com. **Description:** Manufactures rubber, plastic, and silicone products. Products range from inflatable rubber products to architectural protection products.

SULZER-METCO INC.
1101 Prospect Avenue, Westbury NY 11590-0201. 516/334-1300. **Contact:** Human Resources. **E-mail address:** hr-us@sulzermetco.com. **World Wide Web address:** http://www.sulzermetco.com. **Description:** Develops a thermal spray coating process that is used on industrial surfaces to increase resistance. **International locations:** Germany; the Netherlands; Switzerland.

SUPERIOR PRINTING INK COMPANY, INC.
70 Bethune Street, New York NY 10014-1768. 212/741-3600. **Contact:** Hal Rubin, Controller. **World Wide Web address:** http://www.superiorink.com. **Description:** Manufactures inks and pigments used in lithographic and other printing processes.

UNIFLEX, INC.
383 West John Street, Hicksville NY 11802. 516/932-2000. **Contact:** Human Resources. **World Wide Web address:** http://www.uniflexinc.com. **Description:** Designs, manufactures, and markets a broad line of customized plastic packaging for sales and advertising promotions; clear bags for apparel and soft goods manufacturers; and specialized, recyclable bags and other products for use in hospitals, medical laboratories, and emergency care centers. Medical products include patented, disposable bags for the safe handling of specimens, and general purpose bags for personal belongings. Specialty advertising products include handle bags, drawstring bags, tote bags, and litter bags. The Haran Packaging Division manufactures and markets custom flexible plastic for the health care, food, financial, and other markets. Tamper-evident security bags are sold to banks, retailers, casino operations, stockbrokers, and courier firms that have security concerns for cash and other valuables. **Corporate headquarters location:** This location. **Other area locations:** Westbury NY. **Other U.S.**

locations: Albuquerque NM. **Subsidiaries include:** The Cycle Plastics produces and markets jumbo flexible loop handle bags, double drawstring bags, and reclosable, resealable, Trac-Loc bags. These products are sold to retailers, cosmetics firms, food packing companies, and medical/health care supply firms.

UNILEVER CORPORATION
390 Park Avenue, New York NY 10022. 212/888-1260. **Contact:** Human Resources. **World Wide Web address:** http://www.unilever.com. **Description:** An international consumer products firm manufacturing a wide range of soaps, toiletries, and foods. **Corporate headquarters location:** This location. **Parent company:** Unilever NV (Netherlands). **Listed on:** New York Stock Exchange. **Stock exchange symbol:** UN.

COMMUNICATIONS: TELECOMMUNICATIONS AND BROADCASTING

You can expect to find the following types of companies in this chapter:

Cable/Pay Television Services • Communications Equipment • Radio and Television Broadcasting Systems • Telephone, Telegraph, and other Message Communications

ABC, INC.
77 West 66th Street, New York NY 10023. 212/456-7777. **Contact:** Human Resources. **World Wide Web address:** http://www.abc.com. **Description:** Engaged in television and radio broadcasting, providing cable television service to subscribers, and specialized newspaper publishing. Broadcasting operations include ABC Television Network Group, the Broadcast Group, the Cable and International Broadcast Group, and the Multimedia Group. In addition to its network operation, the Broadcasting segment consists of 8 network-affiliated television stations, 10 radio stations, cable television systems providing service to subscribers in 16 states, and the developing of multimedia video-by-wire business. Publishing operations consist of 8 daily newspapers, 78 weekly newspapers, 63 shopping guides, and other specialized publications. **Other U.S. locations:** Los Angeles CA; New Haven CT; Clifton NJ.

ACTV INC.
233 Park Avenue South, 10th Floor, New York NY 10003. 212/262-2570. **Contact:** Human Resources. **E-mail address:** jobs@actv.com. **World Wide Web address:** http://www.actv.com. **Description:** Engaged in individual television programming. The company's primary markets are in-home entertainment and education. **Corporate headquarters location:** This location. **Other U.S. locations:** Los Angeles CA. **Operations at this facility include:** Administration; Research and Development; Sales; Service. **Listed on:** NASDAQ. **Stock exchange symbol:** IATV. **Annual sales/revenues:** Less than $5 million. **Number of employees at this location:** 15. **Number of employees nationwide:** 25.

CBS INC.
51 West 52nd Street, 19th Floor, New York NY 10019. 212/975-4321. **Contact:** Human Resources Department. **World Wide Web address:** http://www.cbs.com. **Description:** A broad-based entertainment and communications company that operates one of the country's major commercial television networks and two nationwide radio networks. **Special programs:** Internships. **Internship information:** The company offers unpaid, full-time, summer internship positions for students. **Corporate headquarters location:** This location. **Parent company:** Viacom Inc. **Listed on:** New York Stock Exchange. **Stock exchange symbol:** VIA.

CNN (CABLE NEWS NETWORK)
5 Penn Plaza, 20th Floor, New York NY 10001. 212/714-7800. **Contact:** Human Resources. **World Wide Web address:** http://www.cnn.com. **Description:** A cable news network. CNN has 28 bureaus worldwide and provides 24-hour news programming worldwide. Programming includes international, domestic, and business news; sports; weather; special reports;

and topical programming. **Corporate headquarters location:** Atlanta GA. **Other U.S. locations:** Washington DC.

CABLEVISION SYSTEMS CORPORATION
1111 Stewart Avenue, Bethpage NY 11714. 516/803-2300. **Fax:** 516/803-3065. **Contact:** Personnel. **E-mail address:** careers@cablevision.com. **World Wide Web address:** http://www.cablevision.com. **Description:** Owns and operates cable television systems serving customers in the Boston, Cleveland, and New York markets. **Common positions include:** Accountant/Auditor; Attorney; Blue-Collar Worker Supervisor; Broadcast Technician; Budget Analyst; Buyer; Cashier; Computer Operator; Computer Programmer; Customer Service Representative; Department Manager; Employment Interviewer; Financial Analyst; Graphic Artist; Human Resources Manager; Industrial Engineer; Marketing Specialist; Payroll Clerk; Public Relations Specialist; Purchasing Agent/Manager; Radio/TV Announcer/Broadcaster; Receptionist; Reporter; Services Sales Representative; Statistician; Systems Analyst. **Special programs:** Internships. **Corporate headquarters location:** This location. **Operations at this facility include:** Administration. **Listed on:** New York Stock Exchange. **Stock exchange symbol:** CVC. **Number of employees at this location:** 700. **Number of employees nationwide:** 6,000.

CLEAR CHANNEL ENTERTAINMENT
220 West 42nd Street, New York NY 10036. 917/421-5100. **Contact:** Human Resources. **World Wide Web address:** http://www.cc.com. **Description:** Acquires, owns, and operates radio stations in small- and medium-sized markets in the eastern United States. Clear Channel Entertainment's stations are WHMP-FM, WHMP-AM, and WPKX-FM, each operating in the Springfield/Northampton MA market; WYAK-FM and WYAK-AM, operating in the Myrtle Beach SC market; and WKBG-FM and WRXR-FM, each operating in the Augusta GA market. The company also sells broadcasting and advertising to WVCO-FM. **Corporate headquarters location:** This location. **Parent company:** Clear Channel Communications, Inc. **Listed on:** New York Stock Exchange. **Stock exchange symbol:** CCU.

COMTECH TELECOMMUNICATIONS CORPORATION
105 Baylis Road, Melville NY 11747-3833. 631/777-8900. **Contact:** Linda Compitello, Personnel Manager. **E-mail address:** info@comtechtel.com. **World Wide Web address:** http://www.comtechtel.com. **Description:** Manufactures and markets high-tech microwave and telecommunications products and systems including antennas, frequency converters, and VSAT transceivers and modems. Products are used worldwide in satellite, tropospheric scatter, and wireless communications systems. The company also manufactures high-power amplifiers that are used to test electronic systems for electromagnetic compatibility and susceptibility; for defense systems; and for high power testing of electronic components and systems. Comtech, through its subsidiaries, offers products to customers including domestic and foreign common carriers and telephone companies, defense contractors, medical and automotive suppliers, oil companies, private and wireless networks, broadcasters, utilities, and government entities. **Corporate headquarters location:** This location. **Listed on:** NASDAQ. **Stock exchange symbol:** CMTL.

COMVERSE TECHNOLOGY INC.
170 Crossways Park Drive, Woodbury NY 11797-2048. 516/677-7200. **Contact:** Human Resources. **E-mail address:** resumes@comverse.com. **World Wide Web address:** http://www.comverse.com. **Description:**

Manufactures, markets, and supports specialized telecommunications systems for multimedia communications and information processing applications. The company's systems are used in a broad range of applications by fixed and wireless telephone network operators, government agencies, financial institutions, and other public and commercial organizations worldwide. Products include AUDIODISK, which is a multimedia digital monitoring system; and the ULTRA series, which is a variety of multimedia recording systems. **Corporate headquarters location:** This location. **Other U.S. locations:** Nationwide. **International locations:** Worldwide. **Subsidiaries include:** Comverse Network Systems; Comverse Infosys; Ulticom; and Startel. Founded in 1984. **Listed on:** NASDAQ. **Stock exchange symbol:** CMVT. **Annual sales/revenues:** More than $100 million.

COPYTELE, INC.
900 Walt Whitman Road, Suite 203C, Melville NY 11747. 631/549-5900. **Contact:** Ms. Anne Rotondo, Corporate Secretary. **World Wide Web address:** http://www.copytele.com. **Description:** Designs, develops, and markets encryption products, multifunctional telecommunications products, high-resolution flat panel displays, and specialty printers. **Corporate headquarters location:** This location. **Listed on:** NASDAQ. **Stock exchange symbol:** COPY.

CRESCENT TELEPHONE COMPANY
6 Nevada Drive, Building C, Lake Success NY 11042. 516/326-0517. **Contact:** Human Resources. **Description:** Provides telecommunication services for operator-assisted and long-distance telephone calls.

DHB INDUSTRIES, INC.
P.O. Box 269, Old Westbury NY 11568. 516/997-1155. **Physical address:** 555 Westbury Avenue, Carle Place NY 11514. **Contact:** Human Resources. **World Wide Web address:** http://www.dhbt.com. **Description:** DHB Industries is a diversified holding company. **Subsidiaries include:** PACA manufactures and distributes bullet-, bomb-, and projectile-resistant garments; NDL manufactures and distributes protective sports apparel and fitness products and related items; Intelligent Data Corporation develops sophisticated telecommunications systems for remote document signature and authentication; Zydacron designs and manufactures video teleconferencing codecs; Darwin Molecular Corporation develops novel drugs to treat cancer and AIDS. **Corporate headquarters location:** This location. **Listed on:** American Stock Exchange. **Stock exchange symbol:** DHB.

FOX NEWS CHANNEL
1211 Avenue of the Americas, New York NY 10036. 212/556-2400. **Contact:** Human Resources Department. **World Wide Web address:** http://www.foxnews.com. **Description:** A television broadcasting company. **NOTE:** Jobseekers should send resumes to Fox Broadcasting Company, Human Resources, P.O. Box 900, Beverly Hills CA 90213. **Corporate headquarters location:** This location. **Parent company:** Fox Entertainment Group Inc. **Listed on:** New York Stock Exchange. **Stock exchange symbol:** FOX.

GRANITE BROADCASTING CORPORATION
767 Third Avenue, 34th Floor, New York NY 10017. 212/826-2530. **Contact:** Dolores Perez, Personnel Manager. **World Wide Web address:** http://www.granitetv.com. **Description:** Granite Broadcasting Corporation

owns and operates eight network-affiliated television stations. ABC affiliates include KNTV-TV Channel 11 (San Jose/Monterey CA); WPTA-TV Channel 21 (Fort Wayne IN); and WKBW-TV Channel 7 (Buffalo NY). NBC affiliates include KBJR-TV Channel 6 (Duluth MN and Superior WI); KSEE-TV Channel 24 (Fresno CA); and WEEK-TV Channel 25 (Peoria/Bloomington IL). CBS affiliates include WWMT-TV Channel 3 (Grand Rapids/Battle Creek MI); WTVH-TV Channel 5 (Syracuse NY); and KBVO-TV Channel 42 (Austin TX). **Listed on:** NASDAQ. **Stock exchange symbol:** GBTVK.

HEARST-ARGYLE TELEVISION, INC.
888 Seventh Avenue, 27th Floor, New York NY 10106. 212/887-6800. **Fax:** 212/887-6835. **Contact:** Human Resources Department. **World Wide Web address:** http://www.hearstargyle.com. **Description:** Owns and manages 26 network affiliated television stations nationwide and manages seven radio stations. The company's television stations comprise one of the largest non-network-owned television station groups. Hearst-Argyle Television, Inc.'s television stations include: WCVB-TV (ABC affiliate in Boston MA); WTAE-TV (ABC affiliate in Pittsburgh PA); WBAL-TV (NBC affiliate in Baltimore MD); WLWT-TV (NBC affiliate in Cincinnati OH); WISN-TV (ABC affiliate in Milwaukee WI); KMBC-TV (ABC affiliate in Kansas City MO); KCCI-TV (CBS affiliate in Des Moines IA); KCRA-TV (NBC affiliate in Sacramento CA); KQCA-TV (WB affiliate in Sacramento/Stockton/Modesto CA); KSBW-TV (NBC affiliate in Monterey/Salinas CA); KOCO-TV (ABC affiliate in Oklahoma City OK); WNAC-TV (Fox affiliate in Providence RI); WDTN-TV (ABC affiliate in Dayton OH); KITV-TV (ABC affiliate in Honolulu HI); WYFF-TV (NBC affiliate in Greenville/Spartanburg SC); WNNE-TV (NBC affiliate in Burlington VT); WAPT-TV (ABC affiliate in Jackson MS); KHBS-TV (ABC affiliate in Fort Smith AR); and KHOG-TV (ABC affiliate in Fayetteville AR). Hearst-Argyle Television also provides management services for WWWB-TV (WB affiliate in Tampa FL); WPBF-TV (ABC affiliate in West Palm Beach FL); KCWB-TV (UPN affiliate in Kansas City MO); WBAL-AM (radio station in Baltimore MD); and WIYY-FM (radio station in Baltimore MD). In addition, Hearst-Argyle Television, Inc. in partnership with Internet Broadcasting Systems, Inc. is involved in convergence of local TV broadcasts with interactivity capabilities on the Internet. **Corporate headquarters location:** This location. **Subsidiaries include:** Hearst-Argyle Television Productions. **Listed on:** New York Stock Exchange. **Stock exchange symbol:** HTV.

KING WORLD PRODUCTIONS
1700 Broadway, 33rd Floor, New York NY 10019. 212/315-4000. **Contact:** Human Resources. **World Wide Web address:** http://www.kingworld.com. **Description:** A broadcasting company engaged in the syndication of television. **Parent company:** CBS Enterprises.

LORAL SPACE & COMMUNICATIONS LTD.
600 Third Avenue, 38th Floor, New York NY 10016. 212/697-1105. **Contact:** Human Resources Department. **World Wide Web address:** http://www.loral.com. **Description:** A satellite communications company operating through three subsidiaries. **Corporate headquarters location:** This location. **Other U.S. locations:** Washington DC. **Subsidiaries include:** Space Systems/Loral (Palo Alto CA) manufactures communications and weather satellites used by companies and NASA; Globalstar enables wireless service providers to offer services in every area of the world through a network of 48 low-Earth-orbit satellites; Skyne operates the Telstar network, which provides direct-to-home subscription and pay-per-view television via satellite systems, and leases transponder capacity in order to

distribute network programming to local television affiliates. **Listed on:** New York Stock Exchange. **Stock exchange symbol:** LOR. **Number of employees nationwide:** 40,000.

LUCENT TECHNOLOGIES INC.

5 Penn Plaza, 10th Floor, New York NY 10001. 212/290-5900. **Contact:** Human Resources. **World Wide Web address:** http://www.lucent.com. **Description:** Manufactures communications products including switching, transmission, fiber-optic cable, wireless systems, and operations systems, to supply the needs of telephone companies and other communications services providers. **NOTE:** Interested jobseekers should send resumes to Lucent Technologies, Inc., 600 Mountain Avenue, Murray Hill NJ 07974. **Corporate headquarters location:** Murray Hill NJ. **Listed on:** New York Stock Exchange. **Stock exchange symbol:** LU.

LYNCH INTERACTIVE CORPORATION

401 Theodore Fremd Avenue, Rye NY 10580. 914/921-7601. **Contact:** Manager of Human Resources Department. **World Wide Web address:** http://www.lynchinteractivecorp.com. **Description:** A holding company with subsidiaries involved in multimedia services and manufacturing. **Subsidiaries include:** Telecommunications operations consist of six exchange companies: Western New Mexico Telephone Company (NM); Inter-Community Telephone Company (ND); Cuba City Telephone Exchange Company (WI); Belmont Telephone Company (WI); Bretton Woods Telephone Company (NH); and J.B.N. Telephone Company, Inc. (KS). Services offered include local network, network access, and long distance. Lynch Entertainment Corporation and Lombardo Communications are the general partners of Coronet Communications Company, which owns a CBS-affiliated television station (WHBF-TV) serving Rock Island and Moline IL, and Davenport and Bettendorf IA. Capital Communications Corporation operates WOI-TV, an ABC affiliate broadcasting to Des Moines IA. The Morgan Group Inc. (IN), Lynch Corporation's only service subsidiary, provides services to the manufactured housing and recreational vehicle industries. Lynch Manufacturing Corporation and its subsidiary, Lynch Machinery-Miller Hydro, Inc. (GA), manufacture glass-forming machines and packaging machinery, as well as replacement parts for each. M-tron Industries, Inc. (SD) manufactures, imports, and distributes quartz crystal products and clock oscillator modules used for clocking digital circuits, precision time base references, and frequency- and time-related circuits. Safety Railway Service Corporation and its subsidiary, Entoleter, Inc. (CT), produce various capital equipment including granulators, air scrubbers, and shredders. **Corporate headquarters location:** This location. **Listed on:** American Stock Exchange. **Stock exchange symbol:** LIC. **Number of employees nationwide:** 600.

NBC (NATIONAL BROADCASTING COMPANY, INC.)

30 Rockefeller Plaza, New York NY 10112. 212/664-4444. **Contact:** Human Resources. **World Wide Web address:** http://www.nbc.com. **Description:** A national television broadcasting communications firm. **Corporate headquarters location:** This location. **Parent company:** General Electric Corporation. **Listed on:** New York Stock Exchange. **Stock exchange symbol:** GE.

NICE SYSTEMS INC.

116 John Street, Suite 1601, New York NY 10038. 646/836-6900. **Contact:** Human Resources. **World Wide Web address:** http://www.nice.com. **Description:** Develops, designs, manufactures, markets, and services digital

voice recording systems. The company's products are used in a variety of telemarketing applications. **Listed on:** NASDAQ. **Stock exchange symbol:** NICE.

PORTA SYSTEMS CORPORATION

575 Underhill Boulevard, Syosset NY 11791. 516/364-9300. **Fax:** 516/682-4655. **Contact:** Personnel Department. **World Wide Web address:** http://www.portasystems.com. **Description:** Designs, manufactures, and markets telecommunications equipment, software, and systems to customers worldwide. Products are used for the connection, testing, management, and security of telecommunications and computer networks and systems. Porta Systems Corporation is comprised of three operating divisions: Operations Support Systems (OSS); Connection/Protection; and Signal Processing. **Common positions include:** Accountant/Auditor; Attorney; Buyer; Computer Programmer; Credit Manager; Customer Service Representative; Department Manager; Draftsperson; Electrical/Electronics Engineer; Financial Analyst; General Manager; Human Resources Manager; Industrial Engineer; Industrial Production Manager; Marketing Specialist; Mechanical Engineer; Operations/Production Manager; Purchasing Agent/Manager; Quality Control Supervisor; Systems Analyst; Technical Writer/Editor. **Corporate headquarters location:** This location. **Operations at this facility include:** Administration; Manufacturing; Research and Development; Sales. **Listed on:** American Stock Exchange. **Stock exchange symbol:** PSI.

ROANWELL CORPORATION

2564 Park Avenue, Bronx NY 10451. 718/401-0288. **Contact:** Human Resources. **World Wide Web address:** http://www.roanwellcorp.com. **Description:** Manufactures terminal voice communication equipment. **Corporate headquarters location:** This location.

TIME WARNER CABLE

One Cablevision Center, 2nd Floor, Suite 2, Ferndale NY 12734. 845/295-2650. **Fax:** 845/295-2451. **Contact:** Kerry Madison, Director of Human Resources. **World Wide Web address:** http://www.twcnyc.com. **Description:** Time Warner Cable is one of the largest cable television operators in the United States. The company owns or manages 64 cable television systems in 18 states, serving a total of 1.3 million subscribers. The company owns and operates 50 cable television systems in 15 states, principally in New York, Pennsylvania, Massachusetts, Florida, California, North Carolina, South Carolina, and Louisiana. The company's systems offer subscribers packages of basic and cable programming services consisting of television signals available off-air; a limited number of television signals from distant cities; numerous satellite-delivered, nonbroadcast channels such as CNN, MTV, USA Network, ESPN, A&E, TNT, and Nickelodeon; displays of information such as time, news, weather and stock market reports; and public, governmental, and educational access channels. **Common positions include:** Customer Service Representative; Installer; Marketing Specialist; Sales Executive; Technician. **Special programs:** Summer Jobs. **Parent company:** AOL Time Warner, Inc. **Listed on:** New York Stock Exchange. **Stock exchange symbol:** AOL. **Number of employees at this location:** 380. **Number of employees nationwide:** 27,000.

VIACOM INC.

1515 Broadway, 31st Floor, New York NY 10036. 212/258-6000. **Contact:** Human Resources. **World Wide Web address:** http://www.viacom.com.

Description: A diversified entertainment and communications company with operations in four principal segments: Networks, Entertainment, Cable Television, and Broadcasting. Viacom Networks operates three advertiser-supported basic cable television program services: MTV (Music Television including MTV Europe and MTV Latino), VH-1/Video Hits One, and Nickelodeon/Nick at Nite; and three premium subscription television services: SHOWTIME, The Movie Channel, and FLIX. Viacom Entertainment distributes television series, feature films, made-for-television movies, miniseries, and movies for prime time broadcast network television; acquires and distributes television series for initial exhibition on a first-run basis; and develops, produces, distributes, and markets interactive software for multimedia markets. Viacom Cable Television owns and operates cable television systems in California, the Pacific Northwest, and the Midwest. Viacom Broadcasting owns and operates five network-affiliated television stations and 14 radio stations. **Corporate headquarters location:** This location. **Listed on:** New York Stock Exchange. **Stock exchange symbol:** VIA.

COMPUTER HARDWARE, SOFTWARE, AND SERVICES

You can expect to find the following types of companies in this chapter:

Computer Components and Hardware Manufacturers • Consultants and Computer Training Companies • Internet and Online Service Providers • Networking and Systems Services • Repair Services/Rental and Leasing • Resellers, Wholesalers, and Distributors • Software Developers/Programming Services • Web Technologies

AMI (ADVANCED MEDIA INC.)
80 Orville Drive, Bohemia NY 11716. 631/244-1616. **Contact:** Office Manager. **Description:** Provides professional multimedia development products, services, and proprietary technologies to corporate accounts. AMI's services include Website designing and redesigning.

AJILON SERVICES INC.
One Penn Plaza, Suite 4701-13, New York NY 10119. 212/695-6611. **Contact:** Human Resources Department. **World Wide Web address:** http://www.ajilon.com. **Description:** Offers computer consulting services, project support, and end user services. **Corporate headquarters location:** Towson MD. **Other U.S. locations:** Nationwide.

ANALYSTS INTERNATIONAL CORPORATION (AIC)
7 Penn Plaza, Suite 300, New York NY 10001. 212/465-1660. **Fax:** 212/465-1724. **Contact:** Recruiter. **World Wide Web address:** http://www.analysts.com. **Description:** AiC is an international computer consulting firm. The company assists clients in developing systems in a variety of industries using different programming languages and software. **Corporate headquarters location:** Minneapolis MN. **Other U.S. locations:** Nationwide. **International locations:** Cambridge, England; Toronto, Canada. **Listed on:** NASDAQ. **Stock exchange symbol:** ANLY.

BANCTEC SYSTEMS, INC.
888 Veterans Memorial Highway, Suite 515, Hauppauge NY 11788. 631/234-5353. **Contact:** Human Resources Department. **E-mail address:** jobs@banctec.com. **World Wide Web address:** http://www.banctec.com. **Description:** BancTec is engaged in systems integration and specializes in document management solutions. The company also provides network support services and develops image management software. Founded in 1972. **NOTE:** Resumes should be sent to P.O. Box 660204, Dallas TX 75266-0204. **Corporate headquarters location:** Dallas TX. **Number of employees worldwide:** 4,000.

CAM GRAPHICS COMPANY INC.
206 New Highway, Amityville NY 11701. 631/842-3400. **Contact:** Human Resources. **World Wide Web address:** http://www.camgraphics.com. **Description:** CAM Graphics Company supplies businesses and manufacturers with assorted memory-related devices.

CAP GEMINI ERNST & YOUNG
5 Times Square, 9th Floor, New York NY 10036. 917/934-8000. **Contact:** Human Resources. **World Wide Web address:** http://www.cgey.com. **Description:** Provider of management consulting services including business strategy, operations, and people and information management. Services include systems integration; application design, development, and documentation; systems conversions and migrations; and information technology consulting. **NOTE:** Jobseekers are encouraged to apply online. **Other U.S. locations:** Nationwide. **International locations:** Worldwide. **Number of employees nationwide:** 3,000.

CAP GEMINI ERNST & YOUNG
1114 Avenue of the Americas, 29th Floor, New York NY 10036. 212/944-6464. **Contact:** Human Resources Department. **World Wide Web address:** http://www.usa.capgemini.com. **Description:** Provider of management consulting services including business strategy, operations, and people and information management. Services include systems integration; application design, development, and documentation; systems conversions and migrations; and information technology consulting. **NOTE:** Jobseekers are encouraged to apply online. **Other U.S. locations:** Nationwide. **International locations:** Worldwide. **Number of employees nationwide:** 3,000.

COMPUTER ASSOCIATES INTERNATIONAL, INC.
One Computer Associates Plaza, Islandia NY 11749. **Toll-free phone:** 800/454-3788. **Fax:** 800/962-9224. **Contact:** Global Recruiting Department. **E-mail address:** joinca@ca.com. **World Wide Web address:** http://www.ca.com. **Description:** This location houses the corporate offices. Overall, Computer Associates International is one of the world's leading developers of client/server and distributed computing software. The company develops, markets, and supports enterprise management, database and applications development, business applications, and consumer software products for a broad range of mainframe, midrange, and desktop computers. Computer Associates International serves major business, government, research, and educational organizations. Founded in 1976. **Common positions include:** Account Manager; Administrative Assistant; Computer Operator; Computer Programmer; Consultant; Customer Service Representative; Daycare Worker; Project Manager; Sales Executive; Sales Manager; Sales Representative; Systems Analyst; Systems Manager; Teacher/Professor; Technical Writer/Editor. **Special programs:** Internships. **Corporate headquarters location:** This location. **Other U.S. locations:** Nationwide. **Operations at this facility include:** Administration; Research and Development; Sales. **Listed on:** New York Stock Exchange. **Stock exchange symbol:** CA. **Annual sales/revenues:** More than $100 million. **Number of employees at this location:** 2,500.

COMPUTER HORIZONS CORPORATION
747 Third Avenue, 15th Floor, New York NY 10017. 212/371-9600. **Contact:** Recruiting Department. **World Wide Web address:** http://www.computerhorizons.com. **Description:** A full-service technology solutions company offering contract staffing, outsourcing, re-engineering, migration, downsizing support, and network management. The company has a worldwide network of 33 offices. Founded in 1969. **Common positions include:** Computer Programmer; Management Analyst/Consultant; Software Engineer; Systems Analyst. **Corporate headquarters location:** Mountain Lakes NJ. **Other U.S. locations:** Nationwide. **Subsidiaries include:** Birla Horizons International Ltd.; Horizons Consulting, Inc.;

Strategic Outsourcing Services, Inc.; Unified Systems Solutions, Inc. **Operations at this facility include:** Administration; Sales. **Listed on:** NASDAQ. **Stock exchange symbol:** CHRZ. **Annual sales/revenues:** More than $100 million. **Number of employees nationwide:** 1,500. **Number of employees worldwide:** 3,000.

CYBER DIGITAL, INC.
400 Oser Avenue, Suite 1650, Hauppauge NY 11788-3641. 631/231-1200. **Fax:** 631/231-1446. **Contact:** Human Resources Department. **E-mail address:** cybd@cyberdigitalinc.com. **World Wide Web address:** http://www.cyberdigitalinc.com. **Description:** Cyber Digital designs, develops, manufactures, and markets digital switching and networking systems that enable simultaneous communication of voice and data to a large number of users. The company's systems are based on its proprietary software technology that permits the modemless transmission of data between a variety of incompatible and dissimilar end user equipment including computers, printers, workstations, and data terminals over standard telephone lines. **Common positions include:** Design Engineer; Electrical/Electronics Engineer; Purchasing Agent/Manager; Telecommunications Manager. **Corporate headquarters location:** This location. **Annual sales/revenues:** Less than $5 million.

CYBERCHRON CORPORATION
P.O. Box 160, 2700 Route 9, Cold Spring NY 10516. 845/265-3700. **Contact:** Human Resources Department. **World Wide Web address:** http://www.cyberchron.com. **Description:** Cyberchron manufactures computers that are made to withstand environmental extremes. The military is one user of Cyberchron's products.

DESIGN STRATEGY CORPORATION
600 Third Avenue, 25th Floor, New York NY 10016. 212/370-0392. **Contact:** Human Resources Department. **World Wide Web address:** http://www.designstrategy.com. **Description:** Develops and markets inventory control software.

DICE INC.
3 Park Avenue, 33rd Floor, New York NY 10016. 212/725-6550. **Contact:** Human Resources. **World Wide Web address:** http://www.dice.com. **Description:** Provides online services to IT companies. The technical resources offered include hundreds of technical books, a retail store, and information on the newest technologies. Founded in 1994. **Corporate headquarters location:** This location. **Listed on:** NASDAQ. **Stock exchange symbol:** DICE.

DIGITAL SYSTEMS
44Q West Jefryn Boulevard, Deer Park NY 11729. 631/274-0320. **Contact:** Human Resources. **Description:** Manufactures, installs, and supports computer networking systems and provides total systems solutions. **Operations at this facility include:** Sales.

DIRECT INSITE CORPORATION
80 Orville Drive, Suite 100, Bohemia NY 11716. 631/244-1500. **Contact:** Human Resources. **World Wide Web address:** http://www.directinsite.com. **Description:** Direct Insite Corp. designs, markets, and supports information delivery software products including end user data access tools for personal computers and client/server environments, and systems management software products for corporate mainframe data centers. Products include

d.b.Express, which offers methods of searching, organizing, analyzing, and utilizing information contained in databases; systems management software products, which improve mainframe system performance, reduce hardware expenditures, and enhance the reliability and availability of the data processing environment; client/server products, which develop client/server relational database administration and programmer productivity tools. **Corporate headquarters location:** This location.

ESLS
545 Eighth Avenue, Suite 401, New York NY 10018. 212/868-1126. **Contact:** Human Resources. **Description:** Provides computer consulting services for Macintosh systems.

ELECTROGRAPH SYSTEMS INC.
175 Commerce Drive, Hauppauge NY 11788. 631/436-5050. **Contact:** Personnel. **World Wide Web address:** http://www.electrograph.com. **Description:** Distributes microcomputer peripherals, components, and accessories throughout the East Coast of the United States. Electrograph Systems distributes national brand names such as Mitsubishi, Sony, Hitachi, Magnavox, Toshiba, and Idex. The company's products include monitors, printers, large-screen televisions, CD-ROMs, computer video products, optical storage products, notebook computers, and personal computers. Founded in 1982. **Other U.S. locations:** Garden Grove CA; Madeira Beach FL; Woodridge IL; Olathe KS; Timonium MD; Plano TX. **Parent company:** Manchester Equipment.

GP STRATEGIES CORPORATION
9 West 57th Street, Suite 4170, New York NY 10019. 212/230-9500. **Contact:** Human Resources. **Description:** A holding company for computer training and consulting firms. **Corporate headquarters location:** This location. **Subsidiaries include:** General Physics Corporation is a computer consulting and training firm that evaluates and resolves performance problems. Learning Technologies provides computer training and consulting services. Specialised Technical Services Limited (United Kingdom) provides language and technical training services. The Deltapoint Corporation (Seattle WA) is a management consulting firm specializing in large-scale systems changes. **Listed on:** New York Stock Exchange. **Stock exchange symbol:** GPX. **Number of employees worldwide:** 2,100.

HAUPPAUGE COMPUTER WORKS INC.
91 Cabot Court, Hauppauge NY 11788. 631/434-1600. **Fax:** 631/434-3198. **Contact:** Human Resources Department. **World Wide Web address:** http://www.hauppauge.com. **Description:** Manufactures PC circuit boards. **Corporate headquarters location:** This location. **Listed on:** NASDAQ. **Stock exchange symbol:** HAUP. **Annual sales/revenues:** $51 - $100 million.

IBM CORPORATION
2455 South Road, Poughkeepsie NY 12601-5400. 845/433-1234. **Recorded jobline:** 800/964-4473. **Contact:** IBM Staffing Services Center, M/SP911. **World Wide Web address:** http://www.ibm.com. **Description:** This location is an administration facility. Overall, IBM (International Business Machines) is a developer, manufacturer, and marketer of advanced information processing products, including computers and microelectronic technology, software, networking systems, and information technology-related services. The company operates in the United States, Canada, Europe/Middle East/Africa, Latin America, and Asia Pacific. **Corporate headquarters location:** Armonk NY. **Subsidiaries include:** IBM Credit Corporation; IBM

Instruments, Inc.; IBM World Trade Corporation. **Listed on:** New York Stock Exchange. **Stock exchange symbol:** IBM.

IBM CORPORATION
New Orchard Road, Armonk NY 10504. 914/765-1900. **Recorded jobline:** 800/964-4473. **Contact:** IBM Staffing Services Center. **World Wide Web address:** http://www.ibm.com. **Description:** A developer, manufacturer, and marketer of advanced information processing products including computers and microelectronic technology, software, networking systems, and information technology-related services. **Corporate headquarters location:** This location. **International locations:** Worldwide. **Subsidiaries include:** IBM Credit Corporation; IBM Instruments, Inc.; IBM World Trade Corporation. **Listed on:** New York Stock Exchange. **Stock exchange symbol:** IBM.

IPC INFORMATION SYSTEMS
516 West 19th Street, New York NY 10011. 212/367-3600. **Contact:** Human Resources. **World Wide Web address:** http://www.ipc.com. **Description:** This location is involved in systems engineering. Overall, IPC Information Systems provides network communications solutions for the financial industry. Through its Information Transport Systems (ITS) business, the company provides its customers with voice, data, and video solutions through the design, integration, implementation, and support of local and wide area networks. ITS solutions incorporate the latest technology and are supported by a team of systems engineers. Founded in 1973. **Common positions include:** Electrical/Electronics Engineer; General Manager; Software Engineer. **Corporate headquarters location:** New York NY. **International locations:** Asia; Europe. **Number of employees at this location:** 70. **Number of employees nationwide:** 775.

IPC INFORMATION SYSTEMS
Wall Street Plaza, 88 Pine Street, New York NY 10005. 212/825-9060. **Contact:** Human Resources Department. **World Wide Web address:** http://www.ipc.com. **Description:** Provides network communications solutions for the financial industry. Through its Information Transport Systems (ITS) business, the company provides its customers with voice, data, and video solutions through the design, integration, implementation, and support of local and wide area networks. ITS solutions incorporate the latest technology and are supported by a team of systems engineers. Founded in 1973. **Corporate headquarters location:** This location. **International locations:** Asia; Europe. **Number of employees nationwide:** 775.

ITT INDUSTRIES
4 West Red Oak Lane, White Plains NY 10604. 914/641-2000. **Contact:** Human Resources. **World Wide Web address:** http://www.ittind.com. **Description:** Designs and engineers software for satellite communications under government contracts. **Corporate headquarters location:** This location. **Listed on:** New York Stock Exchange. **Stock exchange symbol:** ITT.

INFOGRAMES ENTERTAINMENT
417 Fifth Avenue, 8th Floor, New York NY 10016. 212/726-6500. **Fax:** 212/726-6533. **Contact:** Manager of Human Resources Department. **E-mail address:** recruiter@us.infogrames.com. **World Wide Web address:** http://www.infogrames.com. **Description:** Infogrames Entertainment creates,

wholesales, and markets a wide variety of software including interactive games. **Other U.S. locations:** CA; MD; MA; MN; TX; VA; WA.

INFORMATION BUILDERS INC.
2 Penn Plaza, New York NY 10121. 212/736-4433. **Fax:** 212/967-6406. **Contact:** Personnel. **E-mail address:** employment_opportunities@ibi.com. **World Wide Web address:** http://www.ibi.com. **Description:** A software development firm. Products include FOCUS, EDA, and SmartMart software for various platforms. **Common positions include:** Accountant/Auditor; Customer Service Representative; Operations/Production Manager; Systems Analyst; Technical Writer/Editor. **Corporate headquarters location:** This location. **Other U.S. locations:** Nationwide. **Operations at this facility include:** Administration; Divisional Headquarters; Research and Development. **Listed on:** Privately held. **Number of employees at this location:** 800. **Number of employees nationwide:** 1,500.

INTERNET COMMERCE CORPORATION
805 Third Avenue, 9th Floor, New York NY 10022. 212/271-7640. **Contact:** Human Resources. **E-mail address:** info@icc.net. **World Wide Web address:** http://www.icc.net. **Description:** Manufactures computer systems that enable protection, retrieval, and monitoring of digital information use. **Corporate headquarters location:** This location. **Other area locations:** Setauket NY. **Listed on:** NASDAQ. **Stock exchange symbol:** ICCA.

INVESTMENT TECHNOLOGY GROUP, INC. (ITG)
380 Madison Avenue, 4th Floor, New York NY 10017. 212/444-6300. **Contact:** Human Resources. **E-mail address:** itg_hr@itginc.com. **World Wide Web address:** http://www.itginc.com. **Description:** Provides automated securities trade execution and analysis services to institutional equity investors. ITG's two main services are POSIT, one of the largest automated stock crossing systems operated during trading hours, and QuantEX, a proprietary software to enhance customers' trading efficiencies, access to market liquidity, and portfolio analysis capabilities. **Corporate headquarters location:** This location. **Other U.S. locations:** Los Angeles CA; Boston MA. **International locations:** London, England. **Listed on:** New York Stock Exchange. **Stock exchange symbol:** ITG.

JUNO ONLINE SERVICES, INC.
1540 Broadway, 27th Floor, New York NY 10036. 212/597-9000. **Contact:** Human Resources. **World Wide Web address:** http://www.juno.com. **Description:** A leading Internet access provider offering a variety of online services. Founded in 1996. **Common positions include:** Account Representative; Administrative Assistant; Advertising Executive; Applications Engineer; Computer Engineer; Computer Programmer; Computer Support Technician; Computer Technician; Content Developer; Customer Service Representative; Database Administrator; Database Manager; Financial Analyst; Help-Desk Technician; Human Resources Manager; Internet Services Manager; Intranet Developer; Market Research Analyst; Marketing Manager; Marketing Specialist; MIS Specialist; Multimedia Designer; Network Engineer; Network/Systems Administrator; Online Sales Manager; Public Relations Specialist; Sales Representative; Secretary; Software Engineer; SQL Programmer; Systems Analyst; Systems Manager; Technical Writer/Editor; Web Advertising Specialist; Webmaster; Website Developer. **Special programs:** Internships. **Office hours:** Monday - Friday, 9:00 a.m. - 6:00 p.m. **Parent company:** United Online, Inc. **Corporate headquarters**

location: Westlake Village CA. **Listed on:** NASDAQ. **Stock exchange symbol:** UNTD.

KANTEK INC.
3460 Hampton Road, Oceanside NY 11572. 516/593-3212. **Contact:** Human Resources Department. **E-mail address:** info@kantek.com. **World Wide Web address:** http://www.kantek.com. **Description:** Manufactures glare reduction screens for computer monitors.

KEANE, INC.
290 Broadhollow Road, Melville NY 11747. 631/351-7000. **Contact:** Human Resources. **World Wide Web address:** http://www.keane.com. **Description:** This location provides technical support to consumers for software. Overall, Keane offers businesses a variety of computer consulting services. Keane also develops, markets, and manages software for its clients and assists in project management. Founded in 1965. **Common positions include:** Accountant/Auditor; Computer Operator; Computer Programmer; Database Manager; MIS Specialist; Operations/Production Manager; Registered Nurse; Sales Representative; Systems Analyst. **Corporate headquarters location:** Boston MA. **Other U.S. locations:** Nationwide. **Operations at this facility include:** Divisional Headquarters. **Listed on:** American Stock Exchange. **Stock exchange symbol:** KEA. **Annual sales/revenues:** More than $100 million. **Number of employees at this location:** 75. **Number of employees worldwide:** 4,500.

MAINTECH
560 Lexington Avenue, 15th Floor, New York NY 10022. 212/704-2400. **Contact:** Human Resources. **E-mail address:** info@maintech.com. **World Wide Web address:** http://www.maintech.com. **Description:** Provides on-site computer maintenance services. **Corporate headquarters location:** Wallington NJ. **Parent company:** Volt Information Services, Inc. **Listed on:** New York Stock Exchange. **Stock exchange symbol:** VOL.

MANCHESTER TECHNOLOGIES, INC.
160 Oser Avenue, Hauppauge NY 11788. 631/435-1199. **Toll-free phone:** 800/632-9880. **Contact:** Human Resources. **E-mail address:** staffing@mecnet.com. **World Wide Web address:** http://www.mecnet.com. **Description:** A network integrator and reseller of computer systems, software, and peripherals. Founded in 1973. **Listed on:** NASDAQ. **Stock exchange symbol:** MANC.

MERCURY INTERACTIVE CORPORATION
317 Madison Avenue, 10th Floor, New York NY 10017-5201. 212/687-4646. **Contact:** Human Resources Department. **World Wide Web address:** http://www.mercuryinteractive.com. **Description:** This location is a sales and technical support office. Overall, Mercury Interactive is a provider of automated software quality (ASQ) tools for enterprise applications testing. The company's products are used to isolate software and system errors prior to application deployment. **Corporate headquarters location:** Sunnyvale CA. **Other U.S. locations:** Nationwide. **International locations:** Worldwide. **Listed on:** NASDAQ. **Stock exchange symbol:** MERQ. **Annual sales/revenues:** More than $100 million.

MOBIUS MANAGEMENT SYSTEMS
120 Old Post Road, Rye NY 10580. 914/921-7200. **Contact:** Milly Rivera, Human Resources. **E-mail address:** staffing@mobius.com. **World Wide Web address:** http://www.mobius.com. **Description:** Develops and sells

business-related software products including a report distribution program and an automated balance program. **Other U.S. locations:** Nationwide. **Listed on:** NASDAQ. **Stock exchange symbol:** MOBI.

MUZE INC.
304 Hudson Street, 8th Floor, New York NY 10013. 212/824-0300. **Contact:** Jeanne Petras, Director of Personnel. **World Wide Web address:** http://www.muze.com. **Description:** Muze is a multimedia company that develops software for touch-screen, point-of-sales terminals that allow users access to a musical database. **Common positions include:** Accountant/Auditor; Administrative Manager; Budget Analyst; Computer Programmer; Financial Analyst; Human Resources Manager; Purchasing Agent/Manager; Sales Executive; Sales Manager; Sales Representative; Software Engineer; Systems Analyst. **Special programs:** Internships. **Corporate headquarters location:** This location. **International locations:** United Kingdom. **Parent company:** MetroMedia. **Operations at this facility include:** Administration; Manufacturing; Research and Development; Sales; Service. **Listed on:** Privately held. **Number of employees at this location:** 120.

NEXTSOURCE
462 Seventh Avenue, 4th Floor, New York NY 10018. 212/736-5870. **Contact:** Human Resources. **World Wide Web address:** http://www.nextsource.com. **Description:** Develops and offers instructor-led and computer-based personal computer training programs and provides consulting services, primarily to large businesses and public sector organizations. The company's instructor-led training programs include a wide range of introductory and advanced classes in operating systems including MS/DOS, Microsoft Windows, and Macintosh systems; word processing; spreadsheets; databases; communications; executive overviews; integrated software packages; computer graphics; and desktop publishing. The company's computer-based training programs include offerings on Lotus Notes, CC Mail, Microsoft Office, and Lotus Smartsuite. The consulting division provides computer personnel on a temporary basis.

OM TECHNOLOGIES
140 Broadway, 25th Floor, New York NY 10005. 646/428-2800. **Contact:** Human Resources. **World Wide Web address:** http://www.om.com. **Description:** OM Technologies develops software for the securities and brokerage industries.

ORACLE CORPORATION
100 Summit Lake Drive, Valhalla NY 10595. 914/747-2900. **Contact:** Human Resources. **World Wide Web address:** http://www.oracle.com. **Description:** Designs and manufactures database and information management software for business and provides consulting services. **NOTE:** Resumes should be sent to Human Resources, 500 Oracle Parkway, Redwood Shores CA 94065. **Corporate headquarters location:** Redwood Shores CA. **Other U.S. locations:** Nationwide. **Listed on:** NASDAQ. **Stock exchange symbol:** ORCL. **Number of employees worldwide:** 30,000.

PENCOM SYSTEMS INC.
40 Fulton Street, 18th Floor, New York NY 10038-1850. 212/513-7777. **Fax:** 212/227-1854. **Contact:** Tom Morgan, Recruiting. **E-mail address:** career@pencom.com. **World Wide Web address:** http://www.pencom.com. **Description:** Provides computer consulting services including open systems management and software consulting.

ROYALBLUE TECHNOLOGIES INC.
17 State Street, 42nd Floor, New York NY 10004-1501. 212/269-9000. **Contact:** Human Resources Department. **World Wide Web address:** http://www.royalblue.com. **Description:** Develops software for the NASDAQ stock exchange. **International locations:** China; France; Japan; United Kingdom.

SIEMENS BUSINESS SERVICES, INC.
6 International Drive, 2nd Floor, Rye Brook NY 10573. 914/935-3600. **Fax:** 914/935-3038. **Contact:** Human Resources. **World Wide Web address:** http://www.sba-usa.siemens.com. **Description:** Provides systems integration, help desk, and PC repair services to *Fortune* 1000 companies and federal clients. Siemens Business Services also resells hardware and software products. **Common positions include:** Account Manager; Accountant; Applications Engineer; Computer Engineer; Computer Support Technician; Computer Technician; Network/Systems Administrator; Operations Manager; Sales Engineer; Sales Manager; Systems Manager. **Corporate headquarters location:** Munich, Germany. **Other U.S. locations:** Nationwide. **Parent company:** Siemens AG. **Listed on:** New York Stock Exchange. **Stock exchange symbol:** SI.

STANDARD MICROSYSTEMS CORPORATION
80 Arkay Drive, P.O. Box 18047, Hauppauge NY 11788. 631/435-6000. **Fax:** 631/273-5550. **Contact:** Human Resources. **E-mail address:** hr@smsc.com. **World Wide Web address:** http://www.smsc.com. **Description:** This location houses the VLSI circuit design and LAN hub and switch engineering centers, marketing, customer support, and wafer fabrication, as well as operations and administrative staff. The company's Component Products Division supplies MOS/VLSI circuits for personal computers and embedded control systems. These include input/output devices for disk drive control, communications interface, power management and other PC motherboard functions, Ethernet and Fast Ethernet controllers for local area network applications, and ARCNET controllers for embedded networking applications. The System Products Division provides a broad range of networking solutions for scaling, managing, and controlling LANs. Its products include network adapters, hubs, switches, and network management software. This division has an installed base of over 12 million nodes. Standard Microsystems uses internally developed integrated circuits. Founded in 1971. **NOTE:** Entry-level positions and second and third shifts are offered. **Common positions include:** Account Manager; Accountant/Auditor; Administrative Assistant; Computer Programmer; Customer Service Representative; Design Engineer; Electrical/Electronics Engineer; Financial Analyst; Manufacturing Engineer; Market Research Analyst; Marketing Manager; Marketing Specialist; Mechanical Engineer; MIS Specialist; Project Manager; Public Relations Specialist; Purchasing Agent/Manager; Quality Control Supervisor; Sales Engineer; Sales Representative; Secretary; Software Engineer; Systems Analyst; Systems Manager; Technical Writer/Editor. **Special programs:** Internships. **Corporate headquarters location:** This location. **Other U.S. locations:** Irvine CA; San Jose CA; Danvers MA; Austin TX. **International locations:** Worldwide. **Listed on:** NASDAQ. **Stock exchange symbol:** SMSC. **Annual sales/revenues:** More than $100 million. **Number of employees at this location:** 500. **Number of employees worldwide:** 800.

SUNBURST TECHNOLOGY
101 Castleton Street, Suite 201, Pleasantville NY 10570. 914/747-3310. **Contact:** Human Resources. **E-mail address:** hr-us@sunburst.com. **World**

Wide Web address: http://www.sunburst.com. **Description:** Develops and markets educational videos and software. **Common positions include:** Computer Animator; Computer Programmer; Customer Service Representative; Editor; Software Engineer; Technical Writer/Editor. **Special programs:** Internships. **Office hours:** Monday - Friday, 8:00 a.m. - 5:00 p.m. **Corporate headquarters location:** This location. **Listed on:** Privately held. **Annual sales/revenues:** $21 - $50 million. **Number of employees at this location:** 150.

SYMBOL TECHNOLOGIES INC.
One Symbol Plaza, Holtsville NY 11742-1300. 631/738-2400. **Contact:** Human Resources. **E-mail address:** jobopps@symbol.com. **World Wide Web address:** http://www.symbol.com. **Description:** This location manufactures barcode and data capture equipment. Overall, Symbol Technologies designs, manufactures, and markets integrated products based on barcode laser scanning, hand-held computing, and wireless LANs. **Corporate headquarters location:** Costa Mesa CA. **Operations at this facility include:** Customer Service. **Listed on:** New York Stock Exchange. **Stock exchange symbol:** SBL.

SYSTEMAX INC.
22 Harbor Park Drive, Port Washington NY 11050. 516/608-7000. **Fax:** 516/608-7111. **Contact:** Human Resources Department. **World Wide Web address:** http://www.systemax.com. **Description:** A direct marketer of brand-name and private-label computer, office, and industrial products targeting mid-range and major corporate accounts, small office/home customers, and value-added resellers. Founded in 1949. **NOTE:** Entry-level positions are offered. **Common positions include:** Account Representative; Accountant; Administrative Assistant; Advertising Executive; Applications Engineer; Auditor; Buyer; Computer Operator; Computer Programmer; Computer Support Technician; Computer Technician; Customer Service Representative; Database Administrator; Database Manager; Desktop Publishing Specialist; Graphic Artist; Industrial Engineer; Internet Services Manager; Market Research Analyst; Marketing Manager; Marketing Specialist; MIS Specialist; Network/Systems Administrator; Sales Representative; Software Engineer; Systems Analyst; Technical Writer/Editor; Transportation/Traffic Specialist; Webmaster. **Special programs:** Internships; Summer Jobs. **Corporate headquarters location:** This location. **Other U.S. locations:** CA; FL; GA; IL; NJ; NC; OH. **Subsidiaries include:** Global Computer Supplies; Midwest Micro Corp.; Misco America, Inc.; Misco Canada Inc.; TigerDirect Inc. **Listed on:** New York Stock Exchange. **Stock exchange symbol:** SYX. **Annual sales/revenues:** More than $100 million. **Number of employees at this location:** 500. **Number of employees nationwide:** 2,000. **Number of employees worldwide:** 4,000.

TSR INC.
400 Oser Avenue, Suite 150, Hauppauge NY 11788. 631/231-0333. **Contact:** Human Resources Department. **World Wide Web address:** http://www.tsrconsulting.com. **Description:** Provides computer consulting services. **Corporate headquarters location:** This location. **Listed on:** NASDAQ. **Stock exchange symbol:** TSRI.

TRACK DATA
56 Pine Street, New York NY 10005. 212/943-4555. **Contact:** Human Resources. **World Wide Web address:** http://www.trackdata.com. **Description:** Electronically provides trading information, news, and third-party database services on stocks, bonds, commodities, and other securities

through its Dial/Data service. The company's AIQ Systems division produces expert systems software for individual and professional investors. **Listed on:** NASDAQ. **Stock exchange symbol:** TRAC.

TRIZETTO GROUP, INC.
1700 Broadway, New York NY 10019. 212/765-8500. **Contact:** Human Resources Department. **World Wide Web address:** http://www.trizetto.com. **Description:** Develops health management software for insurance agencies and health care providers. **NOTE:** Interested jobseekers should send resumes to 1085 Morris Avenue, Union NJ 07083. **Corporate headquarters location:** Newport Beach CA. **Listed on:** NASDAQ. **Stock exchange symbol:** TZIX.

VESON INC.
29 Broadway, Suite 1002, New York NY 10006. 212/422-0300. **Contact:** Personnel. **World Wide Web address:** http://www.veson.com. **Description:** Develops computer software for the shipping industry.

WEN TECHNOLOGY CORPORATION
999 Central Park Avenue, Yonkers NY 10704. 914/376-5435. **Fax:** 914/376-7092. **Contact:** Human Resources. **E-mail address:** info@wentech.com. **World Wide Web address:** http://www.wentech.com. **Description:** Manufactures computer monitors and displays. **NOTE:** Entry-level positions are offered. **Common positions include:** Account Manager; Account Representative; Administrative Assistant; Applications Engineer; Buyer; Chief Financial Officer; Credit Manager; Customer Service Representative; Design Engineer; Designer; Electrical/Electronics Engineer; Industrial Engineer; Manufacturing Engineer; Mechanical Engineer; Multimedia Designer; Project Manager; Purchasing Agent/Manager; Quality Control Supervisor; Sales Engineer; Sales Executive; Sales Manager; Sales Representative; Secretary; Systems Manager. **Corporate headquarters location:** This location. **Listed on:** Privately held. **Annual sales/revenues:** $51 - $100 million. **Number of employees at this location:** 40.

WILCO SYSTEMS, INC.
17 State Street, 8th Floor, New York NY 10004. 212/589-2000. **Fax:** 212/589-2001. **Contact:** Linda Chui, Human Resources Manager. **E-mail address:** info@wilco-int.com. **World Wide Web address:** http://www.wilco-int.com. **Description:** Develops computer systems and software products for the financial and communications industries. Founded in 1970. **Common positions include:** Computer Programmer; Project Manager. **International locations:** Geneva; Hong Kong; London. **Listed on:** Privately held. **President:** Roy Staines. **Number of employees at this location:** 105. **Number of employees worldwide:** 525.

EDUCATIONAL SERVICES

You can expect to find the following types of facilities in this chapter:

*Business/Secretarial/Data Processing Schools •
Colleges/Universities/Professional Schools • Community
Colleges/Technical Schools/Vocational Schools • Elementary and
Secondary Schools • Preschool and Child Daycare Services*

AFS INTERCULTURAL PROGRAMS, INC.
198 Madison Avenue, 8th Floor, New York NY 10016. 212/299-9000. **Fax:** 212/299-9090. **Contact:** Human Resources Department. **World Wide Web address:** http://www.afs.org/usa. **Description:** An international exchange organization that provides intercultural learning opportunities for high school students, families, and teachers. The agency operates programs in approximately 55 countries via an international network of volunteers. **Common positions include:** Admissions Officer; Communications Specialist; Computer Programmer; Fundraising Specialist; Marketing Specialist; Public Relations Specialist.

ADELPHI UNIVERSITY
One South Avenue, Garden City NY 11530. 516/877-3222. **Toll-free phone:** 800/ADELPHI. **Fax:** 516/877-4970. **Contact:** Ms. Jane Fisher, Employment Manager. **World Wide Web address:** http://www.adelphi.edu. **Description:** A private university with approximately 7,000 undergraduate and graduate students enrolled. Founded in 1896. **NOTE:** Entry-level positions are offered. **Common positions include:** Administrative Assistant; Computer Programmer; Secretary; Teacher/Professor. **Corporate headquarters location:** This location. **Number of employees at this location:** 1,300.

ATELIER ESTHETIQUE INC.
386 Park Avenue South, Suite 1409, New York NY 10016. 212/725-6130. **Contact:** Human Resources Department. **World Wide Web address:** http://www.aeinstitute.net. **Description:** A wholesaler of cosmetic products and equipment. This location also houses a beauty school.

BARNARD COLLEGE
3009 Broadway, New York NY 10027-6598. 212/854-2551. **Fax:** 212/854-2100. **Contact:** Human Resources Department. **World Wide Web address:** http://www.barnard.edu. **Description:** An independent college of liberal arts and sciences for women, affiliated with Columbia University. Barnard College has an enrollment of approximately 2,200 undergraduates from more than 40 countries. Barnard offers approximately 50 majors in the humanities, social sciences, arts, and natural sciences. Double- and joint-degree programs with Columbia (dentistry, engineering, international and public policy, law, and administration), Juilliard, and the Jewish Theological Seminary are offered. Founded in 1889.

BARUCH COLLEGE
THE CITY UNIVERSITY OF NEW YORK (CUNY)
17 Lexington Avenue, Box D-0202, New York NY 10010. 212/802-2000. **Fax:** 212/802-2745. **Contact:** Ms. Ronny Widener, Director of Human Resources. **World Wide Web address:** http://www.baruch.cuny.edu.

Description: A college offering undergraduate and graduate programs through its School of Business, School of Liberal Arts and Sciences, and School of Public Affairs. **Common positions include:** Computer Programmer; Education Administrator; Human Resources Manager; Librarian; Public Relations Specialist; Purchasing Agent/Manager; Systems Analyst; Teacher/Professor. **Other area locations:** Bronx NY; Brooklyn NY; Flushing NY; Jamaica NY; Staten Island NY. **Operations at this facility include:** Administration; Research and Development; Service. **Number of employees at this location:** 1,800.

THE CITY COLLEGE OF NEW YORK
THE CITY UNIVERSITY OF NEW YORK (CUNY)
138th Street and Convent Avenue, New York NY 10031. 212/650-7000. **Contact:** Human Resources Department. **World Wide Web address:** http://www.ccny.cuny.edu. **Description:** A public, coeducational college offering both undergraduate and graduate programs of study in a wide variety of disciplines. **Other area locations:** Bronx NY; Brooklyn NY; Flushing NY; Jamaica NY; Staten Island NY.

COLUMBIA UNIVERSITY
475 Riverside Drive, Interchurch Center, Room 1901, New York NY 10115. 212/870-2403. **Contact:** Department of Human Resources. **World Wide Web address:** http://www.cc.columbia.edu. **Description:** A private university comprised of 15 schools and 71 academic departments and divisions. The university is affiliated with Barnard College, Teachers College, and Union Theological Seminary. There are approximately 20,000 students enrolled at the university including 11,800 graduate and professional, 5,600 undergraduate, and 2,500 nondegree students. Founded in 1754. **NOTE:** Interested jobseekers should send resumes to P.O. Box 920, Burlington MA 01803. **Common positions include:** Administrative Assistant; Administrative Manager; Budget Analyst; Computer Programmer; Editor; Education Administrator; Librarian; Library Technician; Systems Analyst; Typist/Word Processor. **Corporate headquarters location:** This location.

DOWLING COLLEGE
150 Idle Hour Boulevard, Oakdale NY 11769-1999. 631/244-3020. **Fax:** 631/589-6123. **Contact:** Bridget Carroll, Human Resources Department. **E-mail address:** carrollb@dowling.edu. **World Wide Web address:** http://www.dowling.edu. **Description:** Dowling College is an independent, comprehensive, coeducational college. The college serves approximately 6,000 full- and part-time students, offering undergraduate programs leading to bachelor of arts, bachelor of science, and bachelor of business administration degrees. Graduate program degrees include master of science in reading and special education, master of business administration, and master of education with the following concentrations: elementary education, secondary education, special education, life-span special services, and reading. Founded in 1968. **Common positions include:** Accountant/Auditor; Administrative Assistant; Budget Analyst; Controller; Counselor; Editor; ESL Teacher; Financial Analyst; Graphic Artist; Librarian; Purchasing Agent/Manager; Secretary; Teacher/Professor; Typist/Word Processor. **Corporate headquarters location:** This location. **Number of employees at this location:** 900.

FASHION INSTITUTE OF TECHNOLOGY
7th Avenue at 27th Street, New York NY 10001. 212/217-7999. **Contact:** Human Resources. **World Wide Web address:** http://www.fitnyc.suny.edu.

Description: A fashion institute offering degrees in art and design or business and technology.

FLIGHTSAFETY INTERNATIONAL, INC.
Marine Air Terminal, LaGuardia Airport, Flushing NY 11371. 718/565-4140. **Fax:** 718/565-4169. **Contact:** Human Resources Department. **E-mail address:** laguardia@flightsafety.com. **World Wide Web address:** http://www.flightsafety.com. **Description:** FlightSafety International provides high-technology training to operators of aircraft and ships. Total training systems are used including simulators and training devices, computer-based training, and professional instructors. The company's worldwide clients include corporations, airlines, the military, and government agencies. **Common positions include:** Computer Programmer; Operations/Production Manager; Software Engineer; Systems Analyst; Technical Writer/Editor. **Other U.S. locations:** Nationwide. **Number of employees nationwide:** 2,000.

FORDHAM UNIVERSITY
441 East Fordham Road, Bronx NY 10458. 718/817-1000. **Contact:** Angela Cioffi, Employment Manager. **World Wide Web address:** http://www.fordham.edu. **Description:** A university offering bachelor's and master's degrees. **Common positions include:** Administrator; Computer Programmer; Counselor; Department Manager; Instructor/Trainer; Systems Analyst; Teacher/Professor. **Special programs:** Internships. **Operations at this facility include:** Administration.

HOFSTRA UNIVERSITY
205 Hofstra University, Human Resources Center, Hempstead NY 11549. 516/463-6600. **Contact:** Human Resources Department. **World Wide Web address:** http://www.hofstra.edu. **Description:** A private, four-year university offering both undergraduate and graduate degree programs. The university enrolls over 12,800 students.

HUNTER COLLEGE
THE CITY UNIVERSITY OF NEW YORK (CUNY)
695 Park Avenue, East Building, 1502, New York NY 10021. 212/772-4000. **Contact:** Personnel Department. **World Wide Web address:** http://www.hunter.cuny.edu. **Description:** One of the largest coeducational colleges of CUNY. Hunter College offers undergraduate and graduate programs in arts and sciences, education, health sciences, nursing, and social work. Founded in 1870. **Other area locations:** Bronx NY; Brooklyn NY; Flushing NY; Jamaica NY; Staten Island NY.

IONA COLLEGE
715 North Avenue, New Rochelle NY 10801. 914/633-2000. **Contact:** Donald Herring, Personnel Director. **World Wide Web address:** http://www.iona.edu. **Description:** A four-year Catholic college offering bachelor's and master's degree programs.

JOHN JAY COLLEGE OF CRIMINAL JUSTICE
THE CITY UNIVERSITY OF NEW YORK (CUNY)
555 West 57th Street, Suite 612, New York NY 10019. 212/237-8517. **Contact:** Donald J. Gray, Director of Human Resources Department. **World Wide Web address:** http://www.jjay.cuny.edu. **Description:** A college with undergraduate and graduate programs of study concentrating in criminal justice.

KATHARINE GIBBS SCHOOLS INC.
50 West 40th Street, 1st Floor, New York NY 10138-1347. 212/867-9300.
Contact: Department of Human Resources. **World Wide Web address:**
http://www.katharinegibbs.com. **Description:** One of the nation's foremost
business instruction schools.

LEHMAN COLLEGE
THE CITY UNIVERSITY OF NEW YORK (CUNY)
250 Bedford Park Boulevard West, Shuster Hall, Room 230, Bronx NY
10468. 718/960-8181. **Contact:** Human Resources Department. **World
Wide Web address:** http://www.lehman.cuny.edu. **Description:** A public
coeducational liberal arts college offering over 90 undergraduate and
graduate programs.

LONG ISLAND UNIVERSITY
C.W. Post Campus, 720 Northern Boulevard, Brookville NY 11548.
516/299-2504. **Contact:** Human Resources. **World Wide Web address:**
http://www.liunet.edu. **Description:** A university offering undergraduate
and graduate programs of study. The university's programs of study are
offered through its six schools: College of Liberal Arts & Sciences; School of
Education; College of Management; School of Health Professions; School of
Visual & Performing Arts; and the Palmer School of Library & Information
Sciences. **Common positions include:** Accountant/Auditor; Attorney;
Biological Scientist; Blue-Collar Worker Supervisor; Chemist; Claim
Representative; Department Manager; Draftsperson; Economist; Financial
Analyst; Geographer; Geologist/Geophysicist; Human Resources Manager;
Industrial Production Manager; Marketing Specialist; Public Relations
Specialist; Systems Analyst; Technical Writer/Editor. **Special programs:**
Internships. **Corporate headquarters location:** This location. **Other area
locations:** Brentwood NY; Brooklyn NY; Greenvale NY; Southampton NY.
Operations at this facility include: Administration. **Number of employees
nationwide:** 2,000.

MARIST COLLEGE
3399 North Road, Poughkeepsie NY 12601-1387. 845/575-3000. **Contact:**
Carol Coogan Wing, Director of Human Resources. **World Wide Web
address:** http://www.marist.edu. **Description:** A liberal arts college with an
enrollment of 3,300 undergraduate and 600 graduate students. Marist
College offers a variety of academic programs including business
management, communication, computer science and information systems,
behavioral sciences, science, and the humanities.

MERCY COLLEGE
555 Broadway, Dobbs Ferry NY 10522. 914/693-4500. **Contact:** Theresa
Morgan, Human Resources Director. **World Wide Web address:**
http://www.mercynet.edu. **Description:** A private commuter college
offering a wide range of undergraduate, graduate, associate, and certificate
programs.

MOUNT ST. MARY COLLEGE
330 Powell Avenue, Newburgh NY 12550. 845/561-0800. **Contact:**
Human Resources. **World Wide Web address:** http://www.msmc.edu.
Description: A Judeo-Christian liberal arts college. Mount St. Mary College
is an independent and coeducational institution with approximately 1,800
students. Founded in 1960.

NASSAU COMMUNITY COLLEGE
One Education Drive, Tower 702, Garden City NY 11530. 516/572-7500. **Contact:** Human Resources Department. **World Wide Web address:** http://www.sunynassau.edu. **Description:** A two-year college that is part of the State University of New York educational system. **Common positions include:** Blue-Collar Worker Supervisor; Buyer; Custodian; Education Administrator; Librarian; Library Technician. **Special programs:** Internships. **Number of employees at this location:** 2,500.

NEW YORK INSTITUTE OF TECHNOLOGY
P.O. Box 8000, Old Westbury NY 11568-8000. 516/686-7667. **Fax:** 516/686-7929. **Contact:** Manager of Human Resources Department. **E-mail address:** humanresources@nyit.edu. **World Wide Web address:** http://www.nyit.edu. **Description:** A technical university offering associate, bachelor's, and master's degree programs in health and life sciences, architecture, arts/sciences, education, technology, and management.

NEW YORK UNIVERSITY
7 East 12th Street, Main Floor, New York NY 10003-4475. 212/998-1250. **Fax:** 212/995-4229. **Contact:** Personnel Department. **World Wide Web address:** http://www.nyu.edu/hr. **Description:** A state university. **Common positions include:** Accountant/Auditor; Administrative Worker/Clerk; Administrator; Computer Programmer; Editor; Human Resources Manager; Purchasing Agent/Manager; Systems Analyst; Technical Writer/Editor.

PACE UNIVERSITY
One Pace Plaza, New York NY 10038-1598. 212/346-1200. **Contact:** Human Resources. **World Wide Web address:** http://www.pace.edu. **Description:** A university with three campus locations. **Common positions include:** Account Manager; Administrator; Computer Programmer; Mechanical Engineer; Purchasing Agent/Manager. **Other area locations:** Pleasantville NY; White Plains NY.

QUEENS COLLEGE
THE CITY UNIVERSITY OF NEW YORK (CUNY)
65-30 Kissena Boulevard, Flushing NY 11367-1597. 718/997-4455. **Fax:** 718/997-5799. **Contact:** Human Resources Department. **World Wide Web address:** http://www.qc.edu. **Description:** A liberal arts commuter college. Founded in 1937.

ST. JOHN'S UNIVERSITY
8000 Utopia Parkway, Jamaica NY 11439. 718/990-6161. **Contact:** Human Resources. **E-mail address:** employment@stjohns.edu. **World Wide Web address:** http://www.stjohns.edu. **Description:** A private, four-year university. St. John's University offers bachelor's and master's degrees. Founded in 1870.

SARAH LAWRENCE COLLEGE
One Mead Way, Bronxville NY 10708. 914/337-0700. **Contact:** Human Resources. **World Wide Web address:** http://www.slc.edu. **Description:** Sarah Lawrence College is a four-year, liberal arts college that emphasizes independent study through undergraduate and graduate programs. Founded in 1926.

STATE UNIVERSITY OF NEW YORK AT NEW PALTZ
Human Resources Department, 75 South Manheim Boulevard, Suite 9, New Paltz NY 12561-2433. 845/257-2121. **Contact:** Director, Human

Resources. **World Wide Web address:** http://www.newpaltz.edu.
Description: SUNY at New Paltz offers bachelor's, master's, and doctoral
degrees. The university has over 9,000 students. Founded in 1828.

STATE UNIVERSITY OF NEW YORK AT STONY BROOK
390 Administration, Stony Brook NY 11794-0751. 631/689-6000. **Fax:**
631/632-6168. **Recorded jobline:** 631/632-9222. **Contact:** Human
Resources. **World Wide Web address:** http://www.sunysb.edu/hr.
Description: A state university that offers bachelor's, master's, and doctoral
degrees. The university has over 17,000 students enrolled. Founded in
1957.

TASA (TOUCHSTONE APPLIED SCIENCE ASSOCIATES, INC.)
P.O. Box 382, 4 Hardscrabble Heights, Brewster NY 10509-0382. 845/277-
8100. **Fax:** 845/277-3548. **Contact:** Human Resources. **E-mail address:**
tasa@tasa.com. **World Wide Web address:** http://www.tasa.com.
Description: TASA designs, develops, publishes, and distributes educational
tests, instructional materials, and microcomputer software to elementary
and secondary schools, colleges, and universities. The educational tests,
known as Primary, Standard, and Advanced Degrees of Reading Power tests
and Degrees of Word Meaning tests, are components on the company's
Degrees of Literacy Power program. **Corporate headquarters location:** This
location.

VASSAR COLLEGE
124 Raymond Avenue, Poughkeepsie NY 12604. 845/437-7000. **Fax:**
845/437-7298. **Contact:** Human Resources. **E-mail address:**
careers@vassar.edu. **World Wide Web address:** http://www.vassar.edu.
Description: Vassar College is a four-year undergraduate college focusing
on the liberal arts. Student enrollment is approximately 2,250. Founded in
1860. **Common positions include:** Administrative Assistant; Clerical
Supervisor; Computer Programmer; Licensed Practical Nurse; Secretary;
Typist/Word Processor. **Annual sales/revenues:** $51 - $100 million. **Number
of employees at this location:** 1,000.

ELECTRONIC/INDUSTRIAL ELECTRICAL EQUIPMENT

You can expect to find the following types of companies in this chapter:

Electronic Machines and Systems • Semiconductor Manufacturers

ADEMCO (ALARM DEVICE MANUFACTURING COMPANY)
178 Michael Drive, Syosset NY 11791. 516/921-6704. **Contact:** Human Resources Department. **E-mail address:** opportunities@ademco.com. **World Wide Web address:** http://www.ademco.com. **Description:** Ademco manufactures alarm and security products. Products include smoke detectors, glass break detectors, and other home invasion alarms. Ademco's automated manufacturing facility processes more than 4 million printed circuit boards per year. The company also runs a quality service laboratory that conducts UL certified testing. **Common positions include:** Electrical/Electronics Engineer; Industrial Engineer; Mechanical Engineer. **Corporate headquarters location:** Chicago IL. **Parent company:** Pittway Corporation. **Operations at this facility include:** Divisional Headquarters.

AMERICAN MEDICAL ALERT CORPORATION
3265 Lawson Boulevard, P.O. Box 40, Oceanside NY 11572. 516/536-5850. **Toll-free phone:** 800/645-3244. **Contact:** Human Resources. **World Wide Web address:** http://www.amacalert.com. **Description:** A manufacturer and distributor of the Personal Emergency Response System for the home health industry. The Personal Emergency Response System is an in-home safety device used by the chronically ill or physically impaired allowing them to communicate with emergency care providers using digital-wireless technology. **NOTE:** Entry-level positions are offered. **Common positions include:** Administrative Assistant; Electrical/Electronics Engineer; Marketing Specialist; Sales Representative; Telecommunications Manager. **Corporate headquarters location:** This location. **Other U.S. locations:** Parker CO; Decatur GA; Tinley Park IL. **Operations at this facility include:** Administration; Sales; Service. **Listed on:** NASDAQ. **Stock exchange symbol:** AMAC. **Annual sales/revenues:** $5 - $10 million. **Number of employees at this location:** 70. **Number of employees nationwide:** 80.

AMERICAN TECHNICAL CERAMICS CORPORATION (ATC)
One Norden Lane, Huntington Station NY 11746. 631/622-4774. **Contact:** Human Resources Manager. **E-mail address:** hr@atceramics.com. **World Wide Web address:** http://www.atceramics.com. **Description:** American Technical Ceramics Corporation (ATC) is a high-technology firm engaged in the design, development, and manufacture of ceramic and porcelain capacitors. ATC's processing technology creates high-performance capacitors for critical applications in both the commercial and military markets including missile systems, satellite broadcasting equipment, mobile telephones, medical electronics, and aircraft radar and navigation systems. **Corporate headquarters location:** This location. **Other U.S. locations:** Jacksonville FL. **International locations:** Sussex, England. **Listed on:** American Stock Exchange. **Stock exchange symbol:** AMK.

ANDREA ELECTRONICS CORPORATION
45 Melville Park Road, Melville NY 11747. 631/719-1800. **Contact:** Personnel. **World Wide Web address:** http://www.andreaelectronics.com.

Description: Andrea Electronics Corporation designs, develops, and produces electronic audio systems, intercommunication systems, and related equipment for military and industrial companies. **Corporate headquarters location:** This location. **Listed on:** American Stock Exchange. **Stock exchange symbol:** AND.

ARROW/ZEUS ELECTRONICS
2900 Westchester Avenue, Suite 401, Purchase NY 10577. 914/701-7400. **Fax:** 914/701-4283. **Contact:** Human Resources Department. **World Wide Web address:** http://www.arrow.com. **Description:** Distributes and designs electronic components to military and aerospace contractors. **Common positions include:** Marketing Specialist; Services Sales Representative. **Corporate headquarters location:** Melville NY. **Parent company:** Arrow Electronics. **Operations at this facility include:** Sales. **Listed on:** New York Stock Exchange. **Stock exchange symbol:** ARW. **Number of employees at this location:** 65. **Number of employees nationwide:** 180.

ASTREX, INC.
205 Express Street, Plainview NY 11803. 516/433-1700. **Toll-free phone:** 800/633-6360. **Fax:** 516/433-1796. **Contact:** Human Resources. **World Wide Web address:** http://www.astrex.net. **Description:** Distributes electronic components used to connect, control, regulate, or store electricity in equipment. Products assembled and sold by Astrex include connectors, relays, switches, and LEDs. Founded in 1960. **Common positions include:** Administrative Assistant; Assistant Manager; Blue-Collar Worker Supervisor; Credit Manager; Customer Service Representative; Purchasing Agent/Manager; Sales Executive; Sales Manager; Sales Representative. **Corporate headquarters location:** This location. **Other U.S. locations:** Woburn MA; Endwell NY; Willow Grove PA. **Annual sales/revenues:** $11 - $20 million. **Number of employees at this location:** 40. **Number of employees nationwide:** 60.

AVNET, INC.
390 Rabro Drive, Hauppauge NY 11788. 631/434-7470. **Contact:** Human Resources. **World Wide Web address:** http://www.avnet.com. **Description:** One of the nation's largest distributors of electronic components and computer products for industrial and military customers. The company also manufactures and distributes other electronic, electrical, and video communications products. **NOTE:** Resumes must be sent to Avnet, Inc., Human Resources, 2211 South 47th Street, Phoenix AZ 85034. Resumes can be faxed to 602/643-4670. **Corporate headquarters location:** Phoenix AZ. **Listed on:** New York Stock Exchange. **Stock exchange symbol:** AVT.

BAE SYSTEMS
One Hazelteen Way, Greenlawn NY 11740. 631/261-7000. **Contact:** Human Resources. **World Wide Web address:** http://www.baesystems.com. **Description:** Designs, develops, and manufactures information electronics systems that acquire, protect, enhance, communicate, and display information for the defense and technically related markets. **Common positions include:** Accountant/Auditor; Buyer; Computer Programmer; Designer; Draftsperson; Electrical/Electronics Engineer; Human Resources Manager; Industrial Engineer; Mechanical Engineer; Software Engineer; Systems Analyst; Technical Writer/Editor. **Corporate headquarters location:** Rockville MD. **Other U.S. locations:** Nationwide. **International locations:** Worldwide. **Number of employees at this location:** 925.

BAE SYSTEMS

One Ridge Hill, Mail Stop 9, Yonkers NY 10710-5598. 914/964-2579. **Fax:** 914/964-3913. **Contact:** Human Resources Department. **World Wide Web address:** http://www.baesystems.com. **Description:** Designs, manufactures, and sells flight simulators, weapon systems, tactical air defense systems, small arms, and training devices for the U.S. government, as well as commercial and international customers. BAE Systems also develops simulation-based devices for the entertainment industry. The company also provides a variety of simulator-related training services at customer-owned facilities, its Tampa training center, and the British Aerospace-owned Dulles training facility. BAE Systems conducts business through its three primary operating segments: Training Devices, Training Services, and Systems Management. **Common positions include:** Aerospace Engineer; Budget Analyst; Buyer; Computer Programmer; Designer; Draftsperson; Editor; Electrical/Electronics Engineer; Financial Analyst; Human Resources Manager; Industrial Engineer; Mechanical Engineer; Purchasing Agent/Manager; Quality Control Supervisor; Software Engineer; Systems Analyst. **Corporate headquarters location:** Rockville MD. **Other U.S. locations:** Nationwide. **International locations:** Worldwide.

BAE SYSTEMS

300 Robbins Lane, Syosset NY 11791. 516/349-4947. **Contact:** Human Resources. **World Wide Web address:** http://www.baesystems.com. **Description:** Designs, manufactures, and sells flight simulators, weapon systems, tactical air defense systems, small arms, and training devices for the U.S. government, as well as commercial and international customers. BAE Systems also develops simulation-based devices for the entertainment industry. The company also provides a variety of simulator-related training services at customer-owned facilities, its Tampa training center, and the British Aerospace-owned Dulles training facility. BAE Systems conducts business through its three primary operating segments: Training Devices, Training Services, and Systems Management. **Corporate headquarters location:** Rockville MD. **Other U.S. locations:** Nationwide. **International locations:** Worldwide.

CHYRON CORPORATION

5 Hub Drive, Melville NY 11747. 631/845-2069. **Fax:** 631/845-2090. **Contact:** Human Resources. **E-mail address:** careers@chyron.com. **World Wide Web address:** http://www.chyron.com. **Description:** Designs, manufactures, and markets worldwide digital equipment, software, systems, and solutions that facilitate the production and enhance the presentation of live and programmed television content. Chyron also provides comprehensive solutions that address the management and routing of video and data signals prior to transmission. **NOTE:** Entry-level positions are offered. **Common positions include:** Administrative Assistant; Computer Programmer; Computer Support Technician; Customer Service Representative; Electrical/Electronics Engineer; Help-Desk Technician; Software Engineer; Website Developer. **Special programs:** Internships. **Corporate headquarters location:** This location. **Other U.S. locations:** Santa Clara CA. **Operations at this facility include:** Administration; Manufacturing; Research and Development; Sales; Service. **President/CEO:** Roger Henderson. **Annual sales/revenues:** $21 - $50 million. **Number of employees at this location:** 120. **Number of employees nationwide:** 160. **Number of employees worldwide:** 350.

COOPER WIRING DEVICES

45-31 Court Square, Long Island City NY 11101. 718/937-8000. **Contact:** Human Resources. **E-mail address:** recruit@cooperindustries.com. **World Wide Web address:** http://www.cooperwiringdevices.com. **Description:** Manufactures electrical wiring devices. **Common positions include:** Administrator; Advertising Clerk; Blue-Collar Worker Supervisor; Commercial Artist; Computer Programmer; Credit Manager; Customer Service Representative; Draftsperson; Electrical/Electronics Engineer; Human Resources Manager; Industrial Engineer; Mechanical Engineer; Purchasing Agent/Manager; Quality Control Supervisor; Transportation/Traffic Specialist. **Corporate headquarters location:** Houston TX. **Parent company:** Cooper Industries. **Listed on:** New York Stock Exchange. **Stock exchange symbol:** CBE.

DATA DEVICE CORPORATION

105 Wilbur Place, Bohemia NY 11716. 631/567-5600. **Fax:** 631/567-6357. **Contact:** Christine Ortize, Human Resources Supervisor. **World Wide Web address:** http://www.ddc-web.com. **Description:** A manufacturer of high-performance microelectronic components for military, aerospace, and industrial applications. **Common positions include:** Accountant/Auditor; Design Engineer; Draftsperson; Electrical/Electronics Engineer; Human Resources Manager; Operations/Production Manager. **Special programs:** Internships. **Corporate headquarters location:** This location. **Subsidiaries include:** Beta Transformer Technology Corp. **Operations at this facility include:** Manufacturing; Research and Development. **Listed on:** Privately held. **Annual sales/revenues:** $5 - $10 million. **Number of employees at this location:** 500. **Number of employees nationwide:** 800.

DEL GLOBAL TECHNOLOGIES CORPORATION

One Commerce Park, Valhalla NY 10595. 914/686-3600. **Contact:** Human Resources. **World Wide Web address:** http://www.delglobaltech.com. **Description:** Del Global Technologies Corporation is comprised of five operations that are engaged in the design, manufacture, and distribution of electronic components, assemblies, and systems for medical, industrial, and defense markets. Products are sold throughout the world to a broad range of OEM customers, distributors, radiologists, and defense agencies. The Dynarad subsidiary manufactures and markets mobile medical imaging systems, mammography equipment, portable dental X-ray units, and advanced neonatal imaging systems. Del Medical Systems markets medical diagnostic products on a worldwide basis. The Power Conversion Division provides standard and custom high-voltage power supplies, transformers, and custom low-voltage power supplies. The Bertan subsidiary designs and manufactures precision high-voltage power supplies and high-voltage instrumentation. The RFI subsidiary designs and manufactures electronic noise suppression filters, high-voltage capacitors, pulse transformers, and specialty magnetics.

DEUTSCH RELAYS INC.

55 Engineers Road, Hauppauge NY 11788. 631/342-1700. **Contact:** Diane Goerz, Human Resources Manager. **World Wide Web address:** http://www.deutschrelays.com. **Description:** Manufactures miniature electronic relays. **Corporate headquarters location:** This location.

DIONICS INC.

65 Rushmore Street, Westbury NY 11590. 516/997-7474. **Fax:** 516/997-7479. **Contact:** Human Resources Department. **World Wide Web address:** http://www.dionics-usa.com. **Description:** Dionics Inc. designs,

manufactures, and sells silicon semiconductor electronic products as individual discrete components, multicomponent integrated circuits, and multicomponent hybrid circuits.

EDO CORPORATION
ELECTRONIC SYSTEMS GROUP
455 Commack Road, Deer Park NY 11729. 631/595-5000. **Contact:** Human Resources. **World Wide Web address:** http://www.edocorp.com. **Description:** Engaged in the engineering and manufacturing of electronic systems including defensive avionics, ATC radar, satellite communications systems, and components. **Common positions include:** Accountant/Auditor; Buyer; Computer Programmer; Electrical/Electronics Engineer; Human Resources Manager; Industrial Engineer; Mechanical Engineer; Purchasing Agent/Manager; Teacher/Professor; Technical Writer/Editor. **Corporate headquarters location:** New York NY. **Operations at this facility include:** Administration; Manufacturing; Research and Development. **Listed on:** New York Stock Exchange. **Stock exchange symbol:** EDO. **Number of employees at this location:** 1,700.

ELECTRIC FUEL CORPORATION
632 Broadway, Suite 301, New York NY 10012. 212/529-9200. **Fax:** 212/529-5800. **Contact:** Human Resources. **E-mail address:** info@electric-fuel.com. **World Wide Web address:** http://www.electric-fuel.com. **Description:** Electric Fuel Corporation researches, develops, and commercializes zinc-air, battery-based systems for consumer electronic devices such as cellular phones, computers, medical devices, and PDAs, as well as electric vehicles. Founded in 1990. **Corporate headquarters location:** This location. **International locations:** Jerusalem, Israel. **Listed on:** NASDAQ. **Stock exchange symbol:** EFCX.

FIRECOM, INC.
39-27 59th Street, Woodside NY 11377. 718/899-6100. **Fax:** 718/899-1932. **Contact:** Human Resources. **E-mail address:** info@firecominc.com. **World Wide Web address:** http://www.firecominc.com. **Description:** Designs, manufactures, and distributes fire alarm and communication systems used for safety in large commercial buildings, primarily in the metropolitan New York area. Founded in 1978. **Corporate headquarters location:** This location. **Subsidiaries include:** Commercial Radio-Sound Corp. (NY); Fire Controls, Inc. (NY). **Annual sales/revenues:** $11 - $20 million. **Number of employees at this location:** 120.

FOSTER WHEELER LTD.
9431 Foster Wheeler Road, Dansville NY 14437. 716/335-3131. **Contact:** Human Resources. **World Wide Web address:** http://www.fwc.com. **Description:** Engaged in three business segments: process plants segment, consisting primarily of the design, engineering, and construction of process plants and fired heaters for oil refiners and chemical producers; a utility and engine segment, consisting primarily of the design and fabrication of steam generators, condensers, feedwater heaters, electrostatic precipitators, and other pollution abatement equipment; and an industrial segment that supplies pressure vessels and internals, electrical copper products, industrial insulation, welding wire, and electrodes. **Corporate headquarters location:** Clinton NJ. **Other U.S. locations:** Nationwide. **International locations:** Worldwide. **Listed on:** New York Stock Exchange. **Stock exchange symbol:** FWC.

JACO ELECTRONICS, INC.
145 Oser Avenue, Hauppauge NY 11788. 631/273-5500. **Contact:** Diane Ecknoff, Human Resources Director. **World Wide Web address:** http://www.jacoelectronics.com. **Description:** Jaco Electronics distributes computer systems, computer subsystems, electronic components, and electromechanical devices produced by other companies. Active products include computer subsystems and semiconductors, and passive products include capacitors, electromechanical devices, and motors and resistors. **Corporate headquarters location:** This location. **Subsidiaries include:** Nexus Custom Electronics, Inc. is a contract manufacturer of printed circuit board assemblies and complete systems from print to final product. Nexus offers surface-mount, thru-hole, and mixed PCB technologies; global test resources; and total systems integration. **Listed on:** NASDAQ. **Stock exchange symbol:** JACO.

L-3 COMMUNICATIONS CORPORATION
SATELLITE NETWORKS
125 Kennedy Drive, Hauppauge NY 11788. 631/231-1919. **Contact:** Human Resources. **World Wide Web address:** http://www.l-3com.com. **Description:** Manufactures and installs satellite Earth station ground communication equipment and systems. **Corporate headquarters location:** This location. **Other U.S. locations:** Melbourne FL. **Parent company:** L-3 Communications Holdings, Inc. **Listed on:** New York Stock Exchange. **Stock exchange symbol:** LLL. **Number of employees at this location:** 340. **Number of employees nationwide:** 460.

LSI COMPUTER SYSTEMS INC.
1235 Walt Whitman Road, Melville NY 11747-3010. 631/271-0400. **Contact:** Roberta Williams, Personnel Manager. **E-mail address:** hr@lsicsi.com. **World Wide Web address:** http://www.lsicsi.com. **Description:** Manufactures integrated circuits and microchips.

THE LECROY CORPORATION
700 Chestnut Ridge Road, Chestnut Ridge NY 10977-6499. 845/425-2000. **Fax:** 845/578-4461. **Contact:** Corporate Staffing. **E-mail address:** hrweb@lecroy.com. **World Wide Web address:** http://www.lecroy.com. **Description:** The LeCroy Corporation is a leading manufacturer of digital oscilloscopes and related products for the electronics, computer, and communications markets. Founded in 1964. **NOTE:** Entry-level positions are offered. **Common positions include:** Applications Engineer; Customer Service Representative; Design Engineer; Electrical/Electronics Engineer; Hardware Engineer; Manufacturing Engineer; Marketing Specialist; Sales Engineer; Software Engineer; Technical Writer/Editor. **Corporate headquarters location:** This location. **International locations:** Geneva, Switzerland. **Listed on:** NASDAQ. **Stock exchange symbol:** LCRY. **Annual sales/revenues:** More than $100 million. **Number of employees at this location:** 200. **Number of employees worldwide:** 500.

LEVITON MANUFACTURING COMPANY
59-25 Little Neck Parkway, Little Neck NY 11362-2591. 718/229-4040. **Contact:** Human Resources. **World Wide Web address:** http://www.leviton.com. **Description:** Manufactures electrical wiring devices. Leviton produces more than 80,000 variations of light switches, sockets, and plugs for both consumer and industrial customers. Products are used in small appliances, lamps, and similar products. Founded in 1906. **NOTE:** Entry-level positions are offered. **Common positions include:** Account Manager; Account Representative; Accountant; Administrative

Assistant; Applications Engineer; Budget Analyst; Computer Operator; Computer Programmer; Cost Estimator; Credit Manager; Electrical/Electronics Engineer; Finance Director; Financial Analyst; Human Resources Manager; Industrial Engineer; Industrial Production Manager; Manufacturing Engineer; Marketing Manager; Marketing Specialist; Mechanical Engineer; MIS Specialist; Software Engineer; Systems Analyst; Systems Manager. **Corporate headquarters location:** This location. **Other U.S. locations:** Atlanta GA; Chicago IL; Coffeyville KS; Sparks NV; Pawtucket RI; Bothell WA. **International locations:** Canada; Mexico. **Subsidiaries include:** Electricord Company; Leviton Telcom. **Listed on:** Privately held. **Annual sales/revenues:** More than $100 million.

MICROWAVE DISTRIBUTORS COMPANY
500 Johnson Avenue, Suite A, Bohemia NY 11716-2675. 631/589-8000. **Contact:** Human Resources Department. **World Wide Web address:** http://www.microwavedistributors.com. **Description:** A distributor of microwave and RF components. **Common positions include:** Accountant/Auditor; Customer Service Representative; Design Engineer. **Corporate headquarters location:** This location.

NAPCO SECURITY GROUP
333 Bayview Avenue, Amityville NY 11701. 631/842-9400. **Contact:** Human Resources Department. **World Wide Web address:** http://www.napcosecurity.com. **Description:** Manufactures electronic security equipment. The company's products are used in residential, commercial, institutional, and industrial installations. **Corporate headquarters location:** This location. **Subsidiaries include:** Alarm Lock manufactures and distributes a variety of door security hardware. **Listed on:** NASDAQ. **Stock exchange symbol:** NSSC.

NEW ENGLAND LAMINATE COMPANY INC.
40 Governor Drive, Newburgh NY 12550. 845/567-6200. **Contact:** Tama Murphy, Director of Human Resources. **Description:** Manufactures computer laminates that are integrated with circuits and then used in the manufacturing of computers and pagers. **Number of employees at this location:** 400.

ORBIT INTERNATIONAL CORPORATION
80 Cabot Court, Hauppauge NY 11788. 631/435-8300. **Contact:** Lynn Cooper, Human Resources Manager. **World Wide Web address:** http://www.orbitintl.com. **Description:** Manufactures electronic devices for the aerospace industry. Founded in 1957. **Common positions include:** Accountant; Administrative Assistant; Design Engineer; Draftsperson; Electrical/Electronics Engineer; Mechanical Engineer; Production Manager; Quality Control Supervisor; Sales Engineer; Secretary. **Special programs:** Summer Jobs. **Corporate headquarters location:** This location. **Subsidiaries include:** Behlman Electronics, Inc., through its military division, designs and manufactures power conversion devices and electronic products for measurement and display. The commercial products division of Behlman produces distortion-free commercial power units and low-noise, uninterruptable power sources. **Listed on:** NASDAQ. **Stock exchange symbol:** ORBT. **President:** Dennis Sunshine. **Annual sales/revenues:** $11 - $20 million. **Number of employees at this location:** 120.

PHILIPS ELECTRONICS NORTH AMERICA CORPORATION
1251 Avenue of the Americas, New York NY 10020. 212/536-0500. **Contact:** Denise Townsen, Supervisor of Human Resources. **World Wide**

Web address: http://www.philips.com. **Description:** This location provides services including intellectual property, legal, tax, customs, employee benefits, communications and processing, government affairs, manufacturing technology, purchasing, travel, environmental affairs, audit, compensation, training, and development to Philips companies nationwide. Overall, Philips Electronics North America is a multimarket manufacturing organization with nationwide locations and various subsidiaries, concentrating its efforts primarily in the fields of consumer electronics, consumer products, electrical and electronics components, and professional equipment. **Common positions include:** Accountant/Auditor; Attorney; Computer Programmer; Financial Analyst; Human Resources Manager; Systems Analyst. **Corporate headquarters location:** This location. **Operations at this facility include:** Administration. **Listed on:** New York Stock Exchange. **Stock exchange symbol:** PHG. **Number of employees at this location:** 230.

PHILIPS RESEARCH
345 Scarborough Road, Briarcliff Manor NY 10510. 914/945-6000. **Fax:** 914/945-6400. **Contact:** Human Resources. **World Wide Web address:** http://www.research.philips.com. **Description:** This location conducts research in microelectronics, High Definition TV (HDTV), medical imaging, lighting, integrated circuit design, software engineering, materials engineering, and manufacturing automation to support Philips' international business interests. **Parent company:** Philips Electronics North America is a multimarket manufacturing organization with nationwide locations and various subsidiaries. The company concentrates its efforts primarily in the fields of consumer electronics, consumer products, electrical and electronics components, and professional equipment. **Listed on:** New York Stock Exchange. **Stock exchange symbol:** PHG.

PHOTOCIRCUITS CORPORATION
31 Sea Cliff Avenue, Glen Cove NY 11542. 516/674-1000. **Contact:** Personnel. **World Wide Web address:** http://www.photocircuits.com. **Description:** A manufacturer of printed circuit boards. **Common positions include:** Buyer; Chemical Engineer; Customer Service Representative; Electrical/Electronics Engineer; Electrician; Industrial Engineer; Industrial Production Manager; Mechanical Engineer; Operations/Production Manager; Purchasing Agent/Manager; Quality Control Supervisor; Software Engineer. **Special programs:** Internships. **Corporate headquarters location:** This location. **Other U.S. locations:** Peachtree City GA. **Operations at this facility include:** Administration; Manufacturing; Sales. **Listed on:** Privately held. **Number of employees at this location:** 1,525.

PRAXAIR MRC
560 Route 303, Orangeburg NY 10962. 845/398-8307. **Contact:** Human Resources. **World Wide Web address:** http://www.praxairmrc.com. **Description:** Designs and manufactures thin-film coating and etching systems used in the manufacture of integrated circuits for sale to the semiconductor, computer, and telecommunications industries. The company also processes and fabricates ultra-high-purity metals and metal alloys, principally for thin-film purposes. Praxair MRC's thin-film technology products are also used in nonelectronic applications such as protective coatings for corrosion and wear resistance in razor blades and various automotive products. The company operates in three segments: Sputtering Equipment, Associated Target Materials, and Other High-Purity Materials. **Common positions include:** Buyer; Computer Programmer; Designer; Electrical/Electronics Engineer; Financial Analyst; General Manager; Human

Resources Manager; Industrial Engineer; Industrial Production Manager; Materials Engineer; Mechanical Engineer; Metallurgical Engineer; Operations/Production Manager; Physicist; Purchasing Agent/Manager; Science Technologist; Software Engineer; Systems Analyst; Technical Writer/Editor. **Special programs:** Internships. **Corporate headquarters location:** This location. **International locations:** France; Korea; Taiwan. **Parent company:** Praxair, Inc. **Listed on:** New York Stock Exchange. **Stock exchange symbol:** PX. **Number of employees at this location:** 550.

RICHARDSON ELECTRONICS
701-1 Koehler Avenue, Ronkonkoma NY 11779. **Toll-free phone:** 800/348-5580. **Contact:** Sales Manager. **World Wide Web address:** http://www.rell.com. **Description:** An international distributor of electronic components including turn-key microwave generators. **Corporate headquarters location:** La Fox IL. **Listed on:** NASDAQ. **Stock exchange symbol:** RELL.

SIEMENS CORPORATION
153 East 53rd Street, 56th Floor, New York NY 10022-4611. 212/258-4000. **Contact:** Human Resources Department. **World Wide Web address:** http://www.usa.siemens.com. **Description:** This location is the United States management and administrative headquarters for one of the world's leading companies in the electrical and electronics industry. Overall, Siemens operates internationally through the following groups: power engineering and automation; electrical installations; communications; medical engineering; data systems; and components. **Parent company:** Siemens AG (Munich, Germany). **Listed on:** New York Stock Exchange. **Stock exchange symbol:** SI.

SIGNAL TRANSFORMER COMPANY, INC.
500 Bayview Avenue, Inwood NY 11096-1792. 516/239-5777. **Contact:** Joe Dairo, Engineering Director. **World Wide Web address:** http://www.signaltransformer.com. **Description:** Manufactures and distributes transformers for a wide range of applications, from printed circuit board requirements to rectifiers and chokes. **Common positions include:** Accountant/Auditor; Blue-Collar Worker Supervisor; Buyer; Credit Manager; Customer Service Representative; Electrical/Electronics Engineer; General Manager; Industrial Engineer; Mechanical Engineer; Operations/Production Manager; Purchasing Agent/Manager; Quality Control Supervisor. **Corporate headquarters location:** Columbus OH. **Parent company:** Insilco Technologies Group. **Operations at this facility include:** Manufacturing; Sales.

SYSKA HENNESSY GROUP
11 West 42nd Street, New York NY 10036-2300. 212/921-2300. **Contact:** Human Resources. **E-mail address:** info@syska.com. **World Wide Web address:** http://www.syska.com. **Description:** An electrical engineering company.

VISHAY INTERTECHNOLOGY, INC.
10 Melville Park Road, Melville NY 11747-3113. 631/847-3000. **Contact:** Human Resources. **World Wide Web address:** http://www.vishay.com. **Description:** Manufactures transistors, transient voltage suppressors, diodes, and rectifiers. **Listed on:** New York Stock Exchange. **Stock exchange symbol:** VSH.

ENVIRONMENTAL AND WASTE MANAGEMENT SERVICES

You can expect to find the following types of companies in this chapter:

Environmental Engineering Firms • Sanitary Services

ATC ASSOCIATES INC.
104 East 25th Street, New York NY 10010. 212/353-8280. **Contact:** Human Resources. **World Wide Web address:** http://www.atc-enviro.com. **Description:** An environmental consulting firm that provides asbestos, lead, water, and soil testing. **Corporate headquarters location:** Woburn MA.

ARCADIS G&M, INC.
88 Duryea Road, Melville NY 11747. 631/249-7600. **Contact:** Human Resources. **World Wide Web address:** http://www.arcadis-us.com. **Description:** A consulting firm that provides environmental and engineering services. The company focuses on the environmental, building, and infrastructure markets. Founded in 1888. **NOTE:** Interested jobseekers are encouraged to apply online. **Corporate headquarters location:** Arnhem, Netherlands. **Other U.S. locations:** Nationwide. **Listed on:** NASDAQ. **Stock exchange symbol:** ARCAF. **Annual sales/revenues:** More than $100 million. **Number of employees worldwide:** 6,700.

COMMODORE APPLIED TECHNOLOGIES, INC.
150 East 58th Street, Suite 3238, New York NY 10155-0035. 212/308-5800. **Contact:** Personnel Department. **World Wide Web address:** http://www.commodore.com. **Description:** Develops technologies to destroy PCBs, chemical weapons, dioxins, and pesticides. Commodore Applied Technologies also salvages and resells cross-contaminated CFCs, and acquires and cleans up environmentally distressed properties. **Corporate headquarters location:** Alexandria VA. **Subsidiaries include:** Commodore Advanced Sciences, Inc.; Commodore Separation Technologies, Inc.; Commodore Solution Technologies, Inc.; Teledyne-Commodore LLC. **Listed on:** American Stock Exchange. **Stock exchange symbol:** CXI.

FOSTER WHEELER LTD.
9431 Foster Wheeler Road, Dansville NY 14437. 716/335-3131. **Contact:** Human Resources. **World Wide Web address:** http://www.fwc.com. **Description:** Engaged in three business segments: process plants segment, consisting primarily of the design, engineering, and construction of process plants and fired heaters for oil refiners and chemical producers; a utility and engine segment, consisting primarily of the design and fabrication of steam generators, condensers, feedwater heaters, electrostatic precipitators, and other pollution abatement equipment; and an industrial segment that supplies pressure vessels and internals, electrical copper products, industrial insulation, welding wire, and electrodes. **Corporate headquarters location:** Clinton NJ. **Other U.S. locations:** Nationwide. **International locations:** Worldwide. **Listed on:** New York Stock Exchange. **Stock exchange symbol:** FWC.

HUDSON TECHNOLOGIES, INC.

275 North Middletown Road, Pearl River NY 10965. 845/735-6000. **Contact:** Human Resources Department. **World Wide Web address:** http://www.hudsontech.com. **Description:** Hudson provides services for the recovery and reclamation of refrigerants in response to the requirements of the United States Clean Air Act. The company's services consist of removing used refrigerants from air conditioning and refrigeration systems and transferring them into cylinders for collection. Hudson's reclamation services consist of cleaning used refrigerants to remove impurities and contaminants and returning them to their original purity standards. **Listed on:** NASDAQ. **Stock exchange symbol:** HDSN.

FABRICATED/PRIMARY METALS AND PRODUCTS

You can expect to find the following types of companies in this chapter:

Aluminum and Copper Foundries • Die-Castings • Iron and Steel Foundries • Steel Works, Blast Furnaces, and Rolling Mills

DAYTON T. BROWN INC.
1175 Church Street, Bohemia NY 11716. 631/589-6300. **Fax:** 631/589-6300. **Contact:** Angela Chewening, Human Resources Representative. **World Wide Web address:** http://www.daytontbrown.com. **Description:** Engaged in sheet metal fabrication. Dayton T. Brown also offers engineering and testing services for industrial and commercial companies. **Common positions include:** Accountant/Auditor; Administrator; Attorney; Blue-Collar Worker Supervisor; Computer Programmer; Credit Manager; Customer Service Representative; Draftsperson; Electrical/Electronics Engineer; Human Resources Manager; Mechanical Engineer; Operations/Production Manager; Purchasing Agent/Manager; Technical Writer/Editor. **Corporate headquarters location:** This location.

FAIR-RITE PRODUCTS CORPORATION
P.O. Box J, One Commercial Row, Wallkill NY 12589. 845/895-2055. **Fax:** 845/895-9441. **Contact:** Debra A. Sherman, Director of Human Resources. **E-mail address:** shermand@fair-rite.com. **World Wide Web address:** http://www.fair-rite.com. **Description:** A manufacturer of ferrite components used in electronics. **Common positions include:** Ceramics Engineer; Customer Service Rep.; Electrical/Electronics Engineer; Industrial Production Manager; Metallurgical Engineer. **Special programs:** Internships. **Corporate headquarters location:** This location. **Other U.S. locations:** Flat Rock IL; Springfield VT. **Listed on:** Privately held. **Number of employees at this location:** 200. **Number of employees nationwide:** 300.

NIAGARA CORPORATION
667 Madison Avenue, 11th Floor, New York NY 10021. 212/317-1000. **Contact:** Human Resources. **Description:** Manufactures, processes, and distributes cold drawn steel bars. Niagara Corporation sells its products primarily to steel service centers in the United States and Canada. Founded in 1993. **Corporate headquarters location:** This location. **Subsidiaries include:** LaSalle Steel Company (Griffith IN; Hammond IN); Niagara LaSalle Corporation (Buffalo NY, Chattanooga TN, Midlothian TX). **Listed on:** NASDAQ. **Stock exchange symbol:** NIAG. **President/CEO:** Michael J. Scharf. **Number of employees nationwide:** 645.

PRAXAIR MRC
560 Route 303, Orangeburg NY 10962. 845/398-8307. **Contact:** Human Resources. **World Wide Web address:** http://www.praxairmrc.com. **Description:** Designs and manufactures thin-film coating and etching systems used in the manufacture of integrated circuits for sale to the semiconductor, computer, and telecommunications industries. The company also processes and fabricates ultra-high-purity metals and metal alloys, principally for thin-film purposes. Praxair MRC's thin-film technology products are also used in nonelectronic applications such as protective coatings for corrosion and wear resistance in razor blades and various

automotive products. The company operates in three segments: Sputtering Equipment, Associated Target Materials, and Other High-Purity Materials. **Common positions include:** Buyer; Computer Programmer; Designer; Electrical/Electronics Engineer; Financial Analyst; General Manager; Human Resources Manager; Industrial Engineer; Industrial Production Manager; Materials Engineer; Mechanical Engineer; Metallurgical Engineer; Operations/Production Manager; Physicist; Purchasing Agent/Manager; Science Technologist; Software Engineer; Systems Analyst; Technical Writer/Editor. **Special programs:** Internships. **Corporate headquarters location:** This location. **International locations:** France; Korea; Taiwan. **Parent company:** Praxair, Inc. **Listed on:** New York Stock Exchange. **Stock exchange symbol:** PX. **Number of employees at this location:** 550.

TIFFEN COMPANY
80 Oser Avenue, Hauppauge NY 11788. 631/273-2500. **Contact:** Human Resources. **World Wide Web address:** http://www.tiffen.com. **Description:** Engaged in sheet metal fabrication used to manufacture photographic-related products and accessories.

FINANCIAL SERVICES

You can expect to find the following types of companies in this chapter:

Consumer Finance and Credit Agencies • Investment Specialists •
Mortgage Bankers and Loan Brokers •
Security and Commodity Brokers, Dealers, and Exchanges

ALLIANCE CAPITAL MANAGEMENT
1345 Avenue of the Americas, New York NY 10105. 212/969-1000. **Contact:** Human Resources Department. **World Wide Web address:** http://www.alliancecapital.com. **Description:** Alliance Capital Management manages mutual funds for corporations and individual investors.

AMBAC INC.
One State Street Plaza, 15th Floor, New York NY 10004. 212/668-0340. **Contact:** Human Resources Department. **World Wide Web address:** http://www.ambac.com. **Description:** AMBAC Inc. is a holding company that provides, through its affiliates, financial guarantee insurance, financial services, and health care information services to both public and private clients throughout the United States. **Subsidiaries include:** AMBAC Indemnity Corporation, a leading financial guarantee insurance company; AMBAC Capital Management, Inc., a provider of municipal investment contracts; AMBAC Financial Services, L.P., a provider of interest rate swaps to municipalities; HCIA Inc., a health care information company. **Corporate headquarters location:** This location. **Listed on:** New York Stock Exchange. **Stock exchange symbol:** ABK.

AMERICAN EXPRESS COMPANY
American Express Tower C, 3 World Financial Center, 200 Vesey Street, New York NY 10285. 212/640-2000. **Contact:** Staffing Department. **World Wide Web address:** http://www.americanexpress.com. **Description:** American Express Company is a diversified travel and financial services company. Founded in 1850. **Common positions include:** Administrative Assistant; Administrative Manager; Assistant Manager; Computer Programmer; Database Manager; Economist; Financial Analyst; Graphic Artist; Human Resources Manager; Industrial Engineer; Market Research Analyst; Marketing Manager; Marketing Specialist; MIS Specialist; Multimedia Designer; Online Content Specialist; Operations Manager; Public Relations Specialist; Purchasing Agent/Manager; Quality Control Supervisor; Software Engineer; Statistician; Typist/Word Processor. **Corporate headquarters location:** This location. **Other U.S. locations:** Nationwide. **International locations:** Worldwide. **Subsidiaries include:** American Express Travel Related Services offers consumers the Personal, Gold, and Platinum Cards, as well as revolving credit products such as Optima Cards, which allow customers to extend payments. Other products include the American Express Corporate Card, which helps businesses manage their travel and entertainment expenditures; and the Corporate Purchasing Card, which helps businesses manage their expenditures on supplies, equipment, and services. American Express Travel Related Services also offers American Express Traveler's Cheques and travel services including trip planning, reservations, ticketing, and management information. American Express Financial Advisors provides a variety of financial products and services to help individuals, businesses, and

institutions meet their financial goals. American Express Financial Advisors has a staff of more than 8,000 in the United States and offers products and services that include financial planning; annuities; mutual funds; insurance; investment certificates; and institutional investment advisory trust, tax preparation, and retail securities brokerage services. **Listed on:** New York Stock Exchange. **Stock exchange symbol:** AXP. **Annual sales/revenues:** More than $100 million. **Number of employees at this location:** 5,000. **Number of employees nationwide:** 95,000.

AMERICAN STOCK EXCHANGE
86 Trinity Place, New York NY 10006. 212/306-1215. **Contact:** Human Resources Department. **E-mail address:** career@amex.com. **World Wide Web address:** http://www.amex.com. **Description:** One of the nation's largest stock exchanges, the American Stock Exchange is one of the only primary marketplaces for both stocks and derivative securities. The American Stock Exchange also handles surveillance, legal, and regulatory functions that are related to the stock exchange. **Common positions include:** Compliance Analyst; Financial Analyst; Public Relations Specialist; Research Assistant; Sales Representative; Systems Analyst. **Special programs:** Internships. **Corporate headquarters location:** This location. **Operations at this facility include:** Administration; Marketing. **Number of employees at this location:** 700.

ATALANTA SOSNOFF CAPITAL CORPORATION
101 Park Avenue, 6th Floor, New York NY 10178-0002. 212/867-5000. **Contact:** Kevin Kelly, Chief Financial Officer. **World Wide Web address:** http://www.atalantasosnoff.com. **Description:** Atalanta Sosnoff Capital Corporation provides discretionary investment management and brokerage services. **Corporate headquarters location:** This location. **Listed on:** New York Stock Exchange. **Stock exchange symbol:** ATL.

BEAR, STEARNS & COMPANY, INC.
THE BEAR STEARNS COMPANIES INC.
383 Madison Avenue, 30th Floor, New York NY 10179. 212/272-2000. **Contact:** Human Resources Department. **World Wide Web address:** http://www.bearstearns.com. **Description:** A leading worldwide investment banking, securities trading, and brokerage firm. **Corporate headquarters location:** This location. **Other U.S. locations:** Nationwide. **International locations:** Worldwide. **Subsidiaries include:** Bear, Stearns & Company, Inc. is an investment banking and brokerage firm; Bear, Stearns Securities Corporation provides professional and correspondent clearing services including securities lending; Custodial Trust Company provides master trust, custody, and government securities services. **Listed on:** New York Stock Exchange. **Stock exchange symbol:** BSC. **Annual sales/revenues:** More than $100 million. **Number of employees nationwide:** 9,200.

BERNSTEIN INVESTMENT RESEARCH & MANAGEMENT
1345 Avenue of the Americas, New York NY 10105. 212/486-5800. **Contact:** Human Resources. **E-mail address:** resumes@bernstein.com. **World Wide Web address:** http://www.bernstein.com. **Description:** An investment management research company that conducts research on specific companies and provides investment banking services for both private and institutional clients. **Corporate headquarters location:** This location. **Other U.S. locations:** Nationwide. **Parent company:** Alliance Capital Management L.P. **Listed on:** New York Stock Exchange. **Stock exchange symbol:** AC.

BROWN BROTHERS HARRIMAN & COMPANY
63 Wall Street, New York NY 10005. 212/483-1818. **Contact:** Human Resources. **E-mail address:** jobs@bbh.com. **World Wide Web address:** http://www.bbh.com. **Description:** Provides commercial banking, brokerage, and investment advisory services. **Other U.S. locations:** Boston MA; Jersey City NJ.

CIT GROUP, INC.
1211 Sixth Avenue, New York NY 10036. 212/382-7000. **Contact:** Human Resources. **World Wide Web address:** http://www.citgroup.com. **Description:** This division provides factoring services to a wide range of customers as a subsidiary of CIT Financial Services. Overall, CIT Group is a diversified financial services organization providing flexible funding alternatives, secured business lending, and financial advisory services for corporations, manufacturers, and dealers. Founded in 1908. **International locations:** Worldwide. **Number of employees nationwide:** 2,500.

CAMERON ASSOCIATES
640 Fifth Avenue, 15th Floor, New York NY 10019. 212/245-8800. **Contact:** Human Resources. **E-mail address:** mail@cameronassoc.com. **World Wide Web address:** http://www.cameronassoc.com. **Description:** An investor relations firm providing financial services for public companies. Cameron Associates also offers corporate communications services.

CANTOR FITZGERALD SECURITIES CORPORATION
299 Park Avenue, 32nd Floor, New York NY 10171. 212/821-6710. **Contact:** Human Resources Department. **World Wide Web address:** http://www.cantor.com. **Description:** An institutional brokerage firm dealing in fixed income securities, equities, derivatives, options, eurobonds, and emerging markets. Founded in 1945. **Common positions include:** Broker. **Special programs:** Internships; Training. **Corporate headquarters location:** This location. **Other U.S. locations:** Los Angeles CA; Chicago IL; Boston MA; Dallas TX. **International locations:** Germany; China; England; Italy; France; Japan. **Listed on:** Privately held. **Number of employees at this location:** 1,300. **Number of employees nationwide:** 1,500. **Number of employees worldwide:** 2,000.

CITIGROUP INC.
399 Park Avenue, New York NY 10043. 212/559-1000. **Contact:** Human Resources. **World Wide Web address:** http://www.citigroup.com. **Description:** A holding company offering a wide range of financial services through its subsidiaries. **Corporate headquarters location:** This location. **Subsidiaries include:** Citibank; CitiFinancial; Global Corporate & Investment Banking; Primerica Financial Services; Salomon Smith Barney; SSB Citi Asset Management Group; Travelers Life & Annuity; Travelers Property Casualty Corp. **Listed on:** New York Stock Exchange. **Stock exchange symbol:** C.

CREDIT SUISSE FIRST BOSTON
11 Madison Avenue, New York NY 10010. 212/325-2000. **Contact:** Recruiting. **World Wide Web address:** http://www.csfb.com. **Description:** A diversified financial services firm serving as underwriters, distributors, and investment dealers. **International locations:** Switzerland; United Kingdom.

DEUTSCHE BANK
31 West 52nd Street, New York NY 10019. 212/250-2500. **Contact:** Human Resources. **World Wide Web address:** http://www.deutsche-

bank.com. **Description:** A merchant investment bank. Deutsche Bank also manages index funds. **Corporate headquarters location:** This location. **Listed on:** New York Stock Exchange. **Stock exchange symbol:** DB.

DREYFUS CORPORATION
200 Park Avenue, 7th Floor, New York NY 10166. 212/922-6000. **Contact:** Linda Vanwart, Human Resources Representative. **World Wide Web address:** http://www.dreyfus.com. **Description:** A nationwide investment corporation managing over 150 mutual funds. **NOTE:** Entry-level positions are offered. **Common positions include:** Accountant; Administrative Assistant; Customer Service Representative; Secretary. **Corporate headquarters location:** This location. **Parent company:** Mellon Financial Corporation. **Listed on:** New York Stock Exchange. **Stock exchange symbol:** MEL. **Annual sales/revenues:** More than $100 million. **Number of employees at this location:** 2,400.

FAHNESTOCK & COMPANY
125 Broad Street, 16th Floor, New York NY 10004. 212/668-8000. **Contact:** Human Resources Representative. **World Wide Web address:** http://www.fahnestock.com. **Description:** A stock brokerage firm serving corporate clients and individual investors. **Parent company:** Fahnestock Viner Holdings Inc.

FIDUCIARY TRUST COMPANY INTERNATIONAL
600 Fifth Avenue, New York NY 10020. 212/632-3000. **Contact:** Human Resources. **World Wide Web address:** http://www.ftci.com. **Description:** Provides global investment management and custody services for institutional and individual clients. **Common positions include:** Administrative Assistant; Financial Analyst; Investment Manager; Systems Analyst. **Other U.S. locations:** Los Angeles CA; Washington DC; Wilmington DE; Miami FL. **International locations:** Australia; Geneva; Hong Kong; London; Tokyo. **Parent company:** Franklin Templeton Investments. **Operations at this facility include:** Administration. **Number of employees at this location:** 600. **Number of employees nationwide:** 700.

FIRST INVESTORS CORPORATION
95 Wall Street, 23rd Floor, New York NY 10005. 212/858-8000. **Fax:** 212/858-8099. **Contact:** Manager of Human Resources Department. **E-mail address:** hr@firstinvestors.com. **World Wide Web address:** http://www.firstinvestors.com. **Description:** Specializes in the distribution and management of investment programs for individuals and corporations, as well as retirement plans. First Investors operates through several area locations in Westchester County, New Jersey, and Long Island. **Common positions include:** Accountant/Auditor; Attorney; Computer Programmer; Customer Service Representative; Financial Analyst; Management Trainee; Securities Sales Representative. **Corporate headquarters location:** This location.

GILMAN & CIOCIA INC.
475 Northern Boulevard, Suite 25, Great Neck NY 11021. 516/482-4860. **Contact:** Thomas Povinelli, CEO. **E-mail address:** resumes@gilcio.com. **World Wide Web address:** http://www.e1040.com. **Description:** Provides income tax and financial planning. **Listed on:** NASDAQ. **Stock exchange symbol:** GTAX.

GOLDMAN SACHS & COMPANY
85 Broad Street, New York NY 10004. 212/902-1000. **Contact:** Recruiting Department. **World Wide Web address:** http://www.gs.com. **Description:** An investment banking firm. **NOTE:** Interested jobseekers should send resumes to 180 Maiden Lane, 23rd Floor, New York NY 10038. **Corporate headquarters location:** This location. **Other U.S. locations:** Nationwide. **International locations:** Worldwide.

GRUNTAL & CO., LLC
650 Madison Avenue, 10th Floor, New York NY 10022. 212/407-0500. **Contact:** Human Resources. **World Wide Web address:** http://www.gruntal.com. **Description:** A financial services firm offering retail clients investment banking, trading, insurance, retirement plans, investment advisory services, fixed income research, and brokerage accounts. **Common positions include:** Accountant/Auditor; Attorney; Brokerage Clerk; Budget Analyst; Financial Analyst; Paralegal; Research Analyst; Telecommunications Manager; Typist/Word Processor. **Corporate headquarters location:** This location. **Other U.S. locations:** Nationwide. **Parent company:** Ryan, Beck & Co., LLC. **Listed on:** Privately held. **Number of employees at this location:** 600. **Number of employees nationwide:** 1,500.

HSBC BANK USA
452 Fifth Avenue, 12th Floor, New York NY 10018. 212/525-5000. **Fax:** 877/248-4722. **Recorded jobline:** 888/HRHELP4. **Contact:** Human Resources. **World Wide Web address:** http://www.banking.us.hsbc.com. **Description:** An international banking institution that provides a wide range of individual and commercial services. **Corporate headquarters location:** London, England. **Parent company:** HSBC Holdings plc. **Listed on:** New York Stock Exchange. **Stock exchange symbol:** HBC.

ING
1325 Avenue of the Americas, New York NY 10019. 646/424-6000. **Contact:** Human Resources Department. **World Wide Web address:** http://www.ing.com. **Description:** A nationwide investment banking firm.

INVESTEC ERNST & COMPANY
One Battery Park Plaza, 2nd Floor, New York NY 10004. 212/898-6200. **Contact:** Human Resources. **E-mail address:** info@investec.com. **World Wide Web address:** http://www.investecernst.com. **Description:** A securities brokerage firm. Investec Ernst & Company is one of the largest financial clearinghouses in New York City, with over 80 correspondents.

J.P. MORGAN CHASE & COMPANY
270 Park Avenue, New York NY 10017. 212/270-6000. **Contact:** Employment. **World Wide Web address:** http://www.jpmorganchase.com. **Description:** Specializes in global financial services and retail banking. J.P. Morgan Chase and Company's services include asset management, cardmember services, community development, commercial banking for middle market companies, diversified consumer lending, global markets, home finance, investment banking, private banking, private equity, regional consumer and small business banking, and treasury and securities services. **Special programs:** Internships; Co-ops.

J.P. MORGAN CHASE & COMPANY
60 Wall Street, New York NY 10260-0060. 212/483-2323. **Contact:** Personnel. **World Wide Web address:** http://www.jpmorganchase.com.

Description: Specializes in global financial services and retail banking. J.P. Morgan Chase and Company's services include asset management, cardmember services, community development, commercial banking for middle market companies, diversified consumer lending, global markets, home finance, investment banking, private banking, private equity, regional consumer and small business banking, and treasury and securities services. Founded in 1838. **Special programs:** Internships; Co-ops.

J.P. MORGAN CHASE & COMPANY
2 Chase Manhattan Plaza, New York NY 10081-0001. 212/270-6000. **Contact:** Human Resources Department. **World Wide Web address:** http://www.jpmorganchase.com. **Description:** Specializes in global financial services and retail banking. J.P. Morgan Chase and Company's services include asset management, cardmember services, community development, commercial banking for middle market companies, diversified consumer lending, global markets, home finance, investment banking, private banking, private equity, regional consumer and small business banking, and treasury and securities services. **Special programs:** Internships; Co-ops.

J.P. MORGAN PARTNERS
1221 6th Avenue, 39th & 40th Floors, New York City NY 10020-1080. 212/899-3400. **Fax:** 212/899-3401. **Contact:** Human Resources. **World Wide Web address:** http://www.jpmorganpartners.com. **Description:** Provides equity and other financial services.

JEFFERIES & COMPANY, INC.
520 Madison Avenue, 12th Floor, New York NY 10022. 212/284-2300. **Contact:** Human Resources Department. **World Wide Web address:** http://www.jefco.com. **Description:** Jefferies & Company is engaged in equity, convertible debt and taxable fixed income securities brokerage and trading, and corporate finance. Jefferies is one of the leading national firms engaged in the distribution and trading of blocks of equity securities and conducts such activities primarily in the third market, which refers to transactions in listed equity securities effected away from national securities exchanges. Founded in 1962. **Corporate headquarters location:** This location. **Other U.S. locations:** Nationwide. **International locations:** Worldwide. **Parent company:** Jefferies Group, Inc. is a holding company which, through Jefferies & Company and its three other primary subsidiaries, Investment Technology Group, Inc., Jefferies International Limited, and Jefferies Pacific Limited, is engaged in securities brokerage and trading, corporate finance, and other financial services. **Listed on:** New York Stock Exchange. **Stock exchange symbol:** JEF.

LEHMAN BROTHERS HOLDINGS
745 Seventh Avenue, New York NY 10019. 212/526-7000. **Contact:** Human Resources. **World Wide Web address:** http://www.lehman.com. **Description:** A stock brokerage and investment banking firm. **Corporate headquarters location:** This location. **Annual sales/revenues:** More than $100 million.

MERRILL LYNCH
4 World Financial Center, North Tower, New York NY 10080. 212/449-1000. **Contact:** Human Resources. **World Wide Web address:** http://www.ml.com. **Description:** One of the largest securities brokerage firms in the United States, Merrill Lynch provides financial services in the following areas: securities, extensive insurance, and real estate and related

services. The company also brokers commodity futures, commodity options, and corporate and municipal securities. In addition, Merrill Lynch is engaged in investment banking activities. **NOTE:** Jobseekers are asked to call for specific information on where to mail resumes. **Corporate headquarters location:** This location. **Other U.S. locations:** Nationwide. **International locations:** Worldwide. **Listed on:** New York Stock Exchange. **Stock exchange symbol:** MER. **Annual sales/revenues:** More than $100 million. **Number of employees worldwide:** 63,800.

THE MONY GROUP
1740 Broadway, New York NY 10019. 212/708-2000. **Contact:** Human Resources Department. **E-mail address:** monyjobs@mony.com. **World Wide Web address:** http://www.mony.com. **Description:** A mutual life insurer. The MONY Group offers life insurance, disability income, and annuities. The company also operates investment subsidiaries engaged in the management of mutual funds and the distribution of securities. **Special programs:** Internships. **Corporate headquarters location:** This location. **Operations at this facility include:** Administration. **Listed on:** New York Stock Exchange. **Stock exchange symbol:** MNY.

MORGAN STANLEY DEAN WITTER & COMPANY
1221 Avenue of the Americas, New York NY 10020. 212/762-7100. **Contact:** Human Resources Director. **World Wide Web address:** http://www.msdw.com. **Description:** One of the largest investment banking firms in the United States. Services include financing, financial advisory services, real estate services, corporate bond services, equity services, government and money market services, merger and acquisition services, investment research services, investment management services, and individual investor services. **NOTE:** Resumes should be sent to the corporate headquarters: Human Resources, 1585 Broadway, New York NY 10036. 212/761-4000.

MORGAN STANLEY DEAN WITTER & COMPANY
1585 Broadway, New York NY 10036. 212/761-4000. **Contact:** Human Resources. **World Wide Web address:** http://www.msdw.com. **Description:** One of the largest investment banking firms in the United States. Services include financing, financial advisory services, real estate services, corporate bond services, equity services, government and money market services, merger and acquisition services, investment research services, investment management services, and individual investor services. **Corporate headquarters location:** This location.

NATIONAL ASSOCIATION OF SECURITIES DEALERS, INC. (NASD)
One Liberty Plaza, 165 Broadway, New York NY 10006. 212/858-4000. **Contact:** Human Resources Department. **World Wide Web address:** http://www.nasd.com. **Description:** The self-regulatory organization of the securities industry, overseeing the over-the-counter market. Through its subsidiary, NASDAQ, Inc., the company owns and operates the nationwide, electronic NASDAQ system, which serves one of the fastest-growing and second-largest securities markets in the United States. Working closely with the Securities and Exchange Commission, NASD sets the standards for NASDAQ securities and market makers, and provides ongoing surveillance of trading activities. NASD also provides key services for its membership and NASDAQ companies, particularly through its cooperative efforts with governmental and other agencies on policies and legislation that affect the investment banking and securities business. **Common positions include:** Accountant/Auditor; Attorney; Systems Analyst. **Special programs:**

Internships. **Corporate headquarters location:** Washington DC. **Other U.S. locations:** Trumbull CT; Rockville MD. **Number of employees at this location:** 350. **Number of employees nationwide:** 2,500.

NEW YORK STOCK EXCHANGE
11 Wall Street, New York NY 10005. 212/656-2266. **Contact:** Ms. Dale Bernstein, Managing Director of Staffing and Training. **World Wide Web address:** http://www.nyse.com. **Description:** The principal securities trading marketplace in the United States, serving a broad range of industries within and outside of the securities industry. More than 2,500 corporations, accounting for approximately 40 percent of American corporate revenues, are listed on the exchange. The New York Stock Exchange is engaged in a wide range of public affairs and economic research programs. **Common positions include:** Accountant/Auditor; Administrative Manager; Assistant Manager; Attorney; Blue-Collar Worker Supervisor; Branch Manager; Broadcast Technician; Budget Analyst; Cashier; Claim Representative; Computer Operator; Computer Programmer; Customer Service Representative; Department Manager; Economist; Editor; Education Administrator; Electrician; Financial Manager; General Manager; Human Resources Manager; Library Technician; Management Trainee; Market Research Analyst; Marketing Manager; Operations Research Analyst; Paralegal; Payroll Clerk; Photographer/Camera Operator; Postal Clerk/Mail Carrier; Property and Real Estate Manager; Public Relations Specialist; Purchasing Agent/Manager; Radio/TV Announcer/Broadcaster; Receptionist; Secretary; Software Engineer; Stenographer; Systems Analyst; Technical Writer/Editor; Typist/Word Processor. **Corporate headquarters location:** This location. **Number of employees at this location:** 1,550.

PARAGON CAPITAL MARKETS
7 Hanover Square, 2nd Floor, New York NY 10004. 212/742-1500. **Contact:** Human Resources Department. **World Wide Web address:** http://www.paragonmarkets.com. **Description:** A full-service securities brokerage firm offering a diverse range of financial products and services. Founded in 1986. **Common positions include:** Broker. **Corporate headquarters location:** This location. **Other U.S. locations:** Nationwide. **Operations at this facility include:** Administration; Sales; Service. **Listed on:** Privately held. **Annual sales/revenues:** $11 - $20 million. **Number of employees at this location:** 100. **Number of employees nationwide:** 150.

PRUDENTIAL SECURITIES INC.
199 Water Street, New York NY 10292. 212/778-1000. **Contact:** Director of Personnel. **World Wide Web address:** http://www.prudential.com. **Description:** An international securities brokerage and investment firm. The company offers clients more than 70 investment products including stocks, options, bonds, commodities, tax-favored investments, and insurance, as well as several specialized financial services. **Corporate headquarters location:** This location. **Parent company:** Prudential Financial, Inc. **Listed on:** New York Stock Exchange. **Stock exchange symbol:** PRU.

QUICK AND REILLY, INC.
299 Park Avenue, New York NY 10171-0002. 212/747-5000. **Contact:** Human Resources Department. **World Wide Web address:** http://www.quickandreilly.com. **Description:** A nationwide securities brokerage firm serving retail customers and institutional investors. **Parent company:** FleetBoston Financial Corporation. **Listed on:** New York Stock Exchange. **Stock exchange symbol:** FBF.

SG COWEN SECURITIES CORPORATION

1221 Avenue of the Americas, 9th Floor, New York NY 10020. 212/278-6000. **Contact:** Human Resources Department. **World Wide Web address:** http://www.sgcowen.com. **Description:** An investment banking firm. **Common positions include:** Financial Analyst; Investment Manager; Researcher; Sales Executive; Systems Analyst. **Corporate headquarters location:** This location. **Other area locations:** Albany NY. **Other U.S. locations:** Phoenix AZ; San Francisco CA; Chicago IL; Boston MA; Cleveland OH; Dayton OH; Philadelphia PA; Houston TX. **International locations:** Canada; France; Switzerland; United Kingdom. **Parent company:** Societe Generale Group (Paris, France). **Number of employees at this location:** 1,000. **Number of employees nationwide:** 1,400.

SALOMON SMITH BARNEY

388 Greenwich Street, New York NY 10013. 800/634-9855. **Contact:** Human Resources Representative. **World Wide Web address:** http://www.salomonsmithbarney.com. **Description:** An international investment banking, market making, and research firm serving corporations, state, local, and foreign governments, central banks, and other financial institutions. **Parent company:** Citigroup. **Listed on:** New York Stock Exchange. **Stock exchange symbol:** C.

SCHONFELD SECURITIES

650 Madison Avenue, 20th Floor, New York NY 10022. 212/832-0900. **Contact:** Human Resources. **Description:** A securities trading firm.

SCUDDER INVESTMENTS

345 Park Avenue, New York NY 10154. 212/326-6200. **Contact:** Human Resources. **Description:** An investment firm with principal operations in securities brokerage. **Parent company:** Deutsche Asset Management.

TD WATERHOUSE SECURITIES, INC.

100 Wall Street, New York NY 10005. 212/806-3500. **Contact:** Human Resources. **World Wide Web address:** http://www.tdwaterhouse.com. **Description:** TD Waterhouse Securities, Inc. provides brokerage and banking services for individuals that manage their own investments and financial affairs. **Common positions include:** Accountant/Auditor; Brokerage Clerk; Computer Programmer; Computer Support Technician; Customer Service Representative; Financial Services Sales Representative; Human Resources Manager; Securities Sales Representative; Software Engineer. **Corporate headquarters location:** This location. **Other U.S. locations:** Nationwide. **Parent company:** TD Waterhouse Investor Services. **Operations at this facility include:** Administration; Divisional Headquarters; Regional Headquarters; Service. **Listed on:** New York Stock Exchange. **Number of employees at this location:** 250. **Number of employees nationwide:** 800.

THOMSON FINANCIAL

195 Broadway, New York NY 10007. 646/822-2000. **Contact:** Personnel Manager. **World Wide Web address:** http://www.thomsonfinancial.com. **Description:** Provides financial information to the investment industry through its many business units. American Banker/Bond Buyer publishes banking and financial industry information in a variety of publications. Rainmaker Information provides software products to help members of the sales and investment industries.

UBS PAINEWEBBER INC.
1285 Avenue of the Americas, 3rd Floor, New York NY 10019. 212/713-2000. **Contact:** Personnel Department. **World Wide Web address:** http://www.ubspainewebber.com. **Description:** A full-service securities firm with over 300 offices nationwide. Services include investment banking, asset management, merger and acquisition consulting, municipal securities underwriting, estate planning, retirement programs, and transaction management. Clients include corporations, governments, institutions, and individuals. Founded in 1879. **Common positions include:** Accountant/Auditor; Brokerage Clerk; Computer Programmer; Payroll Clerk; Secretary; Systems Analyst. **Corporate headquarters location:** This location. **Other U.S. locations:** Nationwide. **Annual sales/revenues:** More than $100 million.

UBS WARBURG LLC
299 Park Avenue, New York NY 10171-0026. 212/821-3000. **Fax:** 212/821-3285. **Contact:** Human Resources Department. **World Wide Web address:** http://www.ubswarburg.com. **Description:** A national investment banking firm serving corporate clients. **Parent company:** UBS AG. **Listed on:** New York Stock Exchange. **Stock exchange symbol:** UBS.

UNITED STATES TRUST COMPANY OF NEW YORK
114 West 47th Street, New York NY 10036. 212/852-1000. **Contact:** Human Resources. **World Wide Web address:** http://www.ustrust.com. **Description:** An investment management, private banking, and securities services firm. Service categories include investment management; estate and trust administration; financial planning; and corporate trust. **Common positions include:** Accountant/Auditor; Administrator; Computer Programmer; Financial Analyst; Operations/Production Manager; Systems Analyst. **Corporate headquarters location:** This location.

VALUE LINE
220 East 42nd Street, 6th Floor, New York NY 10017. 212/907-1500. **Contact:** Human Resources Department. **World Wide Web address:** http://www.valueline.com. **Description:** An investment advisory firm. **Corporate headquarters location:** This location. **Listed on:** NASDAQ. **Stock exchange symbol:** VALU.

FOOD AND BEVERAGES/ AGRICULTURE

You can expect to find the following types of companies in this chapter:

Crop Services and Farm Supplies • Dairy Farms • Food Manufacturers/Processors and Agricultural Producers • Tobacco Products

BALCHEM CORPORATION
P.O. Box 175, Slate Hill NY 10973-0175. 845/355-5300. **Contact:** Human Resources. **World Wide Web address:** http://www.balchem.com. **Description:** A leader in the manufacturing and marketing of encapsulated food ingredients for a variety of industries. The company is also a leading supplier of ethylene oxide, a packaging sterilant. Founded in 1967. **Corporate headquarters location:** This location. **Listed on:** American Stock Exchange. **Stock exchange symbol:** BCP.

DOMINO SUGAR
One Federal Street, Yonkers NY 10702. 914/963-2400. **Contact:** Human Resources. **World Wide Web address:** http://www.dominosugar.com. **Description:** Refines raw sugar and distributes it to major national clients in the soft drink, confectionery, and baking industries. **Common positions include:** Accountant/Auditor; Biological Scientist; Blue-Collar Worker Supervisor; Buyer; Chemical Engineer; Chemist; Clinical Lab Technician; Computer Programmer; Credit Manager; Customer Service Representative; Department Manager; Electrical/Electronics Engineer; Financial Analyst; Food Scientist/Technologist; Human Resources Manager; Industrial Engineer; Manufacturer's/Wholesaler's Sales Rep.; Marketing Specialist; Mechanical Engineer; Operations/Production Manager; Purchasing Agent/Manager; Systems Analyst. **Corporate headquarters location:** This location. **Listed on:** Privately held. **Number of employees at this location:** 400.

FINK BAKING COMPANY
5-35 54th Avenue, Long Island City NY 11101. 718/392-8300. **Contact:** Human Resources. **World Wide Web address:** http://www.finkbaking.com. **Description:** Produces a full-line of bakery products. Fink also supplies bread and rolls to airlines, restaurants, steamship operators, hotels, and other institutional customers. **Corporate headquarters location:** This location.

THE HAIN CELESTIAL GROUP
58 South Service Road, Suite 250, Melville NY 11747. 516/237-6200. **Contact:** Human Resources. **World Wide Web address:** http://www.hain-celestial.com. **Description:** Markets and distributes organic, natural, and specialty food and beverage products. Specialty products include kosher foods, low calorie and diet foods and beverages, snack foods, and dietetic foods. **Corporate headquarters location:** This location. **Subsidiaries include:** Celestial Seasonings; The Hain Food Group, Inc. **Listed on:** NASDAQ. **Stock exchange symbol:** HAIN. **Annual sales/revenues:** More than $100 million.

KRASDALE FOODS INC.
65 West Red Oak Lane, White Plains NY 10604. 718/378-1100. **Contact:** Personnel. **World Wide Web address:** http://www.krasdalefoods.com. **Description:** Engaged in the wholesale distribution of canned goods and other processed food products. **Corporate headquarters location:** This location.

PEPSI-COLA BOTTLING COMPANY
867 East Gate Boulevard, Garden City NY 11530. 516/228-8201. **Contact:** Human Resources. **World Wide Web address:** http://www.pepsico.com. **Description:** A division of Pepsi-Cola Company that produces Pepsi, Diet Pepsi, A&W Root Beer, Slice, Orange Slice, and Mountain Dew. **NOTE:** Interested applicants should send resumes to 550 New Horizon Boulevard, Amityville NY 11701. **Parent company:** PepsiCo, Inc. (Purchase NY) consists of Frito-Lay Company, Pepsi-Cola Company, The Quaker Oats Company, and Tropicana Products, Inc. **Listed on:** New York Stock Exchange. **Stock exchange symbol:** PEP.

PEPSICO, INC.
700 Anderson Hill Road, Purchase NY 10577. 914/253-2000. **Contact:** Staffing Director. **World Wide Web address:** http://www.pepsico.com. **Description:** Operates on a worldwide basis within four companies which include Frito-Lay Company, Pepsi-Cola Company, The Quaker Oats Company, and Tropicana Products, Inc. Pepsi-Cola Company primarily markets its brands worldwide and manufactures concentrates for its brands for sale to franchised bottlers worldwide. The segment also operates bottling plants and distribution facilities located in the United States and key international markets. **Common positions include:** Accountant/Auditor; Attorney; Computer Programmer; Department Manager; Financial Analyst; General Manager; Human Resources Manager; Public Relations Specialist. **Corporate headquarters location:** This location. **International locations:** Canada; Mexico; United Kingdom. **Listed on:** New York Stock Exchange. **Stock exchange symbol:** PEP.

PHILIP MORRIS COMPANIES INC.
PHILIP MORRIS INC.
120 Park Avenue, New York NY 10017. 212/880-5000. **Contact:** Human Resources. **World Wide Web address:** http://www.philipmorris.com. **Description:** Philip Morris Companies is a holding company. Its principal wholly-owned subsidiaries are Philip Morris Inc. (also at this location), Philip Morris U.S.A., Philip Morris International Inc., Kraft Foods, Inc., and Philip Morris Capital Corporation. In the tobacco industry, Philip Morris U.S.A. and Philip Morris International together form one of the largest international cigarette operations in the world. U.S. brand names include Marlboro, Parliament, Virginia Slims, Benson & Hedges, and Merit. In the food industry, Kraft Foods, Inc. is one of the largest producers of packaged grocery products in North America. Major brands include Jell-O, Post, Kool-Aid, Crystal Light, Entenmann's, Miracle Whip, Stove Top, and Shake 'n Bake. Kraft markets a number of products under the Kraft brand including natural and process cheeses and dry packaged dinners. The Oscar Mayer unit markets processed meats, poultry, lunch combinations, and pickles under the Oscar Mayer, Louis Rich, Lunchables, and Claussen brand names. Kraft is also one of the largest coffee companies with principal brands including Maxwell House, Sanka, Brim, and General Foods International Coffees. Kraft Foods Ingredients Corporation manufactures private-label and industrial food products for sale to other food processing companies. Philip Morris Capital Corporation is engaged in financial

services and real estate. **Corporate headquarters location:** This location. **Other area locations:** Rye Brook NY. **Other U.S. locations:** Stamford CT; Richmond VA. **International locations:** Australia; Brazil; Hong Kong; Japan; Switzerland. **Listed on:** New York Stock Exchange. **Stock exchange symbol:** MO. **Number of employees nationwide:** 155,000.

PHILIP MORRIS INTERNATIONAL INC.
800 Westchester Avenue, Rye Brook NY 10573. 914/335-5000. **Contact:** Personnel. **World Wide Web address:** http://www.philipmorris.com. **Description:** In the tobacco industry, Philip Morris U.S.A. and Philip Morris International together form one of the largest international cigarette operations in the world. U.S. brand names include Marlboro, Parliament, Virginia Slims, Benson & Hedges, and Merit. **Corporate headquarters location:** This location. **Parent company:** Philip Morris Companies Inc. (New York NY). **Listed on:** New York Stock Exchange. **Stock exchange symbol:** MO. **Number of employees nationwide:** 155,000.

SARA LEE COFFEE AND TEA
500 Mamaroneck Avenue, 5th Floor, Harrison NY 10528. 212/532-0300. **Contact:** Vince Pellettiere, Human Resources Representative. **E-mail address:** recruiting@saralee.com. **World Wide Web address:** http://www.saralee.com. **Description:** Produces a nationally distributed brand of premium coffee. The company also operates a chain of cafes and drive-thru restaurants. **Common positions include:** Accountant/Auditor; Blue-Collar Worker Supervisor; Branch Manager; Computer Programmer; Manufacturer's/Wholesaler's Sales Rep.; Quality Control Supervisor; Restaurant/Food Service Manager; Systems Analyst. **Corporate headquarters location:** Chicago IL. **Other U.S. locations:** Nationwide. **Subsidiaries include:** Cain's Coffee Company; Greenwich Mills Company. **Parent company:** Sara Lee Corporation. **Operations at this facility include:** Administration; Divisional Headquarters; Sales. **Listed on:** New York Stock Exchange. **Stock exchange symbol:** SLE.

SCHIEFFELIN & SOMERSET COMPANY
2 Park Avenue, 17th Floor, New York NY 10016. 212/251-8200. **Fax:** 212/251-8390. **Contact:** Human Resources Department. **E-mail address:** hrstaffing@schieffelin-somerset.com. **World Wide Web address:** http://www.trade-pages.com. **Description:** Sells and markets premium alcoholic beverages. **Common positions include:** Accountant/Auditor; Administrative Manager; Attorney; Budget Analyst; Computer Programmer; Human Resources Manager; Public Relations Specialist; Sales Representative; Systems Analyst. **Corporate headquarters location:** This location. **Other U.S. locations:** San Francisco CA; Coral Gables FL; Chicago IL. **Parent company:** MoetHennessyLouisVuitton/Diageo. **Operations at this facility include:** Administration; Sales. **Listed on:** NASDAQ/NYSE. **Stock exchange symbol:** LVMHY/DEO. **Number of employees at this location:** 100. **Number of employees nationwide:** 200.

TOPPS COMPANY
One Whitehall Street, New York NY 10004. 212/376-0300. **Contact:** Human Resources. **World Wide Web address:** http://www.topps.com. **Description:** Internationally manufactures and markets a variety of chewing gum, candy, and other similar products. Topps also licenses its technology and trademarks and sells its chewing gum base and flavors to other overseas manufacturers. The company is best known for its internationally registered trademark Bazooka and its perennial Topps Baseball Bubble Gum picture cards. Topps is a leading marketer, under exclusive licenses, of collectible

picture cards, albums, and stickers for baseball, football, and hockey. The company is also a leading producer and distributor of cards and stickers featuring pictures of popular motion picture, television, and cartoon characters, also under exclusive licenses. **Corporate headquarters location:** This location. **Other U.S. locations:** Duryea PA. **International locations:** Ireland. **Listed on:** NASDAQ. **Stock exchange symbol:** TOPP.

GEORGE WESTON BAKERIES, INC.
55 Paradise Lane, Bayshore NY 11706. 631/273-6000. **Contact:** Human Resources. **Description:** Produces and distributes a variety of food products including soups, sauces, and bouillons; dressings including Hellmann's mayonnaise; starches and syrups; bread spreads including Skippy peanut butter; desserts and baking aids; and pasta. **Corporate headquarters location:** This location.

GOVERNMENT

You can expect to find the following types of agencies in this chapter:

Courts • Executive, Legislative, and General Government • Public Agencies (Firefighters, Military, Police) • United States Postal Service

ECONOMIC OPPORTUNITY COUNCIL OF SUFFOLK
475 East Main Street, Suite 206, Patchogue NY 11772. 631/289-2124. **Contact:** Songhi Scott, Chief Financial Officer/Human Resources. **World Wide Web address:** http://www.eoc-suffolk.com. **Description:** A county agency responsible for various social programs in Suffolk County. The council provides counseling in energy conservation, outreach, summer work, health and education, housing, and employment training. **Common positions include:** Accountant/Auditor; Branch Manager; Counselor; Financial Analyst; Human Service Worker; Instructor/Trainer; Social Worker. **Special programs:** Internships. **Corporate headquarters location:** This location. **Operations at this facility include:** Administration. **Listed on:** Privately held. **Number of employees at this location:** 10. **Number of employees nationwide:** 50.

NEW YORK STATE DEPARTMENT OF HEALTH
5 Penn Plaza, New York NY 10001. 212/268-7001. **Contact:** Human Resources. **World Wide Web address:** http://www.health.state.ny.us. **Description:** Provides health regulatory, public health, mental health/addictions, environmental health, and medico-public health laboratory services on a statewide basis. **Common positions include:** Biological Scientist; Chemist; Computer Programmer; Counselor; Database Manager; Dietician/Nutritionist; Economist; Financial Analyst; Health Services Worker; Licensed Practical Nurse; Medical Records Technician; Mental Health Worker; MIS Specialist; Network Engineer; Occupational Therapist; Pharmacist; Physical Therapist; Physician; Psychologist; Recreational Therapist; Registered Nurse; Respiratory Therapist; Social Worker; Speech-Language Pathologist; Statistician; Systems Analyst.

U.S. ENVIRONMENTAL PROTECTION AGENCY (EPA)
290 Broadway, 28th Floor, New York NY 10007. 212/637-3000. **Contact:** Human Resources. **World Wide Web address:** http://www.epa.gov. **Description:** The EPA is dedicated to improving and preserving the quality of the environment, both nationally and globally, and protecting human health and the productivity of natural resources. The agency is committed to ensuring that federal environmental laws are implemented and enforced effectively; U.S. policy, both foreign and domestic, encourages the integration of economic development and environmental protection so that economic growth can be sustained over the long term; and public and private decisions affecting energy, transportation, agriculture, industry, international trade, and natural resources fully integrate considerations of environmental quality. Founded in 1970. **Special programs:** Internships. **Corporate headquarters location:** Washington DC. **Other U.S. locations:** Nationwide. **Number of employees nationwide:** 19,000.

U.S. POSTAL SERVICE
149 East 23rd Street, New York NY 100010-3765. 212/673-3771. **Contact:** Human Resources. **World Wide Web address:** http://www.usps.com. **Description:** A post office. **Other U.S. locations:** Nationwide.

HEALTH CARE: SERVICES, EQUIPMENT, AND PRODUCTS

You can expect to find the following types of companies in this chapter:

Dental Labs and Equipment • Home Health Care Agencies • Hospitals and Medical Centers • Medical Equipment Manufacturers and Wholesalers • Offices and Clinics of Health Practitioners • Residential Treatment Centers/Nursing Homes • Veterinary Services

AFP IMAGING CORPORATION

250 Clearbrook Road, Elmsford NY 10523. 914/592-6100. **Fax:** 914/592-6148. **Contact:** Human Resources. **E-mail address:** afp@afpimaging.com. **World Wide Web address:** http://www.afpimaging.com. **Description:** Provides medical equipment utilized by radiologists, cardiologists, and other medical professionals for generating, recording, processing, and viewing hard copy diagnostic images. The company's products are applied in medical diagnostics X-ray inspection. Products are marketed under the AFP, DENT-X, and SENS-A-RAY 2000 brand names. **Corporate headquarters location:** This location. **Subsidiaries include:** Regam Medical Systems International AB, Sundsvall, Sweden. **Chairman of the Board:** David Vozick. **Annual sales/revenues:** $21 - $50 million.

ALL METRO HEALTH CARE

50 Broadway, Lynbrook NY 11563. 516/887-1200. **Toll-free phone:** 800/225-1200. **Fax:** 516/593-2848. **Contact:** Human Resources. **E-mail address:** all-metro@aol.com. **Description:** A home health care provider. Plaza Domestic Agency and Caregivers on Call also operate out of this facility. Founded in 1955. **Common positions include:** Accountant; Branch Manager; Certified Nurses Aide; Chief Financial Officer; Clerical Supervisor; Computer Programmer; Computer Support Technician; Computer Technician; Controller; Customer Service Representative; Home Health Aide; Human Resources Manager; Licensed Practical Nurse; Marketing Manager; MIS Specialist; Nanny; Occupational Therapist; Physical Therapist; Purchasing Agent/Manager; Registered Nurse; Sales Manager; Sales Representative; Secretary. **Office hours:** Sunday - Saturday, 8:30 a.m. - 8:30 p.m. **Corporate headquarters location:** This location. **Other area locations:** Mount Vernon NY; New York NY. **Other U.S. locations:** FL; MO; NJ. **Listed on:** Privately held. **Annual sales/revenues:** $21 - $50 million. **Number of employees at this location:** 2,000. **Number of employees nationwide:** 3,000.

ALLEGIANCE HEALTHCARE CORPORATION

500 Neely Town Road, Montgomery NY 12549. 845/457-2000. **Contact:** Human Resources. **World Wide Web address:** http://www.allegiance.net. **Description:** This location distributes medical supplies and equipment to hospitals. Overall, Allegiance Healthcare is a producer, developer, and distributor of medical products and technologies for use in hospitals and other health care settings. The company operates through two industry segments: medical specialties, and medical/laboratory products and distribution. **Corporate headquarters location:** Dublin OH. **Parent company:** Cardinal Health. **Listed on:** New York Stock Exchange. **Stock exchange symbol:** CAH.

AMERICUS DENTAL LABS LP

150-15 Hillside Avenue, Jamaica NY 11432. 718/658-6655. **Contact:** Human Resources. **E-mail address:** info@americuslab.com. **World Wide Web address:** http://www.americuslab.com. **Description:** A dental lab that manufactures crowns, bridges, and other dental products.

ANIMAL MEDICAL CENTER
THE E&M BOBST HOSPITAL

510 East 62nd Street, New York NY 10021. 212/838-8100. **Fax:** 212/758-8157. **Contact:** Human Resources. **World Wide Web address:** http://www.amcny.org. **Description:** A full-service, nonprofit animal hospital with a staff of over 80 veterinarians. Founded in 1910.

BARKSDALE HOME CARE SERVICES CORPORATION

327 Fifth Avenue, Pelham NY 10803. 914/738-5600. **Fax:** 914/738-0658. **Contact:** Rosa K. Barksdale, CEO. **Description:** A home health care agency. **Common positions include:** Home Health Aide; Licensed Practical Nurse; Registered Nurse.

BAYER DIAGNOSTICS

511 Benedict Avenue, Tarrytown NY 10591-5097. 914/631-8000. **Fax:** 914/524-2132. **Contact:** Human Resources Department. **World Wide Web address:** http://www.bayerdiag.com. **Description:** Develops, manufactures, and sells clinical diagnostic systems. Bayer Diagnostics specializes in critical care, laboratory, and point-of-care testing. **Common positions include:** Accountant/Auditor; Attorney; Biological Scientist; Biomedical Engineer; Budget Analyst; Buyer; Chemist; Clinical Lab Technician; Computer Programmer; Customer Service Representative; Designer; Draftsperson; Electrical/Electronics Engineer; Electrician; Financial Analyst; Human Resources Manager; Librarian; Mathematician; Mechanical Engineer; Medical Records Technician; Public Relations Specialist; Purchasing Agent/Manager; Science Technologist; Services Sales Representative; Software Engineer; Statistician; Systems Analyst; Technical Writer/Editor. **Corporate headquarters location:** Bayerwerk, Germany. **Other U.S. locations:** CA; IN; MA; NC. **International locations:** Worldwide. **Parent company:** Bayer AG. **Operations at this facility include:** Administration; Divisional Headquarters; Manufacturing; Research and Development; Sales; Service. **Listed on:** New York Stock Exchange. **Stock exchange symbol:** BAY. **Number of employees at this location:** 800. **Number of employees nationwide:** 4,500.

BETH ISRAEL HEALTH CARE SYSTEM

First Avenue at 16th Street, New York NY 10003. 212/420-2000. **Contact:** Human Resources. **World Wide Web address:** http://www.bethisraelny.org. **Description:** An integrated health care system providing a full continuum of primary, acute, tertiary, and long-term care. The system also operates New York HealthCare/Doctors' Walk In, the Japanese Medical Practice, Schnurmacher Nursing Home of Beth Israel Medical Center, Robert Mapplethorpe Residential Treatment Facility, Phillips Beth Israel School of Nursing, Karpas Health Information Center, and D-O-C-S, a multisite, private, group medical practice in the suburbs. **NOTE:** Resumes should be sent to Human Resources, 555 West 57th Street, New York NY 10019. **Corporate headquarters location:** This location.

CVS PROCARE

80 Air Park Drive, Ronkonkoma NY 11779. 631/981-0034. **Fax:** 631/981-0722. **Contact:** Personnel Department. **World Wide Web address:**

http://www.cvsprocare.com. **Description:** A national provider of outpatient drug therapies and a broad array of distribution, case management, and support services to meet the ongoing needs of patients with chronic medical conditions, the health professionals who care for them, and the third-party payers responsible for such care. The company's services include distribution of prescription drug therapies, drug utilization review programs, patient compliance monitoring, psycho-social support services, and assistance in insurance investigation, verification, and reimbursement. **Parent company:** CVS Corporation. **Corporate headquarters location:** Woonsocket RI. **Other U.S. locations:** Nationwide. **Listed on:** New York Stock Exchange. **Stock exchange symbol:** CVS.

CENTER FOR VETERINARY CARE
236 East 75th Street, New York NY 10021. 212/734-7480. **Contact:** Human Resources. **Description:** A full-service animal hospital offering medical and surgical procedures.

COMMUNITY GENERAL HOSPITAL/SULLIVAN COUNTY
P.O. Box 800, Bushville Road, Harris NY 12742-0800. 845/794-3300. **Contact:** Human Resources. **Description:** A 300-bed hospital. Community General Hospital's services include oncology, treatment of biochemical dependence, mental health services, a diabetes unit, a cardiac care unit and a maternity ward. **Number of employees at this location:** 800.

CURATIVE HEALTH SERVICES
150 Motor Parkway, 4th Floor, Hauppauge NY 11788. 631/232-7000. **Contact:** Director of Human Resources. **World Wide Web address:** http://www.curative.com. **Description:** Curative Health Services primarily manages, on behalf of hospital clients, a nationwide network of wound-care centers. Most of the wound-care centers managed by Curative Health Services are outpatient, although a small portion are inpatient. The company is also engaged in the research and development of therapeutic products for wound-healing applications. **Corporate headquarters location:** St. Louis Park MN. **Other U.S. locations:** Nationwide. **Listed on:** NASDAQ. **Stock exchange symbol:** CURE.

FISHKILL HEALTH CENTER
22 Robert R. Kasin Way, Beacon NY 12508-1560. 845/831-8704. **Fax:** 845/831-1124. **Contact:** Human Resources. **Description:** A 160-bed, skilled care nursing home. **NOTE:** Entry-level positions and second and third shifts are offered. **Common positions include:** Activity Director; Certified Nurses Aide; Dietician/Nutritionist; Licensed Practical Nurse; Occupational Therapist; Physical Therapist; Registered Nurse; Social Worker. **Special programs:** Internships; Training; Summer Jobs. **Office hours:** Monday - Friday, 8:30 a.m. - 8:00 p.m. **Corporate headquarters location:** This location. **Other U.S. locations:** Wappingers Falls NY. **Listed on:** Privately held. **Owner:** Lynn Kasin. **Number of employees at this location:** 300. **Number of employees nationwide:** 400.

FLUSHING HOSPITAL MEDICAL CENTER
45th Avenue at Parsons Boulevard, Flushing NY 11355. 718/670-5000. **Recorded jobline:** 718/670-JOBS. **Contact:** Human Resources. **World Wide Web address:** http://www.flushinghospital.org. **Description:** A 428-bed hospital. Flushing Hospital Medical Center is a major teaching affiliate of The Albert Einstein School of Medicine. **Number of employees at this location:** 2,400.

HANGER ORTHOPEDIC GROUP, INC.
151 Hempstead Turnpike, West Hempstead NY 11552. 516/481-9670. **Contact:** Human Resources. **World Wide Web address:** http://www.hanger.com. **Description:** A provider of orthotic and prosthetic rehabilitation services. **Corporate headquarters location:** Bethesda MD. **Other U.S. locations:** Nationwide. **Listed on:** New York Stock Exchange. **Stock exchange symbol:** HGR. **Number of employees nationwide:** 125.

HERON HOME & HEALTH CARE AGENCY
168-30 89th Avenue, Queens NY 11432. 516/292-6200. **Contact:** Director. **Description:** A home health care agency. **Common positions include:** Licensed Practical Nurse; Occupational Therapist; Physical Therapist; Registered Nurse; Respiratory Therapist; Social Worker; Speech-Language Pathologist.

IMPATH INC.
521 West 57th Street, 5th Floor, New York NY 10019. 212/698-0300. **Contact:** Human Resources. **E-mail address:** hr@impath.com. **World Wide Web address:** http://www.impath.com. **Description:** Maintains a database of over 620,000 cancer patients' profiles. IMPATH assists physicians, pharmaceutical companies, and managed care providers in the diagnosis, prognosis, and treatment of cancer. **Corporate headquarters location:** This location. **Other U.S. locations:** Phoenix AZ; Los Angeles CA. **Listed on:** NASDAQ. **Stock exchange symbol:** IMPH. **Annual sales/revenues:** $51 - $100 million.

INTEGRAMED AMERICA, INC.
One Manhattanville Road, Purchase NY 10577. 914/253-8000. **Contact:** Rita Gruber, Human Resources Director. **World Wide Web address:** http://www.integramed.com. **Description:** Manages and provides services to clinical facilities and physician practices that provide assisted reproductive technology (ART) and/or infertility services. ART services consist of medical, psychological, and financial consultations and administration of the appropriate ART services and techniques. Infertility services provided include diagnostic testing, fertility drug therapy, tubal surgery, and intrauterine insemination. **Corporate headquarters location:** This location. **Other area locations:** Long Island NY; North Tarrytown NY; Port Chester NY. **Other U.S. locations:** Boston MA; Hackensack NJ; Livingston NJ. **Listed on:** NASDAQ. **Stock exchange symbol:** INMD.

J&K HEALTH CARE
140 Huguenot Street, New Rochelle NY 10801. 914/633-7810. **Contact:** Manager. **Description:** A home health care agency. **Common positions include:** Certified Nurses Aide; Home Health Aide; Licensed Practical Nurse; Registered Nurse.

JACOBI MEDICAL CENTER
1400 Pelham Parkway, Building 2, Room 101, Bronx NY 10461. 718/918-3533. **Contact:** Barbara Juliano, Employment Manager. **World Wide Web address:** http://www.ci.nyc.ny.us/html/hhc/jacobi/home.html. **Description:** A major medical center with over 700 beds. **Common positions include:** Accountant/Auditor; Adjuster; Administrative Manager; Architect; Attorney; Biomedical Engineer; Blue-Collar Worker Supervisor; Budget Analyst; Buyer; Chemist; Clerical Supervisor; Clinical Lab Technician; Computer Programmer; Construction and Building Inspector; Construction Contractor; Counselor; Credit Manager; Customer Service Representative; Dental Assistant/Dental Hygienist; Dentist; Dietician/Nutritionist; Draftsperson;

Education Administrator; EEG Technologist; EKG Technician; Electrical/Electronics Engineer; Electrician; Emergency Medical Technician; Environmental Engineer; Financial Analyst; Food Scientist/Technologist; General Manager; Health Services Manager; Human Resources Manager; Human Service Worker; Insurance Agent/Broker; Landscape Architect; Librarian; Library Technician; Licensed Practical Nurse; Management Analyst/Consultant; Management Trainee; Materials Engineer; Mechanical Engineer; Medical Records Technician; Nuclear Medicine Technologist; Occupational Therapist; Operations/Production Manager; Pharmacist; Physical Therapist; Physician; Physicist; Preschool Worker; Property and Real Estate Manager; Psychologist; Public Relations Specialist; Purchasing Agent/Manager; Quality Control Supervisor; Recreational Therapist; Registered Nurse; Respiratory Therapist; Restaurant/Food Service Manager; Social Worker; Speech-Language Pathologist; Stationary Engineer; Statistician; Structural Engineer; Systems Analyst; Teacher/Professor; Technical Writer/Editor; Transportation/Traffic Specialist; Wholesale and Retail Buyer. **Special programs:** Internships. **Corporate headquarters location:** New York NY. **Parent company:** New York Health and Hospitals Corporation. **Operations at this facility include:** Administration; Regional Headquarters; Service. **Number of employees at this location:** 5,000. **Number of employees nationwide:** 60,000.

KINGSTON HOSPITAL
396 Broadway, Kingston NY 12401. 845/331-3131. **Fax:** 845/334-2850. **Contact:** Human Resources Department. **World Wide Web address:** http://www.kingstonhospital.org. **Description:** A 150-bed, acute care hospital. **Common positions include:** Biomedical Engineer; Clerical Supervisor; Computer Programmer; Counselor; Dietician; EEG Technologist; EKG Technician; Electrical/Electronics Engineer; Electrician; Food Scientist; Health Services Manager; Human Resources Manager; Human Service Worker; Librarian; Licensed Practical Nurse; Mechanical Engineer; Medical Records Technician; Nuclear Medicine Technologist; Occupational Therapist; Pharmacist; Physical Therapist; Public Relations Specialist; Radiological Technologist; Registered Nurse; Respiratory Therapist; Social Worker; Surgical Technician; Systems Analyst. **Parent company:** Kingston Regional Health Care System. **Number of employees at this location:** 680.

MANHATTAN EYE, EAR & THROAT HOSPITAL
210 East 64th Street, New York NY 10021. 212/605-3708. **Fax:** 212/605-3765. **Contact:** Recruitment Manager. **Description:** A nonprofit hospital specializing in problems of the eye, ear, and throat. Founded in 1825. **NOTE:** Entry-level positions are offered. **Common positions include:** Account Manager; Administrative Assistant; Biochemist; Certified Nurses Aide; Clinical Lab Technician; MIS Specialist. **Operations at this facility include:** Administration; Research and Development; Service. **Listed on:** Privately held. **Annual sales/revenues:** $51 - $100 million. **Number of employees at this location:** 450.

MARY IMMACULATE HOSPITAL
SAINT VINCENT CATHOLIC MEDICAL CENTERS
152-11 89th Avenue, Jamaica NY 11432. 718/558-2000. **Contact:** Human Resources Department. **World Wide Web address:** http://www.svcmc.org. **Description:** A medical center. **Common positions include:** Computer Operator; Computer Programmer; Controller; Database Manager; Dietician/Nutritionist; EEG Technologist; EKG Technician; Emergency Medical Technician; Environmental Engineer; Finance Director; Financial

Analyst; Human Resources Manager; Librarian; Licensed Practical Nurse; Marketing Specialist; Medical Records Technician; MIS Specialist; Nuclear Medicine Technologist; Occupational Therapist; Pharmacist; Physical Therapist; Physician; Project Manager; Psychologist; Public Relations Specialist; Purchasing Agent/Manager; Quality Control Supervisor; Radiological Technologist; Registered Nurse; Respiratory Therapist; Secretary; Speech-Language Pathologist; Surgical Technician; Systems Manager; Telecommunications Manager; Transportation/Traffic Specialist; Typist/Word Processor.

NATIONAL HOME HEALTH CARE CORPORATION
700 White Plains Road, Suite 275, Scarsdale NY 10583. 914/722-9000. **Contact:** Human Resources Department. **World Wide Web address:** http://www.nhhc.net. **Description:** National Home Health Care, through its subsidiaries, is a national provider of a variety of health related services including home care, general care, nurses, and therapists. **Corporate headquarters location:** This location. **Subsidiaries include:** Health Acquisition Corporation provides home health care services, primarily through certified home health aides and personal care aides in the New York metropolitan area; Brevard Medical Center, Inc. provides both primary and specialty outpatient medical services in Brevard County FL; First Health, Inc. provides primary care outpatient medical services in Volusia County FL. **Listed on:** NASDAQ. **Stock exchange symbol:** NHHC.

THE NEW YORK EYE AND EAR INFIRMARY
310 East 14th Street, Second Avenue, New York NY 10003. 212/979-4000. **Contact:** Human Resources Department. **World Wide Web address:** http://www.nyee.edu. **Description:** A hospital specializing in ocular and auditory care. **Common positions include:** Accountant/Auditor; Clinical Lab Technician; Dentist; Dietician/Nutritionist; Electrical/Electronics Engineer; Electrician; Human Resources Manager; Licensed Practical Nurse; Mechanical Engineer; Medical Records Technician; Pharmacist; Physician; Purchasing Agent/Manager; Radiological Technologist; Registered Nurse; Respiratory Therapist; Social Worker; Speech-Language Pathologist. **Number of employees at this location:** 600.

NEW YORK METHODIST HOSPITAL
506 Sixth Street, Brooklyn NY 11215. 718/768-4305. **Fax:** 718/768-4324. **Contact:** Human Resources Department. **World Wide Web address:** http://www.nym.org. **Description:** An acute-care teaching hospital. **Common positions include:** Accountant/Auditor; Budget Analyst; Clerical Supervisor; Clinical Lab Technician; Dietician/Nutritionist; EEG Technologist; EKG Technician; Emergency Medical Technician; Licensed Practical Nurse; Medical Records Technician; Occupational Therapist; Physical Therapist; Physician; Radiological Technologist; Recreational Therapist; Registered Nurse; Respiratory Therapist; Social Worker; Speech-Language Pathologist; Surgical Technician. **Operations at this facility include:** Administration; Research and Development. **Number of employees nationwide:** 2,300.

NEW YORK UNIVERSITY MEDICAL CENTER
560 First Avenue, 32nd Street, New York NY 10016. 212/263-1999. **Contact:** Employment Recruitment Services Department. **World Wide Web address:** http://www.med.nyu.edu. **Description:** A nonprofit medical center engaged in patient care, research, and education. The central component of New York University Medical Center is Tisch Hospital, a 726-bed acute care facility and a major center for specialized procedures in cardiovascular

services, neurosurgery, AIDS, cancer treatment, reconstructive surgery, and transplantation. The medical center also includes the Rusk Institute of Rehabilitation Medicine, the Hospital of Joint Diseases, and several medical schools. The Rusk Institute of Rehabilitation Medicine, a 152-bed unit, is one of the world's largest university-affiliated centers for the treatment and training of physically disabled adults and children, as well as for research in rehabilitation medicine. The Hospital of Joint Diseases, with 226 beds, is dedicated solely to neuromusculoskeletal diseases. The School of Medicine, the Post-Graduate Medical School, and the Skirball Institute of Biomolecular Medicine are also part of the medical center. **NOTE:** Entry-level positions are offered. **Common positions include:** Account Representative; Accountant; Administrative Assistant; Administrative Manager; Biological Scientist; Budget Analyst; Buyer; Certified Nurses Aide; Claim Representative; Clerical Supervisor; Clinical Lab Technician; Computer Operator; Customer Service Representative; Database Manager; Dietician/Nutritionist; Financial Analyst; General Manager; Human Resources Manager; MIS Specialist; Network/Systems Administrator; Occupational Therapist; Pharmacist; Physical Therapist; Project Manager; Psychologist; Purchasing Agent/Manager; Registered Nurse; Respiratory Therapist; Secretary; Social Worker; Speech-Language Pathologist; Systems Analyst; Systems Manager; Typist/Word Processor; Website Developer. **Special programs:** Internships; Summer Jobs. **Corporate headquarters location:** This location. **Annual sales/revenues:** More than $100 million. **Number of employees at this location:** 8,000.

NORTHERN DUTCHESS HOSPITAL
6511 Springbrook Avenue, P.O. Box 5002, Rhinebeck NY 12572-5002. 845/871-3335. **Fax:** 845/871-3252. **Contact:** Human Resources. **World Wide Web address:** http://www.ndhosp.com. **Description:** A hospital. Northern Dutchess Hospital's staff treats the physiological, psychological, social, and spiritual needs of the geriatric and physically challenged by using a multidisciplinary approach. The Thompson House, a 100-bed, skilled nursing facility, was established in 1994. Residents with Alzheimer's disease and related dementia diagnoses receive therapeutic services in The Thompson House's 20-bed Special Care Unit. Wells Manor, founded in 1987, is a senior citizen housing project that has five separate buildings with 19 efficiency apartments and 55 one-bedroom units. The Neugarten Family Birth Center, established in 1985, was the first hospital-based birthing center in New York. Since 1978, Northern Dutchess Hospital has primary health care centers in five New York communities: Beacon Community Dental (Beacon NY); Germantown Community Dental (Germantown NY); Hyde Park Medical/Dental (Hyde Park NY); Rhinebeck Community Dental (Rhinebeck NY); and Stanfordville Medical/Dental (Stanfordville NY).

OLYMPUS AMERICA INC.
2 Corporate Center Drive, Melville NY 11747-3157. 631/844-5000. **Contact:** Human Resources. **E-mail address:** staffing@olympus.com. **World Wide Web address:** http://www.olympus.com. **Description:** This location houses administrative offices only. Overall, Olympus America manufactures and markets cameras and imaging equipment as well as a variety of surgical and medical instruments. **Corporate headquarters location:** This location.

PARK EAST ANIMAL HOSPITAL
52 East 64th Street, New York NY 10021. 212/832-8417. **Fax:** 212/355-3620. **Contact:** Ms. Vicki Ungar, Office Manager. **World Wide Web address:** http://www.parkeastanimalhospital.com. **Description:** A 24-hour

small animal hospital offering medical, nursing, and surgical services for pets. This location also hires seasonally. Founded in 1961. **NOTE:** Entry-level positions and second and third shifts are offered. **Common positions include:** Administrative Assistant; Administrative Manager; EEG Technologist; EKG Technician; Medical Assistant; Medical Records Technician; Medical Secretary; Radiological Technologist; Surgical Technician; Veterinarian. **Special programs:** Internships; Training; Summer Jobs. **Corporate headquarters location:** This location. **President:** Dr. Lewis Berman. **Annual sales/revenues:** Less than $5 million. **Number of employees at this location:** 25.

PFIZER
235 East 42nd Street, New York NY 10017. 212/573-2323. **Recorded jobline:** 212/733-4150. **Contact:** Employee Resources. **E-mail address:** resumes@pfizer.com. **World Wide Web address:** http://www.pfizer.com. **Description:** A leading pharmaceutical company that distributes products concerning cardiovascular health, central nervous system disorders, infectious diseases, and women's health worldwide. The company's brand-name products include Benadryl, Ben Gay, Cortizone, Desitin, Halls, Listerine, Sudafed, and Zantac 75. **Company slogan:** We're part of the cure. **Corporate headquarters location:** This location. **International locations:** Worldwide. **Subsidiaries include:** Pfizer Animal Health Group; Pfizer Consumer Products Division; Pfizer Hospital Products Group; Pfizer International; Pfizer Pharmaceutical Group; Pfizer Specialty Chemicals. **Listed on:** New York Stock Exchange. **Stock exchange symbol:** PFE. **Annual sales/revenues:** More than $100 million. **Number of employees worldwide:** 46,000.

QUANTRONIX
41 Research Way, East Setauket NY 11733. 631/784-6100. **Fax:** 631/246-9742. **Contact:** Human Resources. **E-mail address:** hr@quantron.com. **World Wide Web address:** http://www.quantron.com. **Description:** Manufactures laser systems for dental and medical uses. The company also manufactures lasers for industrial purposes. **International locations:** Germany; Malaysia.

RICHMOND CHILDREN'S CENTER
100 Corporate Drive, Yonkers NY 10701. 914/968-7170. **Contact:** Nancy Morris, Director of Human Resources. **Description:** A nonprofit, intermediate care facility (residential to long-term) for individuals with severe to profound physical and developmental disabilities. Services in the main facility include medical care; recreational services; and physical, language, occupational, and speech therapies. Richmond Children's Center offers other services in the community including case management, early intervention, group homes, and respite programs (for children with special needs who are cared for at home). **NOTE:** Entry-level positions and second and third shifts are offered. **Common positions include:** Certified Nurses Aide; Licensed Practical Nurse; Registered Nurse; Social Worker; Speech-Language Pathologist. **Executive Director:** Richard Bloom. **Number of employees at this location:** 325.

SACHEM ANIMAL HOSPITAL
227 Union Avenue, Holbrook NY 11741. 631/467-2121. **Contact:** Manager of Human Resources Department. **World Wide Web address:** http://www.members.aol.com/sachemah/index.html. **Description:** Sachem Animal Hospital provides general medical and surgical services, dental

services, and boarding for domestic and exotic pets. The hospital also specializes in reproduction and infertility services.

ST. LUKE'S CORNWALL HOSPITAL
19 Laurel Avenue, Cornwall NY 12518. 845/534-7711. **Contact:** Human Resources. **Description:** A 125-bed acute care, community-based, nonprofit hospital. St. Luke's Cornwall Hospital has 20 additional beds devoted to mental health care. **Number of employees at this location:** 500.

ST. LUKE'S-ROOSEVELT HOSPITAL CENTER
1111 Amsterdam Avenue, New York NY 10025. 212/523-4000. **Contact:** Recruitment. **World Wide Web address:** http://www.wehealnewyork.org. **Description:** A 1,315-bed, teaching hospital associated with Columbia University. **NOTE:** Resumes should be sent to Human Resources, 555 West 57th Street, 19th Floor, New York NY 10019. 212/523-2011. **Common positions include:** Clinical Lab Technician; Housekeeper; Medical Records Technician; Occupational Therapist; Pharmacist; Physical Therapist; Recreational Therapist; Respiratory Therapist; Secretary; Social Worker. **Parent company:** Continuum Health Partners, Inc. **Number of employees at this location:** 6,000.

HENRY SCHEIN, INC.
135 Duryea Road, Melville NY 11747. 631/843-5500. **Fax:** 631/843-5658. **Contact:** Human Resources Department. **World Wide Web address:** http://www.henryschein.com. **Description:** Manufactures and distributes dental and medical instruments. Henry Schein, Inc. serves the dental, medical, and veterinary markets. **Common positions include:** Accountant/Auditor; Advertising Clerk; Buyer; Computer Programmer; Customer Service Representative; Dental Assistant/Dental Hygienist; Sales Representative; Systems Analyst; Telemarketer. **Corporate headquarters location:** This location. **Other U.S. locations:** Nationwide. **Operations at this facility include:** Sales. **Listed on:** NASDAQ. **Stock exchange symbol:** HSIC. **Number of employees at this location:** 1,000. **Number of employees nationwide:** 1,700.

SOUTH BEACH PSYCHIATRIC CENTER
777 Seaview Avenue, Staten Island NY 10305. 718/667-2726. **Fax:** 718/667-2467. **Contact:** Human Resources. **Description:** South Beach Psychiatric Center is a New York State Office of Mental Health outpatient facility that is organized to deliver comprehensive mental health services to people in West Brooklyn, Staten Island, and New York City. **Common positions include:** Dietician/Nutritionist; Human Service Worker; Medical Records Technician; Occupational Therapist; Pharmacist; Physician; Psychologist; Registered Nurse; Social Worker; Stationary Engineer. **Corporate headquarters location:** Albany NY. **Operations at this facility include:** Administration. **Number of employees at this location:** 1,100.

STATE UNIVERSITY OF NEW YORK DOWNSTATE MEDICAL CENTER UNIVERSITY HOSPITAL AND HEALTH SCIENCE CENTER AT BROOKLYN
151 East 34th Street, Room 103, Brooklyn NY 11203. 718/270-1000. **Physical address:** 450 Clarkson Avenue, Brooklyn NY 11203. **Fax:** 718/270-1815. **Contact:** Human Resources. **Description:** An academic medical center that includes colleges of medicine, nursing, and health-related professions and a school of graduate studies as well as University Hospital of Brooklyn.

TENDER LOVING CARE/STAFF BUILDERS

1983 Marcus Avenue, Suite 200, Lake Success NY 11042. 516/358-1000. **Fax:** 516/358-2465. **Contact:** Human Resources Department. **World Wide Web address:** http://www.tlcathome.com. **Description:** A home health care agency. **Common positions include:** Accountant/Auditor; Budget Analyst; Claim Representative; Clerical Supervisor; Computer Programmer; Credit Manager; Dietician/Nutritionist; Financial Analyst; Licensed Practical Nurse; Medical Records Technician; Purchasing Agent/Manager; Registered Nurse; Systems Analyst. **Corporate headquarters location:** This location. **Other U.S. locations:** Nationwide. **Operations at this facility include:** Administration. **Number of employees at this location:** 300. **Number of employees nationwide:** 20,000.

TENDER LOVING CARE/STAFF BUILDERS

99 Railroad Station Plaza, Suite 100, Hicksville NY 11801-2898. 516/935-3737. **Contact:** Human Resources Department. **World Wide Web address:** http://www.tlcathome.com. **Description:** A home health care agency. **Common positions include:** Accountant/Auditor; Budget Analyst; Claim Representative; Clerical Supervisor; Computer Programmer; Credit Manager; Dietician/Nutritionist; Financial Analyst; Licensed Practical Nurse; Medical Records Technician; Purchasing Agent/Manager; Registered Nurse; Systems Analyst. **Corporate headquarters location:** Lake Success NY. **Other U.S. locations:** Nationwide.

WATERVIEW NURSING CARE CENTER

119-15 27th Avenue, Flushing NY 11354. 718/461-5000. **Fax:** 718/321-1984. **Contact:** Manager of Human Resources Department. **World Wide Web address:** http://www.healthlistings.com/waterview. **Description:** A 200-bed facility that offers specialized, long-term nursing care to chronically ill individuals of all ages. Waterview's in-house medical staff provides care in areas that include psychiatry, psychotherapy, dentistry, podiatry, otolaryngology, physiatry, ophthalmology, hematology, urology, neurology, optometry, portable X-rays, and lab work. Founded in 1989. **NOTE:** Entry-level positions and second and third shifts are offered. **Company slogan:** A special place for special people. **Common positions include:** Administrative Assistant; Certified Nurses Aide; Dietician/Nutritionist; Licensed Practical Nurse; Occupational Therapist; Physical Therapist; Physician; Registered Nurse; Secretary; Social Worker. **Special programs:** Training; Summer Jobs. **Office hours:** Monday - Friday, 9:00 a.m. - 5:00 p.m. **Listed on:** Privately held. **President:** Larry I. Slatky. **Annual sales/revenues:** $11 - $20 million. **Number of employees at this location:** 280.

WEIGHT WATCHERS INTERNATIONAL INC.

175 Crossways Park West, Woodbury NY 11797. 516/390-1400. **Contact:** Brian Powers, General Manager of Human Resources. **World Wide Web address:** http://www.weightwatchers.com. **Description:** Conducts and supervises franchised weight-control classes in 21 countries, markets packaged products through its food licensees, and publishes the *Weight Watchers* magazine in three countries. **Corporate headquarters location:** This location. **Listed on:** New York Stock Exchange. **Stock exchange symbol:** WTW.

WESTSIDE VETERINARY CENTER

220 West 83rd Street, New York NY 10024. 212/580-1800. **Contact:** Human Resources. **Description:** An animal hospital offering medical, surgical, and dental services.

HOTELS AND RESTAURANTS

You can expect to find the following types of companies in this chapter:

Casinos • Dinner Theaters • Hotel/Motel Operators •
Resorts • Restaurants

ARK RESTAURANTS CORPORATION
85 Fifth Avenue, 14th Floor, New York NY 10003. 212/206-8800. **Contact:** Marilyn Guy, Manager of Human Resources Department. **World Wide Web address:** http://www.arkrestaurants.com. **Description:** Ark Restaurants Corporation and its subsidiaries own, operate, or manage 27 restaurants nationwide. **Corporate headquarters location:** This location. **Listed on:** NASDAQ. **Stock exchange symbol:** ARKR.

CARLYLE HOTEL
35 East 76th Street, New York NY 10021. 212/744-1600. **Contact:** Personnel. **World Wide Web address:** http://www.rosewoodhotels.com. **Description:** A luxury hotel offering 180-rooms, three restaurants, and banquet/meeting facilities. **Corporate headquarters location:** This location. **Parent company:** Rosewood Hotels & Resorts.

COURTYARD BY MARRIOTT
475 White Plains Road, Tarrytown NY 10591. 914/631-1122. **Contact:** General Manager. **World Wide Web address:** http://www.courtyard.com. **Description:** A hotel with 139 guest rooms and two meeting rooms. **Corporate headquarters location:** Bethesda MD. **Parent company:** Marriott International. **Listed on:** New York Stock Exchange. **Stock exchange symbol:** MAR.

CROWNE PLAZA
66 Hale Avenue, White Plains NY 10601. 914/682-0050. **Contact:** Human Resources. **World Wide Web address:** http://www.crowneplaza.com. **Description:** A 401-room hotel with 13 meeting rooms. **Parent company:** Six Continents plc. **Listed on:** New York Stock Exchange. **Stock exchange symbol:** SXC.

DORAL ARROWWOOD
975 Anderson Hill Road, Rye Brook NY 10573. 914/939-5500. **Contact:** Personnel. **World Wide Web address:** http://www.arrowwood.com. **Description:** A hotel and conference center with 272 guest rooms and 36 meeting rooms.

ESSEX HOUSE
160 Central Park South, New York NY 10019. 212/247-0300. **Contact:** Human Resources. **World Wide Web address:** http://www.essexhouse.com. **Description:** Operates a hotel with 597 guest rooms and 150 condominiums. **Corporate headquarters location:** White Plains NY. **Parent company:** Starwood Hotels & Resorts Worldwide. **Listed on:** New York Stock Exchange. **Stock exchange symbol:** HOT.

GURNEY'S INN
290 Old Montauk Highway, Montauk NY 11954. 631/668-1770. **Fax:** 631/668-1881. **Contact:** Human Resources. **World Wide Web address:** http://www.gurneys-inn.com. **Description:** A 109-room hotel featuring fine

dining and rooms with an ocean view. **NOTE:** Entry-level positions are offered. **Common positions include:** Accountant; Administrative Assistant; Blue-Collar Worker Supervisor; Controller; Finance Director; Registered Nurse; Restaurant/Food Service Manager; Typist/Word Processor. **Special programs:** Internships; Apprenticeships; Summer Jobs. **Office hours:** Monday - Friday, 9:00 a.m. - 5:00 p.m. **Corporate headquarters location:** This location. **Listed on:** Privately held. **Annual sales/revenues:** $5 - $10 million. **Number of employees at this location:** 250.

HELMSLEY PARK LANE HOTEL
36 Central Park South, New York NY 10019. 212/371-4000. **Fax:** 212/935-5489. **Contact:** Personnel Department. **World Wide Web address:** http://www.helmsleyhotels.com. **Description:** Operates a 650-room, luxury hotel with a wide range of lodging, lounge, dining, and meeting rooms. **Common positions include:** Blue-Collar Worker Supervisor; Customer Service Representative; Food Service Manager; General Manager; Hotel Manager; Human Resources Manager; Purchasing Agent/Manager. **Corporate headquarters location:** This location. **Parent company:** Helmsley Hotels Group. **Operations at this facility include:** Administration; Sales; Service.

HILTONS OF WESTCHESTER
699 Westchester Avenue, Rye Brook NY 10573. 914/934-2519. **Fax:** 914/939-7374. **Contact:** Human Resources. **World Wide Web address:** http://www.hilton.com. **Description:** Hiltons of Westchester is comprised of two separate Hilton hotels: a 444-room facility in Rye Brook and a 252-room facility in Tarrytown. Founded in 1919. **NOTE:** Entry-level positions, part-time jobs, and second and third shifts are offered. **Common positions include:** Accountant; Administrative Assistant; Assistant Manager; Electrician; Human Resources Manager; Purchasing Agent/Manager; Sales Manager; Sales Representative. **Corporate headquarters location:** Beverly Hills CA. **Other U.S. locations:** Nationwide. **International locations:** Worldwide. **Parent company:** Hilton Hotels Corp. **Listed on:** New York Stock Exchange. **Stock exchange symbol:** HLT. **Annual sales/revenues:** $21 - $50 million. **Number of employees at this location:** 500.

HOTEL INTER-CONTINENTAL NEW YORK
111 East 48th Street, New York NY 10017. 212/755-5900. **Contact:** Human Resources. **World Wide Web address:** http://www.interconti.com. **Description:** A hotel with 682 rooms. **Common positions include:** Administrator; Customer Service Representative; Hotel Manager; Management Trainee; Purchasing Agent/Manager. **Special programs:** Internships. **Corporate headquarters location:** London, England. **Parent company:** Six Continents plc. **Listed on:** New York Stock Exchange. **Stock exchange symbol:** SXC. **Number of employees at this location:** 500.

LOEWS CORPORATION
655 Madison Avenue, 7th Floor, New York NY 10021. 212/521-2000. **Contact:** Human Resources. **E-mail address:** hrmgr@newposition.com. **World Wide Web address:** http://www.loews.com. **Description:** A holding company. **Corporate headquarters location:** This location. **Subsidiaries include:** CNA Financial Corporation, which provides insurance services; Lorillard, Inc., which produces tobacco products; Loews Hotels, which owns and operates a nationwide chain of hotels; Diamond Offshore Drilling, Inc., an offshore drilling company; and Bulova Corporation, which distributes watches and clocks. **Listed on:** New York Stock Exchange. **Stock exchange symbol:** LTR. **Annual sales/revenues:** More than $100 million.

MARRIOTT EASTSIDE

525 Lexington Avenue, New York NY 10017. 212/755-4000. **Contact:** Personnel. **World Wide Web address:** http://www.marriotthotels.com. **Description:** Operates a luxury hotel with 652 guest rooms and dining, meeting, and sales function facilities. **Parent company:** Marriott International, Inc. **Listed on:** New York Stock Exchange. **Stock exchange symbol:** MAR.

NEW HUNTINGTON TOWN HOUSE INC.

124 East Jericho Turnpike, Huntington Station NY 11746. 631/427-8485. **Contact:** Vice President. **Description:** A general service catering company specializing in weddings, organizational functions, bar mitzvahs, anniversaries, and special parties through over 25 area locations including the New York City area. **Corporate headquarters location:** This location.

THE NEW YORK HELMSLEY HOTEL

212 East 42nd Street, New York NY 10017. 212/490-8900. **Contact:** Marilyn O'Brien, Human Resources Director. **World Wide Web address:** http://www.helmsleyhotels.com. **Description:** Operates a 793-room luxury hotel facility with a wide range of lodging, dining, meeting, and other facilities. **Common positions include:** Accountant/Auditor; Department Manager; General Manager; Hotel Manager; Management Trainee; Restaurant/Food Service Manager; Sales Manager. **Parent company:** Helmsley Hotels Group.

PARK CENTRAL HOTEL

870 Seventh Avenue, New York NY 10019-4038. 212/247-8000. **Contact:** Manager of Human Resources Department. **World Wide Web address:** http://www.parkcentralny.com. **Description:** A 1,260-room hotel with restaurant, lounge, banquet, convention, and meeting facilities. **Common positions include:** Accountant/Auditor; Computer Programmer; Customer Service Representative; Electrical/Electronics Engineer; Hotel Manager; Mechanical Engineer; Purchasing Agent/Manager; Sales Executive. **Corporate headquarters location:** Hampton NH. **Parent company:** Omni/Donley Hotel Group. **Operations at this facility include:** Sales; Service.

RENAISSANCE WESTCHESTER HOTEL

80 West Red Oak Lane, White Plains NY 10604. 914/694-5400. **Contact:** Personnel. **World Wide Web address:** http://www.renaissancehotels.com. **Description:** A hotel with 364 guest rooms and 18 meeting rooms. **Parent company:** Marriott International Inc. **Listed on:** New York Stock Exchange. **Stock exchange symbol:** MAR.

RESTAURANT ASSOCIATES CORPORATION

36 West 44th Street, 5th Floor, New York NY 10036. 212/789-7900. **Fax:** 212/789-8196. **Contact:** Manager of Recruitment. **World Wide Web address:** http://www.restaurantassociates.com. **Description:** A broad-based company that operates 60 restaurants in major cities, cultural centers, and leisure attractions along the East Coast. Private food service facilities are also offered to corporations, institutions, and clubs. **Common positions include:** Chef/Cook/Kitchen Worker; Restaurant/Food Service Manager. **Special programs:** Internships. **Corporate headquarters location:** This location. **Operations at this facility include:** Divisional Headquarters.

SARA LEE COFFEE AND TEA
500 Mamaroneck Avenue, 5th floor, Harrison NY 10528. 212/532-0300. **Contact:** Mr. Vince Pellettiere, Recruiting Department Representative. **E-mail address:** recruiting@saralee.com. **World Wide Web address:** http://www.saralee.com. **Description:** Produces a nationally distributed brand of premium coffee. The company also operates a chain of cafes and drive-thru restaurants. **Common positions include:** Accountant/Auditor; Blue-Collar Worker Supervisor; Branch Manager; Computer Programmer; Manufacturer's/Wholesaler's Sales Rep.; Quality Control Supervisor; Restaurant/Food Service Manager; Systems Analyst. **Corporate headquarters location:** Chicago IL. **Other U.S. locations:** Nationwide. **Subsidiaries include:** Cain's Coffee Company; Greenwich Mills Company. **Parent company:** Sara Lee Corporation. **Operations at this facility include:** Administration; Divisional Headquarters; Sales. **Listed on:** New York Stock Exchange. **Stock exchange symbol:** SLE.

STARWOOD HOTELS & RESORTS WORLDWIDE, INC.
1111 Westchester Avenue, White Plains NY 10604. 914/640-8100. **Fax:** 914/640-8310. **Contact:** Human Resources Department. **World Wide Web address:** http://www.starwoodhotels.com. **Description:** Manages and operates hotels under the names Westin, Sheraton, Four Points, St. Regis, and others. **Corporate headquarters location:** This location. **Listed on:** New York Stock Exchange. **Stock exchange symbol:** HOT.

TARRYTOWN HOUSE
East Sunnyside Lane, Tarrytown NY 10591. 914/591-8200. **Contact:** Sue Burnie, Human Resources Director. **Description:** A historic hotel and conference center with 148 guest rooms, 30 meeting rooms, and eight private dining areas. Founded in 1981. **Common positions include:** Account Manager; Account Representative; Accountant/Auditor; Administrative Assistant; Assistant Manager; Chief Financial Officer; Computer Operator; Controller; Customer Service Representative; Finance Director; Financial Analyst; General Manager; Human Resources Manager; Management Trainee; Marketing Manager; Marketing Specialist; Mechanical Engineer; Operations/Production Manager; Purchasing Agent/Manager; Sales Executive; Sales Manager; Sales Representative; Typist/Word Processor. **Special programs:** Internships; Training. **Internship information:** Internships are available year round in sales/marketing, accounting, human resources, operations, and the culinary arts. **Corporate headquarters location:** This location. **Other U.S. locations:** CT; NJ; OR; TX; WA. **International locations:** Canada; France. **Parent company:** Dolce International. **Listed on:** Privately held. **Number of employees at this location:** 235. **Number of employees worldwide:** 2,500.

INSURANCE

You can expect to find the following types of companies in this chapter:

Commercial and Industrial Property/Casualty Insurers • Health Maintenance Organizations (HMOs) • Medical/Life Insurance Companies

AMALGAMATED LIFE INSURANCE COMPANY
730 Broadway, New York NY 10003-9511. 212/473-5700. **Contact:** Human Resources. **E-mail address:** generalinfo@amalgamatedlife.com. **World Wide Web address:** http://www.amalgamatedlife.com. **Description:** A nonprofit insurance firm handling claims service and group medical, life, and health maintenance policies for the national textile workers union. **Common positions include:** Accountant/Auditor; Computer Programmer; Technical Writer/Editor. **Corporate headquarters location:** This location.

AMERICAN INTERNATIONAL GROUP, INC.
70 Pine Street, New York NY 10270. 212/770-7000. **Contact:** Human Resources. **E-mail address:** aig.hr@aig.com. **World Wide Web address:** http://www.aig.com. **Description:** American International Group, Inc. (AIG) is a leading U.S.-based international insurance organization and one of the nation's largest underwriters of commercial and industrial coverage. Member companies write property, casualty, marine, life, and financial services insurance in approximately 130 countries and jurisdictions. The company is also engaged in a broad range of financial businesses. AIG's General Insurance operations group is composed of Domestic General-Brokerage, which markets property and casualty insurance products through brokers to large corporate buyers and other commercial customers; Domestic Personal Lines, which is in the business of U.S. personal lines, principally personal auto; and Foreign General, which comprises AIG's overseas property and casualty operations. **Corporate headquarters location:** This location. **Listed on:** New York Stock Exchange. **Stock exchange symbol:** AIG.

AON RISK SERVICES
685 Third Avenue, New York NY 10017. 212/792-9200. **Contact:** Human Resources Department. **World Wide Web address:** http://www.aon.com. **Description:** An insurance brokerage that specializes in property and casualty insurance. **Corporate headquarters location:** Chicago IL. **Parent company:** Aon Corporation. **Listed on:** New York Stock Exchange. **Stock exchange symbol:** AOC.

ARISTA INSURANCE COMPANY
116 John Street, New York NY 10038. 212/964-2150. **Contact:** Peter Norton, Human Resources Manager. **Description:** Arista Insurance Company is engaged in the sale and underwriting of statutory disability insurance for corporations. **Parent company:** Arista Investor Corporation.

ATLANTIC MUTUAL COMPANIES
140 Broadway, 33rd Floor, New York NY 10005-1101. 212/227-3500. **Contact:** Lisa M. Resciniti, Manager of Human Resources Department. **World Wide Web address:** http://www.atlanticmutual.com. **Description:** Operates two multiple-line insurance companies that write property,

liability, and marine insurance. **Subsidiaries include:** Atlantic Mutual Insurance Company and its wholly-owned subsidiary, Centennial Insurance Company, share the same offices and staff. Services are sold primarily through independent insurance agents and brokers. Another subsidiary is Atlantic Lloyd's Insurance Company of Texas. **Other U.S. locations:** Nationwide. **International locations:** Canada; England.

CNA INSURANCE COMPANIES
40 Wall Street, New York NY 10005. 212/440-3000. **Contact:** Human Resources Manager. **World Wide Web address:** http://www.cna.com. **Description:** A property and casualty insurance writer offering commercial and personal policies.

THE CENTRE GROUP
One Chase Manhattan Plaza, New York NY 10005. 212/898-5300. **Fax:** 212/898-5400. **Contact:** Human Resources Department. **World Wide Web address:** http://www.entercentre.com. **Description:** A reinsurance company that offers finite risk reinsurance, insurance, and financial solutions ranging from workers' compensation and product liability coverage to managed environmental impairment liabilities and post-closure reclamation. **International locations:** Australia; China; France; Ireland; Switzerland; United Kingdom. **Parent company:** Zurich Financial Services Group.

EMPIRE BLUE CROSS AND BLUE SHIELD
11 West 42nd Street, New York NY 10036. 212/476-1000. **Contact:** Staffing. **World Wide Web address:** http://www.empirehealthcare.com. **Description:** A nonprofit health insurance company offering coverage that includes comprehensive hospital, medical, prescription drug, and dental plans, as well as programs supplemental to Medicare. **Corporate headquarters location:** This location.

FIDELITY NATIONAL TITLE INSURANCE COMPANY OF NEW YORK
2 Park Avenue, Suite 300, New York NY 10016. 212/481-5858. **Contact:** Human Resources. **World Wide Web address:** http://www.fntic.com. **Description:** Provides title insurance and escrow services nationwide. **Common positions include:** Accountant/Auditor; Administrator; Attorney; Branch Manager; Computer Programmer; General Manager; Marketing Specialist; Operations/Production Manager; Public Relations Specialist; Services Sales Representative; Systems Analyst; Underwriter/Assistant Underwriter.

FINANCIAL GUARANTY INSURANCE COMPANY
125 Park Avenue, 6th Floor, New York NY 10017. 212/312-3000. **Contact:** Human Resources. **World Wide Web address:** http://www.fgic.com. **Description:** A leading insurer of debt securities. FGIC also guarantees a variety of nonmunicipal structured obligations such as mortgage-backed securities. **Parent company:** General Electric Capital Corporation. **Listed on:** New York Stock Exchange. **Stock exchange symbol:** GE.

FINANCIAL SECURITY ASSURANCE INC.
350 Park Avenue, New York NY 10021. 212/826-0100. **Contact:** Human Resources. **World Wide Web address:** http://www.fsa.com. **Description:** A monoline financial guaranty insurer of municipal bonds and asset-backed securities, including residential mortgage-backed securities. **Other U.S. locations:** CA; TX. **International locations:** France; Spain; United Kingdom. **Parent company:** Financial Security Assurance Holdings Ltd. **Listed on:** New York Stock Exchange. **Stock exchange symbol:** FSA.

FRONTIER INSURANCE GROUP
195 Lake Louise Marie Road, Rock Hill NY 12775-8000. 845/796-2100. **Fax:** 845/796-1925. **Contact:** Human Resources. **World Wide Web address:** http://www.frontier.com. **Description:** Frontier Insurance Group is an underwriter and creator of specialty insurance products. Founded in 1934. **NOTE:** Entry-level positions are offered. **Common positions include:** Accountant/Auditor; Adjuster; Administrative Assistant; Administrative Manager; Attorney; Budget Analyst; Claim Representative; Clerical Supervisor; Computer Operator; Computer Programmer; Controller; Customer Service Representative; Database Manager; Education Administrator; Finance Director; Financial Analyst; Human Resources Manager; Librarian; MIS Specialist; Paralegal; Secretary; Software Engineer; Statistician; Systems Analyst; Typist/Word Processor; Underwriter/Assistant Underwriter. **Special programs:** Internships. **Corporate headquarters location:** This location. **Other U.S. locations:** La Jolla CA; Orlando FL; Atlanta GA; Louisville KY; Charlotte NC; Bedford Hills NY. **Operations at this facility include:** Divisional Headquarters; Regional Headquarters. **Listed on:** New York Stock Exchange. **Stock exchange symbol:** FTR. **Annual sales/revenues:** More than $100 million. **Number of employees at this location:** 430.

GEICO (GOVERNMENT EMPLOYEES INSURANCE COMPANY)
750 Woodbury Road, Woodbury NY 11797. 516/496-5208. **Toll-free phone:** 800/841-3000. **Fax:** 516/496-5769. **Contact:** Human Resources Department. **E-mail address:** jobs@geico.com. **World Wide Web address:** http://www.geico.com. **Description:** A multiple-line property and casualty insurer offering private passenger automobile, homeowners, fire, and extended coverage; professional and comprehensive personal liability; and boat owners insurance. **NOTE:** Entry-level positions are offered. **Common positions include:** Adjuster; Claim Representative; Customer Service Representative; Services Sales Representative. **Corporate headquarters location:** Washington DC. **Other U.S. locations:** Nationwide. **Parent company:** GEICO Corporation. **Operations at this facility include:** Regional Headquarters; Sales; Service. **Listed on:** Privately held. **Number of employees at this location:** 1,800.

GENERALCOLOGNE RE
120 Broadway, 31st Floor, New York NY 10271-0067. 212/341-8000. **Contact:** Human Resources Department. **World Wide Web address:** http://www.gcr.com. **Description:** Provides property and casualty reinsurance to primary insurers on a direct basis. The company markets reinsurance directly to these insurers through its own sales team. Reinsurance is marketed and underwritten on both a treaty and facultative basis. Treaty marketing efforts are focused on small to medium-sized regional and specialty property and casualty insurers. The company does not underwrite businesses that involve aviation, ocean marine, and professional liability. **Corporate headquarters location:** Omaha NE. **Parent company:** Berkshire Hathaway Inc. **Listed on:** New York Stock Exchange. **Stock exchange symbol:** BRK. **Number of employees nationwide:** 240.

GROUP HEALTH INCORPORATED (GHI)
441 Ninth Avenue, New York NY 10001. 212/615-0000. **Fax:** 212/563-8563. **Contact:** Employment Manager. **World Wide Web address:** http://www.ghi.com. **Description:** One of the largest, nonprofit health services corporations operating throughout New York. The company provides insurance benefits and third-party administrative services. Founded in 1937. **Common positions include:** Account Representative; Accountant;

Case Manager; Claim Representative; Customer Service Representative; MIS Specialist; Network/Systems Administrator; Quality Control Supervisor; Systems Manager. **Corporate headquarters location:** This location. **Other area locations:** Albany NY; Buffalo NY; Garden City NY; Long Island NY; Rochester NY; Syracuse NY; Tarrytown NY. **Operations at this facility include:** Administration; Sales; Service. **Number of employees nationwide:** 2,200.

THE GUARDIAN LIFE INSURANCE COMPANY OF AMERICA
7 Hanover Square, New York NY 10004. 212/598-8000. **Contact:** Human Resources. **World Wide Web address:** http://www.glic.com. **Description:** Provides health and life insurance, as well as some financial services. **Corporate headquarters location:** This location.

HEALTH NET OF THE NORTHEAST, INC.
Crosswest Office Center, 399 Knollwood Road, Suite 113, White Plains NY 10603. 888/747-4090. **Contact:** Human Resources Department. **World Wide Web address:** http://www.phshealthplans.com. **Description:** A managed care health insurance company. **NOTE:** Send resumes to One Far Mill Crossing, P.O. Box 904, Shelton CT 06484. 203/381-6400.

HIP HEALTH PLAN OF GREATER NEW YORK
7 West 34th Street, 7th Floor, New York NY 10001-8190. 212/630-5000. **Fax:** 212/630-0060. **Recorded jobline:** 212/630-8300. **Contact:** Human Resources Department. **E-mail address:** career_ops@hipusa.com. **World Wide Web address:** http://www.hipusa.com. **Description:** A health maintenance organization marketing a comprehensive prepaid health plan with care delivered by independent medical groups and coverage provided for hospitalization. **Common positions include:** Accountant/Auditor; Buyer; Claim Representative; Computer Programmer; Customer Service Representative; Department Manager; Financial Analyst; Health Services Manager; Marketing Specialist; Secretary; Services Sales Representative; Systems Analyst. **Corporate headquarters location:** This location. **Number of employees at this location:** 1,000.

JUNIPER GROUP, INC.
111 Great Neck Road, Suite 604, Great Neck NY 11021. 516/829-4670. **Fax:** 516/829-4691. **Contact:** Personnel. **World Wide Web address:** http://www.junipergroup.com. **Description:** Juniper Group operates in two segments: health care and entertainment. The company's principal revenues are generated from health care, which consists of management for hospitals and health care cost containment for health care payers. The entertainment segment acquires and distributes film rights to various media including home video, pay-per-view, pay television, cable television, networks, ad-hoc networks, and independent syndicated television stations. Founded in 1989. **Corporate headquarters location:** This location. **Subsidiaries include:** Juniper Medical Systems, Inc. with subsidiaries that include Diversified Health Affiliates, Inc. and Juniper Healthcare Containment Systems, Inc. Diversified Health Affiliates operates Juniper Group's management business while Juniper Healthcare Containment Systems conducts health care cost containment service operations. **Listed on:** NASDAQ. **Stock exchange symbol:** JUNI.

KEMPER INSURANCE COMPANIES
30 Rockefeller Plaza, 12th Floor, New York NY 10112. 646/710-7000. **Contact:** Human Resources Department. **World Wide Web address:** http://www.kemperinsurance.com. **Description:** Provides a wide range of

commercial and personal property/casualty insurance in the United States and foreign markets. **Common positions include:** Loss Prevention Specialist; Underwriter/Assistant Underwriter. **Corporate headquarters location:** Long Grove IL. **Other U.S. locations:** Nationwide. **Annual sales/revenues:** More than $100 million. **Number of employees at this location:** 250. **Number of employees nationwide:** 9,500.

LAWYERS TITLE INSURANCE CORPORATION
10 Bank Street, Suite 1120, White Plains NY 10606. 914/682-3900. **Contact:** Human Resources Department. **World Wide Web address:** http://www.landam.com. **Description:** Provides title insurance and other real estate-related services on commercial and residential transactions in the United States, Canada, the Bahamas, Puerto Rico, and the U.S. Virgin Islands. Lawyers Title Insurance Corporation also provides search and examination services and closing services for a broad-based customer group that includes lenders, developers, real estate brokers, attorneys, and homebuyers. This location covers New Jersey, New York, and Pennsylvania. Founded in 1925. **Corporate headquarters location:** Richmond VA. **Other U.S. locations:** Pasadena CA; Tampa FL; Chicago IL; Boston MA; Troy MI; Westerville OH; Memphis TN; Dallas TX. **Subsidiaries include:** Datatrace Information Services Company, Inc. (Richmond VA) markets automated public record information for public and private use; Genesis Data Systems, Inc. (Englewood CO) develops and markets computer software tailored specifically to the title industry; and Lawyers Title Exchange Company functions as an intermediary for individual and corporate investors interested in pursuing tax-free property exchanges. **Parent company:** LandAmerica Financial Group, Inc. **Listed on:** New York Stock Exchange. **Stock exchange symbol:** LFG.

LEUCADIA NATIONAL CORPORATION
315 Park Avenue South, New York NY 10010. 212/460-1900. **Contact:** Human Resources. **Description:** Leucadia National is a diversified company with subsidiaries involved in the insurance, manufacturing, banking, investment, and incentive service industries. The insurance business offers property, casualty, and life insurance nationwide. **Corporate headquarters location:** This location. **Subsidiaries include:** Charter, CPL; Empire Group; Intramerica. **Listed on:** New York Stock Exchange. **Stock exchange symbol:** LUK.

LIBERTY INTERNATIONAL UNDERWRITERS
61 Broadway, 25th Floor, New York NY 10006-2802. 212/208-4100. **Contact:** Personnel. **E-mail address:** resume@libertyinternational.com. **World Wide Web address:** http://www.libertyiu.com. **Description:** A property and casualty insurance company with some specialty lines including marine and nonstandard automotive. Founded in 1999. **Parent company:** Liberty Mutual Insurance Company.

LIBERTY MUTUAL INSURANCE GROUP
1133 Avenue of the Americas, 27th Floor, New York NY 10036. 212/391-7500. **Contact:** Human Resources Department. **World Wide Web address:** http://www.libertymutual.com. **Description:** A full-line insurance firm offering life, medical, and business insurance, as well as investment and retirement plans. **Common positions include:** Adjuster; Assistant Manager; Attorney; Branch Manager; Claim Representative; Customer Service Representative; Department Manager; Financial Analyst; Financial Services Sales Representative; Human Resources Manager; Insurance Agent/Broker; Loss Prevention Specialist; Underwriter/Assistant Underwriter. **Special**

programs: Internships. **Corporate headquarters location:** Boston MA. **Operations at this facility include:** Administration; Sales; Service. **Number of employees at this location:** 1,650.

MBIA INSURANCE CORPORATION

113 King Street, Armonk NY 10504. 914/273-4545. **Contact:** Human Resources. **World Wide Web address:** http://www.mbia.com. **Description:** A leading insurer of municipal bonds including new issues and bonds traded in the secondary market. The company also guarantees asset-backed transactions offered by financial institutions and provides investment management services for school districts and municipalities. **Common positions include:** Accountant/Auditor; Administrator; Computer Programmer; Financial Analyst; Marketing Specialist; Public Relations Specialist; Underwriter/Assistant Underwriter. **Corporate headquarters location:** This location. **Other area locations:** New York NY. **Other U.S. locations:** San Francisco CA. **International locations:** Australia; England; France; Japan; Singapore; Spain. **Parent company:** MBIA Inc. **Listed on:** New York Stock Exchange. **Stock exchange symbol:** MBI.

MARSH & McLENNAN COMPANIES, INC.

1166 Avenue of the Americas, New York NY 10036. 212/345-6000. **Contact:** Human Resources Department. **World Wide Web address:** http://www.mmc.com. **Description:** Provides consulting services worldwide through an insurance brokerage and risk management firm, reinsurance intermediary facilities, and a consulting and financial services group, to clients concerned with the management of assets and risks. Specific services include insurance and risk management services, reinsurance, consulting and financial services, merchandising, and investment management. Founded in 1871. **Corporate headquarters location:** This location. **Other U.S. locations:** Nationwide. **International locations:** Worldwide. **Listed on:** New York Stock Exchange. **Stock exchange symbol:** MMC. **Annual sales/revenues:** More than $100 million. **Number of employees worldwide:** 39,000.

METROPOLITAN LIFE INSURANCE COMPANY (METLIFE)

One Madison Avenue, Corporate Staffing Area 1-F, New York NY 10010-3690. 212/578-2211. **Contact:** Corporate Staffing. **World Wide Web address:** http://www.metlife.com. **Description:** A national insurance and financial services company that offers a wide range of individual and group insurance including life, annuity, disability, and mutual finds. **Corporate headquarters location:** This location. **Other U.S. locations:** Nationwide. **Listed on:** New York Stock Exchange. **Stock exchange symbol:** MET. **Number of employees nationwide:** 13,500.

THE MONY GROUP

1740 Broadway, New York NY 10019. 212/708-2000. **Contact:** Human Resources Department. **E-mail address:** monyjobs@mony.com. **World Wide Web address:** http://www.mony.com. **Description:** A mutual life insurer. The MONY Group offers life insurance, disability income, and annuities. The company also operates investment subsidiaries engaged in the management of mutual funds and the distribution of securities. **Special programs:** Internships. **Corporate headquarters location:** This location. **Operations at this facility include:** Administration. **Listed on:** New York Stock Exchange. **Stock exchange symbol:** MNY.

MUTUAL OF AMERICA

320 Park Avenue, New York NY 10022. 212/224-1045. **Fax:** 212/224-2500. **Contact:** Human Resources Department. **World Wide Web address:** http://www.mutualofamerica.com. **Description:** A life insurance company that offers pension plans, tax-deferred annuities, IRAs, deferred compensation plans, individual life insurance and thrift plans, funding agreements, guaranteed interest contracts, group life insurance, and group long-term disability income insurance to nonprofit, tax-exempt employers. Mutual of America also sells 401(k) products nationally. Services include actuarial (annual valuations, cost proposals, and reports to auditors); administrative (preparation of documents, monthly billings, maintenance of employee records, benefit payment services, development of administrative manuals, calculation of benefit estimates, and annual participant benefit statements); assistance with government filings (preparation and release of ERISA Information Bulletins and distribution of employer kits for qualifying pension plans); communications (Mutual of America Report, audio/visual presentations, and annual reports); investments (17 investment funds); and field consulting. **Common positions include:** Accountant/Auditor; Actuary; Claim Representative; Computer Support Technician; Computer Technician; Customer Service Representative; Financial Analyst; Human Resources Manager; Intranet Developer; Management Trainee; Network Engineer; Network/Systems Administrator; Sales Representative; Systems Analyst; Underwriter/Assistant Underwriter. **Corporate headquarters location:** This location. **Other U.S. locations:** Nationwide. **Subsidiaries include:** Capital Management Corporation. **Operations at this facility include:** Administration; Service. **Number of employees at this location:** 650. **Number of employees nationwide:** 1,050.

NATIONAL BENEFIT LIFE INSURANCE COMPANY

333 West 34th Street, 10th Floor, New York NY 10001. 212/615-7500. **Contact:** Human Resources. **Description:** A nationally licensed insurance firm dealing primarily in health and life insurance. **Corporate headquarters location:** This location.

NEW YORK LIFE INSURANCE COMPANY

51 Madison Avenue, Room 151, New York NY 10010. 212/576-7000. **Fax:** 212/447-4292. **Contact:** Employment Department. **World Wide Web address:** http://www.newyorklife.com. **Description:** New York Life Insurance Company, its subsidiaries, and affiliates offer a wide variety of products and services. Services include life, health, and disability insurance; annuities; mutual funds; health care management services; and commercial mortgage financing. The company's Asset Management operation (including pensions, mutual funds, and NYLIFE Securities) is located in Parsippany NJ. Founded in 1845. **NOTE:** In addition to job opportunities offered at the home office and in Parsippany, the company also recruits for sales positions through local offices. **Common positions include:** Accountant/Auditor; Computer Programmer; Customer Service Representative; Financial Analyst. **Corporate headquarters location:** This location. **Other U.S. locations:** Nationwide. **Operations at this facility include:** Administration; Service. **Annual sales/revenues:** More than $100 million. **Number of employees at this location:** 3,500. **Number of employees nationwide:** 7,185.

ONEBEACON INSURANCE GROUP

201 North Service Road, P.O. Box 9088, Melville NY 11747. 631/423-4400. **Contact:** Personnel. **E-mail address:** careers@onebeacon.com. **World Wide Web address:** http://www.onebeacon.com. **Description:** A carrier of property, casualty, and life insurance, licensed in all 50 states, with offices

throughout the country. **Corporate headquarters location:** Boston MA. **Parent company:** White Mountain Insurance Group Ltd. **Listed on:** New York Stock Exchange. **Stock exchange symbol:** WTM.

RADIAN REINSURANCE INC.
335 Madison Avenue, 25th Floor, New York NY 10017. 212/983-3100. **Contact:** Human Resources Department. **World Wide Web address:** http://www.radiangroupinc.com. **Description:** Radian Reinsurance Inc. provides financial guaranty insurance and reinsurance. **Corporate headquarters location:** Philadelphia PA. **Parent company:** Radian Group Inc. **Listed on:** New York Stock Exchange. **Stock exchange symbol:** RDN.

SECURITY MUTUAL LIFE INSURANCE COMPANY OF NEW YORK
P.O. Box 1625, Binghamton NY 13902. 607/723-3551. **Physical address:** 100 Court Street, Binghamton NY 13901. **Contact:** Janet Vanek, Human Resources Director. **World Wide Web address:** http://www.securitymutual-ny.com. **Description:** Provides life insurance.

TIAA-CREF
730 Third Avenue, New York NY 10017-3206. 212/490-9000. **Contact:** Human Resources. **World Wide Web address:** http://www.tiaa-cref.org. **Description:** Provides insurance and investment options for current and retired teachers. **Corporate headquarters location:** This location.

TRANSATLANTIC HOLDINGS, INC.
80 Pine Street, 7th Floor, New York NY 10005. 212/770-2000. **Contact:** Human Resources. **World Wide Web address:** http://www.transre.com. **Description:** An insurance holding company providing property and casualty reinsurance through its subsidiaries. **Subsidiaries include:** Transatlantic Reinsurance Company and Putnam Reinsurance Company provide general liability, fire, inland marine, workers' compensation, automobile liability, and medical malpractice insurance. **Listed on:** New York Stock Exchange. **Stock exchange symbol:** TRH.

UNIVERSAL AMERICAN FINANCIAL CORPORATION
6 International Drive, Suite 190, Rye Brook NY 10573. 914/934-5200. **Contact:** Human Resources. **World Wide Web address:** http://www.uafc.com. **Description:** Underwrites life and accident insurance and health insurance to seniors. **Corporate headquarters location:** This location. **Listed on:** NASDAQ. **Stock exchange symbol:** UHCO. **Annual sales/revenues:** More than $100 million.

WILLIS OF NEW YORK, INC.
7 Hanover Square, New York NY 10004-2594. 212/344-8888. **Contact:** Human Resources. **World Wide Web address:** http://www.willis.com. **Description:** Provides insurance and risk management services to a broad range of commercial clients. Subsidiaries at this location include Willis Corroon Aerospace and Willis Corroon Americas.

LEGAL SERVICES

You can expect to find the following types of companies in this chapter:

Law Firms • Legal Service Agencies

AMERICAN ARBITRATION ASSOCIATION
335 Madison Avenue, 10th Floor, New York NY 10017. 212/716-5800. **Fax:** 212/716-5912. **Contact:** Ms. Morag Rollins, Vice President of Human Resources. **World Wide Web address:** http://www.adr.org. **Description:** A private, nonprofit organization dedicated to establishing and maintaining fair and impartial procedures of dispute resolution as an effective alternative to the court system. The association helps parties with disputes by encouraging them to settle differences through friendly negotiations, mediation, or arbitration. Founded in 1926. **Other U.S. locations:** Nationwide.

CADWALADER WICKERSHAM & TAFT
100 Maiden Lane, New York NY 10038. 212/504-6000. **Contact:** Tracey Breslin, Manager of Human Resources. **E-mail address:** cwtinfo@cwt.com. **World Wide Web address:** http://www.cwt.com. **Description:** A law firm specializing in corporate law, tax, real estate, trusts, and estates. **Other U.S. locations:** Washington DC; Charlotte NC. **International locations:** London, England.

CAHILL GORDON & REINDEL
80 Pine Street, 17th Floor, New York NY 10005-1702. 212/701-3000. **Contact:** Joyce Hilly, Hiring Coordinator. **E-mail address:** jhilly@cahill.com. **World Wide Web address:** http://www.cahill.com. **Description:** A corporate law firm also specializing in real estate, trusts, and estates. **Corporate headquarters location:** This location.

CARTER, LEDYARD & MILBURN
2 Wall Street, New York NY 10005. 212/732-3200. **Contact:** Recruitment Manager. **E-mail address:** info@clm.com. **World Wide Web address:** http://www.clm.com. **Description:** A law firm specializing in business, litigation, real estate, tax, and trust and estate law. **Common positions include:** Attorney; Paralegal. **Other U.S. locations:** Washington DC; New York NY.

CERTILMAN BALIN ADLER & HYMAN, LLP
90 Merrick Avenue, East Meadow NY 11554. 516/296-7000. **Contact:** Personnel. **World Wide Web address:** http://www.certilmanbalin.com. **Description:** A law firm with over 100 attorneys practicing in all areas of law.

COUDERT BROTHERS LLP
1114 Avenue of the Americas, New York NY 10036-7794. 212/626-4400. **Contact:** Mary Simpson, Manager of Human Resources. **World Wide Web address:** http://www.coudert.com. **Description:** A law firm specializing in international business transactions and dispute resolution. **Corporate headquarters location:** This location. **International locations:** Worldwide.

CRAVATH, SWAINE & MOORE

825 Eighth Avenue, New York NY 10019-7475. 212/474-3062. **Fax:** 212/474-3095. **Contact:** Employment. **World Wide Web address:** http://www.cravath.com. **Description:** A corporate law firm specializing in litigation, trusts and estates, and taxation. **Common positions include:** Data Processor; Legal Assistant; Legal Secretary. **Corporate headquarters location:** This location. **Listed on:** Privately held. **Number of employees at this location:** 1,200.

DEBEVOISE & PLIMPTON

919 Third Avenue, New York NY 10022. 212/909-6000. **Contact:** Ethel Leichti, Director of Recruiting. **E-mail address:** recruit@debevoise.com. **World Wide Web address:** http://www.debevoise.com. **Description:** An international law firm specializing in corporate litigation, tax, trust, estates, and real estate law. **Corporate headquarters location:** This location.

DEWEY BALLANTINE LLP

1301 Avenue of the Americas, New York NY 10019. 212/259-7328. **Contact:** William Davis, Recruiting Department. **E-mail address:** nyrecruitment@deweyballantine.com. **World Wide Web address:** http://www.deweyballantine.com. **Description:** An international law firm with a range of law specialties including corporate, estates groups, litigation, real estate, tax, and trust. **Common positions include:** Attorney; Paralegal. **Special programs:** Internships; Summer Jobs. **Corporate headquarters location:** This location. **Other U.S. locations:** Los Angeles CA; Washington DC. **International locations:** Budapest; Hong Kong; London; Prague; Warsaw. **Managing Partner:** Everett Jassy. **Number of employees at this location:** 645. **Number of employees nationwide:** 920. **Number of employees worldwide:** 950.

FRIED, FRANK, HARRIS, SHRIVER & JACOBSON

One New York Plaza, New York NY 10004. 212/859-8000. **Contact:** Gwen Robinson, Human Resources Manager. **World Wide Web address:** http://www.ffhsj.com. **Description:** A law firm specializing in corporate law, litigation, real estate, estates, trusts, and pension. **Common positions include:** Attorney; Paralegal. **Corporate headquarters location:** This location. **Other U.S. locations:** Washington DC. **International locations:** London, England.

KAYE SCHOLER LLP

425 Park Avenue, 12th Floor, New York NY 10022-3598. 212/836-8365. **Fax:** 212/836-8689. **Contact:** Human Resources Representative. **World Wide Web address:** http://www.kayescholer.com. **Description:** A law firm specializing in a variety of areas including corporate, finance, real estate, and tax law. Founded in 1917. **NOTE:** Entry-level positions, part-time jobs, and second and third shifts are offered. **Common positions include:** Accountant; Attorney; Biochemist; Computer Operator; Computer Programmer; Computer Support Technician; Computer Technician; Controller; Database Manager; Finance Director; General Manager; Human Resources Manager; Librarian; Paralegal; Systems Analyst. **Corporate headquarters location:** This location. **Other U.S. locations:** Los Angeles CA; Washington DC; West Palm Beach FL; Chicago IL. **International locations:** China; Germany; United Kingdom. **Operations at this facility include:** Administration. **Listed on:** Privately held. **Number of employees at this location:** 600. **Number of employees nationwide:** 825.

MILBANK, TWEED, HADLEY & McCLOY

One Chase Manhattan Plaza, 56th Floor, New York NY 10005. 212/530-5000. **Fax:** 212/530-0156. **Contact:** Personnel. **E-mail address:** info@milbank.com. **World Wide Web address:** http://www.milbank.com. **Description:** A law firm specializing in litigation, corporate law, trusts and estates, and tax law. **Common positions include:** Accountant/Auditor; Attorney; Computer Programmer; Financial Analyst; Human Resources Manager; Librarian; Library Technician; Operations/Production Manager; Paralegal; Systems Analyst. **Corporate headquarters location:** This location. **Other U.S. locations:** Los Angeles CA; Washington DC. **Operations at this facility include:** Administration; Service. **Number of employees at this location:** 600.

PATTERSON, BELKNAP, WEBB & TYLER LLP

1133 Avenue of the Americas, New York NY 10036. 212/336-2000. **Contact:** Recruiting. **World Wide Web address:** http://www.pbwt.com. **Description:** A law firm. **NOTE:** Jobseekers interested in an attorney's position should contact Ms. Robin Klum, Director of Professional Development. **Common positions include:** Attorney; Paralegal.

PILLSBURY WINTHROP LLP

One Battery Park Plaza, New York NY 10004-1490. 212/858-1000. **Contact:** Human Resources Department. **World Wide Web address:** http://www.pillsburywinthrop.com. **Description:** An international law firm with a broad-based practice including corporate law, litigation, real estate, and tax law. **Corporate headquarters location:** This location.

SIMPSON THATCHER & BARTLETT

425 Lexington Avenue, New York NY 10017-3954. 212/455-2000. **Contact:** Eric Edelson, Director of Human Resources. **Description:** An international corporate law firm. **Corporate headquarters location:** This location.

SQUIRE SANDERS & DEMPSEY

350 Park Avenue, 15th Floor, New York NY 10022-6022. 212/872-9800. **Contact:** Nancy Christopher, Office Manager. **World Wide Web address:** http://www.ssd.com. **Description:** A law firm whose areas of practice include corporate, environmental, and tax law.

WEIL GOTSHAL & MANGES

767 Fifth Avenue, New York NY 10153. 212/310-8000. **Contact:** Pat Bowers, Human Resources Director. **World Wide Web address:** http://www.weil.com. **Description:** A law firm specializing in corporate, real estate, and tax law. **Other U.S. locations:** DC; FL; TX. **International locations:** London, England.

WHITE & CASE LLP

1155 Avenue of the Americas, New York NY 10036-2787. 212/819-8200. **Contact:** Human Resources Director. **World Wide Web address:** http://www.whitecase.com. **Description:** A general law firm specializing in international law, as well as 30 other practice areas.

MANUFACTURING:
MISCELLANEOUS CONSUMER

You can expect to find the following types of companies in this chapter:

Art Supplies • Batteries • Cosmetics and Related Products • Household Appliances and Audio/Video Equipment • Jewelry, Silverware, and Plated Ware • Miscellaneous Household Furniture and Fixtures • Musical Instruments • Tools • Toys and Sporting Goods

ADVANCE INTERNATIONAL INC.
1200 Zerega Avenue, Bronx NY 10462. 718/892-3460. **Contact:** Human Resources. **Description:** Produces, imports, and exports holiday lighting sets, craft items, and other plastic products. **Common positions include:** Collections Agent; Customer Service Representative; Data Entry Clerk. **Corporate headquarters location:** This location. **Operations at this facility include:** Administration; Manufacturing; Sales.

AMERICAN TACK & HARDWARE COMPANY INC.
25 Robert Pitt Drive, Monsey NY 10952. 845/352-2400. **Fax:** 845/425-3554. **Contact:** Human Resources. **Description:** Manufactures a broad range of decorative hardware items. **Common positions include:** Accountant/Auditor; Administrative Manager; Budget Analyst; Buyer; Computer Operator; Computer Programmer; Credit Manager; Customer Service Representative; Designer; Electrician; Financial Manager; Industrial Engineer; Inspector/Tester/Grader; Machinist; Market Research Analyst; Marketing Manager; Mechanical Engineer; Payroll Clerk; Postal Clerk/Mail Carrier; Purchasing Agent/Manager; Quality Control Supervisor; Receptionist; Secretary; Services Sales Representative; Stock Clerk; Systems Analyst; Tool and Die Maker; Truck Driver. **Corporate headquarters location:** This location. **Operations at this facility include:** Administration; Manufacturing; Marketing; Sales. **Number of employees at this location:** 225.

ART LEATHER
GROSS NATIONAL PRODUCT
45-10 94th Street, Elmhurst NY 11373. 718/699-9696. **Fax:** 718/699-9621. **Contact:** Julio C. Barreneche, Human Resources Director. **World Wide Web address:** http://www.artleather.com. **Description:** A manufacturer of photo albums and folios. Partnered with Art Leather, Gross National Product manufactures photo image box display cases. **Common positions include:** Advertising Clerk; Buyer; Civil Engineer; Clerical Supervisor; Computer Programmer; Credit Manager; Customer Service Representative; General Manager; Human Resources Manager; Purchasing Agent/Manager. **Corporate headquarters location:** This location. **Operations at this facility include:** Administration; Manufacturing; Sales; Service. **Number of employees at this location:** 540.

BULOVA CORPORATION
One Bulova Avenue, Woodside NY 11377. 718/204-3384. **Contact:** Human Resources. **World Wide Web address:** http://www.bulova.com. **Description:** Manufactures and sells a wide variety of watches, clocks, and

jewelry for the consumer market. **Common positions include:** Accountant/Auditor; Computer Programmer; Systems Analyst. **Corporate headquarters location:** This location. **Operations at this facility include:** Administration; Divisional Headquarters; Manufacturing; Regional Headquarters; Service. **Number of employees at this location:** 350. **Number of employees nationwide:** 410.

BUTTERICK COMPANY, INC.
11 Penn Plaza, New York NY 10001. 212/465-6800. **Contact:** Human Resources. **World Wide Web address:** http://www.butterick.com. **Description:** Manufactures two lines of clothing patterns for the home sewing market and produces related fashion publications including *Weddings, Butterick Home Catalog, Vogue Patterns Magazine, and Vogue Knitting Magazine.* **Common positions include:** Apparel Worker; Editorial Assistant; Fashion Designer; Human Resources Manager; Public Relations Specialist; Technical Writer/Editor. **Special programs:** Internships. **Corporate headquarters location:** This location. **Operations at this facility include:** Administration; Financial Offices; Research and Development; Sales; Service.

COLGATE-PALMOLIVE COMPANY
300 Park Avenue, New York NY 10022. 212/310-2000. **Contact:** Human Resources. **World Wide Web address:** http://www.colgate.com. **Description:** Colgate-Palmolive Company manufactures and markets a wide variety of products in the United States and around the world in two distinct business segments: Oral, Personal, and Household Care; and Specialty Marketing. Oral, Personal, and Household Care products include toothpastes, oral rinses, toothbrushes, bar and liquid soaps, shampoos, conditioners, deodorants and antiperspirants, baby products, shaving products, laundry and dishwashing detergents, fabric softeners, cleansers and cleaners, and bleach. Specialty Marketing products include pet dietary care products, crystal tableware, and portable fuel for warming food. Principal global trademarks and tradenames include Colgate, Palmolive, Mennen, Ajax, Fab, and Science Diet. **Corporate headquarters location:** This location. **Other U.S. locations:** Kansas City KS; Cambridge MA. **Listed on:** New York Stock Exchange. **Stock exchange symbol:** CL.

COMBE INC.
1101 Westchester Avenue, White Plains NY 10604. 914/694-5454. **Contact:** Employee Relations Manager. **World Wide Web address:** http://www.combe.com. **Description:** A manufacturer of over-the-counter personal care products including hair care and color products, feminine hygiene products, lotions, and creams. Brand names include Just for Men, Odor Eaters, and Sea Bond. Combe also manufactures some dog care and veterinary products.

DEL LABORATORIES, INC.
178 EAB Plaza, West Tower, 8th Floor, Uniondale NY 11556. 516/844-2020. **Fax:** 631/293-7091. **Contact:** Human Resources. **E-mail address:** resume@dellabs.com. **World Wide Web address:** http://www.dellabs.com. **Description:** A fully-integrated manufacturer and marketer of packaged consumer products including cosmetics, toiletries, beauty aids, and proprietary pharmaceuticals. Products are distributed to chain and independent drug stores, mass merchandisers, and supermarkets. Divisions include Commerce Drug Company, Del International, Natural Glow, La Cross, La Salle Laboratories, Nutri-Tonic, Naturistics, Rejuvia, and Sally Hansen. **NOTE:** Entry-level positions and second and third shifts are offered.

Common positions include: Account Manager; Account Representative; Accountant; Administrative Assistant; Advertising Clerk; AS400 Programmer Analyst; Blue-Collar Worker Supervisor; Budget Analyst; Buyer; Chemist; Clerical Supervisor; Computer Operator; Customer Service Representative; Database Administrator; Electrician; Environmental Engineer; Event Planner; Financial Analyst; Graphic Artist; Help-Desk Technician; Industrial Engineer; Internet Services Manager; Intranet Developer; Manufacturing Engineer; Marketing Manager; Media Planner; MIS Specialist; Network/Systems Administrator; Production Manager; Public Relations Specialist; Quality Control Supervisor; Sales Manager; Sales Representative; Secretary; Systems Analyst; Systems Manager; Webmaster; Website Developer. **Corporate headquarters location:** This location. **Other area locations:** Farmingdale NY. **Other U.S. locations:** Rocky Point NC. **Operations at this facility include:** Administration; Divisional Headquarters; Manufacturing; Regional Headquarters; Research and Development; Service. **Listed on:** American Stock Exchange. **Stock exchange symbol:** DLI. **Annual sales/revenues:** More than $100 million.

EMPIRE SCIENTIFIC CORPORATION
87 East Jefryn Boulevard, Deer Park NY 11729. 631/595-9206. **Fax:** 631/595-9093. **Contact:** Personnel. **World Wide Web address:** http://www.empirebat.com. **Description:** Manufactures camcorder batteries and related video accessories. **Common positions include:** Welder. **Corporate headquarters location:** This location.

ESSELTE CORPORATION
48 South Service Road, Suite 400, Melville NY 11747. 516/741-3200. **Fax:** 631/675-3456. **Contact:** Personnel. **World Wide Web address:** http://www.esselte.com. **Description:** Manufactures and distributes filing and marking systems, storage systems, and other office materials. Primary products are paper-based filing products, mainly suspension filing systems. The company operates production and sales facilities in the United States and Canada. **Common positions include:** Accountant/Auditor; Blue-Collar Worker Supervisor; Buyer; Claim Representative; Computer Programmer; Draftsperson; Human Resources Manager; Industrial Designer; Industrial Engineer; Manufacturer's/Wholesaler's Sales Rep.; Marketing Specialist; Mechanical Engineer; Operations/Production Manager. **Special programs:** Internships. **Corporate headquarters location:** This location. **Other U.S. locations:** Moonachie NJ; New York NY. **Parent company:** Esselte AB is a Swedish-based firm engaged in industrial production, trade, and services, primarily in the fields of office equipment, stationery and price marking, custom printing and binding, consumer and transport packaging, textbooks and instructional materials, cartography, publishing, and bookstores. **Operations at this facility include:** Administration; Manufacturing; Research and Development; Sales. **Number of employees worldwide:** 15,000.

THE ESTEE LAUDER COMPANIES INC.
767 Fifth Avenue, New York NY 10153. 212/572-4200. **Contact:** Human Resources. **World Wide Web address:** http://www.elcompanies.com. **Description:** Manufactures, markets, and distributes cosmetics and skin and hair care products. Founded in 1946. **Corporate headquarters location:** This location. **Listed on:** New York Stock Exchange. **Stock exchange symbol:** EL.

EX-CELL HOME FASHIONS INC.
295 Fifth Avenue, Suite 612, New York NY 10016. 212/213-8000. **Contact:** Human Resources. **Description:** Manufactures and distributes home furnishing products including shower curtains, pillows, tablecloths, and bathroom accessories. **Corporate headquarters location:** This location.

4KIDS ENTERTAINMENT, INC.
1414 6th Avenue, New York NY 10019. 212/758-7666. **Fax:** 212/980-0933. **Contact:** Human Resources. **E-mail address:** skeefner@4kidsent.com. **World Wide Web address:** http://www.4kidsentertainmentinc.com. **Description:** A vertically integrated merchandising and entertainment company. 4Kids Entertainment is involved in merchandise licensing, toy design, and TV, movie, and music production. **Corporate headquarters location:** This location. **Subsidiaries include:** 4Kids Productions Inc.; Leisure Concepts UK; Leisure Concepts, Inc.; Technology 4Kids; The Summit Media Group, Inc. **Listed on:** NASDAQ. **Stock exchange symbol:** KIDE.

GARY PLASTIC PACKAGING CORPORATION
1340 Viele Avenue, Bronx NY 10474-7124. 718/893-2200. **Contact:** Mark Varella, Human Resources Director. **World Wide Web address:** http://www.plasticboxes.com. **Description:** Manufactures plastic display and storage boxes for collectibles. Founded in 1963. **Corporate headquarters location:** This location.

GEM ELECTRIC MANUFACTURING COMPANY INC.
20 Commerce Drive, Hauppauge NY 11788. **Contact:** Personnel Department. **Description:** Manufactures electrical wiring devices, fuses, extension cords, and consumer electric products such as Christmas tree lights. **Corporate headquarters location:** This location.

GREAT NECK SAW MANUFACTURERS INC.
165 East Second Street, Mineola NY 11501-3523. 516/746-5352. **Contact:** Mr. Sydney Jacuff, President. **World Wide Web address:** http://www.greatnecksaw.com. **Description:** Manufactures a wide range of consumer and shop-quality hand tools. Founded in 1919. **Corporate headquarters location:** This location.

GRIFFIN CORPORATION
100 Jericho Quadrangle, Jericho NY 11753. 516/938-5544. **Contact:** Personnel Manager. **Description:** Operates through four business segments: Home Furnishings and Furniture-Related Products (bedding products, drapery hardware, and synthetic products); Specialty Hardware (industrial hardware and related components); Electronic Communications Equipment (communication, control, service, and entertainment systems for the aerospace industry); and Other Products (commercial lighting, truck bodies, postal lock boxes, torque converters, and special purpose clutches). **Corporate headquarters location:** This location. **Subsidiaries include:** Buildex Inc.; Lightron Corporation; Telephonics Corporation.

IMPERIAL SCHRADE CORPORATION
7 Schrade Court, P.O. Box 7000, Ellenville NY 12428. 845/647-7600. **Fax:** 845/210-8669. **Contact:** Manager of Human Resources Department. **E-mail address:** hr@schradeknives.com. **World Wide Web address:** http://www.schradeknives.com. **Description:** Produces a large line of sporting knives and cutlery. **NOTE:** Entry-level positions and second and third shifts are offered. **Common positions include:** Account Manager; Account Representative; Accountant; Advertising Executive; Applications

Engineer; Blue-Collar Worker Supervisor; Buyer; Chief Financial Officer; Clerical Supervisor; Computer Programmer; Controller; Cost Estimator; Credit Manager; Database Manager; Design Engineer; Draftsperson; General Manager; Graphic Designer; Human Resources Manager; Industrial Engineer; Industrial Production Manager; Manufacturing Engineer; Marketing Manager; Marketing Specialist; Mechanical Engineer; MIS Specialist; Operations Manager; Production Manager; Project Manager; Purchasing Agent/Manager; Quality Control Supervisor; Registered Nurse; Sales Executive; Sales Manager; Sales Representative; Secretary; Systems Analyst. **Special programs:** Apprenticeships; Co-ops; Summer Jobs. **Corporate headquarters location:** This location. **Listed on:** Privately held. **Annual sales/revenues:** $51 - $100 million. **Number of employees at this location:** 650.

JEAN PHILIPPE FRAGRANCES, INC.
551 Fifth Avenue, Suite 1500, New York NY 10176-0198. 212/983-2640. **Contact:** Human Resources. **Description:** Jean Philippe is a manufacturer and distributor of fragrances, cosmetics, and personal care products including alternative designer fragrances, international moderately priced fragrances, brand-name and licensed fragrances, and mass-market cosmetics. The alternative designer fragrance line consists of over 120 different fragrances, 40 varieties of body sprays, 15 varieties of men's deodorant sticks, and 12 ladies' roll-on deodorants. Brand-name fragrances include Intimate, Chaz, Burberry's, Jordache, and Regine's. Mass-market cosmetics include Cutex nail care and lip color products, Jordache nail care and lip color products, and Aziza eye color products.

KOLMAR LABORATORIES INC.
P.O. Box 1111, Port Jervis NY 12771. 845/856-5311. **Contact:** Human Resources. **World Wide Web address:** http://www.kolmar.com. **Description:** Manufactures all types of color cosmetics for the face, as well as various personal care and beauty items. Kolmar's products include skin care treatments, bath care, and spa items. **Parent company:** Outsourcing Services Group.

LIFETIME HOAN CORPORATION
One Merrick Avenue, Westbury NY 11590. 516/683-6000. **Contact:** Personnel. **World Wide Web address:** http://www.lifetime.hoan.com. **Description:** Lifetime Hoan Corporation designs, markets, and distributes household cutlery, kitchen tools and gadgets, and other houseware products. The company manufactures a variety of carving knives under the Tristar, Old Homestead, and LC Germain brand names. Lifetime Hoan Corporation also produces a deluxe line for Farberware, the cookware company owned by Hanson plc, as well as utensil lines sold under the Disney and Pillsbury names. **Listed on:** NASDAQ. **Stock exchange symbol:** LCUT. **Number of employees at this location:** 285. **Number of employees nationwide:** 445.

MICHAEL ANTHONY JEWELERS, INC.
115 South MacQuesten Parkway, Mount Vernon NY 10550. 914/699-0000. **Contact:** Human Resources. **E-mail address:** recruit@michaelanthony.com. **World Wide Web address:** http://www.michaelanthony.com. **Description:** A designer, manufacturer, and distributor of gold jewelry. The company sells its jewelry directly to retailers, wholesalers, mass merchandisers, discount stores, catalogue distributors, and television home shopping. Michael Anthony Jewelers' largest product line is an extensive selection of gold charms and pendants that include religious symbols; popular sayings

(talking charms); sport themes and team logos; animal motifs; nautical, seashore, western, musical, zodiac, and other thematic figures; initials; and abstract artistic creations. The manufacturing division manufactures gold rope chain and designs gold tubing and bangle blanks used in the production of gold bracelets. The Jardinay product line consists of gold chains, earrings, and watches. **Corporate headquarters location:** This location. **Listed on:** American Stock Exchange. **Stock exchange symbol:** MAJ.

MONARCH LUGGAGE COMPANY INC.
475 Fifth Avenue, 3rd Floor, New York NY 10017. 212/686-6900. **Contact:** Human Resources. **Description:** Manufactures and distributes a wide range of luggage products including briefcases, tote bags, athletic bags, attache cases, and related accessories. **Corporate headquarters location:** This location.

MR. CHRISTMAS INC.
41 Madison Avenue, 38th Floor, New York NY 10010. 212/889-7220. **Contact:** Ms. Joan Gilford, Manager. **World Wide Web address:** http://www.mrchristmas.com. **Description:** Manufactures and imports Christmas items including light sets, artificial Christmas trees, and many other Christmas novelties. **Corporate headquarters location:** This location.

OLYMPUS AMERICA INC.
2 Corporate Center Drive, Melville NY 11747-3157. 631/844-5000. **Contact:** Human Resources. **E-mail address:** staffing@olympus.com. **World Wide Web address:** http://www.olympus.com. **Description:** This location houses administrative offices only. Overall, Olympus America manufactures and markets cameras and imaging equipment as well as a variety of surgical and medical instruments. **Corporate headquarters location:** This location.

PERFECT FIT INDUSTRIES, INC.
261 Fifth Avenue, New York NY 10016. 212/679-6656. **Contact:** Human Resources. **Description:** Manufactures bedding products such as mattress pads, decorative products, and related accessories.

RAND INTERNATIONAL
51 Executive Boulevard, Farmingdale NY 11735. 631/249-6000. **Contact:** Eileen Singer, Director of Human Resources Department. **World Wide Web address:** http://www.randinternational.com. **Description:** Manufactures a complete line of bicycles, from tricycles to racing bikes, for international distribution. **Corporate headquarters location:** This location.

REVLON, INC.
625 Madison Avenue, 8th Floor, New York NY 10022. 212/527-4000. **Contact:** Human Resources. **E-mail address:** jobs.mail@revlon.com. **World Wide Web address:** http://www.revlon.com. **Description:** Manufactures and distributes a line of skin care products, fragrances, and other cosmetics internationally. **Corporate headquarters location:** This location. **Listed on:** New York Stock Exchange. **Stock exchange symbol:** REV.

SIMPLICITY PATTERN COMPANY INC.
2 Park Avenue, 12th Floor, New York NY 10016. 212/372-0500. **Contact:** Personnel Manager. **World Wide Web address:** http://www.simplicity.com. **Description:** A manufacturer of clothing patterns. **Common positions include:** Apparel Worker; Technical Writer/Editor. **Special programs:**

Internships. **Corporate headquarters location:** This location. **Operations at this facility include:** Administration.

STEINWAY & SONS

One Steinway Place, Long Island City NY 11105. 718/721-2600. **Contact:** Michael Anesta, Director of Personnel Department. **World Wide Web address:** http://www.steinway.com. **Description:** A manufacturer and distributor of pianos.

SWANK INC.

90 Park Avenue, 13th Floor, New York NY 10016. 212/867-2600. **Contact:** Office Manager. **Description:** This location houses the executive, national, and international sales offices. Overall, Swank is a manufacturer and distributor of men's and women's jewelry. **Corporate headquarters location:** This location.

UNILEVER CORPORATION

390 Park Avenue, New York NY 10022. 212/888-1260. **Contact:** Human Resources. **World Wide Web address:** http://www.unilever.com. **Description:** An international consumer products firm manufacturing a wide range of soaps, toiletries, and foods. **Corporate headquarters location:** This location. **Parent company:** Unilever NV (Netherlands). **Listed on:** New York Stock Exchange. **Stock exchange symbol:** UN.

VICTORIA & COMPANY

385 Fifth Avenue, 4th Floor, New York NY 10016. 212/725-0600. **Contact:** Office Manager. **Description:** Manufactures costume jewelry. **Corporate headquarters location:** This location.

MANUFACTURING: MISCELLANEOUS INDUSTRIAL

You can expect to find the following types of companies in this chapter:

Ball and Roller Bearings • Commercial Furniture and Fixtures • Fans, Blowers, and Purification Equipment • Industrial Machinery and Equipment • Motors and Generators/Compressors and Engine Parts • Vending Machines

ALLIED DEVICES CORPORATION

P.O. Box 841, Hicksville NY 11802. 516/935-1300. **Physical address:** 325 Duffy Avenue, Hicksville NY 11801. **Contact:** Human Resources Department. **E-mail address:** info@allieddevices.com. **World Wide Web address:** http://www.allieddevices.com. **Description:** Allied Devices is a broad-line manufacturer and distributor of high precision mechanical components used in the manufacture and maintenance of industrial and commercial instruments and equipment. The company's major product groups include precision servo and drivetrain assemblies; instrument related fasteners; gears and gear products; and other components and subassemblies. Allied Devices' customers are primarily original equipment manufacturers. **Listed on:** NASDAQ. **Stock exchange symbol:** ALDV.

AMERICAN FELT & FILTER COMPANY

361 Walsh Avenue, New Windsor NY 12553. 845/561-3560. **Fax:** 845/561-0967. **Contact:** Jack Gibbons, Director of Personnel. **World Wide Web address:** http://www.affco.com. **Description:** Manufactures a line of filter products including bags, cartridges, pressure filters, molded filter media, and nonwoven filter media for air, gas, and liquid filtration. **Common positions include:** Accountant/Auditor; Credit Manager; Customer Service Representative; Electrician; Industrial Engineer; Machinist; Manufacturer's/Wholesaler's Sales Rep.; Market Research Analyst; Marketing Manager; Mechanical Engineer. **Corporate headquarters location:** This location. **Other U.S. locations:** Westerly RI. **Operations at this facility include:** Administration; Manufacturing; Research and Development; Sales. **Number of employees nationwide:** 225.

ARKWIN INDUSTRIES, INC.

686 Main Street, Westbury NY 11590. 516/333-2640. **Contact:** L. Henry, Personnel Manager. **E-mail address:** humanresources@arkwin.com. **World Wide Web address:** http://www.arkwin.com. **Description:** Designs and manufactures fluid power control components, including hydraulics, for a wide range of industries. **Common positions include:** Aerospace Engineer; Blue-Collar Worker Supervisor; Buyer; Computer Programmer; Department Manager; Draftsperson; Human Resources Manager; Industrial Engineer; Management Trainee; Manufacturer's/Wholesaler's Sales Rep.; Marketing Specialist; Mechanical Engineer; Operations/Production Manager; Purchasing Agent/Manager; Statistician; Systems Analyst; Technical Writer/Editor. **Corporate headquarters location:** This location. **Operations at this facility include:** Administration; Manufacturing; Research and Development; Sales; Service.

CVD EQUIPMENT CORPORATION
1881 Lakeland Avenue, Ronkonkoma NY 11779. 631/981-7081. **Contact:** Human Resources. **E-mail address:** hr@cvdequipment.com. **World Wide Web address:** http://www.cvdequipment.com. **Description:** CVD manufactures chemical vapor deposition equipment, customized gas control systems, and hydrogen annealing and brazing furnaces. These products are primarily used to produce semiconductors and other electronic components. **Listed on:** American Stock Exchange. **Stock exchange symbol:** CVV.

CANON U.S.A., INC.
One Canon Plaza, Lake Success NY 11042. 516/328-5050. **Fax:** 516/328-4669. **Contact:** Jennifer Monahan, Human Resources Administrator. **World Wide Web address:** http://www.usa.canon.com. **Description:** A manufacturer of consumer and business imaging systems products including copy machines, facsimiles, printers, computers, cameras, camcorders, broadcasting lenses, and medical equipment. **Common positions include:** Account Representative; Accountant; Administrative Assistant; AS400 Programmer Analyst; Auditor; Computer Operator; Customer Service Representative; Database Manager; Electrical/Electronics Engineer; Event Planner; Human Resources Manager; Market Research Analyst; Marketing Manager; Marketing Specialist; Network/Systems Administrator; Public Relations Specialist; Sales Representative; Secretary; Systems Analyst; Technical Writer/Editor; Transportation/Traffic Specialist. **Special programs:** Internships. **Corporate headquarters location:** This location. **Other U.S. locations:** Nationwide. **International locations:** Worldwide. **Parent company:** Canon Inc. **Listed on:** New York Stock Exchange. **Stock exchange symbol:** CAJ. **Annual sales/revenues:** More than $100 million. **Number of employees at this location:** 800. **Number of employees nationwide:** 12,000.

COX & COMPANY INC.
200 Varick Street, New York NY 10014. 212/366-0200. **Contact:** John Matuzsa, Personnel Director. **E-mail address:** hrresources@coxandco.com. **World Wide Web address:** http://www.coxandco.com. **Description:** Manufactures heating and cooling temperature control systems. **Corporate headquarters location:** This location.

DOVER CORPORATION
280 Park Avenue, Suite 34-W, New York NY 10017. 212/922-1640. **Contact:** Human Resources. **World Wide Web address:** http://www.dovercorporation.com. **Description:** Dover is a diversified producer of specialized industrial equipment and components for the petroleum, aerospace, construction, and electronics markets. Divisions include: Dover Technologies, which manufactures electronic circuitry assembly equipment, radio frequency filters, microwave filters, and other equipment; Dover Resources, which makes pumps, compressors, rods, valves, fittings, liquid filtration systems, and gas nozzles; Dover Industries and Dover Diversified manufacture products such as auto lifts, food preparation equipment, solid waste compaction systems, and electromechanical actuators. **Corporate headquarters location:** This location. **Listed on:** New York Stock Exchange. **Stock exchange symbol:** DOV.

EMBASSY INDUSTRIES, INC.
P&F INDUSTRIES, INC.
300 Smith Street, Farmingdale NY 11735. 631/694-1800. **Contact:** Human Resources. **World Wide Web address:** http://www.embassyind.com. **Description:** A manufacturing firm specializing in the production of portable pneumatic tools, baseboard heating equipment, hardware, and sheet metal contracting. **Corporate headquarters location:** This location. **Other U.S. locations:** Boynton Beach FL; New Hyde Park NY. **Parent company:** P&F Industries, Inc. (also at this location). **Listed on:** NASDAQ. **Stock exchange symbol:** PFIN.

FOSTER WHEELER LTD.
9431 Foster Wheeler Road, Dansville NY 14437. 716/335-3131. **Contact:** Human Resources. **World Wide Web address:** http://www.fwc.com. **Description:** Engaged in three business segments: process plants segment, consisting primarily of the design, engineering, and construction of process plants and fired heaters for oil refiners and chemical producers; a utility and engine segment, consisting primarily of the design and fabrication of steam generators, condensers, feedwater heaters, electrostatic precipitators, and other pollution abatement equipment; and an industrial segment that supplies pressure vessels and internals, electrical copper products, industrial insulation, welding wire, and electrodes. **Corporate headquarters location:** Clinton NJ. **Other U.S. locations:** Nationwide. **International locations:** Worldwide. **Listed on:** New York Stock Exchange. **Stock exchange symbol:** FWC.

GATEWAY COMMUNITY INDUSTRIAL INC.
P.O. Box 5002, Kingston NY 12402. 845/331-1261. **Physical address:** One Amy Kay Parkway, Kingston NY 12401. **Fax:** 845/331-2112. **Contact:** Else Fitzpatrick, Personnel Manager. **World Wide Web address:** http://www.gatewayindustries.org. **Description:** Engaged in the manufacturing, packing, and assembling of various products. **Number of employees at this location:** 1,200.

GENERAL BEARING CORPORATION
44 High Street, West Nyack NY 10994. 845/358-6000. **Fax:** 845/348-9016. **Contact:** Ms. Fran Garner, Director of Human Resources Department. **E-mail address:** fran_garner@gbc.gnrl.com. **World Wide Web address:** http://www.generalbearing.com. **Description:** A manufacturer of ball bearings. **Common positions include:** Accountant/Auditor; Administrator; Advertising Clerk; Computer Programmer; Credit Manager; Customer Service Representative; Draftsperson; General Manager; Industrial Engineer; Management Trainee; Mechanical Engineer; Quality Control Supervisor. **Corporate headquarters location:** This location. **Operations at this facility include:** Manufacturing; Sales. **Listed on:** NASDAQ. **Stock exchange symbol:** GNRL.

GRIFFIN CORPORATION
100 Jericho Quadrangle, Jericho NY 11753. 516/938-5544. **Contact:** Personnel Manager. **Description:** Operates through four business segments: Home Furnishings and Furniture-Related Products (bedding products, drapery hardware, and synthetic products); Specialty Hardware (industrial hardware and related components); Electronic Communications Equipment (communication, control, service, and entertainment systems for the aerospace industry); and Other Products (commercial lighting, truck bodies, postal lock boxes, torque converters, and special purpose clutches).

Corporate headquarters location: This location. **Subsidiaries include:** Buildex Inc.; Lightron Corporation; Telephonics Corporation.

GUSSCO MANUFACTURING INC.
5112 Second Avenue, Brooklyn NY 11232. 718/492-7900. **Contact:** Diane Crosby, Human Resources Manager. **World Wide Web address:** http://www.gussco.com. **Description:** A manufacturer of office filing supplies, cabinets, and systems. **Corporate headquarters location:** This location.

LYNCH INTERACTIVE CORPORATION
401 Theodore Fremd Avenue, Rye NY 10580. 914/921-7601. **Contact:** Manager of Human Resources Department. **World Wide Web address:** http://www.lynchinteractivecorp.com. **Description:** A holding company with subsidiaries involved in multimedia services and manufacturing. **Subsidiaries include:** Telecommunications operations consist of six exchange companies: Western New Mexico Telephone Company (NM); Inter-Community Telephone Company (ND); Cuba City Telephone Exchange Company (WI); Belmont Telephone Company (WI); Bretton Woods Telephone Company (NH); and J.B.N. Telephone Company, Inc. (KS). Services offered include local network, network access, and long distance. Lynch Entertainment Corporation and Lombardo Communications are the general partners of Coronet Communications Company, which owns a CBS-affiliated television station (WHBF-TV) serving Rock Island and Moline IL, and Davenport and Bettendorf IA. Capital Communications Corporation operates WOI-TV, an ABC affiliate broadcasting to Des Moines IA. The Morgan Group Inc. (IN), Lynch Corporation's only service subsidiary, provides services to the manufactured housing and recreational vehicle industries. Lynch Manufacturing Corporation and its subsidiary, Lynch Machinery-Miller Hydro, Inc. (GA), manufacture glass-forming machines and packaging machinery, as well as replacement parts for each. M-tron Industries, Inc. (SD) manufactures, imports, and distributes quartz crystal products and clock oscillator modules used for clocking digital circuits, precision time base references, and frequency- and time-related circuits. Safety Railway Service Corporation and its subsidiary, Entoleter, Inc. (CT), produce various capital equipment including granulators, air scrubbers, and shredders. **Corporate headquarters location:** This location. **Listed on:** American Stock Exchange. **Stock exchange symbol:** LIC. **Number of employees nationwide:** 600.

OTIS ELEVATOR COMPANY
521 Fifth Avenue, 7th Floor, New York NY 10175. 212/557-5700. **Contact:** Human Resources. **World Wide Web address:** http://www.nao.otis.com. **Description:** Produces and distributes a line of elevators and escalators for commercial and industrial use. **Corporate headquarters location:** Farmington CT. **Other U.S. locations:** Nationwide. **Parent company:** United Technologies Corporation. **Listed on:** New York Stock Exchange. **Stock exchange symbol:** UTX.

PALL CORPORATION
2200 Northern Boulevard, East Hills NY 11548-1289. 516/484-5400. **Contact:** Patricia Lowy, Human Resources. **World Wide Web address:** http://www.pall.com. **Description:** Pall Corporation is a leader in filtration technology, specializing in fluid clarification and high-end separation. The company's overall business is organized into three segments: Health Care, Aeropower, and Fluid Processing. **Common positions include:** Accountant/Auditor; Biological Scientist; Biomedical Engineer; Chemist;

Draftsperson; Operations/Production Manager; Public Relations Specialist. **Corporate headquarters location:** This location. **Other area locations:** Cortland NY; Glen Cove NY; Hauppauge NY; Port Washington NY. **Other U.S. locations:** Putnam CT; Fort Myers FL; New Port Richey FL; Pinellas Park FL. **Subsidiaries include:** Pall Gelman Sciences Inc. **Operations at this facility include:** Administration; Manufacturing; Research and Development; Sales. **Listed on:** New York Stock Exchange. **Stock exchange symbol:** PLL. **Number of employees nationwide:** 6,500.

PALL CORPORATION
25 Harbor Park Drive, Port Washington NY 11050. 516/484-3600. **Contact:** Human Resources Department. **World Wide Web address:** http://www.pall.com. **Description:** A world leader in filtration technology, specializing in fluid clarification and high-end separation. The company's overall business is organized into three segments: Health Care, Aeropower, and Fluid Processing. In the fluid clarification market, Pall sells disposable cartridges that fit into filter houses it has sold to clients. In the separations market, the company sells complete systems, which include both semi-permanent filters and systems that regularly consume disposable cartridges. **Corporate headquarters location:** East Hills NY. **Other area locations:** Cortland NY; Glen Cove NY; Hauppauge NY. **Other U.S. locations:** Putnam CT; Fort Myers FL; New Port Richey FL; Pinellas Park FL. **Listed on:** New York Stock Exchange. **Stock exchange symbol:** PLL. **Number of employees nationwide:** 6,500.

PALL CORPORATION
225 Marcus Boulevard, Hauppauge NY 11788. 631/273-0911. **Contact:** Rita DiStephano, Human Resources Director. **World Wide Web address:** http://www.pall.com. **Description:** A world leader in filtration technology, specializing in fluid clarification and high-end separation. The company's overall business is organized into three segments: Health Care, Aeropower, and Fluid Processing. Pall Corporation products offer reliable solutions for customers, whether the client is involved in the beginning, middle, or end process of a project. In the fluid clarification market, Pall sells disposable cartridges that fit into filter houses it has sold to clients. In the separations market, the company sells complete systems, which include both semipermanent filters and systems that regularly consume disposable cartridges. **Corporate headquarters location:** East Hills NY. **Other area locations:** Cortland NY; Port Washington NY. **Other U.S. locations:** Putnam CT; Fort Myers FL; New Port Richey FL; Pinellas Park FL. **Listed on:** New York Stock Exchange. **Stock exchange symbol:** PLL. **Number of employees nationwide:** 6,500.

PARKER HANNIFIN CORPORATION
300 Marcus Boulevard, P.O. Box 9400, Smithtown NY 11787. 631/231-3737. **Contact:** Human Resources Manager. **World Wide Web address:** http://www.parker.com. **Description:** This location manufactures and distributes aerospace instrumentation and equipment including fuel flow instruments. Overall, Parker Hannifin makes motion control products including fluid power systems, electromechanical controls, and related components. The Motion and Control Group makes hydraulic pumps, power units, control valves, accumulators, cylinders, actuators, and automation devices to remove contaminants from air, fuel, oil, water, and other fluids. The Fluid Connectors Group makes connectors, tube and hose fittings, hoses, and couplers that transmit fluid. The Seal Group makes sealing devices, gaskets, and packing that insure leak-proof connections. The Automotive and Refrigeration Groups make components for use in

industrial and automotive air conditioning and refrigeration systems. Principal products of the aerospace segment are hydraulic, pneumatic, and fuel systems and components. **Corporate headquarters location:** Cleveland OH. **Listed on:** New York Stock Exchange. **Stock exchange symbol:** PH.

PRECISION VALVE CORPORATION
700 Nepperhan Avenue, Yonkers NY 10703. 914/969-6500. **Fax:** 914/966-4401. **Contact:** Manager. **E-mail address:** jobs@precision-valve.com. **World Wide Web address:** http://www.precision-valve.com. **Description:** An international manufacturer of aerosol valves. **Common positions include:** Accountant/Auditor; Blue-Collar Worker Supervisor; Buyer; Computer Programmer; Customer Service Representative; Designer; Draftsperson; General Manager; Human Resources Manager; Manufacturer's/Wholesaler's Sales Rep.; Operations/Production Manager; Purchasing Agent/Manager; Quality Control Supervisor; Services Sales Representative; Systems Analyst. **Corporate headquarters location:** This location. **Other U.S. locations:** Greenville SC. **Operations at this facility include:** Administration; Manufacturing; Research and Development; Sales; Service. **Number of employees at this location:** 390. **Number of employees nationwide:** 575.

VAW OF AMERICA INC.
9 Aluminum Drive, P.O. Box 667, Ellenville NY 12428. 845/647-7510. **Contact:** Lois Cronick, Personnel Manager. **World Wide Web address:** http://www.vawusa.com. **Description:** VAW manufactures aluminum extrusions such as pipes, conduits, and ladder steps. Founded in 1966.

VEECO INSTRUMENTS INC.
One Terminal Drive, Plainview NY 11803. 516/349-8300. **Contact:** Human Resources. **World Wide Web address:** http://www.veeco.com. **Description:** Designs, manufactures, markets, and services a broad line of precision ion beam etching and surface measurement systems used to manufacture microelectronic products. Veeco produces and sells its ion beam etching systems under the Microtech brand name. The company also sells leak detection/vacuum equipment, which is used for the precise identification of leaks in sealed components. Leak detectors are used in a broad range of electronics, aerospace, and transportation products, ranging from air conditioning components to fiber-optic cables. Veeco's surface measurement products include surface profilers, atomic force microscopy measurement systems, and X-ray fluorescence thickness measurement systems. **Corporate headquarters location:** This location. **Listed on:** NASDAQ. **Stock exchange symbol:** VECO.

THOMAS C. WILSON, INC.
21-11 44th Avenue, Long Island City NY 11101-5088. 718/729-3360. **Fax:** 718/361-2872. **Contact:** Personnel Department. **World Wide Web address:** http://www.tcwilson.com. **Description:** A manufacturer of tube cleaners and tube expanders for the boiler and condenser industry. **Corporate headquarters location:** This location. **Operations at this facility include:** Manufacturing; Sales.

MINING/GAS/PETROLEUM/ENERGY RELATED

You can expect to find the following types of companies in this chapter:

Anthracite, Coal, and Ore Mining • Mining Machinery and Equipment • Oil and Gas Field Services • Petroleum and Natural Gas

AMERADA HESS CORPORATION
1185 Avenue of the Americas, 38th Floor, New York NY 10036. 212/536-8167. **Fax:** 212/536-8318. **Recorded jobline:** 800/947-HESS. **Contact:** Larry Fox, Director of Human Resources. **World Wide Web address:** http://www.hess.com. **Description:** Extracts, refines, and markets petroleum. **Common positions include:** Accountant/Auditor; Chemical Engineer; Financial Analyst; Manager of Information Systems; Marketing Specialist; Mechanical Engineer; Sales Representative. **Corporate headquarters location:** This location. **Other U.S. locations:** Woodbridge NJ. **International locations:** Worldwide. **Listed on:** New York Stock Exchange. **Stock exchange symbol:** AHC.

BESICORP GROUP INC.
1151 Flatbush Road, Kingston NY 12401. 845/336-7700. **Contact:** Human Resources. **World Wide Web address:** http://www.besicorp.com. **Description:** A leading alternative energy and independent power generation company. **Corporate headquarters location:** This location.

COLUMBIA PROPANE CORPORATION
69 Denton Avenue South, New Hyde Park NY 11040. 516/352-6500. **Contact:** Human Resources Department. **World Wide Web address:** http://www.columbiapropane.com. **Description:** A propane distribution company. **Corporate headquarters location:** Richmond VA. **Parent company:** Columbia Energy Group.

GETTY PETROLEUM MARKETING INC.
1500 Hampstead Turnpike, East Meadow NY 11590. 516/542-4900. **Contact:** Carolann Gaites, Human Resources Manager. **World Wide Web address:** http://www.getty.com. **Description:** A large, independent wholesaler and retailer of gasoline and petroleum products. The company also stores and distributes petroleum and gasoline products. Service stations operate under the names Getty and Power Test. Principal products for resale include gasoline, oil, diesel fuel, and kerosene. **NOTE:** Entry-level positions are offered. **Common positions include:** Accountant/Auditor; Administrative Assistant; Attorney; Computer Programmer; Controller; Human Resources Manager; Real Estate Agent. **Corporate headquarters location:** This location. **Other U.S. locations:** CT; ME; MD; NJ; PA; RI.

SCHLUMBERGER LTD.
153 East 53rd Street, 57th Floor, New York NY 10022. 212/350-9400. **Contact:** Human Resources Department. **World Wide Web address:** http://www.schlumberger.com. **Description:** Schlumberger provides oil field services including logging, testing, seismic, MWD, LWD, drilling, cementing, and stimulation; CAD/CAM; automatic test equipment; electricity, water, and gas metering and measurement; and fuel dispensing and monitoring systems. **NOTE:** Recruiting focuses on recent graduates with B.S., M.S., and Ph.D. degrees. **Other U.S. locations:** Sugar Land TX. **Listed on:** New York Stock Exchange. **Stock exchange symbol:** SLB.

SITHE ENERGIES, INC.

335 Madison Avenue, 28th Floor, New York NY 10017. 212/351-0000. **Contact:** Human Resources. **E-mail address:** info@sithe.com. **World Wide Web address:** http://www.sithe.com. **Description:** Develops, builds, owns, and operates electricity-generating facilities throughout the United States and Canada. Revenues are derived primarily from the sale of electricity produced by natural gas-fired cogeneration plants under long-term agreements with major electric utilities. The company also sells thermal energy to the government, industries, and other users. **International locations:** China; France; Philippines; Thailand.

PAPER AND WOOD PRODUCTS

You can expect to find the following types of companies in this chapter:
Forest and Wood Products and Services • Lumber and Wood Wholesale • Millwork, Plywood, and Structural Members • Paper and Wood Mills

IMPERIAL PAPER BOX CORPORATION

252 Newport Street, Brooklyn NY 11212. 718/346-6100. **Contact:** Steven Sukoff, Human Resources Director. **World Wide Web address:** http://www.imperialpaperbox.com. **Description:** A manufacturer of paper containers including boxes and packaging materials. **Corporate headquarters location:** This location.

INTERNATIONAL PAPER COMPANY

1185 Avenue of the Americas, Suite 1701, New York NY 10036-2601. 212/771-1500. **Contact:** Human Resources Department. **World Wide Web address:** http://www.internationalpaper.com. **Description:** International Paper is one of the world's largest forest products companies, with over 300 locations worldwide. International Paper is a manufacturer of pulp and paper, packaging, and wood products as well as a range of specialty products. Millions of acres of timberland are controlled by International Paper, making it one of the largest private landowners in the United States. The company is organized into five business segments including Printing Papers, in which principal products include uncoated papers, coated papers, bristles, and pulp; Packaging, which includes industrial packaging, consumer packaging, and kraft and specialty papers; Distribution, which includes sales of printing papers, graphic arts equipment and supplies, packaging materials, industrial supplies, and office products; Specialty Products, which includes imaging products, specialty panels, nonwovens, chemicals, and minerals; and Forest Products, including logs and wood products. **Corporate headquarters location:** Stamford CT. **Subsidiaries include:** Champion Papel e Celulose (Brazil); Weldwood of Canada. **Listed on:** New York Stock Exchange. **Stock exchange symbol:** IP. **Number of employees worldwide:** 72,500.

MEADWESTVACO

299 Park Avenue, New York NY 10171. 212/688-5000. **Contact:** Human Resources. **World Wide Web address:** http://www.meadwestvaco.com. **Description:** A producer of paper packaging and specialty chemicals. Worldwide, MeadWestvaco operates 50 facilities including paper and paperboard mills, converting plants, chemical plants, lumber mills, research and development laboratories, and real estate operations. **Common positions include:** Accountant/Auditor; Buyer; Computer Programmer; Designer; Electrician; Financial Analyst; Human Resources Manager; Management Trainee; Marketing Manager; Marketing Specialist; Mechanical Engineer; Production Manager; Purchasing Agent/Manager; Quality Control Supervisor. **Corporate headquarters location:** Stamford CT. **Operations at this facility include:** Administration; Sales. **Listed on:** New York Stock Exchange. **Stock exchange symbol:** MWV. **Number of employees nationwide:** 14,000.

NEW YORK ENVELOPE CORPORATION
29-10 Hunters Point Avenue, Long Island City NY 11101. 718/786-0300.
Contact: Human Resources. **Description:** Manufactures a wide range of envelopes for distribution to wholesalers. **Corporate headquarters location:** This location.

STANDARD FOLDING CARTONS
85th Street & 24th Avenue, Jackson Heights NY 11370. 718/335-5500.
Contact: Human Resources. **Description:** A manufacturer of folding boxes. **Corporate headquarters location:** This location.

PRINTING AND PUBLISHING

You can expect to find the following types of companies in this chapter:

Book, Newspaper, and Periodical Publishers • Commercial Photographers • Commercial Printing Services • Graphic Designers

AOL TIME WARNER, INC.
75 Rockefeller Plaza, New York NY 10019. 212/484-8000. **Contact:** Personnel. **World Wide Web address:** http://www.aoltimewarner.com. **Description:** Publishes and distributes books and magazines including the weekly *Time* magazine. Time Warner also produces, distributes, licenses, and publishes recorded music; owns and administers music copyrights; produces, finances, and distributes motion pictures and television programming; distributes videocassettes; produces and distributes pay television and cable programming; and operates and manages cable television systems. **Corporate headquarters location:** This location. **Listed on:** New York Stock Exchange. **Stock exchange symbol:** AOL.

ADVANCE PUBLICATIONS INC.
950 Fingerboard Road, Staten Island NY 10305. 718/981-1234. **Contact:** Mr. Richard Diamond, Publisher. **World Wide Web address:** http://www.advance.net. **Description:** Publishes the *Staten Island Advance,* a daily local newspaper. The paper has a weekday circulation of 80,000 and a Sunday circulation of 95,000. Founded in 1886. **Corporate headquarters location:** This location. **Parent company:** Newhouse Newspapers Group. **Number of employees at this location:** 450.

AMERICAN BANK NOTE HOLOGRAPHICS, INC.
399 Executive Boulevard, Elmsford NY 10523. 914/592-2355. **Fax:** 914/592-3248. **Contact:** Human Resources. **Description:** One of the world's largest producers of the laser-generated, three-dimensional images that appear on credit cards and products requiring proof of authenticity. **Corporate headquarters location:** This location. **President/CEO:** Kenneth H. Traub.

AMERICAN BIBLE SOCIETY
1865 Broadway, 6th Floor, New York NY 10023. 212/408-1200. **Contact:** Personnel. **World Wide Web address:** http://www.americanbible.org. **Description:** Translates, publishes, and distributes the Bible and portions of the Scriptures, without doctrinal note or comment, in more than 180 nations. Founded in 1816. **Common positions include:** Accountant/Auditor; Administrator; Customer Service Representative; Department Manager; Editor; Financial Analyst; General Manager; Manufacturer's/Wholesaler's Sales Rep.; Operations/Production Manager; Public Relations Specialist; Purchasing Agent/Manager; Secretary; Systems Analyst. **Corporate headquarters location:** This location. **Operations at this facility include:** Administration; Manufacturing; Sales; Service. **Number of employees at this location:** 300.

AMERICAN SOCIETY OF COMPOSERS, AUTHORS & PUBLISHERS (ASCAP)
One Lincoln Plaza, New York NY 10023. 212/595-3050. **Fax:** 212/874-8480. **Contact:** Human Resources Department. **E-mail address:** jobline@ascap.com. **World Wide Web address:** http://www.ascap.com.

Description: An international service organization serving the music, publishing, and other creative industries. The organization provides a wide range of services to members including the supervision and enforcement of copyrights. **Corporate headquarters location:** This location.

APPLIED GRAPHICS TECHNOLOGIES (AGT)/SEVEN
450 West 33rd Street, 11th Floor, New York NY 10001. 212/716-6600. **Contact:** Human Resources Department. **World Wide Web address:** http://www.agt.com. **Description:** Applied Graphics Technologies (AGT)/Seven is one of the largest providers of integrated graphic communications services to advertising agencies, magazine and catalog publishers, and corporate clients in various industries worldwide. The company's services include commercial printing, color separation and retouching, facilities management, photo CD and digital image archiving, electronic imaging services, flexo/packaging services, publication and catalog services, satellite transmission services, creative design services, technical support and training services, and black and white ad production. **Corporate headquarters location:** This location. **Other area locations:** Rochester NY. **Other U.S. locations:** Nationwide. **Listed on:** American Stock Exchange. **Stock exchange symbol:** AGD.

APPLIED GRAPHICS TECHNOLOGIES (AGT)/SEVEN
1775 Broadway, 12th Floor, New York NY 10019. 212/333-4111. **Fax:** 212/333-7921. **Contact:** Human Resources. **World Wide Web address:** http://www.agt.com. **Description:** This location provides publication and catalog services, four-color facsimile or digital transmittal, desktop service bureau, satellite transmission services, and advertising agency services. Overall, Applied Graphics Technologies (AGT)/Seven is one of the largest providers of integrated graphic communications services to advertising agencies, magazine and catalog publishers, and corporate clients in various industries worldwide. The company's services include commercial printing, color separation and retouching, facilities management, photo CD and digital image archiving, electronic imaging services, flexo/packaging services, publication and catalog services, satellite transmission services, creative design services, technical support and training services, and black and white ad production. **NOTE:** All hiring is conducted through the corporate headquarters. Interested jobseekers should address all inquiries to Applied Graphics Technologies/Seven, 450 West 33rd Street, 11th Floor, New York NY 10001. 212/716-6600. **Corporate headquarters location:** New York NY. **Listed on:** American Stock Exchange. **Stock exchange symbol:** AGD.

THE ASSOCIATED PRESS
50 Rockefeller Plaza, 7th Floor, New York NY 10020. 212/621-1500. **Fax:** 212/621-5447. **Contact:** Human Resources. **E-mail address:** apjobs@ap.org. **World Wide Web address:** http://www.ap.org. **Description:** One of the largest independent news-gathering organizations in the world. Founded in 1848. **Corporate headquarters location:** This location. **Other U.S. locations:** Nationwide. **International locations:** Worldwide.

BP INDEPENDENT REPROGRAPHICS
853 Broadway, New York NY 10003. 212/777-1110. **Fax:** 212/777-0880. **Contact:** Ms. Jessie Matias, Manager of Human Resources. **World Wide Web address:** http://www.bpirepro.com. **Description:** Provides blueprinting services, blueprint supplies, printing services, and photo services. **Parent company:** American Reprographics Company (ARC).

BOWNE OF NEW YORK CITY, INC.

345 Hudson Street, 10th Floor, New York NY 10014. 212/924-5500. **Fax:** 212/229-3400. **Contact:** Ellen McLynch, Human Resources Manager. **E-mail address:** jobs.bowne@bowne.com. **World Wide Web address:** http://www.bowne.com. **Description:** Provides nationwide information management and compliance documentation services through principal business segments. Printing activities are divided into four segments: financial, corporate, commercial, and legal printing. Services in the legal printing segment include the typesetting and printing of compliance documentation relating to corporate and municipal financing, mergers, and acquisitions; the dissemination of information by companies through annual and interim reports and proxy material; and the printing of materials unrelated to compliance such as business forms and reports, newsletters, promotional aids, market letters, sales literature, and legal printing products. Founded in 1775. **NOTE:** Entry-level positions and second and third shifts are offered. **Company slogan:** Empowering your information. **Common positions include:** Accountant; Administrative Assistant; Administrative Manager; Advertising Clerk; Applications Engineer; AS400 Programmer Analyst; Computer Operator; Computer Programmer; Controller; Credit Manager; Customer Service Representative; Database Manager; Electrician; Finance Director; Financial Analyst; Fund Manager; Human Resources Manager; Intranet Developer; Marketing Manager; Marketing Specialist; MIS Specialist; Network/Systems Administrator; Operations Manager; Production Manager; Project Manager; Public Relations Specialist; Purchasing Agent/Manager; Quality Control Supervisor; Sales Executive; Sales Manager; Sales Representative; Secretary; Systems Analyst; Systems Manager; Transportation/Traffic Specialist; Typist/Word Processor; Vice President of Sales; Web Advertising Specialist; Website Developer. **Special programs:** Internships; Training; Co-ops; Summer Jobs. **Corporate headquarters location:** This location. **Other U.S. locations:** Nationwide. **International locations:** Worldwide. **Parent company:** Bowne & Company. **Listed on:** New York Stock Exchange. **Stock exchange symbol:** BNE. **CEO:** Robert Johnson. **Annual sales/revenues:** More than $100 million. **Number of employees at this location:** 900. **Number of employees nationwide:** 6,000. **Number of employees worldwide:** 7,800.

BUTTERICK COMPANY, INC.

11 Penn Plaza, New York NY 10001. 212/465-6800. **Contact:** Human Resources. **World Wide Web address:** http://www.butterick.com. **Description:** Manufactures two lines of clothing patterns for the home sewing market and produces related fashion publications including *Weddings, Butterick Home Catalog, Vogue Patterns Magazine, and Vogue Knitting Magazine.* **Common positions include:** Apparel Worker; Editorial Assistant; Fashion Designer; Human Resources Manager; Public Relations Specialist; Technical Writer/Editor. **Special programs:** Internships. **Corporate headquarters location:** This location. **Operations at this facility include:** Administration; Financial Offices; Research and Development; Sales; Service.

CMP MEDIA LLC

600 Community Drive, Manhasset NY 11030. 516/562-5000. **Fax:** 516/562-5564. **Contact:** Human Resources. **World Wide Web address:** http://www.cmp.com. **Description:** Publishes high-tech, computer-related magazines and trade publications. **Common positions include:** Advertising Clerk; Art Director; Artist; Customer Service Representative; Editor; Reporter; Sales Representative; Systems Analyst. **Special programs:** Internships. **Corporate headquarters location:** This location. **Other U.S.**

locations: CA; GA; KS; MA; NH. **Operations at this facility include:** Sales.
Listed on: Privately held. **Number of employees at this location:** 1,000.
Number of employees nationwide: 1,400.

CAMBRIDGE UNIVERSITY PRESS
40 West 20th Street, New York NY 10011-4211. 212/924-3900. **Contact:**
Carol New, Personnel Director. **E-mail address:** jobs@cup.org. **World Wide
Web address:** http://www.cup.org. **Description:** Cambridge University Press
publishes an average of 1,300 nonfiction books a year.

CONDE NAST PUBLICATIONS INC.
4 Times Square, New York NY 10036. 212/286-2860. **Contact:** Human
Resources. **World Wide Web address:** http://www.condenast.com.
Description: Publishes a broad range of nationally distributed magazines
including *Mademoiselle, Glamour, House & Garden, Vogue, Self,* and
Gentleman's Quarterly.

DSA COMMUNITY PUBLISHING
250 Miller Place, Hicksville NY 11801. 516/393-9300. **Contact:** Human
Resources. **World Wide Web address:** http://www.dsapub.com.
Description: A regional publisher involved in the publishing, printing, and
distribution of weekly free-circulation newspapers, as well as circulars and
other promotional and printed material. DSA's publications include *The
Pennysaver, Shoppers Guide, Yankee Trader, Marketeer, Pocket Mailer,* and
Value Mailer. **Common positions include:** Account Representative;
Accountant/Auditor; Advertising Clerk; Blue-Collar Worker Supervisor;
Commercial Artist; Computer Programmer; Customer Service
Representative; Department Manager; General Manager; Marketing
Manager; Operations/Production Manager; Printing Press Operator;
Promotion Manager; Telemarketer. **Corporate headquarters location:** This
location. **Operations at this facility include:** Administration; Manufacturing;
Sales; Service.

DOW JONES & COMPANY, INC.
World Financial Center, 12th Floor, 200 Liberty Street, New York NY
10281. 212/416-2000. **Contact:** Human Resources Department. **E-mail
address:** djcareers@dowjones.com. **World Wide Web address:**
http://www.dowjones.com. **Description:** A highly diversified publishing
and communications firm. Publishing operations include *The Wall Street
Journal,* an international business daily newspaper; *The Asian Wall Street
Journal;* and the weekly investor's newspaper, *Barron's.* The company offers
a wide range of information services including an online library of news
and financial information, an online sports information service, a real-time
financial market data service, and a newswire service. **NOTE:** This building
is currently under repair. Interested jobseekers should send resumes to P.O.
Box 300, Princeton NJ 08543-0300. **Corporate headquarters location:** This
location. **Other U.S. locations:** Nationwide. **Listed on:** New York Stock
Exchange. **Stock exchange symbol:** DJ.

FACTS ON FILE, INC.
132 West 31st Street, 17th Floor, New York NY 10001. 212/967-8800.
Contact: Human Resources Department. **World Wide Web address:**
http://www.factsonfile.com. **Description:** Facts on File is a reference book
publisher that specializes in books for public and school libraries.

FAIRCHILD PUBLICATIONS, INC.

7 West 34th Street, 6th Floor, New York NY 10001. 212/630-4300. **Contact:** Human Resources Department. **World Wide Web address:** http://www.fairchildpub.com. **Description:** A business and professional publisher. Fairchild Publications' primary focus is on the fashion industry. **Common positions include:** Accountant/Auditor; Advertising Clerk; Designer; Editor; Reporter. **Special programs:** Internships. **Corporate headquarters location:** This location. **Other U.S. locations:** Los Angeles CA; Washington DC; Chicago IL; Boston MA; Dallas TX. **Operations at this facility include:** Administration; Divisional Headquarters; Sales. **Number of employees at this location:** 550. **Number of employees nationwide:** 750.

FARRAR, STRAUS AND GIROUX

19 Union Square West, New York NY 10003. 212/741-6900. **Contact:** Peggy Miller, Human Resources Manager. **World Wide Web address:** http://www.fsgbooks.com. **Description:** Farrar, Straus and Giroux is a general trade book publisher. Founded in 1946.

FORBES INC.

60 Fifth Avenue, New York NY 10011. 212/620-2200. **Contact:** Human Resources. **World Wide Web address:** http://www.forbes.com. **Description:** One of the nation's leading book and magazine publishers. **Common positions include:** Accountant/Auditor; Advertising Clerk; Editor. **Special programs:** Internships. **Corporate headquarters location:** This location. **Operations at this facility include:** Administration; Divisional Headquarters; Sales. **Number of employees at this location:** 450.

SAMUEL FRENCH INC.

45 West 25th Street, 2nd Floor, New York NY 10010-2751. 212/206-8990. **Fax:** 212/206-1429. **Contact:** Ms. Alleen Hussung, Personnel Director. **World Wide Web address:** http://www.samuelfrench.com. **Description:** A publishing firm engaged in the production and distribution of plays and books relating to the theater. **Other U.S. locations:** Hollywood CA. **International locations:** Toronto, Canada; London, England.

GANNETT COMPANY, INC.

535 Madison Avenue, New York NY 10022. 212/715-5300. **Contact:** Human Resources. **World Wide Web address:** http://www.gannett.com. **Description:** Gannett Company, Inc. is one of the largest news and information organizations in the United States. Gannett Company is involved in newspaper publishing, radio and television broadcasting, cable television, television entertainment programming, and outdoor advertising. The company owns and operates 15 television stations, 7 FM radio stations, and 6 AM radio stations. The company's cable division provides service to 458,000 subscribers. Gannett Outdoor Advertising operates in 19 major U.S. markets, as well as in Canada. The company has also diversified into areas such as alarm security services; commercial printing; data services; marketing; news programming; and newswire service, with operations in 44 states, as well as Washington DC, Canada, Guam, and the U.S. Virgin Islands. Average circulation of Gannett's 92 U.S. daily and nondaily newspapers and publications is approximately 6.6 million. Founded in 1906. **Common positions include:** Accountant/Auditor; Administrative Manager; Advertising Clerk; Advertising Manager; Editor; Financial Analyst; General Manager; Market Research Analyst; Radio/TV Announcer/Broadcaster; Reporter; Services Sales Representative; Systems Analyst. **Corporate headquarters location:** McLean VA. **Other U.S. locations:** CA; CO; CT; MI; MO; NJ; NC; TX. **International locations:**

Canada. **Operations at this facility include:** Administration; Divisional Headquarters; Sales. **Listed on:** New York Stock Exchange. **Stock exchange symbol:** GCI. **Annual sales/revenues:** $51 - $100 million. **Number of employees at this location:** 250. **Number of employees nationwide:** 40,000.

GARLAND PUBLISHING
29 West 35th Street, 10th Floor, New York NY 10001. 917/351-7100. **Contact:** Human Resources Department. **World Wide Web address:** http://www.garlandpub.com. **Description:** Publishes scholarly books in the areas of science textbooks, literary manuscripts, architecture, music, and encyclopedias. **Parent company:** Taylor & Francis Group.

GENERAL MEDIA, INC.
11 Penn Plaza, 12th Floor, New York NY 10001. 212/702-6000. **Contact:** Human Resources. **Description:** Engaged in the publication and sale of men's and automotive magazines and produces various entertainment products. The publishing segment publishes *Penthouse* magazine and six other affiliated men's magazines. The company also publishes four domestic automotive titles, *Four Wheeler, Stock Car, Open Wheel*, and *Super Stock and Drag Illustrated*, that have a combined average monthly circulation of approximately 700,000 copies. The entertainment segment produces a number of adult-oriented entertainment products including pay-per-call telephone lines, videocassettes, pay-per-view programming, and CD-ROM interactive products. **Number of employees nationwide:** 250.

GOLDEN BOOKS, INC.
888 Seventh Avenue, New York NY 10106. 212/547-6700. **Contact:** Manager of Human Resources Department. **World Wide Web address:** http://www.randomhouse.com/golden. **Description:** A publisher of children's books and family entertainment products. Titles include *The Poky Little Puppy, Pat the Bunny*, and *Little LuLu*. **Parent company:** Random House, Inc.

HARCOURT
15 East 26th Street, New York NY 10010. 212/592-1000. **Contact:** Human Resources. **World Wide Web address:** http://www.harcourt.com. **Description:** A publishing company. The operations are divided into Elementary and Secondary Education, and University and Professional Education. Elementary and Secondary Education publishes textbooks and other instructional materials, publishes and scores achievement and aptitude tests, and manufactures and markets school and office supplies and equipment. University and Professional Education publishes textbooks and other instructional materials for higher education, scientific and medical books and journals, and general fiction and nonfiction; publishes books and conducts courses and seminars for law, accounting, and business; and provides outplacement counseling services. **Corporate headquarters location:** Orlando FL.

HARPERCOLLINS PUBLISHERS
10 East 53rd Street, New York NY 10022. 212/207-7000. **Contact:** Human Resources. **World Wide Web address:** http://www.harpercollins.com. **Description:** HarperCollins Publishers is one of the largest book publishers in the world. Titles include fiction, nonfiction, and children's books. **Corporate headquarters location:** This location. **Other U.S. locations:** San Francisco CA. **Parent company:** News Corporation. **Number of employees at this location:** 600.

HEARST PUBLICATIONS
224 West 57th Street, 10th Floor, New York NY 10019. 212/649-2000. **Contact:** Human Resources. **E-mail address:** hearstmagazines@hearst.com. **World Wide Web address:** http://www.hearst.com. **Description:** Operates a book and business publishing group, which includes the William Morrow publishing line. As a broadcaster, the company operates television stations and Hearst Broadcasting Productions. The broadcasting group also runs six radio stations. The company's Newspaper Group publishes 12 newspapers around the country in major markets. The Newspaper Group also operates the Associated Publishing Company, an independent Yellow Pages directory publisher. The company also publishes popular magazines including *Cosmopolitan, Country Living,* and *Redbook.* The New Media Group is actively developing products for CD-ROM and online distribution. Hearst's Entertainment and Syndication operations produce movies, animated shows, documentaries, and syndicates pieces for newspapers. Hearst also is a part owner of both the A&E and Lifetime Television cable channels. **NOTE:** E-mail address is for resume submissions only.

HIPPOCRENE BOOKS INC.
171 Madison Avenue, Suite 1602, New York NY 10016. 212/685-4371. **Contact:** Human Resources Department. **World Wide Web address:** http://www.hippocrenebooks.com. **Description:** Publishes foreign language dictionaries, ethnic cookbooks, Jewish and Polish interest books, and military history books.

LEBHAR-FRIEDMAN INC.
425 Park Avenue, 5th Floor, New York NY 10022. 212/756-5000. **Contact:** Human Resources Department. **E-mail address:** info@lf.com. **World Wide Web address:** http://www.lf.com. **Description:** A publisher of retail business publications including newspapers, magazines, and retail directories. **Common positions include:** Advertising Executive; Editor; Reporter; Secretary; Telemarketer. **Corporate headquarters location:** This location.

LIPPINCOTT WILLIAMS & WILKINS
345 Hudson Street, 16th Floor, New York NY 10014. 212/886-1200. **Contact:** Human Resources Department. **World Wide Web address:** http://www.lww.com. **Description:** Publishes the *American Journal of Nursing.* **Common positions include:** Customer Service Representative; Editor; Human Resources Manager; Librarian; Reporter; Technical Writer/Editor. **Other U.S. locations:** MD; PA. **International locations:** Australia; China; United Kingdom. **Operations at this facility include:** Administration; Sales; Service. **Number of employees at this location:** 75.

MARCEL DEKKER, INC.
270 Madison Avenue, New York NY 10016-0602. 212/696-9000. **Fax:** 212/685-4540. **Contact:** Jennifer Foo, Human Resources Recruiter. **World Wide Web address:** http://www.dekker.com. **Description:** An international publisher of scientific, technological, and medical books, journals, and encyclopedias in the following fields: agriculture; biology; food science; chemistry; engineering; environmental science and pollution control; library information science and technology; material science and physics; mathematics; statistics; medicine; social science; business and economics; packaging and converting; and technology. Marcel Dekker distributes to libraries, societies, public institutions, hospitals, colleges, universities, and professionals. **Common positions include:** Accountant; Acquisitions Editor; Administrative Assistant; Designer; Editorial Assistant; Financial Analyst;

Production Editor. **Corporate headquarters location:** This location. **Other area locations:** Monticello NY. **International locations:** Switzerland.

MARVEL ENTERPRISES
10 East 40th Street, 9th Floor, New York NY 10016. 212/576-4000. **Contact:** Human Resources Department. **World Wide Web address:** http://www.marvel.com. **Description:** Marvel Enterprises is a youth entertainment company. Operations and products include Marvel Comics, one of the largest comic book publishers in North America; Marvel character-based consumer products licensing; Fleer, a marketer of sports picture cards; Dubble Bubble confectionery products; and ToyBiz. **Corporate headquarters location:** This location. **Listed on:** New York Stock Exchange. **Stock exchange symbol:** MVL. **Number of employees at this location:** 775. **Number of employees nationwide:** 1,600.

THE McGRAW-HILL COMPANIES, INC.
1221 Avenue of the Americas, New York NY 10020. 212/512-2000. **Contact:** Human Resources Department. **World Wide Web address:** http://www.mcgraw-hill.com. **Description:** McGraw-Hill is a provider of information and services through books, magazines, newsletters, software, CD-ROMs, and online data, fax, and TV broadcasting services. The company operates four network-affiliated TV stations and also publishes Business Week magazine and books for the college, medical, international, legal, and professional markets. McGraw-Hill also offers financial services including Standard & Poor's, commodity items, and international and logistics management products and services. **Corporate headquarters location:** This location. **Listed on:** New York Stock Exchange. **Stock exchange symbol:** MHP. **Annual sales/revenues:** More than $100 million.

METRO CREATIVE GRAPHICS
519 Eighth Avenue, 18th Floor, New York NY 10018. 212/947-5100. **Fax:** 212/967-4602. **Contact:** Human Resources Department. **World Wide Web address:** http://www.metrocreativegraphics.com. **Description:** Provides camera-ready graphics, editorial, and professional production services to the newspaper and graphic communication industries. **NOTE:** When submitting a resume, computer illustrators and artists should include nonreturnable samples of computer artwork. Some testing may be required. **Common positions include:** Computer Graphics Specialist; Copywriter; Customer Service Representative; Editor; Human Resources Manager; Sales Representative. **Corporate headquarters location:** This location. **Operations at this facility include:** Administration; Divisional Headquarters; Regional Headquarters; Research and Development; Sales; Service. **Number of employees at this location:** 60.

NYP HOLDINGS, INC.
1211 Sixth Avenue, 10th Floor, New York NY 10036-8790. 212/930-8500. **Contact:** Human Resources Department. **World Wide Web address:** http://www.nypostonline.com. **Description:** Publishes the New York Post newspaper. **Common positions include:** Accountant/Auditor; Advertising Clerk; Computer Programmer; Credit Manager; Customer Service Representative; Editor; Financial Analyst; General Manager; Human Resources Manager; Librarian; Reporter; Services Sales Representative; Systems Analyst. **Special programs:** Internships. **Parent company:** News America. **Operations at this facility include:** Administration; Divisional Headquarters; Research and Development; Sales. **Number of employees at this location:** 710.

NATIONAL REVIEW INC.
215 Lexington Avenue, 4th Floor, New York NY 10016. 212/679-7330. **Contact:** Theresa Maloney, Circulation Director. **World Wide Web address:** http://www.nationalreview.com. **Description:** Publishes a nationally distributed conservative magazine focusing on current political issues. **Common positions include:** Editor; Reporter. **Corporate headquarters location:** This location.

THE NEW AMERICAN
THE DAILY CHALLENGE
1195 Atlantic Avenue, Brooklyn NY 11216. 718/636-9500. **Contact:** Thomas H. Watkins, Publisher. **Description:** Publishes a nationally distributed, weekly newspaper (circulation of 130,000) primarily covering cultural, political, and social news of interest to African Americans. **Common positions include:** Accountant/Auditor; Administrator; Advertising Clerk; Computer Programmer; Editor; Human Resources Manager; Management Trainee; Marketing Specialist; Operations/Production Manager; Public Relations Specialist; Reporter; Sales Executive. **Special programs:** Internships. **Corporate headquarters location:** This location. **Operations at this facility include:** Administration; Divisional Headquarters; Regional Headquarters; Research and Development; Sales; Service.

NEW YORK MAGAZINE
444 Madison Avenue, 14th Floor, New York NY 10022. 212/508-0700. **Contact:** Human Resources Department. **World Wide Web address:** http://www.newyorkmetro.com. **Description:** Publishes a features-oriented weekly magazine, with primary emphasis on stories of interest to New York City residents.

NEW YORK TIMES COMPANY
229 West 43rd Street, New York NY 10036. 212/556-1234. **Contact:** Human Resources. **World Wide Web address:** http://www.nytco.com. **Description:** Publishes *The New York Times*, one of the largest newspapers in the world (daily circulation exceeds 887,000 weekdays and 1.4 million on Sundays). In addition to *The New York Times*, this diversified, publicly-owned communications firm publishes 30 dailies and weeklies in various cities; publishes three national magazines; and owns and operates three television stations, two radio stations, and a cable television system. The company also publishes syndicated news and features worldwide. The company also has interests in paper and newsprint manufacturing mills, and a partial interest in *the International Herald Tribune*. Newspaper subsidiaries are located throughout the country and have an average daily circulation of 272,000. **Corporate headquarters location:** This location. **Listed on:** New York Stock Exchange. **Stock exchange symbol:** NYT.

NEWSDAY, INC.
235 Pinelawn Road, Melville NY 11747. 631/843-3561. **Fax:** 631/843-4183. **Contact:** Employment Services. **E-mail address:** jobs@newsday.com. **World Wide Web address:** http://www.newsday.com. **Description:** One of the largest daily newspapers in the United States with a circulation of 750,000. **Common positions include:** Accountant/Auditor; Advertising Clerk; Budget Analyst; Buyer; Clerical Supervisor; Computer Programmer; Customer Service Representative; Editor; Human Resources Manager; Librarian; Operations/Production Manager; Public Relations Specialist; Reporter; Systems Analyst; Technical Writer/Editor; Transportation/Traffic Specialist. **Special programs:** Internships. **Corporate headquarters location:**

This location. **Operations at this facility include:** Administration; Divisional Headquarters; Manufacturing; Sales; Service. **Number of employees at this location:** 3,400.

NEWSWEEK MAGAZINE
251 West 57th Street, New York NY 10019. 212/445-4000. **Fax:** 212/445-4575. **Contact:** Human Resources Department. **World Wide Web address:** http://www.newsweek.com. **Description:** One of the most comprehensive weekly news magazines in the world. The company operates a global network of more than 60 correspondents and numerous stringers, reporting on important developments in politics, national and international affairs, business, technology, science, lifestyles, society, and the arts. In addition to its English language editions, the company also publishes two foreign language editions: *Newsweek Nihon Ban* in Japanese, and *Newsweek Hanuk Pan* in Korean and operates 23 bureaus throughout the United States and abroad. Weekly circulation is more than 4 million internationally, and more than 3 million in the United States. Founded in 1933. **Common positions include:** Art Director; Customer Service Representative; Editor; Marketing Specialist; Reporter; Sales Executive; Writer. **Corporate headquarters location:** This location. **Parent company:** The Washington Post Company. **Listed on:** New York Stock Exchange. **Stock exchange symbol:** WPO.

NOTICIAS DEL MUNDO
38-42 9th Street, Long Island City NY 11101. 718/786-4343. **Contact:** Maria Perez, Human Resources Director. **Description:** Publishes a daily Spanish newspaper. **NOTE:** Entry-level positions and part-time jobs are offered. **Common positions include:** Account Manager; Account Representative; Administrative Assistant; Editor; Graphic Artist; Graphic Designer; Managing Editor; Reporter; Sales Executive; Sales Manager; Sales Representative; Systems Manager. **Special programs:** Internships; Apprenticeships. **Corporate headquarters location:** This location. **Parent company:** News World Communications Inc. **Operations at this facility include:** Administration; Regional Headquarters; Sales; Service. **Listed on:** Privately held. **President:** Phillip V. Sanchez. **Information Systems Manager:** Hildegard Gudmundsen. **Sales Manager:** Hugo Lembert. **Annual sales/revenues:** Less than $5 million. **Number of employees at this location:** 60.

OXFORD UNIVERSITY PRESS
198 Madison Avenue, New York NY 10016-4314. 212/726-6000. **Contact:** Helene Klappert, Personnel Director. **World Wide Web address:** http://www.oup-usa.org. **Description:** Publishes a diverse line of scholarly books.

PARADE PUBLICATIONS INC.
711 Third Avenue, New York NY 10017. 212/450-7000. **Fax:** 212/450-7200. **Contact:** Carol Unger, Vice President/Director of Human Resources. **E-mail address:** carol_unger@parade.com. **World Wide Web address:** http://www.parade.com. **Description:** Publishes weekly magazines, including *Parade* and *React*. **Common positions include:** Support Personnel. **Corporate headquarters location:** This location. **Operations at this facility include:** Administration; Manufacturing; Sales; Service. **Listed on:** Privately held. **Number of employees at this location:** 200.

PENGUIN PUTNAM INC.

375 Hudson Street, New York NY 10014. 212/366-2000. **Fax:** 212/366-2930. **Contact:** Personnel. **E-mail address:** jobs@penguinputnam.com. **World Wide Web address:** http://www.penguinputnam.com. **Description:** One of the nation's largest publishers of trade fiction books. Penguin Putnam is a division of Penguin Group. **NOTE:** Entry-level positions are offered. **Common positions include:** Account Manager; Administrative Assistant; Budget Analyst; Computer Support Technician; Computer Technician; Desktop Publishing Specialist; Editor; Editorial Assistant; Financial Analyst; Graphic Artist; Graphic Designer; Help-Desk Technician; Human Resources Manager; Managing Editor; Marketing Manager; MIS Specialist; Operations Manager; Public Relations Specialist; Sales Manager; Sales Representative. **Special programs:** Internships. **Internship information:** Internship candidates should send resumes to the attention of Iris Milstein in Human Resources. **Corporate headquarters location:** This location. **International locations:** Worldwide. **Parent company:** Pearson plc. is an international media group whose subsidiaries include Penguin Group. **Listed on:** New York Stock Exchange. **Stock exchange symbol:** PSO.

RANDOM HOUSE, INC.

299 Park Avenue, New York NY 10171. 212/751-2600. **Fax:** 212/572-2502. **Contact:** Staffing Department. **World Wide Web address:** http://www.randomhouse.com. **Description:** One of the largest trade publishers in the United States. Trade divisions include Villard Books, Vintage, Times Books, Pantheon/Schocken, and Knopf. Crown Publishing Group includes Crown Adult Books, Clarkson N. Potter, Fodor's Travel Guides, and Orion Books. Ballantine, Fawcett, Del Rey, and Ivy are mass-market imprints. **Common positions include:** Editor; Editorial Assistant; Financial Analyst; Graphic Artist; Graphic Designer; Managing Editor; Marketing Specialist; Public Relations Specialist; Sales Representative. **Corporate headquarters location:** This location. **Other U.S. locations:** Chicago IL; Westminster MD. **International locations:** Worldwide. **Parent company:** Bertelsmann, AG. **Listed on:** Privately held. **Number of employees at this location:** 900. **Number of employees nationwide:** 1,200.

THE READER'S DIGEST ASSOCIATION, INC.

Reader's Digest Road, Pleasantville NY 10570. 914/238-1000. **Contact:** Human Resources Department. **World Wide Web address:** http://www.readersdigest.com. **Description:** A publisher of magazines, books, music, and video products. The flagship publication, *Reader's Digest*, is a monthly general interest magazine published in 17 languages with a circulation of approximately 100 million worldwide. Special interest magazines include *American Woodworker*, *The Family Handyman*, *New Choices*, and *Walking*. **Common positions include:** Accountant/Auditor; Budget Analyst; Computer Programmer; Customer Service Representative; Designer; Economist; Editor; Financial Analyst; General Manager; Human Resources Manager; Management Analyst/Consultant; Public Relations Specialist; Purchasing Agent/Manager; Quality Control Supervisor; Statistician; Systems Analyst. **Special programs:** Internships. **Corporate headquarters location:** This location. **Other U.S. locations:** New York NY. **Subsidiaries include:** Joshua Morris Publishing, Inc.; QSP, Inc. is a U.S. fundraising organization that works with schools and youth groups to raise money for educational enrichment programs. **Operations at this facility include:** Administration; Manufacturing; Regional Headquarters; Research and Development; Sales; Service. **Listed on:** New York Stock Exchange. **Stock exchange symbol:** RDA. **Number of employees at this location:** 1,500. **Number of employees nationwide:** 2,000.

REED BUSINESS INFORMATION

345 Hudson Street, 4th Floor, New York NY 10014. 212/519-7700. **Contact:** Human Resources Department. **World Wide Web address:** http://www.reedbusiness.com. **Description:** This location publishes several magazine titles including *Broadcasting & Cable, Childbirth, Daily Variety, Graphic Arts Monthly, Library Journal, Modern Bride, Motor Boat,* and *Publishers Weekly.* Overall, Reed Business Information is a leading business-to-business magazine publisher with more than 80 specialty publications serving 16 major service and industry sectors including media, electronics, research and technology, computers, food service, and manufacturing. **Common positions include:** Editor; Sales Representative. **Corporate headquarters location:** This location. **Other U.S. locations:** Nationwide. **Parent company:** Reed Elsevier, Inc. **Operations at this facility include:** Divisional Headquarters. **Listed on:** New York Stock Exchange. **Stock exchange symbol:** ENL; RUK. **Number of employees at this location:** 500.

RESEARCH INSTITUTE OF AMERICA GROUP

395 Hudson Street, New York NY 10014. 212/645-4800. **Contact:** Manager of Human Resources. **World Wide Web address:** http://www.riahome.com. **Description:** Publishers of tax and other professional services publications designed for attorneys, accountants, and the business community through print, electronic, and online media. Founded in 1935. **Common positions include:** Accountant/Auditor; Administrator; Attorney; Computer Programmer; Credit Manager; Customer Service Representative; Department Manager; Editor; Editorial Assistant; Financial Analyst; Manufacturer's/Wholesaler's Sales Rep.; Marketing Specialist; MIS Specialist; Paralegal; Reporter; Software Engineer; Systems Analyst. **Corporate headquarters location:** This location. **Other U.S. locations:** CA; DC; IL; NY; VA. **Parent company:** Thomson Corporation. **Number of employees at this location:** 300.

ROUTLEDGE INC.

29 West 35th Street, 10th Floor, New York NY 10001-2299. 212/216-7800. **Fax:** 212/564-7854. **Contact:** Mr. Andrey Hanrahan, Human Resources. **World Wide Web address:** http://www.routledge-ny.com. **Description:** A progressive, international book and journal publisher focused on the humanities and social sciences. **Common positions include:** Editor; Editorial Assistant; Graphic Designer. **Special programs:** Internships. **Office hours:** Monday - Friday, 9:00 a.m. - 5:00 p.m. **Parent company:** Taylor & Francis Group. **President:** Colin Jones.

WILLIAM H. SADLIER, INC.

9 Pine Street, New York NY 10005-1002. 212/227-2120. **Contact:** Francis Marsh, Human Resources Director. **World Wide Web address:** http://www.sadlier.com. **Description:** Publishes textbooks and related workbooks, teachers' guides, and other supplementary materials principally in the subject areas of religion, mathematics, language arts, and social studies. Founded in 1832. **Corporate headquarters location:** This location.

ST. MARTIN'S PRESS

175 Fifth Avenue, New York NY 10010. 212/674-5151. **Contact:** Human Resources Manager. **World Wide Web address:** http://www.stmartins.com. **Description:** A national trade and scholarly book publisher. Founded in 1952. **NOTE:** Entry-level positions are offered. **Common positions include:** Accountant; Administrative Assistant; Advertising Clerk; Database Administrator; Editor; Editorial Assistant; Graphic Artist; Help-Desk

Technician; Marketing Manager; Sales Manager; Technical Writer/Editor. **Corporate headquarters location:** This location. **Parent company:** Holtzbrinck Publishers. **Listed on:** Privately held. **CEO:** John Sargent. **Number of employees nationwide:** 930.

SCHOLASTIC INC.
555 Broadway, 7th Floor, New York NY 10012-3999. 212/343-6912. **Fax:** 212/343-6934. **Contact:** Personnel. **E-mail address:** jobs@scholastic.com. **World Wide Web address:** http://www.scholastic.com. **Description:** Publishes and distributes children's books, classroom and professional magazines, software, CD-ROMs, and other educational materials. Products are generally distributed directly to both children and teachers in elementary and secondary schools. **Common positions include:** Accountant/Auditor; Editor; Software Engineer; Teacher/Professor; Technical Writer/Editor. **Special programs:** Internships. **Corporate headquarters location:** This location. **Other U.S. locations:** Nationwide. **International locations:** Australia; Canada; France; Mexico; New Zealand; United Kingdom. **Operations at this facility include:** Administration; Divisional Headquarters; Manufacturing; Research and Development. **Listed on:** NASDAQ. **Stock exchange symbol:** SCHL. **Number of employees at this location:** 1,400. **Number of employees nationwide:** 5,000.

SCIENTIFIC AMERICAN, INC.
415 Madison Avenue, New York NY 10017. 212/754-0550. **Contact:** Human Resources. **World Wide Web address:** http://www.sciam.com. **Description:** Publishes an international monthly magazine dealing with recent scientific research. **Corporate headquarters location:** This location.

SIMMONS-BOARDMAN PUBLISHING CORP.
345 Hudson Street, 12th Floor, New York NY 10014. 212/620-7200. **Contact:** Human Resources. **Description:** Publishes trade magazines and books. **Common positions include:** Editor; Manufacturer's/Wholesaler's Sales Rep.; Operations/Production Manager; Reporter; Technical Writer/Editor. **Special programs:** Internships. **Corporate headquarters location:** This location. **Operations at this facility include:** Administration; Sales.

SIMON & SCHUSTER, INC.
1230 Avenue of the Americas, New York NY 10020. 212/698-7000. **Fax:** 212/698-7640. **Contact:** Human Resources Department. **World Wide Web address:** http://www.simonandschuster.com. **Description:** Publishes consumer, educational, and professional books. **Common positions include:** Administrative Assistant; Designer; Editor; Marketing Specialist. **Corporate headquarters location:** This location. **Other U.S. locations:** CA; MA; NJ; OH. **Subsidiaries include:** Macmillan; Prentice-Hall. **Parent company:** Viacom. **Operations at this facility include:** Administration; Marketing; Sales. **Listed on:** New York Stock Exchange. **Stock exchange symbol:** VIA. **Number of employees nationwide:** 4,000.

SKILL GRAPHICS INC.
448 West 16th Street, 5th Floor, New York NY 10011. 212/271-2065. **Contact:** Human Resources. **Description:** Provides commercial printing services and offset lithography.

SPRINGER-VERLAG NEW YORK, INC.
175 Fifth Avenue, New York NY 10010. 212/460-1500. **Fax:** 212/473-6272. **Contact:** Human Resources Department. **World Wide Web address:**

http://www.springer-ny.com. **Description:** An international publisher of scientific, technical, and medical books, journals, magazines, and electronic media. Founded in 1842. **NOTE:** Entry-level positions and part-time jobs are offered. **Common positions include:** Accountant; Administrative Assistant; Computer Programmer; Customer Service Representative; Editor; Editorial Assistant; Graphic Designer; Marketing Manager; Product Manager; Production Assistant; Production Editor; Sales Representative; Webmaster. **Special programs:** Internships; Co-ops. **Corporate headquarters location:** This location. **Parent company:** BertelsmannSpringer. **Listed on:** Privately held.

STANDARD & POOR'S CORPORATION
55 Water Street, 37th Floor, New York NY 10041. 212/438-2000. **Contact:** Human Resources Department. **World Wide Web address:** http://www.standardandpoors.com. **Description:** Publishes the Standard & Poor's Register and a number of other financial information products. **Parent company:** McGraw-Hill, Inc. **Listed on:** New York Stock Exchange. **Stock exchange symbol:** MHP.

STERLING PUBLISHING COMPANY
387 Park Avenue South, New York NY 10016. 212/532-7160. **Contact:** Human Resources. **World Wide Web address:** http://www.sterlingpub.com. **Description:** Publishes a wide variety of how-to books.

TV GUIDE
1211 Avenue of the Americas, 4th Floor, New York NY 10036. 212/852-7500. **Contact:** Human Resources. **World Wide Web address:** http://www.tvguide.com. **Description:** Produces a national publication for television viewers. **Corporate headquarters location:** Radnor PA. **Parent company:** Gemstar-TV Guide International. **Listed on:** NASDAQ. **Stock exchange symbol:** GMST.

THOMAS PUBLISHING COMPANY
5 Penn Plaza, New York NY 10001. 212/560-1887. **Contact:** Human Resources. **World Wide Web address:** http://www.thomaspublishing.com. **Description:** Publishes a directory of manufacturers, wholesalers, and distributors. **Common positions include:** Manufacturer's/Wholesaler's Sales Rep. **Corporate headquarters location:** This location. **Operations at this facility include:** Administration; Divisional Headquarters; Sales; Service.

THE TIMES-HERALD RECORD
40 Mulberry Street, P.O. Box 2046, Middletown NY 10940. 845/346-3112. **Contact:** Human Resources Director. **World Wide Web address:** http://www.th-record.com. **Description:** Publishes a daily newspaper, with a circulation of more than 80,000. **Common positions include:** Advertising Clerk; Customer Service Representative; Editor; Human Resources Manager; Manufacturer's/Wholesaler's Sales Rep.; Operations/Production Manager; Reporter. **Corporate headquarters location:** Campbell NY. **Other area locations:** New Paltz NY; Newburgh NY; Port Jervis NY. **Parent company:** Ottaway Newspapers, Inc.

USA WEEKEND
535 Madison Avenue, New York NY 10022. 212/715-2100. **Contact:** Personnel. **World Wide Web address:** http://www.usaweekend.com. **Description:** Publishes a general interest national weekly magazine, sold in syndication as a Sunday newspaper supplement. USA Weekend has approximately 31.6 million readers every weekend. Features include

national affairs, sports, personal care, and other subjects. **Common positions include:** Credit Manager; Customer Service Representative; Department Manager; Graphic Artist; Marketing Specialist; Promotion Manager. **Special programs:** Internships. **Parent company:** Gannett Company, Inc. (Arlington VA). **Operations at this facility include:** Divisional Headquarters. **Listed on:** New York Stock Exchange. **Stock exchange symbol:** GCI.

VNU BUSINESS PUBLICATIONS, INC.

770 Broadway, New York NY 10003-9595. 646/654-5270. **Contact:** Human Resources. **E-mail address:** bmcomm@vnuinc.com. **World Wide Web address:** http://www.vnubusinessmedia.com. **Description:** Publishes a weekly trade periodical covering newspapers and an annual yearbook for the newspaper industry. **Common positions include:** Reporter. **Corporate headquarters location:** This location. **Parent company:** VNU, Inc.

VNU INC.

770 Broadway, New York NY 10003-9595. 646/654-5000. **Contact:** Human Resources. **World Wide Web address:** http://www.vnu.com. **Description:** VNU offers marketing information, media measurement information, business information and directory information. VNU publishes 67 business publications, stages 52 trade shows and conferences, and operates more than 75 business-to-business electronic media sites. **Common positions include:** Accountant/Auditor. **Corporate headquarters location:** This location. **Other U.S. locations:** Nationwide. **International locations:** Worldwide.

JOHN WILEY & SONS, INC.

605 Third Avenue, New York NY 10158. 212/850-6000. **Fax:** 212/850-6049. **Contact:** Human Resources. **E-mail address:** info@wiley.com. **World Wide Web address:** http://www.wiley.com. **Description:** An international publishing house. Wiley publishes in four categories: Educational; Professional; Trade; and Scientific, Technical, and Medical (STM). In Educational, Wiley publishes textbooks and instructional packages for undergraduate and graduate students worldwide. Publishing programs focus on the physical and life sciences, mathematics, engineering, and accounting, with a growing business in economics, finance, business, MIS/CIS, and foreign languages. In Professional, Wiley publishes books and subscription products for lawyers, architects, accountants, engineers, and other professionals. In Trade, Wiley publishes nonfiction books in areas such as business, computers, science, and general interest. In STM, Wiley publishes approximately 260 scholarly and professional journals, as well as encyclopedias, other major reference works, and books for the research and academic communities. Major subject areas include chemistry, the life sciences, and technology. Founded in 1807. **NOTE:** Entry-level positions are offered. **Common positions include:** Account Representative; Administrative Assistant; Applications Engineer; AS400 Programmer Analyst; Computer Programmer; Computer Support Technician; Customer Service Representative; Database Administrator; Database Manager; Editor; Editorial Assistant; Graphic Artist; Internet Services Manager; Managing Editor; Market Research Analyst; Marketing Manager; MIS Specialist; Multimedia Designer; Network/Systems Administrator; Production Manager; Public Relations Specialist; Systems Analyst; Systems Manager; Technical Writer/Editor; Webmaster. **Special programs:** Internships. **Office hours:** Monday - Friday, 8:30 a.m. - 4:30 p.m. **Corporate headquarters location:** This location. **Other U.S. locations:** Colorado Springs CO; Somerset NJ. **International locations:** Asia; Australia; Canada; Europe.

Operations at this facility include: Administration. **Listed on:** New York Stock Exchange. **Stock exchange symbol:** JW. **Number of employees at this location:** 800. **Number of employees nationwide:** 1,200. **Number of employees worldwide:** 2,000.

THE H.W. WILSON COMPANY
950 University Avenue, Bronx NY 10452. 718/588-8400. **Contact:** Harold Regan, President. **World Wide Web address:** http://www.hwwilson.com. **Description:** A publisher of indexes and reference works for libraries covering a broad range of the arts and sciences.

ZIFF-DAVIS MEDIA INC.
28 East 28th Street, New York NY 10016. 212/503-3500. **Contact:** Human Resources. **World Wide Web address:** http://www.ziffdavis.com. **Description:** A magazine publisher whose periodicals are primarily computer related. Ziff-Davis also has minor broadcasting operations. **Corporate headquarters location:** This location.

REAL ESTATE

You can expect to find the following types of companies in this chapter:

Land Subdividers and Developers • Real Estate Agents, Managers, and Operators • Real Estate Investment Trusts

AMREP CORPORATION
641 Lexington Avenue, 6th Floor, New York NY 10022. 212/705-4700.
Contact: Human Resources. **Description:** Amrep Corporation develops land for residential properties. **Corporate headquarters location:** This location. **Listed on:** New York Stock Exchange. **Stock exchange symbol:** AXR.

CENDANT CORPORATION
9 West 57th Street, 37th Floor, New York NY 10019. 212/413-1800.
Contact: Human Resources Department. **World Wide Web address:** http://www.cendant.com. **Description:** Provides a wide range of business services including dining services, hotel franchise management, mortgage programs, and timeshare exchanges. Cendant Corporation's Real Estate Division offers employee relocation and mortgage services through Century 21, Coldwell Banker, ERA, Cendant Mortgage, and Cendant Mobility. The Travel Division provides car rentals, vehicle management services, and vacation timeshares through brand names including Avia, Days Inn, Howard Johnson, Ramada, Travelodge, and Super 8. The Membership Division offers travel, shopping, auto, dining, and other financial services through Travelers Advantage, Shoppers Advantage, Auto Vantage, Welcome Wagon, Netmarket, North American Outdoor Group, and PrivacyGuard. Founded in 1997. **NOTE:** Resumes should be sent to Human Resources, Cendant Corporation, One Campus Drive, Parsippany NJ 07054. **Corporate headquarters location:** This location. **Listed on:** New York Stock Exchange. **Stock exchange symbol:** CD. **Number of employees worldwide:** 28,000.

CENTRAL PARKING SYSTEMS
360 West 31st Street, 12th Floor, New York NY 10001. 212/502-5490.
Contact: Human Resources Department. **World Wide Web address:** http://www.parking.com. **Description:** Operates parking garages and lots throughout New York. **Corporate headquarters location:** This location. **Other U.S. locations:** FL; MA. **Parent company:** Central Parking Corporation.

COLDWELL BANKER
151 North Main Street, New City NY 10956. 845/634-0400. **Contact:** Personnel. **World Wide Web address:** http://www.coldwellbanker.com. **Description:** Coldwell Banker is one of the largest residential real estate companies in the United States and Canada. **Corporate headquarters location:** Mission Viejo CA.

CUSHMAN AND WAKEFIELD, INC.
51 West 52nd Street, 8th Floor, New York NY 10019-6178. 212/841-7500.
Fax: 212/841-5039. **Contact:** Human Resources Department. **E-mail address:** recruiting@cushwake.com. **World Wide Web address:** http://www.cushwake.com. **Description:** This location provides assessment services, corporate services, brokerage services, financial and general administration, research, sales, and valuation advisory services. Overall, Cushman and Wakefield is an international commercial and industrial real

estate services firm with 44 offices in 20 states. The company is engaged in appraisals, financial services, project development, research services, and the management and leasing of commercial office space. **Common positions include:** Accountant/Auditor; Human Resources Manager; Market Research Analyst; Property and Real Estate Manager; Real Estate Broker. **Office hours:** Monday - Friday, 8:30 a.m. - 5:30 p.m. **Corporate headquarters location:** This location. **Other U.S. locations:** Los Angeles CA; San Francisco CA; Chicago IL. **International locations:** Worldwide. **Parent company:** The Rockefeller Group Inc. **Listed on:** Privately held. **Annual sales/revenues:** More than $100 million. **Number of employees at this location:** 500. **Number of employees nationwide:** 5,000.

DVL INC.
70 East 55th Street, 7th Floor, New York NY 10022. 212/350-9900. **Contact:** Human Resources. **Description:** Acquires and develops retirement and resort properties; purchases, collects, and services installment sales contacts originated by national tool companies for automobile mechanics' tools; and manages and services existing real estate properties.

GRUBB & ELLIS NEW YORK, INC.
55 East 59th Street, 10th Floor, New York NY 10012. 212/759-9700. **Contact:** Human Resources. **World Wide Web address:** http://www.grubb-ellis.com. **Description:** A real estate management firm dealing primarily with commercial real estate including shopping centers, office buildings, and similar complexes. **Corporate headquarters location:** Northbrook IL. **Listed on:** New York Stock Exchange. **Stock exchange symbol:** GBE.

HELMSLEY-NOYES COMPANY INC.
230 Park Avenue, Suite 659, New York NY 10169. 212/679-3600. **Contact:** Human Resources. **Description:** A commercial real estate agency engaged in the management of office buildings and a wide range of other institutional buildings including department stores and corporate offices. **Corporate headquarters location:** This location.

HELMSLEY-SPEAR INC.
60 East 42nd Street, 53rd Floor, New York NY 10165. 212/880-0603. **Contact:** Human Resources Department. **World Wide Web address:** http://www.helmsleyspear.com. **Description:** One of the largest real estate service companies in the nation offering leasing (including industrial leasing, and retail and store leasing divisions); sales and brokerage; management; development; appraisals; and financing services. **Common positions include:** Accountant/Auditor; Actuary; Administrator; Assistant Manager; Attorney; Blue-Collar Worker Supervisor; Computer Programmer; Counselor; Electrical/Electronics Engineer; Financial Analyst; General Manager; Industrial Engineer; Industrial Production Manager; Instructor/Trainer; Management Trainee; Mechanical Engineer; Paralegal; Quality Control Supervisor; Real Estate Agent; Sales Executive; Systems Analyst. **Corporate headquarters location:** This location. **Operations at this facility include:** Administration; Research and Development; Sales.

INSIGNIA RESIDENTIAL GROUP
675 Third Avenue, 6th Floor, New York NY 10017. 212/350-2800. **Contact:** Human Resources Department. **World Wide Web address:** http://www.insigniaresidential.com. **Description:** A real estate firm engaged in apartment sales, rentals, and insurance. **Common positions include:** Accountant/Auditor; Administrative Worker/Clerk; Administrator; Computer Programmer; Customer Service Representative; Department Manager;

Operations/Production Manager; Purchasing Agent/Manager; Secretary. **Corporate headquarters location:** This location. **Parent company:** Insignia Financial Group. **Operations at this facility include:** Administration; Sales; Service. **Listed on:** New York Stock Exchange. **Stock exchange symbol:** IFS.

LEXINGTON CORPORATE PROPERTIES
355 Lexington Avenue, 14th Floor, New York NY 10017. 212/692-7260. **Contact:** Human Resources. **E-mail address:** info@lxp.com. **World Wide Web address:** http://www.lxp.com. **Description:** A real estate investment trust that owns and manages office, industrial, and retail properties located in 25 states. Founded in 1993. **Corporate headquarters location:** This location. **Number of employees at this location:** 25.

J.W. MAYS INC.
9 Bond Street, Brooklyn NY 11201. 718/624-7400. **Contact:** Frank Mollo, Personnel Director. **Description:** A real estate company operating commercial properties in Brooklyn, Jamaica, Levittown, Fishkill, and Dutchess County NY, as well as in Circleville OH. **Corporate headquarters location:** This location.

UNITED CAPITAL CORPORATION
United Capital Building, 9 Park Place, 4th Floor, Great Neck NY 11021. 516/466-6464. **Contact:** Anthony Miceli, Human Resources Director. **Description:** United Capital Corporation invests in and manages real estate properties. **Subsidiaries include:** Metex Corporation provides antenna systems and knitted wire products to aviation and automotive markets worldwide. **Corporate headquarters location:** This location. **Listed on:** AMEX. **Stock exchange symbol:** AFP.

RETAIL

You can expect to find the following types of companies in this chapter:

Catalog Retailers • Department Stores; Specialty Stores•
Retail Bakeries • Supermarkets

ANN TAYLOR, INC.
142 West 57th Street, New York NY 10019. 212/541-3300. **Contact:** Human Resources. **Description:** Ann Taylor, Inc. is a leading national specialty retailer of women's apparel, shoes, and accessories sold primarily under the Ann Taylor brand name. The company operates 262 stores in 38 states and the District of Columbia and offers a collection of career and casual separates, dresses, tops, weekend wear, shoes, and accessories. **Listed on:** New York Stock Exchange. **Stock exchange symbol:** ANN.

AVON PRODUCTS INC.
1345 Avenue of the Americas, New York NY 10105. 212/282-5000. **Contact:** Human Resources Department. **E-mail address:** jobs@avon.com. **World Wide Web address:** http://www.avoncareers.com. **Description:** A direct seller of beauty care products, fashion jewelry, gifts, fragrances, and decorative products. Avon, a *Fortune* 500 company, markets its products through a network of 2.8 million independent sales representatives in 135 countries worldwide. **NOTE:** Salespeople are considered independent contractors or dealers and most work part-time. If you are interested in becoming a sales representative, please call 800/FOR-AVON, or visit the company's Website. **Corporate headquarters location:** This location. **Other U.S. locations:** Nationwide. **Listed on:** New York Stock Exchange. **Stock exchange symbol:** AVP.

BARNES & NOBLE BOOKSTORES
1400 Old Country Road, Westbury NY 11590. 516/338-8000. **Contact:** Human Resources. **World Wide Web address:** http://www.bn.com. **Description:** This location houses financial offices. Overall, Barnes & Noble Bookstores is a nationwide bookstore chain. **Corporate headquarters location:** New York NY. **Listed on:** New York Stock Exchange. **Stock exchange symbol:** BKS.

BARNES & NOBLE CORPORATION
122 Fifth Avenue, 2nd Floor, New York NY 10011. 212/633-3300. **Contact:** Melissa Church, Senior Employment Specialist. **World Wide Web address:** http://www.bn.com. **Description:** A nationwide bookstore chain. **Common positions include:** Accountant/Auditor; Administrative Worker/Clerk; Buyer; Customer Service Representative; Financial Analyst; Management Trainee; Store Manager. **Corporate headquarters location:** This location. **Other U.S. locations:** Nationwide. **Listed on:** New York Stock Exchange. **Stock exchange symbol:** BKS.

BARNEYS NEW YORK
660 Madison Avenue, New York NY 10021. 212/593-7800. **Contact:** Human Resources. **World Wide Web address:** http://www.barneys.com. **Description:** A national specialty retailer offering primarily men's and women's apparel collections from both American and international designers. **Common positions include:** Accountant/Auditor; Administrator; Advertising Clerk; Assistant Buyer; Assistant Manager; Buyer; Customer

Service Representative; Department Manager; Human Resources Manager; Operations/Production Manager; Public Relations Specialist; Purchasing Agent/Manager; Sales Executive. **Corporate headquarters location:** This location. **Operations at this facility include:** Administration; Sales; Service.

BLOOMINGDALE'S
1000 Third Avenue, New York NY 10022. 212/705-2000. **Contact:** Human Resources. **World Wide Web address:** http://www.federated-fds.com. **Description:** Operates a chain of department stores. **Common positions include:** Administrator; Advertising Clerk; Blue-Collar Worker Supervisor; Branch Manager; Buyer; Commercial Artist; Customer Service Representative; Department Manager; General Manager; Management Trainee; Operations/Production Manager; Public Relations Specialist; Purchasing Agent/Manager; Quality Control Supervisor; Systems Analyst. **Corporate headquarters location:** This location. **Other U.S. locations:** Washington DC; Boca Raton FL; Miami FL; Palm Beach FL; Chicago IL; Boston MA; Minneapolis MN; Philadelphia PA. **Parent company:** Federated Department Stores Inc. **Operations at this facility include:** Administration; Regional Headquarters; Research and Development; Sales; Service. **Listed on:** New York Stock Exchange. **Stock exchange symbol:** FD.

BROOKS BROTHERS
346 Madison Avenue, New York NY 10017. 212/682-8800. **Contact:** Human Resources. **E-mail address:** hr@brooksbrothers.com. **World Wide Web address:** http://www.brooksbrothers.com. **Description:** Operates over 150 retail stores and factory outlets in the United States. Founded in 1818. **Common positions include:** Advertising Clerk; Architect; Branch Manager; Buyer; Claim Representative; Computer Programmer; Customer Service Representative; Department Manager; Draftsperson; Editor; General Manager; Human Resources Manager; Management Trainee; Operations/Production Manager; Purchasing Agent/Manager; Receptionist; Reporter; Secretary; Stock Clerk; Systems Analyst. **Corporate headquarters location:** This location. **Operations at this facility include:** Administration; Divisional Headquarters; Regional Headquarters; Sales; Service.

CACHE INC.
1460 Broadway, 15th Floor, New York NY 10036-7306. 212/575-3200. **Contact:** Margarita Chroasdaile, Human Resources Manager. **World Wide Web address:** http://www.cache.com. **Description:** Owns and operates 139 women's apparel specialty stores. **Corporate headquarters location:** This location. **Listed on:** NASDAQ. **Stock exchange symbol:** CACH.

D'AGOSTINO SUPERMARKETS INC.
1385 Boston Post Road, Larchmont NY 10538. 914/833-4000. **Fax:** 914/833-4060. **Contact:** Human Resources. **World Wide Web address:** http://www.dagnyc.com. **Description:** A supermarket chain offering a full line of grocery, produce, and meats. The company operates more than 25 stores serving Westchester County, Brooklyn, Riverdale, and Manhattan. **Common positions include:** Accountant/Auditor; Cashier; Customer Service Representative; Management Trainee; Operations/Production Manager; Pharmacist; Retail Sales Worker. **Special programs:** Internships. **Corporate headquarters location:** This location. **Operations at this facility include:** Administration. **Listed on:** Privately held.

THE DRESS BARN, INC.
30 Dunnigan Drive, Suffern NY 10901. 845/369-4500. **Contact:** Human Resources. **World Wide Web address:** http://www.dressbarn.com.

Description: Operates a chain of women's apparel stores. **Corporate headquarters location:** This location. **Listed on:** NASDAQ. **Stock exchange symbol:** DBRN.

FINLAY ENTERPRISES, INC.
529 Fifth Avenue, New York NY 10017. 212/808-2079. **Contact:** Fran Galluccio, Personnel Manager. **World Wide Web address:** http://www.finlayenterprises.com. **Description:** Operates through its subsidiary, Finlay Fine Jewelry Corporation, which sells jewelry through over 950 department store locations in the United States. **Corporate headquarters location:** This location. **Listed on:** NASDAQ. **Stock exchange symbol:** FNLY.

FOOT LOCKER
112 West 34th Street, New York NY 10120. 212/720-3700. **Contact:** Human Resources. **World Wide Web address:** http://www.footlocker.com. **Description:** This location houses the administrative offices. Overall, Foot Locker is a global retailer with stores and related support facilities in 22 countries on four continents. The company retails and distributes a broad range of footwear, apparel, and department store merchandise through more than 7,400 specialty stores and more than 950 general merchandise stores in over 40 formats. The company operates retail units under the following names: Kinney, Foot Locker, Champs Sports, Lady Foot Locker, Northern Reflections, Little Folks, San Francisco Music Box Company, Rx Place, and World Foot Locker. Founded in 1894. **NOTE:** Entry-level positions are offered. **Common positions include:** Accountant/Auditor; Administrative Assistant; Advertising Clerk; Budget Analyst; Buyer; Chief Financial Officer; Draftsperson; Editorial Assistant; Financial Analyst; Human Resources Manager; Secretary; Typist/Word Processor. **Corporate headquarters location:** This location. **International locations:** Australia; the Netherlands. **Listed on:** New York Stock Exchange. **Stock exchange symbol:** Z. **Annual sales/revenues:** More than $100 million. **Number of employees at this location:** 450. **Number of employees nationwide:** 24,000.

FORTUNOFF
1300 Old Country Road, Westbury NY 11590. 516/832-1520. **Contact:** Robyn Ornstein, Personnel Manager. **World Wide Web address:** http://www.fortunoff.com. **Description:** One location of the retail department store chain. Fortunoff offers a wide range of merchandise including home furnishings, fine jewelry, and fine silver. **Common positions include:** Assistant Buyer; Cashier; Clerk; Computer Programmer; Customer Service Representative; Sales Representative; Security Officer; Warehouse/Distribution Worker. **Operations at this facility include:** Sales.

KEY FOOD STORES CO-OPERATIVE INC.
1200 South Avenue, Staten Island NY 10314. 718/370-4200. **Contact:** Ronald Phillips, Controller. **Description:** Operates a chain of food stores. **Corporate headquarters location:** This location.

LERNER NEW YORK
450 West 33rd Street, 5th Floor, New York NY 10001. 212/736-1222. **Fax:** 212/884-2396. **Contact:** Recruitment. **World Wide Web address:** http://www.limited.com. **Description:** This location houses administrative offices. Overall, Lerner New York is a specialty women's clothing retailer. **Common positions include:** Accountant/Auditor; Budget Analyst; Buyer; Computer Programmer; Financial Analyst; Systems Analyst; Wholesale and Retail Buyer. **Special programs:** Internships. **Parent company:** Limited

Brands, Inc. (Columbus OH). **Operations at this facility include:** Divisional Headquarters. **Listed on:** New York Stock Exchange. **Stock exchange symbol:** LTD. **Number of employees at this location:** 300.

LILLIAN VERNON CORPORATION

One Theall Road, Rye NY 10580. 914/925-1200. **Fax:** 914/925-1444. **Contact:** Human Resources Manager. **World Wide Web address:** http://www.lillianvernon.com. **Description:** Lillian Vernon markets gift, household, gardening, decorative, Christmas, and children's products through a variety of specialty catalogs. Catalog titles include: Lillian Vernon; Lillian Vernon Gardening; Neat Ideas; Personalized Gift; Christmas Memories; Lilly's Kids; Favorites; and Private Sale. Founded in 1951. **Common positions include:** Account Manager; Account Representative; Accountant; Administrative Assistant; AS400 Programmer Analyst; Auditor; Bank Officer/Manager; Budget Analyst; Buyer; Chief Financial Officer; Computer Programmer; Controller; Credit Manager; Database Manager; Desktop Publishing Specialist; Editor; Finance Director; Financial Analyst; Graphic Artist; Graphic Designer; Human Resources Manager; Internet Services Manager; Market Research Analyst; Marketing Manager; Marketing Specialist; Network/Systems Administrator; Public Relations Specialist; Purchasing Agent/Manager; Sales Representative; Secretary; Systems Analyst; Systems Manager. **Office hours:** Monday - Friday, 8:30 a.m. - 5:00 p.m. **Corporate headquarters location:** This location. **Other U.S. locations:** Virginia Beach VA. **Listed on:** American Stock Exchange. **Stock exchange symbol:** LVC. **Annual sales/revenues:** More than $100 million. **Number of employees at this location:** 175.

LORD & TAYLOR

424 Fifth Avenue, New York NY 10018. 212/391-3344. **Contact:** Human Resources. **World Wide Web address:** http://www.lordandtaylor.com. **Description:** A full-line department store offering clothing, accessories, home furnishings, and many other retail items. Founded in 1826. **Common positions include:** Branch Manager; Buyer; Credit Manager; Department Manager; Management Trainee. **Corporate headquarters location:** St. Louis MO. **Other U.S. locations:** Nationwide. **Parent company:** The May Department Stores Company. **Listed on:** New York Stock Exchange. **Stock exchange symbol:** MAY. **Operations at this facility include:** Administration; Divisional Headquarters; Research and Development; Sales; Service.

MACY'S

151 West 34th Street, New York NY 10001. 212/695-4400. **Contact:** Human Resources. **World Wide Web address:** http://www.federated-fds.com. **Description:** This location houses administrative offices as well as a department store. **Corporate headquarters location:** This location. **Parent company:** Federated Department Stores. **Listed on:** New York Stock Exchange. **Stock exchange symbol:** FD.

NINE WEST GROUP

Nine West Plaza, 1129 Westchester Avenue, White Plains NY 10604-3529. 914/640-6400. **Fax:** 914/640-3499. **Contact:** Melissa Tavino, Human Resources. **E-mail address:** jobs@ninewest.com. **World Wide Web address:** http://www.ninewest.com. **Description:** A manufacturer and retailer of women's shoes. **Office hours:** Monday - Thursday, 9:00 a.m. - 5:00 p.m.; Friday, 8:30 a.m. - 3:00 p.m. **Parent company:** Jones Apparel Group. **Listed on:** New York Stock Exchange. **Stock exchange symbol:** JNY.

PICK QUICK FOODS INC.
83-10 Rockaway Boulevard, Ozone Park NY 11416. 718/296-9100.
Contact: Krish Malik, Controller. **Description:** A grocery retailer. **Corporate headquarters location:** This location.

QUALITY MARKETS
101 Jackson Avenue, Jamestown NY 14701. 716/664-6010. **Contact:** Human Resources. **World Wide Web address:** http://www.penntraffic.com. **Description:** Regional office of a chain of retail grocery stores. **Parent company:** The Penn Traffic Company (Syracuse NY) is a food retailer, wholesaler, and producer. The company operates over 230 supermarkets in New York, Ohio, Pennsylvania, and West Virginia under the names Big Bear, Insalaco's, Riverside Markets, Quality Markets, P&C Foods, and Bi-Lo Foods. Penn Traffic also wholesales to 249 stores, and operates a dairy and ice cream facility in Pennsylvania, two bakeries in New York and Ohio, and 15 discount department stores. **Listed on:** NASDAQ. **Stock exchange symbol:** PNFT.

SAKS FIFTH AVENUE
611 Fifth Avenue, New York NY 10022. 212/753-4000. **Contact:** Employment. **World Wide Web address:** http://www.saksincorporated.com. **Description:** This location is a part of the nationwide specialty department store chain. Overall, Saks Fifth Avenue is a 62-store chain emphasizing soft-goods products, primarily apparel for men, women, and children. **Corporate headquarters location:** Birmingham AL. **Parent company:** Saks Incorporated is a department store holding company that operates approximately 360 stores in 36 states. The company's stores include Saks Fifth Avenue, Parisian, Proffit's, Younker's, Herberger's, Carson Pirie Scott, Boston Store, Bergner's, and Off 5th, the company's outlet store. Saks Incorporated also operates two retail catalogs and several retail Internet sites. **Listed on:** New York Stock Exchange. **Stock exchange symbol:** SKS.

SOFTWARE ETC.
1120 Avenue of the Americas, New York NY 10036. 212/921-7855. **Contact:** Store Manager. **Description:** Retails computer software, hardware, video games, accessories, and books. **Common positions include:** Management Trainee; Sales Manager; Sales Representative. **Corporate headquarters location:** Dallas TX. **Other U.S. locations:** Nationwide. **International locations:** Worldwide. **Parent company:** Babbage's Etc.

WESTERN BEEF, INC.
47-05 Metropolitan Avenue, Ridgewood NY 11385. 718/417-3770. **Contact:** Human Resources Department. **World Wide Web address:** http://www.westernbeef.com. **Description:** A warehouse supermarket chain in the metropolitan New York area that provides a full-line of value-priced perishable and grocery products. In addition to operating 14 supermarkets, the company is also a meat and poultry distributor.

WESTERN BEEF, INC.
4444 College Point Boulevard, Flushing NY 11355. 718/539-4900. **Contact:** Human Resources Department. **World Wide Web address:** http://www.westernbeef.com. **Description:** A warehouse supermarket chain in the metropolitan New York area that provides a full-line of value-priced perishable and grocery products. In addition to operating 14 supermarkets, the company is also a meat and poultry distributor. **NOTE:** Interested jobseekers should send resumes to 47-05 Metropolitan Avenue, Ridgewood NY 11385.

STONE, CLAY, GLASS, AND CONCRETE PRODUCTS

You can expect to find the following types of companies in this chapter:

Cement, Tile, Sand, and Gravel • Crushed and Broken Stone •
Glass and Glass Products • Mineral Products

FLORAL GLASS
895 Motor Parkway, P.O. Box 18039, Hauppauge NY 11788. 631/234-2200. **Contact:** Personnel Department. **World Wide Web address:** http://www.floralglass.com. **Description:** Manufactures specialty glass products including beveled mirrors.

GEMCO WARE INC.
P.O. Box 18044, Hauppauge NY 11788-8844. 631/851-9501. **Physical address:** 600 Old Willets Path, Hauppauge NY 11788. **Toll-free phone:** 800/735-4362. **Fax:** 631/851-9512. **Contact:** Human Resources Department. **World Wide Web address:** http://www.gemcoware.com. **Description:** Manufactures glass containers. Gemco Ware's products are used primarily to store, process or dispense condiments, spices and other dressings.

MINERALS TECHNOLOGIES INC.
The Chrysler Building, 405 Lexington Avenue, 20th Floor, New York NY 10174-1901. 212/878-1800. **Contact:** Human Resources Department. **World Wide Web address:** http://www.mineralstech.com. **Description:** Minerals Technologies is a resource- and technology-based company that develops and produces performance-enhancing minerals and mineral-based and synthetic mineral products for the paper, steel, polymer, and other manufacturing industries. The company's three businesses include producing and supplying precipitated calcium carbonate to the paper industry; developing and marketing mineral-based monolithic refractory materials that are used to resist the effects of high temperatures and are usually applied as coatings to surfaces exposed to extreme heat; and mining and producing natural mineral-based products including limestone, lime, talc, calcium, and metallurgical wire products. **Corporate headquarters location:** This location. **Listed on:** New York Stock Exchange. **Stock exchange symbol:** MTX.

PECKHAM INDUSTRIES, INC.
20 Haarlem Avenue, White Plains NY 10603. 914/949-2000. **Fax:** 914/949-2075. **Contact:** Human Resources Department. **World Wide Web address:** http://www.peckham.com. **Description:** A supplier of highway building materials. The company maintains blacktop plants, stone quarries, bulk asphalt terminals and liquid plants that stretch from Long Island up the Hudson Valley to Warren County. **Corporate headquarters location:** This location.

TRANSPORTATION/TRAVEL

You can expect to find the following types of companies in this chapter:
Air, Railroad, and Water Transportation Services • Courier Services •
Local and Interurban Passenger Transit • Ship Building and Repair •
Transportation Equipment Travel Agencies • Trucking •
Warehousing and Storage

AIR FRANCE
125 West 55th Street, New York NY 10019. 212/830-4000. **Fax:** 212/830-4191. **Contact:** Personnel. **E-mail address:** mail.resume@airfrance.fr. **World Wide Web address:** http://www.airfrance.com. **Description:** An international airline. This location also hires seasonally. Founded in 1933. **NOTE:** Part-time jobs and second and third shifts are offered. **Common positions include:** Account Manager; Account Representative; Accountant; Administrative Assistant; Computer Programmer; Network/Systems Administrator; Sales Executive; Sales Manager; Sales Representative; Typist/Word Processor; Web Advertising Specialist. **Special programs:** Co-ops. **Office hours:** Monday - Friday, 9:00 a.m. - 5:15 p.m. **Corporate headquarters location:** Paris, France. **Number of employees at this location:** 830. **Number of employees worldwide:** 49,000.

AIR INDIA
570 Lexington Avenue, 15th Floor, New York NY 10022. 212/407-1300. **Fax:** 212/838-9533. **Contact:** Human Resources Department. **World Wide Web address:** http://www.airindia.com. **Description:** An international airline with routes to major cities throughout the world. **Corporate headquarters location:** This location.

AVANT SERVICES CORPORATION
60 East 42nd Street, New York NY 10165. 212/867-6845. **Fax:** 212/370-1452. **Contact:** Timothy Downs, Personnel Manager. **Description:** A delivery company. **NOTE:** Entry-level positions, part-time jobs, and second and third shifts are offered. **Common positions include:** Administrative Assistant; Assistant Manager; Driver; Human Resources Manager. **Special programs:** Summer Jobs.

CAMP SYSTEMS INC. (CSI)
999 Marconi Avenue, Ronkonkoma NY 11779. 631/588-3200. **Contact:** Human Resources Department. **E-mail address:** careers@campsys.com. **World Wide Web address:** http://www.campsys.com. **Description:** Camp Systems Inc. (CSI) performs computerized aircraft maintenance.

CENDANT CORPORATION
9 West 57th Street, 37th Floor, New York NY 10019. 212/413-1800. **Contact:** Human Resources Department. **World Wide Web address:** http://www.cendant.com. **Description:** Provides a wide range of business services including dining services, hotel franchise management, mortgage programs, and timeshare exchanges. Cendant Corporation's Real Estate Division offers employee relocation and mortgage services through Century 21, Coldwell Banker, ERA, Cendant Mortgage, and Cendant Mobility. The Travel Division provides car rentals, vehicle management services, and

vacation timeshares through brand names including Avia, Days Inn, Howard Johnson, Ramada, Travelodge, and Super 8. The Membership Division offers travel, shopping, auto, dining, and other financial services through Travelers Advantage, Shoppers Advantage, Auto Vantage, Welcome Wagon, Netmarket, North American Outdoor Group, and PrivacyGuard. Founded in 1997. **NOTE:** Resumes should be sent to Human Resources, Cendant Corporation, One Campus Drive, Parsippany NJ 07054. **Corporate headquarters location:** This location. **Listed on:** New York Stock Exchange. **Stock exchange symbol:** CD. **Number of employees worldwide:** 28,000.

COURTESY BUS COMPANY
107 Lawson Boulevard, Oceanside NY 11572. 516/766-6740. **Fax:** 516/678-0253. **Contact:** Personnel Office. **Description:** Provides bus service to local school districts, as well as a range of charter services through several area locations. **Common positions include:** Automotive Mechanic; Driver. **Corporate headquarters location:** This location.

EL AL ISRAEL AIRLINES
120 West 45th Street, 18th Floor, New York NY 10036-9998. 212/852-0625. **Contact:** Personnel Department. **World Wide Web address:** http://www.elal.co.il. **Description:** An international air carrier operating a route system that includes major United States cities, and destinations in Israel, Europe, and Africa. **Corporate headquarters location:** This location.

HUDSON GENERAL CORPORATION
111 Great Neck Road, Great Neck NY 11021. 516/487-8610. **Fax:** 516/498-1534. **Contact:** Human Resources. **Description:** A nationwide aviation service company providing contracting services to airlines and airports including loading/unloading, cleaning planes, fueling planes, and cargo services. **Common positions include:** Accountant/Auditor; Administrative Manager; Automotive Mechanic; Customer Service Representative; General Manager. **Special programs:** Internships. **Corporate headquarters location:** This location. **Subsidiaries include:** Hudson Aviation Services, Inc. **Operations at this facility include:** Administration. **Number of employees at this location:** 45. **Number of employees nationwide:** 3,400.

LIBERTY LINES
475 Saw Mill River Road, P.O. Box 624, Yonkers NY 10703. 914/969-6900. **Fax:** 914/376-6440. **Contact:** Neil Erickson, Director of Personnel. **E-mail address:** jobs@libertylines.com. **World Wide Web address:** http://www.libertylines.com. **Description:** One of the largest and most diversified bus services in the Yonkers/Westchester area. Services include commuter and transit bus operations. **Common positions include:** Bus Driver. **Corporate headquarters location:** This location. **Operations at this facility include:** Administration; Service. **President:** Jerry D'Amore.

LINDBLAD SPECIAL EXPEDITIONS
720 Fifth Avenue, 6th Floor, New York NY 10019. 212/261-9000. **Contact:** Personnel. **World Wide Web address:** http://www.specialexpeditions.com. **Description:** An ocean cruise line.

THE LONG ISLAND RAILROAD COMPANY
93-02 Sutphin Boulevard, Jamaica NY 11435. 718/558-7400. **Contact:** Human Resources. **World Wide Web address:** http://www.lirr.org. **Description:** Operates one of the oldest active railroads in the United States. The company has extensive commuter passenger and freight service

railroad operations, primarily between New York City and numerous points on Long Island. The Long island Railroad Company is one of the busiest passenger railroad operators in the United States. **Corporate headquarters location:** This location. **Parent company:** Metropolitan Transportation Authority.

McALLISTER TOWING AND TRANSPORTATION COMPANY
17 Battery Place, Suite 1200, New York NY 10004. 212/269-3200. **Contact:** Nancy Errichiello, Director of Personnel. **Description:** A marine services firm providing ship docking, deep-sea and coastal towing, oil transportation, bulk transportation, special projects such as positioning tunnel and bridge segments and other services for the transportation industry. McAllister also offers full-service, in-house capabilities through a complete packaged transportation service provided to shippers. The company operates one of the largest fleets of tugs and barges on the East Coast and in the Caribbean, with ship docking services in New York NY, Philadelphia PA, Norfolk VA, Charleston SC, Jacksonville FL, Baltimore MD, and Puerto Rico. Marine towing and transportation services are operated along the East Coast, in the Caribbean, through the New York State barge canal system, and in the Great Lakes and the St. Lawrence River. **Common positions include:** Accountant/Auditor; Administrator; Claim Representative; Computer Programmer; Department Manager; Financial Analyst; General Manager; Human Resources Manager; Management Trainee; Operations/Production Manager; Services Sales Representative. **Corporate headquarters location:** This location. **Operations at this facility include:** Service.

METROPOLITAN TRANSPORTATION AUTHORITY (MTA)
347 Madison Avenue, New York NY 10017. 212/878-7000. **Contact:** Human Resources Department. **World Wide Web address:** http://www.mta.nyc.ny.us. **Description:** A public benefit corporation primarily devoted to obtaining funding for mass transportation in the New York City area, as well as serving as the headquarters for the MTA's constituent agencies. **Common positions include:** Accountant/Auditor; Attorney; Computer Operator; Computer Programmer; Economist; Financial Analyst; Financial Manager; Market Research Analyst; Payroll Clerk; Purchasing Agent/Manager; Real Estate Agent; Secretary; Systems Analyst. **Corporate headquarters location:** This location. **Operations at this facility include:** Administration. **Number of employees at this location:** 400.

QUEENS SURFACE CORPORATION
128-15 28th Avenue, Flushing NY 11354. 718/445-3100. **Contact:** Kathleen O'Shea, Director of Human Resources. **World Wide Web address:** http://www.qsbus.com. **Description:** A public transportation firm providing express and local service in Queens and Manhattan with more than 270 buses operating on nearly 20 routes. **Common positions include:** Accountant/Auditor; Automotive Mechanic; Blue-Collar Worker Supervisor; Buyer; Claim Representative; Clerical Supervisor; Computer Programmer; Cost Estimator; Electrician; Human Resources Manager; Purchasing Agent/Manager. **Special programs:** Internships. **Office hours:** Monday - Friday, 8:30 a.m. - 4:30 p.m. **Corporate headquarters location:** This location. **Operations at this facility include:** Administration. **Number of employees at this location:** 700.

SWISSPORT USA
JFK International Airport, Building 151, East Hanger Road, Jamaica NY 11430. 718/995-8405. **Contact:** Human Resources Department. **World

Wide Web address: http://www.swissportusa.com. **Description:** Provides a wide range of ground-handling services for airlines and airports. Services include maintenance, inspections, spare parts inventory, into-plane fueling, cargo handling, cabin cleaning, and ramp services. Swissport USA also operates reservation centers for airlines. **Parent company:** Alpha Airports Group.

TIX INTERNATIONAL GROUP
201 Main Street, Nyack-On-Hudson NY 10960. 845/358-1007. **Fax:** 845/358-1266. **Contact:** Human Resources. **World Wide Web address:** http://www.tixtravel.com. **Description:** A full-service travel agency and ticket broker for concerts, sports, and theater events. **Common positions include:** Travel Agent. **Corporate headquarters location:** This location. **Listed on:** Privately held.

WE TRANSPORT INC.
303 Sunnyside Boulevard, Plainview NY 11803. 516/349-8200. **Contact:** Mary Prioli, Personnel Manager. **Description:** An area school bus and van transportation company. **Common positions include:** Accountant; Accounting Clerk; Administrative Assistant; Bus Driver; Claim Representative; Computer Animator; Computer Engineer; Computer Programmer; Customer Service Representative; Department Manager; Dispatcher; Draftsperson; Human Resources Manager; Operations Manager; Payroll Clerk; Safety Specialist; Transportation/Traffic Specialist; Vice President of Operations. **Special programs:** Internships. **Corporate headquarters location:** This location. **Operations at this facility include:** Administration; Service. **Number of employees at this location:** 70.

UTILITIES: ELECTRIC/GAS/WATER

You can expect to find the following types of companies in this chapter:

Gas, Electric, and Fuel Companies; Other Energy-Producing Companies • Public Utility Holding Companies • Water Utilities

CENTRAL HUDSON GAS AND ELECTRIC

284 South Avenue, Poughkeepsie NY 12601. 845/452-2000. **Contact:** Personnel. **World Wide Web address:** http://www.chenergygroup.com. **Description:** An investor-owned utility, Central Hudson Gas and Electric generates, purchases, and distributes electric energy, and purchases and distributes natural gas. **Parent company:** CH Energy Group, Inc. **CEO:** Paul J. Ganci.

CON EDISON COMPANY OF NEW YORK INC.

4 Irving Place, Room 2215-S, New York NY 10003-3598. 212/460-4600. **Contact:** Human Resources Department. **World Wide Web address:** http://www.coned.com. **Description:** Supplies electric service in New York City and most of Westchester County, a service area with a population of more than 8 million. The company also supplies gas to Manhattan, the Bronx, and parts of Queens and Westchester. **Corporate headquarters location:** This location. **Parent company:** Consolidated Edison, Inc. **Listed on:** New York Stock Exchange. **Stock exchange symbol:** ED.

KEYSPAN ENERGY DELIVERY

One MetroTech Center, Brooklyn NY 11201. 718/403-1000. **Contact:** Human Resources. **E-mail address:** employment@keyspanenergy.com. **World Wide Web address:** http://www.keyspanenergy.com. **Description:** Provides natural gas service and engages in gas exploration, production, and transportation. **Corporate headquarters location:** This location. **Subsidiaries include:** Brooklyn Union Gas Company. **Listed on:** New York Stock Exchange. **Stock exchange symbol:** KSE. **Annual sales/revenues:** More than $100 million.

LONG ISLAND POWER AUTHORITY (LIPA)

333 Earle Ovington Boulevard, Suite 403, Uniondale NY 11553. 516/222-7700. **Toll-free phone:** 877/275-5472. **Contact:** Human Resources Department. **E-mail address:** info@lipower.org. **World Wide Web address:** http://www.lipower.org. **Description:** Supplies electric and gas service in Nassau and Suffolk Counties and the Rockaway Peninsula in Queens County. **Corporate headquarters location:** This location.

ORANGE AND ROCKLAND UTILITIES

71 Dolson Avenue, Middletown NY 10940. 845/342-8940. **Contact:** Human Resources. **World Wide Web address:** http://www.oru.com. **Description:** Orange and Rockland Utilities and its subsidiaries supply electric service to 254,000 customers and gas service to 108,200 customers in southeastern New York, northern New Jersey, and northeastern Pennsylvania. **Corporate headquarters location:** Pearl River NY. **Other U.S. locations:** Spring Valley NY. **Subsidiaries include:** Rockland Electric Company (NJ); Pike County Light and Power (PA). **Parent company:** Consolidated Edison, Inc. **Listed on:** New York Stock Exchange. **Stock exchange symbol:** ED. **Number of employees nationwide:** 1,725.

WATER AUTHORITY OF WESTERN NASSAU COUNTY

58 South Tyson Avenue, Floral Park NY 11001. 516/327-4100. **Contact:** Janice Varley, Director of Human Resources. **Description:** The Water Authority of Western Nassau County supplies and distributes water for residential and commercial use in western Nassau County. **NOTE:** Positions are filled in accordance with Nassau County Civil Service Commission rules. **Corporate headquarters location:** This location.

MISCELLANEOUS WHOLESALING

You can expect to find the following types of companies in this chapter:

Exporters and Importers • General Wholesale Distribution Companies

ACTRADE FINANCIAL TECHNOLOGIES
7 Penn Plaza, Suite 422, New York NY 10001. 212/563-1036. **Fax:** 732/868-1121. **Contact:** Human Resources Department. **E-mail address:** hr@actrade.com. **World Wide Web address:** http://www.actrade.com. **Description:** Provides U.S. companies with foreign markets for their products through the company's own network of buyers, wholesalers, and distributors. The company also provides flexible financing allowing timely payment for sellers and convenient payment terms for buyers. **Corporate headquarters location:** This location. **Subsidiaries include:** Actrade Capital, Inc. **Listed on:** NASDAQ. **Stock exchange symbol:** ACRT. **Annual sales/revenues:** More than $100 million.

ALLOU HEALTH & BEAUTY CARE
50 Emjay Boulevard, Brentwood NY 11717. 631/273-4000. **Contact:** Kathy Calvente, Personnel Manager. **Description:** Distributes health and beauty products such as fragrances, cosmetics, and food items to independent retailers in the metropolitan New York area. **NOTE:** Entry-level positions and second and third shifts are offered. **Corporate headquarters location:** This location. **Listed on:** American Stock Exchange. **Stock exchange symbol:** ALU. **Number of employees at this location:** 200.

ATELIER ESTHETIQUE INC.
386 Park Avenue South, Suite 1409, New York NY 10016. 212/725-6130. **Contact:** Human Resources Department. **World Wide Web address:** http://www.aeinstitute.net. **Description:** A wholesaler of cosmetic products and equipment. This location also houses a beauty school.

DYNAMIC CLASSICS LIMITED
58 Second Avenue, Brooklyn NY 11215. 718/369-4160. **Contact:** Human Resources. **Description:** Dynamic Classics sells and distributes a diverse line of exercise equipment, sport bags, luggage, and gift products, which are distributed nationwide. The majority of sales are to catalog showrooms, drug chains, sporting goods chains, distributors, chain stores, discount stores, and the premium trade.

ITOCHU INTERNATIONAL INC.
335 Madison Avenue, New York NY 10017. 212/818-8000. **Fax:** 212/818-8543. **Contact:** Human Resources. **E-mail address:** recruiting@itochu.com. **World Wide Web address:** http://www.itochu.com. **Description:** A diversified international trading company with markets that include textiles, metals, machinery, foodstuffs, general merchandise, electronics, chemicals, and energy. The company has import/export, distribution, finance, investment, transportation, and joint venture operations, all of which contribute to an annual business volume of over $12 billion. Itochu International is also engaged in direct investments and partnerships in many additional industries including high-technology manufacturing, retailing, fiber optics, satellite communications, and real estate development.

Corporate headquarters location: This location. **Parent company:** Itochu Corporation.

MARUBENI AMERICA CORPORATION
450 Lexington Avenue, 35th Floor, New York NY 10017-3907. 212/450-0100. **Contact:** Human Resources. **E-mail address:** info@marubeni-usa.com. **World Wide Web address:** http://www.marubeni-usa.com. **Description:** An international trading firm that provides importing and exporting services to and from Japan. Operations are conducted through seven groups: Metals & Minerals Group; Machinery Group; Petroleum Group; General Merchandise Group; Chemical & Plastics Group; Textile Group; and Grain, Marine, & Other Products Group. The New York and New Jersey operations involve all groups and offer a wide range of products. **Common positions include:** Attorney; Chemical Engineer; Computer Programmer; Credit Manager; Department Manager; General Manager; Human Resources Manager; Management Trainee; Marketing Specialist; Metallurgical Engineer; Petroleum Engineer; Services Sales Representative. **Corporate headquarters location:** This location. **Other U.S. locations:** Nationwide. **Subsidiaries include:** Don Juan Sportswear Inc.; It Fabrics Inc. **Parent company:** Marubeni Corporation (Japan). **Operations at this facility include:** Accounting/Auditing; Administration; Business Investment; Corporate Planning; Development; Financial Offices; International Finance; Legal/Legal Research; Regional Headquarters; Research and Development; Sales; Service; Systems Planning; Tax; Traffic; Transportation Services.

MITSUBISHI INTERNATIONAL CORPORATION
520 Madison Avenue, 16th Floor, New York NY 10022. 212/605-2000. **Contact:** Human Resources Department. **World Wide Web address:** http://www.mitsubishiintl.com. **Description:** This location is an integrated trading company for one of Japan's largest and most diversified corporations. Overall, Mitsubishi International operates through several trading divisions and related support divisions including Petroleum, Steel, Foods, Chemicals, Machinery, Textile, Non-Ferrous Metals, Ferrous Raw Materials, Lumber and Pulp, and General Merchandise. Regional offices are located throughout the United States. **Common positions include:** Marketing Specialist; Sales Representative; Transportation/Traffic Specialist. **Corporate headquarters location:** This location. **Other U.S. locations:** Nationwide. **Subsidiaries include:** Mitsubishi Trust & Banking Corporation (also at this location, 212/838-7700) is a bank with diverse activities that include real estate and foreign exchange services. **Parent company:** Mitsubishi Corporation of Japan. **Operations at this facility include:** Administration; Sales. **Number of employees at this location:** 400. **Number of employees nationwide:** 850.

MITSUI & COMPANY (USA)
200 Park Avenue, New York NY 10166. 212/878-4000. **Fax:** 212/878-4100. **Contact:** Human Resources. **World Wide Web address:** http://www.mitsui.com. **Description:** An international trading firm engaged in a wide range of import and export activities. **Common positions include:** Accountant/Auditor; Brokerage Clerk; Credit Manager; Economist; Human Resources Manager; Management Trainee; Purchasing Agent/Manager; Transportation/Traffic Specialist. **Corporate headquarters location:** This location. **Other U.S. locations:** Nationwide. **Parent company:** Mitsui Group (Tokyo, Japan) is an international industrial corporation operating in the following areas: cement, chemicals, commerce, construction, energy, engineering, finance and insurance, food, machinery, mining, nonferrous

metals, paper, real estate, steel, synthetic fibers and plastics, transportation, warehousing, and other services. **Operations at this facility include:** Administration; Divisional Headquarters; Regional Headquarters; Sales. **Listed on:** NASDAQ. **Stock exchange symbol:** MITSY. **Number of employees nationwide:** 700.

UOP/XEROX
2344 Flatbush Avenue, Brooklyn NY 11234. 718/252-6500. **Fax:** 718/252-8585. **Contact:** Human Resources. **Description:** Sells and services copiers, fax machines, laser printers, and other types of office equipment. **Common positions include:** Sales Representative.

PRIMARY EMPLOYERS
(Northern New Jersey)

ACCOUNTING AND MANAGEMENT CONSULTING

You can expect to find the following types of companies in this chapter:

Consulting and Research Firms • Industrial Accounting Firms • Management Services • Public Accounting Firms • Tax Preparation Companies

AON CONSULTING
125 Chubb Avenue, Lyndhurst NJ 07071. 201/460-6854. **Contact:** Human Resources. **World Wide Web address:** http://www.aonconsulting.com. **Description:** An international human resources consulting and benefits brokerage firm providing integrated advisory and support services in retirement planning, health care management, organizational effectiveness, compensation, human resources-related communications, and information technologies. **Corporate headquarters location:** Chicago IL.

CAP GEMINI ERNST & YOUNG
100 Walnut Avenue, Clark NJ 07066. 732/382-5400. **Contact:** Human Resources. **World Wide Web address:** http://www.us.cgey.com. **Description:** A leading provider of information technology consulting services with offices nationwide. **Other U.S. locations:** Nationwide.

DELOITTE & TOUCHE
2 Hilton Court, P.O. Box 319, Parsippany NJ 07054-0319. 973/683-7000. **Fax:** 973/683-7459. **Contact:** Human Resources Department. **World Wide Web address:** http://www.us.deloitte.com. **Description:** An international firm of certified public accountants providing professional accounting, auditing, tax, and management consulting services to widely diversified clients. The company has a specialized program consisting of national industry groups and functional groups that cross industry lines. Groups are involved in various disciplines including accounting, auditing, taxation management advisory services, small and growing businesses, mergers and acquisitions, and computer applications. **Corporate headquarters location:** Wilton CT. **Other U.S. locations:** Nationwide. **Parent company:** Deloitte Touche Tohmatsu International is a global leader with nearly 90,000 employees in over 130 countries.

ERNST & YOUNG LLP
125 Chubb Avenue, Lyndhurst NJ 07071. 201/872-2200. **Contact:** Human Resources. **World Wide Web address:** http://www.ey.com. **Description:** A certified public accounting firm that also provides management consulting services. Services include data processing, financial modeling, financial feasibility studies, production planning and inventory management, management sciences, health care planning, human resources, cost accounting, and budgeting systems. **Corporate headquarters location:** New York NY.

JACKSON HEWITT INC.
339 Jefferson Road, Parsippany NJ 07054. 973/496-1040. **Contact:** Human Resources. **World Wide Web address:** http://www.jacksonhewitt.com. **Description:** A full-service company specializing in computerized tax preparation and electronic filing. The foundation of Jackson Hewitt's tax

service is Hewtax, a proprietary software program. The company offers a number of filing options including SuperFast Refund, through which customers receive a refund anticipation loan within one to two days of filing; Accelerated Check Refund, which allows Jackson Hewitt to set up a bank account for the IRS to deposit the taxpayer's refund; and a standard electronically filed returnThe company also operates a travel agency, Campbell Travel.

KPMG
3 Chestnut Ridge Road, Montvale NJ 07645. 201/307-7000. **Contact:** Personnel. **World Wide Web address:** http://www.kpmgcareers.com. **Description:** This location houses the company's administrative offices. Overall, KPMG delivers a wide range of value-added assurance, tax, and consulting services. **Corporate headquarters location:** This location. **Other U.S. locations:** Nationwide. **Parent company:** KPMG International is a leader among professional services firms engaged in capturing, managing, assessing, and delivering information to create knowledge that will help its clients maximize shareholder value.

KEPNER-TREGOE, INC.
P.O. Box 704, Princeton NJ 08542. 609/921-2806. **Physical address:** 17 Research Road, Skillman NJ 08558. **Contact:** Human Resources. **World Wide Web address:** http://www.kepner-tregoe.com. **Description:** A worldwide management consulting firm. Product categories include strategy formulation, systems improvement, skill development, and specific issue resolution. Industry markets served include automotive, information technology, chemicals, financial services, and natural resources. Founded in 1958. **Common positions include:** Administrator; Consultant. **Corporate headquarters location:** This location. **International locations:** Worldwide. **Number of employees worldwide:** 225.

MERCER HUMAN RESOURCE CONSULTING
212 Carnegie Center, 4th Floor, Princeton NJ 08543. 609/520-2500. **Contact:** Personnel. **World Wide Web address:** http://www.mercerhr.com. **Description:** One of the world's largest actuarial and human resources management consulting firms, providing advice to organizations on all aspects of employee/management relationships. Services include retirement, health and welfare, performance and rewards, communication, investment, human resources administration, risk, finance and insurance, and health care provider consulting. **Corporate headquarters location:** New York NY. **Other U.S. locations:** Nationwide. **International locations:** Worldwide. **Parent company:** Marsh & McClennan Companies. **Listed on:** New York Stock Exchange. **Stock exchange symbol:** MMC.

KURT SALMON ASSOCIATES, INC.
103 Carnegie Center, Suite 205, Princeton NJ 08540. 609/452-8700. **Contact:** Director of Recruiting. **World Wide Web address:** http://www.kurtsalmon.com. **Description:** Provides management consulting to logistics and consumer products companies.

SIBSON CONSULTING
600 Alexander Park, Suite 208, Princeton NJ 08540. 609/520-2700. **Contact:** Human Resources Department. **World Wide Web address:** http://www.segalco.com/sibson. **Description:** A management consulting firm. **Corporate headquarters location:** This location. **Parent company:** Segal.

ADVERTISING, MARKETING, AND PUBLIC RELATIONS

You can expect to find the following types of companies in this chapter:

Advertising Agencies • Direct Mail Marketers • Market Research Firms • Public Relations Firms

CLIENTLOGIC
230 Brighton Road, Clifton NJ 07012. 973/778-5588. **Fax:** 973/778-7485. **Contact:** Human Resources. **E-mail address:** cliftonjobs@clientlogic.com. **World Wide Web address:** http://www.clientlogic.com. **Description:** A direct marketing firm. **Common positions include:** Accountant/Auditor; Clerical Supervisor; Computer Programmer; Customer Service Representative; Management Trainee; Systems Analyst. **Corporate headquarters location:** Nashville TN. **Other area locations:** Weehawken NJ. **Parent company:** Onex Corporation.

IMS HEALTH
100 Campus Road, Totowa NJ 07512. 973/790-0700. **Contact:** Human Resources Department. **World Wide Web address:** http://www.ims-health.com. **Description:** Conducts market research on the health care industry for pharmaceutical companies. **Common positions include:** Accountant/Auditor; Administrator; Attorney; Computer Programmer; Customer Service Representative; Department Manager; Financial Analyst; General Manager; Human Resources Manager; Instructor/Trainer; Operations/Production Manager; Public Relations Specialist; Statistician; Systems Analyst; Teacher/Professor; Technical Writer/Editor. **Special programs:** Internships. **Corporate headquarters location:** Plymouth Meeting PA. **Parent company:** Dun & Bradstreet. **Number of employees at this location:** 400.

IMEDIA, INC.
233 South Street, Morristown NJ 07960. 973/267-8500. **Fax:** 973/267-8977. **Contact:** Personnel. **World Wide Web address:** http://www.imedianet.com. **Description:** Provides public relations and technological consulting services for large companies.

MOKRYNSKI & ASSOCIATES
401 Hackensack Avenue, 2nd Floor, Hackensack NJ 07601. 201/488-5656. **Contact:** Human Resources Department. **World Wide Web address:** http://www.mokrynski.com. **Description:** A direct mailing company that manages, acquires, and sells mailing lists for client companies.

TOTAL RESEARCH CORPORATION
5 Independence Way, P.O. Box 5305, Princeton NJ 08543. 609/520-9100. **Fax:** 609/987-8839. **Contact:** Jane Giles, Manager of Human Resources Department. **E-mail address:** trc@totalres.com. **World Wide Web address:** http://www.harrisinteractive.com. **Description:** A full-service marketing research firm that provides information for use in strategic and tactical marketing decisions. **NOTE:** Mail employment correspondence to: Human Resources, Job Code #, 76 Carlson Road, Rochester NY 14610. **Common positions include:** Administrative Assistant; Applications Engineer; Computer Programmer; Market Research Analyst; Network/Systems

Administrator. **Special programs:** Internships. **Corporate headquarters location:** Rochester NY. **Other U.S. locations:** Tampa FL; Chicago IL; Detroit MI; Minneapolis MN. **International locations:** Argentina; England. **Parent company:** Harris Interactive. **Listed on:** NASDAQ. **Stock exchange symbol:** HPOL.

AEROSPACE

You can expect to find the following types of companies in this chapter:

Aerospace Products and Services • Aircraft Equipment and Parts

BREEZE-EASTERN
700 Liberty Avenue, Union NJ 07083. 908/686-4000. **Fax:** 908/686-4279. **Contact:** Ed Chestnut, Director of Human Resources Department. **E-mail address:** echestnut@breeze-eastern.com. **World Wide Web address:** http://www.breeze-eastern.com. **Description:** Designs, develops, manufactures, and services sophisticated lifting and restraining products, principally helicopter rescue hoist and cargo hook systems; winches and hoists for aircraft and weapon systems; and aircraft cargo tie-down systems. **Corporate headquarters location:** This location. **Parent company:** TransTechnology designs, manufactures, sells, and distributes specialty fasteners through several other subsidiaries including: Breeze Industrial Products (Saltsburg PA) manufactures a complete line of standard and specialty gear-driven band fasteners in high-grade stainless steel for use in highly-engineered applications; The Palnut Company (Mountainside NJ) manufactures light- and heavy-duty single and multithread specialty fasteners; Industrial Retaining Ring (Irvington NJ) manufactures a variety of retaining rings made of carbon steel, stainless steel, and beryllium copper; The Seeger Group (Somerville NJ) manufactures retaining clips, circlips, spring pins, and similar components.

DASSAULT FALCON JET CORPORATION
475 Wall Street, Princeton NJ 08540. 609/921-0450. **Contact:** Human Resources Department. **E-mail address:** resumes@falconjet.com. **World Wide Web address:** http://www.falconjet.com. **Description:** This location is a sales office. Overall, Dassault Falcon Jet Corporation manufactures and sells a line of two- and three-engine business aircraft. The company also operates international jet aircraft service and maintenance centers (Falcon Jet Service Centers), engaged in the service, repair, and maintenance of a wide range of jet aircraft engines, airframes, avionics, instruments, and accessories. **Parent company:** Dassault Aviation.

DASSAULT FALCON JET CORPORATION
Teterboro Airport, P.O. Box 2000, South Hackensack NJ 07606. 201/262-0800. **Physical address:** Teterboro Airport, 200 Riser Road, Little Ferry NJ 07643. **Contact:** Mr. Mark Clifford, Career Opportunities Representative. **E-mail address:** resumes@falconjet.com. **World Wide Web address:** http://www.falconjet.com. **Description:** Manufactures and sells a line of two- and three-engine business aircraft. Dassault Falcon Jet also operates international jet aircraft service and maintenance centers (Falcon Jet Service Centers), engaged in the service, repair, and maintenance of a wide range of jet aircraft engines, airframes, avionics, instruments, and accessories. **Parent company:** Dassault Aviation.

GOODRICH CORPORATION
MOTION CONTROLS DIVISION
197 Ridgedale Avenue, Cedar Knolls NJ 07927. 973/267-4500. **Contact:** Human Resources. **World Wide Web address:** http://www.goodrich.com. **Description:** Manufactures aircraft systems and components and provides services for the aerospace industry worldwide. **NOTE:** For employment

information contact: Human Resources, Goodrich Corporation, 100 Panton Road, Vergennes VT 05491. 802/877-2911. **Parent company:** Goodrich Company. **Listed on:** New York Stock Exchange. **Stock exchange symbol:** GR.

HONEYWELL
10 North Avenue East, Elizabeth NJ 07201. 908/354-3215. **Contact:** Human Resources. **World Wide Web address:** http://www.honeywell.com. **Description:** This location manufactures plastic inserts for pill bottles. Overall, Honeywell is engaged in the research, development, manufacture, and sale of advanced technology products and services in the fields of chemicals, electronics, automation, and controls. The company's major businesses are home and building automation and control, performance polymers and chemicals, industrial automation and control, space and aviation systems, and defense and marine systems. **Listed on:** New York Stock Exchange. **Stock exchange symbol:** HON.

HONEYWELL
101 Columbia Road, Morristown NJ 07962-1057. 973/455-2000. **Contact:** Personnel Director. **World Wide Web address:** http://www.honeywell.com. **Description:** Honeywell is engaged in the research, development, manufacture, and sale of advanced technology products and services in the fields of chemicals, electronics, automation, and controls. The company's major businesses are home and building automation and control, performance polymers and chemicals, industrial automation and control, space and aviation systems, and defense and marine systems. **Corporate headquarters location:** This location. **Listed on:** New York Stock Exchange. **Stock exchange symbol:** HON.

HONEYWELL
DEFENSE AND AVIONICS SYSTEMS
699 Route 46 East, Teterboro NJ 07608. 201/288-2000. **Contact:** Human Resources. **World Wide Web address:** http://www.honeywell.com. **Description:** This location develops and manufactures advanced aerospace products under government contract including instrumentation for air and guidance systems. Overall, Honeywell is engaged in the research, development, manufacture, and sale of advanced technology products and services in the fields of chemicals, electronics, automation, and controls. The company's major businesses are home and building automation and control, performance polymers and chemicals, industrial automation and control, space and aviation systems, and defense and marine systems. **Listed on:** New York Stock Exchange. **Stock exchange symbol:** HON.

LYNTON AVIATION
3 Airport Road, Morristown Municipal Airport, Morristown NJ 07960-4624. 973/292-9000. **Fax:** 973/539-6657. **Contact:** Sue Lemen, Human Resources Director. **Description:** Performs aviation services including the management, charter, maintenance, and refueling of corporate helicopters and fixed-wing aircraft, and helicopter support services for industrial and utility applications. Lynton Group also provides aircraft sales and brokerage services worldwide. **Corporate headquarters location:** This location.

R-V METAL FABRICATING INC.
20 Sand Park Road, Cedar Grove NJ 07009. 973/239-8100. **Contact:** Human Resources. **World Wide Web address:** http://www.rvmetal.com. **Description:** Supplies fabricated sheet metal detail parts and assemblies for primarily the aerospace industry.

SMITHS INDUSTRIES
110 Algonquin Parkway, Whippany NJ 07981. 973/428-9898. **Contact:** Russell J. Stehn, Vice President of Human Resources. **World Wide Web address:** http://www.smiths-aerospace.com. **Description:** Engineers and manufactures electro-mechanical actuation control systems for the aerospace and commercial industries. **Common positions include:** Accountant/Auditor; Aerospace Engineer; Blue-Collar Worker Supervisor; Buyer; Computer Programmer; Credit Manager; Customer Service Representative; Department Engineer; Electrical/Electronics Engineer; Financial Analyst; Human Resources Manager; Industrial Engineer; Mechanical Engineer; Operations/Production Manager; Purchasing Agent/Manager; Quality Control Supervisor; Technical Writer/Editor. **Parent company:** Smiths Group. **Operations at this facility include:** Divisional Headquarters; Manufacturing; Research and Development; Sales. **Number of employees at this location:** 250.

APPAREL, FASHION, AND TEXTILES

You can expect to find the following types of companies in this chapter:
Broadwoven Fabric Mills • Knitting Mills • Curtains and Draperies • Footwear • Nonwoven Fabrics • Textile Goods and Finishing • Yarn and Thread Mills

BEACON LOOMS, INC.
411 Alfred Avenue, Teaneck NJ 07666. 201/833-1600. **Contact:** Human Resources Department. **E-mail address:** contact@beaconlooms.com. **World Wide Web address:** http://www.beaconlooms.com. **Description:** Produces a wide range of textiles, primarily for sale to retailers. **Corporate headquarters location:** This location. **Other U.S. locations:** Englewood NJ.

NEIL COOPER LLC
356 Nye Avenue, Irvington NJ 07111. 973/416-8100. **Contact:** Controller. **Description:** Imports and manufactures men's and boys' leather and cloth coats and jackets in the moderate-to-high price range. The company sells coats to department stores and private label distributors, and distributes products worldwide.

S. GOLDBERG & COMPANY, INC.
20 East Broadway, Hackensack NJ 07601. 201/342-1200. **Contact:** Personnel Manager. **Description:** Manufactures house slippers. **Common positions include:** Industrial Engineer. **Corporate headquarters location:** This location.

JACLYN, INC.
5801 Jefferson Street, West New York NJ 07093. 201/868-9400. **Contact:** Personnel. **EWorld Wide Web address:** http://www.jaclyninc.com. **Description:** Designs, manufactures, and sells women's and children's handbag fashions, accessories, specialty items, and ready-to-wear apparel. **Common positions include:** Accountant/Auditor; Administrator; Blue-Collar Worker Supervisor; Buyer; Computer Programmer; Credit Manager; Department Manager; Financial Analyst; General Manager; Human Resources Manager; Operations/Production Manager; Purchasing Agent/Manager; Sales Executive; Transportation/Traffic Specialist. **Corporate headquarters location:** This location.

PHILLIPS-VAN HEUSEN CORPORATION
1001 Frontier Road, Suite 100, Bridgewater NJ 08807-2955. 908/685-0050. **Contact:** Betty Chaves, Director of Human Resources. **World Wide Web address:** http://www.pvh.com. **Description:** Engaged in the manufacture, wholesale, and retail of men's and women's apparel. **Corporate headquarters location:** New York NY. **Other U.S. locations:** AL. **Listed on:** New York Stock Exchange. **Stock exchange symbol:** PVH. **Number of employees nationwide:** 14,000.

SETON COMPANY
849 Broadway, Newark NJ 07104. 973/485-4800. **Contact:** Human Resources Department. **E-mail address:** hr@setonco.com. **World Wide Web address:** http://www.setonleather.com. **Description:** Company operations are conducted primarily through two business segments. The Leather

Division's operations include tanning, finishing, and distributing whole-hide cattle leathers for the automotive and furniture upholstery industries, cattle hide side leathers for footwear, handbag, and other markets, and cattle products for collagen, rawhide pet items, and other applications. The Chemicals and Coated Products Division is engaged in the manufacture and distribution of epoxy and urethane chemicals, specialty leather finishes, industrial and medical tapes, foams, films, and laminates. Other manufacturing facilities are located in Wilmington DE (epoxy, urethane chemicals, leather finishes); Toledo OH (cattle hide processing); Malvern PA (industrial coated products); and Saxton PA (cutting of finished leathers). **Corporate headquarters location:** This location. **Subsidiaries include:** Radel Leather Manufacturing Company; Seton Leather Company.

ARCHITECTURE, CONSTRUCTION, AND ENGINEERING

You can expect to find the following types of companies in this chapter:

Architectural and Engineering Services • Civil and Mechanical Engineering Firms • Construction Products, Manufacturers, and Wholesalers • General Contractors/ Specialized Trade Contractors

ABB INC.

1460 Livingstone Avenue, North Brunswick NJ 08902-6005. 732/932-6000. **Contact:** Human Resources Manager. **World Wide Web address:** http://www.abb.com/us. **Description:** Provides engineering, construction, and sales support services as part of a worldwide engineering firm. Internationally, the company operates through the following business segments: oil field equipment and services; power systems; engineering and construction; process equipment; and industrial products. **Corporate headquarters location:** Norwalk CT. **Other U.S. locations:** New York NY. **Subsidiaries include:** ABB Lumus Global Inc. (Bloomfield NJ); ABB Simcom (Bloomfield NJ); ABB Susa (also at this location). **Parent company:** ABB AG (Baden, Switzerland). **Number of employees worldwide:** 220,000.

ABB LUMMUS GLOBAL INC.

1515 Broad Street, Bloomfield NJ 07003. 973/893-1515. **Contact:** Human Resources. **World Wide Web address:** http://www.abb.com/us. **Description:** An engineering firm serving power plants, chemical plants, and petrochemical and oil refineries, as well as other industries such as aviation and storage. **Parent company:** ABB Inc. (Norwalk CT) provides engineering, construction, and sales support services as part of the worldwide engineering firm. Another subsidiary, ABB Simcon (Bloomfield NJ), specializes in chemical engineering. Internationally, the company operates in five business segments: oil field equipment and services, power systems, engineering and construction, process equipment, and industrial products.

AMERICAN STANDARD COMPANIES INC.

P.O. Box 6820, Piscataway NJ 08854. 732/980-6000. **Physical address:** One Centennial Avenue, Piscataway NJ 08855. **Contact:** Human Resources. **World Wide Web address:** http://www.americanstandard.com. **Description:** A global, diversified manufacturer. The company's operations are comprised of four segments: air conditioning products, plumbing products, automotive products, and medical systems. The air conditioning products segment (through subsidiary The Trane Company) develops and manufactures Trane and American Standard air conditioning equipment for use in central air conditioning systems for commercial, institutional, and residential buildings. The plumbing products segment develops and manufactures American Standard, Ideal Standard, Porcher, Armitage Shanks, Dolomite, and Standard bathroom and kitchen fixtures and fittings. The automotive products segment develops and manufactures truck, bus, and utility vehicle braking and control systems under the WABCO and Perrot brands. The medical systems segment manufactures Copalis, DiaSorin, and Pylori-Chek medical diagnostic products and systems for a variety of diseases including HIV, osteoporosis, and renal disease.

Corporate headquarters location: This location. **International locations:** Worldwide. **Listed on:** New York Stock Exchange. **Stock exchange symbol:** ASD. **Chairman/CEO:** Frederic M. Poses. **Number of employees worldwide:** 57,000.

ARROW GROUP INDUSTRIES, INC.
1680 Route 23 North, P.O. Box 928, Wayne NJ 07474-0928. 973/696-6900. **Fax:** 973/696-8539. **Contact:** Joanne Trezza, Human Resources Director. **World Wide Web address:** http://www.sheds.com. **Description:** Manufactures steel storage buildings. **Corporate headquarters location:** This location. **Other U.S. locations:** Breese IL. **Listed on:** Privately held. **Number of employees at this location:** 115. **Number of employees nationwide:** 330.

BARHAM-McBRIDE COMPANY INC.
80 Park Plaza Newark NJ 07102. 973/430-5640. **Contact:** Human Resources. **World Wide Web address:** http://www.et.pseg.com. **Description:** Mechanical contractors for the architecture and construction industries. **Parent company:** PSEG.

THE LOUIS BERGER GROUP, INC.
100 Halsted Street, East Orange NJ 07018. 973/678-1960. **Fax:** 973/676-0532. **Contact:** Terry Williams, Human Resources Department. **E-mail address:** recruiting@louisberger.com. **World Wide Web address:** http://www.louisberger.com. **Description:** A diversified consulting firm. The company provides cultural, environmental, and transportation-related engineering and planning services in the United States. Louis Berger also aids in urban and rural development projects in Africa, Asia, Latin America, and the Middle East. This location also hires seasonally. Founded in 1940. **NOTE:** Entry-level positions and part-time jobs are offered. **Common positions include:** Accountant; Administrative Assistant; Biological Scientist; Chemical Engineer; Civil Engineer; Design Engineer; Electrical/Electronics Engineer; Environmental Engineer; Financial Analyst; Geographer; Geologist/Geophysicist; Transportation/Traffic Specialist. **Special programs:** Summer Jobs. **Office hours:** Monday - Friday, 8:30 a.m. - 5:15 p.m. **Corporate headquarters location:** This location. **Other U.S. locations:** Washington DC; Chicago IL; Needham MA; Las Vegas NV. **International locations:** Worldwide. **Listed on:** Privately held. **President:** Derish Wolff. **Information Systems Manager:** Michael Stern. **Annual sales/revenues:** More than $100 million. **Number of employees at this location:** 270. **Number of employees nationwide:** 900. **Number of employees worldwide:** 2,000.

BURNS AND ROE ENTERPRISES, INC.
800 Kinderkamack Road, Oradell NJ 07649. 201/265-2000. **Contact:** Human Resources. **World Wide Web address:** http://www.roe.com. **Description:** Engaged in construction, engineering, maintenance, and operation services. The company specializes in the design and engineering of complex facilities. **Common positions include:** Electrical/Electronics Engineer; Environmental Engineer; Industrial Engineer; Manufacturing Engineer; Marketing Manager; Marketing Specialist; Mechanical Engineer; Metallurgical Engineer; MIS Specialist; Project Manager; Purchasing Agent/Manager; Quality Control Supervisor; Secretary; Systems Analyst; Technical Writer/Editor; Transportation/Traffic Specialist. **Special programs:** Internships. **Corporate headquarters location:** This location. **Listed on:** Privately held. **Number of employees at this location:** 600. **Number of employees nationwide:** 1,200. **Number of employees worldwide:** 1,250.

C/S GROUP
3 Werner Way, Lebanon NJ 08833. 908/236-0800. **Fax:** 908/236-0604. **Contact:** Mr. Lee DiRubbo, Director of Human Resources. **E-mail address:** careerops@c-sgroup.com. **World Wide Web address:** http://www.c-sgroup.com. **Description:** Manufactures building materials including wall protection products, sun controls, and fire vents. Founded in 1948. **NOTE:** Entry-level positions and part-time jobs are offered. **Common positions include:** Accountant; Computer Support Technician; Computer Technician; Database Administrator; Draftsperson; Mechanical Engineer; Sales Manager; Sales Representative. **Corporate headquarters location:** This location. **Other U.S. locations:** Garden Grove CA; Muncy PA. **International locations:** France; Spain; United Kingdom. **Listed on:** Privately held. **Annual sales/revenues:** More than $100 million.

CENTEX HOMES
500 Craig Road, Manalapan NJ 07726. 732/780-1800. **Contact:** Human Resources. **World Wide Web address:** http://www.centexhomes.com. **Description:** Centex Homes designs, constructs, and sells homes nationwide. **Other U.S. locations:** Nationwide. **Parent company:** Centex Corporation. **Listed on:** New York Stock Exchange. **Stock exchange symbol:** CTX.

CLAYTON BRICK
2 Porete Avenue, North Arlington NJ 07032. 201/998-7600. **Contact:** Human Resources. **World Wide Web address:** http://www.claytonco.com. **Description:** Engaged in precast concrete panel construction and installation. **NOTE:** For employment information contact the central Clayton Companies office: P.O. Box 3015, 515 Lakewood-New Egypt Road, Lakewood NJ 08701. 732/363-1995.

EDWARDS AND KELCEY INC.
P.O. Box 1936, 299 Madison Avenue, Morristown NJ 07962-1936. 973/267-8830. **Contact:** Harry P. Daley, Human Resources Director. **World Wide Web address:** http://www.ekcorp.com. **Description:** A consulting, engineering, planning, and communications organization whose range of services includes location and economic feasibility studies; valuations and appraisals; cost analyses; computer technology; marketing studies; traffic and transportation studies; soils and foundation analyses; environmental impact studies; master planning; structural surveys; and preliminary and final designs. Services also include preparation of contract documents and observation of construction operations for public transit systems, terminals, railroads, bus depots, parking garages, airports, ports, highways, streets, bridges, tunnels, traffic control systems, military facilities, communications systems, storm and sanitary sewers, water supply and distribution, flood control, and land development. Founded in 1946. **NOTE:** Entry-level positions are offered. **Common positions include:** Accountant; Civil Engineer; Construction Engineer; Cost Estimator; Draftsperson; Electrical/Electronics Engineer; Market Research Analyst; Marketing Specialist; Transportation/Traffic Specialist. **Special programs:** Internships. **Corporate headquarters location:** This location. **Other U.S. locations:** Atlanta GA; Chicago IL; Baltimore MD; Boston MA; Minneapolis MN; Manchester NH; New York NY; Saratoga Springs NY; Cincinnati OH; Chadds Ford PA; West Chester PA; Providence RI; Dallas TX; Houston TX; Leesburg VA; Milwaukee WI. **International locations:** Puerto Rico. **Operations at this facility include:** Administration; Divisional Headquarters. **Listed on:** Privately held. **Annual sales/revenues:** More than

$100 million. **Number of employees at this location:** 200. **Number of employees nationwide:** 730.

FM GLOBAL

400 Interpace Parkway, Building C, 3rd Floor, Parsipanny NJ 07054-1196. 973/402-2200. **Contact:** Human Resources Department. **World Wide Web address:** http://www.fmglobal.com. **Description:** A loss control services organization. The company helps owner company policyholders to protect their properties and occupancies from damage caused by fire, wind, flood, and explosion; boiler, pressure vessel, and machinery accidents; and many other insured hazards. **Corporate headquarters location:** Johnston RI. **Other U.S. locations:** Nationwide. **International locations:** Worldwide.

GAF MATERIALS CORPORATION

1361 Alps Road, Wayne NJ 07470. 973/628-3000. **Toll-free phone:** 800/766-3411. **Contact:** Human Resources Department. **E-mail address:** employment@gaf.com. **World Wide Web address:** http://www.gaf.com. **Description:** Manufactures roofing materials. **Common positions include:** Accountant/Auditor; Industrial Engineer; Industrial Production Manager; Quality Control Supervisor. **Operations at this facility include:** Administration; Manufacturing.

K. HOVNANIAN COMPANIES

10 Highway 35, Red Bank NJ 07701. 732/747-7800. **Contact:** Human Resources. **World Wide Web address:** http://www.khov.com. **Description:** Designs, constructs, and sells condominium apartments, townhouses, and single-family homes in residential communities. The company is also engaged in mortgage banking. Founded in 1959. **Common positions include:** Accountant; Administrative Assistant; Architect; Attorney; Auditor; Civil Engineer; Computer Operator; Computer Programmer; Controller; Financial Analyst; Human Resources Manager; Market Research Analyst; Marketing Manager; Marketing Specialist; MIS Specialist; Online Content Specialist; Real Estate Agent; Sales Manager; Secretary; Systems Analyst; Systems Manager; Technical Writer/Editor; Webmaster. **Corporate headquarters location:** This location. **Other U.S. locations:** CA; FL; NC; NY; PA; VA. **Subsidiaries include:** New Fortis Homes. **Listed on:** New York Stock Exchange. **Stock exchange symbol:** HOV. **Number of employees at this location:** 90. **Number of employees nationwide:** 1,150.

INTERNATIONAL SPECIALTY PRODUCTS

1361 Alps Road, Wayne NJ 07470. 973/628-4000. **Contact:** Gary Schneid, Director of Employee Selection. **E-mail address:** jobs2@ispcorp.com. **World Wide Web address:** http://www.ispcorp.com. **Description:** Manufactures specialty chemicals and building materials. Chemicals include high-pressure acetylene derivatives, industrial organic and inorganic chemicals, GAF filter systems, and GAF mineral products. Building materials include prepared roofing, roll roofing, built-up roofing systems, and single-ply roofing. **Common positions include:** Accountant/Auditor; Advertising Clerk; Attorney; Biological Scientist; Biomedical Engineer; Budget Analyst; Buyer; Chemical Engineer; Chemist; Computer Programmer; Financial Analyst; General Manager; Paralegal; Pharmacist; Systems Analyst. **Corporate headquarters location:** This location. **Listed on:** New York Stock Exchange. **Stock exchange symbol:** ISP. **Number of employees at this location:** 700. **Number of employees nationwide:** 4,300.

MELARD MANUFACTURING CORPORATION

2 Paulison Avenue, Passaic NJ 07055-5703. 973/472-8888. **Contact:** Personnel. **World Wide Web address:** http://www.masco.com. **Description:** Manufactures a broad range of hardware products including bath accessories and plumbing equipment. **Corporate headquarters location:** This location. **Parent company:** Masco Corporation.

JOS. L. MUSCARELLE, INC.

99 West Essex Street, Route 17, Maywood NJ 07607. 201/845-8100. **Contact:** Joseph Muscarelle, Jr., President. **Description:** Engaged in construction and real estate development. **Common positions include:** Civil Engineer; Credit Manager; Draftsperson; Electrical/Electronics Engineer; General Manager; Human Resources Manager; Operations/Production Manager; Project Manager; Purchasing Agent/Manager; Real Estate Agent; Sales Executive; Scheduler.

PATENT CONSTRUCTION SYSTEMS

One Mack Centre Drive, Paramus NJ 07652. 201/261-5600. **Fax:** 201/261-5544. **Contact:** Human Resources and Labor Relations. **E-mail address:** jobs@pcshd.com. **World Wide Web address:** http://www.pcshd.com. **Description:** Manufactures and markets scaffolding as well as concrete forming and shoring products. Founded in 1909. **Parent company:** Harsco Corporation.

PIONEER INDUSTRIES

171 South Newman Street, Hackensack NJ 07601. 201/933-1900. **Contact:** Personnel Director. **Description:** Produces industrial doors, fireproof and theft-proof doors, and other sheet metal specialties. **Corporate headquarters location:** Bloomfield Hills MI. **Parent company:** Core Industries. **Operations at this facility include:** Manufacturing.

SCHIAVONE CONSTRUCTION CO.

150 Meadowlands Parkway, 3rd Floor, Secaucus NJ 07094. 201/867-5070. **Contact:** Recruiting. **World Wide Web address:** http://www.schiavone.com. **Description:** A heavy construction firm engaged in large-scale projects such as highways, tunnels, and bridges. Clients include city, state, and federal governments.

U.S. INDUSTRIES

101 Wood Avenue South, Iselin NJ 08830. 732/767-0700. **Contact:** Human Resources. **Description:** A holding company for four categories of manufacturing companies: bath and plumbing products, hardware and nonelectric tools, commercial and residential lighting, and a variety of consumer products ranging from vacuum cleaners to toys. **Corporate headquarters location:** This location. **Subsidiaries include:** Jacuzzi; Lighting Corporation of America; Selkirk; Spaulding.

ARTS, ENTERTAINMENT, SPORTS, AND RECREATION

You can expect to find the following types of companies in this chapter:
Botanical and Zoological Gardens • Entertainment Groups • Motion Picture and Video Tape Production and Distribution • Museums and Art Galleries • Physical Fitness Facilities • Professional Sports Clubs • Public Golf Courses • Racing and Track Operations • Sporting and Recreational Camps • Theatrical Producers

AUDIO PLUS VIDEO INTERNATIONAL, INC.
235 Pegasus Avenue, Northvale NJ 07647. 201/767-3800. **Contact:** Human Resources. **World Wide Web address:** http://www.apvi.com. **Description:** Services include post-production work and audio and video restoration for a variety of networks including the Children's Television Network (CTW). **Corporate headquarters location:** New York NY. **Parent company:** International Post Ltd. provides a wide range of post-production services, primarily to the television advertising industry, and distributes television programming to the international market through its operating subsidiaries. Other subsidiaries of the parent company include Big Picture/Even Time Limited; Cabana; Manhattan Transfer, Inc.; and The Post Edge, Inc. The company's services include creative editorial services, film-to-tape transfer, electronic video editing, computer-generated graphics, duplication, and audio services, all in multiple standards and formats, as well as network playback operations. The company's services are provided in the New York metropolitan area and South Florida.

CNBC
MSNBC
2200 Fletcher Avenue, 7th Floor, Fort Lee NJ 07024. 201/585-2622. **Fax:** 201/346-6506. **Contact:** Personnel Department. **World Wide Web address:** http://www.cnbc.com. **Description:** Operates all-news networks offering current business and finance news. CNBC and MSNBC are both updated 24 hours a day, seven days a week. **Corporate headquarters location:** This location. **Parent company:** NBC.

INSTRUCTIVISION, INC.
P.O. Box 2004, 16 Chapin Road, Pine Brook NJ 07058. 973/575-9992. **Contact:** Human Resources Department. **World Wide Web address:** http://www.instructivision.com. **Description:** Develops video production and education software. Instructivision also operates a full-service video production facility encompassing a production stage, an interformat digital editing suite, offline editing, 3-D animation, and audio recording equipment.

McCARTER THEATRE
CENTER FOR THE PERFORMING ARTS
91 University Place, Princeton NJ 08540. 609/258-6500. **Fax:** 609/497-0369. **Contact:** General Manager. **World Wide Web address:** http://www.mccarter.org. **Description:** A performing arts center that produces and presents artists in dramatic, musical, dance, and special events. Established in 1963. **Common positions include:** Actor/Actress;

Performer; Artist; Designer; Painter; Tailor. **Special programs:** Internships. **Corporate headquarters location:** This location. **Number of employees at this location:** 200.

MOUNTAIN CREEK
200 Route 94, Vernon NJ 07462. 973/827-2000. **Contact:** Human Resources. **World Wide Web address:** http://www.mountaincreek.com. **Description:** Operates as a water amusement park in the summer and a ski resort in the winter.

NEW JERSEY SHAKESPEARE FESTIVAL
36 Madison Avenue, Madison NJ 07940-1434. 973/408-3278. **Fax:** 973/408-3361. **Contact:** Mr. Joseph Discher, Artistic Associate. **E-mail address:** njsf@njshakespeare.org. **World Wide Web address:** http://www.njshakespeare.org. **Description:** A nonprofit professional theater devoted to producing the works of Shakespeare and other classic masterworks. Founded in 1962. **NOTE:** Entry-level positions are offered. **Common positions include:** Administrative Assistant; General Manager; Graphic Artist; Graphic Designer; Marketing Manager; Production Manager; Public Relations Specialist; Teacher/Professor. **Special programs:** Internships; Apprenticeships; Training.

NEW JERSEY SPORTS & EXPOSITION AUTHORITY
50 Route 120, East Rutherford NJ 07073. 201/935-8500. **Recorded jobline:** 201/460-4265. **Contact:** Gina Klein, Director of Human Resources. **E-mail address:** hr@njsea.com. **World Wide Web address:** http://www.njsea.com. **Description:** A state-appointed agency responsible for coordinating and running sports and entertainment activities at the Meadowlands Sports Complex, which includes Meadowlands Racetrack (harness and thoroughbred racing, as well as other events), Giants Stadium (New York Giants, New York Jets, concerts, and other events), and Continental Airlines Arena (New Jersey Nets, New Jersey Devils, tennis, track, concerts, and other events). **Corporate headquarters location:** This location.

PPI ENTERTAINMENT
88 St. Francis Street, Newark NJ 07105. 973/344-4214. **Contact:** Personnel. **World Wide Web address:** http://www.peterpan.com. **Description:** Manufactures and distributes records, tapes, videos, and CD-ROMs. **Common positions include:** Accountant; Advertising Executive; Editorial Assistant; Graphic Artist; Graphic Designer; Marketing Manager; Production Manager; Public Relations Specialist; Purchasing Agent/Manager; Sales Manager; Sales Representative; Secretary; Video Production Coordinator. **Corporate headquarters location:** This location. **Listed on:** Privately held.

AUTOMOTIVE

You can expect to find the following types of companies in this chapter:

Automotive Repair Shops • Automotive Stampings • Industrial Vehicles and Moving Equipment • Motor Vehicles and Equipment • Travel Trailers and Campers

AMERICAN STANDARD COMPANIES INC.
P.O. Box 6820, Piscataway NJ 08854. 732/980-6000. **Physical address:** One Centennial Avenue, Piscataway NJ 08855. **Contact:** Human Resources. **World Wide Web address:** http://www.americanstandard.com. **Description:** A global, diversified manufacturer. The company's operations are comprised of four segments: air conditioning products, plumbing products, automotive products, and medical systems. The air conditioning products segment (through subsidiary The Trane Company) develops and manufactures Trane and American Standard air conditioning equipment for use in central air conditioning systems for commercial, institutional, and residential buildings. The plumbing products segment develops and manufactures American Standard, Ideal Standard, Porcher, Armitage Shanks, Dolomite, and Standard bathroom and kitchen fixtures and fittings. The automotive products segment develops and manufactures truck, bus, and utility vehicle braking and control systems under the WABCO and Perrot brands. The medical systems segment manufactures Copalis, DiaSorin, and Pylori-Chek medical diagnostic products and systems for a variety of diseases including HIV, osteoporosis, and renal disease. **Corporate headquarters location:** This location. **International locations:** Worldwide. **Listed on:** New York Stock Exchange. **Stock exchange symbol:** ASD. **Chairman/CEO:** Frederic M. Poses. **Number of employees worldwide:** 57,000.

BMW OF NORTH AMERICA, INC.
P.O. Box 964, Hewitt NJ 07461. 201/307-4000. **Physical address:** 300 Chestnut Ridge Road, Woodcliff Lake NJ 07675. **Contact:** Manager of Employment Department. **E-mail address:** bmwna@hreasy.com. **World Wide Web address:** http://www.bmwusa.com. **Description:** BMW of North America is responsible for U.S. marketing operations for BMW's extensive line of motorcycles and automobiles. **Parent company:** BMW-Bayerische Motoren Werke AG (Munich, Germany).

FORD MOTOR COMPANY
698 U.S. Highway 46, Teterboro NJ 07608. 201/288-9400. **Contact:** Manager of Human Resources. **World Wide Web address:** http://www.ford.com/careercenter. **Description:** This location is a parts distribution center. Overall, Ford is engaged in the manufacture, assembly, and sale of cars, trucks, and related parts and accessories. Ford is also one of the largest providers of financial services in the United States. The company's two core businesses are the Automotive Group and the Financial Services Group (Ford Credit, The Associates, USL Capital, and First Nationwide). Ford is also engaged in a number of other businesses, including electronics, glass, electrical and fuel-handling products, plastics, climate control systems, automotive service and replacement parts, vehicle leasing and rental, and land development. **Corporate headquarters**

location: Dearborn MI. **Listed on:** New York Stock Exchange. **Stock exchange symbol:** F.

GENERAL HOSE PRODUCTS INC.
30 Sherwood Lane, Fairfield NJ 07004. 973/228-0500. **Contact:** Diana Taylor, Office Manager. **Description:** Manufactures heavy-duty hose products used primarily by automobile manufacturers in air conditioning systems. General Hose is also engaged in tube fabrication and assemblies. **Common positions include:** Accountant/Auditor; Blue-Collar Worker Supervisor; Manufacturer's/Wholesaler's Sales Rep.; Mechanical Engineer; Operations/Production Manager. **Corporate headquarters location:** This location. **Operations at this facility include:** Manufacturing. **Number of employees at this location:** 25.

KEM MANUFACTURING COMPANY INC.
18-35 River Road, Fair Lawn NJ 07410. 201/796-8000. **Contact:** Personnel. **World Wide Web address:** http://www.kemparts.com. **Description:** Manufactures and markets a wide range of products for distribution to the automotive aftermarket. KEM also produces Perfect Part, a complete general service line. **Common positions include:** Accountant/Auditor; Administrator; Advertising Clerk; Blue-Collar Worker Supervisor; Buyer; Computer Programmer; Credit Manager; Customer Service Representative; Department Manager; Draftsperson; General Manager; Human Resources Manager; Manufacturer's/Wholesaler's Sales Rep.; Mechanical Engineer; Operations/Production Manager; Purchasing Agent/Manager; Quality Control Supervisor. **Corporate headquarters location:** This location. **Operations at this facility include:** Manufacturing.

MERCEDES-BENZ USA, LLC
3 Mercedes Drive, Montvale NJ 07645. 201/573-2235. **Fax:** 201/573-6791. **Contact:** Human Resources. **E-mail address:** careers@mbusa.com. **World Wide Web address:** http://www.mercedesbenzcareers.com. **Description:** An importer of the complete line of Mercedes-Benz automobiles and related components. Mercedes-Benz of North America distributes Mercedes products to dealers throughout the United States. **Common positions include:** Accountant/Auditor; Automotive Engineer; Computer Programmer; Customer Service Representative; Financial Analyst; Instructor/Trainer; Marketing Specialist; Systems Analyst; Technical Writer/Editor. **Corporate headquarters location:** This location. **Parent company:** DaimlerChrysler. **Operations at this facility include:** Administration. **Number of employees nationwide:** 1,500.

VOLVO CARS OF NORTH AMERICA, INC.
6 Volvo Drive, Rockleigh NJ 07647. 201/768-7300. **Contact:** Human Resources. **World Wide Web address:** http://www.volvo.com. **Description:** Supports the sale and service of Volvo automobiles and related parts and accessories for approximately 400 dealers. **Common positions include:** Automotive Engineer. **Corporate headquarters location:** This location.

BANKING/SAVINGS AND LOANS

You can expect to find the following types of companies in this chapter:

Banks • Bank Holding Companies and Associations •
Lending Firms/Financial Services Institutions

BANK OF NEW YORK
385 Rifle Camp Road, West Paterson NJ 07424. 973/357-7405. **Contact:** Personnel. **World Wide Web address:** http://www.bankofny.com. **Description:** A bank that serves individuals, corporations, foreign and domestic banks, governments, and other institutions through banking offices in New York City and foreign branches, representative offices, subsidiaries, and affiliates. **Corporate headquarters location:** New York NY. **Parent company:** Bank of New York Company, Inc. **Listed on:** New York Stock Exchange. **Stock exchange symbol:** BK. **Number of employees nationwide:** 12,000.

FIRST UNION NATIONAL BANK
190 River Road, Summit NJ 07901. 908/598-3449. **Contact:** Human Resources. **World Wide Web address:** http://www.firstunion.com. **Description:** A bank. **Subsidiaries include:** CoreStates Financial Corporation; The Money Store, Inc. **Parent company:** First Union Corporation (Charlotte NC) is one of the nation's largest bank holding companies with subsidiaries that operate over 1,330 full-service bank branches in the south Atlantic states. These subsidiaries provide retail banking, retail investment, and commercial banking services. The corporation provides other financial services including mortgage banking, home equity lending, leasing, insurance, and securities brokerage services from 222 branch locations. The corporation also operates one of the nation's largest ATM networks. **Operations at this facility include:** Regional Headquarters. **Listed on:** New York Stock Exchange. **Stock exchange symbol:** FUR.

FIRST UNION NATIONAL BANK
120 Albany Street Plaza, New Brunswick NJ 08901. 732/843-4200. **Contact:** Human Resources. **World Wide Web address:** http://www.firstunion.com. **Description:** A bank. **Subsidiaries include:** CoreStates Financial Corporation; The Money Store, Inc. **Parent company:** First Union Corporation (Charlotte NC) is one of the nation's largest bank holding companies with subsidiaries that operate over 1,330 full-service bank branches in the south Atlantic states. These subsidiaries provide retail banking, retail investment, and commercial banking services. The corporation provides other financial services including mortgage banking, home equity lending, leasing, insurance, and securities brokerage services from 222 branch locations. The corporation also operates one of the nation's largest ATM networks. **Listed on:** New York Stock Exchange. **Stock exchange symbol:** FUR.

FLEET BANK
One Exchange Place, Jersey City NJ 07302. **Toll-free phone:** 800/841-4000. **Contact:** Human Resources Department. **World Wide Web address:** http://www.fleet.com. **Description:** Operates a full-service bank, serving the commercial and consumer banking needs of individuals, corporation, institutions, and government in the Northeast. **Corporate headquarters**

location: Boston MA. **Parent company:** FleetBoston Financial. **Listed on:** New York Stock Exchange. **Stock exchange symbol:** FBF.

FLEET BANK
301 Carnegie Center, Princeton NJ 08540. 609/987-3200. **Contact:** Staffing. **World Wide Web address:** http://www.fleet.com. **Description:** A full-service financial institution that serves corporate, retail, and private markets. **Corporate headquarters location:** Boston MA. **Parent company:** FleetBoston Financial. **Listed on:** New York Stock Exchange. **Stock exchange symbol:** FBF.

FLEET BANK
55 Challenger Road, Ridgefield Park NJ 07660. 201/296-3000. **Contact:** Human Resources. **World Wide Web address:** http://www.fleet.com. **Description:** A full-service financial institution that serves corporate, retail, and private markets. **Corporate headquarters location:** Boston MA. **Parent company:** FleetBoston Financial. **Listed on:** New York Stock Exchange. **Stock exchange symbol:** FBF.

GREATER COMMUNITY BANCORP
2 Sears Drive, Paramus NJ 07653. 973/942-1111. **Contact:** Human Resources. **World Wide Web address:** http://www.greatercommunity.com. **Description:** A holding company. **Subsidiaries include:** Greater Community Bank conducts general commercial and retail banking. **Listed on:** NASDAQ. **Stock exchange symbol:** GFLS.

HUDSON CITY SAVINGS BANK
West 80 Century Road, Paramus NJ 07652. 201/967-1900. **Contact:** Human Resources Department. **World Wide Web address:** http://www.hudsoncitysavingsbank.com. **Description:** Operates a full-service mutual savings bank with 80 branches in Bergen, Burlington, Camden, Essex, Gloucester, Hudson, Middlesex, Monmouth, Morris, Ocean, Passaic, and Union Counties. Hudson City Savings Bank provides a wide range of traditional banking services, as well as other financial services including IRAs.

HUDSON UNITED BANK
1500 Route 202, Harding Township NJ 07920. 973/425-3000. **Contact:** Human Resources. **E-mail address:** career@hudsonunitedbank.com. **World Wide Web address:** http://www.hudsonunitedbank.com. **Description:** A full-service bank. **NOTE:** Please send resumes to 1000 MacArthur Boulevard, Mahwah NJ 07430. **Corporate headquarters location:** This location.

INTERCHANGE BANK
Park 80 West/Plaza 2, Saddle Brook NJ 07663. 201/703-2265. **Fax:** 201/703-5291. **Contact:** Jane Matheson, Human Resources Director. **E-mail address:** humanresources@interchangebank.com. **World Wide Web address:** http://www.interchangebank.com. **Description:** A full-service bank with locations throughout Bergen County. **Parent company:** Interchange Financial Services Corporation. **Listed on:** NASDAQ. **Stock exchange symbol:** IFCJ.

UNITED TRUST
P.O. Box 6000, Bridgewater NJ 08807. 908/429-2200. **Physical address:** 1130 Route 22 East, Bridgewater NJ 08807. **Fax:** 908/707-8329. **Contact:** Human Resources Department. **E-mail address:** hr@unitedtrust.com. **World**

Wide Web address: http://www.unitedtrust.com. **Description:** Operates a full-service commercial bank offering a wide range of traditional banking, trust, and other financial services. **Corporate headquarters location:** This location.

VALLEY NATIONAL BANK

1455 Valley Road, Wayne NJ 07470. 973/696-4020. **Contact:** Peter Verbout, Director of Human Resources. **Description:** Operates a commercial bank offering a wide range of traditional banking services. **Common positions include:** Bank Officer/Manager; Branch Manager; Computer Programmer; Credit Manager; Customer Service Representative; Department Manager; Financial Analyst; General Manager; Human Resources Manager; Management Trainee. **Corporate headquarters location:** This location. **Parent company:** Valley National Bancorp. **Operations at this facility include:** Administration.

BIOTECHNOLOGY, PHARMACEUTICALS, AND SCIENTIFIC R&D

You can expect to find the following types of companies in this chapter:

Clinical Labs • Lab Equipment Manufacturers
Pharmaceutical Manufacturers and Distributors

ALPHARMA INC.
One Executive Drive, Fort Lee NJ 07024. 201/947-7774. **Fax:** 201/947-0153. **Contact:** Nancy Ryan, Vice President of Human Resources. **World Wide Web address:** http://www.alpharma.com. **Description:** A multinational pharmaceutical company that develops, manufactures, and markets specialty generic and proprietary human pharmaceuticals and animal health products. The U.S. Pharmaceuticals Division is a market leader in liquid pharmaceuticals and a prescription market leader in creams and ointments. The International Pharmaceuticals Division manufactures generic pharmaceuticals and OTC products. Other divisions include the Animal Health Division, which manufactures and markets antibiotics and other feed additives for the poultry and swine industries; the Aquatic Animal Health Division, which serves the aquaculture industry and is a manufacturer and marketer of vaccines for farmed fish; and the Fine Chemicals Division, which is a basic producer of specialty bulk antibiotics. **Corporate headquarters location:** This location. **Listed on:** NASDAQ. **Stock exchange symbol:** ALO.

ALTEON INC.
170 Williams Drive, Ramsey NJ 07446. 201/934-5000. **Fax:** 201/934-0090. **Contact:** Human Resources. **E-mail address:** postings@alteonpharma.com. **World Wide Web address:** http://www.alteonpharma.com. **Description:** A pharmaceutical company engaged in the discovery and development of novel therapeutic and diagnostic products for treating complications associated with diabetes and aging. **Listed on:** NASDAQ. **Stock exchange symbol:** ALT.

AVENTIS PHARMACEUTICALS
300 Somerset Corporation Boulevard, Bridgewater NJ 08807. 908/243-6000. **Contact:** Human Resources Department. **World Wide Web address:** http://www.aventispharma-us.com. **Description:** An international pharmaceutical company working with respiratory, cardiac, and osteopathic medications. **Operations at this facility include:** Marketing; Research and Development.

BASF CORPORATION
KNOLL PHARMACEUTICALS
3000 Continental Drive North, Mount Olive NJ 07828-1234. 973/426-2600. **Contact:** Liz Roman, Director of Human Resources. **World Wide Web address:** http://www.basf.com. **Description:** This location serves as the U.S. headquarters and houses management offices and the pharmaceutical division, Knoll Pharmaceuticals. Overall, BASF Corporation is an international chemical products organization, doing business in five operating groups: Chemicals; Coatings and Colorants; Consumer Products and Life Sciences; Fiber Products; and Polymers. **Common positions include:** Accountant/Auditor; Chemical Engineer; Computer Programmer;

Financial Analyst; Marketing Specialist. **Corporate headquarters location:** This location. **Operations at this facility include:** Administration; Divisional Headquarters; Sales. **Listed on:** New York Stock Exchange. **Stock exchange symbol:** BF. **Number of employees worldwide:** 125,000.

BERLEX LABORATORIES, INC.
300 Fairfield Road, Wayne NJ 07470. 973/694-4100. **Contact:** Human Resources. **World Wide Web address:** http://www.berlex.com. **Description:** Researches, manufactures, and markets ethical pharmaceutical products in the fields of cardiovascular medicine, endocrinology and fertility control, diagnostic imaging, oncology, and central nervous system disorders. Berlex Laboratories has three strategic units: Berlex Drug Development & Technology (New Jersey), Oncology/Central Nervous System (California), and Berlex Biosciences (California). The company also owns Berlex Drug Development and Technology and operates a national sales force. The sales force, which is divided into three geographic regions, markets the complete line of Berlex products including BETASERON, which is used to treat multiple sclerosis. **Corporate headquarters location:** This location. **Parent company:** Schering AG (Germany).

BIO-REFERENCE LABORATORIES
481B Edward H. Ross Drive, Elmwood Park NJ 07407. 201/791-2600. **Contact:** Human Resources. **World Wide Web address:** http://www.bio-referencelabs.com. **Description:** Operates a clinical laboratory. Bio-Reference offers a list of chemical diagnostic tests including blood and urine analysis, blood chemistry, hematology services, serology, radioimmunological analysis, toxicology (including drug screening), Pap smears, tissue pathology (biopsies), and other tissue analyses. Bio-Reference markets its services directly to physicians, hospitals, clinics, and other health facilities. **Corporate headquarters location:** This location. **Listed on:** NASDAQ. **Stock exchange symbol:** BRLI.

BIO-TECHNOLOGY GENERAL CORPORATION
70 Wood Avenue South, Iselin NJ 08830. 732/632-8800. **Fax:** 732/632-8872. **Contact:** Human Resources. **E-mail address:** hr@btgc.com. **World Wide Web address:** http://www.btgc.com. **Description:** Develops, manufactures, and markets novel therapeutic products. The company specializes in preclinical studies, research and development, and biotechnology derived products. **Corporate headquarters location:** This location. **International locations:** Rehovot, Israel. **Listed on:** NASDAQ. **Stock exchange symbol:** BTGC.

BRACCO DIAGNOSTICS INC.
107 College Road East, Princeton NJ 08540. 609/514-2200. **Toll-free phone:** 800/631-5244. **Fax:** 609/514-2452. **Contact:** Human Resources. **World Wide Web address:** http://www.bdi.bracco.com. **Description:** Researches and develops diagnostic pharmaceuticals and nuclear medicine imaging products. **NOTE:** Resumes may be submitted on-line at the above Website. Job listings provide e-mail addresses and contact information. **Common positions include:** Administrative Assistant; Sales Representative; Staff Accountant; Systems Analyst. **Parent company:** Bracco S.p.A. **Number of employees worldwide:** 2,300.

BRADLEY PHARMACEUTICALS, INC.
383 Route 46 West, Fairfield NJ 07004-2402. 973/882-1505. **Fax:** 973/575-5366. **Contact:** Personnel. **E-mail address:** personnel@bradpharm.com. **World Wide Web address:** http://www.bradpharm.com. **Description:**

Manufactures and markets over-the-counter and prescription pharmaceuticals, and health-related products including nutritional, personal hygiene, and internal medicine brands. Founded in 1985. **Corporate headquarters location:** This location. **Subsidiaries include:** Doak Dermatologics Company Inc. (Westbury NY); Kenwood Therapeutics. **Listed on:** NASDAQ. **Stock exchange symbol:** BPRX.

BRISTOL-MYERS SQUIBB COMPANY
P.O. Box 5335, Princeton NJ 08543-5335. 609/252-4000. **Fax:** 609/897-6412. **Contact:** Employment Department. **World Wide Web address:** http://www.bms.com. **Description:** This location is engaged in the research and manufacture of various pharmaceuticals and personal care products. Overall, Bristol-Myers Squibb manufactures pharmaceuticals, medical devices, nonprescription drugs, toiletries, and beauty aids. The company's pharmaceutical products include cardiovascular drugs, anti-infectives, anticancer agents, AIDS therapy treatments, central nervous system drugs, diagnostic agents, and other drugs. Nonprescription products include formulas, vitamins, analgesics, remedies, and skin care products. Nonprescription drug brand names include Bufferin, Excedrin, Nuprin, and Comtrex. Beauty aids include Clairol and Ultress hair care, Nice 'n Easy and Clairesse hair colorings, hair sprays, gels, and deodorants. **Corporate headquarters location:** New York NY. **Listed on:** New York Stock Exchange. **Stock exchange symbol:** BMY.

CELGENE CORPORATION
7 Powder Horn Drive, Warren NJ 07059. 732/271-1001. **Fax:** 732/271-4184. **Contact:** Human Resources. **E-mail address:** hr@celgene.com. **World Wide Web address:** http://www.celgene.com. **Description:** Engaged in the development and commercialization of a broad range of immunotherapeutic drugs designed to control serious disease states. Celgene also manufactures and sells chiral intermediates, key building blocks in the production of advanced therapeutic compounds and certain agrochemical and food-related products. The focus of Celgene's immunotherapeutics program is the development of small molecule compounds that modulate bodily production of tumor necrosis factor alpha, a hormone-like protein. Elevated levels of this cytokine are believed to cause symptoms associated with several debilitating diseases such as HIV and AIDS-related conditions, sepsis, and inflammatory bowel disease. **Corporate headquarters location:** This location. **Listed on:** NASDAQ. **Stock exchange symbol:** CELG.

CELSIS LABORATORY GROUP
165 Fieldcrest Avenue, Edison NJ 08837. 732/346-5100. **Contact:** Human Resources. **World Wide Web address:** http://www.celsislabs.com. **Description:** An independent testing laboratory specializing in toxicology, microbiology, and analytical chemistry. **Common positions include:** Biological Scientist; Chemist; Computer Programmer; Credit Manager; General Manager; Quality Control Supervisor; Science Technologist; Toxicologist. **Number of employees at this location:** 50.

COVANCE INC.
206 Carnegie Center, Princeton NJ 08540. 609/452-4440. **Toll-free phone:** 888/COV-ANCE. **Fax:** 609/452-8520. **Contact:** Human Resources. **World Wide Web address:** http://www.covance.com. **Description:** One of the world's largest and most comprehensive drug development services companies. Covance Inc. provides preclinical testing, health economics consulting, biomanufacturing, and clinical support services. Founded in

1993. **NOTE:** Entry-level positions are offered. **Common positions include:** Administrative Assistant; Computer Support Technician; Data Analyst; Database Administrator; Network/Systems Administrator; Registered Nurse; Research Scientist; Statistician. **Office hours:** Monday - Friday, 8:30 a.m. - 5:00 p.m. **Corporate headquarters location:** This location. **Other U.S. locations:** Berkeley CA; Richmond CA; Walnut Creek CA; Washington DC; Tampa FL; Indianapolis IN; Kalamazoo MI; Research Triangle Park NC; Reno NV; Allentown PA; Denver PA; Radnor PA; Nashville TN; Alice TX; Cumberland VA; Vienna VA; Madison WI. **International locations:** Worldwide. **Subsidiaries include:** Berkeley Antibody Company, Inc. provides a variety of preclinical services. GDXI, Inc. provides electrocardiogram analysis for clinical trials. **Listed on:** New York Stock Exchange. **Stock exchange symbol:** CVD. **President/CEO:** Christopher Kuebler. **Annual sales/revenues:** More than $100 million. **Number of employees at this location:** 1,000. **Number of employees worldwide:** 7,700.

CYTOGEN CORPORATION
600 College Road East, Princeton NJ 08540. **Toll-free phone:** 800/833-3533. **Fax:** 609/750-8130. **Contact:** Director of Human Resources. **E-mail address:** hrdirector@cytogen.com. **World Wide Web address:** http://www.cytogen.com. **Description:** Develops products for the targeted delivery of diagnostic and therapeutic substances directly to sites of disease, using monoclonal antibodies. Proprietary antibody linking technology is used primarily to develop specific cancer diagnostic imaging and therapeutic products. Founded in 1981. **Common positions include:** Accountant/Auditor; Biological Scientist; Chemist; Human Resources Manager; Systems Analyst. **Corporate headquarters location:** This location. **Operations at this facility include:** Administration; Sales. **Listed on:** NASDAQ. **Stock exchange symbol:** CYTO. **Number of employees at this location:** 120.

DERMA SCIENCES, INC.
214 Carnegie Center, Suite 100, Princeton NJ 08540. 609/514-4744. **Contact:** Human Resources Department. **World Wide Web address:** http://www.dermasciences.com. **Description:** Engaged in the development, marketing, and sale of proprietary sprays, ointments, and dressings for the management of certain chronic, nonhealing skin ulcerations such as pressure and venous ulcers, surgical incisions, and burns.

ENZON, INC.
20 Kingsbridge Road, Piscataway NJ 08854-3998. 732/980-4500. **Fax:** 732/980-5911. **Contact:** Human Resources Department. **E-mail address:** hr@enzon.com. **World Wide Web address:** http://www.enzon.com. **Description:** A biopharmaceutical company that develops advanced therapeutics for life threatening diseases, primarily in the area of oncology. **Common positions include:** Administrative Assistant; Biochemist; Biological Scientist; Chemist; Secretary. **Office hours:** Monday - Friday, 8:30 a.m. - 5:00 p.m. **Other area locations:** South Plainfield NJ. **Listed on:** NASDAQ. **Stock exchange symbol:** ENZN. **President/CEO:** Peter Tombros. **Annual sales/revenues:** $11 - $20 million. **Number of employees at this location:** 55. **Number of employees nationwide:** 90.

FISHER SCIENTIFIC COMPANY
One Reagent Lane, Fair Lawn NJ 07410. 201/796-7100. **Contact:** Michelle Valvano, Human Resources Manager. **World Wide Web address:** http://www.fisherscientific.com. **Description:** This location produces

reagents. Overall, Fisher Scientific manufactures, distributes, and sells a wide range of products used in industrial and medical laboratories. Products include analytical and measuring instruments, apparatus, and appliances; reagent chemicals and diagnostics; glassware and plasticware; and laboratory furniture. Customers are primarily industrial laboratories, medical and hospital laboratories, and educational and research laboratories. Manufacturing operations are carried out by six operating divisions in 11 U.S. locations. **Common positions include:** Accountant/Auditor; Administrator; Biological Scientist; Biomedical Engineer; Blue-Collar Worker Supervisor; Buyer; Chemical Engineer; Chemist; Computer Programmer; Customer Service Representative; Department Manager; Draftsperson; Electrical/Electronics Engineer; Financial Analyst; General Manager; Human Resources Manager; Industrial Engineer; Materials Engineer; Mechanical Engineer; Operations/Production Manager; Purchasing Agent/Manager; Quality Control Supervisor; Systems Analyst. **Operations at this facility include:** Administration; Manufacturing; Research and Development. **Listed on:** New York Stock Exchange. **Stock exchange symbol:** FSH.

GENZYME BIOSURGERY
1125 Pleasant View Terrace, Ridgefield NJ 07657. 201/945-9550. **Contact:** Human Resources. **World Wide Web address:** http://www.genzyme.com. **Description:** An international biomedical company that develops and commercializes products for matrix engineering in new medical therapeutic modalities. The company's products are used worldwide in a diverse range of medical applications including viscosurgery, viscosupplementation, and viscoprotection. **Listed on:** NASDAQ. **Stock exchange symbol:** GZBX.

GLAXOSMITHKLINE CORPORATION
257 Cornelison Avenue, Jersey City NJ 07302. 201/434-3000. **Contact:** Human Resources. **World Wide Web address:** http://www.gsk.com. **Description:** Develops, manufactures, and sells products in four general categories: denture, dental care, oral hygiene, and professional dental products; proprietary products; ethical pharmaceutical products; and household products. Dental-related products include Polident denture cleansers. **Listed on:** New York Stock Exchange. **Stock exchange symbol:** GSK.

GLAXOSMITHKLINE CORPORATION
65 Industrial South, Clifton NJ 07012. 973/778-9000. **Contact:** Human Resources. **World Wide Web address:** http://www.gsk.com. **Description:** This location manufactures toothpaste and Massengill products. Overall, GlaxoSmithKline Corporation is a health care company engaged in the research, development, manufacture, and marketing of ethical pharmaceuticals, animal health products, ethical and proprietary medicines, and eye care products. The company is also engaged in many other aspects of the health care field including the production of medical and electronic instruments. **Corporate headquarters location:** Philadelphia PA. **Subsidiaries include:** Menley & James Laboratories products include Contac Cold Capsules, Sine-Off sinus medicine, Love cosmetics, and Sea & Ski outdoor products. **Listed on:** New York Stock Exchange. **Stock exchange symbol:** GSK.

GLAXOSMITHKLINE PHARMACEUTICALS
101 Possumtown Road, Piscataway NJ 08854. 732/469-5200. **Contact:** Human Resources. **World Wide Web address:** http://www.gsk.com. **Description:** Manufactures penicillin. **Corporate headquarters location:**

Philadelphia PA. **Parent company:** GlaxoSmithKline Corporation is health care company engaged in the research, development, manufacture, and marketing of ethical pharmaceuticals, animal health products, ethical and proprietary medicines, and eye care products. **Listed on:** New York Stock Exchange. **Stock exchange symbol:** GSK.

HOFFMANN-LA ROCHE INC.
340 Kingsland Street, Nutley NJ 07110-0119. 973/235-5000. **Contact:** Director of Staffing. **World Wide Web address:** http://www.rocheusa.com. **Description:** An international health care organization that develops and manufactures pharmaceuticals, diagnostics, and vitamins. **NOTE:** Entry-level positions, part-time jobs, and second and third shifts are offered. **Common positions include:** Accountant; Auditor; Computer Programmer; Database Administrator; Financial Analyst; Manufacturing Engineer; Market Research Analyst; Marketing Manager; Network Engineer; Public Relations Specialist; Systems Analyst; Website Developer. **Corporate headquarters location:** This location. **Other U.S. locations:** Nationwide. **International locations:** Worldwide. **Subsidiaries include:** Roche Biomedical Laboratories; Roche Diagnostics (ethical pharmaceuticals); Roche Vitamins Inc. **Parent company:** F. Hoffmann-La Roche Ltd. **Operations at this facility include:** Divisional Headquarters. **Listed on:** Privately held. **Annual sales/revenues:** More than $100 million. **Number of employees at this location:** 6,000. **Number of employees nationwide:** 20,000. **Number of employees worldwide:** 80,000.

HUNTINGDON LIFE SCIENCES
P.O. Box 2360, Mettlers Road, East Millstone NJ 08875. 732/873-2550. **Fax:** 732/873-3992. **Contact:** Cathy Brower, Director of Human Resources Department. **E-mail address:** careers@princeton.huntingdon.com. **World Wide Web address:** http://www.huntingdon.com. **Description:** Provides contract biological safety (toxicological) testing services on a worldwide basis through two laboratories in the United States and the United Kingdom. The toxicology divisions of Huntington Life Sciences conduct studies designed to test pharmaceutical products, biologicals, chemical compounds, and other substances in order to produce the data required to identify, quantify, and evaluate the risks to humans and the environment resulting from the manufacture or use of these substances. These divisions also perform analytical and metabolic chemistry services. Huntington Life Sciences also performs clinical trials of new and existing pharmaceutical and biotechnology products and medical devices. The company is engaged in the clinical development process including analytical chemistry, evaluation of clinical data, data processing, biostatistical analysis, and the preparation of supporting documentation for compliance with regulatory requirements. Founded in 1952. **NOTE:** Entry-level positions, part-time jobs, and second and third shifts are offered. **Common positions include:** Accountant; Administrative Assistant; Advertising Executive; Biochemist; Chemist; Computer Engineer; Computer Support Technician; Computer Technician; Finance Director; Help-Desk Technician; Human Resources Manager; Internet Services Manager; Network/Systems Administrator; Purchasing Agent/Manager; Sales Manager; Sales Representative; Secretary; Systems Analyst; Veterinarian; Vice President. **Special programs:** Summer Jobs. **Office hours:** Monday - Friday, 8:30 a.m. - 5:00 p.m. **Corporate headquarters location:** Cambridgeshire, England. **Parent company:** Huntingdon Life Sciences, Ltd. **President:** Alan Staple. **Annual sales/revenues:** $51 - $100 million. **Number of employees at this location:** 200. **Number of employees worldwide:** 1,500.

HYMEDIX
2245 Route 130, Suite 101, Dayton NJ 08810. 732/274-2288. **Contact:** George Stoy, President. **World Wide Web address:** http://www.hymedix.com. **Description:** Develops medical and skin care body creams.

IVC INDUSTRIES, INC.
500 Halls Mill Road, Freehold NJ 07728. 732/308-3000. **Fax:** 732/761-2837. **Contact:** Human Resources. **World Wide Web address:** http://www.ivcinc.com. **Description:** Manufactures and distributes vitamins, herbs, nonprescription drugs, and nutritional supplements under the brand names Fields of Nature, Pine Brothers throat drops, Rybutol, Nature's Wonder, Synergy Plus, and Liquafil vitamin supplements. **Corporate headquarters location:** This location. **Listed on:** NASDAQ. **Stock exchange symbol:** IVCO.

IMMUNOMEDICS, INC.
300 American Road, Morris Plains NJ 07950. 973/605-8200. **Fax:** 973/605-8282. **Contact:** Personnel. **E-mail address:** hr@immunomedics.com. **World Wide Web address:** http://www.immunomedics.com. **Description:** Manufactures products to treat and detect infectious diseases and cancer. Products include LeukoScan, a diagnostic imaging tool that can scan for cancers such as osteomyelitis. **Listed on:** NASDAQ. **Stock exchange symbol:** IMMU.

IVAX PHARMACEUTICALS INC.
140 LeGrand Avenue, Northvale NJ 07647. 201/767-1700. **Fax:** 201/767-1700. **Contact:** Manager of Human Resources Department. **World Wide Web address:** http://www.ivaxpharmaceuticals.com. **Description:** IVAX Pharmaceuticals produces ethical pharmaceuticals for the cardiovascular, nervous, digestive, and respiratory systems. **Corporate headquarters location:** Miami FL.

LABORATORY CORPORATION OF AMERICA (LABCORP)
116 Millburn Avenue, Suite 211, Millburn NJ 07041. 973/912-8617. **Contact:** Human Resources Department. **World Wide Web address:** http://www.labcorp.com. **Description:** This location is a blood-drawing facility. Overall, the company is one of the nation's leading clinical laboratory companies, providing services primarily to physicians, hospitals, clinics, nursing homes, and other clinical labs nationwide. LabCorp performs tests on blood, urine, and other body fluids and tissue, aiding the diagnosis of disease. **NOTE:** Direct employment correspondence to: LabCorp Human Resources, 309 East Davis Street, Burlington NC 27215. **Corporate headquarters location:** Burlington NC.

LIFECELL CORPORATION
One Millennium Way, Branchburg NJ 08876. 908/947-1100. **Fax:** 908/947-1200. **Contact:** Human Resources. **E-mail address:** hr@lifecell.com. **World Wide Web address:** http://www.lifecell.com. **Description:** Designs, manufactures, and produces products dealing with skin grafts for burn patients and with the preservation of transfusable blood platelets (blood cells that control clotting). LifeCell's main product, AlloDerm, removes the cells in allograft skin (from a cadaveric donor) that the patient's own immune system would normally reject. This technology enables the AlloDerm to become populated with the patient's own skin cells and blood vessels. Founded in 1986. **Listed on:** NASDAQ. **Stock exchange symbol:** LIFC.

THE LIPOSOME COMPANY, INC.
600 College Road East, Princeton NJ 08540-6619. 609/452-7060. **Contact:** Human Resources. **World Wide Web address:** http://www.lipo.com. **Description:** Develops proprietary lipid- and liposome-based pharmaceuticals for the treatment, prevention, and diagnosis of cancer, systemic fungal infections, and inflammatory and vaso-occlusive diseases. **Corporate headquarters location:** This location.

MEDAREX, INC.
707 State Road #206, Princeton NJ 08540-1437. 609/430-2880. **Fax:** 609/430-2850. **Contact:** Human Resources. **World Wide Web address:** http://www.medarex.com. **Description:** Researches and develops antibody-based pharmaceutical products to be used for the treatment of AIDS and other infectious diseases; cancers (including breast, ovarian, prostate, colon, and pancreatic); autoimmune diseases; and cardiovascular disease. These products bind to cells in the immune system and to the diseased cells, then stimulate the immune system to destroy the diseased cells. Founded in 1987. **Corporate headquarters location:** Princeton NJ.

MEDPOINTE INC.
Half Acre Road, P.O. Box 1001, Cranbury NJ 08512. 609/655-6000. **Contact:** Human Resources Department. **World Wide Web address:** http://www.medpointe.com. **Description:** A major manufacturer of ethical drugs and consumer products. Health care products include tranquilizers, laxatives, antibacterials, analgesics, decongestants, and cold and cough remedies. The company also manufactures tests for pregnancy, mononucleosis, rubella, and meningitis. Consumer products include Arrid antiperspirants and deodorants, Trojan condoms, hair lotions, and pet care items. **NOTE:** Entry-level positions and second and third shifts are offered. A move to a new facility in Somerset NJ is anticipated in mid-2002. See Website for current contact information. **Common positions include:** Account Manager; Account Representative; Administrative Assistant; Biochemist; Biological Scientist; Blue-Collar Worker Supervisor; Budget Analyst; Chemist; Clinical Lab Technician; Customer Service Representative; Finance Director; Financial Analyst; Human Resources Manager; Intellectual Property Lawyer; Marketing Manager; Operations/Production Manager; Paralegal; Production Manager; Quality Control Supervisor; Sales and Marketing Manager; Sales Representative; Secretary. **Corporate headquarters location:** This location. **Other U.S. locations:** Decatur IL. **Number of employees nationwide:** 2,200.

MERCK & COMPANY, INC.
126 East Lincoln Avenue, P.O. Box 2000, Rahway NJ 07065. 732/594-4000. **Contact:** Human Resources. **World Wide Web address:** http://www.merck.com. **Description:** A worldwide organization engaged in discovering, developing, producing, and marketing products for health care and the maintenance of the environment. Products include human and animal pharmaceuticals and chemicals sold to the health care, oil exploration, food processing, textile, paper, and other industries. Merck also runs an ethical drug mail-order marketing business. **NOTE:** Applicants should indicate position of interest. **Corporate headquarters location:** Whitehouse Station NJ. **Other U.S. locations:** Albany GA; Montvale NJ; Whitehouse Station NJ; Wilson NC; West Point PA; Elkton VA. **Listed on:** New York Stock Exchange. **Stock exchange symbol:** MRK.

MERCK & COMPANY, INC.

P.O. Box 100, One Merck Drive, Whitehouse Station NJ 08889-0100. 908/423-1000. **Contact:** Human Resources Manager. **World Wide Web address:** http://www.merck.com. **Description:** A worldwide organization engaged in discovering, developing, producing, and marketing products for health care and the maintenance of the environment. Products include human and animal pharmaceuticals and chemicals sold to the health care, oil exploration, food processing, textile, paper, and other industries. Merck also runs an ethical drug mail-order marketing business. **Corporate headquarters location:** This location. **Other U.S. locations:** Albany GA; Montvale NJ; Rahway NJ; Wilson NC; West Point PA; Elkton VA. **Listed on:** New York Stock Exchange. **Stock exchange symbol:** MRK.

NAPP TECHNOLOGIES

299 Market Street, 4th Floor, Saddle Brook NJ 07663. 201/843-4664. **Fax:** 201/843-4737. **Contact:** Personnel Department. **World Wide Web address:** http://www.napptech.com. **Description:** Produces bulk pharmaceuticals, cosmetic raw materials, and fine chemicals. **Corporate headquarters location:** This location.

NOVARTIS PHARMACEUTICALS CORPORATION

556 Morris Avenue, Summit NJ 07901. 908/277-5000. **Contact:** Human Resources. **World Wide Web address:** http://www.novartis.com. **Description:** This location manufactures pharmaceuticals. Overall, Novartis Pharmaceuticals Corporation is one of the largest life science companies in the world. The company has three major divisions: health care, agribusiness, and nutrition. The health care division specializes in pharmaceuticals, both proprietary and generic, and ophthalmic health care. The agribusiness division is involved in seed technology, animal health, and crop protection. The nutrition sector includes medical, health, and infant nutrition. **NOTE:** Resumes should be sent to Human Resources, Novartis Pharmaceuticals Corporation, 59 Route 10, East Hanover NJ 07936. **Corporate headquarters location:** East Hanover NJ.

NOVARTIS PHARMACEUTICALS CORPORATION

59 Route 10, East Hanover NJ 07936. 973/503-7500. **Contact:** Human Resources. **World Wide Web address:** http://www.novartis.com. **Description:** This location houses administrative offices and Novartis Pharmaceuticals' primary research facility. Overall, Novartis Pharmaceuticals Corporation is one of the largest life science companies in the world. The company has three major divisions: health care, agribusiness, and nutrition. The health care division specializes in pharmaceuticals, both proprietary and generic, and ophthalmic health care. The agribusiness division is involved in seed technology, animal health, and crop protection. The nutrition sector includes medical, health, and infant nutrition. **Corporate headquarters location:** This location. **Other area locations:** Summit NJ.

NOVO NORDISK PHARMACEUTICALS INC.

100 College West, Princeton NJ 08540. 609/987-5800. **Fax:** 609/987-3915. **Contact:** Human Resources. **World Wide Web address:** http://www.novo-nordisk.com. **Description:** One of the world's largest producers of industrial enzymes and insulin for the treatment of diabetes. **Parent company:** Novo Nordisk A/S (Baysvaerd, Denmark).

ORGANON INC.
375 Mount Pleasant Avenue, West Orange NJ 07052. 973/325-4500. **Toll-free phone:** 800/241-8812. **Fax:** 973/669-6144. **Contact:** Human Resources. **World Wide Web address:** http://www.organoninc.com. **Description:** A worldwide leader in pharmaceutical research and development in the fields of reproductive medicine, anesthesiology, central nervous system disorders, thrombosis, and immunology. **NOTE:** Entry-level positions and part-time jobs are offered. **Common positions include:** Accountant; Administrative Assistant; Biochemist; Biological Scientist; Chemical Engineer; Chemist; Computer Programmer; Computer Support Technician; Customer Service Representative; Market Research Analyst; Mechanical Engineer; MIS Specialist; Pharmacist; Physician; Public Relations Specialist; Quality Assurance Engineer; Sales Representative; Secretary; SQL Programmer; Statistician; Systems Analyst; Technical Writer/Editor. **Special programs:** Internships; Summer Jobs. **Office hours:** Monday - Friday, 8:00 a.m. - 4:30 p.m. **Corporate headquarters location:** This location. **Parent company:** Akzo Nobel. **Annual sales/revenues:** More than $100 million. **Number of employees at this location:** 1,200.

ORTHO-McNEIL PHARMACEUTICAL
1000 Route 202 South, P.O. Box 300, Raritan NJ 08869-0602. 908/218-6000. **Contact:** Human Resources Department. **World Wide Web address:** http://www.ortho-mcneil.com. **Description:** Develops and sells pharmaceutical products including women's health, infectious disease, and wound healing products. **NOTE:** All hiring is done out of the corporate offices. Resumes should be sent to Johnson & Johnson Recruiting Services, Employment Management Center, Room JH-215, 501 George Street, New Brunswick NJ 08906-6597. **Parent company:** Johnson & Johnson (New Brunswick NJ).

OSTEOTECH INC.
51 James Way, Eatontown NJ 07724. 732/542-2800. **Fax:** 732/542-9312. **Contact:** Charles Jannetti, Human Resources Director. **E-mail address:** hr@osteotech.com. **World Wide Web address:** http://www.osteotech.com. **Description:** Processes human bone and connective tissue for transplantation and develops and manufactures biomaterial and device systems for musculoskeletal surgery. Osteotech is a leader in volume and quality of tissue processing for the American Red Cross and the Musculoskeletal Tissue Foundation. Founded in 1986. **NOTE:** Entry-level positions and second and third shifts are offered. **Company slogan:** Innovators in musculoskeletal tissue science. **Common positions include:** Accountant; Administrative Assistant; Biochemist; Biological Scientist; Biomedical Engineer; Buyer; Chemist; Database Manager; Environmental Engineer; Librarian; Marketing Specialist; Operations Manager; Pharmacist; Physician; Production Manager; Quality Control Supervisor; Sales Executive; Sales Representative; Secretary; Surgical Technician; Systems Analyst; Technical Writer/Editor. **Special programs:** Training. **Office hours:** Monday - Friday, 8:00 a.m. - 5:00 p.m. **Corporate headquarters location:** This location. **Other U.S. locations:** Nationwide. **International locations:** The Netherlands. **Listed on:** NASDAQ. **Stock exchange symbol:** OSTE. **President:** Richard Bauer. **Annual sales/revenues:** $21 - $50 million. **Number of employees at this location:** 180. **Number of employees nationwide:** 200. **Number of employees worldwide:** 225.

PFIZER
201 Tabor Road, Morris Plains NJ 07950. 973/385-2000. **Contact:** Human Resources. **World Wide Web address:** http://www.pfizer.com. **Description:**

A leading pharmaceutical company that distributes products concerning cardiovascular health, central nervous system disorders, infectious diseases, and women's health worldwide. The company's brand-name products include Benadryl, Ben Gay, Cortizone, Desitin, Halls, Listerine, Sudafed, Viagra, and Zantac 75.

PHARMACEUTICAL FORMULATIONS, INC.
P.O. Box 1904, 460 Plainfield Avenue, Edison NJ 08818-1904. 732/985-7100. **Fax:** 732/819-3330. **Contact:** Human Resources. **E-mail address:** pfiresumes@pfiotc.com. **World Wide Web address:** http://www.pfiotc.com. **Description:** Manufactures and distributes over-the-counter, solid-dosage pharmaceutical products in tablet, caplet, and capsule forms. **Common positions include:** Accountant/Auditor; Buyer; Chemical Engineer; Chemist; Customer Service Representative; Electrician; General Manager; Human Resources Manager; Purchasing Agent/Manager; Science Technologist; Services Sales Representative; Transportation/Traffic Specialist. **Corporate headquarters location:** This location. **Operations at this facility include:** Administration; Manufacturing; Research and Development; Sales; Service. **Number of employees at this location:** 320.

PHARMACIA CORPORATION
100 Route 206 North, Peapack NJ 07977. 908/901-8000. **Contact:** Human Resources. **World Wide Web address:** http://www.pharmacia.com. **Description:** This location houses administrative offices. Overall, Pharmacia manufactures and markets agricultural products, performance chemicals used in consumer products, prescription pharmaceuticals, and food ingredients. **Corporate headquarters location:** This location. **Listed on:** New York Stock Exchange. **Stock exchange symbol:** PHA. **Number of employees worldwide:** 60,000.

QMED, INC.
100 Metro Park South, 3rd Floor, Laurence Harbor NJ 08878. 732/566-2666. **Fax:** 732/566-0912. **Contact:** Human Resources. **E-mail address:** jobs@qmedinc.com. **World Wide Web address:** http://www.qmedinc.com. **Description:** Designs, manufactures, and markets testing devices that enable medical professionals to perform minimally invasive diagnostic procedures for certain illnesses, such as silent myocardial ischemia, venous blood flow insufficiencies, and diabetic neuropathy. **Listed on:** NASDAQ. **Stock exchange symbol:** QEKG.

QUEST DIAGNOSTICS INCORPORATED
One Malcolm Avenue, Teterboro NJ 07608. 201/393-5000. **Fax:** 201/462-4715. **Contact:** Personnel Department. **World Wide Web address:** http://www.questdiagnostics.com. **Description:** One of the largest clinical laboratories in North America, providing a broad range of clinical laboratory services to health care clients that include physicians, hospitals, clinics, dialysis centers, pharmaceutical companies, and corporations. The company offers and performs tests on blood, urine, and other bodily fluids and tissues to provide information for health and well-being. **Corporate headquarters location:** This location. **Other U.S. locations:** Nationwide. **Listed on:** New York Stock Exchange. **Stock exchange symbol:** DGX.

ROCHE VITAMINS INC.
45 Waterview Boulevard, Parsippany NJ 07054-1298. 973/257-1063. **Fax:** 800/526-0189. **Contact:** Human Resources. **World Wide Web address:** http://www.roche-vitamins.com. **Description:** A pharmaceutical company that manufactures pharmaceutical drugs, diagnostic kits, and vitamins for

dietary, pharmaceutical, and cosmetic use. **Corporate headquarters location:** This location.

SGS U.S. TESTING COMPANY INC.
291 Fairfield Avenue, Fairfield NJ 07004. 973/575-5252. **Toll-free phone:** 800/777-8378. **Fax:** 973/575-1071. **Contact:** Human Resources Department. **E-mail address:** hrustc@yahoo.com. **World Wide Web address:** http://www.ustesting.sgsna.com. **Description:** An independent laboratory specializing in the testing of a variety of industrial and consumer products. Services include biological, chemical, engineering/materials, environmental, electrical, paper/packaging, textiles, certification programs, and inspections. **Common positions include:** Account Representative; Administrative Assistant; Administrative Manager; Biological Scientist; Chemist; Civil Engineer; Clinical Lab Technician; Customer Service Representative; Electrical/Electronics Engineer; Industrial Engineer; Manufacturing Engineer; Marketing Manager; Marketing Specialist; Mechanical Engineer; Sales Engineer; Sales Representative; Secretary. **Corporate headquarters location:** This location. **Other U.S. locations:** Los Angeles CA; Tulsa OK. **Parent company:** SGS North America. **Operations at this facility include:** Administration; Sales; Service.

SCHERING-PLOUGH CORPORATION
2000 Galloping Hill Road, Kenilworth NJ 07033. 908/298-4000. **Contact:** Human Resources Department. **World Wide Web address:** http://www.schering-plough.com. **Description:** Engaged in the discovery, development, manufacture, and marketing of pharmaceutical and consumer products. Pharmaceutical products include prescription drugs, over-the-counter medicines, eye care products, and animal health products promoted to the medical and allied health professions. The consumer products group consists of proprietary medicines, toiletries, cosmetics, and foot care products. Brand names include Coricidin, Maybelline, Claritin, Coppertone, and Dr. Scholl's. **Corporate headquarters location:** This location. **Other area locations:** Statewide. **International locations:** Worldwide.

SCHERING-PLOUGH CORPORATION
One Giralda Farms, Madison NJ 07940-1000. 973/822-7000. **Contact:** Human Resources Department. **World Wide Web address:** http://www.schering-plough.com. **Description:** Engaged in the discovery, development, manufacture, and marketing of pharmaceutical and consumer products. Pharmaceutical products include prescription drugs, over-the-counter medicines, eye care products, and animal health products. The consumer products group consists of proprietary medicines, toiletries, cosmetics, and foot care products. Brand names include Coricidin, Maybelline, Claritin, Coppertone, and Dr. Scholl's. **Corporate headquarters location:** Kenilworth NJ. **Other area locations:** Statewide. **International locations:** Worldwide.

SYNAPTIC PHARMACEUTICAL CORPORATION
215 College Road, Paramus NJ 07652. 201/261-1331. **Contact:** Human Resources. **World Wide Web address:** http://www.synapticcorp.com. **Description:** This location houses administrative offices and is not involved in the manufacturing process. Overall, Synaptic Pharmaceutical Corporation researches and develops pharmaceuticals. Founded in 1987. **NOTE:** For current job postings and on-line contact information, see the above Website. Part-time jobs are offered. **Common positions include:** Biochemist; Biological Scientist; Chemist; Clinical Lab Technician. **Special programs:**

Summer Jobs. **Corporate headquarters location:** This location. **Listed on:** NASDAQ. **Stock exchange symbol:** SNAP. **Number of employees at this location:** 130.

TEVA PHARMACEUTICALS USA
18-01 River Road, Fair Lawn NJ 07410. 201/703-0400. **Fax:** 201/703-9491. **Contact:** Human Resources Department. **World Wide Web address:** http://www.tevapharmusa.com. **Description:** Manufactures and markets generic pharmaceuticals. The company focuses on therapeutic medicines for the analgesic, cardiovascular, dermatological, and anti-inflammatory markets. **Corporate headquarters location:** This location. **Other area locations:** Elmwood Park NJ; Fairfield NJ; Paterson NJ; Waldwick NJ. **Other U.S. locations:** Mexico MO. **Number of employees nationwide:** 790.

UNIGENE LABORATORIES, INC.
110 Little Falls Road, Fairfield NJ 07004. 973/882-0860. **Fax:** 973/227-6088. **Contact:** William Steinhauer, Controller. **World Wide Web address:** http://www.unigene.com. **Description:** A biopharmaceutical research and manufacturing company that has developed a patented method to produce calcitonin, a leading drug for treating osteoporosis. Founded in 1980. **Corporate headquarters location:** This location. **Other U.S. locations:** Boonton NJ. **Listed on:** NASDAQ. **Stock exchange symbol:** UGNE. **President:** Warren P. Levy, Ph.D. **Annual sales/revenues:** $5 - $10 million. **Number of employees at this location:** 65.

UNILEVER HOME & PERSONAL CARE USA
45 River Road, Edgewater NJ 07020. 201/943-7100. **Contact:** Human Resources. **Description:** Researches and develops household and personal care products. **Common positions include:** Chemical Engineer; Chemist. **Corporate headquarters location:** Greenwich CT. **Annual sales/revenues:** More than $100 million. **Number of employees at this location:** 500.

WATSON PHARMACEUTICALS
360 Mount Kemble Avenue, Morristown NJ 07962. 973/355-8300. **Contact:** Human Resources Department. **World Wide Web address:** http://www.watsonpharm.com. **Description:** Manufactures generic drugs. **Corporate headquarters location:** This location. **Listed on:** New York Stock Exchange. **Stock exchange symbol:** WPI. **Number of employees nationwide:** 1,500.

WYETH CORPORATION
5 Giralda Farms, Madison NJ 07940. 973/660-5000. **Contact:** Human Resources. **World Wide Web address:** http://www.wyeth.com. **Description:** Manufactures and markets prescription drugs and medical supplies, packaged medicines, food products, household products, and housewares. Each division operates through one or more of Wyeth Corporation's subsidiaries. Prescription Drugs and Medical Supplies operates through: Wyeth-Ayerst Laboratories (produces ethical pharmaceuticals, biologicals, nutritional products, over-the-counter antacids, vitamins, and sunburn remedies); Fort Dodge Animal Health (veterinary pharmaceuticals and biologicals); Sherwood Medical (medical devices, diagnostic instruments, test kits, and bacteria identification systems); and Corometrics Medical Systems (medical electronic instrumentation for obstetrics and neonatology). The Packaged Medicines segment operates through Whitehall-Robins Healthcare (produces analgesics, cold remedies, and other packaged medicines). The Food Products segment operates through American Home Foods (canned pasta, canned vegetables, specialty foods, mustard, and

popcorn). The Household Products and Housewares segment operates through: Boyle-Midway (cleaners, insecticides, air fresheners, waxes, polishes, and other items for home, appliance, and apparel care); Dupli-Color Products (touch-up, refinishing, and other car care and shop-use products); Ekco Products (food containers, commercial baking pans, industrial coatings, food-handling systems, foilware, and plasticware); Ekco Housewares (cookware, cutlery, kitchen tools, tableware and accessories, and padlocks); and Prestige Group (cookware, cutlery, kitchen tools, carpet sweepers, and pressure cookers). **Corporate headquarters location:** This location. **Number of employees worldwide:** 53,000.

XENOGEN BIOSCIENCES
5 Cedarbrook Drive, Cranbury NJ 08512. 609/860-0806. **Fax:** 609/860-8977. **Contact:** Employment. **E-mail address:** employment@xenogen.com. **World Wide Web address:** http://www.xenogen.com. **Description:** Offers real-time in vivo imaging services. Xenogen's in vivo biophotonic imaging system assists pharmaceutical companies in drug discovery and development. **Corporate headquarters location:** Alameda CA.

BUSINESS SERVICES AND NON-SCIENTIFIC RESEARCH

You can expect to find the following types of companies in this chapter:

Adjustment and Collection Services • Cleaning, Maintenance, and Pest Control Services • Credit Reporting • Detective, Guard, and Armored Car Services • Miscellaneous Equipment Rental and Leasing • Secretarial and Court Reporting Services

ADT SECURITY SERVICES
290 Veterans Boulevard, Rutherford NJ 07070. 201/804-8600. **Contact:** Personnel. **World Wide Web address:** http://www.adtsecurityservices.com. **Description:** Services more than 15,000 burglar, fire, and other alarm systems. ADT Security Services also manufactures a variety of alarms and monitoring equipment for use in alarm service operations and for sale to commercial and industrial users. **Corporate headquarters location:** Boca Raton FL. **Other U.S. locations:** Orlando FL; St. Petersburg FL; Tampa FL; Atlanta GA; Baltimore MD; Rockville MD. **Parent company:** Tyco.

AUTOMATIC DATA PROCESSING (ADP)
99 Jefferson Road, P.O. Box 450, Parsippany NJ 07054. 973/739-3000. **Contact:** Human Resources Department. **World Wide Web address:** http://www.adp.com. **Description:** One of the world's largest providers of computerized transaction processing, data communications, and information services. ADP pays over 18 million U.S. employees. The company provides payroll processing, payroll tax filing, job costing, labor distribution, automated bill payment, management reports, unemployment compensation management, human resource information, and benefits administration support to over 300,000 businesses. **Common positions include:** Sales Executive. **Special programs:** Internships. **Corporate headquarters location:** Roseland NJ. **Operations at this facility include:** Divisional Headquarters; Research and Development. **Listed on:** New York Stock Exchange. **Stock exchange symbol:** ADP. **Annual sales/revenues:** More than $100 million. **Number of employees nationwide:** 25,000.

AUTOMATIC DATA PROCESSING (ADP)
One ADP Boulevard, Roseland NJ 07068. 973/974-5000. **Contact:** Human Resources. **World Wide Web address:** http://www.adp.com. **Description:** This location houses administrative offices. Overall, ADP is one of the world's largest providers of computerized transaction processing, data communications, and information services. ADP pays over 18 million U.S. employees. The company provides payroll processing, payroll tax filing, job costing, labor distribution, automated bill payment, management reports, unemployment compensation management, human resource information, and benefits administration support to over 300,000 businesses. **Corporate headquarters location:** This location. **Listed on:** New York Stock Exchange. **Stock exchange symbol:** ADP. **Annual sales/revenues:** More than $100 million. **Number of employees nationwide:** 25,000.

CENDANT CORPORATION
One Campus Drive, Parsippany NJ 07054-0642. 973/428-9700. **Fax:** 973/496-5966. **Contact:** Manager of Human Resources Department. **E-mail**

address: cendant.jobs@cendant.com. **World Wide Web address:** http://www.cendant.com. **Description:** Provides a wide range of business services including dining services, hotel franchise management, mortgage programs, and timeshare exchanges. Cendant Corporation's Real Estate Division offers employee relocation and mortgage services through Century 21, Coldwell Banker, ERA, Cendant Mortgage, and Cendant Mobility. The Travel Division provides car rentals, vehicle management services, and vacation timeshares through brand names including Avia, Days Inn, Howard Johnson, Ramada, Travelodge, and Super 8. The Membership Division offers travel, shopping, auto, dining, and other financial services through Travelers Advantage, Shoppers Advantage, Auto Vantage, Welcome Wagon, Netmarket, North American Outdoor Group, and PrivacyGuard. **Common positions include:** Accountant/Auditor; Computer Operator; Computer Programmer; Customer Service Representative; Marketing Manager; Marketing Specialist; Public Relations Specialist; Real Estate Agent; Sales Representative; Secretary. **Corporate headquarters location:** New York NY. **Listed on:** New York Stock Exchange. **Stock exchange symbol:** CD. **President/CEO:** Henry Silverman. **Number of employees at this location:** 1,100. **Number of employees worldwide:** 28,000.

COMPUTER OUTSOURCING SERVICES, INC. (COSI)
2 Christie Heights Street, Leonia NJ 07605. 201/840-4700. **Fax:** 201/363-9675. **Contact:** Human Resources. **World Wide Web address:** http://www.cosi-us.com. **Description:** Provides payroll, data processing, and tax filing services to companies in book publishing, apparel, direct response marketing, and other industries. **Corporate headquarters location:** This location. **Listed on:** NASDAQ. **Stock exchange symbol:** COSI.

DUN & BRADSTREET
One Diamond Hill Road, Murray Hill NJ 07974. 908/665-5000. **Contact:** Human Resources Department. **World Wide Web address:** http://www.dnb.com. **Description:** A holding company. **Common positions include:** Accountant/Auditor; Computer Programmer; Customer Service Representative; Financial Analyst; Human Resources Manager; Marketing Specialist. **Subsidiaries include:** Dun & Bradstreet, Inc. provides information to the business community about other companies including data on credit and marketing. Moody's Investor Services provides ratings and other financial market information to assist individuals and companies in assessing investment opportunities. **Operations at this facility include:** Divisional Headquarters. **Listed on:** New York Stock Exchange. **Stock exchange symbol:** DNB. **Number of employees worldwide:** 12,000.

HOUSEHOLD INTERNATIONAL
200 Somerset Corporate Boulevard, Bridgewater NJ 08807. 908/203-2100. **Contact:** Human Resources Department. **World Wide Web address:** http://www.household.com. **Description:** Provides data processing services for the insurance and banking industries.

GREG MANNING AUCTIONS, INC.
775 Passaic Avenue, West Caldwell NJ 07006. 973/882-0004. **Fax:** 973/882-3499. **Contact:** Personnel Department. **World Wide Web address:** http://www.gregmanning.com. **Description:** Conducts public auctions of rare stamps, stamp collections, and stocks. Items included in the auctions are rare stamps; sports trading cards and sports memorabilia; rare glassware and pottery; pre-Colombian art objects; Egyptian, Middle Eastern, and Far Eastern antiquities; and rare coins. **Corporate headquarters location:** This location. **Listed on:** NASDAQ. **Stock exchange symbol:** GMAI.

MATHEMATICA POLICY RESEARCH, INC.

P.O. Box 2393, Princeton NJ 08543-2393. 609/799-3535. **Contact:** Personnel Department. **E-mail address:** hrnj@mathematica-mpr.com. **World Wide Web address:** http://www.mathematica-mpr.com. **Description:** An employee-owned company that conducts social policy research (both data collection and data analysis) for government agencies, foundations, and private sector clients. The company specializes in health, labor, welfare, education, child care, and food and nutrition. **Common positions include:** Economist; Statistician. **Corporate headquarters location:** This location. **Other U.S. locations:** Washington DC. **Operations at this facility include:** Service. **Number of employees at this location:** 200.

SCIENCE MANAGEMENT LLC
SMC CONSULTING

721 Routes 202/206, Bridgewater NJ 08807. 908/722-0300. **Contact:** Personnel. **World Wide Web address:** http://www.smcmgmt.com. **Description:** Works with IBM to provide disaster recovery services to large corporations. SMC Consulting (also at this location) provides management consulting services. **Common positions include:** Accountant/Auditor; Computer Programmer; Financial Analyst; General Manager; Human Resources Manager; Industrial Engineer; Systems Analyst. **Corporate headquarters location:** This location.

TEAM STAFF, INC.

300 Atrium Drive, Somerset NJ 08873. 732/748-1700. **Fax:** 732/748-3220. **Contact:** Human Resources Department. **World Wide Web address:** http://www.teamstaff.com. **Description:** A full-line provider of human resource management services to employers in a wide variety of industries. Services include professional employer organization (employee leasing) services, placement of temporary and permanent staffing, and payroll and payroll tax service preparation. **Corporate headquarters location:** This location.

CHARITIES AND SOCIAL SERVICES

You can expect to find the following types of organizations in this chapter:

Social and Human Service Agencies • Job Training and Vocational Rehabilitation Services • Nonprofit Organizations

AMERICAN RED CROSS
203 West Jersey Street, Elizabeth NJ 07202. 908/353-2500. **Contact:** Human Resources. **World Wide Web address:** http://www.redcross.org. **Description:** A humanitarian organization that aids disaster victims, gathers blood for crisis distribution, trains individuals to respond to emergencies, educates individuals on various diseases, and raises funds for other charitable establishments. **Other U.S. locations:** Nationwide.

THE ARC OF BERGEN AND PASSAIC COUNTIES, INC.
223 Moore Street, Hackensack NJ 07601. 201/343-0322. **Fax:** 201/343-0401. **Contact:** Human Resources. **E-mail address:** workatarc@aol.com. **World Wide Web address:** http://www.arcbergenpassaic.org. **Description:** A nonprofit organization that works with mentally disabled people to improve their quality of life.

COMMUNITY OPTIONS INC.
16 Farber Road, Princeton NJ 08540. 609/951-9900. **Fax:** 609/499-4407. **Contact:** Recruiter. **E-mail address:** resume@comop.org. **World Wide Web address:** http://www.comop.org. **Description:** A private, nonprofit organization that works with adults who have developmental disabilities to find them housing and employment opportunities. **Corporate headquarters location:** This location. **Other area locations:** Forked River NJ; Morristown NJ; Trenton NJ; Wayne NJ.

HOPE HOUSE
19-21 Belmont Avenue, Dover NJ 07801. 973/361-5555. **Contact:** Human Resources. **World Wide Web address:** http://www.hopehouse.com. **Description:** A nonprofit organization that provides AIDS outpatient, substance abuse, and family counseling; does house cleaning for the elderly; and performs household chores for home-bound individuals. Hope House also operates a 40-bed residential facility for children and adolescents.

HOPES
124 Grand Street, Hoboken NJ 07030. 201/656-3711. **Contact:** Human Resources. **Description:** A nonprofit organization funded by the state of New Jersey that sponsors programs such as Head Start and a medical transportation program for senior citizens.

URBAN LEAGUE OF HUDSON COUNTY
779 Bergen Avenue, Jersey City NJ 07306. 201/451-8888. **Contact:** Manager of Human Resources Department. **World Wide Web address:** http://www.urbanleaguehudsonnj.org. **Description:** A nonprofit organization that sponsors a variety of social programs including employment services and parenting programs.

CHEMICALS/RUBBER AND PLASTICS

You can expect to find the following types of companies in this chapter:

Adhesives, Detergents, Inks, Paints, Soaps, Varnishes • Agricultural Chemicals and Fertilizers • Carbon and Graphite Products • Chemical Engineering Firms • Industrial Gases

ASHLAND SPECIALITY CHEMICAL COMPANY
One Drew Plaza, Boonton NJ 07005. 973/263-7600. **Fax:** 973/263-4487. **Contact:** Personnel. **World Wide Web address:** http://www.ashchem.com. **Description:** This location supplies specialty chemicals and services to the international maritime industry and other industrial markets worldwide. Through its industrial chemical sector, the Drew Division also manufactures and markets products for water management and fuel treatment, as well as specialized chemicals for major industries. The Ameroid Marine Division provides chemical and sealing products and applications technology for these products to the maritime industry. Ashland Chemical Company provides shipboard technical service for more than 15,000 vessels in more than 140 ports around the world. **Common positions include:** Chemical Engineer; Chemist; Computer Programmer; Manufacturer's/Wholesaler's Sales Rep.; Marketing Specialist; Mechanical Engineer; Systems Analyst. **Corporate headquarters location:** Dublin OH. **Parent company:** Ashland Inc. **Operations at this facility include:** Administration; Divisional Headquarters; Manufacturing; Regional Claims Center; Research and Development; Sales; Service. **Listed on:** New York Stock Exchange. **Stock exchange symbol:** ASH.

BASF CORPORATION
KNOLL PHARMACEUTICALS
3000 Continental Drive North, Mount Olive NJ 07828-1234. 973/426-2600. **Contact:** Liz Roman, Director of Human Resources. **World Wide Web address:** http://www.basf.com. **Description:** This location serves as the U.S. headquarters and houses management offices and the pharmaceutical division, Knoll Pharmaceuticals. Overall, BASF Corporation is an international chemical products organization, doing business in five operating groups: Chemicals; Coatings and Colorants; Consumer Products and Life Sciences; Fiber Products; and Polymers. **Common positions include:** Accountant/Auditor; Chemical Engineer; Computer Programmer; Financial Analyst; Marketing Specialist. **Corporate headquarters location:** This location. **Operations at this facility include:** Administration; Divisional Headquarters; Sales. **Listed on:** New York Stock Exchange. **Stock exchange symbol:** BF. **Number of employees worldwide:** 125,000.

BOC GASES
575 Mountain Avenue, Murray Hill NJ 07974. 908/464-8100. **Contact:** Corporate Personnel Department. **World Wide Web address:** http://www.boc.com/gases. **Description:** BOC Gases manufactures industrial, electronic, and medical gases; and cryogenic equipment. **Corporate headquarters location:** This location. **Other U.S. locations:** Nationwide.

BENJAMIN MOORE & COMPANY
51 Chestnut Ridge Road, Montvale NJ 07645. 201/573-9600. **Fax:** 201/573-6631. **Contact:** Human Resources Department. **World Wide Web address:** http://www.benjaminmoore.com. **Description:** Manufactures paints, varnishes, and other coatings. **Common positions include:** Accountant/Auditor; Administrative Manager; Advertising Clerk; Attorney; Budget Analyst; Buyer; Chemist; Computer Programmer; Credit Manager; Customer Service Representative; Economist; Financial Analyst; Human Resources Manager; Human Service Worker; Manufacturer's/Wholesaler's Sales Rep.; Paralegal; Public Relations Specialist; Purchasing Agent/Manager; Transportation/Traffic Specialist. **Corporate headquarters location:** This location. **Other U.S. locations:** Nationwide. **Operations at this facility include:** Administration; Research and Development; Sales; Service. **Listed on:** Privately held. **Number of employees at this location:** 175. **Number of employees nationwide:** 1,800.

CAMBREX CORPORATION
One Meadowlands Plaza, East Rutherford NJ 07073-2150. 201/804-3000. **Fax:** 201/804-9852. **Contact:** Melissa Lesko, Professional Staffing Department. **E-mail address:** human.resources@cambrex.com. **World Wide Web address:** http://www.cambrex.com. **Description:** Manufactures and markets products and provides services to the life sciences industries. Cambrex Corporation operates in four segments: Human Health; Biotechnology; Animal Health and Agriculture; and Specialty Products. Founded in 1981. **Office hours:** Monday - Friday, 8:30 a.m. - 5:00 p.m. **Corporate headquarters location:** This location.

CHEMETALL OAKITE
50 Valley Road, Berkeley Heights NJ 07922. 908/464-6900. **Contact:** Suzanne Watson, Recruiting Department. **World Wide Web address:** http://www.oakite.com. **Description:** Manufactures and markets specialty chemical products used primarily for industrial cleaning, metal conditioning, and surface preparation. **Common positions include:** Accountant/Auditor; Chemist; Manufacturer's/Wholesaler's Sales Rep.; Marketing Specialist. **Corporate headquarters location:** This location. **Other U.S. locations:** Nationwide. **International locations:** Canada

CHURCH & DWIGHT COMPANY, INC.
469 North Harrison Street, Princeton NJ 08543. 609/683-5900. **Contact:** Human Resources. **E-mail address:** jobs@churchdwight.com. **World Wide Web address:** http://www.churchdwight.com. **Description:** Manufactures Arm & Hammer brand products including soaps and detergents. **Listed on:** New York Stock Exchange. **Stock exchange symbol:** CHD.

COLORITE WATERWORKS
COLORITE POLYMERS
101 Railroad Avenue, Ridgefield NJ 07657. 201/941-2900. **Contact:** Mr. Manuel Aneiros, Human Resources Manager. **World Wide Web address:** http://www.tekni-plex.com/companies/colorpoly.html. **Description:** A manufacturer of plastic garden hoses. Colorite Polymers (also at this location) manufactures PVC compounds. **Parent company:** Tekni-Plex Inc.

CREST FOAM INDUSTRIES, INC.
100 Carol Place, Moonachie NJ 07074. 201/807-0809. **Contact:** Human Resources. **World Wide Web address:** http://www.crestfoam.com. **Description:** Manufactures reticulated and specialty foam for a wide variety of industries such as aerospace, electronics, and medical.

DAICOLOR-POPE INC.
33 Sixth Avenue, Paterson NJ 07524. 973/278-5170. **Contact:** Human Resources. **Description:** Manufactures pigments used by printing companies to produce inks.

DEGUSSA CORPORATION
P.O. Box 677, 379 Interpace Parkway, Parsippany NJ 07054-0677. 973/541-8000. **Fax:** 973/541-8013. **Contact:** Personnel Manager. **World Wide Web address:** http://www.degussa-huls.com. **Description:** Manufactures specialty chemicals, polymers, colorants, additives, and raw materials for the coatings industry. **Common positions include:** Accountant; Administrative Assistant; AS400 Programmer Analyst; Attorney; Auditor; Biological Scientist; Chemist; Claim Representative; Computer Operator; Computer Programmer; Controller; Credit Manager; Database Manager; Financial Analyst; General Manager; Human Resources Manager; Industrial Production Manager; Internet Services Manager; Marketing Manager; Marketing Specialist; MIS Specialist; Network/Systems Administrator; Sales Manager; Sales Representative; Secretary; Systems Analyst. **Special programs:** Internships; Co-ops. **Corporate headquarters location:** This location. **Other U.S. locations:** Theodore AL; Pleasanton CA; Piscataway NJ; Lockland OH. **Parent company:** Degussa AG. **Operations at this facility include:** Divisional Headquarters; Regional Headquarters. **Annual sales/revenues:** More than $100 million. **Number of employees at this location:** 350. **Number of employees nationwide:** 875.

FAIRMOUNT CHEMICAL COMPANY, INC.
117 Blanchard Street, Newark NJ 07105. 973/344-5790. **Toll-free phone:** 800/872-9999. **Fax:** 973/690-5298. **Contact:** Human Resources. **Description:** Manufactures and distributes chemical intermediates for the imaging industry; hydrazine salts and derivatives; additives used in the manufacture of plastics; and specialty chemicals, primarily pharmaceutical intermediates.

FISHER SCIENTIFIC COMPANY
One Reagent Lane, Fair Lawn NJ 07410. 201/796-7100. **Contact:** Michelle Valvano, Human Resources Manager. **World Wide Web address:** http://www.fisherscientific.com. **Description:** This location produces reagents. Overall, Fisher Scientific manufactures, distributes, and sells a wide range of products used in industrial and medical laboratories. Products include analytical and measuring instruments, apparatus, and appliances; reagent chemicals and diagnostics; glassware and plasticware; and laboratory furniture. Customers are primarily industrial laboratories, medical and hospital laboratories, and educational and research laboratories. Manufacturing operations are carried out by six operating divisions in 11 U.S. locations. **Common positions include:** Accountant/Auditor; Administrator; Biological Scientist; Biomedical Engineer; Blue-Collar Worker Supervisor; Buyer; Chemical Engineer; Chemist; Computer Programmer; Customer Service Representative; Department Manager; Draftsperson; Electrical/Electronics Engineer; Financial Analyst; General Manager; Human Resources Manager; Industrial Engineer; Materials Engineer; Mechanical Engineer; Operations/Production Manager; Purchasing Agent/Manager; Quality Control Supervisor; Systems Analyst. **Operations at this facility include:** Administration; Manufacturing; Research and Development. **Listed on:** New York Stock Exchange. **Stock exchange symbol:** FSH.

GENERAL CHEMICAL CORPORATION
90 East Halsey Road, Parsippany NJ 07054. 973/515-0900. **Contact:** Human Resources. **World Wide Web address:** http://www.genchem.com. **Description:** Manufactures inorganic chemicals and soda ash. **Common positions include:** Accountant/Auditor; Chemical Engineer; Customer Service Representative; Financial Analyst; Financial Manager; Human Resources Manager; Mining Engineer; Secretary. **Corporate headquarters location:** This location. **Other U.S. locations:** Claymont DE; Syracuse NY; Pittsburgh PA; Green River WY. **Parent company:** The General Chemical Group Inc. (Hampton NH). **Operations at this facility include:** Administration; Manufacturing; Sales; Service. **Number of employees at this location:** 180. **Number of employees nationwide:** 2,000.

HONEYWELL
10 North Avenue East, Elizabeth NJ 07201. 908/354-3215. **Contact:** Human Resources. **World Wide Web address:** http://www.honeywell.com. **Description:** This location manufactures plastic inserts for pill bottles. Overall, Honeywell is engaged in the research, development, manufacture, and sale of advanced technology products and services in the fields of chemicals, electronics, automation, and controls. The company's major businesses are home and building automation and control, performance polymers and chemicals, industrial automation and control, space and aviation systems, and defense and marine systems. **Listed on:** New York Stock Exchange. **Stock exchange symbol:** HON.

HONEYWELL
101 Columbia Road, Morristown NJ 07962-1057. 973/455-2000. **Contact:** Human Resources. **World Wide Web address:** http://www.honeywell.com. **Description:** Honeywell is engaged in the research, development, manufacture, and sale of advanced technology products and services in the fields of chemicals, electronics, automation, and controls. The company's major businesses are home and building automation and control, performance polymers and chemicals, industrial automation and control, space and aviation systems, and defense and marine systems. **Corporate headquarters location:** This location. **Listed on:** New York Stock Exchange. **Stock exchange symbol:** HON.

IFF
1040 Broad Street, Shrewsbury NJ 07702. 732/578-6700. **Contact:** Staffing. **E-mail address:** staffing.manager@iff.com. **World Wide Web address:** http://www.iff.com. **Description:** Manufactures and distributes flavors and fragrances for use in foods, beverages, detergents, cosmetics, and other personal care items. **Other U.S. locations:** Nationwide. **International locations:** Worldwide. **Listed on:** NASDAQ. **Stock exchange symbol:** IFF.

INTERNATIONAL SPECIALTY PRODUCTS
1361 Alps Road, Wayne NJ 07470. 973/628-4000. **Contact:** Gary Schneid, Director of Employee Selection. **E-mail address:** jobs2@ispcorp.com. **World Wide Web address:** http://www.ispcorp.com. **Description:** Manufactures specialty chemicals and building materials. Chemicals include high-pressure acetylene derivatives, industrial organic and inorganic chemicals, GAF filter systems, and GAF mineral products. Building materials include prepared roofing, roll roofing, built-up roofing systems, and single-ply roofing. **Common positions include:** Accountant/Auditor; Advertising Clerk; Attorney; Biological Scientist; Biomedical Engineer; Budget Analyst; Buyer; Chemical Engineer; Chemist; Computer Programmer; Financial Analyst; General Manager; Paralegal; Pharmacist; Systems Analyst. **Corporate**

headquarters location: This location. **Listed on:** New York Stock Exchange. **Stock exchange symbol:** ISP. **Number of employees at this location:** 700. **Number of employees nationwide:** 4,300.

KOHL & MADDEN PRINTING INK CORP.
222 Bridge Plaza South, Suite 701, Fort Lee NJ 07024. 201/886-1203. **Contact:** Human Resources Department. **World Wide Web address:** http://www.kohlmadden.com. **Description:** Produces printing inks, compounds, and varnishes. **Common positions include:** Clinical Lab Technician; Services Sales Representative. **Corporate headquarters location:** This location. **Parent company:** Sun Chemical Corporation. **Operations at this facility include:** Administration; Divisional Headquarters; Sales. **Listed on:** Privately held. **Number of employees at this location:** 25. **Number of employees nationwide:** 450.

MILLENNIUM CHEMICALS, INC.
230 Half Mile Road, Red Bank NJ 07701. 732/933-5000. **Contact:** Human Resources. **E-mail address:** careers@millenniumchem.com. **World Wide Web address:** http://www.millenniumchem.com. **Description:** Produces a range of chemical products including detergents and fragrances. **Corporate headquarters location:** This location. **Subsidiaries include:** Millennium Petrochemicals Inc. **Listed on:** New York Stock Exchange. **Stock exchange symbol:** MCH.

NATIONAL STARCH AND CHEMICAL COMPANY
10 Finderne Avenue, P.O. Box 6500, Bridgewater NJ 08807. 908/685-5000. **Toll-free phone:** 800/366-4031. **Fax:** 908/685-6956. **Contact:** Hope Hurley, Employment Manager. **E-mail address:** nstarch.jobs@nstarch.com. **World Wide Web address:** http://www.nationalstarch.com. **Description:** Manufactures industrial chemicals including adhesives, resins, starches, and specialty chemicals for the packaging, textile, paper, food, furniture, electronic materials, and automotive markets. **NOTE:** Entry-level positions are offered. **Common positions include:** Accountant; Biochemist; Chemical Engineer; Customer Service Representative; Food Scientist/Technologist; MIS Specialist. **Special programs:** Internships; Co-ops. **Corporate headquarters location:** This location. **Other U.S. locations:** Nationwide. **International locations:** Worldwide. **Parent company:** The ICI Group. **Annual sales/revenues:** More than $100 million. **Number of employees nationwide:** 8,500. **Number of employees worldwide:** 10,000.

PVC CONTAINER CORPORATION
2 Industrial Way West, Eatontown NJ 07724-2202. 732/542-0060. **Toll-free phone:** 800/975-2784. **Fax:** 732/544-8007. **Contact:** Personnel. **World Wide Web address:** http://www.novapakcorp.com. **Description:** Designs and manufactures plastic bottles and polyvinyl chloride compounds.

RED DEVIL, INC.
2400 Vauxhall Road, Union NJ 07083. 908/688-6900. **Fax:** 908/688-8872. **Contact:** Maria Janeira, Director of Human Resources. **World Wide Web address:** http://www.reddevil.com. **Description:** Manufactures and distributes paint sundries; hand tools; and a full-line of caulks, sealants, and adhesives for home and professional use. **Corporate headquarters location:** This location. **Number of employees at this location:** 150. **Number of employees nationwide:** 250.

REEDY INTERNATIONAL
25 East Front Street, Suite 200, Key Port NJ 07735. 732/264-1777. **Contact:** Human Resources. **World Wide Web address:** http://www.reedyintl.com. **Description:** Produces chemical components for items such as Styrofoam and car parts.

RHODIA INC.
CN7500, Cranbury NJ 08512-7500. 609/860-4000. **Physical address:** 259 Prospect Plains Road, Cranbury NJ 08512. **Contact:** Human Resources. **World Wide Web address:** http://www.rhodia.com. **Description:** This location houses administrative offices. Overall, Rhodia supplies specialty and intermediate chemicals for consumer and industrial applications. **Other U.S. locations:** Nationwide. **Parent company:** Rhone-Poulenc.

SAINT-GOBAIN PERFORMANCE PLASTICS
150 Dey Road, Wayne NJ 07470. 973/696-4700. **Contact:** Anne Ginestre, Personnel Manager. **World Wide Web address:** http://www.sgppl.com. **Description:** Manufactures a wide range of plastic products and shapes including pipes, rods, sheet, tape, rectangular stock, insulated wire, and coaxial cable core; finished plastic products such as laboratory wire; and nylon products such as rods, tubes, slabs, and custom castings. **Common positions include:** Chemical Engineer; Customer Service Representative. **Special programs:** Internships.

SETON COMPANY
849 Broadway, Newark NJ 07104. 973/485-4800. **Contact:** Human Resources Department. **E-mail address:** hr@setonco.com. **World Wide Web address:** http://www.setonleather.com. **Description:** Company operations are conducted primarily through two business segments. The Leather Division's operations include tanning, finishing, and distributing whole-hide cattle leathers for the automotive and furniture upholstery industries, cattle hide side leathers for footwear, handbag, and other markets, and cattle products for collagen, rawhide pet items, and other applications. The Chemicals and Coated Products Division is engaged in the manufacture and distribution of epoxy and urethane chemicals, specialty leather finishes, industrial and medical tapes, foams, films, and laminates. Other manufacturing facilities are located in Wilmington DE (epoxy, urethane chemicals, leather finishes); Toledo OH (cattle hide processing); Malvern PA (industrial coated products); and Saxton PA (cutting of finished leathers). **Corporate headquarters location:** This location. **Subsidiaries include:** Radel Leather Manufacturing Company; Seton Leather Company.

SIKA CORPORATION
P.O. Box 297, 201 Polito Avenue, Lyndhurst NJ 07071. 201/933-8800. **Fax:** 201/933-6166. **Contact:** Human Resources Department. **World Wide Web address:** http://www.sikausa.com. **Description:** Manufactures specialty chemicals including sealants and adhesives for the construction and transportation industries. Founded in 1937. **NOTE:** Second and third shifts are offered. **Common positions include:** Administrative Assistant; Chemist; Customer Service Representative; Secretary; Services Sales Representative; Systems Analyst. **Corporate headquarters location:** This location. **Parent company:** Sika Finanz AG. **Operations at this facility include:** Administration; Manufacturing; Regional Headquarters; Research and Development; Sales; Service. **Listed on:** Privately held. **Annual sales/revenues:** More than $100 million. **Number of employees at this location:** 200. **Number of employees nationwide:** 700.

STAR-GLO INDUSTRIES L.L.C.
2 Carlton Avenue, East Rutherford NJ 07073. 201/939-6162. **Contact:** Personnel Department. **World Wide Web address:** http://www.starglo.com. **Description:** Manufactures precision-molded rubber and plastic parts, often bonded to metal. Sales are made primarily to original equipment manufacturers in the business machine and computer, welding, food packaging equipment, chemical, and aerospace industries. **Corporate headquarters location:** This location.

STEPAN COMPANY
100 West Hunter Avenue, Maywood NJ 07607. 201/845-3030. **Contact:** Tim O'Donnell, Office Manager. **E-mail address:** stepanhr@stepan.com. **World Wide Web address:** http://www.stepan.com. **Description:** Produces specialty chemicals and food additives. **Common positions include:** Accountant/Auditor; Chemical Engineer; Chemist; Clinical Lab Technician; Financial Manager; Food Scientist/Technologist. **Corporate headquarters location:** Northfield IL. **Operations at this facility include:** Administration; Manufacturing; Research and Development; Sales. **Listed on:** New York Stock Exchange. **Stock exchange symbol:** SCL. **Number of employees at this location:** 100. **Number of employees nationwide:** 1,300.

TICONA
86-90 Morris Avenue, Summit NJ 07901. 908/598-4000. **Contact:** Human Resources Department. **World Wide Web address:** http://www.ticona-us.com. **Description:** Produces and markets chemicals and manufactured fibers for industrial and textile uses. **Parent company:** Hoechst Group.

USA DETERGENTS
1735 Jersey Avenue, North Brunswick NJ 08902. 732/828-1800. **Fax:** 732/246-7733. **Contact:** Human Resources. **Description:** Manufactures laundry detergents, household cleaners, and scented candles.

COMMUNICATIONS: TELECOMMUNICATIONS AND BROADCASTING

You can expect to find the following types of companies in this chapter:

Cable/Pay Television Services • Communications Equipment•
Radio and Television Broadcasting Systems • Telephone, Telegraph,
and other Message Communications

AT&T CORPORATION
295 North Maple Avenue, Basking Ridge NJ 07920. 908/221-6035. **Contact:** Mirian Graddick-Weir, Executive Vice President of Human Resources. **World Wide Web address:** http://www.att.com. **Description:** AT&T is a major long-distance telephone company that provides domestic and international voice and data communications and management services, telecommunications products, and leasing and financial services. The company manufactures data communications products, computer products, switching and transmission equipment, and components. **NOTE:** Please send resumes to the resume scanning center at 1200 Peachtree Street, Room 7075, Promenade 1, Atlanta GA 30309. **Common positions include:** Telecommunications Analyst. **Corporate headquarters location:** New York NY. **Other U.S. locations:** Nationwide. **Subsidiaries include:** AT&T Capital Corporation offers financing and leases and provides consumer credit through its AT&T Universal credit card. **Listed on:** New York Stock Exchange. **Stock exchange symbol:** T.

ARCH WIRELESS
61 South Paramus Road, Paramus NJ 07652. 201/556-4800. **Contact:** Human Resources. **World Wide Web address:** http://www.arch.com. **Description:** A telecommunications service company providing a wide variety of specialized data- and message-processing and communications services. The company operates a nationwide computer-controlled network that electronically receives, processes, and transmits record and data communications. Arch Wireless also operates a radio paging business.

BROADBEAM CORPORATION
100 College Road West, Princeton NJ 08540-5052. 609/734-0300. **Fax:** 609/734-0346. **Contact:** Personnel. **E-mail address:** hr@broadbeam.com. **World Wide Web address:** http://www.broadbeam.com. **Description:** Provides wireless solutions by developing platform and professional services that allow companies to develop, deploy, and manage mobile solutions. **Corporate headquarters location:** This location.

INTEL CORPORATION
1515 Route 10, Parsippany NJ 07054. 973/993-3000. **Contact:** Human Resources. **World Wide Web address:** http://www.intel.com. **Description:** This Intel Corporation business offers computer telephony services that provide telephone network access to computer terminals. **Other U.S. locations:** Nationwide. **International locations:** Worldwide. **Listed on:** NASDAQ. **Stock exchange symbol:** INTC.

LUCENT TECHNOLOGIES INC.
600-700 Mountain Avenue, Murray Hill NJ 07974. 908/582-3000. **Contact:** Employment Manager. **World Wide Web address:** http://www.lucent.com. **Description:** Manufactures communications products including switching, transmission, fiber-optic cable, wireless systems, and operations systems to fulfill the needs of telephone companies and other communications services providers. **Corporate headquarters location:** This location. **Number of employees worldwide:** 141,600.

LUCENT TECHNOLOGIES INC.
283 King George Road, Room B2C36, Warren NJ 07059. 908/559-5000. **Contact:** Human Resources Department. **World Wide Web address:** http://www.lucent.com. **Description:** This location is a research and development center. Overall, Lucent Technologies Inc. manufactures communications products including switching, transmission, fiber-optic cable, wireless systems, and operations systems to fulfill the needs of telephone companies and other communications services providers. **Special programs:** Summer Jobs. **Corporate headquarters location:** Murray Hill NJ.

MIKROS SYSTEMS CORPORATION
707 Alexander Road, Building 2, Suite 208, Princeton NJ 08540. 609/987-1513. **Contact:** Personnel Department. **World Wide Web address:** http://www.mikrossystems.com. **Description:** Develops communications products for the transmission of digital data over AM and FM radio frequencies.

NEXTEL COMMUNICATIONS
2 Industrial Road, Fairfield NJ 07004. 973/276-8200. **Contact:** Human Resources. **World Wide Web address:** http://www.nextel.com. **Description:** This location provides customer service for cellular phones. Overall, Nextel Communications is engaged in the specialized mobile radio (SMR) wireless communications business. These services permit the company's customers to dispatch fleets of vehicles and place calls using their two-way mobile radios to or from any telephone in North America through interconnection with the public switched telephone network. Nextel Communications also sells and rents two-way mobile radio equipment and provides related installation, repair, and maintenance services. **Corporate headquarters location:** Reston VA. **Listed on:** NASDAQ. **Stock exchange symbol:** NXTL.

RCN CORPORATION
105 Carnegie Center, Princeton NJ 08540. 609/734-3700. **Toll-free phone:** 800/746-4726. **Fax:** 609/734-3789. **Contact:** Employment Administrator. **World Wide Web address:** http://www.rcn.com. **Description:** A full-service communications company that provides customers with cable, Internet, long-distance telephone, and local telephone services. **NOTE:** Entry-level positions and second and third shifts are offered. **Common positions include:** Accountant; Administrative Assistant; Computer Programmer; Customer Service Representative; Financial Analyst; General Manager; Graphic Artist; Human Resources Manager; Internet Services Manager; Market Research Analyst; MIS Specialist; Paralegal; Sales Executive; Sales Representative; Typist/Word Processor; Webmaster. **Special programs:** Co-ops. **Corporate headquarters location:** This location. **Other U.S. locations:** DC; MA; NY; PA; VA. **Subsidiaries include:** Starpower LLC. **Listed on:** NASDAQ. **Stock exchange symbol:** RCNC. **Annual sales/revenues:** $51 - $100 million. **Number of employees at this location:** 200. **Number of employees nationwide:** 1,400.

RFL ELECTRONICS INC.
353 Powerville Road, Boonton Township NJ 07005-9151. 973/334-3100. **Fax:** 973/334-3863. **Contact:** Human Resources Department. **E-mail address:** hrmanager@rflelect.com. **World Wide Web address:** http://www.rflelect.com. **Description:** Designs and manufactures a wide range of telecommunication and teleprotection products for the electric, water, gas, and telephone utilities; railroads; mines; pipelines; airlines; oil drilling and refining firms; private contractors; OEMs; and government agencies. **Common positions include:** Accountant/Auditor; Administrator; Applications Engineer; Assembly Worker; Buyer; Draftsperson; Electrical/Electronics Engineer; Electronics Technician; Industrial Engineer; Sales Engineer.

TELCORDIA TECHNOLOGIES
45 Nightsbridge Road, Room PY-5-B153, Piscataway NJ 08854. 732/699-2000. **Contact:** Human Resources. **World Wide Web address:** http://www.telcordia.com. **Description:** Develops, provides, and maintains telecommunications information networking software, and professional services for businesses, governments, and telecommunications carriers.

VERIZON COMMUNICATIONS
540 Broad Street, Newark NJ 07101. 973/649-9900. **Contact:** Human Resources. **World Wide Web address:** http://www.verizon.com. **Description:** A full-service communications services provider. Verizon offers residential local and long distance telephone services and Internet access; wireless service plans, cellular phones, and data services; a full-line of business services including Internet access, data services, and telecommunications equipment and services; and government network solutions including Internet access, data services, telecommunications equipment and services, and enhanced communications services. **Corporate headquarters location:** New York NY. **Listed on:** New York Stock Exchange. **Stock exchange symbol:** VZ.

WESTERN UNION CORPORATION
One Mack Centre Drive, Paramus NJ 07652. 201/818-5000. **Contact:** Personnel. **World Wide Web address:** http://www.westernunion.com. **Description:** Provides telecommunications systems and services to businesses, government agencies, and consumers. The company operates a nationwide communications network that includes Westar satellites in orbit.

COMPUTER HARDWARE, SOFTWARE, AND SERVICES

You can expect to find the following types of companies in this chapter:

Computer Components and Hardware Manufacturers • Consultants and Computer Training Companies • Internet and Online Service Providers • Networking and Systems Services • Repair Services/Rental and Leasing • Resellers, Wholesalers, and Distributors • Software Developers/Programming Services • Web Technologies

ADP/OMR
101 Business Park Drive, Suite 220, Skillman NJ 08558. 609/497-2000. **Contact:** Human Resources Department. **World Wide Web address:** http://www.adp.com. **Description:** Develops trade-processing software for the financial services industry.

AM BEST COMPANY
AM Best Road, Oldwick NJ 08858. 908/439-2200. **Fax:** 908/439-3027. **Contact:** Human Resources. **E-mail address:** hr@ambest.com. **World Wide Web address:** http://www.ambest.com. **Description:** Manufactures products including software, CD-ROMs, and diskette support products for the insurance industry. **Corporate headquarters location:** This location.

AXS-ONE INC.
301 Route 17 North, 12th Floor, Rutherford NJ 07070. 201/935-3400. **Toll-free phone:** 800/828-7660. **Contact:** Human Resources Department. **E-mail address:** careers@axsone.com. **World Wide Web address:** http://www.axsone.com. **Description:** Develops and markets various financial software products.

ACCENTURE
5 Spring Street, Murray Hill NJ 07974. 908/898-5000. **Contact:** Human Resources. **World Wide Web address:** http://www.accenture.com. **Description:** A management and technology consulting firm. Accenture offers a wide range of services including business re-engineering; customer service system consulting; data system design and implementation; Internet sales systems research and design; and strategic planning. **Number of employees nationwide:** 5,600.

AFFINITI GROUP
106 Apple Street, Suite 110, Tinton Falls NJ 07724. 732-747-9600. **Contact:** Human Resources. **E-mail address:** careers@affinitigroup.com. **World Wide Web address:** http://www.affinitigroup.com. **Description:** Provides systems integration and software development services.

ALPHANET SOLUTIONS, INC.
7 Ridgedale Avenue, Cedar Knolls NJ 07927. 973/267-0088. **Fax:** 973/267-8675. **Contact:** Robert Derosa, Vice President of Human Resources. **World Wide Web address:** http://www.alphanetcorp.com. **Description:** A leading systems integrator. The company's services include computer network design, installation, and administration; helpdesk support; technical

education; cabling and telecommunications sales and service; computer product sales and services; and Internet services. Clients include many small and mid-range companies, national and global *Fortune* 1000 companies, and large government agencies. Founded in 1984. **Common positions include:** Computer Programmer; Internet Services Manager; MIS Specialist; Systems Analyst; Systems Manager; Webmaster. **Corporate headquarters location:** This location. **Other U.S. locations:** NY; PA. **Listed on:** NASDAQ. **Stock exchange symbol:** ALPH. **Annual sales/revenues:** More than $100 million.

ANALYSTS INTERNATIONAL CORPORATION (AIC)
111 Wood Avenue South, Iselin NJ 08830. 732/906-0100. **Fax:** 732/906-8808. **Contact:** Human Resources. **World Wide Web address:** http://www.analysts.com. **Description:** AiC is an international computer consulting firm. The company assists clients in analyzing, designing, and developing systems in a variety of industries using different programming languages and software. **Corporate headquarters location:** Minneapolis MN.

ANSOFT CORPORATION
669 River Drive, Suite 200, Elmwood Park NJ 07407-1361. 201/796-2003. **Contact:** Human Resources. **E-mail address:** jobs@ansoft.com. **World Wide Web address:** http://www.ansoft.com. **Description:** Develops and distributes circuit design software. **NOTE:** Send resumes and cover letters to: 4 Station Square, Suite 200, Pittsburgh PA 15219-1119. 412/261-3200. **Corporate headquarters location:** Pittsburgh PA.

ASPECT COMPUTER CORPORATION
21 World's Fair Drive, Somerset NJ 08873. 732/563-1304. **Contact:** Human Resources. **World Wide Web address:** http://www.aspectcom.com. **Description:** Manufactures computers.

AUTOMATED CONCEPTS, INC.
90 Woodbridge Center Drive, Suite 400, Woodbridge NJ 07095. 732/602-0200. **Contact:** Human Resources Department. **World Wide Web address:** http://www.autoconcepts.com. **Description:** Provides systems integration services.

BLUEBIRD AUTO RENTAL SYSTEMS INC.
700 Lanidex Plaza, Parsippany NJ 07054. 973/560-0080. **Contact:** Human Resources. **World Wide Web address:** http://www.barsnet.com. **Description:** Designs computer applications for automobile rental agencies.

CAP GEMINI ERNST & YOUNG
100 Walnut Avenue, Clark NJ 07066. 732/382-5400. **Contact:** Human Resources. **World Wide Web address:** http://www.us.cgey.com. **Description:** A leading provider of information technology consulting services with offices nationwide. **Other U.S. locations:** Nationwide.

CIBER, INC.
Iselin Metro Park, 70 Wood Avenue, Iselin NJ 08830. 732/968-9310. **Fax:** 732/494-2224. **Contact:** Human Resources Department. **World Wide Web address:** http://www.ciber.com. **Description:** Provides consulting for client/server development, mainframe and legacy systems, industry-specific analysis, application-specific analysis, and network development. **Common positions include:** Account Representative; Applications Engineer; Computer Operator; Computer Programmer; Database Manager; Internet

Services Manager; Project Manager; Sales Executive; Sales Manager; Sales Representative; Secretary; Systems Analyst; Systems Manager.

CLARION OFFICE SUPPLIES INC.
101 East Main Street, Little Falls NJ 07424. 973/785-8383. **Contact:** Human Resources. **World Wide Web address:** http://www.clarionofficesupply.com. **Description:** Distributes a wide variety of office supplies including computer hardware. Clarion Office Supplies provides individuals and businesses with most major brands of CPUs and monitors.

COMMVAULT SYSTEMS
2 Crescent Place, P.O. Box 900, Oceanport NJ 07757-0900. 732/870-4000. **Contact:** Human Resources. **E-mail address:** employment@commvault.com. **World Wide Web address:** http://www.commvault.com. **Description:** Develops and sells software for businesses with computer backup systems. **Corporate headquarters location:** This location.

COMPUTER ASSOCIATES INTERNATIONAL, INC.
Route 206 and Orchard Road, Princeton NJ 08543. 908/874-9000. **Fax:** 908/874-9420. **Contact:** Hiring Manager. **E-mail address:** joinca@ca.com. **World Wide Web address:** http://www.cai.com. **Description:** One of the world's leading developers of client/server and distributed computing software. The company develops, markets, and supports enterprise management, database and applications development, business applications, and consumer software products for a broad range of mainframe, midrange, and desktop computers. Computer Associates International serves major business, government, research, and educational organizations. Founded in 1976. **NOTE:** Mail resumes to: CAI Inc., One Computer Associates Plaza, Islandia NY 11749. **Corporate headquarters location:** Islandia NY. **Other U.S. locations:** Nationwide. **Listed on:** New York Stock Exchange. **Stock exchange symbol:** CA. **Annual sales/revenues:** More than $100 million.

COMPUTER ASSOCIATES INTERNATIONAL, INC.
2 Executive Drive, Fort Lee NJ 07024. 201/592-0009. **Contact:** Hiring Manager. **E-mail address:** joinca@ca.com. **World Wide Web address:** http://www.cai.com. **Description:** This location sells software, offers technical support, and is home to the marketing department. Overall, Computer Associates International is one of the world's leading developers of client/server and distributed computing software. The company develops, markets, and supports enterprise management, database and applications development, business applications, and consumer software products for a broad range of mainframe, midrange, and desktop computers. Computer Associates International serves major business, government, research, and educational organizations. Founded in 1976. **NOTE:** Mail resumes to: CAI Inc., One Computer Associates Plaza, Islandia NY 11749. **Corporate headquarters location:** Islandia NY. **Other U.S. locations:** Nationwide. **Listed on:** New York Stock Exchange. **Stock exchange symbol:** CA. **Annual sales/revenues:** More than $100 million.

COMPUTER HORIZONS CORPORATION
49 Old Bloomfield Avenue, Mountain Lakes NJ 07046-1495. 973/299-4000. **Contact:** Human Resources Department. **World Wide Web address:** http://www.computerhorizons.com. **Description:** A full-service technology solutions company offering contract staffing, outsourcing, re-engineering, migration, downsizing support, and network management. Founded in 1969. **Corporate headquarters location:** This location. **Other U.S.**

locations: Nationwide. **Subsidiaries include:** Birla Horizons International Ltd.; Horizons Consulting, Inc.; Strategic Outsourcing Services, Inc.; Unified Systems Solutions, Inc. **Listed on:** NASDAQ. **Stock exchange symbol:** CHRZ. **Number of employees nationwide:** 1,500.

CORPORATE DISK COMPANY
1800 Bloomsbury Avenue, Ocean City NJ 07712. 732/431-5300. **Contact:** Controller. **World Wide Web address:** http://www.disk.com. **Description:** Provides a broad range of integrated software and information distribution options in multiple formats on disk, in print, and online to many industries including the technology, insurance, financial services, pharmaceutical, publishing, government, and transportation communities. **NOTE:** Resumes should be sent to Human Resources, Corporate Disk Company, 1226 Michael Drive, Wood Dale IL 60191.

DRS TECHNOLOGIES
5 Sylvan Way, Suite 60, Parsippany NJ 07054. 973/898-1500. **Fax:** 973/898-4730. **Contact:** Alicia Shelton, Human Resources. **World Wide Web address:** http://www.drs.com. **Description:** A producer of magnetic recording heads for the information processing industry. **Corporate headquarters location:** This location.

DATA SYSTEMS & SOFTWARE INC.
200 Route 17 South, Mahwah NJ 07430. 201/529-2026. **Fax:** 201/529-3163. **Contact:** Human Resources. **World Wide Web address:** http://www.dssiinc.com. **Description:** A leading provider of consulting and development services for computer software and systems to high-technology companies in Israel and the United States, principally in the area of embedded real-time systems.

DATARAM CORPORATION
P.O. Box 7528, Princeton NJ 08543-7528. 609/799-0071. **Physical address:** 186 Route 571, Building 2A, West Windsor 08550. **Toll-free phone:** 800/DAT-ARAM. **Fax:** 609/897-7021. **Contact:** Dawn Craft, Human Resources Administrator. **E-mail address:** hr@dataram.com. **World Wide Web address:** http://www.dataram.com. **Description:** Designs and manufactures memory products that improve the performance of computer systems. Dataram primarily serves HP, DEC, Sun, and IBM users in the manufacturing, finance, government, telecommunications, utilities, research, and education industries. **Common positions include:** Accountant; Design Engineer; Designer; Sales Representative; Test Engineer. **Corporate headquarters location:** This location. **Listed on:** American Stock Exchange. **Stock exchange symbol:** DTM. **Number of employees at this location:** 100. **Number of employees nationwide:** 150.

DATATECH INDUSTRIES INC.
23 Madison Road, Fairfield NJ 07004. 973/808-4000. **Contact:** Human Resources. **Description:** Specializes in installing mainframes and networking hardware for businesses.

DENDRITE INTERNATIONAL, INC.
1200 Mount Kemble Avenue, Morristown NJ 07960. 973/425-1200. **Fax:** 973/425-1919. **Contact:** Personnel. **World Wide Web address:** http://www.dendrite.com. **Description:** Develops software and provides consulting services aimed at optimizing the sales force effectiveness of pharmaceutical and consumer packaged goods companies. **Corporate headquarters location:** This location. **International locations:** Worldwide.

Listed on: NASDAQ. **Stock exchange symbol:** DRTE. **Annual sales/revenues:** More than $100 million.

DESKTOP ENGINEERING INTERNATIONAL, INC.
172 Broadway, Woodcliff Lake NJ 07677. 201/505-9200. **Toll-free phone:** 800/888-8680. **Fax:** 201/505-1566. **Contact:** Human Resources. **World Wide Web address:** http://www.deiusa.com. **Description:** Designs and manufactures software for use in mechanical and structural engineering industries.

EDS
25 Hanover Road, 3rd Floor, Florham Park NJ 07932-1424. 973/301-7502. **Contact:** Human Resources. **World Wide Web address:** http://www.eds.com. **Description:** Provides integrated hardware, software, and network solutions to *Fortune* 500 companies. EDS focuses primarily on international corporations in the service, wholesale, distribution, and transportation industries. **Listed on:** New York Stock Exchange. **Stock exchange symbol:** EDS.

EASTMAN KODAK COMPANY
One Pearl Court, Allendale NJ 07401. 201/760-5500. **Contact:** Lisa Kessler, Staffing Specialist. **E-mail address:** lkessler@kodak.com. **World Wide Web address:** http://www.kodak.com. **Description:** Develops software for client/server image management systems for use with medical ultrasound instrumentation. **NOTE:** Entry-level positions are offered. **Common positions include:** Administrative Assistant; Applications Engineer; Clinical Lab Technician; Computer Engineer; Computer Programmer; Computer Scientist; Computer Technician; Database Administrator; Quality Assurance Engineer; Secretary; Software Engineer. **Special programs:** Internships; Co-ops; Summer Jobs. **Corporate headquarters location:** Rochester NY. **Number of employees at this location:** 85. **Number of employees nationwide:** 125.

FDS INTERNATIONAL
18 West Ridgewood Avenue, Paramus NJ 07652. 201/843-0800. **Contact:** Personnel. **World Wide Web address:** http://www.fdsinternational.com. **Description:** Develops transportation and custom brokerage software.

FUJITSU CONSULTING
333 Thornall Street, Edison NJ 08837. 732/549-4100. **Fax:** 732/549-2375. **Contact:** Recruiting Administrator. **World Wide Web address:** http://consulting.fujitsu.com. **Description:** Provides computer consulting services including outsourcing solutions and systems integration. **Common positions include:** Administrative Assistant; Applications Engineer; AS400 Programmer Analyst; Computer Animator; Computer Engineer; Computer Operator; Computer Programmer; Computer Scientist; Computer Support Technician; Computer Technician; Content Developer; Database Administrator; Database Manager; Financial Analyst; Internet Services Manager; MIS Specialist; Multimedia Designer; Network/Systems Administrator; Software Engineer; SQL Programmer; Systems Analyst; Systems Manager; Webmaster. **Corporate headquarters location:** This location. **Parent company:** Fujitsu Limited. **Number of employees worldwide:** 8,000.

FUJITSU CORPORATION
85 Challenger Road, 3rd Floor, Ridgefield Park NJ 07660. 201/229-4400. **Contact:** Human Resources Department. **World Wide Web address:**

http://www.fujitsu.com. **Description:** This location is engaged in sales, service, and support. Overall, Amdahl designs, develops, manufactures, markets, and services large-scale, high-performance, general purpose computer systems including both hardware and software. Customers are primarily large corporations, government agencies, and large universities with high-volume data processing requirements. Amdahl markets more than 470 different systems. **NOTE:** Mail employment correspondence to: 1250 East Arques Avenue, Sunnyvale CA 94088. **Corporate headquarters location:** Sunnyvale CA.

GLOBAL COMPUTER SUPPLIES
2139 Highway 35 North, Holmdel NJ 07733. 732/264-1000. **Contact:** Personnel. **World Wide Web address:** http://www.globalcomputer.com. **Description:** Resells computer supplies and peripherals including faxes and modems.

GLOBE MANUFACTURING SALES, INC.
1159 U.S. Route 22, Mountainside NJ 07092. 908/232-7301. **Fax:** 908/232-0179. **Contact:** Personnel Department. **World Wide Web address:** http://www.globebrackets.com. **Description:** Manufactures computer brackets that hold computer chips and other plastic parts. **Parent company:** AK Stamping Company, Inc.

HRSOFT, INC.
10 Madison Avenue, 3rd Floor, Morristown NJ 07962. 973/984-6334. **Toll-free phone:** 800/437-6781. **Fax:** 973/984-5427. **Contact:** Human Resources. **World Wide Web address:** http://www.hrsoft.com. **Description:** Develops and provides human resource-related business software and services.

H.F. HENDERSON INDUSTRIES INC.
45 Fairfield Place, West Caldwell NJ 07006. 973/227-9250. **Contact:** Human Resources. **Description:** Manufactures printed circuit boards, harnesses, battery packs, and other computer components.

IBM CORPORATION
1551 South Washington Avenue, 3rd Floor, Piscataway NJ 08854. 732/926-2000. **Recorded jobline:** 800/964-4473. **Contact:** IBM Staffing Services Center. **World Wide Web address:** http://www.ibm.com. **Description:** This location is a marketing office. Overall, IBM develops, manufactures, and markets advanced information processing products including computers and microelectronic technology, software, networking systems, and information technology-related services. IBM operates in the United States, Canada, Europe, Middle East, Africa, Latin America, and Asia Pacific. **NOTE:** Jobseekers should send a resume to IBM Staffing Services Center, 1DPA/051, 3808 Six Forks Road, Raleigh NC 27609. **Corporate headquarters location:** Armonk NY. **Subsidiaries include:** IBM Credit Corporation; IBM Instruments, Inc.; IBM World Trade Corporation. **Number of employees at this location:** 100.

IDT CORPORATION
520 Broad Street, Newark NJ 07102. 973/438-1000. **Toll-free phone:** 800/CAL-LIDT. **Contact:** Human Resources Manager. **World Wide Web address:** http://www.idt.net. **Description:** An Internet access provider that offers dial-up services, Web hosting, and e-mail by phone. Founded in 1990. **NOTE:** Entry-level positions, part-time jobs, and second and third shifts are offered. **Common positions include:** Account Manager; Account

Representative; Accountant; Administrative Assistant; Administrative Manager; Applications Engineer; Assistant Manager; Attorney; Blue-Collar Worker Supervisor; Clerical Supervisor; Computer Operator; Computer Programmer; Computer Support Technician; Computer Technician; Customer Service Representative; Database Administrator; Database Manager; Financial Analyst; General Manager; Help-Desk Technician; Internet Services Manager; Intranet Developer; Management Trainee; Marketing Specialist; MIS Specialist; Multimedia Designer; Network Engineer; Network/Systems Administrator; Online Sales Manager; Operations Manager; Paralegal; Production Manager; Project Manager; Public Relations Specialist; Quality Control Supervisor; Sales Executive; Sales Manager; Sales Representative; Software Engineer; SQL Programmer; Systems Analyst; Systems Manager; Technical Support Manager; Typist/Word Processor; Web Advertising Specialist; Webmaster; Website Developer. **Special programs:** Internships; Apprenticeships; Summer Jobs. **Corporate headquarters location:** This location. **Other U.S. locations:** Nationwide. **International locations:** London, England; Mexico City, Mexico. **Subsidiaries include:** Amerimax; Net2Phone; Union Telecard Alliances. **Listed on:** NASDAQ. **Stock exchange symbol:** IDTC. **Founder:** Howard Jonas. **Annual sales/revenues:** More than $100 million. **Number of employees at this location:** 1,000. **Number of employees nationwide:** 1,200. **Number of employees worldwide:** 1,500.

ITT INDUSTRIES
AEROSPACE/COMMUNICATIONS DIVISION
100 Kingsland Road, Clifton NJ 07014. 973/284-0123. **Contact:** Richard Pilkington, Recruiter. **E-mail address:** richard.pilkington@avionics.itt.com. **World Wide Web address:** http://www.ittind.com. **Description:** Designs and engineers software for satellite communications under government contracts.

IKEGAMI ELECTRONICS INC.
37 Brook Avenue, Maywood NJ 07607. 201/368-9171. **Contact:** Human Resources. **World Wide Web address:** http://www.ikegami.com. **Description:** Manufactures and sells computer and broadcast monitors.

INNODATA CORPORATION
North American Solutions Center, 3 University Plaza Drive, Hackensack NJ 07601. 201/488-1200. **Contact:** Human Resources. **World Wide Web address:** http://www.innodata.com. **Description:** A worldwide electronic publishing company specializing in data conversion for CD-ROM, print, and online database publishers. The company also offers medical transcription services to health care providers through its Statline Division. **Corporate headquarters location:** Brooklyn NY. **Listed on:** NASDAQ. **Stock exchange symbol:** INOD.

INSTRUCTIVISION, INC.
P.O. Box 2004, 16 Chapin Road, Pine Brook NJ 07058. 973/575-9992. **Contact:** Human Resources Department. **World Wide Web address:** http://www.instructivision.com. **Description:** Develops video production and education software. Instructivision also operates a full-service video production facility encompassing a production stage, an interformat digital editing suite, offline editing, 3-D animation, and audio recording equipment.

INTERACTIVE SOLUTIONS, INC.
377 Route 17 South, Hasbrouck Heights NJ 07604. 201/288-6699. **Contact:** Human Resources. **Description:** Develops custom software applications to meet specific client needs. **Common positions include:** Account Representative; Applications Engineer; Computer Programmer; Database Manager; MIS Specialist; Multimedia Designer; Sales Representative; Software Engineer; Systems Analyst; Telecommunications Manager; Typist/Word Processor. **Corporate headquarters location:** This location. **Listed on:** Privately held. **Annual sales/revenues:** $11 - $20 million. **Number of employees at this location:** 120.

ION NETWORKS INC.
1551 South Washington Avenue, Piscataway NJ 08854. 732/529-0100. **Contact:** Human Resources. **E-mail address:** resumes@ion-networks.com. **World Wide Web address:** http://www.ion-networks.com. **Description:** Develops and markets software and hardware for computer security. **Corporate headquarters location:** This location. **International locations:** Belgium; United Kingdom. **Listed on:** NASDAQ. **Stock exchange symbol:** IONN.

ITOX
8 Elkins Road, East Brunswick NJ 08816. 732/390-2815. **Contact:** Human Resources. **World Wide Web address:** http://www.itox.com. **Description:** Manufactures computer components including graphics accelerator boards, motherboards, and sound cards for commercial and industrial systems.

JCC USA
Crossroads Corporate Center, One International Boulevard, Suite 400, Mahwah NJ 07495. 201/512-8835. **Contact:** Human Resources. **World Wide Web address:** http://www.jccusa.com. **Description:** Manufactures and sells computer terminals with various display screens.

KEANE, INC.
100 Walnut Avenue, Suite 202, Clark NJ 07066. 732/396-4321. **Contact:** Human Resources. **World Wide Web address:** http://www.keane.com. **Description:** This location designs, develops, and manages software for corporations and health care facilities. Overall, Keane offers businesses a variety of computer consulting services. Keane also develops, markets, and manages software for its clients and assists in project management. **Corporate headquarters location:** Boston MA. **Other U.S. locations:** Nationwide. **Listed on:** American Stock Exchange. **Stock exchange symbol:** KEA. **Number of employees worldwide:** 4,500.

MDY ADVANCED TECHNOLOGIES
21-00 Route 208 South, Fair Lawn NJ 07410. 201/797-6676. **Fax:** 201/797-6852. **Contact:** Human Resources Department. **World Wide Web address:** http://www.mdy.com. **Description:** Provides computer networking and record management services.

MAINTECH
39 Paterson Avenue, Wallington NJ 07057. 973/614-1700. **Toll-free phone:** 800/426-8324. **Contact:** Personnel Department. **World Wide Web address:** http://www.maintech.com. **Description:** Provides on-site computer maintenance services.

MOTOROLA, INC.
85 Harristown Road, Glenrock NJ 07452. 201/447-7500. **Contact:** Human Resources. **World Wide Web address:** http://www.motorola.com. **Description:** A leading supplier of corporate networking solutions including data, voice, and video interfaces. Motorola also provides platform software and Internet connectivity services.

NETWORK SPECIALISTS INC.
dba NSI SOFTWARE
Baker Waterfront Plaza, 2 Hudson Place, Suite 700, Hoboken NJ 07030. 201/656-2121. **Fax:** 201/656-3865. **Contact:** Human Resources. **World Wide Web address:** http://www.nsisw.com. **Description:** Develops network performance and fault-tolerant software tools. Products are compatible with Novell NetWare, Microsoft Windows NT, and UNIX.

ORACLE CORPORATION
517 Route 1 South, Iselin NJ 08830. 732/636-2000. **Contact:** Human Resources. **World Wide Web address:** http://www.oracle.com. **Description:** This location designs and manufactures business software programs for small companies. Overall, Oracle Corporation designs and manufactures database and information management software for businesses and provides consulting services. **Corporate headquarters location:** Redwood Shores CA. **Other U.S. locations:** Nationwide. **Listed on:** NASDAQ. **Stock exchange symbol:** ORCL. **Number of employees worldwide:** 12,000.

PNY TECHNOLOGIES, INC.
299 Webro Road, Parsippany NJ 07054. 973/515-9700. **Toll-free phone:** 800/234-4597. **Fax:** 973/560-5283. **Contact:** Human Resources. **E-mail address:** hr@pny.com. **World Wide Web address:** http://www.pny.com. **Description:** Manufactures and designs computer memory products. Founded in 1985. **NOTE:** Entry-level positions are offered. **Common positions include:** Account Manager; Account Representative; Design Engineer; Quality Control Supervisor; Sales and Marketing Representative. **Corporate headquarters location:** This location. **Listed on:** Privately held. **Annual sales/revenues:** More than $100 million. **Number of employees at this location:** 250. **Number of employees nationwide:** 320. **Number of employees worldwide:** 420.

PARAGON COMPUTER PROFESSIONALS INC.
20 Commerce Drive, Suite 226, Cranford NJ 07016. 908/709-6767. **Toll-free phone:** 800/462-5582. **Contact:** Human Resources Administrative Assistant. **World Wide Web address:** http://www.paracomp.com. **Description:** Offers computer consulting services to a variety of businesses. **Corporate headquarters location:** This location.

PRINCETON FINANCIAL SYSTEMS INC.
600 College Road East, Princeton NJ 08540. 609/987-2400. **Fax:** 609/514-4798. **Contact:** Cara Verba, Human Resource Manager. **World Wide Web address:** http://www.pfs.com. **Description:** Develops and supports investment management software. Founded in 1969. **NOTE:** Entry-level positions are offered. **Common positions include:** Accountant/Auditor; Computer Programmer; Fund Manager; Sales Manager; Software Engineer; Systems Analyst; Technical Writer/Editor. **Special programs:** Apprenticeships. **Corporate headquarters location:** This location. **International locations:** London; Toronto. **Parent company:** State Street Boston Corporation. **Number of employees at this location:** 150. **Number of employees nationwide:** 185. **Number of employees worldwide:** 200.

PRINCETON INFORMATION
399 Thornall Street, 4th Floor, Edison NJ 08837-2246. 732/906-5660.
Contact: Personnel. **E-mail address:** newjersey@princetoninformation.com.
World Wide Web address: http://www.princetoninformation.com.
Description: Offers computer consulting services.

PRINCETON SOFTECH
111 Campus Drive, Princeton NJ 08540. 609/688-5000. **Toll-free phone:**
800/457-7060. **Fax:** 609/627-7799. **Contact:** Human Resources. **World
Wide Web address:** http://www.princetonsoftech.com. **Description:**
Provides IT professionals with software solutions. Develops, researches,
sells, and markets software products that are focused on intelligent data
migration and database synchronization. The company offers data and
program synchronization tools to solve application development and
database problems. Founded in 1989. **Corporate headquarters location:**
This location. **International locations:** Worldwide. **Parent company:**
Computer Horizons Corporation.

QUALITY SOFTWARE SYSTEMS INC.
200 Centennial Avenue, Suite 110, Piscataway NJ 08854. 732/885-1919.
Contact: Human Resources Department. **World Wide Web address:**
http://www.qssiwarehouse.com. **Description:** Develops software to aid in
warehouse management and development.

RARITAN COMPUTER INC.
400 Cottontail Lane, Somerset NJ 08873. 732/764-8886. **Fax:** 732/764-
8887. **Contact:** Human Resources. **E-mail address:** hr@raritan.com. **World
Wide Web address:** http://www.raritan.com. **Description:** Designs and
manufactures a line of products for sharing PCs and peripherals. Products
include MasterConsole, a keyboard/video/mouse switch; CompuSwitch, a
KVM switch allowing central control for up to four PCs; and Guardian, a
virtual keyboard and mouse device that emulates keyboard and mouse
signals. Founded in 1985. **Common positions include:** Account Manager;
Account Representative; Accountant/Auditor; Administrative Assistant;
Advertising Clerk; Applications Engineer; Buyer; Clerical Supervisor;
Computer Programmer; Customer Service Representative; General
Manager; Human Resources Manager; Internet Services Manager; Marketing
Manager; MIS Specialist; Operations/Production Manager; Project Manager;
Purchasing Agent/Manager; Quality Control Supervisor; Sales Manager;
Sales Representative; Secretary; Software Engineer; Systems Analyst;
Technical Writer/Editor; Telecommunications Manager; Vice President of
Marketing. **Corporate headquarters location:** This location. **International
locations:** Japan; The Netherlands; Taiwan. **Listed on:** Privately held.
Annual sales/revenues: $21 - $50 million. **Number of employees at this
location:** 40. **Number of employees nationwide:** 100. **Number of
employees worldwide:** 175.

SPHERION
9 Polito Avenue, 9th Floor, Lyndhurst NJ 07071. 201/392-0800. **Contact:**
Human Resources. **World Wide Web address:** http://www.spherion.com.
Description: A nationwide computer outsourcing service company,
providing short-run supplemental and long-term contractual support for
computer operations, communications operations, PC help desks, local area
networks, computer programming, and technology training. The company's
computer services are provided from offices strategically located throughout
the United States. The company also provides the expertise for meeting

applications and systems development objectives within information systems organizations. Capabilities extend beyond evaluating computer software and hardware to providing technically qualified professionals for any task in the systems development life cycle – from conception through feasibility analysis, system design, programming, testing, implementation, and full systems maintenance and support. **Corporate headquarters location:** Fort Lauderdale FL. **Other U.S. locations:** Nationwide. **Listed on:** New York Stock Exchange. **Stock exchange symbol:** SFN.

STORAGE ENGINE, INC.
One Sheila Drive, Tinton Falls NJ 07724. 732/747-6995. **Contact:** Sharon Wallace, Director of Human Resources. **World Wide Web address:** http://www.eccs.com. **Description:** Designs and configures computer systems. Storage Engine's mass storage enhancement products include RAID (Redundant Array of Independent Disks) products and technology; external disk, optical, and tape systems; internal disk and tape storage devices; and RAM. The company also provides related technical services. **Corporate headquarters location:** This location.

SUN MICROSYSTEMS, INC.
400 Atrium Drive, Somerset NJ 08873. 732/469-1000. **Contact:** Human Resources. **World Wide Web address:** http://www.sun.com. **Description:** This location is a sales office. Overall, Sun Microsystems produces high-performance computer systems, workstations, servers, CPUs, peripherals, and operating systems software. The company developed its own microprocessor called SPARC. **Corporate headquarters location:** Palo Alto CA. **Subsidiaries include:** Forte Software Inc. manufactures enterprise application integration software. **Listed on:** NASDAQ. **Stock exchange symbol:** SUNW.

SYNCSORT
50 Tice Boulevard, Woodcliff Lake NJ 07677. 201/930-8200. **Contact:** Human Resources. **World Wide Web address:** http://www.syncsort.com. **Description:** Develops operating systems software for businesses.

TELCORDIA TECHNOLOGIES
45 Nightsbridge Road, Room PY-5-B153, Piscataway NJ 08854. 732/699-2000. **Contact:** Human Resources. **World Wide Web address:** http://www.telcordia.com. **Description:** Develops, provides, and maintains telecommunications information networking software, and professional services for businesses, governments, and telecommunications carriers.

EDUCATIONAL SERVICES

You can expect to find the following types of facilities in this chapter:

Business/Secretarial/Data Processing Schools •
Colleges/Universities/Professional Schools • Community
Colleges/Technical Schools/Vocational Schools • Elementary and
Secondary Schools • Preschool and Child Daycare Services

BERGEN COMMUNITY COLLEGE
400 Paramus Road, Paramus NJ 07652-1595. 201/612-5440. **Fax:** 201/251-4987. **Contact:** Human Resources. **World Wide Web address:** http://www.bergen.cc.nj.us. **Description:** A community college enrolling over 12,000 students. The college offers associate degrees in arts, sciences, and applied sciences.

BERLITZ INTERNATIONAL, INC.
400 Alexander Park, Princeton NJ 08540. 609/514-9650. **Contact:** Human Resources. **World Wide Web address:** http://www.berlitz.com. **Description:** A language services firm providing instruction and translation services through 298 language centers in 28 countries around the world. The company also publishes travel guides, foreign language phrase books, and home study materials. **Common positions include:** Accountant/Auditor; Director; Instructor/Trainer; Services Sales Representative. **Corporate headquarters location:** This location. **Operations at this facility include:** Administration. **Number of employees nationwide:** 3,500.

EDUCATIONAL TESTING SERVICE (ETS)
Rosedale Road, Princeton NJ 08541. 609/921-9000. **Fax:** 609/734-5410. **Contact:** Human Resources. **World Wide Web address:** http://www.ets.org. **Description:** An educational research and evaluation service that administers many aptitude and achievement tests including the SAT, CLEP, TOEFL, GRE, GMAT, and AP.

KEAN UNIVERSITY
1000 Morris Avenue, Union NJ 07083. 908/527-2150. **Contact:** Human Resources. **World Wide Web address:** http://www.kean.edu. **Description:** A university offering more than 60 programs of study for graduates and undergraduates. The university has an enrollment of over 12,000 students. Founded in 1855.

MONTCLAIR STATE UNIVERSITY
One Normal Avenue, Box CO 316, Upper Montclair NJ 07043. 973/655-4398. **Fax:** 973/655-7210. **Contact:** Department of Human Resources. **E-mail address:** hr@mail.monclair.edu. **World Wide Web address:** http://www.montclair.edu. **Description:** A state university with an enrollment of 13,500. The university offers over 70 programs of study. **NOTE:** For more information about employment opportunities in the environmental field school, please contact the New Jersey School of Conservation, Human Resources Department, One Wapalanne Road, Branchville NJ 07826. 973/948-4646.

NEW JERSEY CITY UNIVERSITY
2039 Kennedy Boulevard, Hepburn Hall 105, Jersey City NJ 07305. 201/200-2335. **Fax:** 201/200-2219. **Contact:** Robert Piaskowsky, Director of Human Resources. **World Wide Web address:** http://www.njcu.edu. **Description:** A state university with approximately 10,000 students enrolled in undergraduate, graduate, and continuing education programs. **Common positions include:** Education Administrator; Teacher/Professor.

NEW JERSEY INSTITUTE OF TECHNOLOGY
323 Martin Luther King Jr. Boulevard, Cullimore Hall, Room 211, Newark NJ 07102. 973/596-3140. **Fax:** 973/642-4056. **Contact:** Human Resources. **World Wide Web address:** http://www.njit.edu. **Description:** A technical institute of higher learning offering undergraduate and graduate degrees in engineering, architecture, liberal arts/sciences, management, and education.

PRINCETON UNIVERSITY
Office of Human Resources, One New South, Princeton NJ 08544. 609/258-3300. **Contact:** Personnel. **E-mail address:** jobs@princeton.edu. **World Wide Web address:** http://www.princeton.edu/hr. **Description:** A private, four-year university offering bachelor of arts and science degrees, as well as master's and doctoral degrees. Approximately 4,500 undergraduate and 1,800 graduate students attend Princeton.

RUTGERS STATE UNIVERSITY OF NEW JERSEY
56 Bevier Road, Piscataway NJ 08854. 732/445-3020. **Contact:** Personnel Department. **World Wide Web address:** http://www.rutgers.edu. **Description:** A four-year, state university offering undergraduate and graduate programs in a wide variety of disciplines. **Other U.S. locations:** Camden NJ; Newark NJ.

RUTGERS STATE UNIVERSITY OF NEW JERSEY
UNIVERSITY COLLEGE-NEWARK
249 University Avenue, Room 202, Newark NJ 07102. 973/353-5500. **Contact:** RoseAnn Wesley, Human Resources Representative. **E-mail address:** work@andromeda.rutgers.edu. **World Wide Web address:** http://www.rutgers.edu. **Description:** A campus of the state university. **Other U.S. locations:** Brunswick NJ; Camden NJ.

SETON HALL UNIVERSITY
400 South Orange Avenue, Stafford Hall, South Orange NJ 07079. 973/761-9138. **Fax:** 973/761-9007. **Contact:** Aisha Agee, Human Resources Specialist. **E-mail address:** ageeaiash@shu.edu. **World Wide Web address:** http://www.shu.edu. **Description:** A Catholic university offering a wide range of undergraduate and graduate programs.

WILLIAM PATERSON UNIVERSITY OF NEW JERSEY
358 Hamburg Turnpike, College Hall-Room 150, Wayne NJ 07470. 973/720-2605. **Fax:** 973/720-2090. **Contact:** Human Resources. **World Wide Web address:** http://www.wpunj.edu. **Description:** A public university with approximately 9,000 students. Programs include liberal arts, nursing, sciences, English, history, and music.

ELECTRONIC/INDUSTRIAL ELECTRICAL EQUIPMENT

You can expect to find the following types of companies in this chapter:

Electronic Machines and Systems • Semiconductor Manufacturers

ABACUS CONTROLS
P.O. Box 893, Somerville NJ 08876. 908/526-6010. **Physical address:** 80 Readington Road, Somerville NJ 08876. **Toll-free phone:** 888/222-2287. **Fax:** 908/526-6866. **Contact:** Personnel Department. **World Wide Web address:** http://www.abacuscontrols.com. **Description:** Manufactures frequency converters and uninterrupted power supplies.

AGILENT TECHNOLOGIES
140 Green Pond Road, Rockaway NJ 07866. 973/627-6400. **Contact:** Employment Office. **World Wide Web address:** http://www.agilent.com. **Description:** Designs and manufactures test, measurement, and monitoring instruments, systems, and solutions. The company also designs and manufactures semiconductor and optical components. Agilent Technologies serves the communications, electronics, life sciences and health care industries. Founded in 1999. **NOTE:** Send employment correspondence to: Resume Processing Center, 89 Davis Road, Suite 160, Orinda CA 94563. **Corporate headquarters location:** Palo Alto CA. **Other U.S. locations:** Nationwide. **International locations:** Worldwide. **Listed on:** New York Stock Exchange. **Stock exchange symbol:** A. **Number of employees worldwide:** 46,000.

ALPHA WIRE COMPANY
711 Lidgerwood Avenue, Elizabeth NJ 07207. 908/925-8000. **Toll-free phone:** 800/52A-LPHA. **Fax:** 908/925-3346. **Contact:** Human Resources. **World Wide Web address:** http://www.alphawire.com. **Description:** An international distributor of high-tech and high-reliability wire, cable, tubing, and connector products including communications and control cables, shrinkable and nonshrinkable tubing and insulation, instrumentation cables, flat cable and connectors, coaxial and data cables, plenum cable, and hook-up wire used for electrical and electronic equipment. Products are sold to a network of distributors and OEMs. Founded in 1922. **NOTE:** Entry-level positions and part-time jobs are offered. **Common positions include:** Account Representative; Accountant; Administrative Assistant; AS400 Programmer Analyst; Chief Financial Officer; Computer Programmer; Controller; Credit Manager; Customer Service Representative; Design Engineer; Financial Analyst; General Manager; Human Resources Manager; Industrial Engineer; Intranet Developer; Marketing Manager; Marketing Specialist; Purchasing Agent/Manager; Sales Executive; Sales Manager; Secretary; Vice President of Marketing and Sales. **Special programs:** Internships. **Office hours:** Monday - Friday, 8:00 a.m. - 8:00 p.m. **Corporate headquarters location:** St. Louis MO. **Other U.S. locations:** Nationwide. **International locations:** Worldwide. **Operations at this facility include:** Administration; Research and Development; Sales; Service. **General Manager:** Brian O'Connell. **Purchasing Manager:** Ben Ochinegro. **Annual sales/revenues:** $51 - $100 million. **Number of employees at this location:** 120. **Number of employees nationwide:** 180. **Number of employees worldwide:** 185.

AMERICAN GAS & CHEMICAL COMPANY LTD.

220 Pegasus Avenue, Northvale NJ 07647. 201/767-7300. **Toll-free phone:** 800/288-3647. **Fax:** 201/767-1741. **Contact:** Human Resources Department. **E-mail address:** hr@amgas.com. **World Wide Web address:** http://www.amgas.com. **Description:** Manufactures electronic chemical and gas leak detectors. **Common positions include:** Accountant/Auditor; Applications Engineer; Buyer; Chemist; Chief Financial Officer; Clerical Supervisor; Computer Programmer; Customer Service Representative; Design Engineer; Draftsperson; Electrical/Electronics Engineer; Industrial Production Manager; Marketing Manager; Purchasing Agent/Manager; Quality Control Supervisor; Sales Engineer; Sales Manager. **Corporate headquarters location:** This location. **Operations at this facility include:** Administration; Manufacturing; Research and Development; Sales. **Listed on:** Privately held. **Number of employees at this location:** 125.

ARIES ELECTRONICS

P.O. Box 130, 62A Trenton Ave., Frenchtown NJ 08825. 908/996-6841. **Contact:** Personnel. **World Wide Web address:** http://www.arieselec.com. **Description:** Manufactures a wide variety of electronic components including pin grid array footprints, ZIF and test sockets, cable assemblies, DIP/SIP sockets/headers, display sockets, programming devices, and switches.

BEL FUSE INC.

198 Van Vorst Street, Jersey City NJ 07302. 201/432-0463. **Fax:** 201/432-9542. **Contact:** Personnel Department. **World Wide Web address:** http://www.belfuse.com. **Description:** Designs, manufactures, and sells products used in local area networking, telecommunications, business equipment, and consumer electronic applications. Magnetic components manufactured by the company fall into four major groups: pulse transformers; delay lines, filters, and AC/DC converters; power transformers, line chokes, and coils; and packaged modules. The company manufactures miniature and micro fuses for supplementary circuit protection. Bel Fuse sells its products to approximately 550 customers throughout North America, Western Europe, and the Far East. **Other U.S. locations:** CA; IN. **International locations:** France; Hong Kong; Macau. **Listed on:** NASDAQ. **Stock exchange symbol:** BELF.

BLONDER TONGUE LABORATORIES, INC.

One Jake Brown Road, Old Bridge NJ 08857-1000. 732/679-4000. **Fax:** 732/679-4353. **Contact:** Human Resources Department. **E-mail address:** employment@blondertongue.com. **World Wide Web address:** http://www.blondertongue.com. **Description:** Designs and manufactures signal processing equipment for the television industry. Products are used for satellite communications, master antennae systems (MATV), and other systems using RF technology. **Common positions include:** Accountant/Auditor; Buyer; Customer Service Representative; Draftsperson; Electrical/Electronics Engineer; General Manager; Industrial Engineer; Mechanical Engineer. **Corporate headquarters location:** This location. **Operations at this facility include:** Administration; Divisional Headquarters; Manufacturing; Regional Headquarters; Research and Development; Sales; Service. **Listed on:** American Stock Exchange. **Stock exchange symbol:** BDR. **Annual sales/revenues:** $51 - $100 million. **Number of employees at this location:** 500.

CONTINENTAL CONNECTOR COMPANY

53 La France Avenue, Bloomfield NJ 07003. 973/429-8500. **Contact:** Manager of Human Resources Department. **World Wide Web address:** http://www.continentalconnector.com. **Description:** This location manufactures circuit connectors. Overall, Continental Connector Corporation is engaged in the development, manufacture, and sale of a broad line of multiprecision rack and panel circuit connectors. Manufacturing operations consist primarily of the processing and assembly of plated metals, receptacles, and plugs of various types designed and molded from thermosetting molding compounds and other precision connector parts. **Corporate headquarters location:** Las Vegas NV. **Parent company:** ASC Group Inc.

DRS PHOTRONICS

133 Bauer Drive, Oakland NJ 07436. 201/337-3800. **Fax:** 201/337-4775. **Contact:** Human Resources Department. **World Wide Web address:** http://www.drs.com. **Description:** Designs, manufactures, and markets high-technology electronic products used to process, display, and store information for the U.S. Department of Defense, international defense departments, other U.S. prime defense contractors, and industrial corporations. The company's advanced signal processing, display, data storage, trainer, emulation, and electro-optical systems are utilized in numerous applications for military use and for the disk drive and television broadcast industries. Founded in 1968.

DATA DELAY DEVICES, INC.

3 Mount Prospect Avenue, Clifton NJ 07013. 973/773-2299. **Fax:** 973/773-9672. **Contact:** Human Resources. **World Wide Web address:** http://www.datadelay.com. **Description:** Manufactures analog and digital delay lines. The company's products are used by computer, telecommunications, and aerospace firms, as well as the military.

THE DEWEY ELECTRONICS CORPORATION

27 Muller Road, Oakland NJ 07436. 201/337-4700. **Toll-free phone:** 800/888-8680. **Fax:** 201/337-3976. **Contact:** Carol Grofsik, Director of Personnel Administration. **E-mail address:** dewey@deweyelectronics.com. **World Wide Web address:** http://www.deweyelectronics.com. **Description:** Develops, designs, engineers, and manufactures electronics systems for military and civilian customers. **Common positions include:** Buyer; Draftsperson; Electrical/Electronics Engineer; Industrial Engineer; Mechanical Engineer; Quality Control Supervisor. **Corporate headquarters location:** This location. **Operations at this facility include:** Administration; Manufacturing; Research and Development; Sales.

EMR SCHLUMBERGER PHOTOELECTRIC

20 Wallace Road, Princeton Junction NJ 08550. 609/799-1000. **Contact:** Personnel. **World Wide Web address:** http://www.schlumberger.com. **Description:** This location is engaged in the engineering and manufacturing of critical, high-reliability transducers and transducer systems; nuclear sources and detectors for oil field services; and sensors/transducers for high-value measurement and control. Overall, EMR Schlumberger Photoelectric is a research, development, and manufacturing division of Schlumberger Ltd. **Common positions include:** Chemical Engineer; Electrical/Electronics Engineer; Mechanical Engineer; Physicist. **Corporate headquarters location:** This location. **Parent company:** Schlumberger Ltd. **Listed on:** New York Stock Exchange. **Stock exchange symbol:** SLB.

EMCORE CORPORATION
145 Belmont Drive, Somerset NJ 08873. 732/271-9090. **Contact:** Joan Thomas, Manager of Technical Staffing. **World Wide Web address:** http://www.emcore.com. **Description:** Manufactures semiconductors through the metal organic chemical vapor deposition production system. **NOTE:** Entry-level positions and second and third shifts are offered. **Common positions include:** Chemical Engineer; Customer Service Manager; Design Engineer; Electrical/Electronics Engineer; Manufacturing Engineer; Mechanical Engineer; Software Engineer. **Special programs:** Training; Co-ops. **Office hours:** Monday - Friday, 8:00 a.m. - 5:00 p.m. **Corporate headquarters location:** This location. **Listed on:** NASDAQ. **Stock exchange symbol:** EMKR. **Annual sales/revenues:** $21 - $50 million.

EVENTIDE, INC.
One Alsan Way, Little Ferry NJ 07643. 201/641-1200. **Contact:** Human Resources. **World Wide Web address:** http://www.eventide.com. **Description:** Manufactures electronic harmonizers.

KEARFOTT GUIDANCE & NAVIGATION CORPORATION
150 Totowa Road, Mail Code HWA01, Wayne NJ 07474. 973/785-6459. **Fax:** 973/785-6255. **Contact:** Human Resources Department. **E-mail address:** humanresources@kearfott.com. **World Wide Web address:** http://www.kearfott.com. **Description:** Manufactures precision electromechanical and electronic components used to generate, sense, control, and display motion such as synchros, resolvers, cant angle sensors, and servo motors. Founded in 1917. **Common positions include:** Buyer; Electrical/Electronics Engineer; Mechanical Engineer; Software Engineer. **Corporate headquarters location:** This location. **Parent company:** Astronautics Corporation of America. **Listed on:** Privately held. **Number of employees at this location:** 1,300.

KULITE SEMICONDUCTOR PRODUCTS
One Willow Tree Road, Leonia NJ 07605. 201/461-0900. **Contact:** Personnel Department. **World Wide Web address:** http://www.kulite.com. **Description:** Manufactures computerized metering systems for medical applications and for use in aircraft. Sales offices are located throughout the United States. **Corporate headquarters location:** This location.

LAMBDA EMI
405 Essex Road, Neptune NJ 07753. 732/922-9300. **Contact:** Michele Vail, Manager of Human Resources Department. **World Wide Web address:** http://www.emipower.com. **Description:** Manufactures DC power supplies. **Parent company:** Lambda Electronics.

MERRIMAC INDUSTRIES, INC.
41 Fairfield Place, West Caldwell NJ 07006. 973/575-1300. **Fax:** 973/882-5984. **Contact:** Personnel. **E-mail address:** hrdept@merrimacind.com. **World Wide Web address:** http://www.merrimacind.com. **Description:** An international manufacturer of high-reliability signal-processing components. Products include IF-baseband components (used by electronics and military electronics OEMs); RF-microwave components (for military electronics and fiber optics users); high-reliability space and missile products (electronic components used in military satellite and missile programs); integrated microwave products (for the military and commercial communications markets); and satellite reception products (products for the CATV and satellite master antenna systems). **Common positions include:** Accountant/Auditor; Buyer; Computer Programmer; Customer Service

Representative; Draftsperson; Electrical/Electronics Engineer; Industrial Designer; Mechanical Engineer; Operations Manager; Purchasing Agent/Manager; Quality Control Supervisor; Sales Executive; Technical Writer/Editor. **Corporate headquarters location:** This location. **Operations at this facility include:** Administration; Manufacturing; Research and Development; Sales.

NOISE COM
East 64 Midland Avenue, Paramus NJ 07652. 201/261-8797. **Fax:** 201/261-8339. **Contact:** Human Resources. **E-mail address:** jobs@noisecom.com. **World Wide Web address:** http://www.noisecom.com. **Description:** Manufactures test equipment for the wireless telecommunications industry. **Parent company:** Wireless Telecom Group. **Listed on:** American Stock Exchange. **Stock exchange symbol:** WTT.

OKONITE COMPANY
102 Hilltop Road, P.O. Box 340, Ramsey NJ 07446. 201/825-0300. **Fax:** 201/825-2672. **Contact:** Paulette Vita, Personnel Manager. **World Wide Web address:** http://www.okonite.com. **Description:** Manufactures power cable for large-scale users. **Corporate headquarters location:** This location. **Other area locations:** Passaic NJ; Paterson NJ.

PANASONIC INDUSTRIAL COMPANY
One Panasonic Way, Mailstop 3A-5, Secaucus NJ 07094. 201/348-7000. **Fax:** 201/392-6007. **Contact:** Kisha Rand-Hudson, Human Resources. **E-mail address:** hudsonk@panasonic.com. **World Wide Web address:** http://www.panasonic.com. **Description:** This location houses the U.S. headquarters. Overall, Panasonic is one of the world's largest manufacturers of consumer and industrial electronic equipment and components. Brand names include Panasonic, Technics, and Quasar. **Common positions include:** Accountant/Auditor; Chemical Engineer; Clerical Supervisor; Computer Operator; Credit Manager; Electrical/Electronics Engineer; Employment Interviewer; Financial Manager; Human Resources Manager; Industrial Engineer; Manufacturer's/Wholesaler's Sales Rep.; Mechanical Engineer; Nuclear Engineer; Purchasing Agent/Manager; Receptionist; Secretary; Systems Analyst. **Other U.S. locations:** Nationwide. **Parent company:** Matsushita Electronics Corporation of America. **Number of employees at this location:** 300. **Number of employees nationwide:** 10,000.

PHELPS DODGE HIGH PERFORMANCE CONDUCTORS
666 Passaic Avenue, West Caldwell NJ 07006. 973/575-0400. **Fax:** 973/882-1297. **Contact:** Marge Engel, Human Resources Manager. **Description:** One of the world's leading suppliers of conductive wire. **Common positions include:** Ceramics Engineer; Electrical/Electronics Engineer; Electrician; Materials Engineer; Metallurgical Engineer. **Corporate headquarters location:** Inman SC. **Operations at this facility include:** Administration; Manufacturing; Sales. **Number of employees at this location:** 175. **Number of employees nationwide:** 400.

POWERTECH, INC.
0-02 Fair Lawn Avenue, Fair Lawn NJ 07410. 201/791-5050. **Fax:** 201/791-6805. **Contact:** Alex M. Polner, President. **World Wide Web address:** http://www.power-tech.com. **Description:** Manufactures silicon power transistors.

THERMO ELECTRIC COMPANY, INC.

109 North Fifth Street, Saddle Brook NJ 07663. 201/843-5800. **Contact:** Human Resources. **Description:** An international leader in industrial temperature instrumentation. Thermo Electric Company, Inc. provides solutions for temperature control needs worldwide. Products include temperature sensors, instrumentation, and specialty wire and cable. **Common positions include:** Accountant/Auditor; Electrical/Electronics Engineer; Manufacturer's/Wholesaler's Sales Rep.; Mechanical Engineer. **Corporate headquarters location:** This location. **Operations at this facility include:** Administration; Manufacturing; Research and Development; Sales; Service. **Listed on:** Privately held. **Number of employees at this location:** 200. **Number of employees nationwide:** 225.

THOMAS ELECTRONICS, INC.

100 Riverview Drive, Wayne NJ 07470. 973/696-5200. **Contact:** Human Resources. **World Wide Web address:** http://www.thomaselectronics.com. **Description:** Manufactures cathode ray tubes and liquid crystal displays for use by military and industrial OEMs. **Corporate headquarters location:** This location.

ENVIRONMENTAL AND WASTE MANAGEMENT SERVICES

You can expect to find the following types of companies in this chapter:

Environmental Engineering Firms • Sanitary Services

CLEAN HARBORS, INC.
3 Sutton Place, Edison NJ 08817. 732/248-1997. **Toll-free phone:** 800/782-8805. **Fax:** 732/248-4414. **Contact:** Human Resources. **World Wide Web address:** http://www.cleanharbors.com. **Description:** Clean Harbors, Inc., through its subsidiaries, provides comprehensive environmental services in 35 states in the Northeast, Midwest, Central, and Mid-Atlantic regions. Clean Harbors provides a wide range of hazardous waste management and environmental support services to a diversified customer base from over 40 locations. The company's hazardous waste management services include treatment, storage, recycling, transportation, risk analysis, site assessment, laboratory analysis, site closure, and disposal of hazardous materials through environmentally sound methods including incineration. Environmental remediation services include emergency response, surface remediation, groundwater restoration, industrial maintenance, and facility decontamination. **NOTE:** See Website for current job opportunities and contact information. **Corporate headquarters location:** Braintree MA. **Other U.S. locations:** Nationwide. **Number of employees nationwide:** 1,400.

COVANTA ENERGY GROUP
40 Lane Road, Fairfield NJ 07007. 973/882-9000. **Contact:** Human Resources. **World Wide Web address:** http://www.convantaenergy.com. **Description:** Develops waste-to-energy facilities nationwide through its subsidiaries and provides hazardous waste disposal and recycling services. **Number of employees at this location:** 310.

ENVIRON INTERNATIONAL CORPORATION
214 Carnegie Center, Princeton NJ 08540. 609/452-9000. **Contact:** Margaret Breyer, Personnel. **E-mail address:** mbreyer@environcorp.com. **World Wide Web address:** http://www.environcorp.com. **Description:** A multidisciplinary environmental and health sciences consulting firm that provides a broad range of services relating to the presence of hazardous substances found in the environment, consumer products, and the workplace. ENVIRON International provides assessment and management of chemical risk and supports private sector clients with complex, potentially high-liability concerns. **Corporate headquarters location:** Arlington VA. **Other U.S. locations:** Emeryville CA; Irvine CA; Novato CA; Houston TX. **Parent company:** Applied Bioscience International Inc. (Arlington VA).

GROUNDWATER AND ENVIRONMENTAL SERVICES, INC. (GES)
P.O. Box 1750, Wall NJ 07719. 732/919-0100. **Physical address:** 1340 Campus Parkway, Wall NJ 07719. **Fax:** 732/919-0916. **Contact:** Human Resources. **World Wide Web address:** http://www.gesonline.com. **Description:** An environmental engineering firm specializing in groundwater remediation. Founded in 1985.

HAMON RESEARCH-COTTRELL
58-72 East Main Street, Somerville NJ 08876. 908/685-4000. **Contact:** Human Resources Department. **World Wide Web address:** http://www.hamon-researchcottrell.com. **Description:** An environmental treatment and services company that provides a comprehensive range of services and technologies directed at controlling air pollution; protecting the integrity of the nation's water resources; providing services in support of the management and remediation of hazardous waste; and providing services for the operations, maintenance, and management of treatment facilities. **Office hours:** Monday - Friday, 8:00 a.m. - 5:00 p.m. **Parent company:** Hamon Group.

HANDEX ENVIRONMENTAL
500 Campus Drive, Morganville NJ 07751. 732/536-8500. **Contact:** Human Resources. **World Wide Web address:** http://www.handex.com. **Description:** Provides environmental remediation and educational services including comprehensive solutions to contamination of groundwater and soil resulting from leaking underground storage tanks; petroleum distribution systems; refineries; heavy industrial plants; chemical, aerospace, and pharmaceutical facilities; airports; auto and truck fleet facilities; and related contamination sources.

IDM ENVIRONMENTAL CORPORATION
396 Whitehead Avenue, South River NJ 08882. 732/390-9550. **Contact:** George Pasalano, Personnel Director. **Description:** A full-service contractor specializing in environmental remediation, plant decommissioning services, and the relocation/re-erection of processing plants.

THE KILLAM GROUP, INC.
27 Bleeker Street, Millburn NJ 07041. 973/379-3400. **Toll-free phone:** 800/832-3272. **Fax:** 973/912-3354. **Contact:** Personnel. **E-mail address:** personnel@killam.com. **World Wide Web address:** http://www.killam.com. **Description:** An infrastructure engineering, environmental, and industrial process consulting firm that serves both public and private sectors. The company operates within a wide range of areas providing architectural, environmental, outsourcing, transportation engineering, and water resource management services. Founded in 1937. **Common positions include:** Account Manager; Account Representative; Accountant; Administrative Assistant; Administrative Manager; Advertising Clerk; Advertising Executive; Architect; Assistant Manager; Attorney; Auditor; Branch Manager; Budget Analyst; Chemical Engineer; Chief Financial Officer; Civil Engineer; Clerical Supervisor; Computer Operator; Computer Programmer; Controller; Database Manager; Design Engineer; Draftsperson; Editorial Assistant; Electrical/Electronics Engineer; Environmental Engineer; Finance Director; Financial Analyst; General Manager; Geologist/Geophysicist; Graphic Artist; Graphic Designer; Human Resources Manager; Industrial Engineer; Internet Services Manager; Librarian; Management Trainee; Marketing Manager; Marketing Specialist; Mechanical Engineer; MIS Specialist; Paralegal; Project Manager; Purchasing Agent/Manager; Quality Control Supervisor; Sales Engineer; Sales Executive; Sales Manager; Sales Representative; Secretary; Software Engineer; Systems Analyst; Systems Manager; Technical Writer/Editor; Transportation/Traffic Specialist; Typist/Word Processor; Vice President; Webmaster. **Special programs:** Internships. **Internship information:** Internships are offered May through September, as well as during December and January. **Corporate headquarters location:** This location. **Other area locations:** Cape May Court House NJ; Freehold NJ; Hackensack NJ; Randolph NJ; Toms River NJ; Whitehouse NJ. **Other U.S.**

locations: Nationwide. **Subsidiaries include:** BAC Killam, Inc.; Carlan Killam Consulting Group, Inc.; E3-Killam, Inc.; Killam Associates - New England; Killam Management & Operational Services, Inc. **Parent company:** Hatch Mott MacDonald.

MIDCO RESIDENTIAL SERVICES
11 Harmich Road, South Plainfield NJ 07080. 908/561-8380. **Contact:** Human Resources. **Description:** Provides integrated solid waste management services to residential customers concentrated in the Midwestern and mid-South regions of the United States and in Costa Rica.

MORETRENCH AMERICAN CORPORATION
P.O. Box 316, 100 Stickle Avenue, Rockaway NJ 07866. 973/627-2100. **Fax:** 973/627-3950. **Contact:** Personnel Department. **World Wide Web address:** http://www.moretrench.com. **Description:** A nationwide engineering and contracting firm specializing in groundwater control and hazardous waste removal. **Common positions include:** Accountant/Auditor; Civil Engineer; Draftsperson; Geologist/Geophysicist; Human Resources Manager; Purchasing Agent/Manager; Sales Executive. **Corporate headquarters location:** This location.

RECOVERY TECHNOLOGIES GROUP
7000 Boulevard East, Guttenberg NJ 07093. 201/854-7777. **Contact:** Office Manager. **Description:** Develops and owns waste-to-energy facilities that provide a means of disposal of nonhazardous municipal solid waste. **Corporate headquarters location:** This location.

FABRICATED/PRIMARY METALS AND PRODUCTS

You can expect to find the following types of companies in this chapter:

Aluminum and Copper Foundries • Die-Castings • Iron and Steel Foundries • Steel Works, Blast Furnaces, and Rolling Mills

ALPHA METALS, INC.
600 Route 440, Jersey City NJ 07304. 201/434-6778. **Contact:** Human Resources. **World Wide Web address:** http://www.alphametals.com. **Description:** Manufactures specialized alloys, chemicals, and instrumentation for soldering applications used by electronics OEMs throughout the world. The company's consumer division manufactures solders for plumbing and hobbyists.

ATLANTIC METAL PRODUCTS, INC.
21 Fadem Road, Springfield NJ 07081. 973/379-6200. **Contact:** Personnel. **World Wide Web address:** http://www.atlanticmetal.com. **Description:** Manufactures custom precision sheet metal parts for the computer and office equipment industries. **Corporate headquarters location:** This location. **Other U.S. locations:** Hillside NJ.

HUGO NEU SCHNITZER EAST
One Jersey Avenue, Jersey City NJ 07302. 201/333-4300. **Contact:** Barney Marsh-Gessner, Manager of Human Resources Department. **E-mail address:** humanresources@hugoneu.com. **World Wide Web address:** http://www.hugoneu.com. **Description:** A metals recycling firm, engaged primarily in the purchase, sale, and export of scrap metal. **Corporate headquarters location:** This location.

METEX CORPORATION
970 New Durham Road, Edison NJ 08817. 732/287-0800. **Fax:** 732/248-8739. **Contact:** Human Resources. **E-mail address:** hr@metexcorp.com. **World Wide Web address:** http://www.metexcorp.com. **Description:** Manufactures and sells knitted wire mesh and products made from these materials. The company designs and manufactures knitted wire products and components through its Technical Products Division. Products are used in applications that include adverse environment protective materials used primarily as high-temperature gaskets; seals; shock and vibration isolators; noise reduction elements and shrouds; and phase separation devices used as air, liquid, and solid filtering devices. Metex is also an OEM for the automobile industry, supplying automobile manufacturers with exhaust seals and components for use in exhaust emission control devices. **Common positions include:** Blue-Collar Worker Supervisor; Computer Programmer; Cost Estimator; Designer; Electrical/Electronics Engineer; Electrician; Mechanical Engineer; Metallurgical Engineer; Quality Control Supervisor. **Corporate headquarters location:** Great Neck NJ. **Parent company:** United Capital Corporation. **Operations at this facility include:** Administration; Manufacturing; Research and Development; Sales. **Number of employees at this location:** 380.

PEERLESS TUBE COMPANY
58-76 Locust Avenue, Bloomfield NJ 07003. 973/743-5100. **Contact:** Personnel. **World Wide Web address:** http://www.peerlesstube.com. **Description:** Manufactures collapsible metal tubes and one-piece extruded aluminum aerosol containers for the pharmaceutical, cosmetic, toiletries, and household products industries. Peerless Tube also manufactures and sells extruded aluminum shells for marking pens. The company operates a wholly-owned subsidiary in Puerto Rico that manufactures collapsible metal tubes. **Common positions include:** Blue-Collar Worker Supervisor; Computer Programmer; Manufacturer's/Wholesaler's Sales Rep.; Mechanical Engineer; Quality Control Supervisor. **Corporate headquarters location:** This location. **Number of employees at this location:** 500.

TINNERMAN PALNUT ENGINEERED PRODUCTS
152 Glen Road, Mountainside NJ 07092. 908/233-3300. **Fax:** 908/233-6566. **Contact:** Human Resources Manager. **World Wide Web address:** http://www.palnut.com. **Description:** Manufactures light- and heavy-duty single and multithread specialty fasteners. **Corporate headquarters location:** Brunswick OH.

U.S. CAN COMPANY
669 River Drive, Suite 340, Elmwood Park NJ 07407. 201/794-4441. **Contact:** Human Resources Department. **World Wide Web address:** http://www.uscanco.com. **Description:** Manufactures a wide range of steel container products. Principal clients include paint and ink manufacturers. **Common positions include:** Accountant/Auditor; Blue-Collar Worker Supervisor; Electrical/Electronics Engineer; Manufacturer's/Wholesaler's Sales Rep.; Purchasing Agent/Manager. **Corporate headquarters location:** Oak Brook IL. **Operations at this facility include:** Manufacturing.

FINANCIAL SERVICES

You can expect to find the following types of companies in this chapter:

Consumer Finance and Credit Agencies • Investment Specialists • Mortgage Bankers and Loan Brokers • Security and Commodity Brokers, Dealers, and Exchanges

BEAR, STEARNS & COMPANY, INC.
115 South Jefferson Road, Whippany NJ 07981. 973/793-2600. **Fax:** 973/793-2040. **Contact:** Managing Director of Personnel. **World Wide Web address:** http://www.bearstearns.com. **Description:** An investment banking, securities trading, and brokerage firm engaged in corporate finance, mergers, and acquisitions; institutional equities and fixed income sales and trading; individual investor services; asset management; and correspondent clearing. **Common positions include:** Accountant/Auditor; Computer Programmer; Management Trainee. **Corporate headquarters location:** New York NY. **Parent company:** The Bear Stearns Companies Inc. is a leading worldwide investment banking, securities trading, and brokerage firm. **Listed on:** New York Stock Exchange. **Stock exchange symbol:** BSC.

CIT GROUP, INC.
One CIT Drive, Livingston NJ 07039. 973/740-5000. **Contact:** Personnel Officer. **World Wide Web address:** http://www.citgroup.com. **Description:** A diversified financial services organization that provides flexible funding alternatives, secured business lending, and financial advisory services for corporations, manufacturers, and dealers. Founded in 1908. **Corporate headquarters location:** New York NY. **Other U.S. locations:** Nationwide. **International locations:** Worldwide. **Number of employees nationwide:** 2,500.

FIRST MONTAUK FINANCIAL CORPORATION
328 Newman Springs Road, Red Bank NJ 07701. 732/842-4700. **Contact:** Personnel. **World Wide Web address:** http://www.firstmontauk.com. **Description:** A diversified holding company that provides financial services throughout the United States to individuals, corporations, and institutions. **Subsidiaries include:** First Montauk Securities Corporation is a securities broker/dealer with a nationwide network of more than 300 registered representatives in 90 branch offices serving approximately 25,000 retail and institutional clients. Montauk Insurance Services, Inc. is an insurance agency.

J.B. HANAUER & COMPANY
4 Gatehall Drive, Parsippany NJ 07054. **Toll-free phone:** 800/631-1094. **Fax:** 973/829-0565. **Contact:** Human Resources. **World Wide Web address:** http://www.jbh.com. **Description:** A full-service brokerage firm specializing in fixed-income investments. J.B. Hanauer & Company provides a broad range of financial products and services. Founded in 1931. **NOTE:** Entry-level positions are offered. **Special programs:** Internships; Training. **Corporate headquarters location:** This location. **Other U.S. locations:** North Miami FL; Tampa FL; West Palm Beach FL; Princeton NJ; Rye Brook NY; Philadelphia PA. **Listed on:** Privately held. **Annual sales/revenues:** More than $100 million. **Number of employees at this location:** 250. **Number of employees worldwide:** 600.

K. HOVNANIAN COMPANIES
10 Highway 35, Red Bank NJ 07701. 732/747-7800. **Contact:** Human Resources. **World Wide Web address:** http://www.khov.com. **Description:** Designs, constructs, and sells condominium apartments, townhouses, and single-family homes in residential communities. The company is also engaged in mortgage banking. Founded in 1959. **Common positions include:** Accountant; Administrative Assistant; Architect; Attorney; Auditor; Civil Engineer; Computer Operator; Computer Programmer; Controller; Financial Analyst; Human Resources Manager; Market Research Analyst; Marketing Manager; Marketing Specialist; MIS Specialist; Online Content Specialist; Real Estate Agent; Sales Manager; Secretary; Systems Analyst; Systems Manager; Technical Writer/Editor; Webmaster. **Corporate headquarters location:** This location. **Other U.S. locations:** CA; FL; NC; NY; PA; VA. **Subsidiaries include:** New Fortis Homes. **Listed on:** New York Stock Exchange. **Stock exchange symbol:** HOV. **Number of employees at this location:** 90. **Number of employees nationwide:** 1,150.

JEFFERIES & COMPANY, INC.
51 JFK Parkway, 3rd Floor, Short Hills NJ 07078. 973/912-2900. **Contact:** Human Resources. **World Wide Web address:** http://www.jefco.com. **Description:** Engaged in equity, convertible debt and taxable fixed income securities brokerage and trading, and corporate finance. Jefferies & Company is one of the leading national firms engaged in the distribution and trading of blocks of equity securities and conducts such activities primarily in the third market, which refers to transactions in listed equity securities effected away from national securities exchanges. Founded in 1962. **NOTE:** Please send resumes to Human Resources, 11100 Santa Monica Boulevard, Los Angeles CA 90025. 310/445-1199. **Parent company:** Jefferies Group, Inc. is a holding company which, through Jefferies & Company and its three other primary subsidiaries, Investment Technology Group, Inc., Jefferies International Limited, and Jefferies Pacific Limited, is engaged in securities brokerage and trading, corporate finance, and other financial services.

M.H. MEYERSON & COMPANY, INC.
P.O. Box 260, 525 Washington Boulevard, Jersey City NJ 07303. 201/459-9515. **Toll-free phone:** 800/888-8118. **Contact:** Human Resources. **World Wide Web address:** http://www.mhmeyerson.com. **Description:** Markets and trades approximately 2,000 securities. The company is also an active underwriter of small and mid-sized capitalization debt and equity services. M.H. Meyerson is licensed in 38 states and Washington DC and services approximately 8,500 retail accounts through its retail clearing agent, Bear, Stearns Securities Corporation. The company is also engaged in a variety of investment banking, underwriting, and venture capital activities. M.H. Meyerson provides comprehensive planning services to its corporate clients including public offerings and private placements of securities. Founded in 1960. **Corporate headquarters location:** This location. **Other U.S. locations:** North Miami Beach FL. **Listed on:** NASDAQ. **Stock exchange symbol:** MHMY. **CEO:** Martin H. Meyerson. **Number of employees at this location:** 165.

PERSHING
One Pershing Plaza, 9th Floor, Jersey City NJ 07399. 201/413-2000. **Contact:** Personnel Department. **World Wide Web address:** http://www.pershing.com. **Description:** A securities brokerage firm. **Parent company:** Donaldson, Lufkin & Jenrette Securities Corporation.

WASHINGTON MUTUAL HOME LOANS CENTER
One Garret Mountain Plaza, 3rd Floor, West Paterson NJ 07424. 973/881-2360. **Contact:** Human Resources. **World Wide Web address:** http://www.wamu.com. **Description:** A full-service mortgage banking company that originates, acquires, and services residential mortgage loans. **Common positions include:** Accountant/Auditor; Attorney; Bank Officer/Manager; Branch Manager; Brokerage Clerk; Budget Analyst; Computer Programmer; Construction and Building Inspector; Credit Manager; Economist; Financial Analyst; Human Resources Manager; Management Analyst/Consultant; Management Trainee; Paralegal; Securities Sales Representative; Systems Analyst. **Corporate headquarters location:** Pittsburgh PA. **Other U.S. locations:** KY; OH. **Parent company:** PNC Financial Services Group. **Operations at this facility include:** Regional Headquarters. **Listed on:** New York Stock Exchange. **Stock exchange symbol:** WM. **Number of employees nationwide:** 6,000.

FOOD AND BEVERAGES/ AGRICULTURE

You can expect to find the following types of companies in this chapter:

Crop Services and Farm Supplies • Dairy Farms • Food Manufacturers/Processors and Agricultural Producers • Tobacco Products

ANHEUSER-BUSCH, INC.

200 U.S. Highway 1, Newark NJ 07114. 973/645-7700. **Contact:** Human Resources. **World Wide Web address:** http://www.budweiser.com. **Description:** A leading producer of beer. Beer brands include Budweiser, Michelob, Busch, King Cobra, and O'Doul's (nonalcoholic) beverages. **Corporate headquarters location:** St. Louis MO. **Other U.S. locations:** Los Angeles CA; Jacksonville FL; Tampa FL; Merrimack NH; Baldwinsville NY; Columbus OH; Houston TX; Williamsburg VA. **Parent company:** Anheuser-Busch Companies is a diverse company involved in the entertainment, brewing, baking, and manufacturing industries. The company is one of the largest domestic brewers, operating 13 breweries throughout the United States and distributing through over 900 independent wholesalers. Related businesses include can manufacturing, paper printing, and barley malting. Anheuser-Busch Companies is also one of the largest operators of theme parks in the United States, with locations in Florida, Virginia, Texas, Ohio, and California. Through subsidiary Campbell Taggart Inc., Anheuser-Busch Companies is also one of the largest commercial baking companies in the United States, producing foods under the Colonial brand name, among others. Anheuser-Busch Companies also has various real estate interests. **Listed on:** New York Stock Exchange. **Stock exchange symbol:** BUD.

BESTFOODS BAKING COMPANY

700 Sylvan Avenue, Englewood Cliffs NJ 07632. 201/894-4000. **Contact:** Corporate Personnel Department. **World Wide Web address:** http://www.bestfoods.com. **Description:** This location houses the administrative and marketing offices and is also the world headquarters. Overall, Bestfoods produces and distributes a variety of food products including soups, sauces, and bouillons; dressings including Hellmann's mayonnaise; starches and syrups; bread spreads including Skippy peanut butter; desserts and baking aids; and pasta. **Corporate headquarters location:** This location.

DI GIORGIO CORPORATION
WHITE ROSE FOOD

380 Middlesex Avenue, Carteret NJ 07008. 732/541-5555. **Contact:** Jackie Simmons, Director of Human Resources Department. **World Wide Web address:** http://www.whiterose.com. **Description:** A major area distributor of approximately 850 grocery, dairy, and frozen food items. **Corporate headquarters location:** San Francisco CA. **Other U.S. locations:** Farmingdale NY.

THE FRESH JUICE COMPANY

280 Wilson Avenue, Newark NJ 07105. 973/465-7100. **Contact:** Human Resources. **Description:** Markets and sells frozen and fresh-squeezed

Florida orange juice, grapefruit juice, apple juice, and other noncarbonated beverages under the brand name Just Pik't.

INTERBAKE FOODS, INC.
891 Newark Avenue, Elizabeth NJ 07208-3599. 908/527-7000. **Contact:** Human Resources. **World Wide Web address:** http://www.interbake.com. **Description:** This location is a bakery. Overall, Interbake Foods operates in four business segments: Food Service; Grocery Products; Dairy Products; and Girl Scout Products. The Food Service segment offers a line of more than 160 items including crackers, cookies, tart shells, and other products to institutional customers, such as health care institutions, schools and colleges, and commercial establishments; the Dairy Products segment produces wafers for ice-cream manufacturers; the Grocery Products segment includes a wide range of cookies and crackers; and the Girl Scout Products segment manufactures Girl Scout Cookies. **Parent company:** General Biscuits of America, Inc. is the American subsidiary of General Biscuit, S.A. (France).

ORVAL KENT FOOD COMPANY
164 Madison Street, East Rutherford NJ 07073. 973/779-2090. **Fax:** 973/779-7338. **Contact:** Human Resources Department. **World Wide Web address:** http://www.orvalkent.com. **Description:** Manufactures and markets a line of food products, primarily salads. **Common positions include:** Accountant/Auditor; Electrician; General Manager; Human Resources Manager; Purchasing Agent/Manager. **Corporate headquarters location:** Wheeling IL. **Operations at this facility include:** Administration; Manufacturing; Research and Development; Sales; Service. **Number of employees at this location:** 200.

M&M/MARS INC.
800 High Street, Hackettstown NJ 07840. 908/852-1000. **Contact:** Human Resources. **World Wide Web address:** http://www.mmmars.com. **Description:** This location houses administrative offices. Overall, M&M/Mars produces a variety of candy and snack foods. **Corporate headquarters location:** This location. **Other U.S. locations:** Albany GA; Burr Ridge IL.

MCT DAIRIES, INC.
15 Bleeker Street, Millburn NJ 07041. 973/258-9600. **Fax:** 973/258-9222. **Contact:** Human Resources Department. **World Wide Web address:** http://www.mctdairies.com. **Description:** Buys and sells cheeses and other industrial dairy products including bulk domestic and imported cheeses, whey powders, dairy flavorings, and buttermilk. **Corporate headquarters location:** This location.

MARATHON ENTERPRISES INC.
66 East Union Avenue, East Rutherford NJ 07073. 201/935-3330. **Contact:** Personnel Manager. **Description:** Manufactures Sabrett brand hot dogs. **Corporate headquarters location:** This location.

NABISCO FAIR LAWN BAKERY
22-11 State Route 208, Fair Lawn NJ 07410. 201/794-4000. **Contact:** Personnel. **World Wide Web address:** http://www.kraftfoods.com/careers. **Description:** This location is a bakery. Overall, Nabisco is one of the largest consumer foods operations in the country. The company markets a broad line of cookie and cracker products including brand names such as Oreo, Ritz, Premium, Teddy Grahams, Chips Ahoy!, and Wheat Thins. The

company operates 10 cake and cookie bakeries, a flourmill, and a cheese plant. The bakeries produce over 1 billion pounds of finished products each year. Over 150 biscuit brands reach the consumer via one of the industry's largest distribution networks. **Parent company:** Kraft Foods. **Listed on:** New York Stock Exchange. **Stock exchange symbol:** KFT. **Number of employees at this location:** 1,200.

NABISCO GROUP HOLDINGS
7 Campus Drive, P.O. Box 311, Parsippany NJ 07054-0311. 973/682-5000. **Contact:** Human Resources Department. **World Wide Web address:** http://www.kraftfoods.com/careers. **Description:** This location houses administrative offices. Overall, Nabisco is one of the largest consumer foods operations in the country. The company markets a broad line of cookie and cracker products including brand names such as Oreo, Ritz, Premium, Teddy Grahams, Chips Ahoy!, and Wheat Thins. The company operates 10 cake and cookie bakeries, a flourmill, and a cheese plant. The bakeries produce over 1 billion pounds of finished products each year. Over 150 biscuit brands reach the consumer via one of the industry's largest distribution networks. **Parent company:** Kraft Foods. **Listed on:** New York Stock Exchange. **Stock exchange symbol:** KFT. **Annual sales/revenues:** More than $100 million.

NABISCO INC.
100 DeForest Avenue, East Hanover NJ 07936. 973/503-2000. **Contact:** Staffing. **World Wide Web address:** http://www.kraftfoods.com/careers. **Description:** One of the largest consumer foods operations in the country. The company markets a broad line of cookie and cracker products including brand names such as Oreo, Ritz, Premium, Teddy Grahams, Chips Ahoy!, and Wheat Thins. The company operates 10 cake and cookie bakeries, a flourmill, and a cheese plant. The bakeries produce over 1 billion pounds of finished products each year. Over 150 biscuit brands reach the consumer via one of the industry's largest distribution networks. **Common positions include:** Logistics Manager; Marketing Manager; Systems Analyst. **Special programs:** Internships. **Corporate headquarters location:** Northfield IL. **Parent company:** Kraft Foods. **Listed on:** New York Stock Exchange. **Stock exchange symbol:** KFT.

POLAND SPRINGS OF AMERICA
170 West Commercial Avenue, Moonachie NJ 07074. 201/531-2044. **Contact:** Human Resources. **Description:** Distributes bottled spring and distilled drinking water for home and industrial use. The company also provides water coolers, microwave ovens, and similar equipment for installation in commercial and industrial locations. **Common positions include:** Accountant/Auditor; Blue-Collar Worker Supervisor; Branch Manager; Customer Service Representative; Department Engineer; General Manager; Management Trainee; Operations/Production Manager; Sales Executive. **Parent company:** Perrier Group of America (Greenwich CT).

R&R MARKETING
10 Patton Drive, West Caldwell NJ 07006. 973/228-5100. **Contact:** Human Resources. **World Wide Web address:** http://www.rrmarketing.com. **Description:** Engaged in the wholesale importation and distribution of liquors and wines. **Corporate headquarters location:** This location.

RECKITT BENCKISER
1655 Valley Road, Wayne NJ 07470. 973/633-3600. **Contact:** Staffing Supervisor. **World Wide Web address:** http://www.reckitt.com.

Description: Manufactures cleaning and specialty food products including the brand names Easy-Off oven cleaner, French's mustard, Lysol, and Woolite detergent.

SUPREMA SPECIALTIES INC.
P.O. Box 280, Paterson NJ 07543. 973/684-2900. **Contact:** Employment Office. **World Wide Web address:** http://www.supremachez.com. **Description:** Manufactures and markets a variety of premium gourmet natural cheese products from the United States, Europe, and South America. Suprema Specialties' product line encompasses grated and shredded parmesan and pecorino romano cheeses, mozzarella and ricotta cheese products, low-fat versions of these products, and a provolone cheese. **Corporate headquarters location:** This location.

TUSCAN DAIRY FARM
750 Union Avenue, Union NJ 07083. 908/686-1500. **Contact:** Human Resources. **Description:** Produces and distributes milk and related products throughout northern New Jersey and adjacent areas. **Corporate headquarters location:** This location.

UNILEVER FOODS
800 Sylvan Avenue, Englewood Cliffs NJ 07632. 201/567-8000. **Contact:** Personnel. **World Wide Web address:** http://www.unileverna.com. **Description:** An international consumer products firm manufacturing a wide range of soaps, toiletries, and foods. **Other U.S. locations:** Flemington NJ.

WAKEFERN FOOD CORPORATION
600 York Street, Elizabeth NJ 07207. 908/527-3300. **Contact:** Human Resources. **World Wide Web address:** http://www.shoprite.com. **Description:** Operates a retailer-owned, nonprofit food cooperative. The company provides purchasing, warehousing, and distribution services to various grocery retailers throughout the metropolitan area. Many products are distributed under the Shop-Rite name. **Special programs:** Internships.

GOVERNMENT

You can expect to find the following types of agencies in this chapter:

Courts • Executive, Legislative, and General Government • Public Agencies (Firefighters, Military, Police) • United States Postal Service

NEW JERSEY DEPARTMENT OF TRANSPORTATION
REGION 3 CONSTRUCTION
100 Daniels Way, Freehold NJ 07728. 732/409-3263. **Contact:** Human Resources. **Description:** Designs, builds, and maintains roads and highways throughout the state of New Jersey. **Common positions include:** Accountant/Auditor; Administrative Manager; Budget Analyst; Civil Engineer; Electrician; Environmental Engineer; Human Resources Manager; Landscape Architect; Management Analyst/Consultant; Management Trainee; Materials Engineer; Paralegal; Property and Real Estate Manager; Public Relations Specialist; Purchasing Agent/Manager; Structural Engineer; Surveyor; Systems Analyst; Transportation/Traffic Specialist.

NEW JERSEY TURNPIKE AUTHORITY
P.O. Box 1121, New Brunswick NJ 08903. 732/247-0900. **Contact:** Human Resources. **World Wide Web address:** http://www.state.nj.us/turnpike. **Description:** A state mandated, unsubsidized organization responsible for construction, maintenance, repair, and operation on New Jersey Turnpike projects.

UNION, COUNTY OF
Administration Building, 3rd Floor, Elizabeth NJ 07207. 908/527-4030. **Contact:** Personnel. **Description:** Administration offices for Union County.

U.S. POSTAL SERVICE
46 Grove Street, Passaic NJ 07055. 973/779-0277. **Contact:** Human Resources. **World Wide Web address:** http://www.usps.com. **Description:** A post office for the city of Passaic. **Other U.S. locations:** Nationwide.

U.S. POSTAL SERVICE
NEW JERSEY INTERNATIONAL BULK MAIL
80 County Road, Jersey City NJ 07097-9998. 201/714-6390. **Contact:** Human Resources. **Description:** A United States Post Office that processes foreign, military, and general bulk mail for distribution throughout the world. **Other U.S. locations:** Nationwide.

WEST MILFORD, CITY OF
1480 Union Valley Road, West Milford NJ 07480. 973/728-7000. **Contact:** Personnel. **Description:** Administrative offices for the city of West Milford.

WEST ORANGE POLICE DEPARTMENT
66 Main Street, West Orange NJ 07052. 973/325-4000. **Fax:** 973/731-0004. **Contact:** Human Resources. **E-mail address:** wopd@westorangepolice.org. **World Wide Web address:** http://www.westorangepolice.org. **Description:** A local law enforcement agency providing services to the citizens of West Orange. **Common positions include:** Clerical Supervisor; Computer Programmer; Dispatcher; Graphic Artist; Human Resources Manager; Human Service Worker; Payroll Clerk; Police/Law Enforcement Officer; Secretary; Stenographer; Systems Analyst.

HEALTH CARE: SERVICES, EQUIPMENT, AND PRODUCTS

You can expect to find the following types of companies in this chapter:

Dental Labs and Equipment • Home Health Care Agencies • Hospitals and Medical Centers • Medical Equipment Manufacturers and Wholesalers • Offices and Clinics of Health Practitioners • Residential Treatment Centers/Nursing Homes• Veterinary Services

AMERICAN STANDARD COMPANIES INC.
P.O. Box 6820, Piscataway NJ 08854. 732/980-6000. **Physical address:** One Centennial Avenue, Piscataway NJ 08855. **Contact:** Human Resources. **World Wide Web address:** http://www.americanstandard.com. **Description:** A global, diversified manufacturer. The company's operations are comprised of four segments: air conditioning products, plumbing products, automotive products, and medical systems. The air conditioning products segment (through subsidiary The Trane Company) develops and manufactures Trane and American Standard air conditioning equipment for use in central air conditioning systems for commercial, institutional, and residential buildings. The plumbing products segment develops and manufactures American Standard, Ideal Standard, Porcher, Armitage Shanks, Dolomite, and Standard bathroom and kitchen fixtures and fittings. The automotive products segment develops and manufactures truck, bus, and utility vehicle braking and control systems under the WABCO and Perrot brands. The medical systems segment manufactures Copalis, DiaSorin, and Pylori-Chek medical diagnostic products and systems for a variety of diseases including HIV, osteoporosis, and renal disease. **Corporate headquarters location:** This location. **International locations:** Worldwide. **Listed on:** New York Stock Exchange. **Stock exchange symbol:** ASD. **Chairman/CEO:** Frederic M. Poses. **Number of employees worldwide:** 57,000.

C.R. BARD, INC.
730 Central Avenue, Murray Hill NJ 07974. 908/277-8000. **Fax:** 908/277-8412. **Contact:** Human Resources. **World Wide Web address:** http://www.crbard.com. **Description:** Manufactures and distributes disposable medical, surgical, diagnostic, and patient care products. Cardiovascular products include angioplastic recanalization devices such as balloon angioplasty catheters, inflation devices, and developmental atherectomy and laser devices; electrophysiology products such as temporary pacing catheters, diagnostic and therapeutic electrodes, and cardiac mapping systems; a cardiopulmonary system; and blood oxygenators, cardiotomy reservoirs, and other products used in open heart surgery. Urological products include Foley catheters, trays, and related urine contract collection systems used extensively in postoperative bladder drainage. Surgical products include wound and chest drainage systems and implantable blood vessel replacements. **Corporate headquarters location:** This location. **Listed on:** New York Stock Exchange. **Stock exchange symbol:** BCR.

BARNERT HOSPITAL
680 Dr. Martin Luther King, Jr. Way, Paterson NJ 07514. 973/977-6600. **Fax:** 973/279-2924. **Recorded jobline:** 973/977-6824. **Contact:** Human Resources. **World Wide Web address:** http://www.barnerthosp.com. **Description:** A 280-bed hospital. **Common positions include:** Computer Programmer; Dietician/Nutritionist; EKG Technician; Medical Records Technician; Nuclear Medicine Technologist; Occupational Therapist; Pharmacist; Physical Therapist; Physician; Radiological Technologist; Registered Nurse; Respiratory Therapist; Social Worker; Stationary Engineer; Surgical Technician. **Special programs:** Internships. **Operations at this facility include:** Administration; Service. **Number of employees at this location:** 1,000.

BECTON DICKINSON & COMPANY
One Becton Drive, Franklin Lakes NJ 07417. 201/847-6800. **Contact:** Human Resources. **World Wide Web address:** http://www.bd.com. **Description:** A medical company engaged in the manufacture of health care products, medical instrumentation, diagnostic products, and industrial safety equipment. Major medical equipment product lines include hypodermics, intravenous equipment, operating room products, thermometers, gloves, and specialty needles. The company also offers contract packaging services. Founded in 1896. **Corporate headquarters location:** This location. **Listed on:** New York Stock Exchange. **Stock exchange symbol:** BDX. **Number of employees worldwide:** 18,000.

BIOSEARCH MEDICAL PRODUCTS, INC.
35A Industrial Parkway, Somerville NJ 08876. 908/722-5000. **Toll-free phone:** 800/326-5976. **Fax:** 908/722-5024. **Contact:** Human Resources. **World Wide Web address:** http://www.biosearch.com. **Description:** Manufactures specialty medical devices for the gastroenterology, endoscopy, urology, and enteral feeding markets. The company's products are sold directly to hospitals and alternative care centers through domestic and international specialty dealers. Founded in 1978. **NOTE:** Entry-level positions are offered. **Common positions include:** Account Manager; Attorney; Buyer; Chief Financial Officer; Customer Service Representative; Design Engineer; Draftsperson; Human Resources Manager; Manufacturing Engineer; Production Manager; Purchasing Agent/Manager; Quality Control Supervisor; Sales Manager. **Special programs:** Training. **Parent company:** Hydromer Inc. **Listed on:** NASDAQ. **Stock exchange symbol:** BMPI. **Annual sales/revenues:** $5 - $10 million. **Number of employees at this location:** 30.

BON SECOURS & CANTERBURY PARTNERSHIP FOR CARE
25 McWilliams Place, Jersey City NJ 07302. 201/418-2065. **Fax:** 201/418-2063. **Contact:** Personnel. **World Wide Web address:** http://www.bonsecoursnj.com. **Description:** Operates two community hospitals: St. Mary Hospital (Hoboken NJ) and St. Francis Hospital (Jersey City NJ). **NOTE:** Entry-level positions are offered. **Common positions include:** Accountant; Administrative Assistant; Certified Nurses Aide; Clinical Lab Technician; Computer Operator; Credit Manager; Customer Service Representative; Dietician/Nutritionist; Emergency Medical Technician; Food Scientist/Technologist; Human Resources Manager; Licensed Practical Nurse; MIS Specialist; Nuclear Medicine Technologist; Occupational Therapist; Pharmacist; Physical Therapist; Physician; Psychologist; Registered Nurse; Respiratory Therapist; Social Worker; Speech-Language Pathologist. **Special programs:** Internships. **Corporate headquarters location:** This location. **Annual sales/revenues:** $11 - $20 million. **Number of employees at this location:** 1,500.

CANTEL INDUSTRIES, INC.
Overlook at Great Notch, 150 Clove Road, 9th Floor, Little Falls NJ 07424. 973/890-7220-2139. **Contact:** Joanna Albrecht, Assistant Secretary of Human Resources Department. **World Wide Web address:** http://www.cantelmedical.com. **Description:** A holding company. **Subsidiaries include:** Carson Group Inc. (Canada) markets and distributes medical instruments including flexible and rigid endoscopes; precision instruments including microscopes and image analysis systems; and industrial equipment including remote visual inspection devices, laser distance measurement and thermal imaging products, and online optical inspection and quality assurance systems for specialized industrial applications. Carson also offers a full range of photographic equipment and supplies for amateur and professional photographers. **Listed on:** NASDAQ. **Stock exchange symbol:** CNTL.

COMMUNITY MEDICAL CENTER
99 Highway 37 West, Toms River NJ 08755. 732/240-8000. **Contact:** Human Resources. **Description:** An affiliate of Saint Barnabus Health Care System, Community Medical Center is a 596-bed, general, short-term care hospital.

CORDIS CORPORATION
7 Powder Horn Drive, Warren NJ 07059. 908/755-8300. **Contact:** Human Resources. **World Wide Web address:** http://www.cordis.com. **Description:** This location handles administration, research and development, and quality assurance. Overall, Cordis manufactures medical devices such as catheters to treat cardiovascular diseases. **NOTE:** All hiring is done through the parent company. Resumes should be sent to Johnson & Johnson Recruiting Services, Employment Management Center, Room JH-215, 501 George Street, New Brunswick NJ 08906-6597. **Parent company:** Johnson & Johnson (New Brunswick NJ).

DATASCOPE CORPORATION
14 Phillips Parkway, Montvale NJ 07645. 201/391-8100. **Contact:** Human Resources. **E-mail address:** career_opportunities@datascope.com. **World Wide Web address:** http://www.datascope.com. **Description:** Manufactures cardiac assist systems for hospital use in interventional cardiology and cardiac surgery; and patient monitors for use in the operating room, postanesthesia care, and critical care. Datascope's VasoSeal product rapidly seals femoral arterial punctures after catheterization procedures including coronary angioplasty and angiography. Datascope also manufactures a line of collagen hemostats, which are used to control bleeding during surgery. The company's cardiac assist product is an intra-aortic balloon pumping system used for treating cardiac shock, heart failure, and cardiac arrhythmia. The pump can also be used in various procedures including cardiac surgery and coronary angioplasty. Datascope's patient monitoring products comprise a line of multifunction and stand-alone models that measure a broad range of physiological data including blood oxygen saturation, airway carbon dioxide, ECG, and temperature. **Listed on:** NASDAQ. **Stock exchange symbol:** DSCP.

EBI MEDICAL SYSTEMS, INC.
100 Interpace Parkway, Parsippany NJ 07054. 973/299-9300. **Toll-free phone:** 800/526-2579. **Fax:** 973/402-1396. **Contact:** Department of Human Resources. **E-mail address:** humanresources@ebimed.com. **World Wide Web address:** http://www.ebimedical.com. **Description:** Designs, develops, manufactures, and markets products used primarily by orthopedic medical

specialists in both surgical and nonsurgical therapies. Products include electrical bone growth stimulators, orthopedic support devices, spinal fixation devices for spinal fusion, external fixation devices, and cold temperature therapy. Founded in 1977. **NOTE:** Entry-level positions and part-time jobs are offered. **Common positions include:** Accountant; Computer Operator; Computer Programmer; Customer Service Representative; Design Engineer; Electrical/Electronics Engineer; Marketing Manager; Mechanical Engineer; Sales Representative; Secretary. **Special programs:** Internships; Training; Summer Jobs. **Corporate headquarters location:** This location. **Other U.S. locations:** OK. **International locations:** Puerto Rico. **Parent company:** Biomet, Inc. **Listed on:** NASDAQ. **Stock exchange symbol:** BMET. **Number of employees at this location:** 360.

ETHICON, INC.
U.S. Route 22, P.O. Box 151, Somerville NJ 08876. 908/218-0707. **Contact:** Human Resources Department. **World Wide Web address:** http://www.ethiconinc.com. **Description:** Manufactures products for precise wound closure including sutures, ligatures, mechanical wound closure instruments, and related products. The company also makes its own surgical needles and provides needle-suture combinations to surgeons. **Corporate headquarters location:** This location. **Parent company:** Johnson & Johnson (New Brunswick NJ).

GLAXOSMITHKLINE CORPORATION
257 Cornelison Avenue, Jersey City NJ 07302. 201/434-3000. **Contact:** Human Resources. **World Wide Web address:** http://www.gsk.com. **Description:** Develops, manufactures, and sells products in four general categories: denture, dental care, oral hygiene, and professional dental products; proprietary products; ethical pharmaceutical products; and household products. Dental-related products include Polident denture cleansers. **Listed on:** New York Stock Exchange. **Stock exchange symbol:** GSK.

GLAXOSMITHKLINE CORPORATION
65 Industrial South, Clifton NJ 07012. 973/778-9000. **Contact:** Human Resources. **World Wide Web address:** http://www.gsk.com. **Description:** This location manufactures toothpaste and Massengill products. Overall, GlaxoSmithKline Corporation is a health care company engaged in the research, development, manufacture, and marketing of ethical pharmaceuticals, animal health products, ethical and proprietary medicines, and eye care products. The company is also engaged in many other aspects of the health care field including the production of medical and electronic instruments. **Corporate headquarters location:** Philadelphia PA. **Subsidiaries include:** Menley & James Laboratories products include Contac Cold Capsules, Sine-Off sinus medicine, Love cosmetics, and Sea & Ski outdoor products. **Listed on:** New York Stock Exchange. **Stock exchange symbol:** GSK.

HAUSMANN INDUSTRIES
130 Union Street, Northvale NJ 07647. 201/767-0255. **Contact:** Human Resources. **World Wide Web address:** http://www.hausmann.com. **Description:** Manufactures medical examination tables and physical therapy equipment. **Corporate headquarters location:** This location.

HEALTHCARE INTEGRATED SERVICES
733 Route 35, Ocean NJ 07712. 732/774-1411. **Contact:** Personnel. **World Wide Web address:** http://www.healthcareintegrated.com. **Description:**

Operates five fixed-site MRI centers and one fixed-site multimodality imaging center consisting of MRI, ultrasonography, and mammography facilities. **Corporate headquarters location:** This location.

HOOPER HOLMES, INC.
dba PORTAMEDIC
170 Mount Airy Road, Basking Ridge NJ 07920. 908/766-5000. **Contact:** Manager of Human Resources. **E-mail address:** hres@hooperholmes.com. **World Wide Web address:** http://www.hooperholmes.com. **Description:** Performs health exams for insurance companies. Founded in 1899. **Common positions include:** Account Manager; Accountant/Auditor; Administrative Assistant; Administrative Manager; Assistant Manager; Attorney; Chief Financial Officer; Clerical Supervisor; Computer Operator; Computer Programmer; Controller; Credit Manager; Customer Service Representative; Financial Analyst; General Manager; Help-Desk Technician; Human Resources Manager; Licensed Practical Nurse; Marketing Manager; Marketing Specialist; Multimedia Designer; Network/Systems Administrator; Nurse Practitioner; Operations Manager; Paralegal; Purchasing Agent/Manager; Quality Control Supervisor; Registered Nurse; Sales Executive; Sales Manager; Sales Representative; Systems Analyst; Systems Manager; Vice President. **Office hours:** Monday - Friday, 8:30 a.m. - 5:00 p.m. **Corporate headquarters location:** This location. **Other U.S. locations:** Nationwide. **Operations at this facility include:** Administration; Divisional Headquarters; Research and Development; Sales; Service. **Listed on:** American Stock Exchange. **Stock exchange symbol:** HH. **Annual sales/revenues:** More than $100 million. **Number of employees at this location:** 120. **Number of employees nationwide:** 2,500.

HOWMEDICA OSTEONICS
59 Route 17 South, Allendale NJ 07401. 201/825-4900. **Contact:** Human Resources Department. **E-mail address:** hr@howost.com. **World Wide Web address:** http://www.osteonics.com. **Description:** Manufactures medical implants including artificial knees, hips, shoulders, and elbows. **Parent company:** Stryker Corporation.

HUNTERDON DEVELOPMENTAL CENTER
P.O. Box 4003, Clinton NJ 08809-4003. 908/735-4031. **Physical address:** 40 Pittstown Road, Clinton NJ 08060. **Contact:** Human Resources. **Description:** A state-run residential facility for adults with developmental disabilities.

THE MATHENY SCHOOL AND HOSPITAL
P.O. Box 339, Peapack NJ 07977. 908/234-0011. **Fax:** 908/234-9496. **Contact:** Human Resources Department. **World Wide Web address:** http://www.matheny.org. **Description:** A licensed hospital and school for people with severe physical disabilities such as cerebral palsy and spina bifida. **NOTE:** Entry-level positions and second and third shifts are offered. **Common positions include:** Administrative Assistant; Certified Nurses Aide; Chief Financial Officer; Controller; Counselor; Dietician/Nutritionist; Human Resources Manager; Librarian; Licensed Practical Nurse; Medical Records Technician; MIS Specialist; Occupational Therapist; Physical Therapist; Psychologist; Public Relations Specialist; Registered Nurse; Secretary; Social Worker; Speech-Language Pathologist; Teacher/Professor. **Special programs:** Internships; Apprenticeships; Training. **President:** Robert Schonhorn.

MAXIM HEALTHCARE
622 George's Road, North Brunswick NJ 08902. 800/697-2247. **Contact:** Manager. **World Wide Web address:** http://www.maxhealth.com. **Description:** A home health care agency. **Corporate headquarters location:** Lake Success NY. **Other U.S. locations:** Nationwide. **Number of employees nationwide:** 20,000.

MEDICAL RESOURCES, INC.
125 State Street, Suite 200, Hackensack NJ 07601. 201/488-6230. **Fax:** 201/488-8455. **Contact:** Human Resources. **World Wide Web address:** http://www.mrii.com. **Description:** Owns and manages medical diagnostic imaging centers nationwide. The centers offer magnetic resonance imaging (MRI), computerized tomography (CT), nuclear medicine, mammography, ultrasound, and X-ray. **Common positions include:** Accountant; Administrative Assistant; Architect; Attorney; Construction Contractor; Human Resources Manager; Nuclear Medicine Technologist; Public Relations Specialist; Radiological Technologist; Sales Representative. **Listed on:** NASDAQ. **Stock exchange symbol:** MRII. **Annual sales/revenues:** More than $100 million.

MODERN MEDICAL MODALITIES CORPORATION
1719 Route 10, Suite 119, Parsippany NJ 07054. 973/538-9955. **Fax:** 973/267-7359. **Contact:** Human Resources. **Description:** Provides high-tech, diagnostic imaging services to physicians, hospitals, and other health care facilities. The company's primary focus is on Magnetic Resonance Imaging (MRI) and Computer Axial Tomography (CT scan) technologies. Modern Medical Modalities also offers a range of services including full, partial, or joint-venture financing; site selection, design, and construction; equipment supply, maintenance, and operation; personnel placement and training; and facility marketing, management, billing, and collections. **Corporate headquarters location:** This location.

OCEAN COUNTY VETERINARY HOSPITAL
838 River Avenue, Lakewood NJ 08701. 732/363-7202. **Fax:** 732/370-4176. **Contact:** Human Resources. **World Wide Web address:** http://www.ocvh.com. **Description:** Provides health care services to dogs, cats, and exotic pets including surgery, hospitalization, and diagnostic testing.

OVERLOOK HOSPITAL
P.O. Box 220, Summit NJ 07902-0220. 908/522-2241. **Physical address:** 99 Beauvoir Avenue, Summit NJ 07901. **Contact:** Human Resources. **World Wide Web address:** http://www.atlantichealth.org/hospitals/overlook. **Description:** A part of Atlantic Health Systems, Overlook Hospital is a 490-bed, public hospital with extensive facilities for pediatrics, oncology, cardiology, and same-day surgery.

P.S.A. HEALTHCARE
4900 Route 33, Suite 100, Neptune NJ 07753-6804. 732/938-5550. **Fax:** 732/938-6535. **Contact:** Personnel. **World Wide Web address:** http://www.psakids.com. **Description:** Provides infusion therapy, nursing, and other home health care services to clients.

SIEMENS MEDICAL
186 Wood Avenue South, Iselin NJ 08830. 732/321-4500. **Contact:** Personnel Office. **World Wide Web address:** http://www.sms.siemens.com. **Description:** Develops, manufactures, and sells medical systems including

digital X-rays and 3-D ultrasound equipment. Products are used in a variety of areas including cardiology, audiology, surgery, critical care, and oncology. **Corporate headquarters location:** This location.

TRINITAS HOSPITAL
18-20 South Broad Street, Elizabeth NJ 07201. 908/994-5325. **Fax:** 908/527-0195. **Contact:** Human Resources. **World Wide Web address:** http://www.egmc.org. **Description:** A hospital providing treatments for a variety of illnesses including cardiovascular diseases and cancer.

UNIVERSITY HOSPITAL
30 Bergen Street, Building 8, Newark NJ 07107. 973/972-0012. **Contact:** Manager of Human Resources Department. **World Wide Web address:** http://www.theuniversityhospital.com. **Description:** A 466-bed teaching hospital of the University of Medicine and Dentistry of New Jersey.

VITAL SIGNS, INC.
20 Campus Road, Totowa NJ 07512. 973/790-1330. **Fax:** 973/790-4271. **Contact:** Hyat Khan, Director of Human Resources. **World Wide Web address:** http://www.vital-signs.com. **Description:** Manufactures disposable medical products such as face masks, manual resuscitators, anesthesia kits, and other respiratory-related critical care products. **Common positions include:** Computer Programmer; Customer Service Representative; Electrical/Electronics Engineer; Materials Engineer; Operations/Production Manager; Systems Analyst. **Corporate headquarters location:** This location. **Operations at this facility include:** Administration; Manufacturing; Research and Development; Service. **Number of employees at this location:** 350. **Number of employees nationwide:** 450.

WOODBRIDGE DEVELOPMENTAL CENTER
Rahway Avenue, P.O. Box 189, Woodbridge NJ 07001. 732/499-5525. **Contact:** Human Resources. **Description:** A residential treatment facility for adolescents and adults with developmental disabilities.

HOTELS AND RESTAURANTS

You can expect to find the following types of companies in this chapter:
Casinos • Dinner Theaters • Hotel/Motel Operators • Resorts • Restaurants

CANTEEN VENDING SERVICES
6 Pearl Court, Allendale NJ 07401. 201/760-9000. **Contact:** Office Manager. **World Wide Web address:** http://www.canteen-usa.com. **Description:** One of the largest food service companies in the nation. Sales are primarily through food and vending operations, serving more than 800 manual food accounts nationwide, in both office and manufacturing facilities. The Concessions Division serves major accounts including Yankee Stadium and Yellowstone National Park. The Hospital Host Division services school districts, hospitals, nursing homes, universities, and other institutional customers. **Parent company:** Compass Group NA.

CHEFS INTERNATIONAL, INC.
62 Broadway, P.O. Box 1332, Point Pleasant Beach NJ 08742. 732/295-0350. **Contact:** Manager of Human Resources Department. **World Wide Web address:** http://www.jackbakerslobstershanty.com. **Description:** Operates eight Lobster Shanty restaurants in New Jersey and Florida. **Corporate headquarters location:** This location.

HILTON NEWARK AIRPORT
1170 Spring Street, Elizabeth NJ 07201-2114. 908/351-3900. **Contact:** Human Resources. **World Wide Web address:** http://www.hilton.com. **Description:** A 378-room full service hotel adjacent to the Newark International Airport. **Common positions include:** Customer Service Representative; Food and Beverage Service Worker; Hotel/Motel Clerk; Housekeeper. **Other U.S. locations:** Nationwide.

HILTON OF HASBROUCK HEIGHTS
650 Terrace Avenue, Hasbrouck Heights NJ 07604. 201/288-6100. **Contact:** Human Resources Department. **World Wide Web address:** http://www.hilton.com. **Description:** A hotel that provides a wide range of lodging, restaurant, lounge, meeting, and banquet facilities as part of an international chain. **Common positions include:** Customer Service Representative; Food and Beverage Service Worker; Hotel/Motel Clerk; Housekeeper. **Operations at this facility include:** Administration.

PRIME HOSPITALITY CORPORATION
700 Route 46 East, Fairfield NJ 07007. 973/882-1010. **Contact:** Leo Ranieri, Human Resources. **E-mail address:** recruiter@primehospitality.com. **World Wide Web address:** http://www.primehospitality.com. **Description:** An independent hotel operating company with ownership and management of 86 full- and limited-service hotels in 19 states and one resort hotel in the U.S. Virgin Islands. Hotels typically contain 100 to 200 guest rooms or suites and operate under franchise agreements with national hotel chains or under the company's Wellesley Inns or AmeriSuites trade names. Founded in 1961. **Common positions include:** Accountant/Auditor; Administrative Manager; Advertising Executive; Architect; Attorney; Auditor; Budget Analyst; Buyer; Chief Financial Officer; Computer Operator; Construction Contractor; Controller; Credit Manager; Database Manager; General

Manager; Human Resources Manager; Marketing Manager; Quality Control Supervisor; Secretary; Systems Analyst; Systems Manager; Telecommunications Manager; Typist/Word Processor. **Corporate headquarters location:** This location. **Other U.S. locations:** Nationwide. **Operations at this facility include:** Administration. **Listed on:** New York Stock Exchange. **Stock exchange symbol:** PDQ. **Annual sales/revenues:** More than $100 million. **Number of employees at this location:** 190. **Number of employees nationwide:** 6,050.

INSURANCE

You can expect to find the following types of companies in this chapter:
Commercial and Industrial Property/Casualty Insurers • Health Maintenance Organizations (HMOs) • Medical/Life Insurance Companies

AMERICAN RE-INSURANCE COMPANY
555 College Road East, Princeton NJ 08543. 609/243-4649. **Fax:** 609/243-4257. **Contact:** Virginia M. Zdanowicz, Recruiting Director. **World Wide Web address:** http://www.amre.com. **Description:** Underwrites property and casualty reinsurance in both the domestic and international markets. **Common positions include:** Accountant/Auditor; Actuary; Attorney; Claim Representative; Financial Analyst; Human Resources Manager; Paralegal; Software Engineer; Underwriter/Assistant Underwriter. **Corporate headquarters location:** This location. **Other U.S. locations:** Nationwide. **International locations:** Worldwide. **Parent company:** Munich Re Group. **Operations at this facility include:** Administration. **Number of employees at this location:** 800. **Number of employees nationwide:** 1,200.

THE CHUBB GROUP OF INSURANCE COMPANIES
15 Mountain View Road, Warren NJ 07059. 908/903-2000. **Contact:** Human Resources. **World Wide Web address:** http://www.chubb.com. **Description:** A property and casualty insurer with more than 115 offices in 30 countries worldwide. The Chubb Group of Insurance Companies offers a broad range of specialty insurance products and services designed for individuals and businesses, serving industries including high-technology, financial institutions, and general manufacturers. Founded in 1882. **NOTE:** Entry-level positions are offered. **Common positions include:** Accountant; Administrative Assistant; Attorney; Auditor; Claim Representative; Computer Programmer; Computer Support Technician; Customer Service Representative; Database Administrator; Database Manager; Financial Analyst; Human Resources Manager; Internet Services Manager; MIS Specialist; Paralegal; Secretary; Systems Analyst; Systems Manager; Underwriter/Assistant Underwriter; Webmaster. **Special programs:** Internships. **Corporate headquarters location:** This location. **Listed on:** New York Stock Exchange. **Stock exchange symbol:** CB. **Annual sales/revenues:** More than $100 million. **Number of employees worldwide:** 11,000.

FIREMAN'S FUND INSURANCE COMPANY
110 Allen Road, Liberty Corner NJ 07938. **Contact:** Human Resources. **World Wide Web address:** http://www.the-fund.com. **Description:** A holding company for a group of property/liability insurance companies operating primarily in the United States. **Common positions include:** Attorney; Claim Representative; Underwriter/Assistant Underwriter. **Corporate headquarters location:** Novato CA. **Parent company:** Allianz AG.

GAB ROBINS NORTH AMERICA INC.
9 Campus Drive, Suite 7, Parsippany NJ 07054. 973/993-3400. **Contact:** Human Resources. **World Wide Web address:** http://www.gab.com. **Description:** Provides adjustment, inspection, appraisal, and claims

management services to 15,000 insurance industry customers. Specific services include the settlement of claims following major disasters; appraisal, investigation, and adjustment of auto insurance claims; casualty claims; and fire, marine, life, accident, health, and disability claims. **Common positions include:** Accountant/Auditor; Claim Representative; Computer Programmer; Customer Service Representative; Human Resources Manager. **Corporate headquarters location:** This location. **Parent company:** SGS North America. **Number of employees nationwide:** 3,400.

HOME STATE INSURANCE COMPANY
HOME STATE HOLDINGS
900 U.S. Highway - 9 North, Suite 101, Woodbridge NJ 07095-1096. 732/636-0404. **Fax:** 732/636-6929. **Contact:** Human Resources. **Description:** Provides personal and commercial automobile insurance throughout New Jersey. **Corporate headquarters location:** This location. **Parent company:** Home State Holdings (also at this location) is a property and casualty holding company engaged primarily in providing personal and commercial auto insurance through its operating subsidiaries. Home State writes standard and preferred personal auto lines. The company's commercial auto lines focus on public transportation including school buses, charter buses, limousines, and similar transportation risks. Other subsidiaries of Home State Holdings include personal auto and homeowners insurance provided through the company's Home Mutual Insurance Company (Binghamton NY); commercial automobile and commercial multiperil insurance offered through New York Merchant Bankers Insurance Company (NY). The Pinnacle Insurance Company (Carrollton GA) serves as the company's southeastern operations center and offers personal and commercial auto insurance. Quaker City Insurance Company (operating in DC, DE, MD, PA, VA, and WV) and The Westbrook Insurance Company (CT) also provide personal and commercial auto insurance.

JEFFERSON INSURANCE GROUP
525 Washington Boulevard, Jersey City NJ 07310. 201/222-8666. **Fax:** 201/222-9161. **Contact:** Supervisor of Recruitment and Training. **World Wide Web address:** http://www.jeffgroup.com. **Description:** A property and casualty insurance company. Member companies include Jefferson Insurance Company of New York, Monticello Insurance Company, and Jeffco Management Company, Inc. **Common positions include:** Accountant/Auditor; Actuary; Administrative Manager; Attorney; Claim Representative; Clerical Supervisor; Computer Programmer; Human Resources Manager; Human Service Worker; Quality Control Supervisor; Systems Analyst; Underwriter/Assistant Underwriter. **Corporate headquarters location:** This location. **Parent company:** Allianz (Germany). **Operations at this facility include:** Administration. **Listed on:** Privately held.

MERCK-MEDCO MANAGED CARE, L.L.C.
100 Parsons Pond Drive, Franklin Lakes NJ 07417. 201/269-3400. **Contact:** Human Resources. **World Wide Web address:** http://www.merck-medco.com. **Description:** Manages pharmaceutical benefits through contracts with HMOs. **Parent company:** Merck & Company, Inc. (Whitehouse Station NJ) is a worldwide organization engaged in research, development, production, and marketing of products for health care and the maintenance of the environment. Products include human and animal pharmaceuticals and chemicals sold to the health care, oil exploration, food processing, textile, paper, and other industries. **Listed on:** New York Stock

Exchange. **Stock exchange symbol:** MRK. **Number of employees nationwide:** 10,000.

METROPOLITAN LIFE INSURANCE COMPANY (METLIFE)
501 U.S. Highway 22 West, Bridgewater NJ 08807. 908/253-1000. **Contact:** Human Resources Department. **World Wide Web address:** http://www.metlife.com. **Description:** A national insurance and financial services company that offers a wide range of individual and group insurance including life, annuity, disability, and mutual finds. **Listed on:** New York Stock Exchange. **Stock exchange symbol:** MET.

PRESERVER GROUP, INC.
95 Route 17 South, Paramus NJ 07653-0931. 201/291-2000. **Contact:** Human Resources. **World Wide Web address:** http://www.preserver.com. **Description:** Provides automobile, homeowner, and commercial insurance. Founded in 1926. **Common positions include:** Accountant/Auditor; Adjuster; Claim Representative; Clerical Supervisor; Computer Programmer; Human Resources Manager; Insurance Agent/Broker; Systems Analyst; Underwriter/Assistant Underwriter. **Corporate headquarters location:** This location. **Listed on:** NASDAQ. **Stock exchange symbol:** PRES. **Number of employees at this location:** 95.

PRUDENTIAL INSURANCE COMPANY OF AMERICA
23 Main Street, Holmdel NJ 07733. 732/946-5000. **Contact:** Human Resources. **World Wide Web address:** http://www.prudential.com. **Description:** One of the largest insurance and diversified financial services organizations in the world. The company's primary business is to offer a full range of products and services in three areas: insurance, investment, and home ownership for individuals and families; health care management and other benefit programs for employees of companies and members of groups; and asset management for institutional clients and their associates. The company insures or provides other financial services to more than 50 million people worldwide. **NOTE:** Jobseekers should send resumes to the corporate headquarters located at 751 Broad Street, Newark NJ 07102. **Common positions include:** Accountant/Auditor; Actuary; Administrator; Computer Programmer; Purchasing Agent/Manager; Underwriter/Assistant Underwriter. **Corporate headquarters location:** Newark NJ. **Other area locations:** Iselin NJ; Roseland NJ. **Other U.S. locations:** Woodland Hills CA; Jacksonville FL; Minneapolis MN; Philadelphia PA; Houston TX. **Listed on:** New York Stock Exchange. **Stock exchange symbol:** PRU. **Annual sales/revenues:** More than $100 million. **Number of employees worldwide:** 100,000.

PRUDENTIAL INSURANCE COMPANY OF AMERICA
751 Broad Street, Newark NJ 07102. 973/802-8348. **Fax:** 973/802-5825. **Contact:** Human Resources Department. **World Wide Web address:** http://www.prudential.com. **Description:** One of the largest insurance companies in North America and one of the largest diversified financial services organizations in the world. The company offers a full range of products and services in three areas: insurance, investment, and home ownership for individuals and families; health care management and other benefit programs for employees of companies and members of groups; and asset management for institutional clients and their associates. The company insures or provides financial services to more than 50 million people worldwide. **Common positions include:** Accountant/Auditor; Actuary; Administrator; Computer Programmer; Human Resources Manager; Purchasing Agent/Manager; Underwriter/Assistant Underwriter. **Special**

programs: Internships. **Corporate headquarters location:** This location. **Other area locations:** Holmdel NJ; Iselin NJ; Roseland NJ. **Other U.S. locations:** Woodland Hills CA; Jacksonville FL; Minneapolis MN; Philadelphia PA; Houston TX. **Listed on:** New York Stock Exchange. **Stock exchange symbol:** PRU. **Annual sales/revenues:** More than $100 million. **Number of employees worldwide:** 100,000.

PRUDENTIAL INSURANCE COMPANY OF AMERICA
200 Wood Avenue South, Iselin NJ 08830. 732/632-7000. **Contact:** Human Resources. **World Wide Web address:** http://www.prudential.com. **Description:** This location manages health care policies. Overall, Prudential Insurance Company of America is one of the largest insurance companies in North America and one of the largest diversified financial services organizations in the world. The company's primary business is to offer a full range of products and services in three areas: insurance, investment, and home ownership for individuals and families; health care management and other benefit programs for employees of companies and members of groups; and asset management for institutional clients and their associates. The company insures or provides other financial services to more than 50 million people worldwide. **NOTE:** Jobseekers should send resumes to the corporate headquarters located at 751 Broad Street, Newark NJ 07102. company insures or provides financial services to more than 50 million people worldwide. **Common positions include:** Accountant/Auditor; Actuary; Administrator; Computer Programmer; Human Resources Manager; Purchasing Agent/Manager; Underwriter/Assistant Underwriter. **Corporate headquarters location:** Newark NJ. **Other area locations:** Holmdel NJ; Roseland NJ. **Other U.S. locations:** Woodland Hills CA; Jacksonville FL; Minneapolis MN; Philadelphia PA; Houston TX. **Listed on:** New York Stock Exchange. **Stock exchange symbol:** PRU. **Annual sales/revenues:** More than $100 million. **Number of employees worldwide:** 100,000.

PRUDENTIAL INSURANCE COMPANY OF AMERICA
80 Livingston Avenue, Roseland NJ 07068. 973/716-6834. **Contact:** Human Resources. **World Wide Web address:** http://www.prudential.com. **Description:** One of the largest insurance companies in North America and one of the largest diversified financial services organizations in the world. The company's primary business is to offer a full range of products and services in three areas: insurance, investment, and home ownership for individuals and families; health care management and other benefit programs for employees of companies and members of groups; and asset management for institutional clients and their associates. With a sales force of approximately 19,000 agents, 3,400 insurance brokers, and 6,000 financial advisors, the company insures or provides other financial services to more than 50 million people worldwide. **NOTE:** Jobseekers should send resumes to the corporate headquarters located at 751 Broad Street, Newark NJ 07102. **Common positions include:** Accountant/Auditor; Actuary; Administrator; Computer Programmer; Human Resources Manager; Purchasing Agent/Manager; Underwriter/Assistant Underwriter. **Corporate headquarters location:** Newark NJ. **Other area locations:** Holmdel NJ; Iselin NJ. **Other U.S. locations:** Woodland Hills CA; Jacksonville FL; Minneapolis MN; Philadelphia PA; Houston TX. **Listed on:** New York Stock Exchange. **Stock exchange symbol:** PRU. **Annual sales/revenues:** More than $100 million. **Number of employees worldwide:** 100,000.

ROBERT PLAN OF NEW JERSEY
200 Metroplex Drive, Edison NJ 08817-2600. 732/777-5300. **Contact:** Human Resources. **World Wide Web address:** http://www.rpc.com. **Description:** This location houses an automobile claims office. Overall, Robert Plan of New Jersey provides personal lines of insurance.

SELECTIVE INSURANCE COMPANY OF AMERICA
40 Wantage Avenue, Branchville NJ 07890. 973/948-3000. **Contact:** Christopher Williams, Personnel Department Representative. **E-mail address:** christopher.williams@selective.com. **World Wide Web address:** http://www.selectiveinsurance.com. **Description:** Engaged in fire, marine, and casualty insurance.

LEGAL SERVICES

You can expect to find the following types of companies in this chapter:

Law Firms • Legal Service Agencies

GIBBONS, DEL DEO, DOLAN, GRIFFINGER & VECCHIONE
One Riverfront Plaza, Newark NJ 07102-5496. 973/596-4500. **Contact:** Personnel. **World Wide Web address:** http://www.gibbonslaw.com. **Description:** A law firm specializing in corporate and finance law, commercial litigation, intellectual property law, employment and labor law, environmental law, commercial real estate, and bankruptcy and insolvency counseling and business reorganizations. The company is one of the largest law firms in New Jersey employing over 170 attorneys. **Other area locations:** Trenton NJ. **Other U.S. locations:** New York NY.

GREENBAUM, ROWE, SMITH, RAVIN, DAVIS & HIMMEL LLP
Metro Corporate Campus One, 99 Wood Avenue South, P.O. Box 5600, Woodbridge NJ 07095. 732/549-5600. **Fax:** 732/549-1881. **Contact:** Maureen Lugo, Human Resources Department Representative. **E-mail address:** mlugo@greenbaumlaw.com. **World Wide Web address:** http://www.greenbaumlaw.com. **Description:** A law firm with practice areas including environmental, product liability, employment, white collar criminal, real estate, corporate, tax, and estate law.

LEBOEUF, LAMB, GREENE & MACRAE LLP
One Riverfront Plaza, Newark NJ 07102. 973/643-8000. **Contact:** Recruiting. **World Wide Web address:** http://www.llgm.com. **Description:** A law firm specializing in corporate law, international law, and litigation. The firm primarily serves the insurance and utilities industries.

MANDELBAUM, SALSBURG
155 Prospect Street, West Orange NJ 07052. 973/736-4600. **Fax:** 973/325-7467. **Contact:** Human Resources Department. **World Wide Web address:** http://www.mandelbaumsalsburg.lawoffice.com. **Description:** A law firm practicing in the fields of civil and commercial litigation, corporate and banking transactions, real estate and land use, and bankruptcy, as well as criminal and personal matters. Founded in 1930. **Other area locations:** East Brunswick NJ; Elizabeth NJ; Wall NJ.

SCARINCI & HOLLENBECK, LLC
500 Plaza Drive, P.O. Box 3189, Secaucus NJ 07096-3189. 201/392-8900. **Fax:** 201/348-3877. **Contact:** Human Resources. **World Wide Web address:** http://www.njlegalink.com. **Description:** A law firm. The company organized attorneys into the following practice groups: commercial real estate and business law; environmental and land use law; labor and employment law; litigation; public law. **Corporate headquarters location:** This location. **Other area locations:** Hackensack NJ.

SMITH, STRATTON, WISE, HEHER & BRENNAN
600 College Road East, Princeton NJ 08540. 609/924-6000. **Contact:** Janet M. Derr, Personnel. **E-mail address:** jd@sswhb.com. **World Wide Web address:** http://www.sswhb.com. **Description:** A law firm serving the needs of businesses, the investment community, and entrepreneurs. Founded in 1948.

WILENTZ, GOLDMAN & SPITZER
90 Woodbridge Center Drive, Suite 900, Woodbridge NJ 07095. 732/636-8000. **Contact:** Personnel Department. **World Wide Web address:** http://www.newjerseylaw.com. **Description:** A law firm specializing in corporate, employment, environmental, and tax law.

MANUFACTURING: MISCELLANEOUS CONSUMER

You can expect to find the following types of companies in this chapter:

Art Supplies • Batteries • Cosmetics and Related Products • Household Appliances and Audio/Video Equipment • Jewelry, Silverware, and Plated Ware • Miscellaneous Household Furniture and Fixtures • Musical Instruments • Tools •
Toys and Sporting Goods

AGFA CORPORATION
100 Challenger Road, Ridgefield Park NJ 07660-2199. 201/440-2500. **Contact:** Personnel. **World Wide Web address:** http://www.agfa.com. **Description:** This location manufactures photographic imaging equipment and film. Overall, the company produces polyurethane raw materials, polymer thermoplastic resins and blends, coatings, industrial chemicals, and other related products.

BROTHER INTERNATIONAL CORPORATION
100 Somerset Corporate Boulevard, Bridgewater NJ 08807. 908/704-1700. **Contact:** Human Resources Department. **World Wide Web address:** http://www.brother.com. **Description:** One of America's largest manufacturers and distributors of personal word processors and portable electronic typewriters. Brother also markets many industrial products, home appliances, and business machines manufactured by its parent company. Founded in 1954. **Corporate headquarters location:** This location. **Parent company:** Brother Industries, Ltd. (Nagoya, Japan). **Number of employees nationwide:** 1,300.

CASIO INC.
570 Mount Pleasant Avenue, Dover NJ 07801. 973/361-5400. **Fax:** 973/537-8910. **Contact:** Ken Sterzer, Human Resources Manager. **E-mail address:** casioincjobs@casio.com. **World Wide Web address:** http://www.casio.com. **Description:** Manufactures consumer electronics and computer-based products. **NOTE:** Entry-level positions are offered. **Common positions include:** Account Manager; Account Representative; Accountant; Administrative Assistant; Administrative Manager; AS400 Programmer Analyst; Assistant Manager; Budget Analyst; Computer Operator; Computer Programmer; Computer Technician; Credit Manager; Customer Service Manager; Database Administrator; General Manager; Internet Services Manager; Intranet Developer; Marketing Manager; Marketing Specialist; Network/Systems Administrator; Purchasing Agent/Manager; Sales Manager; Sales Representative; Secretary; Systems Analyst; Transportation/Traffic Specialist; Web Advertising Specialist; Webmaster; Website Developer. **Office hours:** Monday - Friday, 9:00 a.m. - 5:00 p.m. **Corporate headquarters location:** This location. **Other U.S. locations:** Glendale Heights IL; Little Ferry NJ. **International locations:** Worldwide. **Parent company:** Casio Computer Company, Ltd. (Tokyo, Japan). **Listed on:** Privately held. **Annual sales/revenues:** More than $100 million. **Number of employees at this location:** 150. **Number of employees nationwide:** 325.

COLGATE-PALMOLIVE COMPANY

191 East Hanover Avenue, Morristown NJ 07962-1928. 973/631-9000. **Contact:** Human Resources Department. **World Wide Web address:** http://www.colgate.com. **Description:** This location manufactures baby products and deodorant. Overall, Colgate-Palmolive Company manufactures and markets a wide variety of products in the United States and around the world in two business segments: Oral, Personal, and Household Care; and Specialty Marketing. Oral, Personal, and Household Care products include toothpastes, oral rinses and toothbrushes, bar and liquid soaps, shampoos, conditioners, deodorants and antiperspirants, baby and shaving products, laundry and dishwashing detergents, fabric softeners, cleansers and cleaners, and bleach. Specialty Marketing products include pet dietary care products, crystal tableware, and portable fuel for warming food. Principal global trademarks and brand names include Colgate, Palmolive, Mennen, Ajax, Fab, and Science Diet, in addition to various regional brand names. **Corporate headquarters location:** New York NY. **Other U.S. locations:** Kansas City KS; Cambridge MA; Piscataway NJ.

COLGATE-PALMOLIVE COMPANY
TECHNOLOGY CENTER

909 River Road, P.O. Box 1343, Piscataway NJ 08855-1343. 732/878-7500. **Contact:** Human Resources Department. **World Wide Web address:** http://www.colgate.com. **Description:** This location houses a research and development facility. Overall, Colgate-Palmolive Company manufactures and markets a wide variety of products in the United States and around the world in two business segments: Oral, Personal, and Household Care; and Specialty Marketing. Oral, Personal, and Household Care products include toothpastes, oral rinses and toothbrushes, bar and liquid soaps, shampoos, conditioners, deodorants and antiperspirants, baby and shaving products, laundry and dishwashing detergents, fabric softeners, cleansers and cleaners, and bleach. Specialty Marketing products include pet dietary care products, crystal tableware, and portable fuel for warming food. Principal global trademarks and brand names include Colgate, Palmolive, Mennen, Ajax, Fab, and Science Diet, in addition to various regional brand names. **NOTE:** When submitting resumes, please include appropriate mail codes, for engineering or research positions, use Mail Code JHO and for secretarial or administrative positions, use Mail Code MG. **Common positions include:** Accountant/Auditor; Biological Scientist; Chemical Engineer; Chemist; Clinical Lab Technician; Computer Programmer; Dental Assistant/Dental Hygienist; Environmental Engineer; Financial Analyst; Human Resources Manager; Mechanical Engineer; Paralegal; Software Engineer; Systems Analyst; Technical Writer/Editor. **Special programs:** Internships. **Corporate headquarters location:** New York NY. **Other U.S. locations:** Kansas City KS; Cambridge MA; Morristown NJ. **Operations at this facility include:** Administration; Manufacturing; Research and Development. **Number of employees at this location:** 1,000.

EFFANBEE DOLL COMPANY

19 Lexington Avenue, East Brunswick NJ 08816. 732/613-3852. **Contact:** Personnel. **World Wide Web address:** http://www.effnbeedolls.com. **Description:** Manufactures dolls. Founded in 1910. **Corporate headquarters location:** This location.

FEDDERS CORPORATION

505 Martinsville Road, P.O. Box 813, Liberty Corner NJ 07938. 908/604-8686. **Fax:** 908/604-8576. **Contact:** Human Resources Department. **World Wide Web address:** http://www.fedders.com. **Description:** Manufactures

room air conditioners. Brand names of the corporation include Airtemp, Emerson Quiet Kool, and Fedders. **Corporate headquarters location:** This location. **Listed on:** New York Stock Exchange. **Stock exchange symbol:** FJC.

GEMINI INDUSTRIES INC.
215 Entin Road, Clifton NJ 07014. 973/471-9050. **Fax:** 973/574-7215. **Contact:** Human Resources. **E-mail address:** hr@gemini-usa.com. **World Wide Web address:** http://www.gemini-usa.com. **Description:** Manufactures PC and cellular telephone accessories, remote controls, and cable.

GLAXOSMITHKLINE CORPORATION
257 Cornelison Avenue, Jersey City NJ 07302. 201/434-3000. **Contact:** Human Resources. **World Wide Web address:** http://www.gsk.com. **Description:** Develops, manufactures, and sells products in four general categories: denture, dental care, oral hygiene, and professional dental products; proprietary products; ethical pharmaceutical products; and household products. Dental-related products include Polident denture cleansers. **Listed on:** New York Stock Exchange. **Stock exchange symbol:** GSK.

GLAXOSMITHKLINE CORPORATION
65 Industrial South, Clifton NJ 07012. 973/778-9000. **Contact:** Human Resources. **World Wide Web address:** http://www.gsk.com. **Description:** This location manufactures toothpaste and Massengill products. Overall, GlaxoSmithKline Corporation is a health care company engaged in the research, development, manufacture, and marketing of ethical pharmaceuticals, animal health products, ethical and proprietary medicines, and eye care products. The company is also engaged in many other aspects of the health care field including the production of medical and electronic instruments. **Corporate headquarters location:** Philadelphia PA. **Subsidiaries include:** Menley & James Laboratories products include Contac Cold Capsules, Sine-Off sinus medicine, Love cosmetics, and Sea & Ski outdoor products. **Listed on:** New York Stock Exchange. **Stock exchange symbol:** GSK.

GUEST SUPPLY INC.
P.O. Box 902, Monmouth Junction NJ 08852-0902. 609/514-9696. **Physical address:** 4301 U.S. Highway One, Monmouth Junction NJ 08852-0902. **Fax:** 609/514-7379. **Contact:** Joan Constanza, Human Resources Manager. **World Wide Web address:** http://www.guestsupply.com. **Description:** Manufactures, packages, and distributes travel-size personal care products, housekeeping supplies, room accessories, and textiles to the lodging industry. The company also manufactures and packages products for major consumer products and retail companies. Founded in 1979. **NOTE:** Entry-level positions and second and third shifts are offered. **Common positions include:** Account Manager; Account Representative; Accountant; Blue-Collar Worker Supervisor; Branch Manager; Buyer; Chemist; Chief Financial Officer; Computer Operator; Controller; Credit Manager; Customer Service Representative; Database Manager; Design Engineer; Finance Director; Financial Analyst; Graphic Artist; Graphic Designer; Human Resources Manager; Industrial Engineer; Industrial Production Manager; Manufacturing Engineer; Marketing Manager; Marketing Specialist; MIS Specialist; Operations Manager; Production Manager; Purchasing Agent/Manager; Quality Control Supervisor; Sales Executive; Sales Manager; Sales Representative; Secretary; Systems Analyst;

Systems Manager; Telecommunications Manager; Transportation/Traffic Specialist; Typist/Word Processor. **Corporate headquarters location:** This location. **Other U.S. locations:** Nationwide. **Subsidiaries include:** Brecken-Ridge-Remy; Guest Distribution; Guest Packaging. **Operations at this facility include:** Divisional Headquarters; Regional Headquarters. **Listed on:** New York Stock Exchange. **Stock exchange symbol:** GSY. **Annual sales/revenues:** More than $100 million. **Number of employees at this location:** 1,000.

HARTZ MOUNTAIN CORPORATION
400 Plaza Drive, 4th Floor, Secaucus NJ 07094. 201/271-4800. **Fax:** 201/271-0164. **Contact:** Human Resources. **E-mail address:** jobopps@hartz.com. **World Wide Web address:** http://www.hartz.com. **Description:** Engaged in the manufacture, packaging, and distribution of consumer products including pet foods, pet accessories, livestock feed and products; chemical products; home carpet-cleaning products; and equipment rentals. **Corporate headquarters location:** This location. **Other area locations:** Bloomfield NJ. **Subsidiaries include:** Cooper Pet Supply; Permaline Manufacturing Corporation; Sternco-Dominion Real Estate Corporation; The Pet Library Ltd.

HOME CARE INDUSTRIES
One Lisbon Street, Clifton NJ 07013. 973/365-1600. **Contact:** Human Resources. **World Wide Web address:** http://www.homecareind.com. **Description:** Manufactures vacuum cleaner bags.

JOHNSON & JOHNSON
One Johnson & Johnson Plaza, New Brunswick NJ 08933. 732/524-0400. **Contact:** Human Resources Department. **World Wide Web address:** http://www.jnj.com. **Description:** A health care products company. Products include pain relievers, contact lenses, pharmaceuticals, bandages, toothbrushes, and surgical instruments under brand names including Reach, Band-Aid, and Acuvue. **NOTE:** Resumes should be sent to Johnson & Johnson Recruiting Services, Employment Management Center, Room JH-215, 501 George Street, New Brunswick NJ 08906-6597. **Corporate headquarters location:** This location. **International locations:** Worldwide.

JOHNSON & JOHNSON CONSUMER PRODUCTS, INC.
199 Grandview Road, Skillman NJ 08558. 908/874-1000. **Contact:** Employment Management Center. **World Wide Web address:** http://www.jnj.com. **Description:** A large and diverse health care products company. Products include pain relievers, contact lenses, pharmaceuticals, bandages, toothbrushes, and surgical instruments under brand names including Reach, Band-Aid, and Acuvue. **NOTE:** Resumes should be sent to Johnson & Johnson Recruiting Services, Employment Management Center, Room JH-215, 501 George Street, New Brunswick NJ 08906-6597. **Corporate headquarters location:** New Brunswick NJ.

KREMENTZ & COMPANY
P.O. Box 94, Newark NJ 07101-0094. 973/621-8300. **Contact:** Grace Reed, Human Resources Director. **World Wide Web address:** http://www.krementzgemstones.com. **Description:** A manufacturer and distributor of fine jewelry and related items.

L'OREAL USA
222 Terminal Avenue, Clark NJ 07066. 732/499-2838. **Contact:** Human Resources. **World Wide Web address:** http://www.loreal.com. **Description:** Manufactures personal care products including hair dyes and shampoo.

MAGLA PRODUCTS INC.
P.O. Box 1934, Morristown NJ 07962-1934. 973/377-0500. **Physical address:** 159 South Street, Morristown NJ 07962. **Contact:** Human Resources. **World Wide Web address:** http://www.magla.com. **Description:** Manufactures kitchen and domestic household products including ironing-board covers, dish towels, oven mitts, rubber gloves, disposable wipe cloths, and cling sheets. **Corporate headquarters location:** This location.

MARCAL PAPER MILLS, INC.
One Market Street, Elmwood Park NJ 07407. 201/796-4000. **Contact:** James H. Nelson, Director of Human Resources Department. **World Wide Web address:** http://www.marcalpaper.com. **Description:** Manufactures and distributes a broad range of nationally advertised paper products including paper towels, toilet tissue, and napkins. **Common positions include:** Accountant/Auditor; Chemical Engineer; Computer Programmer; Customer Service Representative; Mechanical Engineer; Operations/Production Manager. **Corporate headquarters location:** This location. **Operations at this facility include:** Administration; Manufacturing; Research and Development; Sales.

MYRON MANUFACTURING CORPORATION
205 Maywood Avenue, Maywood NJ 07607. 201/843-6464. **Fax:** 201/587-1905. **Contact:** Jenny Supple, Human Resources Department. **World Wide Web address:** http://www.myrononline.com. **Description:** Manufactures a line of custom-made vinyl products including pocket calendars for the office and business markets. This location also hires seasonally. Founded in 1949. **NOTE:** Entry-level positions and second and third shifts are offered. **Common positions include:** Account Representative; Accountant; Administrative Assistant; Administrative Manager; Advertising Clerk; Advertising Executive; AS400 Programmer Analyst; Assistant Manager; Blue-Collar Worker Supervisor; Chief Financial Officer; Clerical Supervisor; Computer Operator; Computer Programmer; Controller; Customer Service Representative; Design Engineer; Editor; Financial Analyst; Graphic Artist; Industrial Engineer; Industrial Production Manager; Internet Services Manager; Manufacturing Engineer; Market Research Analyst; Marketing Manager; MIS Specialist; Production Manager; Purchasing Agent/Manager; Quality Assurance Engineer; Quality Control Supervisor; Sales Executive; Sales Manager; Sales Representative; Transportation/Traffic Specialist; Website Developer. **Special programs:** Internships; Training. **Office hours:** Monday - Friday, 8:00 a.m. - 5:00 p.m. **Corporate headquarters location:** This location. **Operations at this facility include:** Administration; Manufacturing; Sales; Service. **President:** Marie Adler-Kravecas. **Facilities Manager:** Dan Hurtubise. **Information Systems Manager:** Bruce Kalten. **Purchasing Manager:** Jim Ragucci. **Sales Manager:** Terrence Flynn. **Annual sales/revenues:** More than $100 million. **Number of employees at this location:** 600.

NIELSEN & BAINBRIDGE
40 Eisenhower Drive, Paramus NJ 07652. 201/845-6100. **Contact:** Dorothy Uhler, Personnel Director. **World Wide Web address:** http://www.nielsen-bainbridge.com. **Description:** Produces and distributes picture frames. **Common positions include:** Accountant/Auditor; Administrator; Customer

Service Representative; Sales Executive. **Operations at this facility include:** Administration; Divisional Headquarters; Service.

PENTECH INTERNATIONAL INC.
195 Carter Drive, Edison NJ 08817. 732/287-6640. **Contact:** Human Resources. **World Wide Web address:** http://www.pentechintl.com. **Description:** Designs, manufactures, and markets pencils, pens, markers, activity sets, and accessories. **Corporate headquarters location:** This location.

POWER BATTERY COMPANY
25 McLean Boulevard, Paterson NJ 07514-1507. 973/523-8630. **Contact:** Personnel. **World Wide Web address:** http://www.powerbattery.com. **Description:** Manufactures batteries for use in automobiles, computers, and small electronic appliances.

QUEST INTERNATIONAL FRAGRANCES COMPANY
400 International Drive, Mount Olive NJ 07828. 973/691-7100. **Contact:** Human Resources. **World Wide Web address:** http://www.questintl.com. **Description:** Develops cosmetic fragrances. **Corporate headquarters location:** This location. **Operations at this facility include:** Administration; Manufacturing; Marketing; Sales.

RECKITT BENCKISER
1655 Valley Road, Wayne NJ 07470. 973/633-3600. **Contact:** Staffing Supervisor. **World Wide Web address:** http://www.reckitt.com. **Description:** Manufactures cleaning and specialty food products including the brand names Easy-Off oven cleaner, French's mustard, Lysol, and Woolite detergent.

REVLON, INC.
IMPLEMENT DIVISION
196 Coit Street, Irvington NJ 07111-1490. 973/373-5803. **Contact:** Personnel Manager. **World Wide Web address:** http://www.revlon.com. **Description:** Manufactures nail files, scissors, tweezers, and other manicure and pedicure products. **Common positions include:** Accountant/Auditor; Blue-Collar Worker Supervisor; Department Manager; General Manager; Human Resources Manager; Industrial Engineer; Mechanical Engineer; Operations/Production Manager; Purchasing Agent/Manager; Quality Control Supervisor. **Corporate headquarters location:** New York NY. **Listed on:** New York Stock Exchange. **Stock exchange symbol:** REV.

RUSS BERRIE & COMPANY, INC.
111 Bauer Drive, Oakland NJ 07436. 201/337-9000. **Contact:** Human Resource Department. **E-mail address:** careers@russberrie.com. **World Wide Web address:** http://www.russberrie.com. **Description:** Designs and markets a line of more than 10,000 gift items in the United States and abroad. Products include toys, stuffed animals, novelties, and cards. A diverse customer base includes florists, pharmacies, party shops, and stationery stores, as well as hotel, airport, and hospital gift shops. **Common positions include:** Accountant/Auditor; Commercial Artist; Customer Service Representative; Financial Analyst; Manufacturer's/Wholesaler's Sales Rep.; Marketing Specialist. **Corporate headquarters location:** This location. **Operations at this facility include:** Administration. **Listed on:** New York Stock Exchange. **Stock exchange symbol:** RUS. **Number of employees nationwide:** 2,000.

SCHERING-PLOUGH CORPORATION
2000 Galloping Hill Road, Kenilworth NJ 07033. 908/298-4000. **Contact:** Human Resources Department. **World Wide Web address:** http://www.schering-plough.com. **Description:** Engaged in the discovery, development, manufacture, and marketing of pharmaceutical and consumer products. Pharmaceutical products include prescription drugs, over-the-counter medicines, eye care products, and animal health products promoted to the medical and allied health professions. The consumer products group consists of proprietary medicines, toiletries, cosmetics, and foot care products. Brand names include Coricidin, Maybelline, Claritin, Coppertone, and Dr. Scholl's. **Corporate headquarters location:** This location. **Other area locations:** Statewide. **International locations:** Worldwide.

SCHERING-PLOUGH CORPORATION
One Giralda Farms, Madison NJ 07940-1000. 973/822-7000. **Contact:** Human Resources Department. **World Wide Web address:** http://www.schering-plough.com. **Description:** Engaged in the discovery, development, manufacture, and marketing of pharmaceutical and consumer products. Pharmaceutical products include prescription drugs, over-the-counter medicines, eye care products, and animal health products. The consumer products group consists of proprietary medicines, toiletries, cosmetics, and foot care products. Brand names include Coricidin, Maybelline, Claritin, Coppertone, and Dr. Scholl's. **Corporate headquarters location:** Kenilworth NJ. **Other area locations:** Statewide. **International locations:** Worldwide.

SONY ELECTRONICS, INC.
One Sony Drive, Park Ridge NJ 07656. 201/930-1000. **Contact:** Human Resources. **World Wide Web address:** http://www.sony.com. **Description:** This location houses the U.S. headquarters for the international electronics manufacturer. Overall, Sony's U.S. operations include manufacturing, engineering, design, sales, marketing, product distribution, and customer services. **Other area locations:** Moonachie NJ; Paramus NJ; Teaneck NJ. **Other U.S. locations:** New York NY. **Number of employees nationwide:** 24,000.

SPRINGFIELD PRECISION INSTRUMENTS
76 Passaic Street, Wood-Ridge NJ 07075. 973/777-2900. **Contact:** Personnel Manager. **Description:** Manufactures thermometers and barometers for consumer use. **Corporate headquarters location:** This location.

U.S. INDUSTRIES
101 Wood Avenue South, Iselin NJ 08830. 732/767-0700. **Contact:** Human Resources. **Description:** A holding company for four categories of manufacturing companies: bath and plumbing products, hardware and nonelectric tools, commercial and residential lighting, and a variety of consumer products ranging from vacuum cleaners to toys. **Corporate headquarters location:** This location. **Subsidiaries include:** Jacuzzi; Lighting Corporation of America; Selkirk; Spaulding.

WOMEN'S GOLF UNLIMITED
18 Gloria Lane, Fairfield NJ 07004. 973/227-7783. **Contact:** Personnel. **World Wide Web address:** http://www.womensgolfunlimited.com. **Description:** Manufactures and markets a proprietary line of golf equipment including golf clubs, golf bags, golf balls, and accessories. The company

markets these products under the trademarks Square Two, S2, PCX, XGR, ZCX, ONYX, Totally Matched, and Posiflow. Square Two Golf is also the exclusive golf club licensee of the LPGA. **Corporate headquarters location:** This location. **Listed on:** NASDAQ. **Stock exchange symbol:** GOLF.

WYETH CORPORATION

5 Giralda Farms, Madison NJ 07940. 973/660-5000. **Contact:** Human Resources. **World Wide Web address:** http://www.wyeth.com. **Description:** Manufactures and markets prescription drugs and medical supplies, packaged medicines, food products, household products, and housewares. Each division operates through one or more of Wyeth Corporation's subsidiaries. Prescription Drugs and Medical Supplies operates through: Wyeth-Ayerst Laboratories (produces ethical pharmaceuticals, biologicals, nutritional products, over-the-counter antacids, vitamins, and sunburn remedies); Fort Dodge Animal Health (veterinary pharmaceuticals and biologicals); Sherwood Medical (medical devices, diagnostic instruments, test kits, and bacteria identification systems); and Corometrics Medical Systems (medical electronic instrumentation for obstetrics and neonatology). The Packaged Medicines segment operates through Whitehall-Robins Healthcare (produces analgesics, cold remedies, and other packaged medicines). The Food Products segment operates through American Home Foods (canned pasta, canned vegetables, specialty foods, mustard, and popcorn). The Household Products and Housewares segment operates through: Boyle-Midway (cleaners, insecticides, air fresheners, waxes, polishes, and other items for home, appliance, and apparel care); Dupli-Color Products (touch-up, refinishing, and other car care and shop-use products); Ekco Products (food containers, commercial baking pans, industrial coatings, food-handling systems, foilware, and plasticware); Ekco Housewares (cookware, cutlery, kitchen tools, tableware and accessories, and padlocks); and Prestige Group (cookware, cutlery, kitchen tools, carpet sweepers, and pressure cookers). **Corporate headquarters location:** This location. **Number of employees worldwide:** 53,000.

MANUFACTURING: MISCELLANEOUS INDUSTRIAL

You can expect to find the following types of companies in this chapter:

Ball and Roller Bearings • Commercial Furniture and Fixtures • Fans, Blowers, and Purification Equipment • Industrial Machinery and Equipment • Motors and Generators/Compressors and Engine Parts • Vending Machines

AMERICAN STANDARD COMPANIES INC.
P.O. Box 6820, Piscataway NJ 08854. 732/980-6000. **Physical address:** One Centennial Avenue, Piscataway NJ 08855. **Contact:** Human Resources. **World Wide Web address:** http://www.americanstandard.com. **Description:** A global, diversified manufacturer. The company's operations are comprised of four segments: air conditioning products, plumbing products, automotive products, and medical systems. The air conditioning products segment (through subsidiary The Trane Company) develops and manufactures Trane and American Standard air conditioning equipment for use in central air conditioning systems for commercial, institutional, and residential buildings. The plumbing products segment develops and manufactures American Standard, Ideal Standard, Porcher, Armitage Shanks, Dolomite, and Standard bathroom and kitchen fixtures and fittings. The automotive products segment develops and manufactures truck, bus, and utility vehicle braking and control systems under the WABCO and Perrot brands. The medical systems segment manufactures Copalis, DiaSorin, and Pylori-Chek medical diagnostic products and systems for a variety of diseases including HIV, osteoporosis, and renal disease. **Corporate headquarters location:** This location. **International locations:** Worldwide. **Listed on:** New York Stock Exchange. **Stock exchange symbol:** ASD. **Chairman/CEO:** Frederic M. Poses. **Number of employees worldwide:** 57,000.

ARROW FASTENER COMPANY
271 Mayhill Street, Saddle Brook NJ 07663. 201/843-6900. **Contact:** Plant Manager. **World Wide Web address:** http://www.arrowfastener.com. **Description:** Produces stapling machines and similar products.

BMH CHRONOS RICHARDSON INC.
2 Stewart Place, Fairfield NJ 07004. 973/227-3522. **Contact:** Personnel. **World Wide Web address:** http://www.bmhchronosrichardson.com. **Description:** Manufactures bagging equipment and batching systems for the food, chemical, rubber, and minerals market. **Office hours:** Monday - Friday, 8:30 a.m. - 5:00 p.m.

BELCO TECHNOLOGIES, INC.
7 Entin Road, Parsippany NJ 07054. 973/884-4700. **Contact:** Personnel. **World Wide Web address:** http://www.belcotech.com. **Description:** A worldwide manufacturer of processes and equipment for the removal of air and water pollutants. Pollution control equipment includes electrostatic precipitators and related components. **Common positions include:** Accountant/Auditor; Administrator; Blue-Collar Worker Supervisor; Chemical Engineer; Draftsperson; Electrical/Electronics Engineer; General

Manager; Human Resources Manager; Manufacturer's/Wholesaler's Sales Rep.; Mechanical Engineer; Operations/Production Manager; Purchasing Agent/Manager; Quality Control Supervisor. **Corporate headquarters location:** This location.

BERES INDUSTRIES, INC.
1785 Swarthmore Avenue, Lakewood NJ 08701. 732/367-5700. **Contact:** Human Resources. **Description:** Designs, manufactures, and assembles precision engineered molds for use in the manufacture of molded plastic products and parts. **Subsidiaries include:** Athenia Plastic Mold Corporation; Supply Dynamics, Inc.

BOBST GROUP, INC.
146 Harrison Avenue, Roseland NJ 07068. 973/226-8000. **Contact:** Personnel. **World Wide Web address:** http://www.bobstgroup.com. **Description:** Produces a line of equipment for the converting, printing, and publishing industries. The company operates in the United States through three groups: Bobst, Bobst Champlain, and Bobst Registron. Products include die cutter/creasers, folder/gluers, flexo and gravure presses, electronic controls, and other sheet and web-fed equipment. The company is also a manufacturer of converting equipment for the folding carton industry. **Common positions include:** Accountant/Auditor; Administrator; Advertising Clerk; Buyer; Credit Manager; Customer Service Representative; Department Manager; Draftsperson; Electrical/Electronics Engineer; General Manager; Human Resources Manager; Marketing Specialist; Mechanical Engineer; Operations/Production Manager; Systems Analyst; Transportation/Traffic Specialist. **Parent company:** Bobst S.A. (Lausanne, Switzerland).

CSM WORLDWIDE, INC.
ENVIRONMENTAL SYSTEMS DIVISION
200 Sheffield Street, Mountainside NJ 07092. 908/233-2882. **Contact:** Personnel. **World Wide Web address:** http://www.csmworldwide.com. **Description:** Markets, designs, manufactures, and installs air pollution control systems containing catalysts, blowers, burners, analyzers, heat exchangers, and other treatment and monitoring components. These air pollution control systems for hydrocarbon oxidation and nitrogen oxides reduction are used in a wide variety of industrial manufacturing and chemical processing applications. Environmental regulatory compliance, turnkey installation, and after-sale maintenance services are also provided. The company is a leader in supplying controls for commercial bakeries, chemical plants, the pharmaceutical industry, and can and metal coating operations. The company also sells to worldwide markets through the combination of a direct sales force and manufacturer representatives.

CANTEL INDUSTRIES, INC.
Overlook at Great Notch, 150 Clove Road, 9th Floor, Little Falls NJ 07424. 973/890-7220-2139. **Contact:** Joanna Albrecht, Assistant Secretary of Personnel. **World Wide Web address:** http://www.cantelmedical.com. **Description:** A holding company. **Subsidiaries include:** Carson Group Inc. (Canada) markets and distributes medical instruments including flexible and rigid endoscopes; precision instruments including microscopes and image analysis systems; and industrial equipment including remote visual inspection devices, laser distance measurement and thermal imaging products, and online optical inspection and quality assurance systems for specialized industrial applications. Carson also offers a full range of

photographic equipment and supplies for amateur and professional photographers. **Listed on:** NASDAQ. **Stock exchange symbol:** CNTL.

CERTIFIED LABORATORIES INC.
34 Stouts Lane, Monmouth Junction 08852. 732/329-8117. **Contact:** Personnel. **World Wide Web address:** http://www.certifiedlabs.com. **Description:** Manufactures and sells industrial and maintenance supplies.

COOPER ALLOY CORPORATION
201 Sweetland Avenue, Hillside NJ 07205. 908/688-4120. **Contact:** Personnel. **Description:** Manufactures and distributes a line of plastic pumps to OEMs.

CURTISS-WRIGHT CORPORATION
1200 Wall Street West, Lyndhurst NJ 07071. 201/896-8400. **Contact:** Joyce Quinlan, Corporate Executive Director of Human Resources. **World Wide Web address:** http://www.curtisswright.com. **Description:** A diversified, multinational manufacturing and service company that designs, manufactures, and overhauls precision components and systems and provides highly-engineered services to the aerospace, automotive, shipbuilding, oil, petrochemical, agricultural equipment, power generation, metal working, and fire and rescue industries. Curtiss-Wright's principal operations include five North American manufacturing facilities; several metal improvement service facilities located in North America and Europe; and four component overhaul facilities located in Florida, North Carolina, Singapore, and Denmark. **Common positions include:** Accountant/Auditor; Administrator; Aerospace Engineer; Computer Programmer; Draftsperson; Electrical/Electronics Engineer; Financial Analyst; Human Resources Manager; Industrial Engineer; Mechanical Engineer; Metallurgical Engineer; Operations/Production Manager; Quality Control Supervisor; Systems Analyst. **Corporate headquarters location:** This location. **Subsidiaries include:** Curtiss-Wright Flight Systems, Inc.; Curtiss-Wright Flow Control Corporation; Metal Improvement Company, Inc. **Operations at this facility include:** Administration; Service. **Listed on:** New York Stock Exchange. **Stock exchange symbol:** CW. **Number of employees worldwide:** 2,350.

JOHN DUSENBERY COMPANY INC.
220 Franklin Road, Randolph NJ 07869. 973/366-7500. **Contact:** Connie Krupa, Controller. **Description:** Manufactures machinery for the paper, film, and foil industries. **Corporate headquarters location:** This location.

EDWARDS ENGINEERING CORPORATION
101 Alexander Avenue, P.O. Box 487, Pompton Plains NJ 07444-0487. 973/835-2800. **Fax:** 973/835-2805. **Contact:** Rich Lewin, Personnel and Material Manager. **World Wide Web address:** http://www.edwards-eng.com. **Description:** Manufactures coaxial condensers, coaxial evaporators, and vapor recovery systems using refrigeration and liquid nitrogen, baseboard heat, valance heating/cooling, liquid chillers, and hydronic control valves. **Common positions include:** Accountant/Auditor; Buyer; Chemical Engineer; Chemist; Computer Programmer; Draftsperson; Electrical/Electronics Engineer; Electrician; Financial Analyst; Machinist; Manufacturer's/Wholesaler's Sales Rep.; Mechanical Engineer; Payroll Clerk; Purchasing Agent/Manager; Receptionist; Sheet-Metal Worker; Software Engineer; Stock Clerk; Systems Analyst; Tool and Die Maker; Typist/Word Processor; Welder. **Corporate headquarters location:** This location. **Operations at this facility include:** Administration; Manufacturing;

Research and Development; Sales; Service. **Number of employees at this location:** 150.

FALSTROM COMPANY
P.O. Box 118, One Falstrom Court, Passaic NJ 07055. 973/777-0013. **Contact:** Human Resources. **Description:** Manufactures steel cabinets for various clients including the defense industry.

FOSTER WHEELER CORPORATION
Perryville Corporate Park, Clinton NJ 08809-4000. 908/730-4000. **Fax:** 908/713-3490. **Contact:** Tom Cucchiara, Personnel Department. **E-mail address:** tom_cucchiara@fwc.com. **World Wide Web address:** http://www.fwc.com. **Description:** Foster Wheeler has three business segments: Process Plants segment designs, engineers, and constructs process plants and fired heaters for oil refiners and chemical producers; the Utility and Engine segment designs and fabricates steam generators, condensers, feedwater heaters, electrostatic precipitators, and other pollution abatement equipment; the Industrial segment that supplies pressure vessels and internals, electrical copper products, industrial insulation, welding wire, and electrodes. **Common positions include:** Accountant/Auditor; Chemical Engineer; Civil Engineer; Computer Programmer; Draftsperson; Electrical/Electronics Engineer; Financial Analyst; Industrial Designer; Mechanical Engineer. **Corporate headquarters location:** This location. **International locations:** Worldwide. **Listed on:** New York Stock Exchange. **Stock exchange symbol:** FWC.

STEPHEN GOULD CORPORATION
35 South Jefferson Road, Whippany NJ 07981. 973/428-1500. **Contact:** Personnel. **World Wide Web address:** http://www.stephengould.com. **Description:** Designs, produces, and supplies packaging including plastic, paper, and metal for a variety of materials industries. **Corporate headquarters location:** This location. **Other U.S. locations:** Nationwide.

HANOVIA/COLITE, INC.
825 Lehigh Avenue, Union NJ 07083. 908/688-0050. **Contact:** Rosemary McCann, Director of Human Resources. **World Wide Web address:** http://www.hanovia-uv.com. **Description:** Designs, develops, produces, and markets plasma arc lamps and related equipment including commercial and industrial ultraviolet products and accessories; produces various phosphorescent pigments, compounds, and films; and designs, develops, manufactures, assembles, and markets high-intensity lighting equipment. **Common positions include:** Ceramics Engineer; Electrical/Electronics Engineer; Mechanical Engineer; Metallurgical Engineer. **Corporate headquarters location:** This location. **Operations at this facility include:** Manufacturing; Research and Development.

HAYWARD INDUSTRIES
620 Division Street, Elizabeth NJ 07207. 908/351-5400. **Fax:** 908/351-0604. **Contact:** Human Resources Department. **World Wide Web address:** http://www.haywardnet.com. **Description:** Manufactures swimming pool equipment. The company is engaged in all aspects of production including design and sales. Clients use equipment in the construction, repair, and maintenance of private and commercial swimming pools. The company also manufactures and distributes a standard line of industrial pipeline strainers and valves. **Corporate headquarters location:** This location. **International locations:** Belgium. **Operations at this facility include:** Administration; Manufacturing; Research and Development; Sales; Service.

Barnes & Noble Bookseller
675 6th Ave
New York, NY 10010
212 727-1227
08-04-03 S02538 R004

CUSTOMER RECEIPT COPY

New York JobBank, 18th E   16.95
1580628168

SUB TOTAL   16.95
SALES TAX   1.46
TOTAL   18.41
AMOUNT TENDERED
DISCOVER   18.41
CARD #:   ************5369
AMOUNT   18.41
AUTH CODE   004728

TOTAL PAYMENT   18.41
        Thank you for shopping at
        Barnes & Noble booksellers
Shop online 24 hours a day www.bn.com
#374072 08-04-03 01:59P JTLLEN

Valid photo ID required for all returns, exchanges and to receive and redeem store credit. With a receipt, a full refund in the original form of payment will be issued for new and unread books and unopened music within 14 days from any Barnes & Noble store. For merchandise purchased with a check, a store credit will be issued. **Without an original receipt**, a store credit issued by mail will be offered at the lowest selling price. With a receipt, returns of new and unread books and unopened music from bn.com can be made for store credit. A gift receipt or exchange receipt serves as proof of purchase only.

Valid photo ID required for all returns, exchanges and to receive and redeem store credit. With a receipt, a full refund in the original form of payment will be issued for new and unread books and unopened music within 14 days from any Barnes & Noble store. For merchandise purchased with a check, a store credit will be issued. **Without an original receipt**, a store credit issued by mail will be offered at the lowest selling price. With a receipt, returns of new and unread books and unopened music from bn.com can be made for store credit. A gift receipt or exchange receipt serves as proof of purchase only.

Valid photo ID required for all returns, exchanges and to receive and redeem store credit. With a receipt, a full refund in the

HOLOPAK TECHNOLOGIES, INC.

15 Cotters Lane, East Brunswick NJ 08816. 732/238-1800. **Fax:** 732/238-3018. **Contact:** Bonnie Eichel, Human Resources Director. **World Wide Web address:** http://www.foilmark.com/en. **Description:** HoloPak, through its subsidiaries Transfer Print Foils, Inc. and Alubec Industries Inc., is a producer and distributor of hot stamping foils, holographic foils, metallized paper, and technical coatings. Hot stamping foils are elements of the graphics and packaging industries, and are used to decorate a wide variety of products. Holographic foils are high-precision images embossed into specialized coatings, which are used to discourage counterfeiting and provide specialty decorative effects. **Parent company:** Foilmark Inc. **Corporate headquarters location:** Newburyport MA. **Other U.S. locations:** Nationwide. **International locations:** Canada.

HONEYWELL

10 North Avenue East, Elizabeth NJ 07201. 908/354-3215. **Contact:** Human Resources. **World Wide Web address:** http://www.honeywell.com. **Description:** This location manufactures plastic inserts for pill bottles. Overall, Honeywell is engaged in the research, development, manufacture, and sale of advanced technology products and services in the fields of chemicals, electronics, automation, and controls. The company's major businesses are home and building automation and control, performance polymers and chemicals, industrial automation and control, space and aviation systems, and defense and marine systems. **Listed on:** New York Stock Exchange. **Stock exchange symbol:** HON.

HONEYWELL

101 Columbia Road, Morristown NJ 07962-1057. 973/455-2000. **Contact:** Human Resources. **World Wide Web address:** http://www.honeywell.com. **Description:** Honeywell is engaged in the research, development, manufacture, and sale of advanced technology products and services in the fields of chemicals, electronics, automation, and controls. The company's major businesses are home and building automation and control, performance polymers and chemicals, industrial automation and control, space and aviation systems, and defense and marine systems. **Corporate headquarters location:** This location. **Listed on:** New York Stock Exchange. **Stock exchange symbol:** HON.

HOSOKAWA MICRON POWDER SYSTEMS

10 Chatham Road, Summit NJ 07901. 908/273-6360. **Contact:** Human Resources. **World Wide Web address:** http://www.hosokawa.com. **Description:** Develops and manufactures air pollution control and process equipment. Products are used by the primary metals, nonmetallic minerals, powder, protective coatings, paper, fertilizer, chemical, pharmaceutical, and food processing industries. **Common positions include:** Accountant/Auditor; Administrator; Buyer; Computer Programmer; Department Engineer; Draftsperson; Electrical/Electronics Engineer; Human Resources Manager; Mechanical Engineer; Operations/Production Manager; Purchasing Agent/Manager; Quality Control Supervisor; Sales Executive. **Corporate headquarters location:** New York NY. **Parent company:** Hosokawa Micron International Inc. **Operations at this facility include:** Administration; Manufacturing; Research and Development; Sales; Service.

INGERSOLL-RAND COMPANY

200 Chestnut Ridge Road, Woodcliff Lake NJ 07677. 201/573-0123. **Contact:** Human Resources Department. **World Wide Web address:** http://www.ingersoll-rand.com. **Description:** Manufactures compressors,

pumps, and other nonelectrical industrial equipment and machinery. Ingersoll-Rand Company's products include air compression systems, antifriction systems, construction equipment, air tools, bearings, locks, tools, and pumps. **Corporate headquarters location:** This location. **Other U.S. locations:** Nationwide. **Subsidiaries include:** IR Torrington Company. **Listed on:** New York Stock Exchange. **Stock exchange symbol:** IR.

KYOCERA MITA AMERICA, INC.
225 Sand Road, Fairfield NJ 07004. 973/808-8444. **Contact:** Human Resources. **World Wide Web address:** http://www.kyoceramita.com. **Description:** One of the world's largest manufacturers of copy machines. Kyocera MITA also offers computer peripherals such as fax machines, imaging systems, and laser printers. **Corporate headquarters location:** This location.

MAGNETIC TICKET & LABEL CORPORATION
151 Cortlandt Avenue, Belleville NJ 07109. 973/759-6500. **Fax:** 973/450-4703. **Contact:** Nancy Nesto, Human Resources Manager. **World Wide Web address:** http://www.magticket.com. **Description:** Manufactures plastic and paper airline baggage tags. **Other U.S. locations:** Los Angeles CA; San Francisco CA; Nashville TN; Dallas TX. **Operations at this facility include:** Manufacturing. **Listed on:** Privately held. **Number of employees at this location:** 80. **Number of employees nationwide:** 4,000.

MAROTTA SCIENTIFIC CONTROLS INC.
P.O. Box 427, Montville NJ 07045-0427. 973/334-7800. **Physical address:** 78 Boonton Avenue, Montville NJ 07045. **Contact:** Robert Cooper, Personnel Manager. **Description:** Manufactures high-pressure valves for pneumatic and hydraulic equipment. The company is also a custom manufacturer of fluid control products. **Common positions include:** Mechanical Engineer. **Corporate headquarters location:** This location.

MIKRON INSTRUMENT COMPANY, INC.
16 Thornton Road, Oakland NJ 07436. 201/891-7330. **Contact:** Human Resources. **World Wide Web address:** http://www.mikroninst.com. **Description:** Develops, manufactures, markets, and services equipment and instruments for noncontact temperature measurement. The company's products are typically used to measure the temperature of moving objects; of stationary objects in environments or situations where contact temperature measurement would be difficult, hazardous, or impractical; and wherever rapid temperature changes must be accurately tracked instantaneously. The company also manufactures and/or markets calibration sources and a variety of accessories and optional equipment for its infrared thermometers. **Listed on:** NASDAQ. **Stock exchange symbol:** MIKR.

MINOLTA CORPORATION
101 Williams Drive, Ramsey NJ 07446. 201/825-4000. **Fax:** 201/825-7567. **Contact:** Personnel Department. **World Wide Web address:** http://www.minoltausa.com. **Description:** Markets, sells, and distributes photographic and business equipment, as well as document imaging systems. **Common positions include:** Accountant/Auditor; Credit Manager; Customer Service Representative; Software Engineer. **Corporate headquarters location:** This location. **Parent company:** Minolta Co., Ltd. (Osaka, Japan). **Operations at this facility include:** Administration; Sales; Service. **Listed on:** Privately held. **Number of employees at this location:** 500.

OHAUS CORPORATION
19A Chapin Road, P.O. Box 2033, Pine Brook NJ 07058. 973/377-9000. **Contact:** Human Resources. **E-mail address:** hr@ohaus.com. **World Wide Web address:** http://www.ohaus.com. **Description:** One of the world's largest manufacturers of precision weighing equipment for use in laboratory, education, and specialty markets. **Corporate headquarters location:** This location.

OLIVETTI OFFICE USA
P.O. Box 6945, Bridgewater NJ 08807-0945. 908/526-8200. **Physical address:** 765 U.S. Highway 202 North, Bridgewater NJ 08807. **Contact:** Personnel. **World Wide Web address:** http://www.olivettiofficeusa.com. **Description:** Manufactures and distributes a broad line of electronic office products including typewriters, calculators, word processors, cash registers, copiers, personal and small computers, business computers, complete data processing systems, teleprinters, video terminals, telephone-switching systems, minicomputers, automatic tellers, and associated equipment. **Corporate headquarters location:** This location.

PERMACEL
P.O. Box 671, New Brunswick NJ 08903-0671. 732/418-2455. **Contact:** Human Resources Department. **World Wide Web address:** http://www.permacel.com. **Description:** Manufactures pressure-sensitive tape. **Common positions include:** Accountant/Auditor; Administrator; Blue-Collar Worker Supervisor; Chemical Engineer; Chemist; Computer Programmer; Credit Manager; Customer Service Representative; Department Manager; Economist; Electrical/Electronics Engineer; Financial Analyst; General Manager; Human Resources Manager; Industrial Engineer; Manufacturer's/Wholesaler's Sales Rep.; Marketing Specialist; Mechanical Engineer; Operations/Production Manager; Quality Control Supervisor; Systems Analyst; Transportation/Traffic Specialist. **Corporate headquarters location:** This location. **Operations at this facility include:** Administration; Manufacturing; Research and Development; Sales; Service. **Listed on:** Privately held. **Number of employees at this location:** 500.

ST PRODUCTION SYSTEMS INC.
100 Central Avenue, Farmingdale NJ 07727. 732/919-2420. **Fax:** 732/919-2455. **Contact:** Manager of Human Resources Department. **World Wide Web address:** http://www.stproductionsystems.com. **Description:** Engaged in prime and subcontract manufacturing of weapons, missile systems, test equipment, airborne systems, communication systems, and EW and ASW systems. **Common positions include:** Accountant; Administrative Assistant; Buyer; Clerical Supervisor; Computer Operator; Controller; Design Engineer; Draftsperson; Finance Director; Financial Analyst; Industrial Engineer; Manufacturing Engineer; Mechanical Engineer; Project Manager; Purchasing Agent/Manager; Secretary; Software Engineer; Typist/Word Processor. **Corporate headquarters location:** This location. **Operations at this facility include:** Administration; Manufacturing; Research and Development; Sales. **Listed on:** Privately held. **Number of employees at this location:** 250.

SEALED AIR CORPORATION
Park 80 East, Saddle Brook NJ 07663. 201/791-7600. **Contact:** Manager of Human Resources Department. **World Wide Web address:** http://www.sealedaircorp.com. **Description:** This location produces specialized protective packaging materials and systems that reduce or eliminate the damage to products that may occur during shipping. Overall,

Sealed Air Corporation is a diversified worldwide enterprise consisting of specialty and agricultural chemicals, energy production and services, retailing, restaurants, and other businesses. The firm operates over 2,500 facilities worldwide. **Corporate headquarters location:** This location. **Other U.S. locations:** Danbury CT; Holyoke MA; Scotia NY. **Listed on:** New York Stock Exchange. **Stock exchange symbol:** SEE. **Number of employees at this location:** 35. **Number of employees nationwide:** 2,000.

TRANSTECHNOLOGY CORPORATION
150 Allen Road, Liberty Corner NJ 07938. 908/903-1600. **Contact:** Human Resources. **World Wide Web address:** http://www.transtechnology.com. **Description:** Designs, manufactures, sells, and distributes specialty fasteners. **Corporate headquarters location:** This location. **Subsidiaries include:** Breeze-Eastern (Union NJ) designs, develops, manufactures, and services sophisticated lifting and restraining products, principally helicopter rescue hoist and cargo hook systems, winches and hoists for aircraft and weapon systems, and aircraft cargo tie-down systems. Breeze Industrial Products (PA) manufactures a complete line of standard and specialty gear-driven band fasteners in high-grade stainless steel for use in highly-engineered applications. Industrial Retaining Ring (Irvington NJ) manufactures a variety of retaining rings made of carbon steel, stainless steel, and beryllium copper. The Palnut Company (Mountainside NJ) manufactures light- and heavy-duty single- and multithread specialty fasteners. The Seeger Group (Somerville NJ) manufactures retaining clips, circlips, spring pins, and similar components.

TRANSTECHNOLOGY ENGINEERED RINGS
70 East Willow Street, Millburn NJ 07041. 973/926-5002. **Contact:** Human Resources. **Description:** Manufactures a variety of retaining rings made of carbon steel, stainless steel, and beryllium copper.

VICTORY/YSI INC.
118 Victory Road, P.O. Box 710, Springfield NJ 07081. 973/379-5900. **Contact:** Personnel. **World Wide Web address:** http://www.ysi.com/veco. **Description:** Manufactures and distributes thermistors, varistors, and specialty temperature sensing assemblies. **Common positions include:** Accountant/Auditor; Administrator; Blue-Collar Worker Supervisor; Chemist; Department Manager; Electrical/Electronics Engineer; Human Resources Manager; Manufacturer's/Wholesaler's Sales Rep.; Operations/Production Manager; Purchasing Agent/Manager; Quality Control Supervisor. **Corporate headquarters location:** This location. **Parent company:** YSI Incorporated.

WEISS-AUG COMPANY INC.
P.O. Box 520, East Hanover NJ 07936. 973/887-7600. **Fax:** 973/887-6924. **Contact:** Mary Dante, Director of Personnel. **World Wide Web address:** http://www.weiss-aug.com. **Description:** Manufactures stampings, moldings, insert moldings, and assemblies. Industries served include automotive, telecommunications, electronic and electrical connector, medical, and several specialty markets. Services include design, tooling, production, and quality control. Founded in 1972. **NOTE:** Part-time jobs and second and third shifts are offered. **Common positions include:** Account Manager; Accountant; Administrative Assistant; Chief Financial Officer; Customer Service Representative; Design Engineer; Environmental Engineer; Human Resources Manager; Industrial Engineer; Manufacturing Engineer; Marketing Specialist; Mechanical Engineer; Production Manager; Purchasing Agent/Manager; Quality Assurance Engineer; Systems Manager.

Special programs: Apprenticeships; Training; Co-ops. **Corporate headquarters location:** This location. **Operations at this facility include:** Administration; Manufacturing; Regional Headquarters; Sales; Service. **Listed on:** Privately held. **President:** Dieter Weissenrieden. **Annual sales/revenues:** $21 - $50 million. **Number of employees at this location:** 200.

MINING/GAS/PETROLEUM/ENERGY RELATED

You can expect to find the following types of companies in this chapter:

Anthracite, Coal, and Ore Mining • Mining Machinery and Equipment • Oil and Gas Field Services • Petroleum and Natural Gas

AMERADA HESS CORPORATION
One Hess Plaza, Woodbridge NJ 07095-1229. 732/636-3000. **Contact:** Human Resources. **World Wide Web address:** http://www.hess.com. **Description:** Extracts, refines, and markets petroleum. **Corporate headquarters location:** New York NY. **Listed on:** New York Stock Exchange. **Stock exchange symbol:** AHC.

BEL-RAY COMPANY, INC.
P.O. Box 526, Farmingdale NJ 07727. 732/938-2421. **Physical address:** 1201 Bowman Avenue, Wall NJ 07719. **Fax:** 732/938-4232. **Contact:** Personnel Department. **E-mail address:** employment@belray.com. **World Wide Web address:** http://www.belray.com. **Description:** Manufactures lubricants used in the aerospace, automotive, food, marine, mining, steel, and textiles industries.

CASTROL NORTH AMERICA, INC.
1500 Valley Road, Wayne NJ 07470. 973/633-2200. **Fax:** 973/633-5305. **Contact:** Mary Thompson, Director of Personnel. **E-mail address:** hrjobs@cnacm.com. **World Wide Web address:** http://www.castrolna.com. **Description:** Manufactures and markets lubricants and petroleum products. **Common positions include:** Petroleum Engineer. **Corporate headquarters location:** This location. **Parent company:** Burmah Castrol USA, Inc. **Number of employees at this location:** 200.

CHEVRON CORPORATION
1200 State Street, Perth Amboy NJ 08861. 732/738-2000. **Contact:** Human Resources. **World Wide Web address:** http://www.chevron.com. **Description:** This location operates as part of the asphalt division. An international oil firm with operations in more than 90 countries. Chevron Corporation is engaged in worldwide integrated petroleum operations including the exploration and production of crude oil and natural gas reserves; the transportation of crude oil, natural gas, and petroleum products by pipeline, tanker, and motor equipment; the operation of oil-refining complexes; and the wholesale and retail marketing of petroleum products. **Parent company:** ChevronTexaco Corporation. **Listed on:** New York Stock Exchange. **Stock exchange symbol:** CVX.

EXXONMOBIL CORPORATION
P.O. Box 3140, Edison NJ 08818. 732/321-6100. **Contact:** Human Resources. **Description:** An integrated oil company engaged in petroleum and chemical products marketing, refining, manufacturing, exploration, production, transportation, and research and development worldwide. Other products include fabricated plastics, films, food bags, housewares, garbage bags, and building materials. The company also has subsidiaries involved in real estate development and mining operations. **Corporate headquarters location:** Irving TX. **Listed on:** New York Stock Exchange. **Stock exchange symbol:** XOM.

PHILLIPS PETROLEUM COMPANY
1400 Park Avenue, Linden NJ 07036. 908/523-5000. **Contact:** Professional Employment. **World Wide Web address:** http://www.phillips66.com. **Description:** Refines oil. **NOTE:** Mail employment correspondence to: Professional Employment, 180 Plaza Office Building, Bartlesville OK 74004.

WILSHIRE OIL COMPANY
921 Bergen Avenue, Jersey City NJ 07306. 201/420-2796. **Contact:** Human Resources. **Description:** A diversified corporation engaged in oil and gas exploration and production, real estate operations, and investment activities. **Corporate headquarters location:** This location.

PAPER AND WOOD PRODUCTS

You can expect to find the following types of companies in this chapter:
Forest and Wood Products and Services • Lumber and Wood Wholesale • Millwork, Plywood, and Structural Members • Paper and Wood Mills

BALTEK CORPORATION
P.O. Box 195, 108 Fairway Court, Northvale NJ 07647. 201/767-1400. **Fax:** 201/387-6631. **Contact:** Personnel Department. **World Wide Web address:** http://www.baltek.com. **Description:** Manufactures wood panels and other balsa wood products for marine and industrial use. **Corporate headquarters location:** This location.

BERLIN & JONES COMPANY, INC.
2 East Union Avenue, East Rutherford NJ 07073. 201/933-5900. **Fax:** 201/933-4242. **Contact:** Walt Lypowy, Controller. **Description:** Manufactures envelopes. **Corporate headquarters location:** This location.

HOBOKEN FLOORS
70 Demarest Drive, Wayne NJ 07470. 973/694-2888. **Contact:** Personnel. **World Wide Web address:** http://www.hobokenfloors.com. **Description:** Manufactures hardwood flooring. **Corporate headquarters location:** This location.

INTERNATIONAL PAPER COMPANY
3 Paragon Drive, Montvale NJ 07645. 201/391-1776. **Contact:** Personnel. **World Wide Web address:** http://www.internationalpaper.com. **Description:** This location houses sales offices for paperboard and paper products. Overall, International Paper Company manufactures pulp and paper, packaging, wood products, and a range of specialty products. The company is organized into five business segments: Printing Papers, whose principal products include uncoated papers, coated papers, bristles, and pulp; Packaging, which includes industrial packaging, consumer packaging, and kraft and specialty papers; Distribution, including the sale of printing papers, graphic arts equipment and supplies, packaging materials, industrial supplies, and office products; Specialty Products, which includes imaging products, specialty panels, nonwovens, chemicals, and minerals; and Forest Products which includes logging and wood products. **Corporate headquarters location:** Stamford CT. **Number of employees worldwide:** 72,500.

MAIL-WELL ENVELOPE
25 Linden Avenue East, Jersey City NJ 07305. 201/434-2100. **Toll-free phone:** 800/526-3020. **Fax:** 201/434-4048. **Contact:** Human Resources. **World Wide Web address:** http://www.mail-well.com. **Description:** Manufactures and prints envelopes and tags. Primary customers are publishing houses, insurance agencies, banks, direct mail companies, pharmaceutical companies, brokers, and jobbers. **NOTE:** A college education is required of all applicants. Sales experience with industrial accounts is preferred. **Common positions include:** Customer Service Representative; Manufacturer's/Wholesaler's Sales Rep.; Marketing Specialist. **Corporate headquarters location:** Englewood CO. **Operations at**

this facility include: Administration; Manufacturing; Research and Development; Sales. **Listed on:** New York Stock Exchange. **Stock exchange symbol:** MWL.

MARCAL PAPER MILLS, INC.
One Market Street, Elmwood Park NJ 07407. 201/796-4000. **Contact:** James H. Nelson, Director of Human Resources Department. **World Wide Web address:** http://www.marcalpaper.com. **Description:** Manufactures and distributes a broad range of nationally advertised paper products including paper towels, toilet tissue, and napkins. **Common positions include:** Accountant/Auditor; Chemical Engineer; Computer Programmer; Manufacturer's/Wholesaler's Sales Rep.; Mechanical Engineer; Operations/Production Manager. **Corporate headquarters location:** This location. **Operations at this facility include:** Administration; Manufacturing; Research and Development; Sales.

SCHIFFENHAUS INDUSTRIES
2013 McCarter Highway, Newark NJ 07104. 973/484-5000. **Contact:** Human Resources. **World Wide Web address:** http://www.schifpack.com. **Description:** Manufactures corrugated boxes and flexographic, preprinted liner board. **Common positions include:** Accountant/Auditor; Blue-Collar Worker Supervisor; Computer Programmer; Customer Service Representative; Manufacturer's/Wholesaler's Sales Rep.; Marketing Specialist; Operations/Production Manager; Purchasing Agent/Manager; Quality Control Supervisor. **Corporate headquarters location:** This location. **Number of employees at this location:** 165.

PRINTING AND PUBLISHING

You can expect to find the following types of companies in this chapter:

Book, Newspaper, and Periodical Publishers • Commercial Photographers • Commercial Printing Services • Graphic Designers

ALEXANDER HAMILTON INSTITUTE, INC.
70 Hilltop Road, Ramsey NJ 07446. **Toll-free phone:** 800/879-2441. **Fax:** 201/825-8696. **Contact:** Personnel. **World Wide Web address:** http://www.ahipubs.com. **Description:** Publishes newsletters and manuals focused on employment law.

APPLIED GRAPHICS TECHNOLOGIES (AGT)
463 Barell Avenue, Carlstadt NJ 07072. 201/935-3200. **Fax:** 201/935-5108. **Contact:** Human Resources. **World Wide Web address:** http://www.agt.com. **Description:** This location offers publication and catalog services, satellite transmission services, a desktop service bureau, four-color facsimile or digital transmittal, and packaging services. Overall, Applied Graphics Technologies (AGT) is one of the largest providers of integrated graphic communications services to advertising agencies, magazine and catalog publishers, and corporate clients in various industries. The company's services include commercial printing, color separation and retouching, facilities management, photo CD and digital image archiving, electronic imaging services, flexo/packaging services, publication and catalog services, satellite transmission services, creative design services, technical support and training services, and black and white ad production. **NOTE:** All of the hiring is conducted through the corporate headquarters. Interested jobseekers should address all inquiries to Applied Graphics Technologies, 450 West 33rd Street, 11th Floor, New York NY 10001. 212/716-6600. **Corporate headquarters location:** New York NY.

APPLIED PRINTING TECHNOLOGIES
77 Moonachie Avenue, Moonachie NJ 07074. 201/896-6600. **Fax:** 201/896-1893. **Contact:** Personnel. **World Wide Web address:** http://www.appliedprinting.com. **Description:** Offers commercial printing services, bindery services, a desktop service bureau, and advertising agency services. **Corporate headquarters location:** This location.

THE ASBURY PARK PRESS
3601 Highway 66, P.O. Box 1550, Neptune NJ 07754. 732/922-6000. **Contact:** Human Resources Department. **World Wide Web address:** http://www.app.com. **Description:** Publishes a daily local newspaper. **Common positions include:** Advertising Clerk; Blue-Collar Worker Supervisor; Branch Manager; Broadcast Technician; Computer Programmer; Credit Manager; Customer Service Representative; Electrician; General Manager; Human Resources Manager; Industrial Engineer; Management Analyst/Consultant; Management Trainee; Manufacturer's/Wholesaler's Sales Rep.; Operations/Production Manager; Property and Real Estate Manager; Public Relations Specialist; Purchasing Agent/Manager; Radio/TV Announcer/Broadcaster; Services Sales Representative; Technical Writer/Editor; Transportation/Traffic Specialist; Travel Agent. **Special programs:** Internships. **Corporate headquarters location:** This location. **Other U.S. locations:** Orlando FL. **Operations at this facility include:**

Administration; Sales; Service. **Listed on:** Privately held. **Number of employees nationwide:** 1,900.

BAKER & TAYLOR

1120 Highway 22 East, Bridgewater NJ 08807-0885. 908/541-7000. **Contact:** Human Resources Department. **World Wide Web address:** http://www.btol.com. **Description:** A leading full-line distributor of books, videos, and music products. Customers include online and traditional retailers and institutional customers. Baker & Taylor also provides customers with value-added proprietary data products and customized management and outsourcing services. Founded in 1828. **NOTE:** Entry-level positions and second and third shifts are offered. **Common positions include:** Administrative Assistant; Blue-Collar Worker Supervisor; Buyer; Computer Operator; Customer Service Representative; Industrial Engineer; Sales Representative; Secretary; Systems Analyst. **Corporate headquarters location:** Charlotte NC. **Listed on:** Privately held. **Number of employees worldwide:** 2,500.

BERLITZ INTERNATIONAL, INC.

400 Alexander Park, Princeton NJ 08540. 609/514-9650. **Contact:** Human Resources Department. **World Wide Web address:** http://www.berlitz.com. **Description:** A language services firm providing instruction and translation services through 298 language centers in 28 countries around the world. The company also publishes travel guides, foreign language phrase books, and home study materials. **Common positions include:** Accountant/Auditor; Director; Instructor/Trainer; Services Sales Representative. **Corporate headquarters location:** This location. **Operations at this facility include:** Administration. **Number of employees nationwide:** 3,500.

BOOKAZINE COMPANY INC.

75 Hook Road, Bayonne NJ 07002. 201/339-7777. **Contact:** Richard Kallman, Vice President. **E-mail address:** staff@bookazine.com. **World Wide Web address:** http://www.bookazine.com. **Description:** A general trade book wholesaler serving retail bookstores with an inventory of over 100,000 titles. Founded in 1928. **Corporate headquarters location:** This location. **President/CEO:** Robert Kallman.

CAHNERS TRAVEL GROUP

500 Plaza Drive, Secaucus NJ 07094. 201/902-2000. **Contact:** Staffing Manager. **World Wide Web address:** http://www.cahnerstravelgroup.com. **Description:** A print and online publisher of travel books and maps. **Common positions include:** Designer; Editor; Systems Analyst. **Special programs:** Internships. **Corporate headquarters location:** Newton MA. **Operations at this facility include:** Sales.

THE DAILY RECORD INC.

800 Jefferson Road, Parsippany NJ 07054. 973/428-6200. **Fax:** 973/884-5768. **Contact:** Mike Owen, Human Resources Representative. **E-mail address:** mowen@morristo.gannett.com. **World Wide Web address:** http://www.dailyrecord.com. **Description:** Publishes a morning newspaper, the *Daily Record*. Circulation is approximately 63,000 on weekdays and 72,000 on Sundays. **Common positions include:** Account Representative; Accountant/Auditor; Administrative Manager; Advertising Clerk; Credit Manager; Customer Service Representative; Editor; General Manager; Graphic Artist; Reporter; Sales Representative. **Corporate headquarters location:** Arlington VA. **Parent company:** Gannett Company. **Listed on:**

New York Stock Exchange. **Stock exchange symbol:** GSI. **Number of employees at this location:** 300.

DELUXE FINANCIAL SERVICES
105 Route 46 West, Mountain Lakes NJ 07046-1645. 973/334-8000. **Fax:** 973/334-4292. **Contact:** Russ Perry, Personnel Director. **World Wide Web address:** http://www.deluxe.com. **Description:** Engaged in the printing and selling of checks, deposit tickets, and related forms to banks and other financial institutions. The company also manufactures documents printed with magnetic ink. Printing operations are carried out at more than 15 plants throughout the United States. **Corporate headquarters location:** Shoreview MN. **Parent company:** Deluxe Corporation provides check printing, electronic funds transfer processing services, and related services to the financial industry; check authorization and collection services to retailers; and electronic benefit transfer services to state governments. Deluxe Corporation also produces forms, specialty papers, and other products for small businesses, professional practices, and medical/dental offices; and provides tax forms and electronic tax filing services to tax preparers. Through the direct-mail channel, Deluxe sells greeting cards and gift wrap. **Listed on:** New York Stock Exchange. **Stock exchange symbol:** DLX.

DOW JONES & COMPANY, INC.
P.O. Box 300, Princeton NJ 08543-0300. 609/520-4000. **Physical address:** 4300 North Route 1, South Brunswick NJ 08852. **Fax:** 609/520-7401. **Contact:** Mary Pergament, Human Resources Department. **World Wide Web address:** http://www.dowjones.com. **Description:** A financial news service and publishing company. Publications include the *Wall Street Journal, National Business Employment Weekly,* and Barron's educational book services. **Internship information:** Summer internships are offered for undergraduate and graduate students. See the above Website for program information and application schedule.

THE ECONOMICS PRESS, INC.
12 Daniel Road, Fairfield NJ 07004-2565. 973/227-1224. **Toll-free phone:** 800/526-2554. **Fax:** 973/227-3558. **Contact:** Human Resources. **World Wide Web address:** http://www.epinc.com. **Description:** A publisher of books, audio and video programs, and computer programs focused on employee training, motivation, and business information.

HOME NEWS TRIBUNE
35 Kennedy Boulevard, East Brunswick NJ 08816. 732/246-5500. **Contact:** Personnel. **World Wide Web address:** http://www.injersey.com/hnt. **Description:** A daily newspaper with a weekday circulation of more than 51,000. **Parent company:** Gannett Company, Inc.

THE JERSEY JOURNAL
30 Journal Square, Jersey City NJ 07306. 201/653-1000. **Contact:** Managing Editor. **World Wide Web address:** http://www.nj.com/jjournal/today. **Description:** Publishes a daily morning newspaper with a circulation of more than 55,000. **Parent company:** Newhouse Newspapers Group.

McBEE SYSTEMS, INC.
299 Cherry Hill Road, Parsippany NJ 07054-1111. 973/263-3225. **Fax:** 973/263-8165. **Contact:** Personnel Department. **World Wide Web address:** http://www.mcbeesystems.com. **Description:** Manufactures business forms designed specifically for small businesses and professional offices. **Common**

positions include: Customer Service Representative; Sales Representative. **Corporate headquarters location:** This location. **Parent company:** Romo Corporation. **Operations at this facility include:** Administration. **Number of employees nationwide:** 530.

PANTONE
590 Commerce Boulevard, Carlstadt NJ 07072. 201/935-5500. **Fax:** 201/804-9219. **Contact:** Human Resources. **World Wide Web address:** http://www.pantone.com. **Description:** Produces color charts and color specification materials. **Common positions include:** Accountant/Auditor; Assistant Manager; Blue-Collar Worker Supervisor; Chemist; Credit Manager; Customer Service Representative; General Manager; Human Resources Manager; Manufacturer's/Wholesaler's Sales Rep.; Marketing Manager; Operations/Production Manager; Public Relations Specialist. **Corporate headquarters location:** This location. **Operations at this facility include:** Administration; Manufacturing; Research and Development; Sales.

PEARSON EDUCATION
PRENTICE HALL INC.
One Lake Street, Upper Saddle River NJ 07458. 201/236-7000. **Contact:** Human Resources Department. **World Wide Web address:** http://www.pearsoneducation.com. **Description:** This location houses corporate offices. Overall, Pearson Education publishes consumer, educational, and professional books. Prentice Hall (also at this location) specializes in business and professional books, as well as college-level resource materials. **Subsidiaries include:** Macmillan. **Parent company:** Viacom. **Number of employees nationwide:** 4,000.

PERMANENT LABEL
790 Bloomfield Avenue, Clifton NJ 07012. 973/471-6617. **Contact:** Human Resources. **Description:** Engaged in decorating and printing labels for plastic products, primarily bottles. **Corporate headquarters location:** This location.

QUALEX, INC.
16-31 Route 208, Fair Lawn NJ 07410. 201/797-0600. **Contact:** Karen Mergenthaler, Senior Personnel Manager. **World Wide Web address:** http://www.kodak.com. **Description:** A photofinishing company providing processing services for print and reversal type films. **Common positions include:** Administrative Worker/Clerk; Customer Service Representative; Electronics Technician; Maintenance Technician; Photographic Process Worker; Print Coordinator. **Corporate headquarters location:** Durham NC. **Parent company:** Eastman Kodak Company. **Operations at this facility include:** Administration; Customer Service; Sales; Service.

THE RECORD
NORTH JERSEY MEDIA GROUP
150 River Street, Hackensack NJ 07601-7172. 201/646-4000. **Contact:** Human Resources. **World Wide Web address:** http://www.bergen.com. **Description:** A daily newspaper with a circulation of 150,000 and 203,000 for the Sunday edition.

REED ELSEVIER NEW PROVIDENCE
121 Chanlon Road, New Providence NJ 07974. 908/464-6800. **Contact:** Human Resources. **World Wide Web address:** http://www.reed-elsevier.com. **Description:** A reference publisher of marketing, advertising,

and corporate directories. **Subsidiaries include:** Lexis-Nexis Business Information Services; Marquis Who's Who; Martindale-Hubbel.

THE STAR-LEDGER
One Star Ledger Plaza, Newark NJ 07102. 973/877-4141. **Contact:** Human Resources. **World Wide Web address:** http://www.nj.com/starledger. **Description:** Publishes a large circulation daily newspaper covering local news.

L.P. THEBAULT COMPANY
249 Pomeroy Road, P.O. Box 169, Parsippany NJ 07054. 973/884-1300. **Contact:** Human Resources Department. **World Wide Web address:** http://www.thebault.com. **Description:** One of the largest commercial printing companies in the United States. The company specializes in the print-buying market, with projects ranging from annual reports to promotional pieces. **Common positions include:** Management Trainee. **Special programs:** Internships. **Corporate headquarters location:** This location. **Other U.S. locations:** Detroit MI; New York NY. **Subsidiaries include:** LPT Express Graphics. **Operations at this facility include:** Administration; Manufacturing; Sales. **Number of employees nationwide:** 400.

THOMSON MEDICAL ECONOMICS COMPANY
5 Paragon Drive, Montvale NJ 07645. 201/358-7500. **Fax:** 201/722-2668. **Contact:** Human Resources. **E-mail address:** hr_postings@medec.com. **World Wide Web address:** http://www.medec.com. **Description:** Publishes medical books and journals. **Common positions include:** Accountant/Auditor; Advertising Clerk; Artist; Commercial Artist; Computer Operator; Computer Programmer; Customer Service Representative; Designer; Editor; Financial Manager; Human Resources Manager; Librarian; Marketing Specialist; Receptionist; Services Sales Representative; Systems Analyst; Technical Writer/Editor; Typist/Word Processor. **Special programs:** Internships. **Corporate headquarters location:** This location. **Other U.S. locations:** DC; IL; KS. **Operations at this facility include:** Administration; Divisional Headquarters; Research and Development; Sales; Service. **Number of employees at this location:** 425. **Number of employees nationwide:** 510.

UNIMAC GRAPHICS
350 Michele Place, Carlstadt NJ 07072. 201/372-1000. **Fax:** 201/372-1241. **Contact:** Human Resources Department. **World Wide Web address:** http://www.unimacgraphics.com. **Description:** Provides a full range of commercial printing services.

JOHN WILEY & SONS, INC.
One Wiley Drive, Somerset NJ 08875. 732/469-4400. **Toll-free phone:** 800/225-5945. **Contact:** Human Resources Department. **World Wide Web address:** http://www.wiley.com. **Description:** This location houses the U.S. distribution center. Overall, John Wiley & Sons, Inc. is an international publishing house that publishes in four categories: Educational; Professional; Trade; and Scientific, Technical, and Medical (STM). In Educational, Wiley publishes textbooks and instructional packages for undergraduate and graduate students in the United States and internationally. Publishing programs focus on the physical and life sciences, mathematics, engineering, and accounting, with an increasing emphasis on economics, finance, business, MIS/CIS, and foreign languages. In Professional, Wiley publishes books and subscription products for lawyers,

architects, accountants, engineers, and other professionals. In Trade, Wiley publishes nonfiction books in areas such as business, computers, science, and general interest. In STM, Wiley publishes approximately 260 scholarly and professional journals, as well as encyclopedias, other major reference works, and books for the research and academic communities. Major subject areas include chemistry, the life sciences, and technology. **Corporate headquarters location:** New York NY. **Other U.S. locations:** Colorado Springs CO. **Number of employees nationwide:** 1,200.

WORRALL COMMUNITY NEWSPAPERS INCORPORATED
P.O. Box 3109, 1291 Stuyvesant Avenue, Union NJ 07083. 908/686-7700. **Contact:** Human Resources. **Description:** A publisher of 18 weekly newspapers in Union and Essex Counties with a total circulation of over 40,000.

REAL ESTATE

You can expect to find the following types of companies in this chapter:

Land Subdividers and Developers • Real Estate Agents, Managers, and Operators • Real Estate Investment Trusts

CB RICHARD ELLIS
61 South Paramus Road, 4th Floor, Paramus NJ 07652. 201/556-5000. **Fax:** 201/556-5100. **Contact:** Personnel. **E-mail address:** opps@cbre.com. **World Wide Web address:** http://www.cbrichardellis.com. **Description:** A real estate services company offering property sales and leasing, property and facility management, mortgage banking, and investment management services. **Corporate headquarters location:** Los Angeles CA. **Number of employees worldwide:** 9,000.

CENDANT CORPORATION
One Campus Drive, Parsippany NJ 07054-0642. 973/428-9700. **Fax:** 973/496-5966. **Contact:** Manager of Human Resources Department. **E-mail address:** cendant.jobs@cendant.com. **World Wide Web address:** http://www.cendant.com. **Description:** Provides a wide range of business services including dining services, hotel franchise management, mortgage programs, and timeshare exchanges. Cendant Corporation's Real Estate Division offers employee relocation and mortgage services through Century 21, Coldwell Banker, ERA, Cendant Mortgage, and Cendant Mobility. The Travel Division provides car rentals, vehicle management services, and vacation timeshares through brand names including Avia, Days Inn, Howard Johnson, Ramada, Travelodge, and Super 8. The Membership Division offers travel, shopping, auto, dining, and other financial services through Travelers Advantage, Shoppers Advantage, Auto Vantage, Welcome Wagon, Netmarket, North American Outdoor Group, and PrivacyGuard. **Common positions include:** Accountant/Auditor; Computer Operator; Computer Programmer; Customer Service Representative; Marketing Manager; Marketing Specialist; Public Relations Specialist; Real Estate Agent; Sales Representative; Secretary. **Corporate headquarters location:** New York NY. **Listed on:** New York Stock Exchange. **Stock exchange symbol:** CD. **President/CEO:** Henry Silverman. **Number of employees at this location:** 1,100. **Number of employees worldwide:** 28,000.

CHELSEA GCA REALTY, INC.
103 Eisenhower Parkway, Roseland NJ 07068. 973/228-6111. **Contact:** Human Resources. **World Wide Web address:** http://www.cpgi.com. **Description:** A self-administered and self-managed real estate investment trust engaged in the development, leasing, marketing, and management of upscale and fashion-oriented manufacturers' outlet centers. **Listed on:** New York Stock Exchange. **Stock exchange symbol:** CPG.

K. HOVNANIAN COMPANIES
10 Highway 35, Red Bank NJ 07701. 732/747-7800. **Contact:** Human Resources. **World Wide Web address:** http://www.khov.com. **Description:** Designs, constructs, and sells condominium apartments, townhouses, and single-family homes in residential communities. The company is also engaged in mortgage banking. Founded in 1959. **Common positions include:** Accountant; Administrative Assistant; Architect; Attorney; Auditor; Civil Engineer; Computer Operator; Computer Programmer; Controller;

Financial Analyst; Human Resources Manager; Market Research Analyst; Marketing Manager; Marketing Specialist; MIS Specialist; Online Content Specialist; Real Estate Agent; Sales Manager; Secretary; Systems Analyst; Systems Manager; Technical Writer/Editor; Webmaster. **Corporate headquarters location:** This location. **Other U.S. locations:** CA; FL; NC; NY; PA; VA. **Subsidiaries include:** New Fortis Homes. **Listed on:** New York Stock Exchange. **Stock exchange symbol:** HOV. **Number of employees at this location:** 90. **Number of employees nationwide:** 1,150.

WEICHERT REALTORS
1625 Route 10 East, Morris Plains NJ 07950. 973/267-7777. **Contact:** Human Resources. **World Wide Web address:** http://www.weichert.com. **Description:** A commercial real estate agency. **NOTE:** Jobseekers should specify a department of interest when applying. **Corporate headquarters location:** This location.

RETAIL

You can expect to find the following types of companies in this chapter:

Catalog Retailers • Department Stores; Specialty Stores • Retail Bakeries • Supermarkets

EPSTEIN, INC.
P.O. Box 902, Morristown NJ 07963-0902. 973/538-5000. **Contact:** Personnel. **Description:** A department store offering a wide range of fashions and other soft and hard goods. **Common positions include:** Accountant/Auditor; Administrator; Advertising Clerk; Credit Manager; Department Manager; General Manager. **Corporate headquarters location:** Cedar Knolls NJ. **Other U.S. locations:** Bridgewater NJ; Princeton NJ; Shrewsbury NJ. **Operations at this facility include:** Sales.

FOOD CITY MARKETS INC.
440 Sylvan Avenue, Suite 120, Englewood Cliffs NJ 07632. 201/569-4849. **Contact:** Barry Schwartz, Supervisor of Store Operations. **Description:** Operates a chain of supermarkets. **Corporate headquarters location:** This location.

FOODARAMA SUPERMARKETS
922 Highway 33, Building 6, Suite 1, Freehold NJ 07728. 732/462-4700. **Contact:** Bob Spires, Vice President of Personnel. **Description:** Foodarama operates supermarkets in the states of New Jersey, New York, and Pennsylvania. **Common positions include:** Accountant/Auditor; Management Trainee. **Corporate headquarters location:** This location.

THE GREAT ATLANTIC & PACIFIC TEA COMPANY
2 Paragon Drive, Montvale NJ 07645. 201/573-9700. **Contact:** Personnel. **World Wide Web address:** http://www.aptea.com. **Description:** This location houses administrative offices for one of the nation's largest supermarket chains. Overall, The Great Atlantic & Pacific Tea Company maintains approximately 1,000 retail supermarkets throughout the East Coast, the Mid-Atlantic region, and Canada. **Common positions include:** Accountant/Auditor; Computer Programmer; Draftsperson; Financial Analyst; Systems Analyst. **Corporate headquarters location:** This location. **Listed on:** New York Stock Exchange. **Stock exchange symbol:** GAP. **Number of employees at this location:** 650. **Number of employees nationwide:** 85,000.

HANOVER DIRECT, INC.
115 River Road, Building 10, Edgewater NJ 07020. 201/863-7300. **Fax:** 201/272-3280. **Contact:** Personnel Department. **World Wide Web address:** http://www.hanoverdirect.com. **Description:** A direct marketing company that sells products manufactured by other companies through its 12 core catalogs structured into operating groups. **NOTE:** Entry-level positions are offered. **Common positions include:** Accountant/Auditor; Buyer; Fashion Designer; Financial Analyst; Industrial Engineer; Market Research Analyst; Telemarketer. **Corporate headquarters location:** This location. **Other U.S. locations:** San Diego CA; San Francisco CA; Hanover PA; De Soto TX; Roanoke VA; La Crosse WI. **Operations at this facility include:** Administration; Divisional Headquarters; Sales. **Listed on:** American Stock Exchange. **Stock exchange symbol:** HNV. **Annual sales/revenues:** More

than $100 million. **Number of employees at this location:** 250. **Number of employees nationwide:** 3,000.

KMART CORPORATION
7401 Tonnelle Avenue, North Bergen NJ 07047. 201/868-1960. **Contact:** Human Resources. **World Wide Web address:** http://www.kmartcorp.com. **Description:** One of the largest nonfood retailers in the United States. The company operates over 2,000 stores nationwide under the Kmart name, with more than 50 Kmart stores located in the New York metropolitan area. All stores offer a broad range of discounted general merchandise, both soft and hard goods. **Common positions include:** Accountant/Auditor; Computer Operator; Computer Programmer; Distribution Manager; Human Resources Manager; Systems Analyst. **Corporate headquarters location:** Troy MI. **Operations at this facility include:** Administration; Divisional Headquarters; Service. **Listed on:** New York Stock Exchange. **Stock exchange symbol:** KM. **Number of employees at this location:** 1,700. **Number of employees nationwide:** 330,000.

LINENS 'N THINGS
6 Brighton Road, Clifton NJ 07015. 973/778-1300. **Fax:** 973/815-2990. **Contact:** Personnel. **World Wide Web address:** http://www.lnthings.com. **Description:** A specialty retailer selling linens, home furnishings, and domestics. Linens 'n Things operates over 230 stores nationwide. **Common positions include:** Assistant Manager; Shipping and Receiving Clerk; Store Manager. **Corporate headquarters location:** This location.

MICRO WAREHOUSE, INC.
1720 Oak Street, Lakewood NJ 08701. 732/370-3801. **Fax:** 732/886-0567. **Contact:** Human Resources Department. **World Wide Web address:** http://www.warehouse.com. **Description:** A catalog retailer of brand-name Macintosh and IBM-compatible personal computer software, accessories, and peripherals. **Common positions include:** Blue-Collar Worker Supervisor; Credit Manager; Customer Service Representative; Human Resources Manager; Systems Analyst. **Corporate headquarters location:** South Norwalk CT. **Other U.S. locations:** Gibbsboro NJ; Wilmington OH. **International locations:** Canada; England; France; Germany; Mexico; Sweden; The Netherlands. **Operations at this facility include:** Sales; Service. **Number of employees at this location:** 600. **Number of employees nationwide:** 2,400.

PATHMARK STORES INC.
200 Milik Street, Carteret NJ 07008. 732/499-3000. **Fax:** 732/499-9250. **Contact:** Ms. Louise Hyland, Human Resources Department. **E-mail address:** lhyland@pathmark.com. **World Wide Web address:** http://www.pathmark.com. **Description:** A diversified retailer engaged primarily in the operation of large supermarket/drug stores. The company operates one of the largest supermarket chains in the country. Its Rickel Home Center division is among the largest do-it-yourself home center chains in the nation. The company's retail stores are located in the Mid-Atlantic and New England. **Corporate headquarters location:** This location.

POPULAR CLUB PLAN
22 Lincoln Place, Garfield NJ 07026. 973/471-4300. **Contact:** Human Resources. **World Wide Web address:** http://www.popularclub.com. **Description:** Operates a full-service, mail-order catalog operation offering apparel, housewares, personal care products, jewelry and related items. **Corporate headquarters location:** This location.

STRAUSS DISCOUNT AUTO

9A Brick Plant Road, South River NJ 08882. 732/390-9000. **Contact:** Human Resources Administrator. **World Wide Web address:** http://www.straussauto.com. **Description:** Engaged in the retail trade of automotive aftermarket products. **Common positions include:** Accountant/Auditor; Advertising Clerk; Automotive Mechanic; Budget Analyst; Buyer; Computer Programmer; Construction Contractor; Customer Service Representative; Draftsperson; Human Resources Manager; Management Trainee; Property and Real Estate Manager; Systems Analyst. **Corporate headquarters location:** This location. **Operations at this facility include:** Administration. **Listed on:** Privately held. **Number of employees at this location:** 200. **Number of employees nationwide:** 2,200.

SYMS CORPORATION

One Syms Way, Secaucus NJ 07094. 201/902-9600. **Contact:** John Tyzbir, Director of Human Resources Department. **World Wide Web address:** http://www.symsclothing.com. **Description:** This location houses a retail location and a distribution center. Overall, Syms Corporation operates a chain of over 45 off-priced apparel stores located throughout the Northeast, Midwest, Southeast, and Southwest. All stores offer men's tailored clothing; women's dresses, suits, and separates; and children's apparel. **Corporate headquarters location:** This location.

TOYS 'R US

461 From Road, Paramus NJ 07652. 201/262-7800. **Contact:** Director of Employment. **World Wide Web address:** http://www.toysrus.com. **Description:** One of the largest children's specialty retailers in the world. The company operates over 1,450 stores worldwide. Founded in 1948. **NOTE:** Entry-level positions are offered. **Common positions include:** Accountant; Administrative Assistant; Assistant Manager; Computer Programmer; Financial Analyst; Management Trainee; MIS Specialist; Secretary; Systems Analyst. **Special programs:** Training. **Corporate headquarters location:** This location. **Other U.S. locations:** Nationwide. **Subsidiaries include:** Babies 'R Us; Kids 'R Us. **Listed on:** New York Stock Exchange. **Stock exchange symbol:** TOY. **Annual sales/revenues:** More than $100 million. **Number of employees at this location:** 1,400. **Number of employees worldwide:** 94,000.

UNITED RETAIL GROUP, INC.

365 West Passaic Street, Rochelle Park NJ 07662. 201/845-0880. **Contact:** Human Resources Manager. **World Wide Web address:** http://www.unitedretail.com. **Description:** A leading nationwide specialty retailer of plus-size women's apparel and accessories. The company operates 502 stores in 36 states, principally under the names The Avenue and Sizes Unlimited. New/remodeled stores will bear the name Avenue Plus. Founded in 1987. **Corporate headquarters location:** This location. **Subsidiaries include:** United Retail Incorporated. **CEO:** Raphael Benaroya.

UNITEDAUTO GROUP, INC.

One Harmon Plaza, 9th Floor, Secaucus NJ 07094. 201/325-3300. **Contact:** Human Resources. **World Wide Web address:** http://www.unitedauto.com. **Description:** Operates car dealerships. **Corporate headquarters location:** This location. **Listed on:** New York Stock Exchange. **Stock exchange symbol:** UAG.

VILLAGE SUPERMARKET, INC.
733 Mountain Avenue, Springfield NJ 07081. 973/467-2200. **Contact:** John Jay Sumas, Personnel Director. **Description:** Operates 20 supermarkets, 17 of which are located in north central New Jersey and three of which are in eastern Pennsylvania. Village Supermarket offers traditional grocery, meat, produce, dairy, frozen food, bakery, and delicatessen departments, as well as health and beauty aids, housewares, stationery, and automotive and paint supplies. Six stores contain prescription pharmacy departments, and the company also owns and operates two retail package liquor stores and one variety store. **Corporate headquarters location:** This location. **Other area locations:** Bernardsville NJ; Chester NJ; Florham Park NJ; Livingston NJ; Morristown NJ; The Orchards NJ; Union NJ. **Parent company:** Wakefern Food Corporation.

STONE, CLAY, GLASS, AND CONCRETE PRODUCTS

You can expect to find the following types of companies in this chapter:

Cement, Tile, Sand, and Gravel • Crushed and Broken Stone • Glass and Glass Products • Mineral Products

ANCHOR GLASS CONTAINER CORPORATION
One Bethany Road, Suite 74, Building 5, Hazlet NJ 07730. 732/335-8303. **Contact:** Human Resources. **E-mail address:** webhr@anchorglass.com. **World Wide Web address:** http://www.anchorglass.com. **Description:** Manufactures glassware, commercial and institutional chinaware, decorative and convenience hardware, glass containers, and metal and plastic closures. Operations encompass over 20 divisions and subsidiaries, with 40 plants and distribution centers worldwide. **Common positions include:** Accountant/Auditor; Administrator; Attorney; Buyer; Chemical Engineer; Civil Engineer; Computer Programmer; Credit Manager; Customer Service Representative; Department Manager; Draftsperson; Electrical/Electronics Engineer; Financial Analyst; General Manager; Human Resources Manager; Industrial Engineer; Management Trainee; Mechanical Engineer; Metallurgical Engineer; Quality Control Supervisor; Systems Analyst; Transportation/Traffic Specialist. **Corporate headquarters location:** Tampa FL.

BARRETT PAVING MATERIALS INC.
3 Becker Farm Road, Roseland NJ 07068-1748. 973/533-1001. **Fax:** 973/533-1020. **Contact:** Joann Gooding, Director of Human Resources. **E-mail address:** bpmicorp@aol.com. **World Wide Web address:** http://www.barrettpaving.com. **Description:** This location houses administrative offices. Overall, Barrett Paving Materials is engaged in the manufacture of road construction materials and the construction and paving of roads, airports, parking lots, race tracks, driveways, and bike paths. Founded in 1903. **NOTE:** Entry-level positions are offered. **Common positions include:** Accountant; Civil Engineer; Controller; Cost Estimator; Management Trainee; Mechanical Engineer; Project Manager; Quality Control Supervisor; Sales Manager; Sales Representative; Secretary; Typist/Word Processor. **Special programs:** Training; Co-ops; Summer Jobs. **Corporate headquarters location:** This location. **Other U.S. locations:** Hebron CT; Richmond IN; Bangor ME; Ypsilanti MI; Hooksett NH; Bridgewater NJ; East Syracuse NY; Norwood NY; Utica NY; Cincinnati OH; Piqua OH. **International locations:** Worldwide. **Parent company:** Colas Inc. **Annual sales/revenues:** More than $100 million. **Number of employees at this location:** 1,000.

RALPH CLAYTON & SONS
P.O. Box 3015, 515 Lakewood-New Egypt Road, Lakewood NJ 08701. 732/363-1995. **Contact:** Human Resources Department. **World Wide Web address:** http://www.claytonco.com. **Description:** Manufactures concrete. **Parent company:** The Clayton Companies.

INRAD INC.
181 Legrand Avenue, Northvale NJ 07647. 201/767-1910. **Fax:** 201/767-9644. **Contact:** Human Resources Department. **World Wide Web address:**

http://www.inrad.com. **Description:** Manufactures and finishes synthetic crystals.

TILCON, INC.
P.O. Box 407, Stonehouse Road, Millington NJ 07946. 908/580-3910. **Contact:** Human Resources Department. **World Wide Web address:** http://www.tilconnj.com. **Description:** Manufactures and sells paving equipment and supplies to contract service companies and asphalt companies. **Other U.S. locations:** Nationwide.

TRANSPORTATION/TRAVEL

You can expect to find the following types of companies in this chapter:

Air, Railroad, and Water Transportation Services • Courier Services • Local and Interurban Passenger Transit • Ship Building and Repair • Transportation Equipment Travel Agencies • Trucking • Warehousing and Storage

CENDANT CORPORATION
One Campus Drive, Parsippany NJ 07054-0642. 973/428-9700. **Fax:** 973/496-5966. **Contact:** Manager of Human Resources Department. **E-mail address:** cendant.jobs@cendant.com. **World Wide Web address:** http://www.cendant.com. **Description:** Provides a wide range of business services including dining services, hotel franchise management, mortgage programs, and timeshare exchanges. Cendant Corporation's Real Estate Division offers employee relocation and mortgage services through Century 21, Coldwell Banker, ERA, Cendant Mortgage, and Cendant Mobility. The Travel Division provides car rentals, vehicle management services, and vacation timeshares through brand names including Avia, Days Inn, Howard Johnson, Ramada, Travelodge, and Super 8. The Membership Division offers travel, shopping, auto, dining, and other financial services through Travelers Advantage, Shoppers Advantage, Auto Vantage, Welcome Wagon, Netmarket, North American Outdoor Group, and PrivacyGuard. **Common positions include:** Accountant/Auditor; Computer Operator; Computer Programmer; Customer Service Representative; Marketing Manager; Marketing Specialist; Public Relations Specialist; Real Estate Agent; Sales Representative; Secretary. **Corporate headquarters location:** New York NY. **Listed on:** New York Stock Exchange. **Stock exchange symbol:** CD. **President/CEO:** Henry Silverman. **Number of employees at this location:** 1,100. **Number of employees worldwide:** 28,000.

DPT
1200 Paco Way, Lakewood NJ 08701. 732/367-9000. **Contact:** Personnel. **World Wide Web address:** http://www.dptlabs.com. **Description:** Packages and ships pharmaceutical products manufactured by other companies.

HARBOUR INTERMODAL LTD.
1177 McCarter Highway, Newark NJ 07104. 973/481-6474. **Contact:** Human Resources. **Description:** Provides local intermodal transportation services in the greater New York Harbor area. The company also develops and sells equipment for intermodal services including waterborne vessels and mobile and fixed heavy materials handling equipment for transporting and sorting containers, trailers, and general cargo.

THE HERTZ CORPORATION
225 Brae Boulevard, Park Ridge NJ 07656. 201/307-2000. **Fax:** 201/307-2644. **Contact:** Director of Personnel. **World Wide Web address:** http://www.hertz.com. **Description:** A large rental company that leases new and used cars and industrial and construction equipment in 130 countries worldwide. The company also sells used cars in the United States, Australia, New Zealand, and Europe. The fleet of cars consists of 283,000

automobiles, which are leased through 5,300 offices. **Corporate headquarters location:** This location.

LAIDLAW TRANSIT
LAIDLAW EDUCATIONAL SERVICES
3349 Highway 138, Building 1, Unit D, Wall NJ 07719. 732/449-3530. **Contact:** Human Resources. **Description:** This location houses administrative offices. Overall, Laidlaw Educational Services provides school bus transportation services. **NOTE:** Entry-level positions and part-time jobs are offered. **Company slogan:** Laidlaw - we carry the nation's future. **Common positions include:** Accountant; Administrative Assistant; Administrative Manager; Blue-Collar Worker Supervisor; General Manager; Management Trainee; Secretary; Transportation/Traffic Specialist. **Special programs:** Apprenticeships; Training. **Corporate headquarters location:** Lawrenceville NJ. **Other U.S. locations:** Nationwide. **Listed on:** New York Stock Exchange. **Annual sales/revenues:** $21 - $50 million. **Number of employees nationwide:** 60,000.

MAERSK-SEALAND
Giralda Farms, Madison Avenue, P.O. Box 880, Madison NJ 07940-0880. 973/514-5000. **Contact:** Human Resources Department. **World Wide Web address:** http://www.maersksealand.com. **Description:** This location houses the northeast regional headquarters operations. Overall, Maersk-Sealand ships large containers. **Parent company:** A.P. Moller Group.

TITAN GLOBAL TECHNOLOGIES, LTD.
85 Chestnut Ridge Road, P.O. Box 617, Montvale NJ 07645. 201/930-0300. **Contact:** Human Resources. **World Wide Web address:** http://www.titan-global-tech.com. **Description:** Designs, manufactures, and installs monorail transportation systems. **Common positions include:** Accountant/Auditor; Administrative Manager; Advertising Clerk; Architect; Civil Engineer; Computer Operator; Computer Programmer; Cost Estimator; Electrical/Electronics Engineer; Mechanical Engineer; Quality Control Supervisor; Systems Analyst; Transportation/Traffic Specialist. **Corporate headquarters location:** This location. **Operations at this facility include:** Administration; Research and Development.

UNITED AIR LINES, INC.
Newark International Airport, Newark NJ 07114. **Toll-free phone:** 800/241-6522. **Contact:** Human Resources. **World Wide Web address:** http://www.ual.com. **Description:** An air carrier that provides transportation of people and goods through more than 1,100 daily scheduled flights at 100 airports in the United States, Canada, and Mexico. **NOTE:** Resumes should be sent to United Air Lines-WHQES, P.O. Box 66100, Chicago IL 60666. **Corporate headquarters location:** Elk Grove Township IL. **Parent company:** UAL, Inc. **Listed on:** New York Stock Exchange. **Stock exchange symbol:** UAL.

UNITED PARCEL SERVICE (UPS)
One Clover Place, Edison NJ 08837. **Toll-free phone:** 800/622-3593. **Contact:** Human Resources Department. **World Wide Web address:** http://www.upsjobs.com. **Description:** This location is a package-handling center. Overall, UPS provides package delivery services nationwide.

UTILITIES: ELECTRIC/GAS/WATER

You can expect to find the following types of companies in this chapter:

Gas, Electric, and Fuel Companies; Other Energy-Producing Companies • Public Utility Holding Companies • Water Utilities

ELIZABETHTOWN GAS COMPANY/NUI
P.O. Box 1450, Union NJ 07207. 908/289-5000. **Physical address:** 1085 Morris Road, Union NJ 07083. **Contact:** Human Resources. **E-mail address:** hr@nui.com. **World Wide Web address:** http://www.nui.com. **Description:** Through several area locations, Elizabethtown Gas Company is engaged in the distribution of natural gas through its subsidiaries and investments in joint ventures. The company serves more than 240,000 customers. **Subsidiaries include:** Energy Marketing Exchange. **Parent company:** NUI Corporation (Bedminster NJ).

FIRSTENERGY CORPORATION
300 Madison Avenue, P.O. Box 1911, Morristown NJ 07962-1911. 973/263-6500. **Contact:** Manager of Human Resources Department. **World Wide Web address:** http://www.firstenergycorp.com. **Description:** An electric utility holding company with several operating subsidiaries. **Common positions include:** Accountant/Auditor; Administrator; Electrical/Electronics Engineer; Human Resources Manager; Industrial Engineer; Systems Analyst. **Corporate headquarters location:** Akron OH. **Operations at this facility include:** Administration. **Listed on:** New York Stock Exchange. **Stock exchange symbol:** FE.

NEW JERSEY RESOURCES CORPORATION
1415 Wyckoff Road, Wall NJ 07719. 732/938-1480. **Contact:** Human Resources. **World Wide Web address:** http://www.njresources.com. **Description:** A holding company for natural gas and energy companies. **Subsidiaries include:** New Jersey Natural Gas Company distributes natural gas to over 400,000 customers in Monmouth and Ocean Counties, and parts of Morris and Middlesex Counties. Other subsidiaries are engaged in exploration for natural gas and oil, real estate development, and the development of cogeneration projects.

PASSAIC VALLEY WATER COMMISSION
1525 Main Avenue, Clifton NJ 07011. 973/349-4309. **Contact:** Jim Gallagher, Human Resources Director. **World Wide Web address:** http://www.pvwc.com. **Description:** Provides water utility services. **Corporate headquarters location:** This location.

PUBLIC SERVICE ENTERPRISE GROUP (PSEG)
80 Park Plaza, Newark NJ 07101. 973/430-7000. **Contact:** Human Resources. **World Wide Web address:** http://www.pseg.com. **Description:** An electric and gas utility holding company. **Corporate headquarters location:** This location. **Other area locations:** Hancock's Bridge NJ. **Subsidiaries include:** Public Service Electric & Gas Company provides nuclear, coal, gas, oil, and purchased and interchanged power to industrial and commercial customers. **Listed on:** New York Stock Exchange. **Stock exchange symbol:** PEG.

UNITED WATER RESOURCES, INC.
200 Old Hook Road, Harrington Park NJ 07640. 201/784-9434. **Fax:** 201/767-7142. **Contact:** Carol Ike, Recruiting Department. **World Wide Web address:** http://www.unitedwater.com. **Description:** A holding company for regulated water utilities. **Subsidiaries include:** United Water New Jersey supplies water service to over 750,000 customers in 60 communities in Hudson County and Bergen County NJ.

MISCELLANEOUS WHOLESALING

You can expect to find the following types of companies in this chapter:

Exporters and Importers • General Wholesale Distribution Companies

CCA INDUSTRIES INC.
200 Murray Hill Parkway, East Rutherford NJ 07073. 201/330-1400. **Contact:** Human Resources Department. **World Wide Web address:** http://www.ccaindustries.com. **Description:** Distributes a wide variety of health and beauty products manufactured by other companies using CCA's formulations. The majority of its sales are made to retail drug and food chains and mass merchandisers. Nail treatment products are sold under the name Nutra Nail; hair treatment products are sold under the names Pro Perm, Wash 'n Curl, Wash 'n Tint, and Wash 'n Straight; depilatory products are sold under the Hair Off label; skin care products are sold under the Sudden Change name; oral hygiene products are sold under the Plus+White trademark; meal replacement products are sold under the trademark Eat 'n Lose; and diet products under the trademarks Hungrex and Permathene. **Listed on:** NASDAQ. **Stock exchange symbol:** CCAM.

McMASTER-CARR SUPPLY COMPANY
P.O. Box 440, New Brunswick NJ 08903. 732/329-6666. **Contact:** Recruiting Department. **E-mail address:** recruiting@mcmaster.com. **World Wide Web address:** http://www.mcmaster.com. **Description:** Distributes industrial products and supplies primarily through catalog sales. Products are sold worldwide. **NOTE:** Mail employment correspondence to: Recruiting, McMaster Supply Company, P.O. Box 4355, Chicago IL 60680-4355. **Common positions include:** Management Trainee. **Corporate headquarters location:** Elmhurst IL. **Operations at this facility include:** Service.

RIVIERA TRADING CORPORATION
80 Sea View Drive, Secaucus NJ 07096. 201/864-8686. **Contact:** Human Resources. **Description:** Imports and distributes hair accessories and sunglasses. **Common positions include:** Accountant/Auditor; Administrator; Branch Manager; Customer Service Representative; Department Manager; General Manager; Human Resources Manager; Management Trainee; Marketing Specialist; Operations/Production Manager; Purchasing Agent/Manager. **Operations at this facility include:** Manufacturing; Service.

VAN LEEUWEN
20 Harmich Road, South Plainfield NJ 07080. 908/226-0700. **Contact:** Human Resources. **Description:** Distributes pipes, valves, and fittings, serving both domestic and overseas customers. **NOTE:** If applying for a warehouse position, please contact Martin Curley, Operations Manager; for an office position, contact Jim Gallagher, Regional Manager. **Corporate headquarters location:** This location.

INDEX OF PRIMARY EMPLOYERS
(Includes: New York City, Long Island, Rockland County, Westchester County)

ACCOUNTING & MANAGEMENT CONSULTING

Arthur Andersen LLP/54
Cap Gemini Ernst & Young/54
Deloitte & Touche/54
Ernst & Young LLP/55
FIND/SVP, Inc./55
KPMG/55
Mercer Human Resource Consulting/55
PricewaterhouseCoopers/55, 56
Towers Perrin/56

ADVERTISING, MARKETING, AND PUBLIC RELATIONS

Associated Merchandising Corporation (AMC)/57
BBDO Worldwide Inc./57
Bates USA/57
Blair Television/57
Bozell Worldwide/58
Burson-Marsteller/58
Citigate Dewe Rogerson/58
DDB Worldwide, Inc./58
R.H. Donnelley/58
Doremus & Company, Inc./59
Earle Palmer Brown/59
FCB Worldwide/59
Gotham Inc./59
Hill and Knowlton Inc./59
The Interpublic Group of Companies, Inc./60
The Kaplan Thaler Group, Ltd./60
Katz Media/60
Lowe/60

Lyons Lavey Nickel Swift Inc./60
McCann-Erickson Worldwide/61
Arnold McGrath Worldwide/61
The Medicus Group/61
Mickelberry Communications/61
Moss Dragoti/62
The NPD Group, Inc./62
Nielsen Media Research Company/62
Ogilvy & Mather/62
Posterloid Corporation/62
Publishers Clearing House/62
Ruder-Finn, Inc./63
Saatchi & Saatchi Advertising/63
Sudler & Hennessey Inc./63
Systemax Inc./63
TBWA/Chiat/Day/64
J. Walter Thompson Company/64
Viacom Outdoor/64
Jane Wesman Public Relations, Inc./64
Wunderman/64
Young & Rubicam, Inc./64

AEROSPACE

Aeroflex, Inc./65
CPI Aerostructures, Inc./65
Ellanef Manufacturing Corporation/65
K&F Industries Inc./65
Northrop Grumman Corporation/65
Parker Hannifin Corporation/66
Stellex Monitor Aerospace Corporation/66

Cine Magnetics Video &
   Digital Laboratories/80
City Center of Music and
   Drama Inc. (CCMD)/80
The Cloisters/80
Comedy Central/80
Court TV/80
DuArt Film and Video/80
HBO (Home Box Office)/80
The Hudson River Museum
   of Westchester/Andrus
   Planetarium/81
Juniper Group, Inc./81
Lincoln Center for the Arts,
   Inc./ New York City
   Ballet/81
MGM/United Artists/
   Orion Pictures
   Corporation/81
Madison Square Garden,
   L.P./81
The Metropolitan Museum of
   Art/82
The Metropolitan Opera/82
Multimedia Tutorial Services,
   Inc./82
Museum of Modern Art/83
New Line Cinema/83
The New York Botanical
   Garden/83
The New York Racing
   Association/83
New York Shakespeare
   Festival/83
Oxygen Media, Inc./83
Paramount Center for the
   Arts/83
Radio City Entertainment/84
RIOT Manhattan/84
Roundabout Theatre
   Company, Inc./84
Showtime Networks Inc./84
Shubert Organization, Inc./84
Sony Pictures
   Entertainment/84
South Street Seaport
   Museum/85

Staten Island Institute of Arts
   and Sciences/85
Time Warner Cable/85
USA Interactive/86
Universal Music Group/86
Warner Bros. Inc./86
Wildlife Conservation Society
   (WCS)/Bronx Zoo/86
William Morris Agency,
   Inc./86
Yonkers Raceway/86

AUTOMOTIVE

Arlen Corporation/87
Audiovox Corporation/87
Standard Motor Products
   Inc./87

BANKING/SAVINGS & LOANS/ OTHER DEPOSITORY INSTITUTIONS (MISC.)

Apple Bank for Savings/88
Astoria Federal Savings
   Bank/88
Astoria Financial
   Corporation/
   Astoria Federal Savings &
   Loan Association/88
Bank of New York/89
Bank of Tokyo Mitsubishi/89
Barclays Bank/89
Bridgehampton National
   Bank/90
Citibank/90
Citibank, N.A./90
Dime Savings Bank of
   Williamsburg/90
Emigrant Savings Bank/90
Financial Federal Credit
   Inc./90
First of Long Island
   Corporation/91
Greenpoint Bank/91
HSBC Bank USA/91

BIOTECHNOLOGY/ PHARMACEUTICALS/ SCIENTIFIC R&D (MISC.)

BUSINESS SERVICES/ NON-SCIENTIFIC RESEARCH

CHARITIES/SOCIAL SERVICES

CHEMICALS/RUBBER AND PLASTICS

NextSOURCE/131
OM Technologies/131
Oracle Corporation/131
Pencom Systems Inc./131
Royalblue Technologies
 Inc./132
Siemens Business Services,
 Inc./132
Standard Microsystems
 Corporation/132
Sunburst Technology/132
Symbol Technologies
 Inc./133
Systemax Inc./133
TSR Inc./133
Track Data/133
TriZetto Group, Inc./134
Veson Inc./134
WEN Technology
 Corporation/134
Wilco Systems, Inc./134

EDUCATIONAL SERVICES

AFS Intercultural Programs,
 Inc./135
Adelphi University/135
Atelier Esthetique Inc./135
Barnard College/135
Baruch College/The City
 University of New York
 (CUNY)/135
The City College of New
 York/The City University of
 New York (CUNY)/136
Columbia University/136
Dowling College/136
Fashion Institute of
 Technology/136
FlightSafety International,
 Inc./137
Fordham University/137
Hofstra University/137
Hunter College/The City
 University of New York
 (CUNY)/137
Iona College/137

John Jay College of Criminal
 Justice/The City University
 of New York (CUNY)/137
Katharine Gibbs Schools
 Inc./138
Lehman College/The City
 University of New York
 (CUNY)/138
Long Island University/138
Marist College/138
Mercy College/138
Mount St. Mary College/138
Nassau Community
 College/139
New York Institute of
 Technology/139
New York University/139
Pace University/139
Queens College/The City
 University of New York
 (CUNY)/139
St. John's University/139
Sarah Lawrence College/139
State University of New York
 at New Paltz/139
State University of New York
 at Stonybrook/140
TASA (Touchstone Applied
 Science Associates,
 Inc.)/140
Vassar College/140

ELECTRONIC/INDUSTRIAL ELECTRICAL EQUIPMENT AND COMPONENTS

ADEMCO (Alarm Device
 Manufacturing
 Company)/141
American Medical Alert
 Corporation/141
American Technical
 Ceramics Corporation
 (ATC)/141
Andrea Electronics
 Corporation/141
Arrow/Zeus Electronics/142

**ENVIRONMENTAL &
WASTE MANAGEMENT
SERVICES**

**FABRICATED METAL
PRODUCTS AND
PRIMARY METALS**

**FINANCIAL SERVICES
(MISC.)**

Cantor Fitzgerald Securities
Corporation/156
Citigroup Inc./156
Credit Suisse First Boston/156
Deutsche Bank/156
Dreyfus Corporation/157
Fahnestock & Company/157
Fiduciary Trust Company
International/157
First Investors
Corporation/157
Gilman & Ciocia Inc./157
Goldman Sachs &
Company/158
Gruntal & Co., LLC/158
HSBC Bank USA/158
ING/158
Investec Ernst &
Company/158
J.P. Morgan Chase &
Company/158,159
J.P. Morgan Partners/159
Jefferies & Company,
Inc./159
Lehman Brothers
Holdings/159
Merrill Lynch/159
The MONY Group/160
Morgan Stanley Dean Witter
& Company/160
National Association of
Securities Dealers, Inc.
(NASD)/160
New York Stock
Exchange/161
Paragon Capital Markets/161
Prudential Securities Inc./161
Quick and Reilly, Inc./161
SG Cowen Securities
Corp./162
Salomon Smith Barney/162
Schonfeld Securities/162
Scudder Investment/162
TD Waterhouse Securities,
Inc./162
Thomson Financial/162
UBS Painewebber Inc./163

UBS Warburg LLC/163
United States Trust Company
of New York/163
Value Line/163

FOOD AND BEVERAGES/ AGRICULTURE

Balchem Corporation/164
Domino Sugar/164
Fink Baking Company/164
The Hain Celestial
Group/164
Krasdale Foods Inc./165
Pepsi-Cola Bottling
Company/165
PepsiCo, Inc./165
Philip Morris Companies
Inc./ Philip Morris Inc./165
Philip Morris International
Inc./166
Sara Lee Coffee and Tea/166
Schieffelin & Somerset
Company/166
Topps Company/166
George Weston Bakeries,
Inc./167

GOVERNMENT

Economic Opportunity
Council of Suffolk/168
New York State Department
of Health/168
U.S. Environmental
Protection Agency
(EPA)/168
U.S. Postal Service/168

HEALTH CARE: SERVICES, EQUIPMENT, AND PRODUCTS (MISC.)

AFP Imaging Corporation/169
All Metro Health Care/169
Allegiance Healthcare
Corporation/169

HOTELS AND RESTAURANTS

The New York Helmsley
  Hotel/181
Park Central Hotel/181
Renaissance Westchester
  Hotel/181
Restaurant Associates
  Corporation/181
Sara Lee Coffee and Tea/182
Starwood Hotels & Resorts
  Worldwide, Inc./182
Tarrytown House/182

INSURANCE

Amalgamated Life
  Insurance/183
American International
  Group, Inc./183
Aon Risk Services/183
Arista Insurance
  Company/183
Atlantic Mutual
  Companies/183
CNA Insurance
  Companies/184
The Centre Group/184
Empire Blue Cross and Blue
  Shield/184
Fidelity National Title
  Insurance Company/184
Financial Guaranty Insurance
  Company/184
Financial Security Assurance
  Inc./184
Frontier Insurance Group/185
GEICO (Government
  Employees Insurance
  Company)/185
GeneralCologne Re/185
Group Health Incorporated
  (GHI)/185
The Guardian Life Insurance
  Company of America/186
Health Net of the Northeast,
  Inc./186
HIP Health Plan of Greater
  New York/186

Juniper Group, Inc./186
Kemper Insurance
  Companies/186
Lawyers Title Insurance
  Corporation/187
Leucadia National
  Corporation/187
Liberty International
  Underwriters/187
Liberty Mutual Insurance
  Group/187
MBIA Insurance
  Corporation/188
Marsh & McLennan
  Companies, Inc./188
Metropolitan Life Insurance
  (MetLife)/188
The MONY Group/188
Mutual of America/189
National Benefit Life
  Insurance/189
New York Life Insurance
  Company/189
OneBeacon Insurance
  Group/189
Radian Reinsurance Inc./190
Security Mutual Life
  Insurance Company of New
  York/190
TIAA-CREF/190
Transatlantic Holdings,
  Inc./190
Universal American Financial
  Corporation/190
Willis of New York, Inc./190

LEGAL SERVICES

American Arbitration
  Association/191
Cadwalader Wickersham &
  Taft/191
Cahill Gordon & Reindel/191
Carter, Ledyard &
  Milburn/191
Certilman Balin Adler &
  Hyman, LLP/191

MANUFACTURING: MISCELLANEOUS CONSUMER

MANUFACTURING: MISCELLANEOUS INDUSTRIAL

MINING/GAS/PETROLEUM/ ENERGY RELATED

PAPER AND WOOD PRODUCTS

PRINTING AND PUBLISHING

REAL ESTATE

RETAIL

Lord & Taylor/233
Macy's/233
Nine West Group/233
Pick Quick Foods Inc./234
Quality Markets/234
Saks Fifth Avenue/234
Software Etc./234
Western Beef, Inc./234

STONE, CLAY, GLASS, AND CONCRETE PRODUCTS

Floral Glass/235
Gemco Ware, Inc./235
Minerals Technologies Inc./235
Peckham Industries, Inc./235

TRANSPORTATION/TRAVEL

Air France/236
Air India/236
Avant Services Corporation/236
Camp Systems Inc. (CSI)/236
Cendant Corporation/236
Courtesy Bus Company/237
El Al Israel Airlines/237
Hudson General Corporation/237
Liberty Lines/237
Lindblad Special Expeditions/237
The Long Island Railroad Company/237
McAllister Towing and Transportation Company/238
Metropolitan Transportation Authority (MTA)/238

Queens Surface Corporation/238
Swissport USA/238
Tix International Group/239
We Transport Inc./239

UTILITIES: ELECTRIC/GAS/WATER

Central Hudson Gas and Electric/240
Con Edison Company of New York Inc./240
KeySpan Energy Delivery/240
Long Island Power Authority (LIPA)/240
Orange and Rockland Utilities/240
Water Authority of Western Nassau County/241

MISC. WHOLESALING

Actrade Financial Technologies/242
Allou Health & Beauty Care/242
Atelier Esthetique Inc./242
Dynamic Classics Limited/242
Itochu International Inc./242
Marubeni America Corporation/243
Mitsubishi International Corporation/243
Mitsui & Company (USA)/243
UOP/Xerox/244

INDEX OF PRIMARY EMPLOYERS
(Northern New Jersey)

IVAX Pharmaceuticals
  Inc./273
Laboratory Corporation of
  America (LabCorp)/273
LifeCell Corporation/273
The Liposome Company,
  Inc./274
Medarex, Inc./274
MedPointe Inc./274
Merck & Company,
  Inc./274,275
Napp Technologies/275
Novartis Pharmaceuticals
  Corporation/275
Novo Nordisk
  Pharmaceuticals Inc./275
Organon Inc./276
Ortho-McNeil
  Pharmaceutical/276
Osteotech Inc./276
Pfizer/276
Pharmaceutical Formulations,
  Inc./277
Pharmacia Corporation/277
QMED, Inc./277
Quest Diagnostics
  Incorporated/277
Roche Vitamins Inc./277
SGS U.S. Testing Company
  Inc./278
Schering-Plough
  Corporation/278
Synaptic Pharmaceutical
  Corporation/278
Teva Pharmaceuticals
  USA/279
Unigene Laboratories,
  Inc./279
Unilever Home & Personal
  Care USA/279
Watson Pharmaceuticals/279
Wyeth Corporation/279
Xenogen Biosciences/280

BUSINESS SERVICES/ NON-SCIENTIFIC RESEARCH

ADT Security Services/281
Automatic Data Processing
  (ADP)/281
Cendant Corporation/281
Computer Outsourcing
  Services, Inc. (COSI)/282
Dun & Bradstreet/282
Household International/282
Greg Manning Auctions,
  Inc./282
Mathematica Policy
  Research, Inc./283
Science Management
  LLC/SMC Consulting/283
Team Staff, Inc./283

CHARITIES/SOCIAL SERVICES

American Red Cross/284
The Arc of Bergen and
  Passaic Counties, Inc./284
Community Options Inc./284
Hope House/284
Hopes/284
Urban League of Hudson
  County/284

CHEMICALS/RUBBER AND PLASTICS

Ashland Speciality Chemical
  Company/285
BASF Corporation/
  Knoll Pharmaceuticals/285
BOC Gases/285
Benjamin Moore &
  Company/286
Cambrex Corporation/286
Chemetall Oakite/286

COMMUNICATIONS: TELECOMMUNICATIONS/ BROADCASTING

COMPUTERS (MISC.)

EDUCATIONAL SERVICES

ELECTRONIC/INDUSTRIAL ELECTRICAL EQUIPMENT AND COMPONENTS

M&M/Mars Inc./323
MCT Dairies, Inc./323
Marathon Enterprises
  Inc./323
Nabisco Fair Lawn
  Bakery/323
Nabisco Group Holdings/324
Nabisco Inc./324
Poland Springs of
  America/324
R&R Marketing/324
Reckitt Benckiser/324
Suprema Specialties Inc./325
Tuscan Dairy Farm/325
Unilever Foods/325
Wakefern Food
  Corporation/325

GOVERNMENT

New Jersey Department of
  Transportation/Region 3
  Construction/326
New Jersey Turnpike
  Authority/326
Union, County of/326
U.S. Postal Service/326
U.S. Postal Service/New
  Jersey International Bulk
  Mail/326
West Milford, City of/326
West Orange Police
  Department/326

HEALTH CARE: SERVICES, EQUIPMENT, AND PRODUCTS (MISC.)

American Standard
  Companies/327
C.R. Bard, Inc./327
Barnert Hospital/328
Becton Dickinson &
  Company/328
Biosearch Medical
  Products/328

Bon Secours & Canterbury
  Partnership for Care/328
Cantel Industries, Inc./329
Community Medical
  Center/329
Cordis Corporation/329
Datascope Corporation/329
EBI Medical Systems,
  Inc./329
Ethicon, Inc./330
GlaxoSmithKline
  Corporation/330
Hausmann Industries/330
HealthCare Integrated
  Services/330
Hooper Holmes, Inc./
  dba Portamedic/331
Howmedica Osteonics/331
Hunterdon Developmental
  Center/331
The Matheny School and
  Hospital/331
Maxim Healthcare/332
Medical Resources, Inc./332
Modern Medical Modalities
  Corporation/332
Ocean County Veterinary
  Hospital/332
Overlook Hospital/332
P.S.A. HealthCare/332
Siemens Medical/332
Trinitas Hospital/333
University Hospital/333
Vital Signs, Inc./333
Woodbridge Developmental
  Center/333

HOTELS AND RESTAURANTS

Canteen Vending
  Services/334
Chefs International, Inc./334
Hilton Newark Hotel/334
Hilton of Hasbrouck
  Heights/334

United Air Lines, Inc./379
United Parcel Service
(UPS)/379

UTILITIES: ELECTRIC/GAS/WATER

Elizabethtown Gas
Company/NUI/380
FirstEnergy Corporation/380
New Jersey Resources
Corporation/380
Passaic Valley Water
Commission/380

Public Service Enterprise
Group (PSEG)/380
United Water Resources,
Inc./381

MISC. WHOLESALING

CCA Industries Inc./382
McMaster-Carr Supply
Company/382
Riviera Trading
Corporation/382
Van Leeuwen/382

Your Job Hunt
Your Feedback

*Comments, questions, or suggestions? We want to hear from you!
Please complete this questionnaire and mail it to:*

The JobBank Staff
Adams Media Corporation
57 Littlefield Street
Avon, MA 02322

*Did this book provide helpful advice and valuable information which you used in
your job search? What did you like about it?*

*How could we improve this book to help you in your job search? Is there a
specific company we left out or an industry you'd like to see more of in a future
edition? No suggestion is too small or too large.*

Would you recommend this book to a friend beginning a job hunt?

Name: _____

Occupation: _____

Which JobBank did you use? _____

Mailing address: _____

E-mail address: _____

Daytime phone: _____

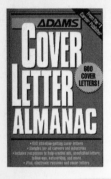
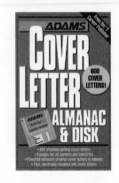